PEARSON CUSTOM BUSINESS RESOURCES

The Pennsylvania State University
Hospitality Decision Making
and Information Systems
HM 350

ISBN 10: 1-269-69807-9
ISBN 13: 978-1-269-69807-8

PEARSON

Table of Contents

1. Using Operations to Compete
Lee J. Krajewski/Larry P. Ritzman/Manoj K. Malhotra   **1**

2. Project Management
Lee J. Krajewski/Larry P. Ritzman/Manoj K. Malhotra   **31**

3. Process Strategy
Lee J. Krajewski/Larry P. Ritzman/Manoj K. Malhotra   **71**

4. Process Analysis
Lee J. Krajewski/Larry P. Ritzman/Manoj K. Malhotra   **101**

5. Quality and Performance
Lee J. Krajewski/Larry P. Ritzman/Manoj K. Malhotra   **141**

6. Constraint Management
Lee J. Krajewski/Larry P. Ritzman/Manoj K. Malhotra   **185**

7. Forecasting
Lee J. Krajewski/Larry P. Ritzman/Manoj K. Malhotra   **217**

8. Supplement: Decision Making
Lee J. Krajewski/Larry P. Ritzman/Manoj K. Malhotra   **261**

9. Supplement: Waiting Lines
Lee J. Krajewski/Larry P. Ritzman/Manoj K. Malhotra   **279**

Index   **297**

USING OPERATIONS TO COMPETE

The seventh novel in the Harry Potter series was released on July 21, 2007 and became an instant best seller around the globe. Because the book had to be delivered in a tight time window to the customers, Scholastic coordinated its publishing and distribution processes in USA months in advance of the release date.

Scholastic and Harry Potter

Scholastic is the world's largest publisher and distributor of children's books and educational materials. Founded in 1920, it had $1.9 billion in revenues in fiscal 2011 with offices in 16 countries including North America, Europe, Southeast Asia, Latin America, the Middle East, Australia, New Zealand, and Africa. Scholastic started planning in early 2007 for the worldwide release of the eagerly awaited seventh book *Harry Potter and the Deathly Hallows* in the acclaimed series by J.K. Rowling on the boy wizard. When the author finished the book in spring 2007, Scholastic's printers R.R. Donnelly & Sons and Quebecor World worked around the clock to make sure that the book would be ready by the release date. To save time in loading and unloading, Scholastic bypassed its own warehouses and required its truckers, Yellow Transportation and JB Hunt Transport Services, to use the same size trailers and pallets to ship books directly from six printing sites to big retailers like Barnes & Noble and Amazon.com. This fleet of trucks, if lined up bumper-to-bumper, would stretch for 15 miles. GPS transponders were used to alert Scholastic by e-mail if the driver or the trailer veered off the designated routes. The timing was particularly tricky for e-tailers, who had to directly ship books in advance for individual orders to arrive simultaneously around the country in order to minimize the risk of someone leaking the book's ending.

From Chapter 1 of *Operations Management: Processes and Supply Chains*, Tenth Edition. Lee J. Krajewski, Larry P. Ritzman, Manoj K. Malhotra. Copyright © 2013 by Pearson Education, Inc. All rights reserved.

Since close to 90 percent of sales of such special books occur in the first week, they get special treatment to save time, money, space, and work. Scholastic had to customize, coordinate, and synchronize its operations and supply chain processes across multiple partners at the printing, warehousing, distribution, and retailing locations to ensure that the last book in the Harry Potter series reached the final customers no more than a few hours before the scheduled July 21, 12:01 A.M. release deadline. Not bad for a bunch of Muggles who transported 12 million copies in a short time window without the magical floo powder, portkeys, and broomsticks!

Source: Dean Foust, "Harry Potter and the Logistical Nightmare," *Business Week* (August 6, 2007), p. 9; Michelle Regenold, "Shipping Harry Potter: How Do They Do That?" **www.go-explore-trans.org/2007/mar-apr/shipping_HP.cfm; www.scholastic.com**, 2011.

LEARNING GOALS *After reading this chapter, you should be able to:*

1. Describe operations and supply chains in terms of inputs, processes, outputs, information flows, suppliers, and customers.

2. Define an operations strategy and its linkage to corporate strategy, as well as the role it plays as a source of competitive advantage in a global marketplace.

3. Identify nine competitive priorities used in operations strategy, and their linkage to marketing strategy.

4. Explain how operations can be used as a competitive weapon.

5. Identify the global trends and challenges facing operations management.

operations management

The systematic design, direction, and control of processes that transform inputs into services and products for internal, as well as external, customers.

process

Any activity or group of activities that takes one or more inputs, transforms them, and provides one or more outputs for its customers.

operation

A group of resources performing all or part of one or more processes.

supply chain

An interrelated series of processes within and across firms that produces a service or product to the satisfaction of customers.

supply chain management

The synchronization of a firm's processes with those of its suppliers and customers to match the flow of materials, services, and information with customer demand.

Operations management refers to the systematic design, direction, and control of processes that transform inputs into services and products for internal, as well as external customers.

A **process** is any activity or group of activities that takes one or more inputs, transforms them, and provides one or more outputs for its customers. For organizational purposes, processes tend to be clustered together into operations. An **operation** is a group of resources performing all or part of one or more processes. Processes can be linked together to form a **supply chain**, which is the interrelated series of processes within a firm and across different firms that produce a service or product to the satisfaction of customers.[1] A firm can have multiple supply chains, which vary by the product or service provided. **Supply chain management** is the synchronization of a firm's processes with those of its suppliers and customers to match the flow of materials, services, and information with customer demand. For example, Scholastic must schedule the printing of a very large quantity of books in a timely fashion, receive orders from its largest customers, directly load and dispatch a fleet of trucks by specific destination while bypassing regular warehouses, keep track of their progress using technology, and finally, bill their customers and collect payment. The operational planning at Scholastic, along with internal and external coordination within its supply chain, provides one example of designing customized processes for competitive operations.

Operations and Supply Chain Management across the Organization

Broadly speaking, operations and supply chain management underlie all departments and functions in a business. Whether you aspire to manage a department or a particular process within it, or you just want to understand how the process you are a part of fits into the overall fabric of the business, you need to understand the principles of operations and supply chain management.

Operations serve as an excellent career path to upper management positions in many organizations. The reason is that operations managers are responsible for key decisions that affect the success of the organization. In manufacturing firms, the head of operations usually holds the

---

[1]The terms *supply chain* and *value chain* are sometimes used interchangeably.

title chief operations officer (COO) or vice president of manufacturing (or of production or operations). The corresponding title in a service organization might be COO or vice president (or director) of operations. Reporting to the head of operations are the managers of departments, such as customer service, production and inventory control, and quality assurance.

Figure 1 shows operations as one of the key functions within an organization. The circular relationships in Figure 1 highlight the importance of the coordination among the three mainline functions of any business, namely, (1) operations, (2) marketing, and (3) finance. Each function is unique and has its own knowledge and skill areas, primary responsibilities, processes, and decision domains. From an external perspective, finance generates resources, capital, and funds from investors and sales of its goods and services in the marketplace. Based on business strategy, the finance and operations functions then decide how to invest these resources and convert them into physical assets and material inputs. Operations subsequently transforms these material and service inputs into product and service outputs. These outputs must match the characteristics that can be sold in the selected markets by marketing. Marketing is responsible for producing sales revenue of the outputs, which become returns to investors and capital for supporting operations. Functions such as accounting, information systems, human resources, and engineering make the firm complete by providing essential information, services, and other managerial support.

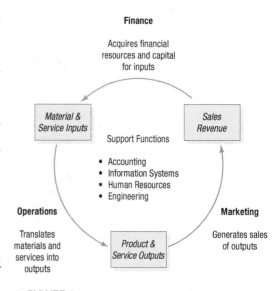

▲ **FIGURE 1**
Integration between Different Functional Areas of a Business

These relationships provide direction for the business as a whole, and are aligned to the same strategic intent. It is important to understand the entire circle, and not just the individual functional areas. How well these functions work together determines the effectiveness of the organization. Functions should be integrated and should pursue a common strategy. Success depends on how well they are able to do so. No part of this circle can be dismissed or minimized without loss of effectiveness, and regardless of how departments and functions are individually managed, they are always linked together through processes. Thus, a firm competes not only by offering new services and products, creative marketing, and skillful finance, but also through its unique competencies in operations and sound management of core processes.

Historical Evolution of Operations and Supply Chain Management

The history of modern operations and supply chain management is rich and over two hundred years old, even though its practice has been around in one form or another for centuries. James Watt invented the steam engine in 1785. The subsequent establishment of railroads facilitated efficient movement of goods throughout Europe, and eventually even in distant colonies such as India. With the invention of the cotton gin in 1794, Eli Whitney introduced the concept of interchangeable parts. It revolutionized the art of machine-based manufacturing, and coupled with the invention of the steam engine, lead to the great industrial revolution in England and the rest of Europe. The textile industry was one of the earliest industries to be mechanized. The industrial revolution gradually spread to the United States and the rest of the world in the nineteenth century, and was accompanied by such great innovations as the internal combustion engine, steam-powered ships, metallurgy of iron making, large-scale production of chemicals, and invention of machine tools, among others. The foundations of modern manufacturing and technological breakthroughs were also inspired by the creation of a mechanical computer

Henry Ford with a Model T in Buffalo, New York, in 1921. The Ford Motor Company, founded in 1903, produced about one million Model T's in 1921.

by Charles Babbage in the early part of the nineteenth century. He also pioneered the concept of division of labor, which laid the foundation for scientific management of operations and supply chain management that was further improved upon by Frederick Taylor in 1911.

Three other landmark events from the twentieth century define the history of operations and supply chain management. First is the invention of the assembly line for the Model T car by Henry Ford in 1909. The era of mass production was born, where complex products like automobiles could be manufactured in large numbers at affordable prices through repetitive manufacturing. Second, Alfred Sloan in the 1930s introduced the idea of strategic planning for achieving product proliferation and variety, with the newly founded General Motors Corporation offering "a car for every purse and purpose." Finally, with the publication of the Toyota Production System in 1978, Taiichi Ohno laid the groundwork for removing wasteful activities from an organization, a concept that we explore further in this book while learning about lean systems.

The recent history of operations and supply chains over the past three decades has been steeped in technological advances. The 1980s were characterized by wide availability of computer aided design (CAD), computer aided manufacturing (CAM), and automation. Information technology applications started playing an increasingly important role in 1990s, and started connecting the firm with its extended enterprise through Enterprise Resource Planning Systems and outsourced technology hosting for supply chain solutions. Service organizations like Federal Express, United Parcel Service (UPS), and Walmart also became sophisticated users of information technology in operations, logistics, and management of supply chains. The new millennium has seen an acceleration of this trend, along with an increased focus on sustainability and the natural environment. We cover all these ideas and topical areas in greater detail throughout this book.

A Process View

You might wonder why we begin by looking at processes, rather than at departments or even the firm. The reason is that a process view of the firm provides a much more relevant picture of the way firms actually work. Departments typically have their own set of objectives, a set of resources with capabilities to achieve those objectives, and managers and employees responsible for performance. Some processes, such as billing, may be so specific that they are contained wholly within a single department, such as accounting.

The concept of a process, however, can be much broader. A process can have its own set of objectives, involve a work flow that cuts across departmental boundaries, and require resources from several departments. You will see examples throughout this text of companies that discovered how to use their processes to gain a competitive advantage. You will notice that the key to success in many organizations is a keen understanding of how their processes work, since an organization is only as effective as its processes. Therefore, operations management is relevant and important for all students, regardless of major, because all departments have processes that must be managed effectively to gain a competitive advantage.

How Processes Work

Figure 2 shows how processes work in an organization. Any process has inputs and outputs. Inputs can include a combination of human resources (workers and managers), capital (equipment and facilities), purchased materials and services, land, and energy. The numbered circles in Figure 2 represent operations through which services, products, or customers pass and where processes are performed. The arrows represent flows, and can cross because one job or customer can have different requirements (and thus a different flow pattern) than the next job or customer.

Processes provide outputs to customers. These outputs may often be services (that can take the form of information) or tangible products. Every process and every person in an organization has customers. Some are **external customers**, who may be end users or intermediaries (e.g., manufacturers, financial institutions, or retailers) buying the firm's finished services or products. Others are **internal customers**, who may be employees in the firm whose process inputs are actually the outputs of earlier processes managed within the firm. Either way, processes must be managed with the customer in mind.

In a similar fashion, every process and every person in an organization relies on suppliers. **External suppliers** may be other businesses or individuals who provide the resources, services, products, and materials for the firm's short-term and long-term needs. Processes also have **internal suppliers**, who may be employees or processes that supply important information or materials.

external customers

A customer who is either an end user or an intermediary (e.g., manufacturers, financial institutions, or retailers) buying the firm's finished services or products.

internal customers

One or more employees or processes that rely on inputs from other employees or processes in order to perform their work.

external suppliers

The businesses or individuals who provide the resources, services, products, and materials for the firm's short-term and long-term needs.

internal suppliers

The employees or processes that supply important information or materials to a firm's processes.

▼ FIGURE 2
Processes and Operations

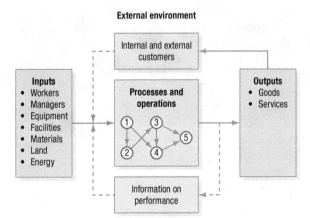

Inputs and outputs vary depending on the service or product provided. For example, inputs at a jewelry store include merchandise, the store building, registers, the jeweler, and customers; outputs to external customers are services and sold merchandise. Inputs to a factory manufacturing blue jeans include denim, machines, the plant, workers, managers, and services provided by outside consultants; outputs are clothing and supporting services. The fundamental role of inputs, processes, and customer outputs holds true for processes at all organizations.

Figure 2 can represent a whole firm, a department, a small group, or even a single individual. Each one has inputs and uses processes at various operations to provide outputs. The dashed lines represent two special types of input: participation by customers and information on performance from both internal and external sources. Participation by customers occurs not only when they receive outputs, but also when they take an active part in the processes, such as when students participate in a class discussion. Information on performance includes internal reports on customer service or inventory levels and external information from market research, government reports, or telephone calls from suppliers. Managers need all types of information to manage processes most effectively.

Nested Processes

Processes can be broken down into subprocesses, which in turn can be broken down further into still more subprocesses. We refer to this concept of a process within a process as a **nested process**. It may be helpful to separate one part of a process from another for several reasons. One person or one department may be unable to perform all parts of the process, or different parts of the process may require different skills. Some parts of the process may be designed for routine work while other parts may be geared for customized work.

nested process
The concept of a process within a process.

Service and Manufacturing Processes

Two major types of processes are (1) service and (2) manufacturing. Service processes pervade the business world and have a prominent place in our discussion of operations management. Manufacturing processes are also important; without them the products we enjoy as part of our daily lives would not exist. In addition, manufacturing gives rise to service opportunities.

Differences   Why do we distinguish between service and manufacturing processes? The answer lies at the heart of the design of competitive processes. While Figure 3 shows several distinctions between service and manufacturing processes along a continuum, the two key differences that we discuss in detail are (1) the nature of their output and (2) the degree of customer contact. In general, manufacturing processes also have longer response times, are more capital intensive, and their quality can be measured more easily than those of service processes.

Manufacturing processes convert materials into goods that have a physical form we call products. For example, an assembly line produces a 350 Z sports car, and a tailor produces an outfit for the rack of an upscale clothing store. The transformation processes change the materials on one or more of the following dimensions:

1.   Physical properties
2.   Shape
3.   Size (e.g., length, breadth, and height of a rectangular block of wood)
4.   Surface finish
5.   Joining parts and materials

The outputs from manufacturing processes can be produced, stored, and transported in anticipation of future demand.

If a process does not change the properties of materials on at least one of these five dimensions, it is considered a service (or nonmanufacturing) process. Service processes tend to produce intangible, perishable outputs. For example, the output from the auto loan process of a bank would be a car loan, and an output of the order fulfillment process of the U.S. Postal Service is the delivery of your letter. The outputs of service processes typically cannot be held in a finished goods inventory to insulate the process from erratic customer demands.

More like a manufacturing process

More like a service process

- Physical, durable output
- Output can be inventoried
- Low customer contact
- Long response time
- Capital intensive
- Quality easily measured

- Intangible, perishable output
- Output cannot be inventoried
- High customer contact
- Short response time
- Labor intensive
- Quality not easily measured

▲ FIGURE 3
Continuum of Characteristics of Manufacturing and Service Processes

A second key difference between service processes and manufacturing processes is degree of customer contact. Service processes tend to have a higher degree of customer contact. Customers may take an active role in the process itself, as in the case of shopping in a supermarket, or they may be in close contact with the service provider to communicate specific needs, as in the case of a medical clinic. Manufacturing processes tend to have less customer contact. For example, washing machines are ultimately produced to meet retail forecasts. The process requires little information from the ultimate consumers (you and me), except indirectly through market surveys and market focus groups. Even though the distinction between service and manufacturing processes on the basis of customer contact is not perfect, the important point is that managers must recognize the degree of customer contact required when designing processes.

Similarities   At the level of the firm, service providers do not just offer services and manufacturers do not just offer products. Patrons of a restaurant expect good service and good food. A customer purchasing a new computer expects a good product as well as a good warranty, maintenance, replacement, and financial services.

Further, even though service processes do not keep finished goods inventories, they do inventory their inputs. For example, hospitals keep inventories of medical supplies and materials needed for day-to-day operations. Some manufacturing processes, on the other hand, do not inventory their outputs because they are too costly. Such would be the case with low-volume customized products (e.g., tailored suits) or products with short shelf lives (e.g., daily newspapers).

When you look at what is being done at the process level, it is much easier to see whether the *process* is providing a service or manufacturing a product. However, this clarity is lost when the whole company is classified as either a manufacturer or a service provider because it often performs both types of processes. For example, the process of cooking a hamburger at a McDonald's is a manufacturing process because it changes the material's physical properties (dimension 1), as is the process of assembling the hamburger with the bun (dimension 5). However, most of the other processes visible or invisible to McDonald's customers are service processes. You can debate whether to call the whole McDonald's organization a service provider or a manufacturer, whereas classifications at the process level are much less ambiguous.

The Supply Chain View

Most services or products are produced through a series of interrelated business activities. Each activity in a process should add value to the preceding activities; waste and unnecessary cost should be eliminated. Our process view of a firm is helpful for understanding how services or products are produced and why cross-functional coordination is important, but it does not shed any light on the strategic benefits of the processes. The missing strategic insight is that processes must add value for customers throughout the supply chain. The concept of supply chains reinforces the link between processes and performance, which includes a firm's internal processes as well as those of its external customers and suppliers. It also focuses attention on the two main types of processes in the supply chain, namely (1) core processes and (2) support processes. Figure 4 shows the links between the core and support processes in a firm and a firm's external customers and suppliers within its supply chain.

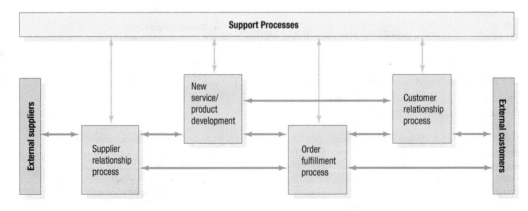

▲ FIGURE 4
Supply Chain Linkages Showing Work and Information Flows

Core Processes

A **core process** is a set of activities that delivers value to external customers. Managers of these processes and their employees interact with external customers and build relationships with them, develop new services and products, interact with external suppliers, and produce the service or product for the external customer. Examples include a hotel's reservation handling, a new car design for an auto manufacturer, or Web-based purchasing for an online retailer like amazon. com. Of course, each of the core processes has nested processes within it.

In this text we focus on four core processes:

1. *Supplier Relationship Process.* Employees in the **supplier relationship process** select the suppliers of services, materials, and information and facilitate the timely and efficient flow of these items into the firm. Working effectively with suppliers can add significant value to the services or products of the firm. For example, negotiating fair prices, scheduling on-time deliveries, and gaining ideas and insights from critical suppliers are just a few of the ways to create value.

2. *New Service/Product Development Process.* Employees in the **new service/product development process** design and develop new services or products. The services or products may be developed to external customer specifications or conceived from inputs received from the market in general.

3. *Order Fulfillment Process.* The **order fulfillment process** includes the activities required to produce and deliver the service or product to the external customer.

4. *Customer Relationship Process,* sometimes referred to as *customer relationship management.* Employees involved in the **customer relationship process** identify, attract, and build relationships with external customers, and facilitate the placement of orders by customers. Traditional functions, such as marketing and sales, may be a part of this process.

Support Processes

A **support process** provides vital resources and inputs to the core processes and is essential to the management of the business. Firms have many support processes. Examples include budgeting, recruiting, and scheduling. Support processes provide key resources, capabilities, or other inputs that allow the core processes to function.

The Human Resources function in an organization provides many support processes such as recruiting and hiring workers who are needed at different levels of the organization, training the workers for skills and knowledge needed to properly execute their assigned responsibilities, and establishing incentive and compensation plans that reward employees for their performance. The legal department puts in place support processes that ensure that the firm is in compliance with the rules and regulations under which the business operates. The Accounting function supports processes that track how the firm's financial resources are being created and allocated over time, while the Information Systems function is responsible for the movement and processing of data and information needed to make business decisions. Support processes from different functional areas like Accounting, Engineering, Human Resources, and Information Systems are therefore vital to the execution of core processes highlighted in Figure 4.

Operations Strategy

Operations strategy specifies the means by which operations implements corporate strategy and helps to build a customer-driven firm. It links long-term and short-term operations decisions to corporate strategy and develops the capabilities the firm needs to be competitive. It is at the heart of managing processes and supply chains. A firm's internal processes are only building blocks: They need to be organized to ultimately be effective in a competitive environment. Operations strategy is the linchpin that brings these processes together to form supply chains that extend beyond the walls of the firm, encompassing suppliers as well as customers. Since customers constantly desire change, the firm's operations strategy must be driven by the needs of its customers.

Developing a customer-driven operations strategy begins with *corporate strategy*, which, as shown in Figure 5, coordinates the firm's overall goals with its core processes. It determines the markets the firm will serve and the responses the firm will make to changes in the environment. It provides the resources to develop the firm's core competencies and core processes, and it identifies the strategy the firm will employ in international markets. Based on corporate strategy, a *market analysis* categorizes the firm's customers, identifies their needs, and assesses competitors' strengths. This information is used to develop *competitive priorities.* These priorities help managers develop the services or products and the processes needed to be competitive in the

---

core process

A set of activities that delivers value to external customers.

supplier relationship process

A process that selects the suppliers of services, materials, and information and facilitates the timely and efficient flow of these items into the firm.

new service/product development process

A process that designs and develops new services or products from inputs received from external customer specifications or from the market in general through the customer relationship process.

order fulfillment process

A process that includes the activities required to produce and deliver the service or product to the external customer.

customer relationship process

A process that identifies, attracts, and builds relationships with external customers, and facilitates the placement of orders by customers, sometimes referred to as *customer relationship management.*

support process

A process that provides vital resources and inputs to the core processes and therefore is essential to the management of the business.

operations strategy

The means by which operations implements the firm's corporate strategy and helps to build a customer-driven firm.

▶ **FIGURE 5**
Connection Between
Corporate Strategy and Key
Operations Management
Decisions

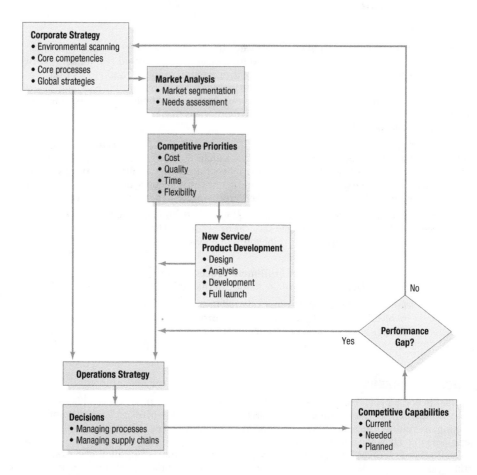

marketplace. Competitive priorities are important to the design of existing as well as new services or products, the processes that will deliver them, and the operations strategy that will develop the firm's capabilities to fulfill them. Developing a firm's operations strategy is a continuous process because the firm's capabilities to meet the competitive priorities must be periodically checked and any gaps in performance must be addressed in the operations strategy.

Corporate Strategy

Corporate strategy provides an overall direction that serves as the framework for carrying out all the organization's functions. It specifies the business or businesses the company will pursue, isolates new opportunities and threats in the environment, and identifies growth objectives.

Developing a corporate strategy involves four considerations: (1) monitoring and adjusting to changes in the business environment, (2) identifying and developing the firm's core competencies, (3) developing the firm's core processes, and (4) developing the firm's global strategies.

Environmental Scanning   The external business environment in which a firm competes changes continually and an organization needs to adapt to those changes. Adaptation begins with *environmental scanning*, the process by which managers monitor trends in the environment (e.g., the industry, the marketplace, and society) for potential opportunities or threats. A crucial reason for environmental scanning is to stay ahead of the competition. Competitors may be gaining an edge by broadening service or product lines, improving quality, or lowering costs. New entrants into the market or competitors that offer substitutes for a firm's service or product may threaten continued profitability. Other important environmental concerns include economic trends, technological changes, political conditions, social changes (i.e., attitudes toward work), and the availability of vital resources. For example, car manufacturers recognize that dwindling oil reserves will eventually require alternative fuels for their cars. Consequently, they have designed prototype cars that use hydrogen or electric power as supplements to gasoline as a fuel.

Developing Core Competencies   Good managerial skill alone cannot overcome environmental changes. Firms succeed by taking advantage of what they do particularly well—that is, the organization's unique strengths. **Core competencies** are the unique resources and strengths that an organization's management considers when formulating strategy. They reflect the collective learning of the organization, especially in how to coordinate processes and integrate technologies. These competencies include the following:

1. *Workforce.* A well-trained and flexible workforce allows organizations to respond to market needs in a timely fashion. This competency is particularly important in service organizations, where customers come in direct contact with employees.

2. *Facilities.* Having well-located facilities (offices, stores, and plants) is a primary advantage because of the long **lead time** needed to build new ones. In addition, flexible facilities that can handle a variety of services or products at different levels of volume provide a competitive advantage.

3. *Market and Financial Know-How.* An organization that can easily attract capital from stock sales, market and distribute its services or products, or differentiate them from similar services or products on the market has a competitive edge.

4. *Systems and Technology.* Organizations with expertise in information systems have an edge in industries that are data intensive, such as banking. Particularly advantageous is expertise in Internet technologies and applications, such as business-to-consumer and business-to-business systems. Having the patents on a new technology is also a big advantage.

core competencies
The unique resources and strengths that an organization's management considers when formulating strategy.

lead time
The elapsed time between the receipt of a customer order and filling it.

Developing Core Processes   A firm's core competencies should drive its core processes: customer relationship, new service/product development, order fulfillment, and supplier relationship. Many companies have all four processes, while others focus on a subset of them to better match their core competencies, since they find it difficult to be good at all four processes and still be competitive. For instance, in the credit card business within the banking industry, some companies primarily specialize in finding customers and maintaining relationships with them. American Airlines's credit card program reaches out and achieves a special affinity to customers through its marketing database. On the other hand, specialized credit card companies, such as CapitalOne, focus on service innovation by creating new features and pricing programs. Finally, many companies are taking over the order fulfillment process by managing the processing of credit card transactions and call centers. The important point is that every firm must evaluate its core competencies and choose to focus on those processes that provide it the greatest competitive strength.

Global Strategies   Identifying opportunities and threats today requires a global perspective. A global strategy may include buying foreign services or parts, combating threats from foreign competitors, or planning ways to enter markets beyond traditional national boundaries. Although warding off threats from global competitors is necessary, firms should also actively seek to penetrate foreign markets. Two effective global strategies are (1) strategic alliances and (2) locating abroad.

One way for a firm to open foreign markets is to create a *strategic alliance.* A strategic alliance is an agreement with another firm that may take one of three forms. One form of strategic alliance is the *collaborative effort,* which often arises when one firm has core competencies that another needs but is unwilling (or unable) to duplicate. Such arrangements commonly arise out of buyer–supplier relationships.

The popular smiling red bee, the mascot of Jollibee, welcomes customers at an outlet in Manila. What began from a two ice cream parlors in Manila in 1975, Jollibee has grown into the biggest Philippines fast-food company employing over 26,000 people in over 1,000 stores in seven countries. By catering to local tastes and preferences, Jollibee took 65 percent of the fiercely competitive Philippine fast-food market, pushing the world giant McDonald's into second place.

Romeo Gacad/AFP/Getty Images/Newscom

Another form of strategic alliance is the *joint venture,* in which two firms agree to produce a service or product jointly. This approach is often used by firms to gain access to foreign markets. For example, to get access to the large Chinese market, General Motors (GM) and Volkswagen (VW) each developed joint ventures with Shanghai Automotive Industry Corporation or SAIC.[2] The Chinese partner is a large manufacturer of automobiles, producing more than 600,000 cars with GM and VW. In 2010, SAIC upped its total share to 51% in Shanghai GM, which is now among the top three passenger vehicle producers in mainland China. Finally, *technology licensing* is a form of strategic alliance in which one company licenses its service or production methods to another. Licenses may be used to gain access to foreign markets.

Another way to enter global markets is to locate operations in a foreign country. However, managers must recognize that what works well in their home country might not work well elsewhere. The economic and political environment or customers' needs may be significantly different. For example, the family-owned chain Jollibee Foods Corporation has become the dominant fast-food chain in the Philippines by catering to a local preference for sweet and spicy flavors, which it incorporates into its fried chicken, spaghetti, and burgers. Jollibee's strength is its creative marketing programs and an understanding of local tastes and claims that its burger is similar to the one a Filipino would cook at home. McDonald's responded by introducing its own Filipino-style spicy burger, but competition is stiff. This example shows that to be successful, corporate strategies must recognize customs, preferences, and economic conditions in other countries.

Locating abroad is a key decision in the design of supply chains because it affects the flow of materials, information, and employees in support of the firm's core processes.

Market Analysis

One key to successfully formulating a customer-driven operations strategy for both service and manufacturing firms is to understand what the customer wants and how to provide it. A *market analysis* first divides the firm's customers into market segments and then identifies the needs of each segment. In this section, we examine the process of market analysis and we define and discuss the concepts of market segmentation and needs assessment.

Market Segmentation *Market segmentation* is the process of identifying groups of customers with enough in common to warrant the design and provision of services or products that the group wants and needs. To identify market segments, the analyst must determine the characteristics that clearly differentiate each segment. The company can then develop a sound marketing program and an effective operating strategy to support it. For instance, The Gap, Inc., a major provider of casual clothes, targets teenagers and young adults while the parents or guardians of infants through 12-year-olds are the primary targets for its GapKids stores. At one time, managers thought of customers as a homogeneous mass market, but now realize that two customers may use the same product for different reasons. Identifying the key factors in each market segment is the starting point in devising a customer-driven operations strategy.

Needs Assessment The second step in market analysis is to make a *needs assessment,* which identifies the needs of each segment and assesses how well competitors are addressing those needs. Each market segment's needs can be related to the service or product and its supply chain. Market needs should include both the tangible and intangible attributes and features of products and services that a customer desires. Market needs may be grouped as follows:

- *Service or Product Needs.* Attributes of the service or product, such as price, quality, and degree of customization.
- *Delivery System Needs.* Attributes of the processes and the supporting systems, and resources needed to deliver the service or product, such as availability, convenience, courtesy, safety, accuracy, reliability, delivery speed, and delivery dependability.
- *Volume Needs.* Attributes of the demand for the service or product, such as high or low volume, degree of variability in volume, and degree of predictability in volume.
- *Other Needs.* Other attributes, such as reputation and number of years in business, after-sale technical support, ability to invest in international financial markets, and competent legal services.

---

[2]Alex Taylor, "Shanghai Auto Wants to Be the World's Next Great Car Company," *Fortune* (October 4, 2004), pp. 103–110.

Once it makes this assessment, the firm can incorporate the needs of customers into the design of the service or product and the supply chain that must deliver it.

Competitive Priorities and Capabilities

A customer-driven operations strategy requires a cross-functional effort by all areas of the firm to understand the needs of the firm's external customers and to specify the operating capabilities the firm requires to outperform its competitors. Such a strategy also addresses the needs of internal customers because the overall performance of the firm depends upon the performance of its core and supporting processes, which must be coordinated to provide the overall desirable outcome for the external customer.

Competitive priorities are the critical operational dimensions a process or supply chain must possess to satisfy internal or external customers, both now and in the future. Competitive priorities are planned for processes and the supply chain created from them. They must be present to maintain or build market share or to allow other internal processes to be successful. Not all competitive priorities are critical for a given process; management selects those that are most important. **Competitive capabilities** are the cost, quality, time, and flexibility dimensions that a process or supply chain actually possesses and is able to deliver. When the capability falls short of the priority attached to it, management must find ways to close the gap or else revise the priority.

We focus on nine broad competitive priorities that fall into the four capability groups of cost, quality, time, and flexibility. Table 1 provides definitions and examples of these competitive priorities, as well as how firms achieve them at the process level.

At times, management may emphasize a cluster of competitive priorities together. For example, many companies focus on the competitive priorities of delivery speed and development speed for their processes, a strategy called **time-based competition**. To implement the strategy, managers carefully define the steps and time needed to deliver a service or produce a product and then critically analyze each step to determine whether they can save time without hurting quality.

To link to corporate strategy, management assigns selected competitive priorities to each process (and the supply chains created from them) that are consistent with the needs of external as well as internal customers. Competitive priorities may change over time. For example, consider a high-volume standardized product, such as color ink-jet desktop printers. In the early stages of the ramp-up period when the printers had just entered the mass market, the manufacturing processes required consistent quality, delivery speed, and volume flexibility. In the later stages of the ramp-up when demand was high, the competitive priorities became low-cost operations, consistent quality, and on-time delivery. Competitive priorities must change and evolve over time along with changing business conditions and customer preferences.

Order Winners and Qualifiers

Competitive priorities focus on what operations can do to help a firm be more competitive, and are in response to what the market wants. Another useful way to examine a firm's ability to be successful in the marketplace is to identify the order winners and order qualifiers. An **order winner** is a criterion that customers use to differentiate the services or products of one firm from those of another. Order winners can include price (which is supported by low-cost operations) and other dimensions of quality, time, and flexibility. However, order winners also include criteria not directly related to the firm's operations, such as after-sale support (Are maintenance service contracts available? Is there a return policy?); technical support (What help do I get if something goes wrong? How knowledgeable are the technicians?); and reputation (How long has this company been in business? Have other customers been satisfied with the service or product?). It may take good performance on a subset of the order-winner criteria, cutting across operational as well as nonoperational criteria, to make a sale.

Order winners are derived from the considerations customers use when deciding which firm to purchase a service or product from in a given market segment. Sometimes customers demand a certain level of demonstrated performance before even contemplating a service or product.

competitive priorities
The critical dimensions that a process or supply chain must possess to satisfy its internal or external customers, both now and in the future.

competitive capabilities
The cost, quality, time, and flexibility dimensions that a process or supply chain actually possesses and is able to deliver.

time-based competition
A strategy that focuses on the competitive priorities of delivery speed and development speed.

The lavish interior lobby decor of the Ritz Carlton resort in Palm Beach, Florida, USA

America/Alamy

order winner
A criterion customers use to differentiate the services or products of one firm from those of another.

TABLE 1 | DEFINITIONS, PROCESS CONSIDERATIONS, AND EXAMPLES OF COMPETITIVE PRIORITIES

Cost	Definition	Processes Considerations	Example
1. **Low-cost operations**	Delivering a service or a product at the lowest possible cost to the satisfaction of external or internal customers of the process or supply chain	To reduce costs, processes must be designed and operated to make them efficient using rigorous process analysis that addresses workforce, methods, scrap or rework, overhead, and other factors, such as investments in new automated facilities or technologies to lower the cost per unit of the service or product.	**Costco** achieves low costs by designing all processes for efficiency, stacking products on pallets in warehouse-type stores, and negotiating aggressively with their suppliers. Costco can provide low prices to its customers because they have designed operations for low cost.
Quality			
2. **Top quality**	Delivering an outstanding service or product	To deliver top quality, a service process may require a high level of customer contact, and high levels of helpfulness, courtesy, and availability of servers. It may require superior product features, close tolerances, and greater durability from a manufacturing process.	**Rolex** is known globally for creating precision timepieces.
3. **Consistent quality**	Producing services or products that meet design specifications on a consistent basis	Processes must be designed and monitored to reduce errors, prevent defects, and achieve similar outcomes over time, regardless of the "level" of quality.	**McDonald's** standardizes work methods, staff training processes, and procurement of raw materials to achieve the same consistent product and process quality from one store to the next.
Time			
4. **Delivery speed**	Quickly filling a customer's order	Design processes to reduce lead time (elapsed time between the receipt of a customer order and filling it) through keeping backup capacity cushions, storing inventory, and using premier transportation options.	**Dell** engineered its customer relationship, order fulfillment, and supplier relationship processes to create an integrated and an agile supply chain that delivers reliable and inexpensive computers to its customers with short lead times.
5. **On-time delivery**	Meeting delivery-time promises	Along with processes that reduce lead time, planning processes (forecasting, appointments, order promising, scheduling, and capacity planning) are used to increase percent of customer orders shipped when promised (95% is often a typical goal).	**United Parcel Services (UPS)** uses its expertise in logistics and warehousing processes to deliver a very large volume of shipments on-time across the globe.
6. **Development speed**	Quickly introducing a new service or a product	Processes aim to achieve cross-functional integration and involvement of critical external suppliers in the service or product development process.	**Zara** is known for its ability to bring fashionable clothing designs from the runway to market quickly.
Flexibility			
7. **Customization**	Satisfying the unique needs of each customer by changing service or product designs	Processes with a customization strategy typically have low volume, close customer contact, and an ability to reconfigure processes to meet diverse types of customer needs.	**Ritz Carlton** customizes services to individual guest preferences.
8. **Variety**	Handling a wide assortment of services or products efficiently	Processes supporting variety must be capable of larger volumes than processes supporting customization. Services or products are not necessarily unique to specific customers and may have repetitive demands.	**Amazon.com** uses information technology and streamlined customer relationship and order fulfillment processes to reliably deliver a vast variety of items to its customers.
9. **Volume flexibility**	Accelerating or decelerating the rate of production of services or products quickly to handle large fluctuations in demand	Processes must be designed for excess capacity and excess inventory to handle demand fluctuations that can vary in cycles from days to months. This priority could also be met with a strategy that adjusts capacity without accumulation of inventory or excess capacity.	**The United States Post Office (USPS)** can have severe demand peak fluctuations at large postal facilities where processes are flexibly designed for receiving, sorting, and dispatching mail to numerous branch locations.

Minimal level required from a set of criteria for a firm to do business in a particular market segment is called an **order qualifier**. Fulfilling the order qualifier will not ensure competitive success; it will only position the firm to compete in the market. From an operations perspective, understanding which competitive priorities are order qualifiers and which ones are order winners is important for the investments made in the design and management of processes and supply chains.

order qualifier
Minimal level required from a set of criteria for a firm to do business in a particular market segment.

Figure 6 shows how order winners and qualifiers are related to achieving the competitive priorities of a firm. If a minimum threshold level is not met for an order-qualifying dimension (consistent quality, for example) by a firm, then it would get disqualified from even being considered further by its customers. For example, there is a level of quality consistency that is minimally tolerable by customers in the auto industry. When the subcompact car Yugo built by Zastava Corporation could not sustain the minimal level of quality, consistency, and reliability expected by customers, it had to exit the U.S. car market in 1991 despite offering very low prices (order winner) of under $4,000. However, once the firm qualifies by attaining consistent quality beyond the threshold, it may only gain additional sales at a very low rate by investing further in improving that order-qualifying dimension. In contrast, for an order-winning dimension (i.e., low price driven by low-cost operations), a firm can reasonably expect to gain appreciably greater sales and market share by continuously lowering its prices as long as the order qualifier (i.e., consistent quality) is being adequately met. Toyota Corolla and Honda Civic have successfully followed this route in the marketplace to become leaders in their target market segment.

▲ FIGURE 6
Relationship of Order Winners and Order Qualifiers to Competitive Priorities

Order winners and qualifiers are often used in competitive bidding. For example, before a buyer considers a bid, suppliers may be required to document their ability to provide consistent quality as measured by adherence to the design specifications for the service or component they are supplying (order qualifier). Once qualified, the supplier may eventually be selected by the buyer on the basis of low prices (order winner) and the reputation of the supplier (order winner).

Using Competitive Priorities: An Airline Example

To get a better understanding of how companies use competitive priorities, let us look at a major airline. We will consider two market segments: (1) first-class passengers and (2) coach passengers. Core services for both market segments are ticketing and seat selection, baggage handling, and transportation to the customer's destination. The peripheral services are quite different across the two market segments. First-class passengers require separate airport lounges; preferred treatment during check-in, boarding, and deplaning; more comfortable seats; better meals and beverages; more personal attention (cabin attendants who refer to customers by name); more frequent service from attendants; high levels of courtesy; and low volumes of passengers (adding to the feeling of being special). Coach passengers are satisfied with standardized services (no surprises), courteous flight attendants, and low prices. Both market segments expect the airline to hold to its schedule. Consequently, we can say that the competitive priorities for the

One of the competitive priorities of airline companies is on-time delivery of their services. Being able to repair and maintain planes rapidly to avoid delays is a crucial aspect of this.

first-class segment are *top quality* and *on-time delivery*, whereas the competitive priorities for the coach segment are *low-cost operations, consistent quality,* and *on-time delivery.*

The airline knows what its collective capabilities must be as a firm, but how does that get communicated to each of its core processes? Let us focus on the four core processes: (1) customer relationship, (2) new service/product development, (3) order fulfillment, and (4) supplier relationship. Competitive priorities are assigned to each core process to achieve the service required to provide complete customer satisfaction. Table 2 shows some possible assignments, just to give you an idea of how this works.

TABLE 2 | COMPETITIVE PRIORITIES ACROSS DIFFERENT CORE PROCESSES FOR AN AIRLINE

	CORE PROCESSES			
Priority	Supplier Relationship	New Service Development	Order Fulfillment	Customer Relationship
Low Cost Operations	Costs of acquiring inputs must be kept to a minimum to allow for competitive pricing.		Airlines compete on price and must keep operating costs in check.	
Top Quality		New services must be carefully designed because the future of the airline industry depends on them.	High quality meal and beverage service delivered by experienced cabin attendants ensures that the service provided to first-class passengers is kept top notch.	High levels of customer contact and lounge service for the first-class passengers.
Consistent Quality	Quality of the inputs must adhere to the required specifications. In addition, information provided to suppliers must be accurate.		Once the quality level is set, it is important to achieve it every time.	The information and service must be error free.
Delivery Speed				Customers want immediate information regarding flight schedules and other ticketing information.
On time delivery	Inputs must be delivered to tight schedules.		The airline strives to arrive at destinations on schedule, otherwise passengers might miss connections to other flights.	
Development Speed		It is important to get to the market fast to preempt the competition.		
Customization		The process must be able to create unique services.		
Variety	Many different inputs must be acquired, including maintenance items, meals and beverages.		Maintenance operations are required for a variety of aircraft models.	The process must be capable of handling the service needs of all market segments and promotional programs.
Volume Flexibility	The process must be able to handle variations in supply quantities efficiently.			

Operations Strategy as a Pattern of Decisions

Operations strategy translates service or product plans and competitive priorities for each market segment into decisions affecting the supply chains that support those market segments. Even if it is not formally stated, the current operations strategy for any firm is really the pattern of decisions that have been made for its processes and supply chains. As we have previously seen in Figure 5, corporate strategy provides the umbrella for key operations management decisions that contribute to the development of the firm's ability to compete successfully in the marketplace. Once managers determine the competitive priorities for a process, it is necessary to assess the *competitive capabilities* of the process. Any gap between a competitive priority and the capability to achieve that competitive priority must be closed by an effective operations strategy.

Developing capabilities and closing gaps is the thrust of operations strategy. To demonstrate how this works, suppose the management of a bank's credit card division decides to embark on a marketing campaign to significantly increase its business, while keeping costs low. A key process in this division is billing and payments. The division receives credit transactions from the merchants, pays the merchants, assembles and sends the bills to the credit card holders, and processes payments. The new marketing effort is expected to significantly increase the volume of bills and payments. In assessing the capabilities, the process must have to serve the bank's customers and to meet the challenges of the new market campaign; management assigns the following competitive priorities for the billing and payments process:

- *Low-Cost Operations.* It is important to maintain low costs in the processing of the bills because profit margins are tight.
- *Consistent Quality.* The process must consistently produce bills, make payments to the merchants, and record payments from the credit card holders accurately.
- *Delivery Speed.* Merchants want to be paid for the credit purchases quickly.
- *Volume Flexibility.* The marketing campaign is expected to generate many more transactions in a shorter period of time.

Management assumed that customers would avoid doing business with a bank that could not produce accurate bills or payments. Consequently, consistent quality is an order qualifier for this process.

Is the billing and payment process up to the competitive challenge? Table 3 shows how to match capabilities to priorities and uncover any gaps in the credit card division's operations strategy. The procedure for assessing an operations strategy begins with identifying good measures for each priority. The more quantitative the measures are, the better. Data are gathered for each measure to determine the current capabilities of the process. Gaps are identified by comparing each capability to management's target values for the measures, and unacceptable gaps are closed by appropriate actions.

The credit card division shows significant gaps in the process's capability for low-cost operations. Management's remedy is to redesign the process in ways that reduce costs but will not impair the other competitive priorities. Likewise, for volume flexibility, management realized that a high level of utilization is not conducive for processing quick surges in volumes while maintaining delivery speed. The recommended actions will help build a capability for meeting more volatile demands.

TABLE 3 | OPERATIONS STRATEGY ASSESSMENT OF THE BILLING AND PAYMENT PROCESS

Competitive Priority	Measure	Capability	Gap	Action
Low-cost operations	■ Cost per billing statement ■ Weekly postage	■ $0.0813 ■ $17,000	■ Target is $0.06 ■ Target is $14,000	■ Eliminate microfilming and storage of billing statements ■ Develop Web-based process for posting bills
Consistent quality	■ Percent errors in bill information ■ Percent errors in posting payments	■ 0.90% ■ 0.74%	■ Acceptable ■ Acceptable	■ No action ■ No action
Delivery speed	■ Lead time to process merchant payments	■ 48 hours	■ Acceptable	■ No action
Volume flexibility	■ Utilization	■ 98%	■ Too high to support rapid increase in volumes	■ Acquire temporary employees ■ Improve work methods

Trends in Operations Management

Several trends are currently having a great impact on operations management: productivity improvement; global competition; and ethical, workforce diversity, and environmental issues. Accelerating change in the form of information technology, e-commerce, robotics, and the Internet is dramatically affecting the design of new services and products as well as a firm's sales, order fulfillment, and purchasing processes. In this section, we look at these trends and their challenges for operations managers.

Productivity Improvement

Productivity is a basic measure of performance for economies, industries, firms, and processes. Improving productivity is a major trend in operations management because all firms face pressures to improve their processes and supply chains so as to compete with their domestic and foreign competitors. **Productivity** is the value of outputs (services and products) produced divided by the values of input resources (wages, cost of equipment, and so on) used:

productivity

The value of outputs (services and products) produced divided by the values of input resources (wages, costs of equipment, and so on).

$$\text{Productivity} = \frac{\text{Output}}{\text{Input}}$$

Manufacturing employment peaked at just below 20 million in mid-1979, and shrunk by nearly 8 million from 1979 to 2011.[3] However, the manufacturing productivity in the United States has climbed steadily, as more manufacturing capacity and output has been achieved efficiently with a leaner work force. It is interesting and even surprising to compare productivity improvements in the service and manufacturing sectors. In the United States, employment in the service sector has grown rapidly, outstripping the manufacturing sector. It now employs about 90 percent of the workforce. But service-sector productivity gains have been much lower. If productivity growth in the service sector stagnates, so does the overall standard of living regardless of which part of the world you live in. Other major industrial countries, such as Japan and Germany, are experiencing the same problem. Yet, signs of improvement are appearing. The surge of investment across national boundaries can stimulate productivity gains by exposing firms to greater competition. Increased investment in information technology by service providers also increases productivity.

Measuring Productivity As a manager, how do you measure the productivity of your processes? Many measures are available. For example, value of output can be measured by what the customer pays or simply by the number of units produced or customers served. The value of inputs can be judged by their cost or simply by the number of hours worked.

Managers usually pick several reasonable measures and monitor trends to spot areas needing improvement. For example, a manager at an insurance firm might measure office productivity as the number of insurance policies processed per employee per week. A manager at a carpet company might measure the productivity of installers as the number of square yards of carpet installed per hour. Both measures reflect *labor productivity*, which is an index of the output per person or per hour worked. Similar measures may be used for *machine productivity*, where the denominator is the number of machines. Accounting for several inputs simultaneously is also possible. *Multifactor productivity* is an index of the output provided by more than one of the resources used in production; it may be the value of the output divided by the sum of labor, materials, and overhead costs. Here is an example:

EXAMPLE 1	Productivity Calculations

MyOMLab

Tutor 1.1 in MyOMLab provides a new example for calculating productivity.

Calculate the productivity for the following operations:

a. Three employees process 600 insurance policies in a week. They work 8 hours per day, 5 days per week.

b. A team of workers makes 400 units of a product, which is sold in the market for $10 each. The accounting department reports that for this job the actual costs are $400 for labor, $1,000 for materials, and $300 for overhead.

---

[3] Paul Wiseman, "Despite China's Might, US Factories Maintain Edge," *The State* and *The Associated Press* (January 31, 2011).

SOLUTION

a. Labor productivity $= \dfrac{\text{Policies processed}}{\text{Employee hours}}$

$= \dfrac{600 \text{ policies}}{(3 \text{ employees})(40 \text{ hours/employee})} = 5 \text{ policies/hour}$

b. Multifactor productivity $= \dfrac{\text{Value of output}}{\text{Labor cost} + \text{Materials cost} + \text{Overhead cost}}$

$= \dfrac{(400 \text{ units})(\$10/\text{unit})}{\$400 + \$1{,}000 + \$300} = \dfrac{\$4{,}000}{\$1{,}700} = 2.35$

DECISION POINT

We want multifactor productivity to be as high as possible. These measures must be compared with performance levels in prior periods and with future goals. If they do not live up to expectations, the process should be investigated for improvement opportunities.

The Role of Management The way processes are managed plays a key role in productivity improvement. Managers must examine productivity from the level of the supply chain because it is the collective performance of individual processes that makes the difference. The challenge is to increase the value of output relative to the cost of input. If processes can generate more output or output of better quality using the same amount of input, productivity increases. If they can maintain the same level of output while reducing the use of resources, productivity also increases.

Global Competition

Most businesses realize that, to prosper, they must view customers, suppliers, facility locations, and competitors in global terms. Firms have found that they can increase their market penetration by locating their production facilities in foreign countries because it gives them a local presence that reduces customer aversion to buying imports. Globalization also allows firms to balance cash flows from other regions of the world when economic conditions are less robust in the home country. Sonoco, a $4-billion-a-year industrial and consumer packaging company in Hartsville, South Carolina, has 335 locations worldwide in Australia, China, Europe, Mexico, New Zealand, and Russia, with 41 industrial product manufacturing facilities and 6 paper mills in Europe alone. These global operations resulted in international sales and income growth even as domestic sales were stumbling during 2007. How did Sonoco do it?[4] Locating operations in countries with favorable tax laws is one reason. Lower tax rates in Italy and Canada helped in padding the earnings margin. Another reason was a weak dollar, whereby a $46 million boost came from turning foreign currencies into dollars as Sonoco exported such items as snack bag packaging, and tubes and cores used to hold tape and textiles, to operations it owned in foreign countries. The exchange

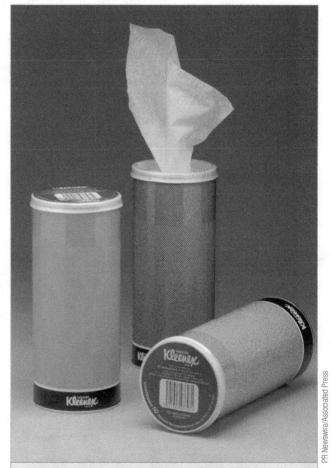

Sonoco is a leading global manufacturer of industrial and consumer packaging goods with more than 300 locations in 35 countries serving 85 nations.

PR Newswire/Associated Press

---

[4] Ben Werner, "Sonoco Holding Its Own," *The State* (February 7, 2008); **www.sonoco.com,** 2008.

rate difference was more than enough to counter the added expense of increased raw materials, shipping, and energy costs in the United States.

Most products today are composites of materials and services from all over the world. Your Gap polo shirt is sewn in Honduras from cloth cut in the United States. Sitting in a Cineplex theater (Canadian), you munch a Nestle's Crunch bar (Swiss) while watching a Columbia Pictures movie (Japanese). Five developments spurred the need for sound global strategies: (1) improved transportation and communications technologies, (2) loosened regulations on financial institutions, (3) increased demand for imported services and goods, (4) reduced import quotas and other international trade barriers due to the formation of regional trading blocks, such as the European Union (EU) and the North American Free Trade Agreement (NAFTA), and (5) comparative cost advantages.

Comparative Cost Advantages   China and India have traditionally been the sources for low-cost, but skilled, labor, even though the cost advantage is diminishing as these countries become economically stronger. In the late 1990s, companies manufactured products in China to grab a foothold in a huge market, or to get cheap labor to produce low-tech products despite doubts about the quality of the workforce and poor roads and rail systems. Today, however, China's new factories, such as those in the Pudong industrial zone in Shanghai, produce a wide variety of products that are sold overseas in the United States and other regions of the world. U.S. manufacturers have increasingly abandoned low profit margin sectors like consumer electronics, shoes, and toys to emerging nations such as China and Indonesia. Instead, they are focusing on making expensive goods like computer chips, advanced machinery, and health care products that are complex and which require specialized labor.

Foreign companies have opened tens of thousands of new facilities in China over the past decade. Many goods the United States imports from China now come from foreign-owned companies with operations there. These companies include telephone makers, such as Nokia and Motorola, and nearly all of the big footwear and clothing brands. Many more major manufacturers are there as well. The implications for competition are enormous. Companies that do not have operations in China are finding it difficult to compete on the basis of low prices with companies that do. Instead, they must focus on speed and small production runs.

What China is to manufacturing, India is to service. As with the manufacturing companies, the cost of labor is a key factor. Indian software companies have grown sophisticated in their applications and offer a big advantage in cost. The computer services industry is also affected. Back-office operations are affected for the same reason. Many firms are using Indian companies for accounting and bookkeeping, preparing tax returns, and processing insurance claims. Many tech companies, such as Intel and Microsoft, are opening significant research and development (R&D) operations in India.

Disadvantages of Globalization   Of course, operations in other countries can have disadvantages. A firm may have to relinquish proprietary technology if it turns over some of its component manufacturing to offshore suppliers or if suppliers need the firm's technology to achieve desired quality and cost goals. Political risks may also be involved. Each nation can exercise its sovereignty over the people and property within its borders. The extreme case is nationalization, in which a government may take over a firm's assets without paying compensation. Exxon and other large multinational oil firms are scaling back operations in Venezuela due to nationalization concerns. Further, a firm may actually alienate customers back home if jobs are lost to offshore operations.

Employee skills may be lower in foreign countries, requiring additional training time. South Korean firms moved much of their sports shoe production to low-wage Indonesia and China, but they still manufacture hiking shoes and in-line roller skates in South Korea because of the greater

Shortage of components from suppliers prevented Nintendo from meeting the customer demand for its popular Wii game system.

MANAGERIAL PRACTICE 1 — Japanese Earthquake and its Supply Chain Impact

Northeast Touhoku district of Japan was struck by a set of massive earthquakes on the afternoon of March 11, 2011, which were soon followed by a huge tsunami that sent waves higher than 33 feet in the port city of Sendai 80 miles away and travelling at the speed of a jetliner. At nearly 9.0 on the Richter scale, it was one of the largest recorded earthquakes to hit Japan. It shifted the Earth's axis by 6 inches with an impact that was felt 250 miles inland in Tokyo, and which moved Eastern Japan 13 feet toward North America. Apart from huge loss of life and hazards of nuclear radiation arising from the crippled Daiichi Nuclear Reactors in Fukushima, the damage to the manufacturing plants in Japan exposed the hazards of interconnected global supply chains and their impact on factories located half way around the globe.

The impact of the earthquake was particularly acute on industries that rely on cutting edge electronic parts sourced from Japan. Shin-Etsu Chemical Company is the world's largest producer of silicon wafers and supplies 20 percent of the global capacity. Its centralized plant located 40 miles from the Fukushima nuclear facility was damaged in the earthquake, causing ripple effects at Intel and Toshiba that purchase wafers from Shin-Etsu. Similarly, a shortage of automotive sensors from Hitachi has slowed or halted production of vehicles in Germany, Spain, and France, while Chrysler is reducing overtime at factories in Mexico and Canada to conserve parts from Japan. Even worse, General Motors stopped production altogether at a plant in Louisiana and Ford closed a truck plant in Kentucky due to the quake. The supply of vehicles such as Toyota's Prius and Lexus will be limited in the United States because of production disruptions in its Japanese factories. China has been affected too, where ZTE Corporation is facing shortages of batteries and LCD screens for its cell phones. Similarly, Lenovo in China is looking at reduced

Following the strong earthquakes and tsunami, flames and smoke rise from a petroleum refining plant next to a heating power station in Shiogama, Miyagi Prefecture, northern Japan, about 220 km north of Tokyo.

supplies of components from Japan for assembly of its tablet computers. These disruptions due to reliance on small concentrated network of suppliers in Japan and globally connected production and logistics systems have caused worker layoffs an increase in prices of affected products, and economic losses that have been felt around the world.

Sources: Don Lee and David Pearson, "Disaster in Japan exposes supply chain weakness," *The State* (April 8, 2011), B6-B7; "Chrysler reduces overtime to help Japan," *The Associated Press* (April 8, 2011) printed in *The State* (April 6, 2011), B7; Krishna Dhir, "From the Editor," *Decision Line*, vol. 42, no. 2, 3.

skills required. In addition, when a firm's operations are scattered globally, customer response times can be longer. These factors should be considered when making decisions about outsourcing. Coordinating components from a wide array of suppliers can be challenging, as Nintendo found out in the production and worldwide distribution of its Wii game systems.[5] Despite twice increasing capacity since April 2007 to 1.8 million Wii's a month, Nintendo could only ship the completed units to retailers like Best Buy, Costco, and Circuit City in limited quantities that did not meet the large demand through the 2007 holiday season and beyond. In addition, as Managerial Practice 1 shows, catastrophic events such as the Japanese earthquake affect production and operations in Europe and United States because connected supply chains can spread disruptions rapidly and quickly across international borders.

Strong global competition affects industries everywhere. For example, U.S. manufacturers of steel, appliances, household durable goods, machinery, and chemicals have seen their market share decline in both domestic and international markets. With the value of world trade in services now at more than $2 trillion per year, banking, data processing, airlines, and consulting services are beginning to face many of the same international pressures. Regional trading blocs, such as EU and NAFTA, further change the competitive landscape in both services and manufacturing. Regardless of which area of the world you live in, the challenge is to produce services or products that can compete in a global market, and to design the processes that can make it happen.

Ethical, Workforce Diversity, and Environmental Issues

Businesses face more ethical quandaries than ever before, intensified by an increasing global presence and rapid technological change. As companies locate new operations and acquire more

---

[5] Peter Svensson, "GameStop to Sell Rain Checks for Wii," *The State* (December 18, 2007).

A Chinese consumer looks at Timberland products at a department store in Shanghai, China, November 11, 2010. Timberland seeks to benefit from rising incomes in the worlds fastest-growing major economy, and will also invest in its Hong Kong shops.

suppliers and customers in other countries, potential ethical dilemmas arise when business is conducted by different rules. Some countries are more sensitive than others about conflicts of interest, bribery, discrimination against minorities and women, minimum-wage levels, and unsafe workplaces. Managers must decide whether to design and operate processes that do more than just meet local standards. In addition, technological change brings debates about data protection and customer privacy. In an electronic world, businesses are geographically far from their customers, so a reputation of trust is paramount.

In the past, many people viewed environmental problems, such as toxic waste, poisoned drinking water, poor air quality, and climate change as quality-of-life issues; now, many people and businesses see them as survival issues. The automobile industry has seen innovation in electric and hybrid cars in response to environmental concerns and economic benefits arising from using less expensive fuels. Industrial nations face a particular burden because their combined populations consume proportionally much larger resources. Just seven nations, including the United States and Japan, produce almost half of all greenhouse gases. Now China and India have added to that total carbon footprint because of their vast economic and manufacturing expansion over the past decade.

Apart from government initiatives, large multinational companies have a responsibility as well for creating environmentally conscious practices, and can do so profitably. For instance, Timberland has over 110 stores in China because of strong demand for its boots, shoes, clothes, and outdoor gear in that country. It highlights its environmental credentials and corporate social responsibility through investments such as the reforestation efforts in northern China's Horqin Desert. Timberland hopes to double the number of stores over the next 3 years by environmentally differentiating itself from the competition.

The challenge is clear: Issues of ethics, workforce diversity, and the environment are becoming part of every manager's job. When designing and operating processes, managers should consider integrity, respect for the individual, and customer satisfaction along with more conventional performance measures such as productivity, quality, cost, and profit.

Operations Management as a Set of Decisions

In this text, we cover the major decisions operations managers make in practice. At the strategic level, operations managers are involved in the development of new capabilities and the maintenance of existing capabilities to best serve the firm's external customers. Operations managers design new processes that have strategic implications, and they are deeply involved in the development and organization of supply chains that link external suppliers and external customers to the firm's internal processes. Operations managers are often responsible for key performance measures such as cost and quality. These decisions have strategic impact because they affect the processes the firm uses to gain a competitive edge.

The operations manager's decisions should reflect corporate strategy. Plans, policies, and actions should be linked to those in other functional areas to support the firm's overall goals and objectives. These links are facilitated by taking a process view of a firm. Regardless of whether you aspire to be an operations manager, or you just want to use the principles of operations management to become a more effective manager, remember that effective management of people, capital, information, and materials is critical to the success of any process and any supply chain.

As you study operations management, keep two principles in mind:

1. Each part of an organization, not just the operations function, must design and operate processes that are part of a supply chain and deal with quality, technology, and staffing issues.

2. Each function of an organization has its own identity and yet is connected with operations through shared processes.

Great strategic decisions lead nowhere if the tactical decisions that support them are wrong. Operations managers are also involved in tactical decisions, including process improvement and performance measurement, managing and planning projects, generating production and staffing plans, managing inventories, and scheduling resources. You will find numerous examples of these decisions, and the implications of making them, throughout this text. You will also learn about the decision-making tools practicing managers use to recognize and define the problem and then choose the best solution.

Computerized Decision-Making Tools

MyOMLab contains a unique set of decision tools we call OM Explorer. This package contains powerful Excel-based computer routines to solve problems often encountered in practice. OM Explorer also has several tutors that provide coaching for all of the difficult analytical techniques in this text, and can be accessed from the drop-down menu. MyOMLab also contains POM for Windows, which is an extensive set of useful decision-making tools to complete your arsenal for solving operations problems, many Active Models (spreadsheets designed to help you learn more about important decision-making techniques), and a spreadsheet-based simulation package called SimQuick.

MyOMLab

Addressing the Challenges in Operations Management

How can firms meet challenges today and in the future? One way is to recognize challenges as opportunities to improve existing processes and supply chains or to create new, innovative ones. The management of processes and supply chains goes beyond designing them; it requires the ability to ensure they achieve their goals. Firms should manage their processes and supply chains to maximize their competitiveness in the markets they serve. We share this philosophy of operations management, as illustrated in Figure 7. We use this figure at the start of each chapter to show how the topic of the chapter fits into our philosophy of operations management. In addition, this text also contains several chapter supplements that are not explicitly shown in Figure 7.

The figure shows that all effective operations decisions follow from a sound operations strategy. Consequently, our text has three major parts: "Part 1: Creating Value through Operations Management," Part 2: "Managing Processes," and "Part 3: Managing Supply Chains." The flow of topics reflects our approach of first understanding how a firm's operations can help provide a solid foundation for competitiveness before tackling the essential process design decisions that will support its strategies. Each part begins with a strategy discussion to support the decisions in that part. Once it is clear how firms design and improve processes, and how they implement those designs, we examine the design and operation of supply chains that link processes, whether they are internal or external to the firm. The performance of the supply chains determines the firm's outcomes, which include the services or products the firm produces, the financial results, and feedback from the firm's customers. These outcomes, which are considered in the firm's strategic plan, are discussed throughout this text.

Supplement "Decision Making," follows this chapter and covers some basic decision techniques.

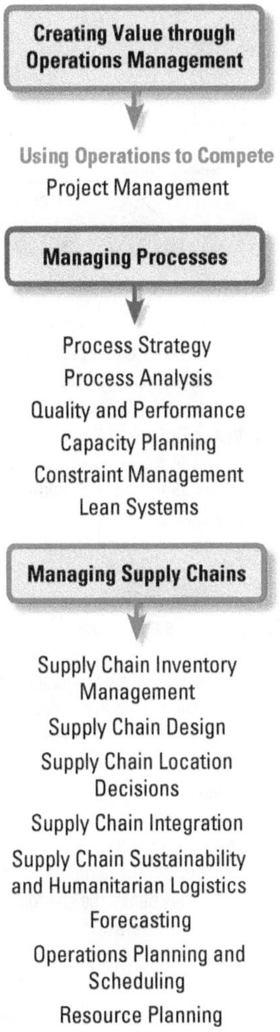

Creating Value through Operations Management

↓

Using Operations to Compete
Project Management

Managing Processes

↓

Process Strategy
Process Analysis
Quality and Performance
Capacity Planning
Constraint Management
Lean Systems

Managing Supply Chains

↓

Supply Chain Inventory Management
Supply Chain Design
Supply Chain Location Decisions
Supply Chain Integration
Supply Chain Sustainability and Humanitarian Logistics
Forecasting
Operations Planning and Scheduling
Resource Planning

▲ FIGURE 7
Managing Processes and Supply Chains

Adding Value with Process Innovation in Supply Chains

It is important to note that the effective operation of a firm and its supply chain is as important as the design and implementation of its processes. Process innovation can make a big difference even in a low-growth industry. Examining processes from the perspective of the value they add is an important part of a successful manager's agenda, as is gaining an understanding of how core processes and related supply chains are linked to their competitive priorities, markets, and the operations strategy of a firm. As illustrated by Progressive Insurance in Managerial Practice 2, who says operations management does not make a difference?

MANAGERIAL PRACTICE 2 — Operational Innovation Is a Competitive Weapon at Progressive Insurance

Progressive Insurance, an automobile insurer that started business in 1937, had approximately $1.3 billion in sales in 1991. By 2011, it was one of the largest U.S. private passenger auto insurance groups with annual premiums in excess of $14 billion. How did it accomplish this amazing growth rate in a 100-year-old industry that traditionally does not experience that sort of growth?

The answer is simple but the implementation was challenging: offer low prices, better service, and more value to customers through operational innovation. *Operational innovation* means designing entirely new processes by dramatically changing the way work is done. For example, Progressive reinvented claims processing to lower costs and increase customer satisfaction and retention. Progressive's agency-dedicated Web site, ForAgentsOnly.com (FAO), lets agents quickly, easily, and securely access payments; view policy, billing, and claims information; and send quote information directly to customers via e-mail. Customers are encouraged to go online to perform routine tasks such as address changes or simple billing inquiries. In addition, Immediate Response Claims Handling allows a claimant to now reach a Progressive representative by telephone 24 hours a day. The representative immediately sends a claims adjuster to inspect the damaged vehicle. The adjuster drives to the vehicle accident site in a mobile claims van, examines the vehicle, prepares an onsite estimate of damage, and if possible, writes a check on the spot. It now takes only 9 hours to complete the cycle, compared with 7–10 days before the changes were made.

The operational innovations to the processes in the customer relationship–order fulfillment supply chain for claims processing produced several benefits. First, claimants received faster service with less hassle, which helped retain them as customers. Second, the shortened cycle time significantly reduced costs. The costs of storing a damaged vehicle and providing a rental car can often wipe out the expected underwriting profit for

Via operational innovations that add value to its products, and catchy promotional advertisements, Progressive Insurance has been able to achieve amazing growth in a low-growth industry.

a six-month policy. This cost becomes significant when you realize that the company processes more than 10,000 claims a day. Third, the new supply chain design requires fewer people for handling the claim, which reduces operational costs. Finally, the operational innovations improved Progressive's ability to detect fraud by arriving on the accident scene quickly and helped to reduce payouts because claimants often accept less money if the payout is quick and hassle-free. Progressive Insurance found a way to differentiate itself in a low-growth industry without compromising profitability, and it accomplished that feat with operational innovation.

Source: Michael Hammer, "Deep Change: How Operational Innovation Can Transform Your Company," *Harvard Business Review* (April 2004), pp. 85–93; http://www.progressive.com/about-progressive-insurance.aspx, 2011.

The topics in this text will help you meet operations challenges and achieve operational innovation regardless of your chosen career path.

LEARNING GOALS IN REVIEW

1 **Describe operations and supply chains in terms of inputs, processes, outputs, information flows, suppliers, and customers.** Review Figure 4 for the important supply chain linkage and information flows. The section "Operations and Supply Chain Management Across the Organization," shows how different functional areas of business come together to create value for a firm.

2 **Define an operations strategy and its linkage to corporate strategy, as well as the role it plays as a source of competitive advantage in a global marketplace.** See the sections on "Operations Strategy" and "Corporate Strategy," and review Figure 5.

3 **Identify nine competitive priorities used in operations strategy, and their linkage to marketing strategy.** The section "Competitive Priorities and Capabilities," discusses the important concept of order winners and qualifiers. Review Table 1 for important

illustrations and examples of how leading edge firms implemented different competitive priorities to create a unique positioning in the marketplace.

4 **Explain how operations can be used as a competitive weapon.** The section "Operations Strategy as a Pattern of Decisions," shows how firms must identify gaps in their competitive priorities and build capabilities through related process and operational changes. Make sure that you review Table 3 that provides a nice illustrative example.

5 **Identify the global trends and challenges facing operations management.** The section "Trends in Operations Management," describes the pressures managers face for achieving productivity improvements, along with managing sustainability and work force diversity related issues in the face of global competition.

MyOMLab helps you develop analytical skills and assesses your progress with multiple problems on labor and multifactor productivity.

MyOMLab Resources	Titles	Link to the Book
Video	*Operations as a Competitive Weapon at Starwood*	A Process View; Operations Strategy as a Pattern of Decisions
Active Model Exercise	1.1 Productivity	Trends in Operations Management; Example 1; Solved Problem 1; Solved Problem 2
OM Explorer Tutors	1.1 Productivity Measures	Trends in Operations Management; Example 1; Solved Problem 1 (p. 24); Solved Problem 2
Tutor Exercises	1.1 Ticket sales	Example 1; Solved Problem 1; Solved Problem 2
Virtual Tours	L'Oréal Cosmetics EDS Industries EDS Services	The Supply Chain View; Trends in Operations Management A Process View; The Supply Chain View A Process View; The Supply Chain View
Internet Exercises	1. Coca-Cola and Nestlé	The Supply Chain View; Operations Strategy as a Pattern of Decisions
	2. Xerox	The Supply Chain View; Competitive Priorities and Capabilities
	3. L'Oréal	A Process View; Trends in Operations Management
	4. Environment, Health, and Safety at Xerox	Trends in Operations Management
Additional Cases	BSB, Inc., The Pizza Wars Come to Campus	A Process View; The Supply Chain View; Competitive Priorities and Capabilities
Key Equations		
Image Library		

Key Equation

1. Productivity is the ratio of output to input:

$$\text{Productivity} = \frac{\text{Output}}{\text{Input}}$$

Key Terms

competitive capabilities
competitive priorities
consistent quality
core competencies
core process
customer relationship process
customization
delivery speed
development speed
external customers
external suppliers
internal customers

internal suppliers
lead time
low-cost operations
nested process
new service/product development
   process
on-time delivery
operation
operations management
operations strategy
order fulfillment process
order qualifier

order winner
process
productivity
supplier relationship process
supply chain
supply chain management
support process
time-based competition
top quality
variety
volume flexibility

Solved Problem 1

Student tuition at Boehring University is $150 per semester credit hour. The state supplements school revenue by $100 per semester credit hour. Average class size for a typical 3-credit course is 50 students. Labor costs are $4,000 per class, materials costs are $20 per student per class, and overhead costs are $25,000 per class.

a. What is the *multifactor* productivity ratio for this course process?

b. If instructors work an average of 14 hours per week for 16 weeks for each 3-credit class of 50 students, what is the *labor* productivity ratio?

SOLUTION

a. Multifactor productivity is the ratio of the value of output to the value of input resources.

$$\text{Value of output} = \left(\frac{50 \text{ students}}{\text{class}}\right)\left(\frac{3 \text{ credit hours}}{\text{students}}\right)\left(\frac{\$150 \text{ tuition} + \$100 \text{ state support}}{\text{credit hour}}\right)$$

$$= \$37,500/\text{class}$$

$$\text{Value of inputs} = \text{Labor} + \text{Materials} + \text{Overhead}$$

$$= \$4,000 + (\$20/\text{student} \times 50 \text{ students/class}) + \$25,000$$

$$= \$30,000/\text{class}$$

$$\text{Multifactor productivity} = \frac{\text{Output}}{\text{Input}} = \frac{\$37,500/\text{class}}{\$30,000/\text{class}} = 1.25$$

b. Labor productivity is the ratio of the value of output to labor hours. The value of output is the same as in part (a), or $37,500/class, so

$$\text{Labor hours of input} = \left(\frac{14 \text{ hours}}{\text{week}}\right)\left(\frac{16 \text{ weeks}}{\text{class}}\right) = 224 \text{ hours/class}$$

$$\text{Labor productivity} = \frac{\text{Output}}{\text{Input}} = \frac{\$37,500/\text{class}}{224 \text{ hours/class}}$$

$$= \$167.41/\text{hour}$$

Solved Problem 2

Natalie Attire makes fashionable garments. During a particular week, employees worked 360 hours to produce a batch of 132 garments, of which 52 were "seconds" (meaning that they were flawed). Seconds are sold for $90 each at Attire's Factory Outlet Store. The remaining 80 garments are sold to retail distribution at $200 each. What is the *labor* productivity ratio of this manufacturing process?

SOLUTION

$$\text{Value of output} = (52 \text{ defective} \times 90/\text{defective}) + (80 \text{ garments} \times 200/\text{garment})$$

$$= \$20,680$$

Labor hours of input = 360 hours

$$\text{Labor productivity} = \frac{\text{Output}}{\text{Input}} = \frac{\$20,680}{360 \text{ hours}}$$

$$= \$57.44 \text{ in sales per hour}$$

Discussion Questions

1. Consider your last (or current) job.

   a. What activities did you perform?

   b. Who were your customers (internal and external), and how did you interact with them?

   c. How could you measure the customer value you were adding by performing your activities?

   d. Was your position in accounting, finance, human resources, management information systems, marketing, operations, or other? Explain.

2. Consider amazon.com, whose Web site enjoys millions of "hits" each day and puts customers in touch with millions of services and products. What are amazon.com's competitive priorities and what should its operations strategy focus on?

3. A local hospital declares that it is committed to provide *care* to patients arriving at the emergency unit in less than 15 minutes and that it will never turn away patients who need to be hospitalized for further medical care. What implications does this commitment have for strategic operations management decisions (i.e., decisions relating to capacity and workforce)?

4. FedEx built its business on quick, dependable delivery of items being shipped by air from one business to another. Its early advantages included global tracking of shipments using Web technology. The advancement of Internet technology enabled competitors to become much more sophisticated in order tracking. In addition, the advent of Web-based businesses put pressure on increased ground transportation deliveries. Explain how this change in the environment has affected FedEx's operations strategy, especially relative to UPS, which has a strong hold on the business-to-consumer ground delivery business.

5. Suppose that you were conducting a market analysis for a new textbook about technology management. What would you need to know to identify a market segment? How would you make a needs assessment? What should be the collection of services and products?

6. Although all nine of the competitive priorities discussed in this chapter are relevant to a company's success in the marketplace, explain why a company should not necessarily try to excel in all of them. What determines the choice of the competitive priorities that a company should emphasize for its key processes?

7. Choosing which processes are core to a firm's competitive position is a key strategic decision. For example, Nike, a popular sports shoe company, focuses on the customer relationship, new product development, and supplier relationship processes and leaves the order fulfillment process to others. Allen Edmonds, a top-quality shoe company, considers all four processes to be core processes. What considerations would you make in determining which processes should be core to your manufacturing company?

8. A local fast-food restaurant processes several customer orders at once. Service clerks cross paths, sometimes nearly colliding, while they trace different paths to fill customer orders. If customers order a special combination of toppings on their hamburgers, they must wait quite some time while the special order is cooked. How would you modify the restaurant's operations to achieve competitive advantage? Because demand surges at lunchtime, volume flexibility is a competitive priority in the fast-food business. How would you achieve volume flexibility?

9. Kathryn Shoemaker established Grandmother's Chicken Restaurant in Middlesburg 5 years ago. It features a unique recipe for chicken, "just like grandmother used to make." The facility is homey, with relaxed and friendly service. Business has been good during the past 2 years, for both lunch and dinner. Customers normally wait about 15 minutes to be served, although complaints about service delays have increased recently. Shoemaker is currently considering whether to expand the current facility or open a similar restaurant in neighboring Uniontown, which has been growing rapidly.

   a. What types of strategic plans must Shoemaker make?

   b. What environmental forces could be at work in Middlesburg and Uniontown that Shoemaker should consider?

   c. What are the possible distinctive competencies of Grandmother's?

10. Wild West, Inc., is a regional telephone company that inherited nearly 100,000 employees and 50,000 retirees from AT&T. Wild West has a new mission: to diversify. It calls for a 10-year effort to enter the financial services, real estate, cable TV, home shopping, entertainment, and cellular communication services markets—and to compete with other telephone companies. Wild West plans to provide cellular and fiber-optic communications services in markets with established competitors, such as the United Kingdom, and in markets with essentially no competition, such as Russia and former Eastern Bloc countries.

   a. What types of strategic plans must Wild West make? Is the "do-nothing" option viable? If Wild West's mission appears too broad, which businesses would you trim first?

   b. What environmental forces could be at work that Wild West should consider?

   c. What are the possible core competencies of Wild West? What weaknesses should it avoid or mitigate?

11. You are designing a grocery delivery business. Via the Internet, your company will offer staples and frozen foods in a large metropolitan area and then deliver them within a customer-defined window of time. You plan to partner with two major food stores in the area. What should be your competitive priorities and what capabilities do you want to develop in your core and support processes?

Problems

The OM Explorer and POM for Windows software is available to all students using the 10th edition of this text. Go to **www.pearsonhighered.com/krajewski** to download these computer packages. If you purchased MyOMLab, you also have access to Active Models software and significant help in doing the following problems. Check with your instructor on how best to use these resources. In many cases, the instructor wants you to understand how to do the calculations by hand. At the least, the software provides a check on your calculations. When calculations are particularly complex and the goal is interpreting the results in making decision, the software entirely replaces the manual calculations.

1. (Refer to Solved Problem 1.) Coach Bjourn Toulouse led the Big Red Herrings to several disappointing football seasons. Only better recruiting will return the Big Red Herrings to winning form. Because of the current state of the program, Boehring University fans are unlikely to support increases in the $192 season ticket price. Improved recruitment will increase overhead costs to $30,000 per class section from the current $25,000 per class section. The university's budget plan is to cover recruitment costs by increasing the average class size to 75 students. Labor costs will increase to $6,500 per 3-credit course. Material costs will be about $25 per student for each 3-credit course. Tuition will be $200 per semester credit, which is supplemented by state support of $100 per semester credit.

   a. What is the multifactor productivity ratio? Compared to the result obtained in Solved Problem 1, did productivity increase or decrease for the course process?

   b. If instructors work an average of 20 hours per week for 16 weeks for each 3-credit class of 75 students, what is the *labor* productivity ratio?

2. Suds and Duds Laundry washed and pressed the following numbers of dress shirts per week.

Week	Work Crew	Total Hours	Shirts
1	Sud and Dud	24	68
2	Sud and Jud	46	130
3	Sud, Dud, and Jud	62	152
4	Sud, Dud, and Jud	51	125
5	Dud and Jud	45	131

   a. Calculate the *labor* productivity ratio for each week.

   b. Explain the labor productivity pattern exhibited by the data.

3. CD players are produced on an automated assembly line process. The standard cost of CD players is $150 per unit (labor, $30; materials, $70; and overhead, $50). The sales price is $300 per unit.

   a. To achieve a 10 percent multifactor productivity improvement by reducing materials costs only, by what percentage must these costs be reduced?

   b. To achieve a 10 percent multifactor productivity improvement by reducing labor costs only, by what percentage must these costs be reduced?

   c. To achieve a 10 percent multifactor productivity improvement by reducing overhead costs only, by what percentage must these costs be reduced?

4. The output of a process is valued at $100 per unit. The cost of labor is $50 per hour including benefits. The accounting department provided the following information about the process for the past four weeks:

	Week 1	Week 2	Week 3	Week 4
Units Produced	1,124	1,310	1,092	981
Labor ($)	12,735	14,842	10,603	9,526
Material ($)	21,041	24,523	20,442	18,364
Overhead ($)	8,992	10,480	8,736	7,848

   a. Use the multifactor productivity ratio to see whether recent process improvements had any effect and, if so, when the effect was noticeable.

   b. Has labor productivity changed? Use the labor productivity ratio to support your answer.

5. Alyssa's Custom Cakes currently sells 5 birthday, 2 wedding, and 3 specialty cakes each month for $50, $150, and $100 each, respectively. The cost of labor is $50 per hour including benefits. It takes 90 minutes to produce a birthday cake, 240 minutes to produce a wedding cake, and 60 minutes to produce a specialty cake. Alyssa's current multifactor productivity ratio is 1.25.

   a. Use the multifactor productivity ratio provided to calculate the average cost of the cakes produced.

   b. Calculate Alyssa's labor productivity ratio in dollars per hour for each type of cake.

   c. Based solely on the labor productivity ratio, which cake should Alyssa try to sell the most?

   d. Based on your answer in part (a), is there a type of cake Alyssa should stop selling?

Advanced Problems

6. The Big Black Bird Company (BBBC) has a large order for special plastic-lined military uniforms to be used in an urgent military operation. Working the normal two shifts of 40 hours each per week, the BBBC production process usually produces 2,500 uniforms per week at a standard cost of $120 each. Seventy employees work the first shift and 30 employees work the second. The contract price is $200 per uniform. Because of the urgent need, BBBC is authorized to use around-the-clock production, 6 days per week. When each of the two shifts works 72 hours per week, production increases to 4,000 uniforms per week but at a cost of $144 each.

   a. Did the multifactor productivity ratio increase, decrease, or remain the same? If it changed, by what percentage did it change?

   b. Did the labor productivity ratio increase, decrease, or remain the same? If it changed, by what percentage did it change?

   c. Did weekly profits increase, decrease, or remain the same?

7. Mack's guitar fabrication shop produces low-cost, highly durable guitars for beginners. Typically, out of the 100 guitars that begin production each month, only 80 percent are considered good enough to sell. The other 20 percent are scrapped due to quality problems that are identified after they have completed the production process. Each guitar sells for $250. Because some of the production process is automated, each guitar only requires 10 labor hours. Each employee works an average 160 hours per month. Labor is paid at $10/hour, materials cost is $40/guitar, and overhead is $4,000.

   a. Calculate the labor and multifactor productivity ratios.

   b. After some study, the operations manager Darren Funk recommends three options to improve the company's multifactor productivity: (1) increase the sales price by 10 percent, (2) improve quality so that only 10 percent are defective, or (3) reduce labor, material, and overhead costs by 10 percent. Which option has the greatest impact on the multifactor productivity measure?

8. Mariah Enterprises makes a variety of consumer electronic products. Its camera manufacturing plant is considering choosing between two different processes, named Alpha and Beta, which can be used to make a component part. To make the correct decision, the managers would like to compare the labor and multifactor productivity of process Alpha with that of process Beta. The value of process output for Alpha and Beta is $175 and $140 per unit, and the corresponding overhead costs are $6,000 and $5,000, respectively.

	PROCESS ALPHA		PROCESS BETA	
Product	A	B	A	B
Output (units)	50	60	30	80
Labor ($)	$1,200	$1,400	$1,000	$2,000
Material ($)	$2,500	$3,000	$1,400	$3,500

   a. Which process, Alpha or Beta, is more productive?

   b. What conclusions can you draw from your analysis?

9. The Morning Brew Coffee Shop sells Regular, Cappuccino, and Vienna blends of coffee. The shop's current daily labor cost is $320, the equipment cost is $125, and the overhead cost is $225. Daily demands, along with selling price and material costs per beverage, are given below.

	Regular Coffee	Cappuccino	Vienna coffee
Beverages sold	350	100	150
Price per beverage	$2.00	$3.00	$4.00
Material ($)	$0.50	$0.75	$1.25

Harald Luckerbauer, the manager at Morning Brew Coffee Shop, would like to understand how adding Eiskaffee (a German coffee beverage of chilled coffee, milk, sweetener, and vanilla ice cream) will alter the shop's productivity. His market research shows that Eiskaffee will bring in new customers and not cannibalize current demand. Assuming that the new equipment is purchased before Eiskaffee is added to the menu, Harald has developed new average daily demand and cost projections. The new equipment cost is $200, and the overhead cost is $350. Modified daily demands, as well as selling price and material costs per beverage for the new product line, are given below.

	Regular Coffee	Cappuccino	Vienna coffee	Eiskaffee
Beverages sold	350	100	150	75
Price per beverage	$2.00	$3.00	$4.00	$5.00
Material ($)	$0.50	$0.75	$1.25	$1.50

   a. Calculate the change in labor and multifactor productivity if Eiskaffee is added to the menu.

   b. If everything else remains unchanged, how many units of Eiskaffee would have to be sold to ensure that the multifactor productivity increases from its current level?

Active Model Exercise

This Active Model appears in MyOMLab. It allows you to evaluate the important elements of labor productivity.

QUESTIONS

1. If the insurance company can process 60 (10 percent) more policies per week, by what percentage will the productivity measure rise?

2. Suppose the 8-hour day includes a 45-minute lunch. What is the revised productivity measure, excluding lunch?

3. If an employee is hired, what will be the weekly number of policies processed if the productivity of five policies per hour is maintained?

4. Suppose that, during the summer, the company works for only 4 days per week. What will be the weekly number of policies processed if the productivity of five policies per hour is maintained?

▶ **ACTIVE MODEL 1.1**
Labor Productivity Using Data from
Example 1

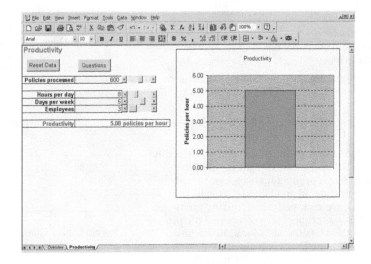

VIDEO CASE | Operations as a Competitive Weapon at Starwood

Starwood is one of the world's largest hotel companies, with more than 750 owned, managed, and franchised properties in more than 80 countries. The company's lodging brands include The Luxury Collection, St. Regis, Sheraton, Westin, Four Points, and W Hotels. Its hotels regularly appear on lists of top hotels around the world. On any given night, guests in the hotels may be individual leisure travelers, independent business guests, or part of a meeting or convention.

In 2002, Starwood standardized its operating processes so that it could measure, improve, and ultimately grow its convention business. Each meeting is assigned a Star Meeting Concierge who works closely with meeting planners.

When guests stay at a Starwood property as part of a meeting or convention, arrangements are typically made by a meeting planner. The meeting planner works with a location to arrange meeting facilities, banquet rooms, lodging, and events for participants. Prior to 2002, the company's individual properties had their own approaches to convention planning, yet no consistent, coordinated program within or across brands made it easy for meeting planners to do business with Starwood. For example, paperwork for confirming program details, rooms, and food and beverage requirements differed between properties and brands. Some hotels had diagrams of meeting space, while others did not. Technology available for meeting rooms varied widely, and a hotel liaison was not always immediately available during the event in case a need arose.

Recognizing that Starwood's future growth and success relied heavily on its relationships with meeting planners, the company held focus groups to gather information about their needs and expectations. One clear priority emerged: consistency in the meeting planning process, whether that meeting was held at the Sheraton in New York, the Westin Kierland in Phoenix, or the W Hotel in Lakeshore, Chicago. Such a program could create consistency across all brands, and generate loyalty and increased revenues from those meeting planners who drive large volumes of business to Starwood properties annually.

As a result of the meetings, Starwood created the Starwood Preferred Planner program. Every hotel property now has the same paperwork for the meeting planning process, and shares that paperwork electronically across properties and brands. Contracts were standardized and new standards created to recognize and reward frequent VIP meeting planners. Each meeting is assigned a "Star Meeting Concierge" whose sole responsibility is to anticipate and fulfill any needs of the meeting planner during the event. Handheld Nextel radio phones are now issued at check-in to the meeting planners at no extra charge so that they have 24-hour access to the concierge.

To measure the performance of the new process, Starwood set high internal targets for scores on the surveys given to meeting planners after their events concluded. For instance, at the Luxury Collection and St. Regis brands, individual meeting scores must be 4.55 on a 5-point scale. At the Westin and W Hotels, scores must be above 4.35 on the 5-point scale. Scores from Sheraton properties must exceed 4.30, and Four Points hotels have a target of 4.25 on the 5-point scale. Because the expectations for an airport location one-day meeting (not held at the St. Regis or Luxury Collection) differ from a multiday resort experience, the targets reflect those expectations.

QUESTIONS

1. What are the key inputs and outputs associated with Starwood's new meeting planning process?
2. How does the meeting planning process at Starwood interact with the following core processes in their hotels?
   a. Customer relationship (internal and external)
   b. New service or product development
   c. Order fulfillment
   d. Supplier relationship

CASE | Chad's Creative Concepts

Chad's Creative Concepts designs and manufactures wood furniture. Founded by Chad Thomas on the banks of Lake Erie in Sandusky, Ohio, the company began by producing custom-made wooden furniture for vacation cabins located along the coast of Lake Erie and on nearby Kelly's Island and Bass Island. Being an "outdoors" type himself, Thomas originally wanted to bring "a bit of the outdoors" inside. Chad's Creative Concepts developed a solid reputation for creative designs and high-quality workmanship. Sales eventually encompassed the entire Great Lakes region. Along with growth came additional opportunities.

Traditionally, the company focused entirely on custom-made furniture, with the customer specifying the kind of wood from which the piece would be made. As the company's reputation grew and sales increased, the sales force began selling some of the more popular pieces to retail furniture outlets. This move into retail outlets led Chad's Creative Concepts into the production of a more standard line of furniture. Buyers of this line were much more price-sensitive and imposed more stringent delivery requirements than did clients for the custom line. Custom-designed furniture, however, continued to dominate sales, accounting for 60 percent of volume and 75 percent of dollar sales. Currently, the company operates a single manufacturing process in Sandusky, where both custom furniture and standard furniture are manufactured. The equipment is mainly general purpose in nature to provide the flexibility needed for producing custom pieces of furniture. The layout puts together saws in one section of the facility, lathes in another, and so on. The quality of the finished product reflects the quality of the wood chosen and the craftsmanship of individual workers. Both custom and standard furniture compete for processing time on the same equipment by the same craftspeople.

During the past few months, sales of the standard line steadily increased, leading to more regular scheduling of this product line. However, when scheduling trade-offs had to be made, custom furniture was always given priority because of its higher sales and profit margins. Thus, scheduled lots of standard furniture pieces were left sitting around the plant in various stages of completion.

As he reviews the progress of Chad's Creative Concepts, Thomas is pleased to note that the company has grown. Sales of custom furniture remain strong, and sales of standard pieces are steadily increasing. However, finance and accounting indicate that profits are not what they should be. Costs associated with the standard line are rising. Dollars are being tied up in inventory, both in raw materials and work-in-process. Expensive public ware-

house space has to be rented to accommodate the inventory volume. Thomas also is concerned with increased lead times for both custom and standard orders, which are causing longer promised delivery times. Capacity is being pushed, and no space is left in the plant for expansion. Thomas begins a careful assessment of the overall impact that the new standard line is having on his manufacturing process.

QUESTIONS

1. What types of decisions must Chad Thomas make daily for his company's operations to run effectively? Over the long run?
2. How did sales and marketing affect operations when they began to sell standard pieces to retail outlets?
3. How has the move to producing standard furniture affected the company's financial structure?
4. What might Chad Thomas have done differently to avoid some of the problems he now faces?

Source: This case was prepared by Dr. Brooke Saladin, Wake Forest University, as a basis for classroom discussion. Copyright © Brooke Saladin. Used with permission.

Selected References

Chase, Richard B., and Uday M. Apte. "A History of Research in Service Operations: What's the Big Idea?" *Journal of Operations Management*, vol. 25, no. 2 (2007), pp. 375–386.

Collis, David J. and Michael G. Rukstad. "Can You Say What Your Strategy Is?" *Harvard Business Review*, vol. 86, no. 4 (2008), pp. 82–90.

Fitzsimmons, James A., and Mona Fitzsimmons. *Service Management.* New York: McGraw-Hill, 2005.

Gaimon, Cheryl. "The Management of Technology: A Production and Operations Management Perspective." *Production and Operations Management*, vol. 17, no. 1 (2008), pp. 1–11.

Hammer, Michael. "Deep Change: How Operational Innovation Can Transform Your Company." *Harvard Business Review* (April 2004), pp. 85–93.

Heineke, Janelle, and Mark Davis. "The Emergence of Service Operations as an Academic Discipline." *Journal of Operations Management*, vol. 25, no. 2 (2007), pp. 364–374.

Hill, Terry. *Manufacturing Strategy: Text and Cases*, 3rd ed. Homewood, IL: Irwin/McGraw-Hill, 2000.

Huckman, Robert S., and Darren E. Zinner. "Does Focus Improve Operational Performance? Lessons from the Management of Clinical Trials." *Strategic Management Journal*, vol. 29 (2008), pp. 173–193.

Karmarkar, Uday. "Will You Survive the Services Revolution?" *Harvard Business Review*, vol. 82 (2004), pp. 100–108.

Kaplan, Robert S., and David P. Norton. *Balanced Scorecard.* Boston, MA: Harvard Business School Press, 1997.

King Jr., Neil. "A Whole New World." *Wall Street Journal* (September 27, 2004).

Meyer, Christopher and Andre Schwager. "Understanding customer experience." *Harvard Business Review*, vol. 85 (2007), pp. 116–126.

Neilson, Gary L., Karla L. Martin, and Elizabeth Powers. "The secrets to successful strategy execution." *Harvard Business Review*, vol. 86, no. 6 (2008), pp. 60–70.

Pande, Peter S., Robert P. Neuman, and Roland R. Cavanagh. *The Six Sigma Way.* New York: McGraw-Hill, 2000.

Porter, Michael. *Competitive Advantage.* New York: The Free Press, 1987.

Porter, Michael E., and Mark R. Kramer. "Strategy and Society: The Link Between Competitive Advantage and Corporate Social Responsibility." *Harvard Business Review*, vol. 84, no. 12 (2006), pp. 78–92.

Powell, Bill. "It's All Made in China Now." *Fortune* (March 4, 2002), pp. 121–128.

Safizadeh, M. Hossein, Larry P. Ritzman, Deven Sharma, and Craig Wood. "An Empirical Analysis of the Product–Process Matrix." *Management Science*, vol. 42, no. 11 (1996), pp. 1576–1591.

Skinner, Wickham. "Manufacturing—Missing Link in Corporate Strategy." *Harvard Business Review* (May–June 1969), pp. 136–145.

Svensson, Peter. "GameStop to Sell Rain Checks for Wii." *The State* (December 18, 2007).

Voss, Chris, Aleda Roth, and Richard Chase. "Experience, Service Operations Strategy, and Services as Destinations: Foundations and Exploratory Investigation" *Production and Operations Management*, vol. 17, no. 3 (2008), pp. 247–266.

Ward, Peter T., and Rebecca Duray. "Manufacturing Strategy in Context: Environment, Competitive Strategy and Manufacturing Strategy." *Journal of Operations Management*, vol. 18 (2000), pp. 123–138.

Wiseman, Paul. "Despite China's might, US factories maintain edge," *The State* and *The Associated Press* (January 31, 2011).

Womack, James P., Daniel T. Jones, and Daniel Roos. *The Machine That Changed the World.* New York: HarperPerennial, 1991.

PROJECT MANAGEMENT

Two boys slug it out in an Xbox 360 wrestling game at the 2011 IT Show in Singapore.

XBOX 360

Four years after the introduction of Xbox, Microsoft needed to quickly design, develop, and produce a new product. Sony's PlayStation 2 was dominating the video game market and Microsoft needed a new product to compete with the impending release of PlayStation 3. Developing such a product is a project of massive proportions. The project consisted of four phases: (1) design, (2) analysis, (3) development, and (4) launch. The result was Xbox 360.

Design

The design of the Xbox 360 was a collaborative effort between Microsoft and many other firms, including Astro Studios in San Francisco, which designed the overall console and controller; IBM, which designed the processor chip; ATI, which designed the graphics chip; and a host of game design firms to develop games for the new product. A key element of the new product was the built-in Internet access that allowed gamers to access online games, buy game add-ons, and access multiplayer games developed exclusively for Xbox 360. Microsoft also included its primary manufacturers, Flextronics and Wistron, in the design process to optimize the production and assembly of the more than 1,000 parts contained in an Xbox 360.

Analysis

Getting an estimate of future sales for a new product is always difficult; however, in this case, the historic patterns for PlayStation 1, PlayStation 2, and Xbox were useful. Analysts found that the peak year for a PlayStation product was 4 years after its introduction and that the life cycle for those products is about 11 years. This information provided a basis for estimating the sales potential of Xbox 360, although actual sales may be limited due to supply constraints. Nonetheless, Microsoft realized that the potential was there to open a new generation of game consoles well ahead of the market.

Development

Microsoft worked closely with Flextronics, Wistron, and the various design firms to iron out manufacturing problems in the early phases of Xbox 360 production. Once initial production was underway, Microsoft brought on Celestica to add production capacity. The decision was made to focus manufacturing operations in China. All told, 10,000 workers in China would be involved in Xbox 360 production.

Launch

Microsoft's Xbox 360 gained an early lead in terms of market share due, in part, to its early launch date, which was one year ahead of its rivals PlayStation 3 and Wii. All told, the product was released in 36 countries in the first year of production, a Herculean effort requiring extensive coordination and a high level of project management skill. Sales of the Xbox 360 exceeded expectations with more than 10 million units sold in the first year alone. Nonetheless, Microsoft experienced difficulties in getting the supply chain to meet customer demands in a timely fashion. The lesson to be learned is that projects can be planned and executed properly; however, the underlying infrastructure that delivers the product is equally important in the ultimate success of the venture.

Source: David Holt, Charles Holloway, and Hau Lee, "Evolution of the Xbox Supply Chain," Stanford Graduate School of Business, Case: GS-49, (April 14, 2006); "Xbox 360," Wikipedia, the free encyclopedia, **http://en.wikipedia.org/wiki/Xbox_360**.

LEARNING GOALS *After reading this chapter, you should be able to:*

1. Define the major activities associated with defining, organizing, planning, monitoring, and controlling projects.

2. Diagram the network of interrelated activities in a project.

3. Identify the sequence of critical activities that determines the duration of a project.

4. Explain how to determine a minimum-cost project schedule.

5. Describe the considerations managers make in assessing the risks in a project and calculate the probability of completing a project on time.

6. Define the options available to alleviate resource problems.

---

project

An interrelated set of activities with a definite starting and ending point, which results in a unique outcome for a specific allocation of resources.

Companies such as Microsoft are experts at managing projects such as Xbox 360. They master the ability to schedule activities and monitor progress within strict time, cost, and performance guidelines. A **project** is an interrelated set of activities with a definite starting and ending point, which results in a unique outcome for a specific allocation of resources.

Projects are common in everyday life as well as in business. Planning weddings, remodeling bathrooms, writing term papers, and organizing surprise parties are examples of small projects in everyday life. Conducting company audits, planning mergers, creating advertising campaigns, reengineering processes, developing new services or products, and establishing a strategic alliance are examples of large projects in business.

The three main goals of any project are (1) complete the project on time or earlier, (2) do not exceed the budget, and (3) meet the specifications to the satisfaction of the customer. When we must undertake projects with some uncertainty involved, it does not hurt to have flexibility with respect to resource availability, deadlines, and budgets. Consequently, projects can be complex and challenging to manage. **Project management**, which is a systemized, phased approach to defining, organizing, planning, monitoring, and controlling projects, is one way to overcome that challenge.

Projects often cut across organizational lines because they need the skills of multiple professions and organizations. Furthermore, each project is unique, even if it is routine, requiring new combinations of skills and resources in the project process. For example, projects for adding a new branch office, installing new computers in a department, or developing a sales promotion may be initiated several times a year. Each project may have been done many times before; however, differences arise with each replication. Uncertainties, such as the advent of new technologies or the activities of competitors, can change the character of projects and require responsive countermeasures. Finally, projects are temporary because personnel, materials, and facilities are organized to complete them within a specified time frame and then are disbanded.

Projects, and the application of project management, facilitate the implementation of strategy. However, the power of this approach goes beyond the focus on one project. Operations strategy initiatives often require the coordination of many interdependent projects. Such a collection of projects is called a **program**, which is an interdependent set of projects with a common strategic purpose. As new project proposals come forward, management must assess their fit to the current operations strategy and ongoing initiatives and have a means to prioritize them because funds for projects are often limited. Projects can be also used to implement changes to processes and supply chains. For example, projects involving the implementation of major information technologies may affect all of a firm's core processes and supporting processes as well as some of their suppliers' and customers' processes. As such, projects are a useful tool for improving processes and supply chains.

Project Management across the Organization

Even though a project may be under the overall purview of a single department, other departments likely should be involved in the project. For example, consider an information systems project to develop a corporate customer database at a bank. Many of the bank's customers are large corporations that require services spanning several departments at the bank. Because no department at the bank knows exactly what services a corporate customer is receiving from other departments, the project would consolidate information about corporate customers from many areas of the bank into one database. From this information, corporate banking services could be designed not only to better serve the corporate customers, but also to provide a basis for evaluating the prices that the bank charges. Marketing is interested in knowing all the services a customer is receiving so that it can package and sell other services that the customer may not be aware of. Finance is interested in how profitable a customer is to the bank and whether the provided services are appropriately priced. The project team, led by the information systems department, should consist of representatives from the marketing and finance departments who have a direct interest in corporate clients. All departments in a firm benefit from sound project management practices, even if the projects remain within the purview of a single department.

Defining and Organizing Projects

A clear understanding of a project's organization and how personnel are going to work together to complete the project are keys to success. In this section, we will address (1) defining the scope and objectives, (2) selecting the project manager and team, and (3) recognizing the organizational structure.

Defining the Scope and Objectives of a Project

A thorough statement of a project's scope, time frame, and allocated resources is essential to managing the project. This statement is often referred to as the *project objective statement*. The scope provides a succinct statement of project objectives and captures the essence of the desired project

project management

A systemized, phased approach to defining, organizing, planning, monitoring, and controlling projects.

program

An interdependent set of projects that have a common strategic purpose.

Creating Value through Operations Management

Using Operations to Compete
Project Management

Managing Processes

Process Strategy
Process Analysis
Quality and Performance
Capacity Planning
Constraint Management
Lean Systems

Managing Supply Chains

Supply Chain Inventory Management
Supply Chain Design
Supply Chain Location Decisions
Supply Chain Integration
Supply Chain Sustainability and Humanitarian Logistics
Forecasting
Operations Planning and Scheduling
Resource Planning

outcomes in the form of major deliverables, which are concrete outcomes of the project. Changes to the scope of a project inevitably increase costs and delay completion. Collectively, changes to scope are called *scope creep* and, in sufficient quantity, are primary causes of failed projects. The time frame for a project should be as specific as possible, as in "the project should be completed by January 1, 2014." Finally, although specifying an allocation of resources to a project may be difficult during the early stages of planning, it is important for managing the project. The allocation should be expressed as a dollar figure or as full-time equivalents of personnel time. A specific statement of allocated resources makes it possible to make adjustments to the scope of the project as it proceeds.

Selecting the Project Manager and Team

Once the project is selected, a project manager must be chosen. The qualities of a good project manager should be well aligned with the roles a project manager must play.

- *Facilitator.* The project manager often must resolve conflicts between individuals or departments to ensure that the project has the appropriate resources for the job to be completed. Successful project managers have good leadership skills and a *systems view*, which encompasses the interaction of the project, its resources, and its deliverables with the firm as a whole.
- *Communicator.* Project progress and requests for additional resources must be clearly communicated to senior management and other stakeholders in a project. The project manager must also frequently communicate with the project team to get the best performance.
- *Decision Maker.* Good project managers will be sensitive to the way the team performs best and be ready to make tough decisions, if necessary. The project manger must organize the team meetings, specify how the team will make decisions, and determine the nature and timing of reports to senior management.

Selecting the project team is just as important as the selection of the project manager. Several characteristics should be considered.

- *Technical Competence.* Team members should have the technical competence required for the tasks to which they will be assigned.
- *Sensitivity.* All team members should be sensitive to interpersonal conflicts that may arise. Senior team members should be politically sensitive to help mitigate problems with upper-level management.
- *Dedication.* Team members should feel comfortable solving project problems that may spill over into areas outside their immediate expertise. They should also be dedicated to getting the project done, as opposed to maintaining a comfortable work schedule.

Recognizing Organizational Structure

The relationship of the project manager to the project team is determined by the firm's organizational structure. Each of the three types of organizational structure described below has its own implications for project management.

- *Functional.* The project is housed in a specific department or functional area, presumably the one with the most interest in the project. Assistance from personnel in other functional areas must be negotiated by the project manager. In such cases, the project manager has less control over project timing than if the entire scope of the project fell within the purview of the department.
- *Pure Project.* The team members work exclusively for the project manager on a particular project. This structure simplifies the lines of authority and is particularly effective for large projects that consist of enough work for each team member to work full time. For small projects, it could result in significant duplication of resources across functional areas.
- *Matrix.* The matrix structure is a compromise between the functional and pure project structures. The project managers of the firm's projects all report to a "program manager" who coordinates resource and technological needs across the functional boundaries. The matrix structure allows each functional area to maintain control over who works on a project and the technology that is used. However, team members, in effect, have two bosses: the project manager and the department manager. Resolving these "line of authority" conflicts requires a strong project manager.

The construction of the 2012 Olympic Stadium in Stratford, East London, required the coordination of materials, equipment, and personnel. Project management techniques played a major role.

Planning Projects

After the project is defined and organized, the team must formulate a plan that identifies the specific work to be accomplished and a schedule for completion. Planning projects involves five steps: (1) defining the work breakdown structure, (2) diagramming the network, (3) developing the schedule, (4) analyzing cost–time trade-offs, and (5) assessing risks.

Defining the Work Breakdown Structure

The **work breakdown structure (WBS)** is a statement of all work that has to be completed. Perhaps, the single most important contributor to delay is the omission of work that is germane to the successful completion of the project. The project manager must work closely with the team to identify all activities. An **activity** is the smallest unit of work effort consuming both time and resources that the project manager can schedule and control. Typically, in the process of accumulating activities, the team generates a hierarchy to the work breakdown. Major work components are broken down to smaller tasks that ultimately are broken down to activities that are assigned to individuals. Figure 1 shows a WBS for a major project involving the relocation of a hospital. In the interest of better serving the surrounding community, the board of St. John's Hospital has decided to move to a new location. The project involves constructing a new hospital and making it operational. The work components at level 1 in the WBS can be broken down into smaller units of work in level 2 that could be further divided at level 3, until the project manager gets to activities at a level of detail that can be scheduled and controlled. For example, "Organizing and Site Preparation" has been divided into six activities at level 2 in Figure 1. We have kept our example simple so that the concept of the WBS can be easily understood. If our activities in the example are divided into even smaller units of work, it is easy to see that the total WBS for a project of this size may include many more than 100 activities. Regardless of the project, care must be taken to include all important activities in the WBS to avoid project delays. Often overlooked are the activities required to plan the project, get management approval at various stages, run pilot tests of new services or products, and prepare final reports.

Each activity in the WBS must have an "owner" who is responsible for doing the work. *Activity ownership* avoids confusion in the execution of activities and assigns responsibility for timely completion. The team should have a defined procedure for assigning activities to team members, which can be democratic (consensus of the team) or autocratic (assigned by the project manager).

work breakdown structure (WBS)

A statement of all work that has to be completed.

activity

The smallest unit of work effort consuming both time and resources that the project manager can schedule and control.

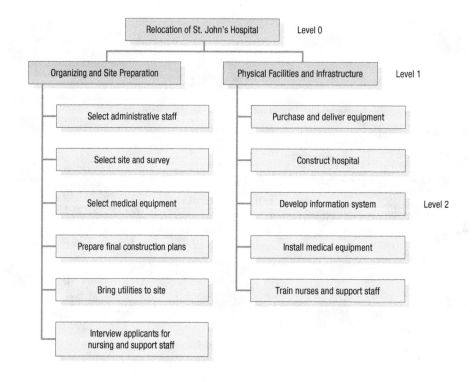

Diagramming the Network

Network planning methods can help managers monitor and control projects. These methods treat a project as a set of interrelated activities that can be visually displayed in a **network diagram**, which consists of nodes (circles) and arcs (arrows) that depict the relationships between activities. Two network planning methods were developed in the 1950s. The **program evaluation and review technique (PERT)** was created for the U.S. Navy's Polaris missile project, which involved 3,000 separate contractors and suppliers. The **critical path method (CPM)** was developed as a means of scheduling maintenance shutdowns at chemical-processing plants. Although early versions of PERT and CPM differed in their treatment of activity time estimates, today the differences are minor. For purposes of our discussion, we refer to them collectively as PERT/CPM. These methods offer several benefits to project managers, including the following:

1. Considering projects as networks forces project teams to identify and organize the data required and to identify the interrelationships between activities. This process also provides a forum for managers of different functional areas to discuss the nature of the various activities and their resource requirements.

2. Networks enable project managers to estimate the completion time of projects, an advantage that can be useful in planning other events and in conducting contractual negotiations with customers and suppliers.

3. Reports highlight the activities that are crucial to completing projects on schedule. They also highlight the activities that may be delayed without affecting completion dates, thereby freeing up resources for other, more critical activities.

4. Network methods enable project managers to analyze the time and cost implications of resource trade-offs.

Diagramming the project network involves establishing precedence relationships and estimating activity times.

Establishing Precedence Relationships   A **precedence relationship** determines a sequence for undertaking activities; it specifies that one activity cannot start until a preceding activity has been completed. For example, brochures announcing a conference for executives must first be designed by the program committee (activity A) before they can be printed (activity B). In other words, activity A must *precede* activity B. For large projects, establishing precedence relationships is essential because incorrect or omitted precedence relationships will result in costly delays. The precedence relationships are represented by a network diagram.

network diagram

A network planning method, designed to depict the relationships between activities, that consists of nodes (circles) and arcs (arrows).

program evaluation and review technique (PERT)

A network planning method created for the U.S. Navy's Polaris missile project in the 1950s, which involved 3,000 separate contractors and suppliers.

critical path method (CPM)

A network planning method developed in the 1950s as a means of scheduling maintenance shutdowns at chemical-processing plants.

precedence relationship

A relationship that determines a sequence for undertaking activities; it specifies that one activity cannot start until a preceding activity has been completed.

Estimating Activity Times   When the same type of activity has been done many times before, time estimates will have a relatively high degree of certainty. Several ways can be used to get time estimates in such an environment. First, statistical methods can be used if the project team has access to data on actual activity times experienced in the past (see MyOMLab Supplement H, "Measuring Output Rates,"). Second, if activity times improve with the number of replications, the times can be estimated using learning curve models (see Supplement I, "Learning Curve Analysis," in MyOMLab). Finally, the times for first-time activities are often estimated using managerial opinions based on similar prior experiences. If the estimates involve a high degree of uncertainty, probability distributions for activity times can be used. We discuss how to incorporate uncertainty in project networks when we address risk assessment later in this chapter. For now, we assume that the activity times are known with certainty.

Using the Activity-On-Node Approach   The diagramming approach we use in this text is referred to as the **activity-on-node (AON) network**, in which nodes represent activities and arcs represent the precedence relationships between them. Some diagramming conventions must be used for AON networks. In cases of multiple activities with no predecessors, it is usual to show them emanating from a common node called *start*. For multiple activities with no successors, it is usual to show them connected to a node called *finish*. Figure 2 shows how to diagram several commonly encountered activity relationships.

MyOMLab

activity-on-node (AON) network

An approach used to create a network diagram, in which nodes represent activities and arcs represent the precedence relationships between them.

◄ **FIGURE 2**
Diagramming Activity Relationships

AON	Activity Relationships
S → T → U	S precedes T, which precedes U.
S, T → U	S and T must be completed before U can be started.
S → T, U	T and U cannot begin until S has been completed.
S, T → U, V	U and V cannot begin until both S and T have been completed.
S → U; T → V	U cannot begin until both S and T have been completed; V cannot begin until T has been completed.
S → T → V; U	T and U cannot begin until S has been completed and V cannot begin until both T and U have been completed.

EXAMPLE 1 | ## Diagramming the St. John's Hospital Project

Judy Kramer, the project manager for the St. John's Hospital project, divided the project into two major modules. She assigned John Stewart the overall responsibility for the Organizing and Site Preparation module and Sarah Walker the responsibility for the Physical Facilities and Infrastructure module. Using the WBS shown in Figure 1, the project team developed the precedence relationships, activity time estimates, and activity responsibilities shown in the following table:

Activity	Immediate Predecessors	Activity Times (wks)	Responsibility
ST. JOHN'S HOSPITAL PROJECT			Kramer
START		0	
ORGANIZING and SITE PREPARATION			Stewart
A. Select administrative staff	Start	12	Johnson
B. Select site and survey	Start	9	Taylor
C. Select medical equipment	A	10	Adams
D. Prepare final construction plans	B	10	Taylor
E. Bring utilities to site	B	24	Burton
F. Interview applicants for nursing and support staff	A	10	Johnson
PHYSICAL FACILITIES and INFRASTRUCTURE			Walker
G. Purchase and deliver equipment	C	35	Sampson
H. Construct hospital	D	40	Casey
I. Develop information system	A	15	Murphy
J. Install medical equipment	E, G, H	4	Pike
K. Train nurses and support staff	F, I, J	6	Ashton
FINISH	K	0	

For purposes of our example, we will assume a work week consists of five work days. Draw the network diagram for the hospital project.

SOLUTION

The network diagram, activities, and activity times for the hospital project are shown in Figure 3. The diagram depicts activities as circles, with arrows indicating the sequence in which they are to be performed. Activities A and B emanate from a *start* node because they have no immediate predecessors. The arrows connecting activity A to activities C, F, and I indicate that all three require completion of activity A before they can begin. Similarly, activity B must be completed before activities D and E can begin, and so on. Activity K connects to a *finish* node because no activities follow it. The start and finish nodes do not actually represent activities; they merely provide beginning and ending points for the network.

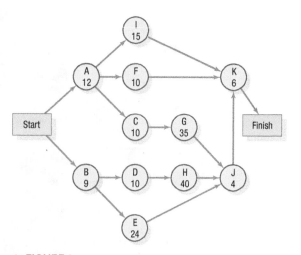

▲ **FIGURE 3**
Network Showing Activity Times for the St. John's Hospital Project

Developing the Schedule

A key advantage of network planning methods is the creation of a schedule of project activities that will help managers achieve the objectives of the project. Managers can (1) estimate the completion time of a project by finding the critical path, (2) identify the start and finish times for each activity for a project schedule, and (3) calculate the amount of slack time for each activity.

Critical Path   A crucial aspect of project management is estimating the time of completion of a project. If each activity in relocating the hospital were done in sequence, with work proceeding on only one activity at a time, the time of completion would equal the sum of the times for all the activities, or 175 weeks. However, Figure 3 indicates that some activities can be carried on simultaneously given adequate resources. We call each sequence of activities between the project's start and finish a **path**. The network describing the hospital relocation project has five paths: (1) A–I–K, (2) A–F–K, (3) A–C–G–J–K, (4) B–D–H–J–K, and (5) B–E–J–K. The **critical path** is the sequence of activities between a project's start and finish that takes the longest time to complete. Thus, the activities along the critical path determine the completion time of the project; that is, if one of the activities on the critical path is delayed, the entire project will be delayed. The estimated times for the paths in the hospital project network are

Path	Estimated Time (weeks)
A–I–K	33
A–F–K	28
A–C–G–J–K	67
B–D–H–J–K	69
B–E–J–K	43

The activity string B–D–H–J–K is estimated to take 69 weeks to complete. As the longest, it constitutes the critical path. Because the critical path defines the completion time of the project, Judy Kramer and the project team should focus on these activities and any other path that is close in length to the critical path.

Project Schedule   The typical objective is to finish the project as early as possible as determined by the critical path. The project schedule is specified by the start and finish times for each activity. For any activity, managers can use the earliest start and finish times, the latest start and finish times (and still finish the project on time), or times in between these extremes.

- **Earliest Start and Earliest Finish Times** The earliest start and earliest finish times are obtained as follows:

  1. The **earliest finish time (EF)** of an activity equals its earliest start time plus its estimated duration, t, or $\text{EF} = \text{ES} + t$.

     The **earliest start time (ES)** for an activity is the earliest finish time of the immediately preceding activity. For activities with more than one preceding activity, ES is the latest of the earliest finish times of the preceding activities.

     To calculate the duration of the entire project, we determine the EF for the last activity on the critical path.

- **Latest Start and Latest Finish Times** To obtain the latest start and latest finish times, we must work backward from the finish node. We start by setting the latest finish time of the project equal to the earliest finish time of the last activity on the critical path.

  1. The **latest finish time (LF)** for an activity is the latest start time of the activity that immediately follows. For activities with more than one activity that immediately follow, LF is the earliest of the latest start times of those activities.

  2. The **latest start time (LS)** for an activity equals its latest finish time minus its estimated duration, t, or $\text{LS} = \text{LF} - t$.

path
The sequence of activities between a project's start and finish.

critical path
The sequence of activities between a project's start and finish that takes the longest time to complete.

earliest finish time (EF)
An activity's earliest start time plus its estimated duration, t, or $\text{EF} = \text{ES} + t$.

earliest start time (ES)
The earliest finish time of the immediately preceding activity.

latest finish time (LF)
The latest start time of the activity that immediately follows.

latest start time (LS)
The latest finish time minus its estimated duration, t, or $\text{LS} = \text{LF} - t$.

Aircraft construction is an example of a large project that requires a sound project schedule because of the capital involved. Here several 747s are under construction at Boeing's plant in Everett, Washington.

George Hall/Corbis

EXAMPLE 2 | **Calculating Start and Finish Times for the Activities**

Calculate the ES, EF, LS, and LF times for each activity in the hospital project. Which activity should Kramer start immediately? Figure 3 contains the activity times.

SOLUTION

To compute the early start and early finish times, we begin at the start node at time zero. Because activities A and B have no predecessors, the earliest start times for these activities are also zero. The earliest finish times for these activities are

$$EF_A = 0 + 12 = 12 \text{ and } EF_B = 0 + 9 = 9$$

Because the earliest start time for activities I, F, and C is the earliest finish time of activity A,

$$ES_I = 12, ES_F = 12, \text{ and } ES_C = 12$$

Similarly,

$$ES_D = 9 \text{ and } ES_E = 9$$

After placing these ES values on the network diagram (see Figure 4), we determine the EF times for activities I, F, C, D, and E:

$$EF_I = 12 + 15 = 27, EF_F = 12 + 10 = 22, EF_C = 12 + 10 = 22,$$
$$EF_D = 9 + 10 = 19, \text{ and } EF_E = 9 + 24 = 33$$

The earliest start time for activity G is the latest EF time of all immediately preceding activities. Thus,

$$ES_G = EF_C = 22, ES_H = EF_D = 19$$
$$EF_G = ES_G + t = 22 + 35 = 57, EF_H = ES_H + t = 19 + 40 = 59$$

▶ **FIGURE 4**

Network Diagram Showing Start and Finish Times and Activity Slack

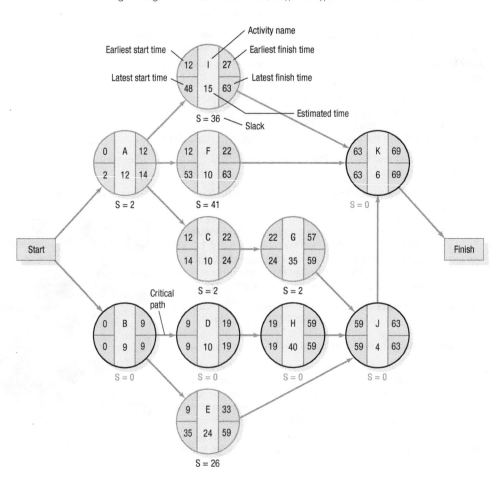

The project team can now determine the earliest time any activity can be started. Because activity J has several predecessors, the earliest time that activity J can begin is the latest of the EF times of any of its preceding activities: EF_G, EF_H, or EF_E. Thus, $EF_J = 59 + 4 = 63$. Similarly, $ES_K = 63$ and $EF_K = 63 + 6 = 69$. Because activity K is the last activity on the critical path, the earliest the project can be completed is week 69. The earliest start and finish times for all activities are shown in Figure 4.

To compute the latest start and latest finish times, we begin by setting the latest finish activity time of activity K at week 69, which is its earliest finish time as determined in Figure 4. Thus, the latest start time for activity K is

$$LS_K = LF_K - t = 69 - 6 = 63$$

If activity K is to start no later than week 63, all its predecessors must finish no later than that time. Consequently,

$$LF_I = 63, LF_F = 63, \text{ and } LF_J = 63$$

The latest start times for these activities are shown in Figure 4 as

$$LS_I = 63 - 15 = 48, LS_F = 63 - 10 = 53, \text{ and } LS_J = 63 - 4 = 59$$

After obtaining LS_J, we can calculate the latest start times for the immediate predecessors of activity J:

$$LS_G = 59 - 35 = 24, LS_H = 59 - 40 = 19, \text{ and } LS_E = 59 - 24 = 35$$

Similarly, we can now calculate the latest start times for activities C and D:

$$LS_C = 24 - 10 = 14 \text{ and } LS_D = 19 - 10 = 9$$

Activity A has more than one immediately following activity: I, F, and C. The earliest of the latest start times is 14 for activity C. Thus,

$$LS_A = 14 - 12 = 2$$

Similarly, activity B has two immediate followers: D and E. Because the earliest of the latest start times of these activities is 9,

$$LS_B = 9 - 9 = 0$$

DECISION POINT

The earliest or latest start times can be used for developing a project schedule. For example, Kramer should start activity B immediately because the latest start time is 0; otherwise, the project will not be completed by week 69. When the LS is greater than the ES for an activity, that activity could be scheduled for any date between ES and LS. Such is the case for activity E, which could be scheduled to start anytime between week 9 and week 35, depending on the availability of resources. The earliest start and earliest finish times and the latest start and latest finish times for all activities are shown in Figure 4.

Activity Slack   The maximum length of time that an activity can be delayed without delaying the entire project is called **activity slack**. Consequently, *activities on the critical path have zero slack*. Information on slack can be useful because it highlights activities that need close attention. In this regard, activity slack is the amount of schedule slippage that can be tolerated for an activity before the entire project will be delayed. Slack at an activity is reduced when the estimated time duration of an activity is exceeded or when the scheduled start time for the activity must be delayed because of resource considerations. Activity slack can be calculated in one of two ways for any activity:

$$S = LS - ES \text{ or } S = LF - EF$$

Computers calculate activity slack and prepare periodic reports for large projects, enabling managers to monitor progress. Using these reports, managers can sometimes manipulate slack to overcome scheduling problems. When resources can be used on several different activities in a project, they can be taken from activities with slack and given to activities that are behind schedule until the slack is used up. The slack for each activity in the hospital project is shown in Figure 4.

Gantt Chart   The project manager, often with the assistance of computer software, creates the project schedule by superimposing project activities, with their precedence relationships and

activity slack

The maximum length of time that an activity can be delayed without delaying the entire project, calculated as $S = LS - ES$ or $S = LF - EF$.

MyOMLab

Active Model 2.1 in MyOMLab provides additional insight on Gantt charts and their uses for the St. John's Hospital project.

	Task Name	Duration	Start	Finish	Predecessors
1	⊟ St John's Hospital Project	69 wks	Mon 9/12/11	Fri 1/4/13	
2	Start	0 wks	Mon 9/12/11	Mon 9/12/11	
3	⊟ Organizing and Site Prep	33 wks	Mon 9/12/11	Fri 4/27/12	
4	A. Select Staff	12 wks	Mon 9/12/11	Fri 12/2/11	2
5	B. Select Site	9 wks	Mon 9/12/11	Fri 11/11/11	2
6	C. Select Equipment	10 wks	Mon 12/5/11	Fri 2/10/12	4
7	D. Construction Plans	10 wks	Mon 11/14/11	Fri 1/20/12	5
8	E. Utilities	24 wks	Mon 11/14/11	Fri 4/27/12	5
9	F. Interviews	10 wks	Mon 12/5/11	Fri 2/10/12	4
10	⊟ Facilities and Infrastructure	57 wks	Mon 12/5/11	Fri 1/4/13	
11	G. Purchase Equipment	35 wks	Mon 2/13/12	Fri 10/12/12	6
12	H. Construct Hospital	40 wks	Mon 1/23/12	Fri 10/26/12	7
13	I. Information System	15 wks	Mon 12/5/11	Fri 3/16/12	4
14	J. Install Equipment	4 wks	Mon 10/29/12	Fri 11/23/12	8,11,12
15	K. Train Staff	6 wks	Mon 11/26/12	Fri 1/4/13	9,13,14
16	Finish	0 wks	Fri 1/4/13	Fri 1/4/13	15

▲ **FIGURE 5**
MS Project Gantt Chart for
the St. John's Hospital Project
Schedule

Gantt chart

A project schedule, usually
created by the project manager
using computer software, that
superimposes project activities,
with their precedence relationships and estimated duration
times, on a time line.

estimated duration times, on a time line. The resulting diagram is called a **Gantt chart**. Figure 5 shows a Gantt chart for the hospital project created with Microsoft Project, a popular software package for project management. The critical path is shown in red. The chart clearly shows which activities can be undertaken simultaneously and when they should be started. Figure 5 also shows the earliest start schedule for the project. Microsoft Project can also be used to show the latest start schedule or to change the definition of the work week to declare Saturday and Sunday as work days, for example. Gantt charts are popular because they are intuitive and easy to construct.

Analyzing Cost–Time Trade-Offs

Keeping costs at acceptable levels is almost always as important as meeting schedule dates. In this section, we discuss the use of PERT/CPM methods to obtain minimum-cost schedules.

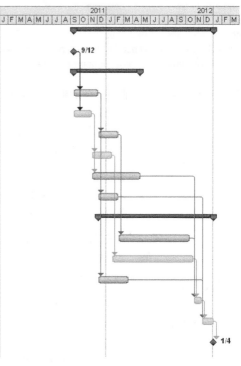
Excavators work on the new Panama Canal project, which has international implications and massive costs.

Mark Eveleigh/Alamy

The reality of project management is that there are always cost–time trade-offs. For example, a project can often be completed earlier than scheduled by hiring more workers or running extra shifts. Such actions could be advantageous if savings or additional revenues accrue from completing the project early. *Total project costs* are the sum of direct costs, indirect costs, and penalty costs. These costs are dependent either on activity times or on project completion time. *Direct costs* include labor, materials, and any other costs directly related to project activities. *Indirect costs* include administration, depreciation, financial, and other variable overhead costs that can be avoided by reducing total project time: The shorter the duration of the project, the lower the indirect costs will be. Finally, a project may incur *penalty costs* if it extends beyond some specific date, whereas *an incentive* may be provided for early completion. Managers can shorten individual activity times by using additional direct resources, such as overtime, personnel, or equipment. Thus, a project manager may consider *crashing*, or expediting, some activities to reduce overall project completion time and total project costs.

Cost to Crash To assess the benefit of crashing certain activities—from either a cost or a schedule perspective—the project manager needs to know the following times and costs:

1. The **normal time (NT)** is the time necessary to complete an activity under normal conditions.

2. The **normal cost (NC)** is the activity cost associated with the normal time.

3. The **crash time (CT)** is the shortest possible time to complete an activity.

4. The **crash cost (CC)** is the activity cost associated with the crash time.

Our cost analysis is based on the assumption that direct costs increase linearly as activity time is reduced from its normal time. This assumption implies that for every week the activity time is reduced, direct costs increase by a proportional amount. For example, suppose that the normal time for activity C in the hospital project is 10 weeks and is associated with a direct cost of $4,000. Also, suppose that we can crash its time to only 5 weeks at a total cost of $7,000; the net time reduction is 5 weeks at a net cost increase of $3,000. We assume that crashing activity C costs $3,000/5 = $600 per week—an assumption of linear marginal costs that is illustrated in Figure 6. Thus, if activity C were expedited by 2 weeks (i.e., its time reduced from 10 weeks to 8 weeks), the estimated direct costs would be $4,000 + 2($600) = $5,200. For any activity, the cost to crash an activity by one week is

$$\text{Cost to crash per period} = \frac{CC - NC}{NT - CT}$$

Table 1 contains direct cost and time data, as well as the costs of crashing per week for the activities in the hospital project.

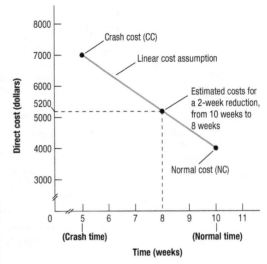

▲ FIGURE 6
Cost-Time Relationships in Cost Analysis

normal time (NT)

In the context of project management, the time necessary to complete an activity under normal conditions.

normal cost (NC)

The activity cost associated with the normal time.

crash time (CT)

The shortest possible time to complete an activity.

crash cost (CC)

The activity cost associated with the crash time.

TABLE 1 | DIRECT COST AND TIME DATA FOR THE ST. JOHN'S HOSPITAL PROJECT

Activity	Normal Time (NT) (weeks)	Normal Cost (NC) ($)	Crash Time (CT) (weeks)	Crash Cost (CC) ($)	Maximum Time Reduction (week)	Cost of Crashing per Week ($)
A	12	$12,000	11	13,000	1	1,000
B	9	50,000	7	64,000	2	7,000
C	10	4,000	5	7,000	5	600
D	10	16,000	8	20,000	2	2,000
E	24	120,000	14	200,000	10	8,000
F	10	10,000	6	16,000	4	1,500
G	35	500,000	25	530,000	10	3,000
H	40	1,200,000	35	1,260,000	5	12,000
I	15	40,000	10	52,500	5	2,500
J	4	10,000	1	13,000	3	1,000
K	6	30,000	5	34,000	1	4,000
	Totals	$1,992,000		$2,209,500		

Minimizing Costs The objective of cost analysis is to determine the project schedule that minimizes total project costs. Suppose that project indirect costs are $8,000 per week. Suppose also that, after week 65, the Regional Hospital Board imposes on St. John's a penalty cost of $20,000 per week if the hospital is not fully operational. With a critical path completion time of 69 weeks, the hospital faces potentially large penalty costs unless the schedule is changed. For every week that the project is shortened—to week 65—the hospital saves one week of penalty *and* indirect costs, or $28,000. For reductions beyond week 65, the savings are only the weekly indirect costs of $8,000.

The minimum possible project duration can be found by using the crash times of each activity for scheduling purposes. However, the cost of that schedule could be prohibitive. Project managers are most interested in minimizing the costs of their projects so that budgets are not exceeded. In determining the **minimum-cost schedule**, we start with the normal time schedule and crash activities along the critical path, whose length equals the length of the project. We want to determine how much we can add in crash costs without exceeding the savings in indirect and penalty costs. The procedure involves the following steps:

minimum-cost schedule

A schedule determined by starting with the normal time schedule and crashing activities along the critical path, in such a way that the costs of crashing do not exceed the savings in indirect and penalty costs.

Step 1. Determine the project's critical path(s).

Step 2. Find the activity or activities on the critical path(s) with the lowest cost of crashing per week.

Step 3. Reduce the time for this activity until (a) it cannot be further reduced, (b) another path becomes critical, or (c) the increase in direct costs exceeds the indirect and penalty cost savings that result from shortening the project. If more than one path is critical, the time for an activity on each path may have to be reduced simultaneously.

Step 4. Repeat this procedure until the increase in direct costs is larger than the savings generated by shortening the project.

EXAMPLE 3	Find a Minimum-Cost Schedule

Determine the minimum-cost schedule for the St. John's Hospital project. Use the information provided in Table 1 and Figure 4.

MyOMLab

Active Model 2.2 in MyOMLab provides additional insight on cost analysis for the St. John's Hospital project.

SOLUTION

The projected completion time of the project is 69 weeks. The project costs for that schedule are $1,992,000 in direct costs, 69($8,000) = $552,000 in indirect costs, and (69 − 65) ($20,000) = $80,000 in penalty costs, for total project costs of $2,624,000. The five paths in the network have the following normal times:

A–I–K:	33 weeks
A–F–K:	28 weeks
A–C–G–J–K:	67 weeks
B–D–H–J–K:	69 weeks
B–E–J–K:	43 weeks

It will simplify our analysis if we can eliminate some paths from further consideration. If all activities on A–C–G–J–K were crashed, the path duration would be 47 weeks. Crashing all activities on B–D–H–J–K results in a project duration of 56 weeks. Because the *normal* times of A–I–K, A–F–K, and B–E–J–K are less than the minimum times of the other two paths, we can disregard those three paths; they will never become critical regardless of the crashing we may do.

STAGE 1

Step 1. The critical path is B–D–H–J–K.

Step 2. The cheapest activity to crash per week is J at $1,000, which is much less than the savings in indirect and penalty costs of $28,000 per week.

Step 3. Crash activity J by its limit of three weeks because the critical path remains unchanged. The new expected path times are

A–C–G–J–K: 64 weeks and B–D–H–J–K: 66 weeks

The net savings are 3 ($28,000) − 3($1,000) = $81,000. The total project costs are now $2,624,000 − $81,000 = $2,543,000.

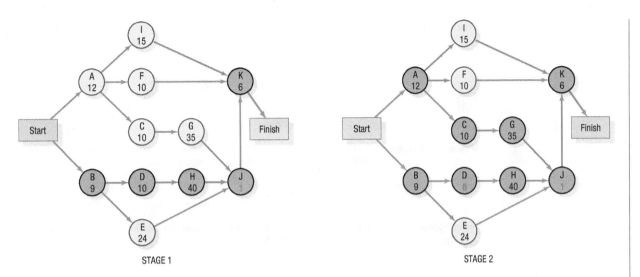

STAGE 1   STAGE 2

STAGE 2

Step 1. The critical path is still B–D–H–J–K.

Step 2. The cheapest activity to crash per week is now D at $2,000.

Step 3. Crash D by two weeks. The first week of reduction in activity D saves $28,000 because it eliminates a week of penalty costs, as well as indirect costs. Crashing D by a second week saves only $8,000 in indirect costs because, after week 65, no more penalty costs are incurred. These savings still exceed the cost of crashing D for a second week. Updated path times are

A–C–G–J–K: 64 weeks and B–D–H–J–K: 64 weeks

The net savings are $28,000 + $8,000 − 2($2,000) = $32,000. Total project costs are now $2,543,000 − $32,000 = $2,511,000.

STAGE 3

Step 1. After crashing D, we now have two critical paths. *Both* critical paths must now be shortened to realize any savings in indirect project costs. If one is shortened and the other is not, the length of the project remains unchanged.

Step 2. Our alternatives are to crash one of the following combinations of activities—(A, B); (A, H); (C, B); (C, H); (G, B); (G, H)—or to crash activity K, which is on both critical paths (J has already been crashed). We consider only those alternatives for which the cost of crashing is less than the potential savings of $8,000 per week. The only viable alternatives are (C, B) at a cost of $7,600 per week and K at $4,000 per week. We choose activity K to crash.

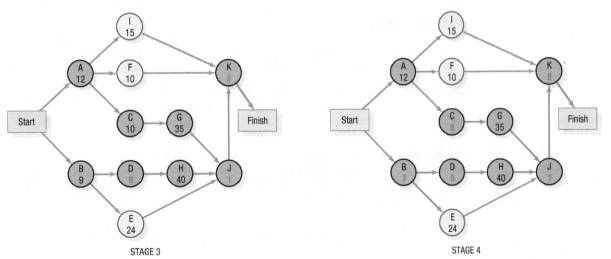

STAGE 3   STAGE 4

Step 3. We crash activity K to the greatest extent possible—a reduction of one week—because it is on both critical paths. Updated path times are

A–C–G–J–K: 63 weeks and B–D–H–J–K: 63 weeks

The net savings are $8,000 − $4,000 = $4,000. Total project costs are $2,511,000 − $4,000 = $2,507,000.

STAGE 4

Step 1. The critical paths are B–D–H–J–K and A–C–G–J–K.

Step 2. The only viable alternative at this stage is to crash activities B and C simultaneously at a cost of $7,600 per week. This amount is still less than the savings of $8,000 per week.

Step 3. Crash activities B and C by two weeks, the limit for activity B. Updated path times are

A–C–G–J–K: 61 weeks and B–D–H–J–K: 61 weeks

Net savings are 2($8,000) − 2($7,600) = $800. Total project costs are $2,507,000 − $800 = $2,506,200. The following table summarizes the analysis:

Stage	Crash Activity	Time Reduction (weeks)	Resulting Critical Path(s)	Project Duration (weeks)	Project Direct Costs, Last Trial ($000)	Crash Cost Added ($000)	Total Indirect Costs ($000)	Total Penalty Costs ($000)	Total Project Costs ($000)
0	—	—	B–D–H–J–K	69	1,992.0	—	552.0	80.0	2,624.0
1	J	3	B–D–H–J–K	66	1,992.0	3.0	528.0	20.0	2,543.0
2	D	2	B–D–H–J–K A–C–G–J–K	64	1,995.0	4.0	512.0	0.0	2,511.0
3	K	1	B–D–H–J–K A–C–G–J–K	63	1,999.0	4.0	504.0	0.0	2,507.0
4	B,C	2	B–D–H–J–K A–C–G–J–K	61	2,003.0	15.2	488.0	0.0	2,506.2

DECISION POINT

Because the crash costs exceed weekly indirect costs, any other combination of activities will result in a net increase in total project costs. The minimum-cost schedule is 61 weeks, with a total cost of $2,506,200. To obtain this schedule, the project team must crash activities B, D, J, and K to their limits and activity C to eight weeks. The other activities remain at their normal times. This schedule costs $117,800 less than the normal-time schedule.

Assessing Risks

Risk is a measure of the probability and consequence of not reaching a defined project goal. Risk involves the notion of uncertainty as it relates to project timing and costs. Often, project teams must deal with uncertainty caused by labor shortages, weather, supply delays, or the outcomes of critical tests. In this section, we discuss risk management plans and the tools managers can use to analyze the risks, such as simulation and statistical analysis, which enable managers to estimate the probability of completing a project on time and the potential for near-critical paths to affect the project completion time.

risk-management plan

A plan that identifies the key risks to a project's success and prescribes ways to circumvent them.

Risk-Management Plans A major responsibility of the project manager at the start of a project is to develop a **risk-management plan**, which identifies the key risks to a project's success and prescribes ways to circumvent them. A good risk-management plan will quantify the risks, predict their impact on the project, and provide contingency plans. Project risk can be assessed by examining four categories:

- **Strategic Fit** The project may not be a good strategic fit in that it may not be clearly linked to the strategic goals of the firm.

- **Service/Product Attributes** If the project involves the development of a new service or product, there may be market, technological, or legal risks. There is a chance that competitors may offer a superior product, or a technological discovery may render the service or product obsolete before it even hits the market. There may also be a legal risk of potential lawsuits or liability that could force a design change after product development has begun.

- **Project Team Capability** The project team may not have the capability to complete the project successfully because of the size and complexity of the project or the technology involved.

- **Operations** There may be an operations risk because of poor information accuracy, lack of communication, missing precedence relationships, or bad estimates for activity times.

These risks should be identified and the significant ones should have contingency plans in case something goes wrong. The riskier a project is, the more likely the project will experience difficulties as Managerial Practice 1 shows.

Simulation PERT/CPM networks can be used to quantify risks associated with project timing. Often, the uncertainty associated with an activity can be reflected in the activity's time duration. For example, an activity in a new product development project might be developing the enabling

---

MANAGERIAL PRACTICE 1 — Boston's Big Dig Project Poses Many Challenges

Boston, Massachusetts, has many noteworthy attractions: the world champion Boston Red Sox baseball team, the Freedom Trail, depicting many historic buildings and sights dating back to the 1600s, and the most ambitious road infrastructure project attempted in the United States. The six-lane elevated highway that ran through the center of the city was designed for 75,000 cars per day, but was forced to accommodate close to 200,000 cars per day. The highway was congested for 10 hours a day; congestion was expected to increase to 16 hours a day by 2010. It was costing residents and businesses $500 million a year in accidents, fuel, and late delivery charges.

Solving the traffic problem would take more than adding a few lanes to the existing highway, which was built in 1953 and whose elevated superstructure was rapidly deteriorating. Rather than fixing the old highway, the decision was made to build an 8-to-10-lane underground highway directly beneath the existing road, culminating at the north end of the city in a 14-lane, 2-bridge crossing of the Charles River. On the south end, a four-lane tunnel was built under South Boston and the Boston Harbor to Logan Airport, leaving no doubt how the project got its "Big Dig" nickname; the project spans 7.8 miles of highway with half in tunnels under a major city and harbor! Planning for the project began in 1983, construction began in 1991, and in spring 2007 it was declared 99 percent complete.

Was the project successful? The answer might depend on whom you ask. The residents of Boston have a much more efficient transportation network that allows for growth for many years into the future. However, from a project management perspective, it missed the three goals of every project: (1) on time, (2) under budget, and (3) meet the specifications. The Big Dig was 9 years late (originally scheduled for completion in 1998), more than $10 billion over the budget (originally projected to be about $4 billion in today's dollars), and required significant repairs for leaks shortly after the tunnels were opened. Much negative publicity in summer 2006 resulted from the failure of ceiling panels in the Seaport Access Tunnel, which fell to the roadway and onto a passing vehicle, resulting in the tragic loss of life. Because the project was funded with taxpayer dollars, it is no wonder that the project is the subject of much debate and controversy.

Why did this project experience problems? The Big Dig is an example of a risky project because it was huge and complex. It was called one of the most complex and controversial engineering projects in human history, rivaling the likes of the Panama Canal, the English Channel Tunnel, and the

A great deal of controversy surrounded the "Big Dig," a massive highway tunnel built under the city of Boston and Boston Harbor. By the time the Big Dig was completed, it was over budget, late, and did not meet the specifications—in part, because no one had ever undertaken such a complex project before.

Trans-Alaska Pipeline. Project managers held many meetings with environmental and permitting agencies, community groups, businesses, and political leaders to gain consensus on how the project would be built. Because of meetings such as these the project scope was modified over time, thereby causing the project plan to change. From an operational perspective, most of the construction companies involved in the project had never done anything of this size and scope before and had difficulty providing good time estimates for their pieces of the project. Delays and cost overruns were inevitable. Further, quality was difficult to achieve because so many contractors were involved in such a complex project. Projects of this size and complexity are inherently risky; contingency plans should cover the most likely disruptions. Schedule and budget problems are not unusual; however, the job of project managers is to manage the risks and minimize the deviations.

Sources: http://en.wikipedia.org/wiki/Big_Dig (2010); www.massturnpike.com/bigdig/updates (2007); Seth Stern, "$14.6 Billion Later, Boston's Big Dig Wraps Up," *Christian Science Monitor* (December 19, 2003); "The Big Dig, Boston, MA, USA," www.roadtraffic-technology.com (2005); "Big Dig Tunnel Is Riddled with Leaks," *Associated Press*, http://abcnews.go.com (November 19, 2004); Michael Roth, "Boston Digs the Big Dig," *Rental Equipment Register* (November 1, 2000), http://rermag.com/ar (2005).

technology to manufacture it, an activity that may take from eight months to a year. To incorporate uncertainty into the network model, probability distributions of activity times can be calculated using two approaches: (1) computer simulation and (2) statistical analysis. With simulation, the time for each activity is randomly chosen from its probability distribution (see MyOMLab Supplement E, "Simulation"). The critical path of the network is determined and the completion date of the project computed. The procedure is repeated many times, which results in a probability distribution for the completion date. We will have more to say about simulation when we discuss near critical paths later in this chapter.

Statistical Analysis   The statistical analysis approach requires that activity times be stated in terms of three reasonable time estimates:

optimistic time (*a*)

The shortest time in which an activity can be completed, if all goes exceptionally well.

most likely time (*m*)

The probable time required to perform an activity.

pessimistic time (*b*)

The longest estimated time required to perform an activity.

1. The **optimistic time** (*a*) is the shortest time in which an activity can be completed, if all goes exceptionally well.

2. The **most likely time** (*m*) is the probable time required to perform an activity.

3. The **pessimistic time** (*b*) is the longest estimated time required to perform an activity.

With three time estimates—the optimistic, the most likely, and the pessimistic—the project manager has enough information to estimate the probability that an activity will be completed on schedule. To do so, the project manager must first calculate the mean and variance of a probability distribution for each activity. In PERT/CPM, each activity time is treated as though it were a random variable derived from a beta probability distribution. This distribution can have various shapes, allowing the most likely time estimate (*m*) to fall anywhere between the pessimistic (*b*) and optimistic (*a*) time estimates. The most likely time estimate is the *mode* of the beta distribution, or the time with the highest probability of occurrence. This condition is not possible with the normal distribution, which is symmetrical, because the normal distribution requires the mode to be equidistant from the end points of the distribution. Figure 7 shows the difference between the two distributions.

▶ **FIGURE 7**
Differences Between Beta and Normal Distributions for Project Risk Analysis

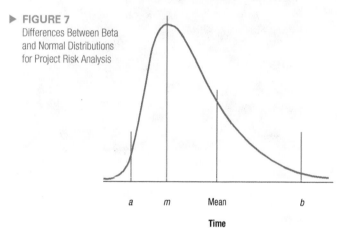

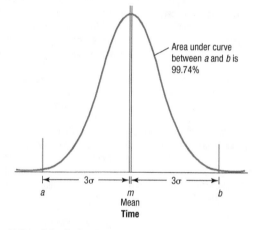

(a) **Beta distribution:** The most likely time (*m*) has the highest probability and can be placed anywhere between the optimistic (*a*) and pessimistic (*b*) times.

(b) **Normal distribution:** The mean and most likely times must be the same. If *a* and *b* are chosen to be 6σ apart, there is a 99.74% chance that the actual activity time will fall between them.

Analysis

Two key assumptions are required. First, we assume that *a*, *m*, and *b* can be estimated accurately. The estimates might best be considered values that define a reasonable time range for the activity duration negotiated between the project manager and the team members responsible for the activities. Second, we assume that the standard deviation, σ, of the activity time is one-sixth the range *b* − *a*. Thus, the chance that actual activity times will fall between *a* and *b* is high. Why does this assumption make sense? If the activity time followed the normal distribution, six standard deviations would span approximately 99.74 percent of the distribution.

Even with these assumptions, derivation of the mean and variance of each activity's probability distribution is complex. These derivations show that the mean of the beta distribution can be estimated by using the following weighted average of the three time estimates:

$$t_e = \frac{a + 4m + b}{6}$$

Note that the most likely time has four times the weight of the pessimistic and optimistic estimates.

The variance of the beta distribution for each activity is

$$\sigma^2 = \left(\frac{b-a}{6}\right)^2$$

The variance, which is the standard deviation squared, increases as the difference between b and a increases. This result implies that the less certain a person is in estimating the actual time for an activity, the greater will be the variance.

| **EXAMPLE 4** | **Calculating Means and Variances** |

Suppose that the project team has arrived at the following time estimates for activity B (Select site and survey) of the St. John's Hospital project:

$$a = 7 \text{ weeks}, m = 8 \text{ weeks, and } b = 15 \text{ weeks}$$

a. Calculate the expected time and variance for activity B.

b. Calculate the expected time and variance for the other activities in the project.

SOLUTION

a. The expected time for activity B is

$$t_e = \frac{7 + 4(8) + 15}{6} = \frac{54}{6} = 9 \text{ weeks}$$

Note that the expected time (9 weeks) does not equal the most likely time (8 weeks) for this activity. These times will be the same only when the most likely time is equidistant from the optimistic and pessimistic times. We calculate the variance for activity B as

$$\sigma^2 = \left(\frac{15-7}{6}\right)^2 = \left(\frac{8}{6}\right)^2 = 1.78$$

b. The following table shows expected activity times and variances for the activities listed in the project description.

	TIME ESTIMATES (WEEKS)			ACTIVITY STATISTICS	
Activity	**Optimistic (a)**	**Most Likely (m)**	**Pessimistic (b)**	**Expected Time (t_e)**	**Variance (σ^2)**
A	11	12	13	12	0.11
B	7	8	15	9	1.78
C	5	10	15	10	2.78
D	8	9	16	10	1.78
E	14	25	30	24	7.11
F	6	9	18	10	4.00
G	25	36	41	35	7.11
H	35	40	45	40	2.78
I	10	13	28	15	9.00
J	1	2	15	4	5.44
K	5	6	7	6	0.11

DECISION POINT

The project team should notice that the greatest uncertainty lies in the time estimate for activity I, followed by the estimates for activities E and G. These activities should be analyzed for the source of the uncertainties and actions should be taken to reduce the variance in the time estimates.

Analyzing Probabilities Because time estimates for activities involve uncertainty, project managers are interested in determining the probability of meeting project completion deadlines. To develop the probability distribution for project completion time, we assume that the duration time of one activity does not depend on that of any other activity. This assumption enables us to estimate the mean and variance of the probability distribution of the time duration of the entire project by summing the duration times and variances of the activities along the critical path. However, if one work crew is assigned two activities that can be done at the same time, the activity times will be interdependent and the assumption is not valid. In addition, if other paths in the network have small amounts of slack, one of them might become the critical path before the project is completed; we should calculate a probability distribution for those paths as well.

Because of the assumption that the activity duration times are independent random variables, we can make use of the central limit theorem, which states that the sum of a group of independent, identically distributed random variables approaches a normal distribution as the number of random variables increases. The mean of the normal distribution is the sum of the expected activity times on the path. In the case of the critical path, it is the earliest expected finish time for the project:

$$T_E = \sum \left(\text{Expected activity times on the critical path} \right) = \text{Mean of normal distribution}$$

Similarly, because of the assumption of activity time independence, we use the sum of the variances of the activities along the path as the variance of the time distribution for that path. That is, for the critical path,

$$\sigma_P^2 = \sum \left(\text{Variances of activities on the critical path} \right)$$

To analyze probabilities of completing a project by a certain date using the normal distribution, we focus on the *critical path* and use the z-transformation formula:

$$z = \frac{T - T_E}{\sigma_P}$$

where

$$T = \text{due date for the project}$$

Given the value of z, we use the Normal Distribution appendix to find the probability that the project will be completed by time T, or sooner. An implicit assumption in this approach is that no other path will become critical during the time span of the project. Example 5, part (a), demonstrates this calculation for the St. John's Hospital project.

The procedure for assessing the probability of completing any activity in a project by a specific date is similar to the one just discussed. However, instead of the critical path, we would use the longest time path of activities from the start node to the activity node in question.

Near-Critical Paths A project's duration is a function of its critical path. However, paths that are close to the same duration as the critical path may ultimately become the critical path over the life of the project. In practice, at the start of the project, managers typically do not know the activity times with certainty and may never know which path was the critical path until the actual activity times are known at the end of the project. Nonetheless, this uncertainty does not reduce the usefulness of identifying the probability of one path or another causing a project to exceed its target completion time; it helps to identify the activities that need close management attention. To assess the chances of near-critical paths delaying the project completion, we can focus on the longest paths in the project network keeping in mind that both duration and variance along the path must be considered. Shorter paths with high variances could have just as much a chance to delay the project as longer paths with smaller variances. We can then estimate the probability that a given path will exceed the project target completion time. We demonstrate that approach using statistical analysis in Example 5, part (b).

Alternatively, simulation can be used to estimate the probabilities. The advantage of simulation is that you are not restricted to the use of the beta distribution for activity times. Also, activity or path dependencies, such as decision points that could involve different groups of activities to be undertaken, can be incorporated in a simulation model much more easily than with the statistical analysis approach. Fortunately, regardless of the approach used, it is rarely necessary to evaluate every path in the network. In large networks, many paths will have both short durations and low variances, making them unlikely to affect the project duration.

EXAMPLE 5	Calculating the Probability of Completing a Project by a Given Date

Calculate the probability that St. John's Hospital will become operational in 72 weeks, using (a) the critical path and (b) near-critical path A–C–G–J–K.

MyOMLab

Active Model 2.3 in MyOMLab provides additional insight on probability analysis for the St. John's Hospital project.

SOLUTION

a. The critical path B–D–H–J–K has a length of 69 weeks. From the table in Example 4, we obtain the variance of path B–D–H–J–K: $\sigma_P^2 = 1.78 + 1.78 + 2.78 + 5.44 + 0.11 = 11.89$. Next, we calculate the z-value:

$$z = \frac{72 - 69}{\sqrt{11.89}} = \frac{3}{3.45} = 0.87$$

Using the Normal Distribution appendix, we go down the left-hand column until we arrive at the value 0.8, and then across until we arrive at the 0.07 column, which shows a tabular value of 0.8078. Consequently, we find that the probability is about 0.81 that the length of path B–D–H–J–K will be no greater than 72 weeks. Because this path is the critical path, there is a 19 percent probability that the project will take longer than 72 weeks. This probability is shown graphically in Figure 8.

b. From the table in Example 4, we determine that the sum of the expected activity times on path A–C–G–J–K is 67 weeks and that $\sigma_P^2 = 0.11 + 2.78 + 7.11 + 5.44 + 0.11 = 15.55$. The z-value is

$$z = \frac{72 - 67}{\sqrt{15.55}} = \frac{5}{3.94} = 1.27$$

The probability is about 0.90 that the length of path A–C–G–J–K will be no greater than 72 weeks.

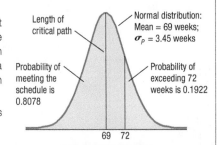

▲ **FIGURE 8**
Probability of Completing the St. John's Hospital Project on Schedule

DECISION POINT

The project team should be aware of the 10 percent chance that path A–C–G–J–K will exceed the target completion date of week 72. Although the probability is not high for that path, activities A, C, and G bear watching during the first 57 weeks of the project to make sure no more than 2 weeks of slippage occurs in their schedules. This attention is especially important for activity G, which has a high time variance.

Monitoring and Controlling Projects

Once project planning is over, the challenge becomes keeping the project on schedule within the budget of allocated resources. In this section, we discuss how to monitor project status and resource usage. In addition, we identify the features of project management software useful for monitoring and controlling projects.

Monitoring Project Status

A good tracking system will help the project team accomplish its project goals. Effective tracking systems collect information on three topics: (1) open issues, (2) risks, and (3) schedule status.

Open Issues and Risks One of the duties of the project manager is to make sure that issues that have been raised during the project actually get resolved in a timely fashion. The tracking system should remind the project manager of due dates for open issues and who was responsible for seeing that they are resolved. Likewise, it should provide the status of each risk to project delays specified in the risk management plan so that the team can review them at each meeting. To be effective, the tracking system requires team members to update information periodically regarding their respective responsibilities.

Schedule Status Even the best laid project plans can go awry. A tracking system that provides periodic monitoring of slack time in the project schedule can help the project manager control activities along the critical path. Periodic updating of the status of ongoing activities in the project allows the tracking system to recalculate activity slacks

Monitoring and controlling shipbuilding projects is critical to keeping these complex projects on schedule. Here a propeller is attached to an ocean-going vessel.

and indicate those activities that are behind schedule or are in danger of using up all of their slack. Management can then focus on those activities and reallocate resources as needed.

Monitoring Project Resources

Experience has shown that the resources allocated to a project are consumed at an uneven rate that is a function of the timing of the schedules for the project's activities. Projects have a *life cycle* that consists of four major phases: (1) definition and organization, (2) planning, (3) execution, and (4) close out. Figure 9 shows that each of the four phases requires different resource commitments.

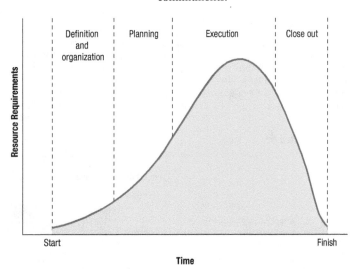

▲ FIGURE 9
Project Life Cycle

We have already discussed the activities associated with the project definition and organization and project planning phases. The phase that takes the most resources is the *execution phase*, during which managers focus on activities pertaining to deliverables. The project schedule becomes very important because it shows when each resource devoted to a given activity will be required. Monitoring the progress of activities throughout the project is important to avoid potential overloading of resources. Problems arise when a specific resource, such as a construction crew or staff specialist, is required on several activities with overlapping schedules. Project managers have several options to alleviate resource problems, including the following:

- *Resource Leveling.* The attempt to reduce the peaks and valleys in resource needs by shifting the schedules of conflicting activities within their earliest and latest start dates. Software packages such as MS Project have algorithms that move activities to avoid violating resource constraints.

- *Resource Allocation.* The assignment of resources to the most important activities. Most popular project management software packages have a few priority rules that can be used to decide which activity a critical resource should be scheduled to perform when conflicts arise. For example, for all the activities requiring a given resource, assign the resource to the one with the earliest start time. An activity slack report identifies potential candidates for resource shifting—shift resources from high slack activities to those behind schedule.

- *Resource Acquisition.* The addition of more of an overloaded resource to maintain the schedule of an activity. Obviously, this tactic is constrained by the project budget.

Controlling Projects

Project managers have the responsibilities of accounting for the effective use of the firm's resources as well as managing the activities to achieve the time and quality goals of the project. The firm's assets include the physical assets, human resources, and financial resources. Physical assets are controlled by the timely maintenance of machines and equipment so that their failure does not delay the project. Inventories must be received, stored for future use, and replenished. Project managers are also responsible for human resource development. Projects provide a rich environment to develop future leaders; project managers can take advantage of the situation by assigning team members important activities to aid in their managerial development. Last, but not least, project managers must control the expenditures of the firm's financial resources. Most project management software packages contain accounting reports, budget reports, capital investment controls, and cash flow reports. Deviations from the project plan, often referred to as variances, must be periodically reported and analyzed for their causes.

Monitoring and controlling projects are ongoing activities throughout the execution phase of the project life cycle. The project **close out**, however, is an activity that many project managers forget to include in their consideration of resource usage. The purpose of this final phase in the project life cycle is to write final reports and complete remaining deliverables. An important aspect of this phase, however, is compiling the team's recommendations for improving the project process of which they were a part. Many team members will be assigned to other projects where they can apply what they learned.

close out

An activity that includes writing final reports, completing remaining deliverables, and compiling the team's recommendations for improving the project process.

LEARNING GOALS IN REVIEW

1 **Define the major activities associated with defining, organizing, planning, monitoring, and controlling projects.** The entire outline of this Chapter revolves around these five very important activities. Nonetheless, be sure to read the opener to the chapter, which shows the four major phases of the project to introduce the new XBOX 360 product, the introduction to the chapter, and the section "Defining and Organizing Projects,".

2 **Diagram the network of interrelated activities in a project.** See "Defining the Work Breakdown Structure," and "Diagramming the Network,". Figure 2 and Example 1 are important for achieving this learning goal.

3 **Identify the sequence of critical activities that determines the duration of a project.** Study the section "Developing the Schedule," and Example 2 for an understanding of the critical path.

4 **Explain how to determine a minimum-cost project schedule.** The section "Analyzing Cost-Time Tradeoffs," and Example 3 demonstrate how the relevant costs must be considered to minimize costs. Figure 6 explains a key assumption in the analysis. Solved Problem 1 contains a detailed solution.

5 **Describe the considerations managers make in assessing the risks in a project and calculate the probability of completing a project on time.** See the section "Assessing Risks," which explains the risks faced by project managers. The section "Analysis," shows how to compute probabilities. Be sure to understand Examples 4 and 5 and Solved Problem 2.

6 **Define the options available to alleviate resource problems.** See the section "Monitoring and Controlling Projects".

MyOMLab helps you develop analytical skills and assesses your progress with multiple problems on identifying the critical path, calculating an activity's slack, expected time, variance, the project's expected completion time, probability of completing it by a certain date, and minimum-cost schedule.

MyOMLab Resources	Titles	Link to the Book
Video	Project Management at the Phoenician Nantucket Nectars: ERP	Entire chapter. Defining and Organizing Projects
Active Model Exercise	2.1 Gantt Chart 2.2 Cost Analysis 2.3 Probability Analysis	Developing the Schedule; Active Model Example Analyzing Cost-Time Trade-Offs; Example 3 Assessing Risks; Exercise 5
OM Explorer Solvers	Single Time Estimates Three Time Estimates Project Budgeting	Developing the Schedule; Example 2 Assessing Risks; Example 4; Solved Problem 2 Monitoring and Controlling Projects
POM for Windows	Single Time Estimates Triple Time Estimates Crashing Cost Budgeting Mean/Standard Deviation Given	Developing the Schedule; Example 2 Assessing Risks; Example 4; Solved Problem 2 Analyzing Cost-Time Trade-Offs; Example 3; Solved Problem 1 Monitoring and Controlling Projects Assessing Risks
SimQuick Simulation Exercises	Software development company	Assessing Risks
Microsoft Project	*Free Trial*	Planning Projects; Figure 5
SmartDraw	*Free Trial*	Diagramming the Network
Virtual Tours	Reiger Orgelbau Pipe Organ Factory and Alaskan Way Viaduct	Planning Projects Assessing Risks; Monitoring and Controlling Projects
MyOMLab Supplements	E. Simulation H. Measuring Output Rates I. Learning Curve Analysis	Assessing Risks Diagramming the Network Diagramming the Network
Internet Exercises	Olympic Movement, London 2012, and Ch2M Hill	Planning Projects Defining and Organizing Projects
Key Equations		
Image Library		

Key Equations

1. Start and finish times:

   t = estimated time duration of the activity

   ES = latest of the EF times of all activities immediately preceding activity

   EF = ES + t

   LF = earliest of the LS times of all activities immediately following activity

   LS = LF − t

2. Activity slack:

   S = LS − ES or S = LF − EF

3. Project costs:

   $$\text{Crash cost per period} = \frac{\text{Crash cost } - \text{ Normal cost}}{\text{Normal time } - \text{ Crash time}}$$

   $$= \frac{\text{CC} - \text{NC}}{\text{NT} - \text{CT}}$$

4. Activity time statistics:

   t_e = mean of an activity's beta distribution

   $$t_e = \frac{a + 4m + b}{6}$$

   σ^2 = variance of the activity time

   $$\sigma^2 = \left(\frac{b - a}{6}\right)^2$$

5. z-transformation formula:

   $$z = \frac{T - T_E}{\sigma_P}$$

   where

   T = due date for the project

   $T_E = \Sigma$ (expected activity times on the critical path)

   $\quad$ = mean of normal distribution of critical path time

   σ_P = standard deviation of critical path time distribution

Key Terms

activity
activity-on-node (AON) network
activity slack
close out
crash cost (CC)
crash time (CT)
critical path
critical path method (CPM)
earliest finish time (EF)
earliest start time (ES)

Gantt chart
latest finish time (LF)
latest start time (LS)
minimum-cost schedule
most likely time (*m*)
network diagram
normal cost (NC)
normal time (NT)
optimistic time (*a*)
path

pessimistic time (*b*)
precedence relationship
program
program evaluation and review
$\quad$ technique (PERT)
project
project management
risk-management plan
work breakdown structure
$\quad$ (WBS)

Solved Problem 1

Your company has just received an order from a good customer for a specially designed electric motor. The contract states that, starting on the thirteenth day from now, your firm will experience a penalty of $100 per day until the job is completed. Indirect project costs amount to $200 per day. The data on direct costs and activity precedence relationships are given in Table 2.

TABLE 2 | ELECTRIC MOTOR PROJECT DATA

Activity	Normal Time (days)	Normal Cost ($)	Crash Time (days)	Crash Cost ($)	Immediate Predecessor(s)
A	4	1,000	3	1,300	None
B	7	1,400	4	2,000	None
C	5	2,000	4	2,700	None
D	6	1,200	5	1,400	A
E	3	900	2	1,100	B
F	11	2,500	6	3,750	C
G	4	800	3	1,450	D, E
H	3	300	1	500	F, G

a. Draw the project network diagram.

b. What completion date would you recommend?

SOLUTION

a. The network diagram, including normal activity times, for this procedure is shown in Figure 10. Keep the following points in mind while constructing a network diagram.

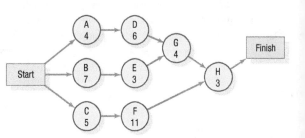

▲ FIGURE 10
Network Diagram for the
Electric Motor Project

 1. Always have start and finish nodes.
 2. Try to avoid crossing paths to keep the diagram simple.
 3. Use only one arrow to directly connect any two nodes.
 4. Put the activities with no predecessors at the left and point the arrows from left to right.
 5. Be prepared to revise the diagram several times before you come up with a correct and uncluttered diagram.

b. With these activity durations, the project will be completed in 19 days and incur a $700 penalty. Determining a good completion date requires the use of the minimum-cost schedule procedure. Using the data provided in Table 2, you can determine the maximum crash-time reduction and crash cost per day for each activity. For example, for activity A

$$\text{Maximum crash time} = \text{Normal time} - \text{Crash time} =$$
$$4 \text{ days} - 3 \text{ days} = 1 \text{ day}$$

$$\text{Crash cost per day} = \frac{\text{Crash cost} - \text{Normal cost}}{\text{Normal time} - \text{Crash time}} = \frac{CC - NC}{NT - CT} =$$

$$\frac{\$1,300 - \$1,000}{4 \text{ days} - 3 \text{ days}} = \$300$$

Activity	Crash Cost per Day ($)	Maximum Time Reduction (days)
A	300	1
B	200	3
C	700	1
D	200	1
E	200	1
F	250	5
G	650	1
H	100	2

Table 3 summarizes the analysis and the resultant project duration and total cost. The critical path is C–F–H at 19 days, which is the longest path in the network. The cheapest of these acvtivities to crash is H, which costs only an extra $100 per day to crash. Doing so saves $200 + $100 = $300 per day in indirect and penalty costs. If you crash this activity for two days (the maximum), the lengths of the paths are now

A–D–G–H: 15 days, B–E–G–H: 15 days, and C–F–H: 17 days

The critical path is still C–F–H. The next cheapest critical activity to crash is F at $250 per day. You can crash F only two days because at that point you will have three critical paths. Further reductions in project duration will require simultaneous crashing of more than one activity (D, E, and F). The cost to do so, $650, exceeds the savings, $300. Consequently, you should stop. Note that every activity is critical. The project costs are minimized when the completion date is day 15. However, some goodwill costs may be associated with disappointing a customer who wants delivery in 12 days.

TABLE 3 | PROJECT COST ANALYSIS

Stage	Crash Activity	Time Reduction (days)	Resulting Critical Path(s)	Project Duration (days)	Project Direct Costs, Last Trial ($)	Crash Cost Added ($)	Total Indirect Costs ($)	Total Penalty Costs ($)	Total Project Costs ($)
0	—	—	C–F–H	19	10,100	—	3,800	700	14,600
1	H	2	C–F–H	17	10,100	200	3,400	500	14,200
2	F	2	A–D–G–H B–E–G–H C–F–H	15	10,300	500	3,000	300	14,100

Solved Problem 2

An advertising project manager developed the network diagram shown in Figure 11 for a new advertising campaign. In addition, the manager gathered the time information for each activity, as shown in the accompanying table.

	TIME ESTIMATES (WEEKS)			
Activity	Optimistic	Most Likely	Pessimistic	Immediate Predecessor(s)
A	1	4	7	—
B	2	6	7	—
C	3	3	6	B
D	6	13	14	A
E	3	6	12	A, C
F	6	8	16	B
G	1	5	6	E, F

▼ FIGURE 11
Network Diagram for the Advertising Project

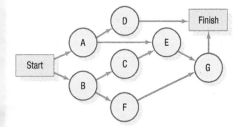

a. Calculate the expected time and variance for each activity.
b. Calculate the activity slacks and determine the critical path, using the expected activity times.
c. What is the probability of completing the project within 23 weeks?

SOLUTION

a. The expected time and variance for each activity are calculated as follows:

$$t_e = \frac{a + 4m + b}{6}$$

Activity	Expected Time (weeks)	Variance (σ^2)
A	4.0	1.00
B	5.5	0.69
C	3.5	0.25
D	12.0	1.78
E	6.5	2.25
F	9.0	2.78
G	4.5	0.69

b. We need to calculate the earliest start, latest start, earliest finish, and latest finish times for each activity. Starting with activities A and B, we proceed from the beginning of the network and move to the end, calculating the earliest start and finish times:

Activity	Earliest Start (weeks)	Earliest Finish (weeks)
A	0	0 + 4.0 = 4.0
B	0	0 + 5.5 = 5.5
C	5.5	5.5 + 3.5 = 9.0
D	4.0	4.0 + 12.0 = 16.0
E	9.0	9.0 + 6.5 = 15.5
F	5.5	5.5 + 9.0 = 14.5
G	15.5	15.5 + 4.5 = 20.0

Based on expected times, the earliest finish for the project is week 20, when activity G has been completed. Using that as a target date, we can work backward through the network, calculating the latest start and finish times (shown graphically in Figure 12):

Activity	Latest Start (weeks)	Latest Finish (weeks)
G	15.5	20.0
F	6.5	15.5
E	9.0	15.5
D	8.0	20.0
C	5.5	9.0
B	0.0	5.5
A	4.0	8.0

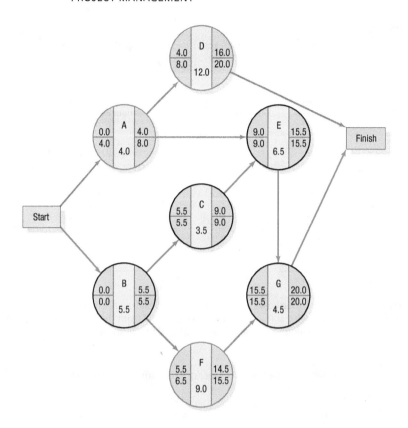

▶ **FIGURE 12**
Network Diagram with
All Time Estimates Needed
to Compute Slack

We now calculate the activity slacks and determine which activities are on the critical path:

| Activity | START (WEEKS) | | FINISH (WEEKS) | | Slack | Critical Activity |
	Earliest	Latest	Earliest	Latest		
A	0.0	4.0	4.0	8.0	4.0	No
B	0.0	0.0	5.5	5.5	0.0	Yes
C	5.5	5.5	9.0	9.0	0.0	Yes
D	4.0	8.0	16.0	20.0	4.0	No
E	9.0	9.0	15.5	15.5	0.0	Yes
F	5.5	6.5	14.5	15.5	1.0	No
G	15.5	15.5	20.0	20.0	0.0	Yes

The paths, and their total expected times and variances, are

Path	Total Expected Time (weeks)	Total Variance (σ_P^2)
A–D	4 + 12 = 16	1.00 + 1.78 = 2.78
A–E–G	4 + 6.5 + 4.5 = 15	1.00 + 2.25 + 0.69 = 3.94
B–C–E–G	5.5 + 3.5 + 6.5 + 4.5 = 20	0.69 + 0.25 + 2.25 + 0.69 = 3.88
B–F–G	5.5 + 9 + 4.5 = 19	0.69 + 2.78 + 0.69 = 4.16

The critical path is B–C–E–G, with a total expected time of 20 weeks. However, path B–F–G is 19 weeks and has a large variance.

c. We first calculate the z-value:

$$z = \frac{T - T_E}{\sigma_P} = \frac{23 - 20}{\sqrt{3.88}} = 1.52$$

Using the Normal Distribution appendix, we find that the probability of completing the project in 23 weeks or fewer is 0.9357. Because the length of path B–F–G is close to that of the critical path and has a large variance, it might well become the critical path during the project.

Discussion Questions

1. One of your colleagues comments that software is the ultimate key to project management success. How would you respond?

2. Explain how to determine the slack for each activity in a project. Why is it important for managers to know where the slack is in their projects?

3. Define risk as it applies to projects. What are the major sources of risk in a project?

Problems

The OM Explorer and POM for Windows software is available to all students using the 10th edition of this text. Go to **www.pearsonhighered.com/krajewski** to download these computer packages. If you purchased MyOMLab, you also have access to Active Models software and significant help in doing the following problems. Check with your instructor on how best to use these resources. In many cases, the instructor wants you to understand how to do the calculations by hand. At the least, the software provides a check on your calculations. When calculations are particularly complex and the goal is interpreting the results in making decisions, the software replaces entirely the manual calculations.

1. Consider the following data for a project:

Activity	Activity Time (days)	Immediate Predecessor(s)
A	2	—
B	4	A
C	5	A
D	2	B
E	1	B
F	8	B, C
G	3	D, E
H	5	F
I	4	F
J	7	G, H, I

a. Draw the network diagram.

b. Calculate the critical path for this project.

c. How much slack is in each of the activities G, H, and I?

2. The following information is known about a project.

Activity	Activity Time (days)	Immediate Predecessor(s)
A	7	—
B	2	A
C	4	A
D	4	B, C
E	4	D
F	3	E
G	5	E

a. Draw the network diagram for this project.

b. Determine the critical path and project duration.

c. Calculate the slack for each activity.

3. A project for improving a billing process has the following precedence relationships and activity times:

Activity	Activity Time (weeks)	Immediate Predecessor(s)
A	3	—
B	11	—
C	7	A
D	13	B, C
E	10	B
F	6	D
G	5	E
H	8	F, G

a. Draw the network diagram.

b. Calculate the slack for each activity. Which activities are on the critical path?

4. The following information is available about a project:

Activity	Activity Time (days)	Immediate Predecessor(s)
A	3	—
B	4	—
C	5	—
D	4	—
E	7	A
F	2	B, C, D
G	4	E, F
H	6	F
I	4	G
J	3	G
K	3	H

    a. Draw the network diagram.

    b. Find the critical path.

5. The following information has been gathered for a project:

Activity	Activity Time (weeks)	Immediate Predecessor(s)
A	4	—
B	7	A
C	9	B
D	3	B
E	14	D
F	10	C, D
G	11	F, E

    a. Draw the network diagram.

    b. Calculate the slack for each activity and determine the critical path. How long will the project take?

6. Consider the following information for a project to add a drive-thru window at Crestview Bank.

Activity	Activity Time (weeks)	Immediate Predecessor(s)
A	5	—
B	2	—
C	6	—
D	2	A, B
E	7	B
F	3	D, C
G	9	E, C
H	11	F, G

    a. Draw the network diagram for this project.

    b. Specify the critical path.

    c. Calculate the slack for activities A and D.

7. Barbara Gordon, the project manager for Web Ventures, Inc., compiled a table showing time estimates for each of the activities of a project to upgrade the company's Web page, including optimistic, most likely, and pessimistic.

    a. Calculate the expected time, t_e, for each activity.

    b. Calculate the variance, σ^2, for each activity.

Activity	Optimistic (days)	Most Likely (days)	Pessimistic (days)
A	3	8	19
B	12	15	18
C	2	6	16
D	4	9	20
E	1	4	7

8. Recently, you were assigned to manage a project for your company. You have constructed a network diagram depicting the various activities in the project (Figure 13). In addition, you have asked your team to estimate the amount of time that they would expect each of the activities to take. Their responses are shown in the following table:

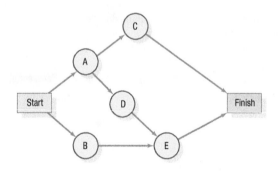

▲ FIGURE 13

Network Diagram for Your Company

Activity	TIME ESTIMATES (DAYS)		
	Optimistic	Most Likely	Pessimistic
A	5	8	11
B	4	8	11
C	5	6	7
D	2	4	6
E	4	7	10

a. What is the expected completion time of the project?

b. What is the probability of completing the project in 21 days?

c. What is the probability of completing the project in 17 days?

9. In Solved Problem 2, estimate the probability that the noncritical path B–F–G will take more than 20 weeks. *Hint:* Subtract from 1.0 the probability that B–F–G will take 20 weeks or less.

10. Consider the following data for a project never before attempted by your company:

Activity	Expected Time t_e (weeks)	Immediate Predecessor(s)
A	5	—
B	3	—
C	2	A
D	5	B
E	4	C, D
F	7	D

a. Draw the network diagram for this project.

b. Identify the critical path and estimate the project's duration.

c. Calculate the slack for each activity.

11. The director of continuing education at Bluebird University just approved the planning for a sales training seminar. Her administrative assistant identified the various activities that must be done and their relationships to each other, as shown in Table 4.

TABLE 4 │ ACTIVITIES FOR THE SALES TRAINING SEMINAR

Activity	Description	Immediate Predecessor(s)
A	Design brochure and course announcement	—
B	Identify prospective teachers	—
C	Prepare detailed outline of course	—
D	Send brochure and student applications	A
E	Send teacher applications	B
F	Select teacher for course	C, E
G	Accept students	D
H	Select text for course	F
I	Order and receive texts	G, H
J	Prepare room for class	G

Because of the uncertainty in planning the new course, the assistant also has supplied the following time estimates for each activity:

	TIME ESTIMATES (DAYS)		
Activity	Optimistic	Most Likely	Pessimistic
A	5	7	8
B	6	8	12
C	3	4	5
D	11	17	25
E	8	10	12
F	3	4	5
G	4	8	9
H	5	7	9
I	8	11	17
J	4	4	4

The director wants to conduct the seminar 47 working days from now. What is the probability that everything will be ready in time?

12. Table 5 contains information about an environmental clean-up project. Shorten the project three weeks by finding the minimum-cost schedule. Assume that project indirect costs and penalty costs are negligible. Identify activities to crash while minimizing the additional crash costs.

TABLE 5 │ ENVIRONMENTAL PROJECT DATA

Activity	Normal Time (weeks)	Crash Time (weeks)	Cost to Crash ($ per week)	Immediate Predecessor(s)
A	7	6	200	None
B	12	9	250	None
C	7	6	250	A
D	6	5	300	A
E	1	1	—	B
F	1	1	—	C, D
G	3	1	200	D, E
H	3	2	350	F
I	2	2	—	G

13. The Advanced Tech Company has a project to design an integrated information database for a major bank. Data for the project are given in Table 6. Indirect project costs amount to $300 per day. The company will incur a $150 per day penalty for each day the project lasts beyond day 14.

a. What is the project's duration if only normal times are used?

b. What is the minimum-cost schedule?

c. What is the critical path for the minimum-cost schedule?

TABLE 6 | DATABASE DESIGN PROJECT DATA

Activity	Normal Time (days)	Normal Cost ($)	Crash Time (days)	Crash Cost ($)	Immediate Predecessor(s)
A	6	1,000	5	1,200	—
B	4	800	2	2,000	—
C	3	600	2	900	A, B
D	2	1,500	1	2,000	B
E	6	900	4	1,200	C, D
F	2	1,300	1	1,400	E
G	4	900	4	900	E
H	4	500	2	900	G

14. You are the manager of a project to improve a billing process at your firm. Table 7 contains the data you will need to conduct a cost analysis of the project. Indirect costs are $1,600 per week, and penalty costs are $1,200 per week after week 12.

a. What is the minimum-cost schedule for this project?

b. What is the difference in total project costs between the earliest completion time of the project using "normal" times and the minimum-cost schedule you derived in part (a)?

15. Table 8 contains data for the installation of new equipment in a manufacturing process at Excello Corporation. Your company is responsible for the installation project. Indirect costs are $15,000 per week, and a penalty cost of $9,000 per week will be incurred by your company for every week the project is delayed beyond week 9.

a. What is the shortest time duration for this project regardless of cost?

b. What is the minimum total cost associated with completing the project in 9 weeks?

c. What is the total time of the minimum-cost schedule?

TABLE 7 | DATA FOR THE BILLING PROCESS PROJECT

Activity	Immediate Predecessor(s)	Normal Time (weeks)	Crash Time (weeks)	Normal Cost ($)	Crash Cost ($)
A	—	4	1	5,000	8,000
B	—	5	3	8,000	10,000
C	A	1	1	4,000	4,000
D	B	6	3	6,000	12,000
E	B, C	7	6	4,000	7,000
F	D	7	6	4,000	7,000

TABLE 8 | DATA FOR THE EQUIPMENT INSTALLATION PROJECT

Activity	Immediate Predecessor(s)	Normal Time (weeks)	Crash Time (weeks)	Normal Cost ($)	Crash Cost ($)
A	—	2	1	7,000	10,000
B	—	2	2	3,000	3,000
C	A	3	1	12,000	40,000
D	B	3	2	12,000	28,000
E	C	1	1	8,000	8,000
F	D, E	5	3	5,000	15,000
G	E	3	2	9,000	18,000

16. Gabrielle Kramer, owner of Pet Paradise, is opening a new store in Columbus, Ohio. Her major concern is the hiring of a manager and several associates who are animal lovers. She also has to coordinate the renovation of a building that was previously owned by a chic clothing store. Kramer has gathered the data shown in Table 9.

   a. How long is the project expected to take?

   b. Suppose that Kramer has a personal goal of completing the project in 14 weeks. What is the probability that it will happen this quickly?

17. The diagram in Figure 14 was developed for a project that you are managing. Suppose that you are interested in finding ways to speed up the project at minimal additional cost. Determine the schedule for completing the project in 25 days at minimum cost. Penalty and project-overhead costs are negligible. Time and cost data for each activity are shown in Table 10.

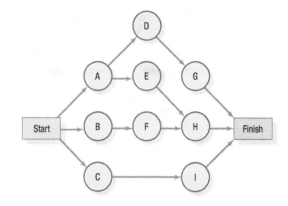

▲ FIGURE 14

Network Diagram for Problem 17

TABLE 9 | DATA FOR THE PET PARADISE PROJECT

Activity	Description	Immediate Predecessor(s)	a	m	b
A	Interview for new manager	—	1	3	6
B	Renovate building	—	6	9	12
C	Place ad for associates and interview applicants	—	6	8	16
D	Have new manager prospects visit	A	2	3	4
E	Purchase equipment for new store and install	B	1	3	11
F	Check employee applicant references and make final selection	C	5	5	5
G	Check references for new manager and make final selection	D	1	1	1
H	Hold orientation meetings and do payroll paperwork	E, F, G	3	3	3

(TIME (WEEKS) spans columns a, m, b)

TABLE 10 | PROJECT ACTIVITY AND COST DATA

Activity	NORMAL Time (days)	NORMAL Cost ($)	CRASH Time (days)	CRASH Cost ($)
A	12	1,300	11	1,900
B	13	1,050	9	1,500
C	18	3,000	16	4,500
D	9	2,000	5	3,000
E	12	650	10	1,100
F	8	700	7	1,050
G	8	1,550	6	1,950
H	2	600	1	800
I	4	2,200	2	4,000

18. Paul Silver, owner of Sculptures International, just initiated a new art project. The following data are available for the project:

Activity	Activity Time (days)	Immediate Predecessor(s)
A	4	—
B	1	—
C	3	A
D	2	B
E	3	C, D

    a. Draw the network diagram for the project.

    b. Determine the project's critical path and duration.

    c. What is the slack for each activity?

19. Reliable Garage is completing production of the J2000 kit car. The following data are available for the project:

Activity	Activity Time (days)	Immediate Predecessor(s)
A	2	—
B	6	A
C	4	B
D	5	C
E	7	C
F	5	C
G	5	F
H	3	D, E, G

    a. Draw the network diagram for the project.

    b. Determine the project's critical path and duration.

    c. What is the slack for each activity?

20. The following information concerns a new project your company is undertaking:

Activity	Activity Time (days)	Immediate Predecessor(s)
A	10	—
B	11	—
C	9	A, B
D	5	A, B
E	8	A, B
F	13	C, E
G	5	C, D
H	10	G
I	6	F, G
J	9	E, H
K	11	I, J

    a. Draw the network diagram for this project.

    b. Determine the critical path and project completion time.

Advanced Problems

21. The project manager of Good Public Relations gathered the data shown in Table 11 for a new advertising campaign.

    a. How long is the project likely to take?

    b. What is the probability that the project will take more than 38 weeks?

    c. Consider the path A–E–G–H–J. What is the probability that this path will exceed 38 weeks?

TABLE 11 | ACTIVITY DATA FOR ADVERTISING PROJECT

Activity	TIME ESTIMATES (WEEKS)			Immediate Predecessor(s)
	Optimistic	Most Likely	Pessimistic	
A	8	10	12	START
B	5	8	17	START
C	7	8	9	START
D	1	2	3	B
E	8	10	12	A, C
F	5	6	7	D, E
G	1	3	5	D, E
H	2	5	8	F, G
I	2	4	6	G
J	4	5	8	H
K	2	2	2	H

22. Consider the office renovation project data in Table 12. A "zero" time estimate means that the activity could take a very small amount of time and should be treated as a numeric zero in the analysis.

a. Based on the critical path, find the probability of completing the office renovation project by 39 days.

b. Find the date by which you would be 90 percent sure of completing the project.

TABLE 12 | DATA FOR THE OFFICE RENOVATION PROJECT

Activity	TIME ESTIMATES (DAYS)			Immediate Predecessor(s)
	Optimistic	Most Likely	Pessimistic	
START	0	0	0	—
A	6	10	14	START
B	0	1	2	A
C	16	20	30	A
D	3	5	7	B
E	2	3	4	D
F	7	10	13	C
G	1	2	3	D
H	0	2	4	G
I	2	2	2	C, G
J	2	3	4	I
K	0	1	2	H
L	1	2	3	J, K
FINISH	0	0	0	E, F, L

23. You are in charge of a project at the local community center. The center needs to remodel one of the rooms in time for the start of a new program. Delays in the project mean that the center must rent other space at a nearby church at additional cost. Time and cost data for your project are contained in Table 13. Your interest is in minimizing the cost of the project to the community center.

a. Using the *normal times* for each activity, what is the earliest date you can complete the project?

b. Suppose the variable overhead costs are $50 per day for your project. Also, suppose that the center must pay $40 per day for a temporary room on day 15 or beyond. Find the minimum-cost project schedule.

TABLE 13 | DATA FOR THE COMMUNITY CENTER PROJECT

Activity	Normal Time (days)	Normal Cost ($)	Crash Time (days)	Crash Cost ($)	Immediate Predecessor(s)
START	0	0	0	0	—
A	10	50	8	150	START
B	4	40	2	200	START
C	7	70	6	160	B
D	2	20	1	50	A, C
E	3	30	3	30	A, C
F	8	80	5	290	B
G	5	50	4	180	D
H	6	60	3	180	E, F
FINISH	0	0	0	0	G, H

24. The information in Table 14 is available for a large fund-raising project.

   a. Determine the critical path and the expected completion time of the project.

   b. Plot the total project cost, starting from day 1 to the expected completion date of the project, assuming the earliest start times for each activity. Compare that result to a similar plot for the latest start times. What implication does the time differential have for cash flows and project scheduling?

25. You are the project manager of the software installation project in Table 15. You would like to find the minimum-cost schedule for your project. There is a $1,000-per-week penalty for each week the project is delayed beyond week 25. In addition, your project team determined that indirect project costs are $2,500 per week.

   a. What would be your target completion week?

   b. How much would you save in total project costs with your schedule?

TABLE 14 | FUND-RAISING PROJECT DATA

Activity	Activity Time (days)	Activity Cost ($)	Immediate Predecessor(s)
A	3	100	—
B	4	150	—
C	2	125	A
D	5	175	B
E	3	150	B
F	4	200	C, D
G	6	75	C
H	2	50	C, D, E
I	1	100	E
J	4	75	D, E
K	3	150	F, G
L	3	150	G, H, I
M	2	100	I, J
N	4	175	K, M
O	1	200	H, M
P	5	150	N, L, O

TABLE 15 | DATA FOR SOFTWARE INSTALLATION PROJECT

Activity	Immediate Predecessors	Normal Time (weeks)	Normal Cost ($)	Crash Time (weeks)	Crash Cost ($)
A	—	5	2,000	3	4,000
B	—	8	5,000	7	8,000
C	A	10	10,000	8	12,000
D	A, B	4	3,000	3	7,000
E	B	3	4,000	2	5,000
F	D	9	8,000	6	14,000
G	E, F	2	2,000	2	2,000
H	G	8	6,000	5	9,000
I	C, F	9	7,000	7	15,000

26. Consider the project described in Table 16.

   a. If you start the project immediately, when will it be finished?

   b. You are interested in completing your project as soon as possible. You have only one option. Suppose you could assign Employee A, currently assigned to activity G, to help Employee B, currently assigned to activity F. Each week that Employee A helps Employee B will result in activity G increasing its time by one week and activity F reducing its time by one week. How many weeks should Employee A work on activity F?

TABLE 16 | PROJECT DATA FOR PROBLEM 26

Activity	Activity Time (weeks)	Immediate Predecessor(s)
START	0	—
A	3	START
B	4	START
C	4	B
D	4	A
E	5	A, B
F	6	D, E
G	2	C, E
FINISH	0	F, G

Active Model Exercise

This Active Model appears in MyOMLab. It allows you to evaluate the sensitivity of the project time to changes in activity times and activity predecessors.

QUESTIONS

1. Activity B and activity K are critical activities. Describe the difference that occurs on the graph when you increase activity B versus when you increase activity K.

2. Activity F is not critical. Use the scroll bar to determine how many weeks you can increase activity F until it becomes critical.

3. Activity A is not critical. How many weeks can you increase activity A until it becomes critical? What happens when activity A becomes critical?

4. What happens when you increase activity A by one week after it becomes critical?

5. Suppose that building codes may change and, as a result, activity C would have to be completed before activity D could be started. How would this affect the project?

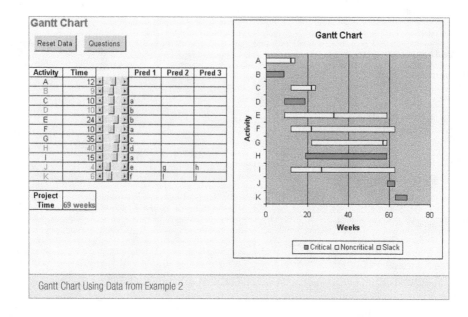

Gantt Chart Using Data from Example 2

VIDEO CASE | Project Management at the Phoenician

The Phoenician in Phoenix, Arizona, is part of Starwood's Luxury Collection and its only AAA Five Diamond Award resort in the southwestern United States. Sophistication, elegance, and excellence only begin to describe the guest experience at the hotel. Guests can dine in one of nine restaurants, relax poolside, play tennis, take in 27 holes of golf on three 9-hole courses, or relax with a variety of soothing spa treatments at the 22,000-square-foot Centre for Well-Being.

The Phoenician recently embarked on an ambitious $38 million spa and golf renovation program. The resort's golf and spa programs historically earned high marks from surveys in their industries over the years, but the environment was changing. Evidence of this change was seen in the explosive growth of new golf courses and spas in the Southwest region. Phoenix alone has over 275 golf courses, and the Southwest boasts the largest concentration of new luxury spas anywhere. The Phoenician's facilities, while world-class and highly rated, were more than 15 years old. The hotel's recently awarded Five Diamond status renewed emphasis on bringing every process and service at the property up to Five Diamond level.

The decision to renovate the golf course and existing spa became not a question of *whether* to undertake the projects, but *to what degree* they needed to be pursued. Key considerations centered on (1) whether to build basic facilities or commit to the grandiose luxury level, (2) having a domestic versus international reputation, and (3) developing creative packaging of the new facilities to attract loyal guests, such as a spa and golf "country club-like" membership program. Such a program would be limited to about 600 spa/golf memberships, with a one-time fee of $65,000 each.

The company's senior management considered three options for the Centre for Well-Being spa. First, the existing space in the heart of the resort could be renovated. This option would require relocating the spa to another part of the resort and offering limited treatments during this time, thereby reducing spa revenues significantly. With option 2, hilly terrain directly behind the resort could be carved out to create a new mountainside facility with sweeping vistas. This option meant the closure of one of the hotel's buildings housing 60 guest rooms and suites during the construction period. The existing spa could remain open, however. Under option 3, a parking structure on existing hotel property could be used, having the least impact on revenues. The first option was seen as a short-term fix, while the remaining two were viewed as having longer-term potential.

Additional discussion centered on the type of spa to be built. Recent acquisition of the Bliss spa brand for Starwood's W Hotels was an option, offering day spa amenities and an indulgence atmosphere. The second option was to remain a holistic resort spa with an emphasis on health and restoration. The third option was to become a destination spa with dedicated guest stays and week-long programs. Day spas are the fastest-growing category, with few destination spas.

The Phoenician management team, with assistance from Starwood Field Operations and Corporate offices, prepared an extensive analysis of strengths, weaknesses, opportunities, and threats to better understand the environment. The result of this analysis was used by the team to identify the set of activities necessary for each option. The Corporate Design and Construction group developed architectural and engineering plans, as

Work Breakdown Structure	Activity Time (days)	Activity Precedence Relationships
Project Conception		
A. Kick-off meeting	2	
B. Creation of spa specifications	30	A
Geotechnical Investigation		
C. Preliminary site characterizations	10	B
D. Subsurface investigation	10	C
E. Laboratory testing	5	D
F. Geologic hazard assessments	10	E
Design Development		
G. Initial designs	70	B
H. Preliminary zoning compliance plan	15	C, G
I. Final designs	18	H
J. Owner approval of designs	5	I
Documentation and Cost Estimation		
K. Construction documentation and landscape package	80	F, I
L. Acquisition of contractor estimates and bids	90	J, K
Decision		
M. Owner approval of one of the three projects	60	L

well as the work breakdown structure and diagrams showing the critical path for the possible project options. The work breakdown structure, activity times, and activity precedence relationships are shown in the table on the previous page.

QUESTIONS

1. Coordinating departments in a major project is always a challenge. Which departments within the Starwood organization likely played a role in each of the following project related activities?
   a. Defining and organizing the project
   b. Planning the project
   c. Monitoring and controlling the project
2. Many times, project decision makers do not rely solely on financial hurdles, such as return on investment or internal rates of return, but place a lot of emphasis on intangible factors. Which are the salient intangible factors associated with selecting one of the three options for the spa?
3. Timing is always a challenge in managing projects. Construct a network diagram for the spa selection process. How soon can The Phoenician management make a decision on the spa?

Pearson

When the Phoenician, a luxury hotel in Phoenix, Arizona, sought to re-design its Center for Well-Being, its management team created a work breakdown structure in order to compare different project options and choose the best one.

CASE | The Pert Mustang

Roberts Auto Sales and Service (RASAS) consists of three car dealerships that sell and service several makes of American and Japanese cars, two auto parts stores, a large body shop and car painting business, and an auto salvage yard. Vicky Roberts, owner of RASAS, went into the car business when she inherited a Ford dealership from her father. She was able to capitalize on her knowledge and experience to build her business into the diversified and successful mini-empire it is today. Her motto, "Sell 'em today, repair 'em tomorrow!" reflects a strategy that she refers to in private as "Get 'em coming and going."

Roberts has always retained a soft spot in her heart for high-performance Mustangs and just acquired a 1965 Shelby Mustang GT 350 that needs a lot of restoration. She also notes the public's growing interest in the restoration of vintage automobiles. Roberts is thinking of expanding into the vintage car restoration business and needs help in assessing the feasibility of such a move. She wants to restore her 1965 Shelby Mustang to mint condition, or as close to mint condition as possible. If she decides to go into the car restoring business, she can use the Mustang as an exhibit in sales and advertising and take it to auto shows to attract business for the new shop.

Roberts believes that many people want the thrill of restoring an old car themselves, but they do not have the time to run down all the old parts. Still, others just want to own a vintage auto because it is different and many of them have plenty of money to pay someone to restore an auto for them.

Roberts wants the new business to appeal to both types of people. For the first group, she envisions serving as a parts broker for NOS ("new old stock"), new parts that were manufactured many years ago and are still packaged in their original cartons. It can be a time-consuming process to find the right part. RASAS could also machine new parts to replicate those that are hard to find or that no longer exist.

In addition, RASAS could assemble a library of parts and body manuals for old cars to serve as an information resource for do-it-yourself restorers. The do-it-yourselfers could come to RASAS for help in compiling parts lists, and RASAS could acquire the parts for them. For others, RASAS would take charge of the entire restoration.

Roberts asked the director of service operations to take a good look at her Mustang and determine what needs to be done to restore it to the condition it was in when it came from the factory more than 40 years ago. She

wants to restore this car in time to exhibit it at the Detroit Auto Show. If the car gets a lot of press, it will be a real public relations coup for RASAS—especially if Roberts decides to enter this new venture. Even if she does not, the car will be a showpiece for the rest of the business.

Roberts asked the director of service operations to prepare a report about what is involved in restoring the car and whether it can be done in time for the Detroit show in 45 working days using PERT/CPM. The parts manager, the body shop manager, and the chief mechanic have provided the following estimates of times and activities that need to be done, as well as cost estimates:

a. Order all needed material and parts (upholstery, windshield, carburetor, and oil pump). Time: 2 days. Cost (telephone calls and labor): $100.

b. Receive upholstery material for seat covers. Cannot be done until order is placed. Time: 30 days. Cost: $2,100.

c. Receive windshield. Cannot be done until order is placed. Time: 10 days. Cost: $800.

d. Receive carburetor and oil pump. Cannot be done until order is placed. Time: 7 days. Cost: $1,750.

e. Remove chrome from body. Can be done immediately. Time: 1 day. Cost: $200.

f. Remove body (doors, hood, trunk, and fenders) from frame. Cannot be done until chrome is removed. Time: 1 day. Cost: $300.

g. Have fenders repaired by body shop. Cannot be done until body is removed from frame. Time: 4 days. Cost: $1,000.

h. Repair doors, trunk, and hood. Cannot be done until body is removed from frame. Time: 6 days. Cost: $1,500.

i. Pull engine from chassis. Do after body is removed from frame. Time: 1 day. Cost: $200.

j. Remove rust from frame. Do after the engine has been pulled from the chassis. Time: 3 days. Cost $900.

k. Regrind engine valves. Do after the engine has been pulled from the chassis. Time: 5 days. Cost: $1,000.

l. Replace carburetor and oil pump. Do after engine has been pulled from chassis and after carburetor and oil pump have been received. Time: 1 day. Cost: $200.

m. Rechrome the chrome parts. Chrome must have been removed from the body first. Time: 3 days. Cost: $210.

n. Reinstall engine. Do after valves are reground and carburetor and oil pump have been installed. Time: 1 day. Cost: $200.

o. Put doors, hood, and trunk back on frame. The doors, hood, and trunk must have been repaired first. The frame must have had its rust removed first. Time: 1 day. Cost: $240.

p. Rebuild transmission and replace brakes. Do so after the engine has been reinstalled and the doors, hood, and trunk are back on the frame. Time: 4 days. Cost: $2,000.

q. Replace windshield. Windshield must have been received. Time: 1 day. Cost: $100.

r. Put fenders back on. The fenders must have been repaired first, the transmission rebuilt, and the brakes replaced. Time: 1 day. Cost: $100.

s. Paint car. Cannot be done until the fenders are back on and windshield replaced. Time: 4 days. Cost: $1,700.

t. Reupholster interior of car. Must have received upholstery material first. Car must have been painted first. Time: 7 days. Cost: $2,400.

u. Put chrome parts back on. Car must have been painted and chrome parts rechromed first. Time: 1 day. Cost: $100.

v. Pull car to the Detroit Auto Show. Must have completed reupholstery of interior and have put the chrome parts back on. Time: 2 days. Cost: $1,000.

Roberts wants to limit expenditures on this project to what could be recovered by selling the restored car. She has already spent $50,000 to acquire the car. In addition, she wants a brief report on some of the aspects of the proposed business, such as how it fits in with RASAS's other businesses and what RASAS's operations task should be with regard to cost, quality, customer service, and flexibility.

In the restoration business there are various categories of restoration. A basic restoration gets the car looking great and running, but a mint condition restoration puts the car back in original condition—as it was "when it rolled off the line." When restored cars are resold, a car in mint condition commands a much higher price than one that is just a basic restoration. As cars are restored, they can also be customized. That is, something is put on the car that could not have been on the original. Roberts wants a mint condition restoration for her Mustang, without customization. (The proposed new business would accept any kind of restoration a customer wanted.)

The total budget cannot exceed $70,000 including the $50,000 Roberts has already spent. In addition, Roberts cannot spend more than $3,600 in any week given her present financial position. Even though much of the work will be done by Roberts's own employees, labor and materials costs must be considered. All relevant costs have been included in the cost estimates.

QUESTIONS

1. Using the information provided, prepare the report that Vicky Roberts requested, assuming that the project will begin immediately. Assume 45 working days are available to complete the project, including transporting the car to Detroit before the auto show begins. Your report should briefly discuss the aspects of the proposed new business, such as the competitive priorities that Roberts asked about.

2. Construct a table containing the project activities using the letter assigned to each activity, the time estimates, and the precedence relationships from which you will assemble the network diagram.

3. Draw a network diagram of the project similar to Figure 4. Determine the activities on the critical path and the estimated slack for each activity.

4. Prepare a project budget showing the cost of each activity and the total for the project. Can the project be completed within the budget? Will the project require more than $3,600 in any week? To answer this question, assume that activities B, C, and D must be paid for when the item is received (the earliest finish time for the activity). Assume that the costs of all other activities that span more than one week can be prorated. Each week contains five work days. If problems exist, how might Roberts overcome them?

Source: This case was prepared by and is used by permission of Dr. Sue P. Siferd, Professor Emerita, Arizona State University (Updated September, 2007).

Selected References

Goldratt, E. M. *Critical Chain.* Great Barrington, MA: North River, 1997.

Hartvigsen, David. *SimQuick: Process Simulation with Excel.* 2nd ed. Upper Saddle River, NJ: Prentice Hall, 2004.

Kerzner, Harold. *Advanced Project Management: Best Practices on Implementation,* 2nd ed. New York: John Wiley & Sons, 2004.

Kerzner, Harold. *Project Management: A Systems Approach to Planning, Scheduling, and Controlling,* 10th ed. New York: John Wiley & Sons, 2009.

Lewis, J. P. *Mastering Project Management,* 2nd ed. New York: McGraw-Hill, 2001.

Mantel Jr., Samuel J., Jack R. Meredith, Scott M. Shafer, and Margaret M. Sutton. *Project Management in Practice,* 3rd ed. New York: John Wiley & Sons, 2007.

Meredith, Jack R., and Samuel J. Mantel, *Project Management: A Managerial Approach,* 6th ed. New York: John Wiley & Sons, 2005.

Muir, Nancy C. *Microsoft Project 2007 for Dummies,* New York: John Wiley & Sons, 2006.

Nicholas, John M, and Herman Stein. *Project Management for Business, Engineering, and Technology,* 3rd ed. Burlington, MA: Butterworth-Heinemann, 2008.

"A Guide to Project Management Body of Knowledge," 2008. Available from the Project Management Institute at www.pmi.org.

Srinivasan, Mandyam, Darren Jones, and Alex Miller. "CORPS Capabilities." *APICS Magazine* (March 2005), pp. 46–50.

Don Ryan/AP Photos

PROCESS STRATEGY

At any given time eBay has approximately 113 million listings worldwide, and yet its workforce consists of just 15,000 employees. The explanation? Customers do most of the work in eBay's buying and selling processes. Here a customer prepares items for shipping from sales on his Ebay account.

eBay

Most manufacturers do not have to contend with customers waltzing around their shop floors, showing up intermittently and unannounced. Such customer contact can introduce considerable variability, disrupting carefully designed production processes. Costs and quality can be adversely affected. While customer contact is an issue even with manufacturers, (each process does have at least one customer), extensive customer contact and involvement are business as usual for many processes of service providers. Customers at restaurants or rental car agencies are directly involved in performing the processes. The area where the sales person interacts with the customer *is* the shop floor.

How much should customers be involved in a process, so as to provide timely delivery and consistent quality, and at sustainable cost? Various ways are available—some accommodate customer-introduced variability and some reduce it. eBay illustrates one way to accommodate variability. As an online auction house, eBay has high volume and request variability. Its customers do not want service at the same time or at times necessarily convenient to the company. They have request variability, seeking to buy and sell an endless number of items. They also have variability in customer capability, some with considerable Internet experience and some needing more handholding. Such variability would greatly complicate workforce scheduling if eBay required its employees to conduct all of its processes. It connects hundreds of millions of people around

From Chapter 3 of *Operations Management: Processes and Supply Chains*, Tenth Edition. Lee J. Krajewski, Larry P. Ritzman, Manoj K. Malhotra. Copyright © 2013 by Pearson Education, Inc. All rights reserved.

the world every day. It has a global presence in 39 markets, with revenue of $9.2 billion in more than 50,000 categories—and only with 15,500 employees. This relatively small workforce is possible in the face of customer-induced variability because its customers perform virtually all of the selling and buying processes through the eBay Web site. When the customer is responsible for much of the work, the right labor is provided at the right moment.

process strategy

The pattern of decisions made in managing processes so that they achieve their competitive priorities.

Source: Frances X. Frei, "Breaking the Trade-Off between Efficiency and Service," *Harvard Business Review* (November 2006), pp. 93–101; **http://en.wikipedia.org/wiki/Ebay** (March 19, 2011).

LEARNING GOALS *After reading this chapter, you should be able to:*

1 Explain why processes exist everywhere in all organizations.

2 Discuss the four major process decisions.

3 Position a process on the customer-contact matrix or product-process matrix.

4 Configure operations into layouts.

5 Define customer involvement, resource flexibility, capital intensity, and economies of scope.

6 Discuss how process decisions should fit together.

7 Define process reengineering and process improvement.

Creating Value through Operations Management

Using Operations to Compete
Project Management

Managing Processes

Process Strategy
Process Analysis
Quality and Performance
Capacity Planning
Constraint Management
Lean Systems

Managing Supply Chains

Supply Chain
Inventory Management

Supply Chain Design

Supply Chain Location
Decisions

Supply Chain Integration

Supply Chain Sustainability and
Humanitarian Logistics

Forecasting

Operations Planning and
Scheduling

Resource Planning

Process decisions, such as the amount of customer involvement allowed at eBay, are strategic in nature: They should further a company's long-term competitive goals. In making process decisions, managers focus on controlling such competitive priorities as quality, flexibility, time, and cost. Process management is an ongoing activity, with the same principles applying to both first-time and redesign choices.

In this chapter, we focus on **process strategy**, which specifies the pattern of decisions made in managing processes so that the processes will achieve their competitive priorities. Process strategy guides a variety of process decisions, and in turn is guided by operations strategy and the organization's ability to obtain the resources necessary to support them. We begin by defining four basic process decisions: (1) process structure (including layout), (2) customer involvement, (3) resource flexibility, and (4) capital intensity. We discuss these decisions for both service and manufacturing processes. We pay particular attention to ways in which these decisions fit together, depending on factors such as competitive priorities, customer contact, and volume. We conclude with two basic change strategies for analyzing and modifying processes: (1) process reengineering and (2) process improvement.

Three principles concerning process strategy are particularly important:

1. The key to successful process decisions is to make choices that fit the situation and that make sense together. They should not work at cross-purposes, with one process optimized at the expense of other processes. A more effective process is one that matches key process characteristics and has a close *strategic fit*.

2. Although this section of the text focuses on individual processes, they are the building blocks that eventually create the firm's whole supply chain. The cumulative effect on customer satisfaction and competitive advantage is huge.

3. Whether processes in the supply chain are performed internally or by outside suppliers and customers, management must pay particular attention to the interfaces between processes. Dealing with these interfaces underscores the need for cross-functional coordination.

Process Strategy across the Organization

Processes are everywhere and are the basic unit of work. Consider the following two major points: (1) supply chains have processes and (2) processes are found throughout the whole organization, and not just in operations.

Supply Chains Have Processes

Managing Processes and Managing Supply Chains are essential aspects of operations management. **Supply chain processes**, are business processes that have external customers or suppliers. Table 1 illustrates some common supply chain processes.

supply chain processes

Business processes that have external customers or suppliers.

TABLE 1 | SUPPLY CHAIN PROCESS EXAMPLES

Process	Description	Process	Description
Outsourcing	Exploring available suppliers for the best options to perform processes in terms of price, quality, delivery time, environmental issues	**Customer Service**	Providing information to answer questions or resolve problems using automated information services as well as voice-to-voice contact with customers
Warehousing	Receiving shipments from suppliers, verifying quality, placing in inventory, and reporting receipt for inventory records	**Logistics**	Selecting transportation mode (train, ship, truck, airplane, or pipeline) scheduling both inbound and outbound shipments, and providing intermediate inventory storage
Sourcing	Selecting, certifying and evaluating suppliers and managing supplier contracts	**Cross-docking**	Packing of products of incoming shipments so they can be easily sorted more economically at intermediate warehouses for outgoing shipments to their final destination

These supply chain processes should be documented and analyzed for improvement, examined for quality improvement and control, and assessed in terms of capacity and bottlenecks. These topics are essential to managing supply chain processes. Supply chain processes will be only as good as the processes within the organization that have only internal suppliers and customers. Each process in the chain, from suppliers to customers, must be designed to achieve its competitive priorities and add value to the work performed.

Processes Are Not Just in Operations

Processes are found in accounting, finance, human resources, management information systems, and marketing. Organizational structure throughout the many diverse industries varies, but for the most part, all organizations perform similar business processes. Table 2 lists a sample of them that are outside the operations area. All of these processes must be managed.

TABLE 2 | ILLUSTRATIVE BUSINESS PROCESSES OUTSIDE OF OPERATIONS

Activity based costing	Employee-development	Payroll
Asset management	Employee-recruiting	Records management
Billing budget	Employee-training	Research and development
Complaint handling	Engineering	Sales
Credit management	Environment	Help desks
Customer-satisfaction	External communications	Disaster recovery
Employee-benefits	Finance	Waste management
Employee-compensation	Security management	Warranty

Managers of these processes must make sure that they are adding as much customer value as possible. They must understand that many processes cut across organizational lines, regardless of whether the firm is organized along functional, product, regional, or process lines.

Process Strategy Decisions

A process involves the use of an organization's resources to provide something of value. No service can be provided and no product can be made without a process, and no process can exist without at least one service or product. One recurring question in managing processes

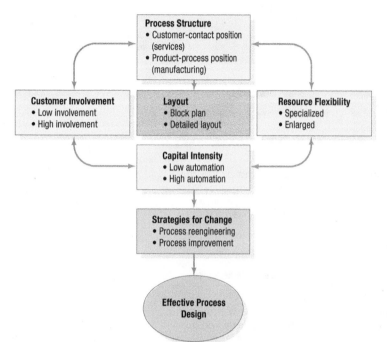

is deciding *how* to provide services or make products. Many different choices are available in selecting human resources, equipment, outsourced services, materials, work flows, and methods that transform inputs into outputs. Another choice is which processes are to be done in-house, and which processes are to be outsourced—that is, done outside the firm and purchased as materials and services. This decision helps to define the supply chain.

Process decisions directly affect the process itself and indirectly the services and the products that it provides. Whether dealing with processes for offices, service providers, or manufacturers, operations managers must consider four common process decisions. Figure 1 shows that they are all important steps toward an effective process design. These four decisions are best understood at the process or subprocess level, rather than at the firm level.

- **Process structure** determines the process type relative to the kinds of resources needed, how resources are partitioned between them, and their key characteristics.

▲ **FIGURE 1**
Major Decisions for Effective Processes

process structure

The process type relative to the kinds of resources needed, how resources are partitioned between them, and their key characteristics.

layout

The physical arrangement of operations created by the various processes.

customer involvement

The ways in which customers become part of the process and the extent of their participation.

resource flexibility

The ease with which employees and equipment can handle a wide variety of products, output levels, duties, and functions.

capital intensity

The mix of equipment and human skills in a process.

A **layout**, which is the physical arrangement of operations created from the various processes, puts these decisions into tangible form.

- **Customer involvement** reflects the ways in which customers become part of the process and the extent of their participation.

- **Resource flexibility** is the ease with which employees and equipment can handle a wide variety of products, output levels, duties, and functions.

- **Capital intensity** is the mix of equipment and human skills in a process. The greater the relative cost of equipment, the greater is the capital intensity.

The concepts that we develop around these four decisions establish a framework within which we can address the appropriate process design in every situation. There is no "how to" element here in this chapter. Instead, we establish the patterns of choices that create a good fit between the four decisions. For example, if you walk through a manufacturing facility where materials flow smoothly from one work station to the next (which we will define later to be a *line* process), you would be tempted to conclude that all processes should be line processes. They seem so efficient and organized. However, if volumes are low and the products made are customized, converting to a line process would be a big mistake. When volumes are low and products are customized, resources must be more flexible to handle a variety of products. The result is a more disorganized appearance with jobs crisscrossing in many different directions depending on the product being made. Despite appearances, this process is the best choice.

Process Structure in Services

One of the first decisions a manager makes in designing a well-functioning process is to choose a process type that best achieves the competitive priorities for that process. Strategies for designing processes can be quite different, depending on whether a service is being provided or a product is being manufactured. We begin with service processes, given their huge implication for workforce resources in industrialized countries.

Nature of Service Processes: Customer Contact

A process strategy that gets customers in and out of a fast-food restaurant quickly would not be the right process strategy for a five-star restaurant, where customers seek a leisurely dining experience. To gain insights, we must start at the process level and recognize key contextual variables associated with the process. A good process strategy for a service process depends first and foremost on the type and amount of customer contact. **Customer contact** is the extent to which the customer is present, is actively involved, and receives personal attention during the service process. Face-to-face interaction, sometimes called a *moment of truth* or *service encounter*, brings the customer and service providers together. At that time, customer attitudes about the quality of the service provided are shaped. Table 3 shows several dimensions of customer contact. Many levels are possible on each of the five dimensions. The nested-process concept applies to customer contact, because some parts of a process can have low contact and other parts of a process can have high contact.

TABLE 3 | DIMENSIONS OF CUSTOMER CONTACT IN SERVICE PROCESSES

Dimension	High Contact	Low Contact
Physical presence	Present	Absent
What is processed	People	Possessions or information
Contact intensity	Active, visible	Passive, out of sight
Personal attention	Personal	Impersonal
Method of delivery	Face-to-face	Regular mail or e-mail

Customer-Contact Matrix

The customer-contact matrix, shown in Figure 2, brings together three elements: (1) the degree of customer contact, (2) customization, and (3) process characteristics. The matrix is the starting point for evaluating and improving a process.

Customer Contact and Customization   The horizontal dimension of the matrix represents the service provided to the customer in terms of customer contact and competitive priorities. A key competitive priority is how much customization is needed. Positions on the left side of the matrix represent high customer contact and highly customized services. The customer is more likely to be present and active. The process is more likely to be visible to the customer, who receives more personal attention. The right side of the matrix represents low customer contact, passive involvement, less personalized attention, and a process out of the customer's sight.

Process Divergence and Flow   The vertical dimension of the customer-contact matrix deals with two characteristics of the process itself: (1) process divergence and (2) flow. Each process can be analyzed on these two dimensions.

   Process divergence is the extent to which the process is highly customized with considerable latitude as to how its tasks are performed. If the process changes with each customer, virtually every performance of the service is unique. Examples of highly divergent service processes where many steps in them change with each customer are found in consulting, law, and architecture. A service with low divergence, on the other hand, is repetitive and standardized. The work is performed exactly the same with all customers, and tends to be less complex. Certain hotel services and telephone services are highly standardized to assure uniformity.

   Closely related to divergence is how the customer, object, or information being processed flows through the service facility. Work progresses through the sequence of steps in a process, which could range from highly diverse to linear. When divergence is considerable, the work flow tends to be more flexible. A **flexible flow** means that the customers, materials, or information move in diverse ways,

customer contact

The extent to which the customer is present, is actively involved, and receives personal attention during the service process.

process divergence

The extent to which the process is highly customized with considerable latitude as to how its tasks are performed.

flexible flow

The customers, materials, or information move in diverse ways, with the path of one customer or job often crisscrossing the path that the next one takes.

◀ **FIGURE 2**
Customer-Contact Matrix for Service Processes

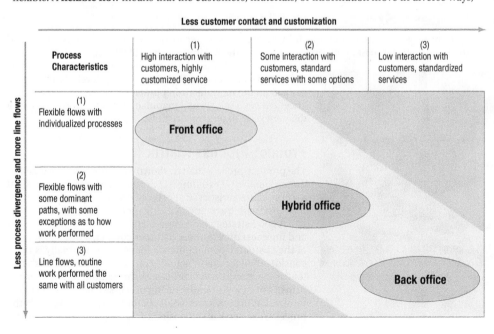

A financial consultant discusses options with a young couple at their home. This process scores high on customer contact, because the customers are present, take an active part in creating the service, receive personal attention, and have face-to-face contact.

line flow

The customers, materials, or information move linearly from one operation to the next, according to a fixed sequence.

front office

A process with high customer contact where the service provider interacts directly with the internal or external customer.

hybrid office

A process with moderate levels of customer contact and standard services with some options available.

back office

A process with low customer contact and little service customization.

with the path of one customer or job often crisscrossing the path that the next one takes. Each one can follow a carefully preplanned path, even though the first impression is one of disorganized, jumbled flows. Such an appearance goes naturally with high process divergence. A **line flow** means that the customers, materials, or information move linearly from one operation to the next, according to a fixed sequence. When diversity is low and the process standardized, line flows are a natural consequence.

Service Process Structuring

Figure 2 shows several desirable positions in the matrix that effectively connect the service product with the process. The manager has three process structures, which form a continuum, to choose from: (1) front office, (2) hybrid office, and (3) back office. It is unlikely that a process can be a top performer if a process lies too far from one of these diagonal positions, occupying instead one of the extreme positions represented by the light blue triangles in the matrix (refer to Figure 2). Such positions represent too much of a disconnect between the service provided and process characteristics.

Front Office   A **front-office** process has high customer contact where the service provider interacts directly with the internal or external customer. Because of the customization of the service and variety of service options, many of the steps in it have considerable divergence. Work flows are flexible, and they vary from one customer to the next. The high-contact service process tends to be adapted or tailored to each customer.

Hybrid Office A hybrid office tends to be in the middle of the five dimensions in Table 3, or perhaps high on some contact measures and low on others. A **hybrid-office** process has moderate levels of customer contact and standard services, with some options available from which the customer chooses. The work flow progresses from one workstation to the next, with some dominant paths apparent.

Back Office   A **back-office** process has low customer contact and little service customization. The work is standardized and routine, with line flows from one service provider to the next until the service is completed. Preparing the monthly client fund balance reports in the financial services industry is a good example. It has low customer contact, low divergence, and a line flow.

Process Structure in Manufacturing

Many processes at a manufacturing firm are actually services to internal or external customers, and so the previous discussion on services applies to them. Similarly, manufacturing processes can be found in service firms. Clarity comes when viewing work at the process level, rather than the organizational level. Here we focus instead on the manufacturing processes. Because of the differences between service and manufacturing processes, we need a different view on process structure.

An employee discusses work with her supervisor. Each employee in this series of work stations are in a back office, because they have low customer contact and little service customization.

Product-Process Matrix

The product-process matrix, shown in Figure 3, brings together three elements: (1) volume, (2) product customization, and (3) process characteristics. It synchronizes the product to be manufactured with the manufacturing process itself.

A good strategy for a manufacturing process depends first and foremost on volume. Customer contact, a primary feature of the customer-contact matrix for services, normally is not a consideration for manufacturing processes (although it *is* a factor for the many service processes throughout manufacturing firms). For many manufacturing processes, high product customization means lower volumes for many of the steps in the process. The vertical dimension of the product-process matrix

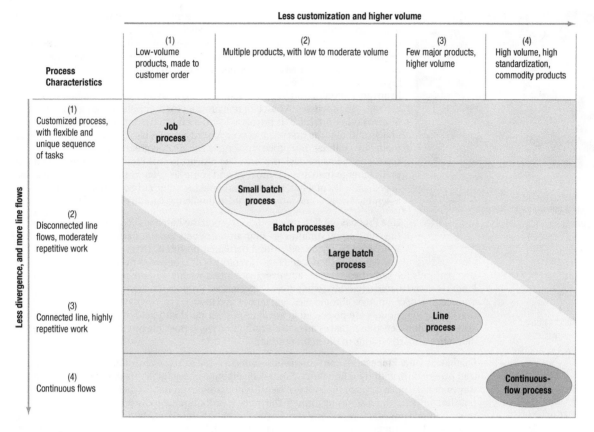

PROCESS STRATEGY

Less customization and higher volume

| Process Characteristics | (1) Low-volume products, made to customer order | (2) Multiple products, with low to moderate volume | (3) Few major products, higher volume | (4) High volume, high standardization, commodity products |

(with vertical axis label: **Less divergence, and more line flows**)

(1) Customized process, with flexible and unique sequence of tasks — **Job process**

(2) Disconnected line flows, moderately repetitive work — **Small batch process**, **Batch processes**, **Large batch process**

(3) Connected line, highly repetitive work — **Line process**

(4) Continuous flows — **Continuous-flow process**

▲ FIGURE 3
Product-Process Matrix for Manufacturing Processes

deals with the same two characteristics in the customer-contact matrix: process divergence and flow. Each manufacturing process should be analyzed on these two dimensions, just as was done for a service process.

Manufacturing Process Structuring

Figure 3 shows several desirable positions (often called *process choices*) in the product-process matrix that effectively connect the manufactured product with the process. **Process choice** is the way of structuring the process by organizing resources around the process or organizing them around the products. Organizing around the process means, for example, that all milling machines are grouped together and process all products or parts needing that kind of transformation. Organizing around the product means bringing together all the different human resources and equipment needed for a specific product and dedicating them to producing just that product. The manager has four process choices, which form a continuum, to choose from: (1) job process, (2) batch process, (3) line process, and (4) continuous-flow process. As with the customer-contact matrix, it is unlikely that a manufacturing process can be a top performer if its position is too far from the diagonal. The fundamental message in Figure 3 is that the best choice for a manufacturing process depends on the volume and degree of customization required of the process. The process choice might apply to an entire manufacturing process or just one subprocess nested within it.

Job Process   A **job process** creates the flexibility needed to produce a wide variety of products in significant quantities, with considerable divergence in the steps performed. Customization is high and volume for any one product is low. The workforce and equipment are flexible to handle considerable task divergence. Companies choosing job processes often bid for work. Typically, they make products to order and do not produce them ahead of time. Each new order is handled as a single unit—as a job. Examples are machining a metal casting for a customized order or producing customized cabinets.

With a job process, all equipment and workers capable of certain types of work are located together. Because customization is high and most jobs have a different sequence of steps, this process choice creates flexible flows through the operations rather than a line flow.

process choice

A way of structuring the process by organizing resources around the process or organizing them around the products.

job process

A process with the flexibility needed to produce a wide variety of products in significant quantities, with considerable divergence in the steps performed.

Batch Process The batch process is by far the most common process choice found in practice, leading to terms such as *small batch* or *large batch* to further distinguish one process choice from another. A **batch process** differs from the job process with respect to volume, variety, and quantity. The primary difference is that volumes are higher because the same or similar products or parts going into them are produced repeatedly. Some of the components going into the final product may be processed in advance. Production lots are handled in larger quantities (or *batches*) than they are with job processes. A batch of one product (or component part going into it or perhaps other products) is processed, and then production is switched to the next one. Eventually, the first product is produced again. A batch process has average or moderate volumes, but process divergence is still too great to warrant dedicating a separate process for each product. The process flow is flexible, but more dominant paths emerge than at a job process, and some segments of the process have a line flow. Examples of a batch process are making standard components that feed an assembly line or some processes that manufacture capital equipment.

Line Process A **line process** lies between the batch and continuous processes on the continuum; volumes are high and products are standardized, which allows resources to be organized around particular products. Divergence is minimal in the process or line flows, and little inventory is held between the processing steps. Each step performs the same process over and over, with little variability in the products manufactured. Production and material handling equipment is specialized. Products created by a line process include the assembly of computers, automobiles, appliances, and toys.

Standard products are produced in advance of their need and held in inventory so that they are ready when a customer places an order. Product variety is possible by careful control of the addition of standard options to the main product.

Continuous Flow Process A **continuous flow process** is the extreme end of high-volume standardized production, with rigid line flows. Process divergence is negligible. Its name derives from the way materials move through the process. Usually, one primary material (such as a liquid, a gas, or a powder) moves without stopping through the process. A continuous-flow process differs from a line process in one important respect: Materials (be they undifferentiated or discrete) flow through the process without stopping until the whole batch is finished. The time span can be several shifts or even several months. Examples of a continuous flow process are petroleum refining; chemical processes; and processes making steel, soft drinks, and food (such as Borden's huge pasta-making plant).

Production and Inventory Strategies

Strategies for manufacturing processes differ from those in services, not only because of low customer contact and involvement, but also because of the ability to use inventories[1]. Make-to-order, assemble-to-order, and make-to-stock strategies are three approaches to inventory that should be coordinated with process choice.

Make-to-Order Strategy Manufacturers that make products to customer specifications in low volumes tend to use the **make-to-order strategy**, coupling it with job or small batch processes. It is a more complex process than assembling a final product from standard components. This strategy provides a high degree of customization and typically uses job or small batch processes. The processes have high divergence. Specialized medical equipment, castings, and expensive homes are suited to the make-to-order strategy.

Assemble-to-Order Strategy The **assemble-to-order strategy** is an approach to producing a wide variety of products from relatively few subassemblies and components after the customer orders are received. Typical competitive priorities are variety and fast delivery times. The assemble-to-order strategy often involves a line process for assembly and a batch process for fabrication. Because they are devoted to manufacturing standardized components and subassemblies in high volumes, the fabrication processes focus on creating appropriate amounts of component inventories for the assembly processes. Once the specific order from the customer is received, the assembly processes create the product from standardized components and subassemblies produced by the fabrication processes.

Stocking finished products would be economically prohibitive because the numerous possible options make forecasting relatively inaccurate. Thus, the principle of **postponement** is applied, whereby the final activities in the provision of a product are delayed until the orders are

A batch of apple fritters roll off one of the pastry lines at the King Soopers's Bakery in Denver to be packaged for transportation. The pastry line is a batch process, and a different kind of pastry will be made next.

batch process

A process that differs from the job process with respect to volume, variety, and quantity.

line process

A process that lies between the batch and continuous processes on the continuum; volumes are high and products are standardized, which allows resources to be organized around particular products.

continuous flow process

The extreme end of high-volume standardized production and rigid line flows, with production not starting and stopping for long time intervals.

make-to-order strategy

A strategy used by manufacturers that make products to customer specifications in low volumes.

assemble-to-order strategy

A strategy for producing a wide variety of products from relatively few subassemblies and components after the customer orders are received.

postponement

The strategy of delaying final activities in the provision of a product until the orders are received.

---

[1]Service firms also hold inventories, but only as purchased material. Manufacturing firms have the additional flexibility of holding inventories as subassemblies or finished products.

received. The assemble-to-order strategy is also linked to **mass customization**, where highly divergent processes generate a wide variety of customized products at reasonably low costs.

Make-to-Stock Strategy Manufacturing firms that hold items in stock for immediate delivery, thereby minimizing customer delivery times, use a **make-to-stock strategy**. This strategy is feasible for standardized products with high volumes and reasonably accurate forecasts. It is the inventory strategy of choice for line or continuous-flow processes. Examples of products produced with a make-to-stock strategy include garden tools, electronic components, soft drinks, and chemicals.

Combining a line process with the make-to-stock strategy is sometimes called **mass production**. It is what the popular press commonly envisions as the classical manufacturing process, because the environment is stable and predictable, with workers repeating narrowly defined tasks with low divergence.

A Chinese manufacturing firm using the make-to-stock strategy has considerable inventory stacked on pallets with rows of shelving racks in the background.

James Hardy/Altopress/Newscom

Layout

Selecting process structures for the various processes housed in a facility is a strategic decision, but must be followed by a more tactical decision—creating a layout. A *layout* is the physical arrangement of operations (or departments) created from the various processes and puts them in tangible form. For organizational purposes, processes tend to be clustered together into operations or departments. An *operation* is a group of human and capital resources performing all or part of one or more processes. For example, an operation could be several customer service representatives in a customer reception area; a group of machines and workers producing cell phones; or a marketing department. Regardless of how processes are grouped together organizationally, many of them cut across departmental boundaries. The flows across departmental lines could be informational, services, or products. Process structures that create more flows across departmental lines, as with job or batch processes, are the most challenging layout problems.

Here we demonstrate an approach to layout design that positions those departments close together that have strong interactions between them. It involves three basic steps, whether the design is for a new layout or for revising an existing layout: (1) gather information, (2) develop a block plan, and (3) design a detailed layout. We illustrate these steps with the Office of Budget Management (OBM), which is a major division in a large state government.

Gather Information

OBM consists of 120 employees assigned to six different departments. Workloads have expanded to the extent that 30 new employees must be hired and somehow housed in the space allocated to OBM. The goal is to improve communication among people who must interact with each other effectively, creating a good work environment.

Three types of information are needed to begin designing the revised layout for OBM: (1) space requirements by center, (2) available space, and (3) closeness factors. OBM has grouped its processes into six different departments: (1) administration, (2) social services, (3) institutions, (4) accounting, (5) education, and (6) internal audit. The exact space requirements of each department, in square feet, are as follows:

Department	Area Needed (ft^2)
1. Administration	3,500
2. Social services	2,600
3. Institutions	2,400
4. Accounting	1,600
5. Education	1,500
6. Internal audit	3,400
	Total 15,000

mass customization

The strategy that uses highly divergent processes to generate a wide variety of customized products at reasonably low costs.

make-to-stock strategy

A strategy that involves holding items in stock for immediate delivery, thereby minimizing customer delivery times.

mass production

A term sometimes used in the popular press for a line process that uses the make-to-stock strategy.

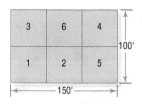

▲ FIGURE 4
Current Block Plan for the
Office of Budget Management

block plan

A plan that allocates space and
indicates placement of each
operation.

closeness matrix

A table that gives a measure of
the relative importance of each
pair of operations being located
close together.

Management must tie space requirements to capacity and staffing plans; calculate the specific equipment and space needs for each center; and allow circulation space, such as aisles and the like. At OBM, a way must be found to include all 150 employees in its assigned area. Consulting with the managers and employees involved can help avoid excessive resistance to change and make the transition smoother.

A **block plan** allocates space and indicates placement of each operation. To describe a new facility layout, the plan need only provide the facility's dimensions and space allocations. When an existing facility layout is being modified, the current block plan is also needed. OBM's available space is 150 feet by 100 feet, or 15,000 square feet. The designer could begin the design by dividing the total amount of space into six equal blocks (2,500 square feet each). The equal-space approximation shown in Figure 4 is sufficient until the detailed layout stage, when larger departments (such as administration) are assigned more space than smaller departments.

The layout designer must also know which operations need to be located close to one another. The table below shows OBM's **closeness matrix**, which gives a measure of the relative importance of each pair of operations being located close together. The metric used depends on the type of processes involved and the organizational setting. It can be a qualitative judgment on a scale from 0 to 10 that the manager uses to account for multiple performance criteria, as in the OBM's case. Only the right-hand portion of the matrix is used. The closeness factors are indicators of the need for proximity based on an analysis of information flows and the need for face-to-face meetings. They give clues as to which departments should be located close together. For example, the most important interaction is between the administration and internal audit departments for OBM, with a score of 10. This closeness factor is given in the first row and last column. Thus, the designer should locate departments 1 and 6 close together, which is not the arrangement in the current layout. Entries in both the columns and rows result in five factor scores for each department.

CLOSENESS FACTORS						
Department	**1**	**2**	**3**	**4**	**5**	**6**
1. Administration	—	3	6	5	6	10
2. Social services		—	8	1	1	
3. Institutions			—	3	9	
4. Accounting				—	2	
5. Education					—	1
6. Internal audit						—

At a manufacturing plant, the closeness factor could be the number of trips (or some other measure of materials movement) between each pair of operations per day. This information can be gleaned by conducting a statistical sampling, polling supervisors and materials handlers, or using the routings and ordering frequencies for typical items made at the plant.

Finally, the information gathered for OBM includes performance criteria that depend not on the relative location of department pairs, but the *absolute* location of a single department. OBM has two such criteria.

1. Education (department 5) should remain where it is because it is next to the office library.

2. Administration (department 1) should remain where it is because that location has the largest conference room, which administration uses often. Relocating the conference room would be costly.

Develop a Block Plan

Having gathered the needed information, the next step is to develop a block plan that best satisfies performance criteria and area requirements. The most elementary way to do so is by trial and error. Because success depends on the designer's ability to spot patterns in the data, this approach does not guarantee the selection of the best or even a nearly best solution. When supplemented by the use of a computer to evaluate solutions, however, research shows that such an approach compares quite favorably with more sophisticated computerized techniques.

Applying the Weighted-Distance Method

weighted-distance method

A mathematical model used to
evaluate layouts (of facility locations) based on closeness factors.

When *relative* locations are a primary concern, such as for effective information flow, communication, material handling, and stockpicking, the weighted-distance method can be used to compare alternative block plans. The **weighted-distance method** is a mathematical model used to evaluate layouts based on closeness factors. A similar approach, sometimes called the *load-distance method*, can be used to evaluate facility locations. The objective is to select a layout (or facility location) that minimizes the total weighted distances. The distance between two points is expressed by assigning the points to grid coordinates on a block diagram or map. An alternative approach is to use time rather than distance.

For a rough calculation, which is all that is needed for the weighted-distance method, either a Euclidean or rectilinear distance measure may be used. **Euclidean distance** is the straight-line distance, or shortest possible path, between two points. To calculate this distance, we create a graph. The distance between two points, say, points A and B, is

$$d_{AB} = \sqrt{(x_A - x_B)^2 + (y_A - y_B)^2}$$

where

d_{AB} = distance between points A and B
x_A = x-coordinate of point A
y_A = y-coordinate of point A
x_B = x-coordinate of point B
y_B = y-coordinate of point B

Rectilinear distance measures the distance between two points with a series of 90-degree turns, as along city blocks. The distance traveled in the x-direction is the absolute value of the difference between the x-coordinates. Adding this result to the absolute value of the difference between the y-coordinates gives

$$d_{AB} = |x_A - x_B| + |y_A - y_B|$$

For assistance in calculating distances using either measure, see Tutor 1 in OM Explorer.

The layout designer seeks to minimize the weighted-distance (*wd*) score by locating centers that have high-closeness ratings close together. To calculate a layout's *wd* score, we use either of the distance measures and simply multiply the proximity scores by the distances between centers. The sum of those products becomes the layout's final *wd* score—the lower the better. The location of a center is defined by its x-coordinate and y-coordinate.

Euclidean distance

The straight-line distance, or shortest possible path, between two points.

rectilinear distance

The distance between two points with a series of 90-degree turns, as along city blocks.

MyOMLab

Tutor 1 in MyOMLab provides an example to calculate both Euclidean and rectilinear distance measures.

EXAMPLE 1	Calculating the Weighted-Distance Score

The block plan in Figure 5 was developed using trial and error. A good place to start was to fix Departments 1 and 5 in their current locations. Then, the department pairs that had the largest closeness factors were located. The rest of the layout fell into place rather easily.

How much better, in terms of the *wd* score, is the proposed block plan shown in Figure 5 than the current plan shown in Figure 4? Use the rectilinear distance measure.

SOLUTION

The accompanying table lists each pair of departments that has a nonzero closeness factor in the closeness matrix. For the third column, calculate the rectilinear distances between the departments in the current layout. For example, departments 3 and 5 in the current plan are in the upper-left corner and bottom-right corner of the building, respectively. The distance between the centers of these blocks is three units (two horizontally and one vertically). For the fourth column, we multiply the weights (closeness factors) by the distances, and then add the results for a total *wd* score of 112 for the current plan. Similar calculations for the proposed plan produce a *wd* score of only 82. For example, between departments 3 and 5 is just one unit of distance (one vertically and zero horizontally).

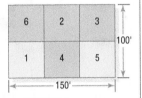

▲ **FIGURE 5**
Proposed Block Plan

MyOMLab

Active Model 1 in MyOMLab allows evaluation of the impact of swapping OBM departmental positions.

Current Plan

3	6	4
1	2	5

Proposed Plan

6	2	3
1	4	5

Department Pair	Closeness Factor (*w*)	CURRENT PLAN		PROPOSED PLAN	
		Distance (*d*)	Weighted-Distance Score (*wd*)	Distance (*d*)	Weighted-Distance Score (*wd*)
1, 2	3	1	3	2	6
1, 3	6	1	6	3	18
1, 4	5	3	15	1	5
1, 5	6	2	12	2	12
1, 6	10	2	20	1	10
2, 3	8	2	16	1	8
2, 4	1	2	2	1	1

Department Pair	Closeness Factor (w)	CURRENT PLAN		PROPOSED PLAN	
		Distance (d)	Weighted-Distance Score (wd)	Distance (d)	Weighted-Distance Score (wd)
2, 5	1	1	1	2	2
3, 4	3	2	6	2	6
3, 5	9	3	27	1	9
4, 5	2	1	2	1	2
5, 6	1	2	2	3	3
			Total 112		Total 82

To be exact, we could multiply the two *wd* total scores by 50 because each unit of distance represents 50 feet. However, the relative difference between the two totals remains unchanged.

DECISION POINT

The *wd* score for the proposed layout makes a sizeable drop from 112 to 82, but management is not sure the improvement outweighs the cost of relocating four of the six departments (i.e., all departments but 1 and 5).

◉ Rectilinear Distances   ◯ Euclidean Distances

Department Pair	Closeness Factor	Distance	Score
1, 6	10	1	10
3, 5	9	1	9
2, 3	8	1	8
1, 3	6	1	6
1, 5	6	2	12
1, 4	5	3	15
1, 2	3	2	6
3, 4	3	2	6
4, 5	2	1	2
2, 4	1	1	1
2, 5	1	2	2
5, 6	1	3	3
	Total		80

6	2	4
1	3	5

▲ **FIGURE 6**
Second Proposed Block Plan
(Analyzed with *Layout* Solver)

Although the *wd* score for the proposed layout in Example 1 represents an almost 27 percent improvement, the designer may be able to improve on this solution. Furthermore, the manager must determine whether the revised layout is worth the cost of relocating four of the six departments. If relocation costs are too high, a less-expensive proposal must be found.

OM Explorer and POM for Windows can help identify some even more attractive proposals. For example, one option is to modify the proposed plan by switching the locations of departments 3 and 4. OM Explorer's output in Figure 6 shows that the *wd* score for this second revision not only drops to 80, but requires that only three departments be relocated compared with the original layout in Figure 4. Perhaps this second proposed plan is the best solution.

Design a Detailed Layout

After finding a satisfactory block plan, the final step translates it into a detailed representation, showing the exact size and shape of each center; the arrangement of elements (e.g., desks, machines, and storage areas); and the location of aisles, stairways, and other service space. These visual representations can be two-dimensional drawings, three-dimensional models, or computer-aided graphics. This step helps decision makers discuss the proposal and problems that might otherwise be overlooked. Such visual representations can be particularly important when evaluating high customer-contact processes.

Customer Involvement

Having covered process structure decisions and how they are translated into a layout, we now turn to a second major decision—customer involvement—shown in Figure 1. Customer involvement reflects the ways in which customers become part of the process and the extent of their participation. It is especially important for many service processes, particularly if customer contact is (or should be) high.

While eBay devised one way to accommodate the variability created by customer involvement, Starbucks faces a different kind of customer variability. The coffee shop chain allows customers to choose among many permutations of sizes, flavors, and preparation techniques in its beverages.

In order to fill orders accurately and efficiently, Starbucks trains its counter clerks to call out orders to beverage makers in a particular sequence. It is even better when customers themselves can do so. Starbucks attempts to teach customers its ordering protocol. First, it provides a "guide-to-ordering pamphlet" for customers to look over. Second, it trains clerks to repeat the order in the correct sequence for the beverage makers, which may not be how the customer presented it. This process not only makes it easier for the beverage makers, but also indirectly "trains" the customers in how to place their orders.

Possible Disadvantages

Customer involvement is not always a good idea. In some cases, giving the customer more active contact in a service process will just be disruptive, making the process less efficient. Managing the timing and volume of customer demands becomes more challenging if the customer is physically present and expects prompt delivery. Exposing the facilities and employees to the customer can have important quality implications (favorable or unfavorable). Such changes make interpersonal skills a prerequisite to the service provider's job, but higher skill levels come at a cost. Revising the facility layout might be a necessary investment, now that managing customer perceptions becomes an important part of the process. It also might mean having many smaller decentralized facilities closer to the various customer concentration areas if the customer comes to the service providers.

The detailed layout becomes a reality. Shown here is part of the office in one of the ABB facilities, a global leader in power and automation technologies. Here the workstations are small and semiprivate, but "outposts" are available. This common area has easy chairs fitted with arms that provide a surface for writing or laptops. People meet comfortably for face-to-face talks, rather than communicating by e-mail.

ABB, Inc.

Possible Advantages

Despite these possible disadvantages, the advantages of a more customer-focused process might increase the net value to the customer. Some customers seek active participation in and control over the service process, particularly if they will enjoy savings in both price and time. The manager must assess whether advantages outweigh disadvantages, judging them in terms of the competitive priorities and customer satisfaction. More customer involvement can mean better quality, faster delivery, greater flexibility, and even lower cost. Self-service is the choice of many retailers, such as gasoline stations, supermarkets, and bank services. Manufacturers of products (such as toys, bicycles, and furniture) may also prefer to let the customer perform the final assembly because product, shipping, and inventory costs frequently are lower. Customer involvement can also help coordinate across the supply chain. Emerging technologies allow companies to engage in an active dialogue with customers and make them partners in creating value and forecasting future demand. Companies can also revise some of their traditional processes, such as pricing and billing systems, to account for their customers' new role. For example, in business-to-business relationships, the Internet changes the roles that companies play with other businesses. Suppliers to automobile companies can be close collaborators in the process of developing new vehicles and no longer are passive providers of materials and services. The same is true for distributors. Walmart does more than just distribute Procter & Gamble's products: It shares daily sales information and works with Procter & Gamble in managing inventories and warehousing operations.

A customer at Starbucks, a large coffee shop chain, places his order in the correct way. By structuring the ordering process for counter clerks and customers, Starbucks can deal efficiently with the variety in products offered, and with no hit on the service experience.

Ramin Talaie/Corbis

Technicians in the parts repair department of this ABB facility must be flexible enough to repair many different parts for automation equipment installed at customer locations in the field. This operation has 30 different workstations configured to perform different types of processes. Workers are cross-trained to move from one station to another, depending on what needs to be done.

flexible workforce

A workforce whose members are capable of doing many tasks, either at their own workstations or as they move from one workstation to another.

MyOMLab

Tutor 2 in MyOMLab demonstrates how to do break-even analysis for equipment selection.

▼ **FIGURE 7**
Relationship Between Process Costs and Product Volume

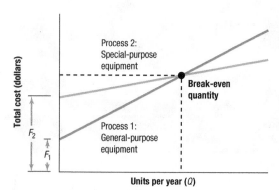

Resource Flexibility

Just as managers must account for customer contact when making customer involvement decisions, so must they account for process divergence and diverse process flows when making resource flexibility decisions in Figure 1. High task divergence and flexible process flows require more flexibility of the process's resources—its employees, facilities, and equipment. Employees need to perform a broad range of duties, and equipment must be general purpose. Otherwise, resource utilization will be too low for economical operations.

Workforce

Operations managers must decide whether to have a **flexible workforce**. Members of a flexible workforce are capable of doing many tasks, either at their own workstations or as they move from one workstation to another. However, such flexibility often comes at a cost, requiring greater skills and thus more training and education. Nevertheless, benefits can be large: Worker flexibility can be one of the best ways to achieve reliable customer service and alleviate capacity bottlenecks. Resource flexibility helps to absorb the feast-or-famine workloads in individual operations that are caused by low-volume production, divergent tasks, flexible flows, and fluid scheduling.

The type of workforce required also depends on the need for volume flexibility. When conditions allow for a smooth, steady rate of output, the likely choice is a permanent workforce that expects regular full-time employment. If the process is subject to hourly, daily, or seasonal peaks and valleys in demand, the use of part-time or temporary employees to supplement a smaller core of full-time employees may be the best solution. However, this approach may not be practical if knowledge and skill requirements are too high for a temporary worker to grasp quickly.

Equipment

Low volumes mean that process designers should select flexible, general-purpose equipment. Figure 7 illustrates this relationship by showing the total cost lines for two different types of equipment that can be chosen for a process. Each line represents the total annual cost of the process at different volume levels. It is the sum of fixed costs and variable costs. When volumes are low (because customization is high), process 1 is the better choice. It calls for inexpensive general-purpose equipment, which keeps investment in equipment low and makes fixed costs (F_1) small. Its variable unit cost is high, which gives its total cost line a relatively steep slope. Process 1 does the job, but not at peak efficiency.

Conversely, process 2 is the better choice when volumes are high and customization is low. Its advantage is low variable unit cost, as reflected in the flatter total cost line. This efficiency is possible when customization is low because the equipment can be designed for a narrow range of products or tasks. Its disadvantage is high equipment investment and, thus, high fixed costs (F_2). When annual volume produced is high enough, spreading these fixed costs over more units produced, the advantage of low variable costs more than compensates for the high fixed costs.

The break-even quantity in Figure 7 is the quantity at which the total costs for the two alternatives are equal. At quantities beyond this point, the cost of process 1 exceeds that of process 2. Unless the firm expects to sell more than the break-even amount, which is unlikely with high customization and low volume, the capital investment of process 2 is not warranted.

Capital Intensity

Capital intensity is the mix of equipment and human skills in the process; the greater the relative cost of equipment, the greater is the capital intensity. As the capabilities of technology increase and its costs decrease, managers face an ever-widening range of choices, from operations utilizing very little automation to those requiring task-specific equipment and little human intervention. **Automation** is a system, process, or piece of equipment that is self-acting and self-regulating. Although automation is often thought to be necessary to gain competitive advantage, it has both advantages and disadvantages. Thus, the automation decision requires careful examination.

Automating Manufacturing Processes

Substituting labor-saving capital equipment and technology for labor has been a classic way of improving productivity and quality consistency in manufacturing processes. If investment costs are large, automation works best when volume is high, because more customization typically means reduced volume. Gillette, for example, spent $750 million on the production lines and robotics that gave it a capacity to make 1.2 billion razor cartridges a year. The equipment is complicated and expensive. Only with such high volumes could this line process produce the product at a price low enough that consumers could afford to buy it.

One big disadvantage of capital intensity can be the prohibitive investment cost for low-volume operations (see Figure 7). Generally, capital-intensive operations must have high utilization to be justifiable. Also, automation does not always align with a company's competitive priorities. If a firm offers a unique product or high-quality service, competitive priorities may indicate the need for hand labor and individual attention rather than new technology. A case in point is the downstream processes in Gillette's supply chain that package and store the razor cartridges. It customizes the packaging for different regions of the world, so that volumes for any one type of package are much lower. As a result of the low volumes, Gillette does not use expensive automation for these processes. In fact, it outsources them. Producing razor cartridges to stock using highly automated processes, and then packaging them in customized fashion at remote locations on demand, is also a good example of the principle of postponement.

Volkswagen aspires to become a full-line manufacturer of cars ranging from the smallest compacts to the largest luxury models. In the United States, for example, it offers the Jetta, GTI, Golf, Passat, CC, Routan, Tiguan, Touareg and Eos. The new VW Phaeton is the latest example of the brand's higher end. It uses a line process dedicated strictly to Phaeton cars. Because of its focus on Phaetons, which are made nowhere else, it enjoys high volumes. This volume justifies the high automation invested in this $208 million plant. The building is located in the heart of Dresden, a city known for its arts and craftsmanship. Its walls are made almost exclusively of glass, and it floors are covered entirely in Canadian maple. There are no smokestacks, no noises, and no toxic byproducts. Parts arrive and luxury cars depart. Of course, such a plant is not always possible, as with a steel mill or foundry. Shown in the photo is the arrival of the body structure that is painted in a plant about 60 miles from Dresden. It is what it looks like when it arrives, before the Phaeton assembly begins. For a photo tour, see http://forums.vwvortex.com/showthread.php?1837641.

Fixed Automation   Manufacturers use two types of automation: (1) fixed and (2) flexible (or programmable). Particularly appropriate for line and continuous-flow process choices, **fixed automation** produces one type of part or product in a fixed sequence of simple operations. Operations managers favor fixed automation when demand volumes are high, product designs are stable, and product life cycles are long. These conditions compensate for the process's two primary drawbacks: (1) large initial investment cost and (2) relative inflexibility. However, fixed automation maximizes efficiency and yields the lowest variable cost per unit if volumes are high.

Flexible Automation   **Flexible (or programmable) automation** can be changed easily to handle various products. The ability to reprogram machines is useful for both low-customization and high-customization processes. In the case of high customization, a machine that makes a variety of products in small batches can be programmed to alternate between products. When a machine has been dedicated to a particular product or family of products, as in the case of low customization and a line flow, and the product is at the end of its life cycle, the machine can simply be reprogrammed with a new sequence of tasks for a new product. An **industrial robot**, which is a versatile, computer-controlled machine programmed to perform various tasks, is a classic example of flexible automation. These "steel-collar" workers operate independently of human control. A robot's arm has up to six standard movements. The robot's "hand" actually does the work. The hand can be changed to perform different tasks, such as materials handling, assembly, and testing. Managerial Practice 1 describes how R.R. Donnelley benefits from more flexible automation, allowing for quick changeovers from one customer order to the next.

Automating Service Processes

Using capital inputs as a labor-saving device is also possible for service processes. In educational services, for example, long-distance learning technology now can supplement or even replace the traditional classroom experience by using books, computers, Web sites, and videos as facilitating goods that go with the service. Justifying technology need not be limited to cost reduction. Sometimes, it can actually allow more task divergence by making available a wide menu of choices to the customer.

automation

A system, process, or piece of equipment that is self-acting and self-regulating.

fixed automation

A manufacturing process that produces one type of part or product in a fixed sequence of simple operations.

flexible (or programmable) automation

A manufacturing process that can be changed easily to handle various products.

industrial robot

Versatile, computer-controlled machine programmed to perform various tasks.

Flexible Automation at Just Born, Inc., a candy company in Pennsylvania (**www.justborn.com**).

On the left, a robot picks up the PEEPS® brand marshmallow yellow bunnies with great speed in groups of four and places them into preformed trays, which then move to automatic shrink-wrapping machines. The trays are then boxed into cases for shipment. Upstream in this line process, the bunnies were extruded in shape on a belt with about 1/2 inch of sugar on it and then cooled as the conveyor moves along. The robot is regularly reprogrammed based on the marshmallow configuration being produced.

On the right, the robot using vacuum cups on the "hand" of its arm picks up boxes of five-pound MIKE AND IKE® bags that are packaged with six bags in a box. The robot reads the bar code, knows the pallet configuration, picks up and places the pallet and a thin cardboard liner on the conveyor, and stacks the boxes until complete. The pallet then comes toward the camera to be picked off the line by a fork truck, and then shrink-wrapped (automatically) and loaded into a 54-foot trailer. PEEPS® and MIKEANDIKE® are registered trademarks of Just Born, Inc. Used with permission.

Technology in the future will surely make possible even a greater degree of customization and variety in services that currently only human providers can now deliver. Beyond cost and variety considerations, management must understand the customer and how much close contact is valued. If the customers seek a visible presence and personal attention, technologies reduced to sorting through a variety of options on the Internet or over the telephone might be a poor choice.

The need for volume to justify expensive automation is just as valid for service processes as for manufacturing processes. Increasing the volume lowers the cost per dollar of sales. Volume is essential for many capital-intensive processes in the transportation, communications, and utilities industries.

Economies of Scope

economies of scope

Economies that reflect the ability to produce multiple products more cheaply in combination than separately.

If capital intensity is high, resource flexibility usually is low. In certain types of manufacturing operations, such as machining and assembly, programmable automation breaks this inverse relationship between resource flexibility and capital intensity. It makes possible both high capital intensity and high resource flexibility, creating economies of scope. **Economies of scope** reflect the ability to produce multiple products more cheaply in combination than separately. In such situations, two conflicting competitive priorities—customization and low price—become more compatible. However, taking advantage of economies of scope requires that a family of parts or products have enough collective volume to utilize equipment fully.

Economies of scope also apply to service processes. Consider, for example, Disney's approach to the Internet. When the company's managers entered the volatile Internet world, their businesses were only weakly tied together. Disney's Infoseek business, in fact, was not even fully owned. However, once its Internet markets became more crystallized, managers at Disney moved to reap the benefits of economies of scope. They aggressively linked their Internet processes with one another and with other parts of Disney. A flexible technology that handles many services together can be less expensive than handling each one separately, particularly when the markets are not too volatile.

Strategic Fit

The manager should understand how the four major process decisions tie together, so as to spot ways of improving poorly designed processes. The choices should fit the situation and each other. When the fit is more *strategic*, the process will be more effective. We examine services and manufacturing processes, looking for ways to test for strategic fit.

| Flexible Automation at R.R. Donnelley

R.R. Donnelley & Sons Company is the largest commercial printer in the United States and the number one printer of books. The industry makes huge capital investments in its printing presses to help drive down the variable unit cost of a book (see Figure 7). Its uses a make-to-order strategy, with customers such as book publishers placing new orders as their inventories became too low. However, the "make-ready" time to prepare for the new order and change over the presses for the next customer order was time-consuming. Keeping such expensive equipment idle for changeovers is costly. These high costs force customers, such as book publishers, to make large, infrequent orders for their books.

Flexible automation at its Roanoke, Virginia, plant allows R.R. Donnelley to take a different course, and it is reaping big rewards. The new process begins when the contents of a book arrive via the Internet as a PDF (portable document format) file and go to the plant's prepress department. The intricate manual operations required to prepare text and pictures for printing traditionally caused the biggest bottlenecks. Roanoke now makes its plates digitally instead of from photographic film. With the elimination of steps, such as duplicating and cleaning the file, a job that once took hours can now be completed in 12 minutes. The all-digital workflow also makes possible the creation of electronic instructions, known as ink presets, which improve productivity and quality. Cleaner and sharper plates are created for the presses because, unlike film, electronic type does not have to be repeatedly handled.

With more flexible automation, the Roanoke plant produces 75 percent of its titles in 2 weeks or less, compared with 4 to 6 weeks for a 4-color book using traditional technology. Management created a culture of continuous improvement at the plant, home of some 300 workers. Overall, Roanoke increased throughput by 20 percent without having to buy an additional press

R.R. Donnelly has been able to achieve flexible automation by receiving books digitally and preparing them to go on press electronically. This allows the company to put books on press more quickly and print smaller, more manageable quantities in a single print run.

and binding line, a savings of $15 million. Its presses run around the clock producing 3.5 million books a month; productivity rose 20 percent, and service improved. Book publishers now enjoy a just-in-time product when they want it.

Decision Patterns for Service Processes

After analyzing a process and determining its position on the customer-contact matrix in Figure 2, it may be apparent that it is improperly positioned, either too far to the left or right, or too far to the top or bottom. Opportunities for improvement become apparent. Perhaps, more customization and customer contact is needed than the process currently provides. Perhaps, instead, the process is too divergent, with unnecessarily flexible flows. Reducing divergence might reduce costs and improve productivity.

The process should reflect its desired competitive priorities. Front offices generally emphasize top quality and customization, whereas back offices are more likely to emphasize low-cost operation, consistent quality, and on-time delivery. The process structure selected then points the way to appropriate choices on customer involvement, resource flexibility, and capital intensity. Figure 8 shows how these key process decisions are tied to customer contact. High customer contact at a front-office service process means:

1. *Process Structure.* The customer (internal or external) is present, actively involved, and receives personal attention. These conditions create processes with high divergence and flexible process flows.

2. *Customer Involvement.* When customer contact is high, customers are more likely to become part of the process. The service created for each customer is unique.

3. *Resource Flexibility.* High process divergence and flexible process flows fit with more flexibility from the process's resources—its workforce, facilities, and equipment.

4. *Capital Intensity.* When volume is higher, automation and capital intensity are more likely. Even though higher volume is usually assumed to be found in the back office, it is just as likely to be in the front office for financial services. Information technology is a major type of automation at many service processes, which brings together both resource flexibility and automation.

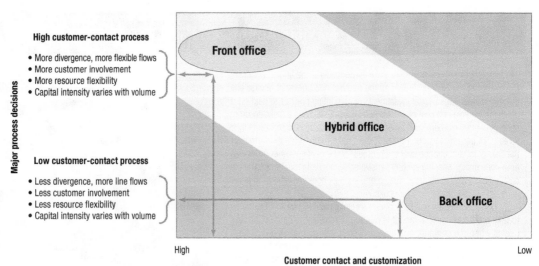

FIGURE 8 ▶
Decision Patterns for
Service Processes

Of course, this list provides general tendencies rather than rigid prescriptions. Exceptions can be found, but these relationships provide a way of understanding how service process decisions can be linked coherently.

Decision Patterns for Manufacturing Processes

Just as a service process can be repositioned in the customer-contact matrix, a manufacturing process can also be moved in the product-process matrix. Changes can be made either in the horizontal direction of Figure 3 by changing the degree of customization and volume, or they can be moved in the vertical direction by changing process divergence. The production and inventory strategy can also be changed. Competitive priorities must be considered when translating strategy into specific manufacturing processes. Figure 9 shows some usual tendencies found in practice. Job and small batch processes are usual choices if top quality, on-time delivery, and flexibility (customization, variety, and volume flexibility) are given primary emphasis. Large batch, line, and continuous-flow processes match up with an emphasis on low-cost operations, consistent quality, and delivery speed.

For production and inventory strategies, the make-to-order strategy matches up with flexibility (particularly customization) and top quality. Because delivery speed is more difficult, meeting due dates and on-time delivery get the emphasis on the time dimension. The assemble-to-order strategy allows delivery speed and flexibility (particularly variety) to be achieved, whereas the make-to-stock strategy is the usual choice if delivery speed and low-cost operations are emphasized. Keeping an item in stock assures quick delivery because it is generally available when needed, without delays in producing it. High volumes open up opportunities to reduce costs.

The process structure selected once again points the way to appropriate choices on customer involvement, resource flexibility, and capital intensity. Figure 10 summarizes the relationships between volume and the four key process decisions. High volumes per part type at a manufacturing process typically mean:

1. *Process Structure.* High volumes, combined with a standard product, make a line flow possible. It is just the opposite where a job process produces to specific customer orders.

2. *Customer Involvement.* Customer involvement is not a factor in most manufacturing processes, except for choices made on product variety and customization. Less discretion is allowed with line or continuous-flow processes in order to avoid the unpredictable demands required by customized orders.

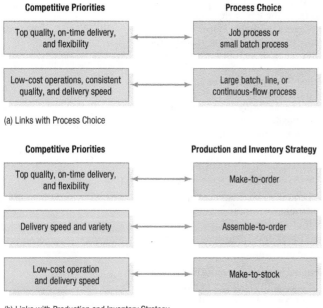

(a) Links with Process Choice

(b) Links with Production and Inventory Strategy

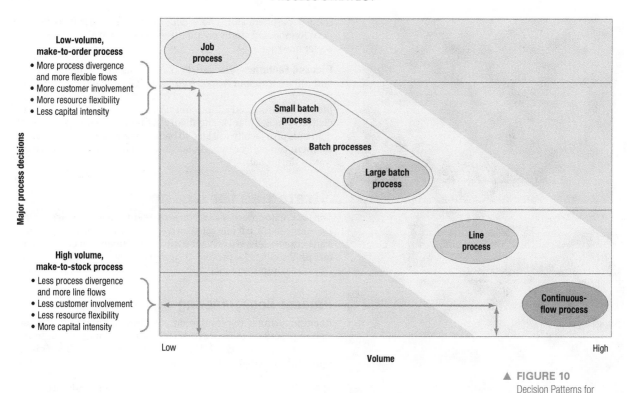

Low-volume, make-to-order process
- More process divergence and more flexible flows
- More customer involvement
- More resource flexibility
- Less capital intensity

Job process

Small batch process

Batch processes

Large batch process

Line process

High volume, make-to-stock process
- Less process divergence and more line flows
- Less customer involvement
- Less resource flexibility
- More capital intensity

Continuous-flow process

Major process decisions

Low   Volume   High

▲ **FIGURE 10**
Decision Patterns for Manufacturing Processes

3. *Resource Flexibility.* When volumes are high and process divergence is low, flexibility is not needed to utilize resources effectively, and specialization can lead to more efficient processes.

4. *Capital Intensity.* High volumes justify the large fixed costs of an efficient operation. The King Soopers's bread line (see *The Big Picture* and the video in MyOMLab) is capital-intensive. It is automated from dough mixing to placement of the product on shipping racks. Expanding this process would be expensive. By way of contrast, the King Soopers's custom cake process is labor-intensive and requires little investment to equip the workers.

MyOMLab

Gaining Focus

In the past, new services or products often were added to a facility in the name of better utilizing fixed costs and keeping everything under the same roof. The result was a jumble of competitive priorities, process structures, and technologies. In the effort to do everything, nothing was done well.

Focus by Process Segments   A facility's operations often can neither be characterized nor actually designed for one set of competitive priorities and one process choice. King Soopers (see *The Big Picture* and video in MyOMLab) had three processes under one roof, but management segmented them into three separate operations that were relatively autonomous. At a services facility, some parts of the process might seem like a front office and other parts like a back office. Such arrangements can be effective, provided that sufficient focus is given to each process.

MyOMLab

  Plants within plants (PWPs) are different operations within a facility with individualized competitive priorities, processes, and workforces under the same roof. Boundaries for PWPs may be established by physically separating subunits or simply by revising organizational relationships. At each PWP, customization, capital intensity volume, and other relationships are crucial and must be complementary. The advantages of PWPs are fewer layers of management, greater ability to rely on team problem solving, and shorter lines of communication between departments.

plants within plants (PWPs)

Different operations within a facility with individualized competitive priorities, processes, and workforces under the same roof.

Focused Service Operations   Service industries also implement the concepts of focus and PWPs. Specialty retailers opened stores with smaller, more accessible spaces. These focused facilities generally chipped away at the business of large department stores. Using the same philosophy, some department stores now focus on specific customers or products. Remodeled stores create the effect of many small boutiques under one roof.

Focused Factories   Hewlett-Packard, Rolls-Royce, Japan's Ricoh and Mitsubishi, and Britain's Imperial Chemical Industries PLC are some of the firms that created **focused factories**, splitting large plants that produced all the company's products into several specialized smaller plants. The theory is that narrowing the range of demands on a facility will lead to better performance because management can concentrate on fewer tasks and lead a workforce toward a single goal.

Strategies for Change

The four major process decisions represent broad, strategic issues. Decisions that are made must be translated into actual process designs or redesigns. We conclude with two different but complementary philosophies for process design: (1) process reengineering and (2) process improvement.

Process Reengineering

Reengineering is the fundamental rethinking and radical redesign of processes to improve performance dramatically in terms of cost, quality, service, and speed. Process reengineering is about reinvention, rather than incremental improvement. It is strong medicine and not always needed or successful. Pain, in the form of layoffs and large cash outflows for investments in information technology, almost always accompanies massive change. However, reengineering processes can have big payoffs. Table 4 lists the key elements of the overall approach.

Reengineering has led to many successes and will continue to do so. However, it is not simple or easily done, nor is it appropriate for all processes or all organizations. The best understanding of a process, and how to improve it, often lies with the people who perform the work each day, not with cross-functional teams or top management.

AP Photo/Mike Wintroath

Focused factories are not just found in manufacturing. This single-speciality facility focuses just on heart surgery and has all of the advanced resources needed that cannot be provided by a general hospital. Another example is the Toronto-based Shouldice Clinic, which focuses just on hernias.

focused factories

The result of a firm's splitting large plants that produced all the company's products into several specialized smaller plants.

reengineering

The fundamental rethinking and radical redesign of processes to improve performance dramatically in terms of cost, quality, service, and speed.

TABLE 4 | KEY ELEMENTS OF REENGINEERING

Element	Description
Critical processes	The emphasis of reengineering should be on core business processes. Normal process-improvement activities can be continued with the other processes.
Strong leadership	Senior executives must provide strong leadership for reengineering to be successful. Otherwise, cynicism, resistance ("we tried that before"), and boundaries between departments can block radical changes.
Cross-functional teams	A team, consisting of members from each functional area affected by the process change, is charged with carrying out a reengineering project. Self-managing teams and employee empowerment are the rule rather than the exception.
Information technology	Information technology is a primary enabler of process engineering. Most reengineering projects design processes around information flows, such as customer order fulfillment.
Clean-slate philosophy	Reengineering requires a "clean-slate" philosophy—that is, starting with the way the customer wants to deal with the company. To ensure a customer orientation, teams begin with internal and external customer objectives for the process.
Process analysis	Despite the clean-slate philosophy, a reengineering team must understand things about the current process: what it does, how well it performs, and what factors affect it. The team must look at every procedure involved in the process throughout the organization.

Process Improvement

Process improvement is the systematic study of the activities and flows of each process to improve it. Its purpose is to "learn the numbers," understand the process, and dig out the details. Once a process is really understood, it can be improved. The relentless pressure to provide better quality at a lower price means that companies must continually review all aspects of their operations. Process improvement goes on, whether or not a process is reengineered. There is always a better way.

An individual or a whole team examines the process, using the tools described in the next chapter. One must look for ways to streamline tasks, eliminate whole processes entirely, cut expensive materials or services, improve the environment, or make jobs safer. One must find the ways to trim costs and delays and to improve customer satisfaction.

process improvement
The systematic study of the activities and flows of each process to improve it.

LEARNING GOALS IN REVIEW

1 **Explain why processes exist everywhere in all organizations.** The "Process Strategy Across the Organization" section, demonstrates that supply chain process exist throughout the supply chain and actually exist in all places throughout the organization. Pay particular attention to Tables 1 and 2.

2 **Discuss the four major process decisions.** The "Process Strategy Decisions" section, identifies the four key decisions around which we develop a vocabulary for understanding operations. Figure 1 shows how they interact in creating an effective process design.

3 **Position a process on the customer-contact matrix or product-process matrix.** The Customer-Contact Matrix for service processes in Figure 2 shows how the degree of customer contact and customization are linked with process divergence and line flows. Three natural positions emerge: the front office, hybrid office, and back office. In manufacturing, the key drivers are customization and volume, which are linked with line flows and the extent of repetitive work. Figure 3 shows these relationships in the form of the Product-Process Matrix, with natural positions ranging from the job process to the continuous flow process.

4 **Configure operations into layouts.** The "Layout" section, puts the process structure into a physical form by showing here each operation is located within the facility. Example 1 shows how to develop a block plan, and evaluate it with the help of the

Layout Solver of OM Explorer. See Solved Problem 1 for another example.

5 **Define customer involvement, resource flexibility, capital intensity, and economies of scope.** These topics are covered in the "Customer Involvement," "Resource Flexibility," "Capital Intensity," and "Economies of Scope" sections. Note that customer involvement has advantages and disadvantages, resource flexibility applies to both workforce and equipment, and economies of scope in certain situations can break the inverse relationship between resource flexibility and capital intensity.

6 **Discuss how process decisions should fit together.** The "Strategic Fit" section, describes how the four major process decisions should tie together. Figures 8 and 9 show the decision patterns in pictorial form. The section concludes with a way to achieve these patterns by gaining focus, either with focused factories or gaining focus by process segments.

7 **Define process reengineering and process improvement.** The "Strategies for Change," describe both approaches to finding better process designs. Table 4 gives the key elements of reengineering. Process improvement is more of an incremental approach.

MyOMLab helps you develop analytic skills and assesses your progress with multiple problems on the break-even analysis in choosing between two different processes, the weighted-distance method, and layout.

MyOMLab Resources	Titles	Link to the Book
Videos	*King Soopers Bakery: Process Choice*	Manufacturing Process Structuring
	Process Choice: Pearson Education Information Technology	Capital Intensity
OM Explorer Solver	Layout	Layout
OM Explorer Tutors	3.1 Distance Measures	Applying the Weighted-Distance Method Example 1
	3.2 Breakeven for Equipment Selection	Resource Flexibility Figure 7
POM for Windows: Layout	Layout	Example 1

MyOMLab Resources	Titles	Link to the Book
Tutor Exercises	3.1—Mt. Mudge	Applying the Weighted-Distance Method Example 1
	3.2—Break-Even for Equipment Selection	Resource Flexibility Figure 7
SmartDraw	Often used to prepare detailed layouts and floor plans	Detailed Layout
Virtual Tours	1. Leannie Company Doll Factory	Process Choice; Production and Inventory Strategy
	2. LA Aluminum Casting Company	Process Choice; Production and Inventory Strategy
Internet Exercises	3.1—United Parcel Service	Service Strategy; Customer Involvement
	3.2—Carnival and Twilight	
	3.3—Timbuk2	
Advanced Problems	3.1 CCI Electronics	Layout
	3.2 Getwell Hospital	Layout
Additional Cases	Car Lube Operations	Layout
	Hightech, Inc.	Layout
	The Pizza Connection	Design a Detailed layout
	Bill's Hardware	Capital Intensity
	The Big Picture: Process Choice at King Soopers Bakery	Manufacturing Process Structuring
Key Equations		
Image Library		

Key Equations

1. Euclidean distance: $d_{AB} = \sqrt{(x_A - x_B)^2 + (y_A - y_B)^2}$
2. Rectilinear distance: $d_{AB} = |x_A - x_B| + |y_A - y_B|$

Key Terms

assemble-to-order strategy
automation
back office
batch process
block plan
capital intensity
closeness matrix
continuous flow process
customer contact
customer involvement
economies of scope
Euclidean distance
fixed automation
flexible (or programmable)
    automation
flexible flow

flexible workforce
focused factories
front office
hybrid office
industrial robot
job process
layout
line flow
line process
make-to-order strategy
make-to-stock strategy
mass customization
mass production

plants within plants (PWPs)
postponement
process choice
process divergence
process improvement
process strategy
process structure
rectilinear distance
reengineering
resource flexibility
supply chain processes
weighted-distance method

Solved Problem 1

A defense contractor is evaluating its machine shop's current layout. Figure 11 shows the current layout, and the table shows the closeness matrix for the facility measured as the number of trips per day between department pairs. Safety and health regulations require departments E and F to remain at their current locations.

	TRIPS BETWEEN DEPARTMENTS					
Department	A	B	C	D	E	F
A	—	8	3		9	5
B		—		3		
C			—		8	9
D				—		3
E					—	3
F						—

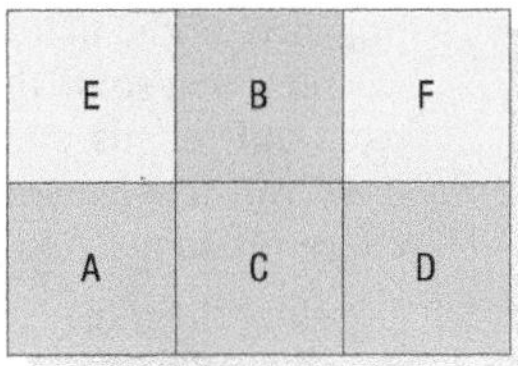

▲ FIGURE 11
Current Layout

a. Use trial and error to find a better layout.

b. How much better is your layout than the current layout in terms of the *wd* score? Use rectilinear distance.

SOLUTION

a. In addition to keeping departments E and F at their current locations, a good plan would locate the following department pairs close to each other: A and E, C and F, A and B, and C and E. Figure 12 was worked out by trial and error and satisfies all these requirements. Start by placing E and F at their current locations. Then, because C must be as close as possible to both E and F, put C between them. Place A below E, and B next to A. All of the heavy traffic concerns have now been accommodated. Department D, located in the remaining space, does not need to be relocated.

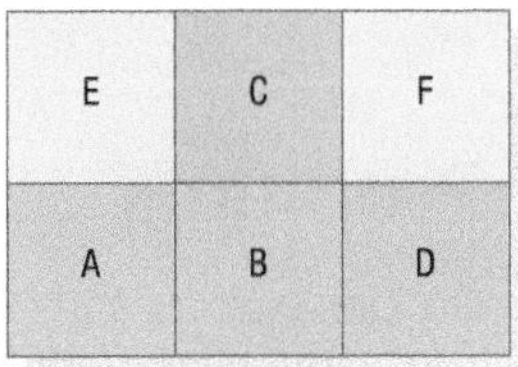

▲ FIGURE 12
Proposed Layout

Department Pair	Number of Trips (1)	CURRENT PLAN		PROPOSED PLAN	
		Distance (2)	*wd* Score (1) × (2)	Distance (3)	*wd* Score (1) × (3)
A, B	8	2	16	1	8
A, C	3	1	3	2	6
A, E	9	1	9	1	9
A, F	5	3	15	3	15
B, D	3	2	6	1	3
C, E	8	2	16	1	8
C, F	9	2	18	1	9
D, F	3	1	3	1	3
E, F	3	2	6	2	6
			wd = 92		*wd* = 67

b. The table reveals that the *wd* score drops from 92 for the current plan to 67 for the revised plan, a 27 percent reduction.

Discussion Questions

1. What processes at manufacturing firms are really service processes that involve considerable customer contact? Can customer contact be high, even if the process only has internal customers?

2. Consider this sign seen in a local restaurant: "To-go orders do NOT include complimentary chips and salsa. If you have any questions, see our management, NOT our employees." What impact does this message have on its employees, their service processes, and customer satisfaction? Contrast this approach with the one taken by a five-star restaurant. Are the differences primarily due to different competitive priorities?

3. How do the process strategies of eBay and McDonald's differ, and how do their choices relate to customer-introduced variability?

4. Medical technology can outfit a patient with an artificial heart, or cure vision defects with the touch of a laser. However, hospitals still struggle with their back-office processes, such as getting X-ray files from radiology on the fourth floor to the first-floor view boxes in the emergency room without having to send a runner. More than 90 percent of the estimated 30 billion health transactions each year are conducted by telephone, fax, or mail. To what extent, and how, can information technology

improve productivity and quality for such processes? Remember that some doctors are not ready to give up their pads and pencils, and many hospitals have strong lines drawn around its departments, such as pharmacy, cardiology, radiology, and pediatrics.

5. Consider the range of processes in the financial services industry. What position on the customer-contact matrix would the process of selling financial services to municipalities occupy? The process of preparing monthly fund balance reports? Explain why they would differ.

6. Performance criteria important in creating a layout can go well beyond communication and materials handling. Identify the types of layout performance criteria that might be most important in the following settings.

   a. Airport

   b. Bank

   c. Classroom

d. Product designers' office

e. Law firm

7. Rate operators at a call center, who respond to queries from customers who call in about the company's product, on each of the five dimensions of customer contact in Table 3. Use a seven-point scale, where 1 = very low and 7 = very high. For example, the operators newer are physically present with the customer, and so they would get a score of 1 for physical presence. Explain your ratings, and then calculate a combined score for the overall customer contact. Did you use equal weights in calculating the combined score? Why or why not? Where is your process positioned on the customer-contact matrix? Is it properly aligned? Why or why not?

8. Select one of the three processes shown in the MyOMLab's video for King Soopers (bread, pastry, or custom cakes). What kind of transformation process, process choice, and inventory strategy are involved? Is the process properly aligned? Explain.

Problems

The OM Explorer and POM for Windows software is available to all students using the 10th edition of this text. Go to **www.pearsonhighered.com/krajewski** to download these computer packages. If you purchased MyOMLab, you also have access to Active Models software and significant help in doing the following problems. Check with your instructor on how best to use these resources. In many cases, the instructor wants you to understand how to do the calculations by hand. At the least, the software provides a check on your calculations. When calculations are particularly complex and the goal is interpreting the results in making decision, the software entirely replaces the manual calculations.

Problems 1 and 2 apply break-even analysis to process decisions.

1. Dr. Gulakowicz is an orthodontist. She estimates that adding two new chairs will increase fixed costs by $150,000, including the annual equivalent cost of the capital investment and the salary of one more technician. Each new patient is expected to bring in $3,000 per year in additional revenue, with variable costs estimated at $1,000 per patient. The two new chairs will allow Dr. Gulakowicz to expand her practice by as many as 200 patients annually. How many patients would have to be added for the new process to break even?

2. Two different manufacturing processes are being considered for making a new product. The first process is less capital-intensive, with fixed costs of only $50,000 per year and variable costs of $700 per unit. The second process has fixed costs of $400,000, but has variable costs of only $200 per unit.

   a. What is the break-even quantity, beyond which the second process becomes more attractive than the first?

   b. If the expected annual sales for the product is 800 units, which process would you choose?

3. Baker Machine Company is a job shop that specializes in precision parts for firms in the aerospace industry. Figure 13 shows the current block plan for the key manufacturing centers of the 75,000-square-foot facility. Refer to the following closeness matrix and use rectilinear

distance (the current distance from inspection to shipping and receiving is three units) to calculate the change in the weighted distance, wd, score if Baker exchanges the locations of the tool crib and inspection.

CLOSENESS MATRIX

Department	Trips Between Departments					
	1	2	3	4	5	6
1. Burr and grind	—	8	3		9	5
2. Numerically controlled (NC) equipment		—		3		
3. Shipping and receiving			—		8	9
4. Lathes and drills				—		3
5. Tool crib					—	3
6. Inspection						—

| 3 | 4 | 2 |
| 1 | 5 | 6 |

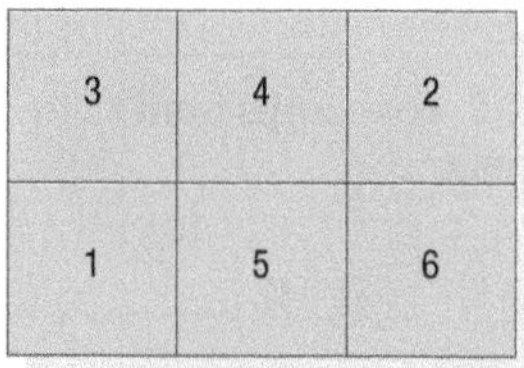

◀ FIGURE 13
Current Layout

4. Baker Machine (see Problem 3) is considering two alternative layouts. Compare the wd scores using rectilinear distance of the following two block plans to determine which alternative layout is better.

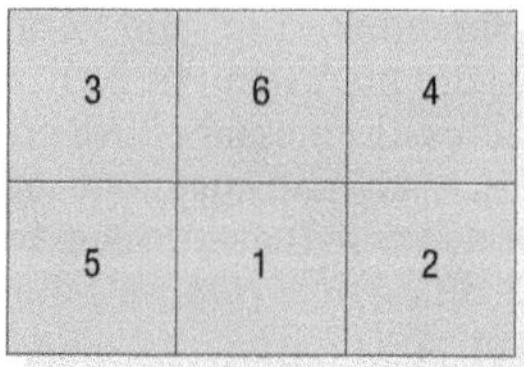

| 3 | 6 | 4 |
| 5 | 1 | 2 |

◀ FIGURE 13(a)
Alternative Layout 1

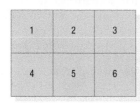

◀ **FIGURE 13(b)**
Alternative Layout 2

5. The head of the information systems group at Conway Consulting must assign six new analysts to offices. The following closeness matrix shows the expected frequency of contact between analysts. The block plan in Figure 14 shows the available office locations (1–6) for the six analysts (A–F). Assume equal-sized offices and rectilinear distance.

CLOSENESS MATRIX

| Analyst | Contacts Between Analysts | | | | | |
	A	B	C	D	E	F
Analyst A	—		6			
Analyst B		—		12		
Analyst C			—	2	7	
Analyst D				—		4
Analyst E					—	
Analyst F						—

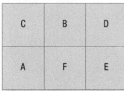

◀ **FIGURE 14**
Conway Consulting's Block Plan

Evaluate the *wd* scores of the following three alternative layouts, again assuming rectilinear distance, and determine which is best.

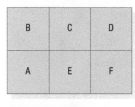

◀ **FIGURE 14(a)**
Alternative Layout 1

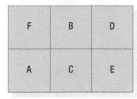

◀ **FIGURE 14(b)**
Alternative Layout 2

◀ **FIGURE 14(c)**
Alternative Layout 3

6. Richard Garber is the head designer for Matthews and Novak Design Company. Garber has been called in to design the layout for a newly constructed office building. From statistical samplings over the past three months, Garber developed the following closeness matrix for daily trips between the department's offices.

CLOSENESS MATRIX

| Department | Trips Between Departments | | | | | |
	A	B	C	D	E	F
A	—	25	90			185
B		—			105	
C			—		125	125
D				—	25	
E					—	105
F						—

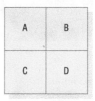

◀ **FIGURE 15**
Alternative Block Plan

a. If other factors are equal, which two offices should be located closest together?

b. Figure 15 shows an alternative layout for the department. What is the total weighted-distance score for this plan based on rectilinear distance and assuming that offices A and B are three units of distance apart?

c. Use the explicit enumeration method of the POM for Windows software to find the block plan that minimize the total weighted-distance score.

7. A firm with four departments has the following closeness matrix and the current block plan shown in Figure 16.

a. What is the weighted-distance score for the current layout (assuming rectilinear distance)?

CLOSENESS MATRIX

| Department | Trips Between Departments | | | |
	A	B	C	D
A	—	12	10	8
B		—	20	6
C			—	0
D				—

◀ **FIGURE 16**
Current Block Plan

b. Develop a better layout. What is its total weighted-distance score?

8. The department of engineering at a university in New Jersey must assign six faculty members to their new offices. The following closeness matrix indicates the expected number of contacts per day between professors. The available office spaces (1–6) for the six faculty members are shown in Figure 17. Assume equal-sized offices. The distance between offices 1 and 2 (and between offices 1 and 3) is 1 unit, whereas the distance between offices 1 and 4 is 2 units.

CLOSENESS MATRIX

Professor	Contacts Between Professors					
	A	B	C	D	E	F
A	—		4			
B		—	12			10
C			—	2	7	
D				—		4
E					—	
F						—

a. Because of their academic positions, Professor A must be assigned to office 1, Professor C must be assigned to office 2, and Professor D must be assigned to office 6. Which faculty members should be assigned to offices 3, 4, and 5, respectively, to minimize the total weighted-distance score (assuming rectilinear distance)?

b. What is the weighted-distance score of your solution?

1	2
3	4
5	6

◀ **FIGURE 17**
Available Space

Active Model Exercise

This Active Model for Example 1 appears in MyOMLab. It allows you to see the effects of performing paired swaps of departments.

QUESTIONS

1. What is the current total weighted-distance score?

2. Use the swap button one swap at a time. If the swap helps, move to the next pair. If the swap does not help, hit the swap button once again to put the departments back. What is the minimum weighted-distance score after all swaps have been tried?

3. Look at the two data tables, and use the yellow-shaded column to put departments in spaces. What space assignments lead to the minimum cost? What is this cost?

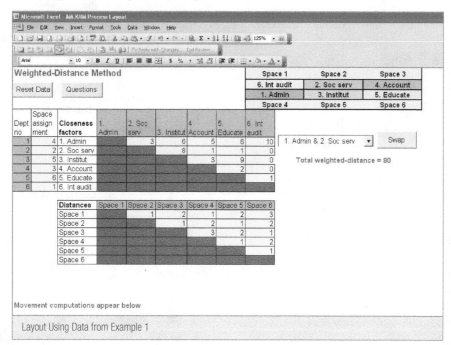

Layout Using Data from Example 1

CASE | Custom Molds, Inc.

Custom Molds, Inc., manufactures custom-designed molds for plastic parts and produces custom-made plastic connectors for the electronics industry. Located in Tucson, Arizona, Custom Molds was founded by the father-and-son-team of Tom and Mason Miller in 1987. Tom Miller, a mechanical engineer, had more than 20 years of experience in the connector industry with AMP, Inc., a large multinational producer of electronic connectors. Mason Miller graduated from the Arizona State University in 1986 with joint degrees in chemistry and chemical engineering.

The company was originally formed to provide manufacturers of electronic connectors with a source of high-quality, custom-designed molds for producing plastic parts. The market consisted mainly of the product design and development divisions of those manufacturers. Custom Molds worked closely with each customer to design and develop molds to be used in the customer's product development processes. Thus, virtually every mold had to meet exacting standards and was somewhat unique. Orders for multiple molds would arrive when customers moved from the design and pilot-run stage of development to large-scale production of newly designed parts.

As the years went by, Custom Molds's reputation grew as a designer and fabricator of precision molds. Building on this reputation, the Millers decided to expand into the limited manufacture of plastic parts. Ingredient-mixing facilities and injection-molding equipment were added, and by the mid-1990s, Custom Molds developed its reputation to include being a supplier of high-quality plastic parts. Because of limited capacity, the company concentrated its sales efforts on supplying parts that were used in limited quantities for research and development efforts and in preproduction pilot runs.

Production Processes

By 2000, operations at Custom Molds involved two distinct processes: one for fabricating molds and one for producing plastic parts. Although different, in many instances these two processes were linked, as when a customer would have Custom Molds both fabricate a mold and produce the necessary parts to support the customer's research and design efforts. All fabrication and production operations were housed in a single facility. The layout was characteristic of a typical job shop, with like processes and similar equipment grouped in various places in the plant. Figure 18 shows a layout of the plant floor. Multiple pieces of various types of high-precision machinery, including milling, turning, cutting, and drilling equipment, were located in the mold-fabrication area.

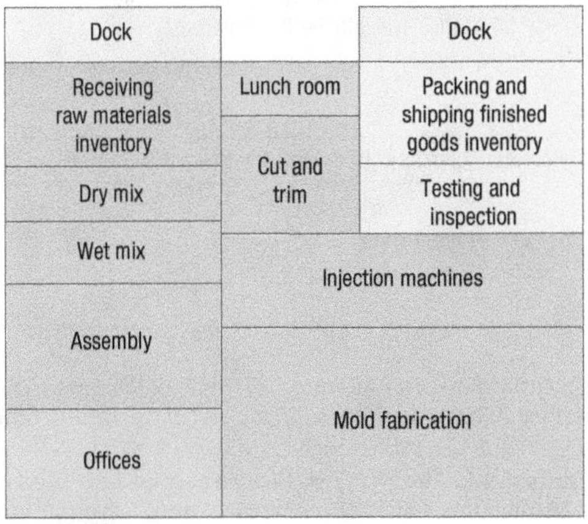

Fabricating molds is a skill-oriented, craftsman-driven process. When an order is received, a design team, comprising a design engineer and one of 13 master machinists, reviews the design specifications. Working closely with the customer, the team establishes the final specifications for the mold and gives them to the master machinist for fabrication. It is always the same machinist who was assigned to the design team. At the same time, the purchasing department is given a copy of the design specifications, from which it orders the appropriate raw materials and special tooling. The time needed to receive the ordered materials is usually three to four weeks. When the materials are received for a particular mold, the plant master scheduler reviews the workload of the assigned master machinist and schedules the mold for fabrication.

Fabricating a mold takes from two to four weeks, depending on the amount of work the machinist already has scheduled. The fabrication process itself takes only three to five days. Upon completion, the mold is sent to the testing and inspection area, where it is used to produce a small number of parts on one of the injection molding machines. If the parts meet the design specifications established by the design team, the mold is passed on to be cleaned and polished. It is then packed and shipped to the customer. One day is spent inspecting and testing the mold and a second day cleaning, polishing, packing, and shipping it to the customer. If the parts made by the mold do not meet design specifications, the mold is returned to the master machinist for retooling and the process starts over. Currently, Custom Molds has a published lead time of nine weeks for delivery of custom-fabricated molds.

The manufacturing process for plastic parts is somewhat different from that for mold fabrication. An order for parts may be received in conjunction with an order for a mold to be fabricated. In instances where Custom Molds has previously fabricated the mold and maintains it in inventory, an order may be just for parts. If the mold is already available, the order is reviewed by a design engineer, who verifies the part and raw material specifications. If the design engineer has any questions concerning the specifications, the customer is contacted and any revisions to specifications are mutually worked out and agreed upon.

Upon acceptance of the part and raw material specifications, raw material orders are placed and production is scheduled for the order. Chemicals and compounds that support plastic-parts manufacturing are typically ordered and received within one week. Upon receipt, the compounds are first dry-mixed and blended to achieve the correct composition. Then, the mixture is wet-mixed to the desired consistency (called *slurry*) for injection into molding machines. When ready, the slurry is transferred to the injection molding area by an overhead pipeline and deposited in holding tanks adjacent to the injection machines. The entire mixing process takes only one day.

When the slurry is staged and ready, the proper molds are secured—from inventory or from the clean and polish operation if new molds were fabricated for the order—and the parts are manufactured. Although different parts require different temperature and pressure settings, the time to produce a part is relatively constant. Custom Molds has the capacity to produce 5,000 parts per day in the injection-molding department; historically, however, the lead time for handling orders in this department has averaged one week. Upon completion of molding, the parts are taken to the cut and trim operation, where they are disconnected and leftover flashing is removed. After being inspected, the parts may be taken to assembly or transferred to the packing and shipping area for shipment to the customer. If assembly of the final parts is not required, the parts can be on their way to the customer two days after being molded.

▲ FIGURE 18
Plant Layout

Sometimes, the final product requires some assembly. Typically, this entails attaching metal leads to plastic connectors. If assembly is necessary, an additional three days are needed before the order can be shipped. Custom Molds is currently quoting a three-week lead time for parts not requiring fabricated molds.

The Changing Environment

In early 2009, Tom and Mason Miller began to realize that the electronics industry they supplied, along with their own business, was changing. Electronics manufacturers had traditionally manufactured their own component parts to reduce costs and ensure a timely supply of parts. By the 1990s, this trend had changed. Manufacturers were developing strategic partnerships with parts suppliers to ensure the timely delivery of high-quality, cost-effective parts. This approach allowed funds to be diverted to other uses that could provide a larger return on investment.

The impact on Custom Molds could be seen in sales figures over the past three years. The sales mix was changing. Although the number of orders per year for mold fabrication remained virtually constant, orders for multiple molds were declining, as shown in the following table:

Order Size	NUMBER OF ORDERS		
	Molds 2006	Molds 2007	Molds 2008
1	80	74	72
2	60	70	75
3	40	51	55
4	5	6	5
5	3	5	4
6	4	8	5
7	2	0	1
8	10	6	4
9	11	8	5
10	15	10	5
Total orders	230	238	231

The reverse was true for plastic parts, for which the number of orders per year had declined, but for which the order sizes were becoming larger, as illustrated in the following table:

Order Size	NUMBER OF ORDERS		
	Parts 2006	Parts 2007	Parts 2008
50	100	93	70
100	70	72	65
150	40	30	35
200	36	34	38
250	25	27	25
500	10	12	14
750	1	3	5
1,000	2	2	8
3,000	1	4	9
5,000	1	3	8
Total orders	286	280	277

During this same period, Custom Molds began having delivery problems. Customers were complaining that parts orders were taking four to five weeks instead of the stated three weeks and that the delays were disrupting production schedules. When asked about the situation, the master scheduler said that determining when a particular order could be promised for delivery was difficult. Bottlenecks were occurring during the production process, but where or when they would occur could not be predicted. The bottlenecks always seemed to be moving from one operation to another.

Tom Miller thought that he had excess labor capacity in the mold-fabrication area. So, to help push through those orders that were behind schedule, he assigned one of the master machinists the job of identifying and expediting those late orders. However, that tactic did not seem to help much. Complaints about late deliveries were still being received. To add to the problems, two orders had been returned recently because of the number of defective parts. The Millers knew that something had to be done. The question was "What?"

QUESTIONS

1. What are the major issues facing Tom and Mason Miller?
2. What are the competitive priorities for Custom Molds's processes and the changing nature of the industry?
3. What alternatives might the Millers pursue? What key factors should they consider as they evaluate these alternatives?

Source: This case was prepared by Dr. Brooke Saladin, Wake Forest University, as a basis for classroom discussion. Copyright © Brooke Saladin. Used with permission.

Selected References

Brink, Harold, Senthiah, and Rajan Naik. "A Better Way to Automate Service Operations." *McKinsey on Business Technology*, no. 20 (Summer, 2010), pp. 1–10.

Baghai, Ramin, Edward H. Levine, and Saumya S. Sutaria. "Service-Line Strategies for US Hospitals." *The McKinsey Quarterly* (July 2008), pp. 1–9.

Booth, Alan. "The Management of Technical Change: Automation in the UK and USA since 1950." *The Economic History Review*, vol. 62, no. 2 (May 2009), pp. 493–494.

Chase, Richard B. and Uday M. Apte. "A History of Research in Service Operations: What's the Big Idea?" *Journal of Operations Management*, vol. 25 (2007), pp. 375–386.

Fisher, Marshall L. "Bob Hayes: Forty Years of Leading Operations Management Into Uncharted Waters." *Production and Operations Management*, vol. 16, no. 2, (March–April 2007), pp. 159–168.

Grover, Varun, and Manoj K. Malhotra. "Business Process Reengineering: A Tutorial on the Concept, Evolution, Method, Technology, and Application." *Journal of Operations Management*, vol. 15, no. 3 (1997), pp. 194–213.

Hayes, Robert. "Operations, Strategy, and Technology: Pursuing the Competitive Edge." *Strategic Direction*, vol. 22, no. 7, (2006).

Johansson, Pontus and Jan Olhger. "Linking Product-Process Matrices for Manufacturing and Industrial Service Operations." *International Journal of Production Economics*, vol. 104 (2006), pp. 615–624.

Hammer, Michael. "Deep Change: How Operational Innovation Can Transform Your Company." *Harvard Business Review*, vol. 82, no. 4 (April 2004), pp. 85–93.

Hill, Terry. *Manufacturing Strategy: Text and Cases*, 3rd ed. Homewood, IL: Irwin/McGraw-Hill, 2000.

Jack, Eric, and John Collis. "Strengthen and Tone: A Flexible Approach to Operations Can Build Some Serious Muscle." *APICS Magazine* (June 2006), pp. 35–38.

Kung, Peter and Claus Hagen. "The Fruits of Business Process Management: An Experience Report from a Swiss Bank." *Business Process Management Journal*, vol. 13, no. 4 (2007), pp. 477–487.

Malhotra, Manoj K., and Larry P. Ritzman. "Resource Flexibility Issues in Multistage Manufacturing." *Decision Sciences*, vol. 21, no. 4 (1990), pp. 673–690.

Metters, Richard, Kathryn King-Metters, and Madeleine Pullman. *Successful Service Operations Management*. Mason, OH: South-Western, 2003.

Prajogo, Daniel. "The Implementation of Operations Management Techniques in Service Organisations." *International Journal of Operations & Production Management*, vol. 26, No. 12 (2006), pp. 1374–1390.

Rayport, Jeffrey F., and Bernard J. Jaworski. "Best Face Forward." *Harvard Business Review*, vol. 82, no. 12 (2003), pp. 47–58.

Safizadeh, M. Hossein, Joy M. Field, and Larry P. Ritzman. "An Empirical Analysis of Financial Services Processes with a Front-Office or Back-Office Orientation." *Journal of Operations Management*, vol. 21, no. 5 (2003), pp. 557–576.

Safizadeh, M. Hossein, Larry P. Ritzman, and Debasish Mallick. "Revisiting Alternative Theoretical Paradigms in Manufacturing." *Production and Operations Management*, vol. 9, no. 2 (2000), pp. 111–127.

Sehgal, Sanjay, B.S. Sahay, and S.K. Goyal. "Reengineering the Supply Chain in a Paint Company." *International Journal of Productivity and Performance Management*, vol. 55, no. 8 (2006), pp. 655–670.

Skinner, Wickham. "Operations Technology: Blind Spot in Strategic Management." *Interfaces*, vol. 14 (January–February 1984), pp. 116–125.

Swink, Morgan and Anand Nair. "Capturing the Competitive Advantages of AMT: Design-Manufacturing Integration as a Complementary Asset." *Journal of Operations Management*, vol. 25 (2007), pp. 736–754.

Zomerdijk, Leonieke G. and Jan de Vries. "Structuring Front Office and Back Office Work in Service Delivery Systems." *International Journal of Operations & Production Management*, vol. 27, no. 1 (2007), pp. 108–131.

McDonald's continually seeks ways to improve its processes so as to provide better quality at a lower cost, with more sustainable resources. This effort combined with innovative menu options pays off. In September, 2011 it delivered its 100th consecutive month of positive global comparable sales. Sales were up by 3.9% in the US and 2.7% in Europe.

McDonald's Corporation

System revenues (company-operated and franchised restaurants) at McDonald's reached a record-high $24 billion in 2010. It has more than 32,000 restaurants around the world and 62 million customers visit them each day. It employs 1.7 million people across the globe. Its stock price in October 2011 was $89.94. Things were not so good in 2002, when customer complaints were growing more frequent and bitter. Its stock price was only $16.08 at the end of 2002. McDonald's is now listening to the customers again, and changing its processes to reflect it. The board brought on a new CEO who had spent 20 years on the operational side of the business. With a zeal for measuring customer satisfaction and sharing the data freely with operators, he pulled off a turnaround that stunned everyone in the business with its speed and scope.

Initiatives were launched to collect performance measures and revamp McDonald's processes to meet customer expectations. McDonald's sends mystery shoppers to restaurants to conduct anonymous reviews using a hard-number scoring system. Mystery diners from outside survey firms jot down on a paper checklist their grades for speed of service; food temperature; presentation and taste; cleanliness of the counter, tables and condiment islands; even whether the counter crewperson smiles at diners. Trailing six-month and year-to-date results are posted on an internal McDonald's Web site so owners can compare their scores with regional averages. Operators could now pinpoint lingering problems, and performance measures focus operators' attention on needed

From Chapter 4 of *Operations Management: Processes and Supply Chains*, Tenth Edition. Lee J. Krajewski, Larry P. Ritzman, Manoj K. Malhotra. Copyright © 2013 by Pearson Education, Inc. All rights reserved.

process changes. Customers now are encouraged to report their experience at a particular U.S. restaurant by e-mail, regular mail, or toll-free telephone call.

Another initiative was to send 900 operations missionaries into the field, each visiting stores multiple times to fine-tune processes while also conducting day-long seminars where store managers could share tips from corporate kitchen gurus—such as where to place staff—that would shave previous seconds off average service times. The process was changed back to toasting buns rather than microwaving them, giving them an even sweeter caramelized flavor. Other initiatives were taken on McDonald's fast lane. Every six seconds shaved off the wait time adds a percentage point to sales growth. Outdoor menu boards now have more pictures and fewer words. An LED display confirms what customers say, reducing confusion later on. Premium sandwiches are put in boxes rather than paper wrappers, saving a few seconds, and boxes are color coded by sandwich to improve speed and accuracy.

Processes are also being changed to be environment friendly, reaching back from the counters of its restaurants into its supply chain. The U.S. menu involves 330 unique consumer package designs, with 83 percent now made from paper or some other wood-fiber material. Its bulk cooking oil delivery system uses reusable containers, eliminating more than 1,500 pounds of packaging waste per restaurant per year. Its commitment to using sustainable resources has it working with its suppliers to improve coatings on its food packaging. It has shifted more than 18,000 metric tons of fish away from unsustainable sources over the past 5 years. It emphasizes reuse and recycling, managing electrical energy, and effective water management. It also seeks certified sustainable sources for its food. For example, it is piloting a three-year beef farm study to investigate the carbon emissions on 350 beef farms.

All in all, performance measurement and process analysis are increasing customer value and paying off on the bottom line.

Source: Daniel Kruger, "You Want Data with That?" *Forbes,* vol. 173, no. 6 (March 2004), pp. 58–60; **http://www.mcdonalds.com**, April 5, 2011.

LEARNING GOALS *After reading this chapter, you should be able to:*

1. Explain a systematic way to analyze processes.
2. Define flowcharts, swim lane flowcharts, service blueprints, and process charts.
3. Describe the various work measurement techniques.
4. Identify metrics for process evaluation.
5. Describe Pareto charts, cause-and-effect diagrams, and process simulation.
6. Create better processes using benchmarking.
7. Identify keys for effective process management.

Processes are perhaps the least understood and managed aspect of a business. No matter how talented and motivated people are, a firm cannot gain competitive advantage with faulty processes. Just as Mark Twain said of the Mississippi River, a process just keeps rolling on—with one big difference. Most processes can be improved if someone thinks of a way and implements it effectively. Indeed, companies will either adapt processes to the changing needs of customers or cease to exist. Long-term success comes from managers and employees who really understand their businesses. But all too often, highly publicized efforts that seem to offer quick-fix solutions fail to live up to expectations over the long haul, be they programs for conceptualizing a business vision, conducting culture transformation campaigns, or providing leadership training.

Within the field of operations management, many important innovations over the past several decades include work-simplification or better-methods programs, statistical process control, optimization techniques, statistical forecasting techniques, material requirements planning, flexible automation, lean manufacturing, total quality management, reengineering, Six Sigma programs, enterprise resource planning, and e-commerce. We cover these important approaches in the following chapters because they can add significant customer value to a process. However, they are best viewed as just part of a total system for the effective management of work processes, rather than cure-alls.

Of course, process analysis is needed for both reengineering and process improvement, but it is also part of monitoring performance over time. In this chapter, we begin with a systematic approach for analyzing a process that identifies opportunities for improvement, documents the current process, evaluates the process to spot performance gaps, redesigns the process to eliminate the gaps, and implements the desired changes. The goal is continual improvement.

Four supporting techniques—(1) flowcharts, (2) service blueprints, (3) work measurement techniques, and (4) process charts—can give good insights into the current process and the proposed changes. Data analysis tools, such as checklists, bar charts, Pareto charts, and cause-and-effect diagrams, allow the analyst to go from problem symptoms to root causes. Simulation is a more advanced technique to evaluate process performance. We conclude with some of the keys to managing processes effectively, to ensuring that changes are implemented and an infrastructure is set up for making continuous improvements. Process analysis, however, extends beyond the analysis of individual processes. It is also a tool for improving the operation of supply chains.

Process Analysis across the Organization

All parts of an organization need to be concerned about process analysis simply because they are doing work, and process analysis focuses on how work is actually done. Are they providing the most value to their customers (internal or external), or can they be improved? Operations and sales departments are often the first areas that come to mind because they are so closely connected with the core processes. However, support processes in accounting, finance, and human resources are crucial to an organization's success as well. Top management also gets involved, as do other departments. During these handoffs of the "baton," disconnects are often the worst and opportunities for improvement the greatest.

A Systematic Approach

Figure 1 shows a six-step blueprint for process analysis. **Process analysis** is the documentation and detailed understanding of how work is performed and how it can be redesigned. Process analysis begins with identifying a new opportunity for improvement and ends with implementing a revised process. The last step goes back to the first step, thus creating a cycle of continual improvement. Other approaches to process improvement are reengineering and value stream mapping and other techniques.

Step 1: Identify Opportunities

In order to identify opportunities, managers must pay particular attention to the four core processes: (1) supplier relationship, (2) new service/product development, (3) order fulfillment, and (4) the customer relationship. Each of these processes, and the subprocesses nested within them, are involved in delivering value to external customers. Are customers currently satisfied with the services or products they receive, or is there room for improvement? How about internal customers? Customer satisfaction must

Creating Value through Operations Management

Using Operations to Compete
Project Management

Managing Processes

Process Strategy
Process Analysis
Quality and Performance
Capacity Planning
Constraint Management
Lean Systems

Managing Supply Chains

Supply Chain Inventory Management
Supply Chain Design
Supply Chain Location Decisions
Supply Chain Integration
Supply Chain Sustainability and Humanitarian Logistics
Forecasting
Operations Planning and Scheduling
Resource Planning

process analysis

The documentation and detailed understanding of how work is performed and how it can be redesigned.

▼ FIGURE 1
Blueprint for Process Analysis

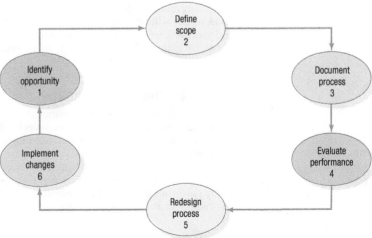

be monitored periodically, either with a formal measurement system or with informal checks or studies. Managers sometimes develop an inventory of their core and support processes that provide a guide for what processes need scrutiny.

Another way to identify opportunities is by looking at the strategic issues. Do gaps exist between a process's competitive priorities and its current competitive capabilities? Do multiple measures of cost, top quality, quality consistency, delivery speed, and on-time delivery meet or exceed expectations? Is there a good *strategic fit* in the process? If the process provides a service, does its position on the customer-contact matrix seem appropriate? How does the degree of customer contact match up with process structure, customer involvement, resource flexibility, and capital intensity? Similar questions should be asked about manufacturing processes regarding the strategic fit between process choice, volume, and product customization.

Employees who actually perform the process or internal suppliers or customers should be encouraged to bring their ideas to managers and staff specialists (such as industrial engineers), or perhaps pass on their ideas through a formal suggestion system. A **suggestion system** is a voluntary system by which employees submit their ideas on process improvements. Usually, a specialist evaluates the proposals, makes sure worthy suggestions are implemented, and provides feedback to those who make the suggestions. Sometimes, the person or team making a good suggestion is rewarded with money or special recognition.

Step 2: Define the Scope

Step 2 establishes the boundaries of the process to be analyzed. Is it a broad process that stretches across the whole organization, involving many steps and many employees, or a more narrowly bracketed nested subprocess that is just part of one person's job? A process's scope can be too narrow or too broad. For example, a broadly defined process that outstrips the resources available, sometimes called "trying to boil the ocean," is doomed because it will increase employee frustration without producing any results.

The resources that management assigns to improving or reengineering a process should match the scope of the process. For a small nested process involving only one employee, perhaps he or she is asked to redesign the process. For a project that deals with a major core process, managers typically establish one or more teams. A **design team** consists of knowledgeable, team-oriented individuals who work at one or more steps in the process, conduct the process analysis, and make the necessary changes. Other resources may be full-time specialists called internal or external *facilitators*. Facilitators know process analysis methodology, and they can guide and train the design team. If the process cuts across several departmental lines, it may benefit from a *steering team* of several managers from various departments, headed by a project manager who oversees the process analysis.

Step 3: Document the Process

Once scope is established, the analyst should document the process. Documentation includes making a list of the process's inputs, suppliers (internal or external), outputs, and customers (internal or external). This information then can be shown as a diagram, with a more detailed breakdown given in a table.

The next part of documentation is understanding the different steps performed in the process, using one or more of the diagrams, tables, and charts described later in this chapter. When breaking down the process into steps, the analyst notes the degrees and types of customer contact and process divergence along the various steps in the process. The analyst also notes what steps are visible to the customer and where in the process work is handed off from one department to the next.

Step 4: Evaluate Performance

It is important to have good performance measures to evaluate a process for clues on how to improve it. **Metrics** are performance measures for the process and the steps within it. A good place to start is with competitive priorities, but they need to be specific. The analyst creates multiple measures of quality, customer satisfaction, time to perform each step or the whole process, cost, errors, safety, environmental measures, on-time delivery, flexibility, and the like.

Once the metrics are identified, it is time to collect information on how the process is currently performing on each one. Measurement can be rough-cut estimates or quite extensive. Techniques for analyzing wait times and delays can provide important information (see MyOMLab

suggestion system

A voluntary system by which employees submit their ideas on process improvements.

design team

A group of knowledgeable, team-oriented individuals who work at one or more steps in the process, conduct the process analysis, and make the necessary changes.

metrics

Performance measures that are established for a process and the steps within it.

Supplement E "Simulation"). Work measurement techniques are also more extensive and are previewed in a later section of this chapter.

Step 5: Redesign the Process

A careful analysis of the process and its performance on the selected metrics should uncover *disconnects*, or gaps, between actual and desired performance. Performance gaps can be caused by illogical, missing, or extraneous steps. They can be caused by metrics that reinforce the silo mentality of individual departments when the process spans across several departments. The analyst or design team should dig deep to find the root causes of performance gaps.

Using analytical and creative thinking, the design team generates a long list of ideas for improvements. These ideas are then sifted and analyzed. Ideas that are justifiable, where benefits outweigh costs, are reflected in a new process design. The new design should be documented "as proposed." Combining the new process design with the documentation of the current process gives the analysts clear before and after pictures. The new documentation should make clear how the revised process will work and the performance expected for the various metrics used.

McDonald's uses mystery shoppers to evaluate its stores. It also sends operations "emissaries" to its stores to help managers fine-tune their processes, while revising processes and its supply chain to be more environmentally friendly.

Step 6: Implement Changes

Implementation is more than developing a plan and carrying it out. Many processes have been redesigned effectively, but never get implemented. People resist change: "We have always done it that way" or "we tried that before." Widespread participation in process analysis is essential, not only because of the work involved but also because it builds commitment. It is much easier to implement something that is partly your own idea. In addition, special expertise may be needed, such as for developing software. New jobs and skills may be needed, involving training and investments in new technology. Implementation brings to life the steps needed to bring the redesigned process online. Management or the steering committee must make sure that the implementation project goes according to schedule.

In the remainder of this chapter, we examine steps in process analysis in detail.

Documenting the Process

Five techniques are effective for documenting and evaluating processes: (1) flowcharts, (2) swim lane flowcharts, (3) service blueprints, (4) work measurement techniques, and (5) process charts. They allow you to "lift the lid and peer inside" to see how an organization does its work. You can see how a process operates, at any level of detail, and how well it is performing. Trying to create one of these charts might even reveal a lack of any established process. It may not be a pretty picture, but it is how work actually gets done. Techniques for documenting the process lend themselves to finding performance gaps, generating ideas for process improvements, and documenting the look of a redesigned process.

flowchart

A diagram that traces the flow of information, customers, equipment, or materials through the various steps of a process.

A consultant discusses the proposal for a new organizational development program with clients during a follow-up meeting. The use of flowcharts can help in understanding this step as just one part of the overall sales process for a consulting company.

Flowcharts

A **flowchart** traces the flow of information, customers, equipment, or materials through the various steps of a process. Flowcharts are also known as flow diagrams, process maps, relationship maps, or blueprints. Flowcharts have no precise format and typically are drawn with boxes (with a brief description of the step inside), and with lines and arrows to show sequencing. The rectangle (□) shape is the usual choice for a box, although other shapes (O, ◯, ◇, ▽, or ▱) can differentiate between different types of steps (e.g., operation, delay, storage, inspection, and so on). Colors and shading can also call attention to different types of steps, such as those particularly high on process divergence. Divergence is also communicated when an outgoing arrow from a step splits into two or more arrows that lead to different boxes. Although many representations are acceptable, there must be agreement on the conventions used. They can be given as a key somewhere in the flowchart, and/or described in accompanying text. It is also important to communicate *what* (e.g., information, customer order, customer, materials, and so on) is being tracked.

You can create flowcharts with several programs. Microsoft PowerPoint offers many different formatting choices for flowcharts (see the Flowchart submenu under AutoShapes). The tutorials "Flowcharting in Excel" and "Flowcharting in PowerPoint" in MyOMLab offer other options, and its live demonstrations of flowcharting in Figures 2 and 3 are instructive. Other powerful software packages for flowcharting and drawing diagrams (such as organization charts and decision trees) are SmartDraw (**www.smartdraw.com**), Microsoft Visio (**www.microsoft.com/office/visio**), and Micrografx (**www.micrografx.com**). Often, free downloads are available at such sites on a trial basis.

Flowcharts can be created for several levels in the organization. For example, at the strategic level, they could show the core processes and their linkages. At this level, the flowcharts would not have much detail; however, they would give a bird's eye view of the overall business. Just identifying a core process is often helpful. Let us now turn to the process level, where we get into the details of the process being analyzed. Figure 2 shows such a process, which consists of many steps that have subprocesses nested within them. Rather than representing everything in one flowchart,

MyOMLab

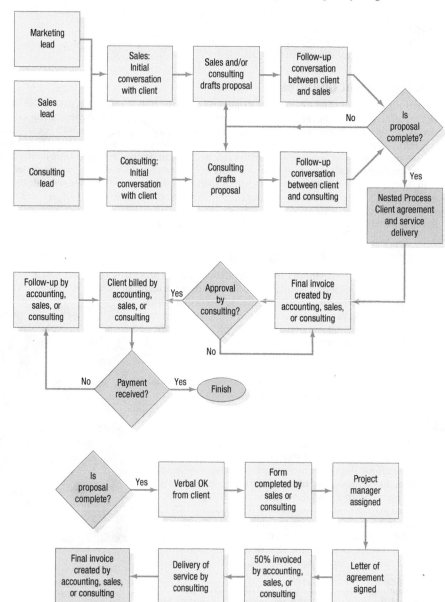

FIGURE 2 ▶
Flowchart of the Sales Process for a Consulting Company

FIGURE 3 ▶
Flowchart of the Nested Subprocess of Client Agreement and Service Delivery

Figure 2 presents an overview of the whole process. It describes the sales process for a consulting firm that specializes in organizational development and corporate education programs. Four different departments (accounting, consulting, marketing, and sales) interact with the external customer (client). The process goes through three main phases: (1) generating business leads, (2) client agreement and service delivery, and (3) billing and collection.

Figure 2 illustrates one other feature. The diamond shape ($\Diamond$) represents a yes/no decision or outcome, such as the results of an inspection or a recognition of different kinds of customer requirements. In Figure 2, the diamond represents three yes/no decision points: (1) whether the proposal is complete, (2) whether consulting approves the invoice, and (3) whether payment is received. These yes/no decision points are more likely to appear when a process is high in divergence.

Sometimes, it is impossible to get the whole flowchart on one page. Figures 2 and 3 show how to create nested processes for steps that can be more aggregated. For example, Figure 3 flowcharts a nested process within the client agreement and service delivery step in Figure 2. Figure 3 brings out more details, such as invoicing the customer for 50 percent of the total estimated cost of the service before the service is delivered, and then putting together a final invoice after the service is finished. This nesting approach often becomes a practical necessity because only so much detail can be shown in any single flowchart.

Swim Lane Flowcharts

The **swim lane flowchart** is a visual representation that groups functional areas responsible for different sub-processes into lanes. It is most appropriate when the business process spans several department boundaries, and where each department or a functional area is separated by parallel lines similar to lanes in a swimming pool. Swim lanes are labeled according to the functional groups they represent, and can be arranged either horizontally or vertically.

The swim lane flowchart in Figure 4 illustrates the order placement and acceptance process at a manufacturing company. The process starts when an order is generated by a customer and

swim lane flowchart

A visual representation that groups functional areas responsible for different sub-processes into lanes. It is most appropriate when the business process spans several department boundaries.

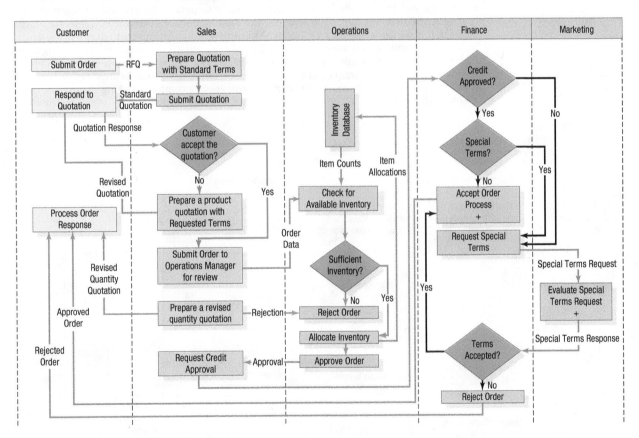

▲ FIGURE 4
Swim Lane Flowchart of the Order-Filling Process Showing Handoffs Between Departments
Source: D. Kroenke, *Using MIS,* 4th ed., 2012, p. 336. Reprinted by permission of Pearson, Upper Saddle River, NJ.

ends when the order is actually rejected, modified, or approved by the company in consultation with the customer. All functions contributing to this process are included in the flowchart. The columns represent different departments or functional areas, and the steps appear in the department column where they are performed. The customer is also shown as one of the column headings. This approach shows the *handoffs* from one department to another when the outgoing arrow from a step goes to another column. Special dotted-line arrows are one way to show handoffs. Handoffs are points where cross-functional coordination is at particular risk due to the silo mentality. Misunderstandings, backlogs, and errors are more likely at these points.

Flowcharts allow the process analyst and managers to look at the horizontal organization, rather than the vertical organization and departmental boundaries implied by a typical organizational chart. Flowcharts show how organizations produce their outputs through cross-functional work processes, and allow the design team to see all the critical interfaces between functions and departments.

Service Blueprints

service blueprint

A special flowchart of a service process that shows which steps have high customer contact.

A good design for service processes depends first and foremost on the type and amount of customer contact. A **service blueprint** is a special flowchart of a service process that shows which steps have high customer contact. It uses a line of visibility to identify which steps are visible to the customer (and thus. more of a front-office process) and those that are not (back office process).

Another approach to creating a service blueprint is to create three levels. The levels clarify how much control the customer has over each step. For example, consider a customer driving into a Fast Lube shop to have their car serviced. Level 1 would be when the customer is in control, such as driving in for service or paying the bill at the end. Level 2 could be when the customer interacts with the service provider, such as making the initial service request, or being notified on what needs to be done. Level 3 could be when the service is removed from the customer's control, such as when the work is performed and the invoice is prepared.

Figure 5 illustrates a fairly complex service blueprint. It not only shows steps with its customers, but also with its consumer's customers. It shows the steps taken by a consulting company that specializes in inventory appraisals and inventory liquidations. Its external customers are large banks that make asset-based loans. The bank's customers, in turn, are customers seeking a loan based on the value of their assets (including inventories). Figure 5 describes the consulting company's current evaluation and appraisal process. This service blueprint not only shows the steps in its current inventory evaluation and appraisal process, but also which steps are visible to its external customers (the banks) and its customers' customers (the company seeking a loan). The steps visible to the banks (salmon boxes) are partitioned with the vertical lines of visibility. The steps

▼ **FIGURE 5**
Service Blueprint of
Consulting Company's
Inventory Appraisal Process

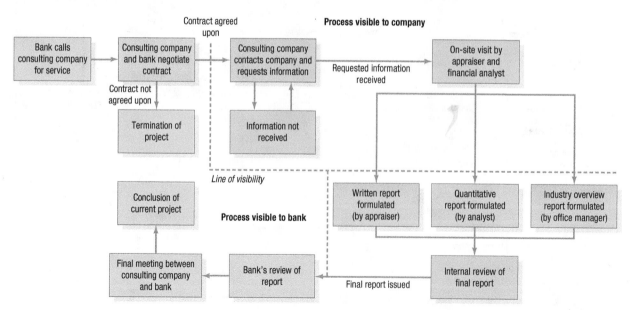

visible to the company seeking a loan (green boxes) are partitioned off by the top left vertical line of visibility and the horizontal line of visibility. The steps in purple are performed by the consulting company and not visible to external customers.

The process begins with a call from a bank seeking the service by the consulting company. There are three main steps in the overall process.

1. The bank contacts the consulting company and they agree on the contract.

2. The consulting company performs the inventory evaluation on the site of the company seeking a loan from the bank.

3. The consulting company prepares the final report and presents it to the bank.

Of course, visibility is just one aspect of customer contact, and it may not adequately capture how actively the customer is involved or how much personal attention is required. A service blueprint can use colors, shading, or box shapes, instead of the lines of visibility, to show the extent and type of customer contact. Another approach to service blueprinting is to tag each step with a number, and then have an accompanying table that describes in detail the customer contact for each numbered step. There is no one "right way" to create a flow chart or service blueprint.

Work Measurement Techniques

Process documentation would not be complete without estimates of the average time each step in the process would take. Time estimates are needed not just for process improvement efforts, but for capacity planning, constraint management, performance appraisal, and scheduling. Estimating task times can be as simple as making a reasoned guess, asking a knowledgeable person, or taking notes while observing the process. More extensive studies involve collecting data for several weeks, consulting cost accounting data, or checking data recorded in information systems.

Formal techniques are also available that rely on the judgment of skilled observers: (1) the time study method, (2) the elemental standard data approach, (3) the predetermined data approach, and (4) work sampling. A fifth method, (5) learning curve analysis, is particularly appropriate when a new product or process is introduced and the time per unit produced has not yet stabilized. The method chosen depends on the purpose of the data, process type (job or line), and degree of product customization. A more comprehensive treatment of these techniques is provided in MyOMLab Supplement H, "Measuring Output Rates" and MyOMLab Supplement I, "Learning Curve Analysis."

Time Study Method　**Time study** uses a trained analyst to perform four basic steps in setting a time standard for a job or process: (1) selecting the work elements (steps in a flowchart or process chart) within the process to be studied, (2) timing the elements, (3) determining the sample size, and (4) setting the final standard. It is essentially the average time observed, adjusted for normal effort and making an allowance for breaks, unavoidable delays, and the like. The analyst records time spent on each element of the process being studied using a stopwatch, and records the time spent on each element for several repetitions. The analyst assigns a performance rating for each element to adjust for normal effort. Some elements may be performed faster or slower than normal, in the analyst's judgment. The allowance is expressed as a proportion or percent of the total *normal* time.

Elemental Standard Data Approach　Another approach is needed when products or services are highly customized, job processes prevail, and process divergence is great. **Elemental standard data** is a database of standards compiled by a firm's analysts for basic elements that they can draw on later to estimate the time required for a particular job. This approach works well when work elements within certain jobs are similar to those in other jobs. Sometimes, the time required for a work element depends on variable characteristics of the jobs, such as the amount of metal to be deposited for a welding process. In such cases, an equation that relates these characteristics to the time required is also stored in the database. Another method, such as time study or past records, still must be used to compile the normal times (before the allowance is added) stored in the database.

EXAMPLE 1	Time Study of Watch Assembly Process

A process at a watch assembly plant has been changed. The process is divided into three work elements. A time study has been performed with the following results. The time standard for the process previously was 14.5 minutes. Based on the new time study, should the time standard be revised?

SOLUTION

The new time study had an initial sample of four observations, with the results shown in the following table. The performance rating factor (RF) is shown for each element (to adjust for normal effort), and the allowance for the whole process is 18 percent of the total *normal* time.

	Obs 1	Obs 2	Obs 3	Obs 4	Average (min)	RF	Normal Time
Element 1	2.60	2.34	3.12	2.86	2.730	1.0	2.730
Element 2	4.94	4.78	5.10	4.68	4.875	1.1	5.363
Element 3	2.18	1.98	2.13	2.25	2.135	0.9	1.922
						Total Normal Time =	**10.015 minutes**

The normal time for an element in the table is its average time, multiplied by the RF. The total normal time for the whole process is the sum of the normal times for the three elements, or 10.015 minutes. To get the standard time (ST) for the process, just add in the allowance, or

$$ST = 10.015(1 + 0.18) = \textbf{11.82} \text{ minutes/watch}$$

DECISION POINT

The time to assemble a watch appears to have decreased considerably. However, based on the precision that management wants, the analyst decided to increase the sample size before setting a new standard. MyOMLab Supplement H, "Measuring Output Rates," gives more information on determining the number of additional observations needed.

MyOMLab

---

predetermined data approach

A database approach that divides each work element into a series of micromotions that make up the element. The analyst then consults a published database that contains the normal times for the full array of possible micromotions.

work sampling

A process that estimates the proportion of time spent by people or machines on different activities, based on observations randomized over time.

Predetermined Data Approach The **predetermined data approach** divides each work element even more, into a series of micromotions that make up the element. The analyst then consults a published database that contains the normal times for the full array of possible micromotions. A process's normal time can then be calculated as the sum of the times given in the database for the elements performed in the process. This approach makes most sense for highly repetitive processes with little process divergence and line flows. The micromotions (such as reach, move, or apply pressure) are very detailed.

Work Sampling Method **Work sampling** estimates the proportion of time spent by people or machines on different activities, based on observations randomized over time. Examples of these activities include working on a service or product, doing paperwork, waiting for instructions, waiting for maintenance, or being idle. Such data can then be used to assess a process's productivity, estimate the allowances needed to set standards for other work measurement methods, and spot areas for process improvement. It is best used when the processes are highly divergent with flexible flows. Figure 6 shows the input data and numerical results for one week of observations. Figure 6 shows an idle time of 23.81 percent for the week. It also reports that 237 more observations are needed to achieve the confidence and precision levels required with the input data. How these conclusions are reached is explained in MyOMLab Supplement H, "Measuring Output Rates".

FIGURE 6 ▼
Work Sampling Study of Admission Clerk at Health Clinic Using OM Explorer's *Time Study* Solver.

(a) Input Data and Numerical Results

Increase Observations		Remove An Observation	

Confidence *z*	1.96	Precision *p*	0.05

Observation Period	Times Busy	Times Idle	Observations
Monday	6	1	7
Tuesday	5	2	7
Wednesday	7	0	7
Thursday	9	2	11
Friday	5	5	10
Total	32	10	42

(b) Idle Time and Observations Required

Portion of idle times	0.2381
Total observations required	279
Additional observations required	237

Learning Curve Analysis   The time estimation techniques just covered assume that the process is stable. If the process is revised, then just repeat the method for the revised process after it stabilizes. Learning curve analysis, on the other hand, takes into account that learning takes place on an ongoing basis, such as when new products or services are introduced frequently. With instruction and repetition, workers learn to perform jobs more efficiently, process improvements are identified, and better administration methods are created. These learning effects can be anticipated with a **learning curve**, a line that displays the relationship between processing time and the cumulative quantity of a product or service produced. The time required to produce a unit or create a service decreases as more units or customers are processed. The learning curve for a process depends on the rate of learning and the actual or estimated time for the first unit processed. Figure 7 demonstrates the learning curve assuming an 80 percent learning rate, with the first unit taking 120,000 hours and the cumulative average time for the first 10 units produced. The learning rate deals with each *doubling* of the output total. The time for the second unit is 80 percent of the first (or $120,000 \times .80 = 96,000$ hours), the time for the fourth unit is 80 percent of the second unit (or $96,000 \times .80 = 76,800$ hours), and so on. Finding the time estimate for a unit that is not an exact doubling (such as the fifth unit), and also the cumulative average time for the first 10 units, is explained in MyOMLab Supplement I, "Learning Curve Analysis".

learning curve

A line that displays the relationship between processing time and the cumulative quantity of a product or service produced.

MyOMLab

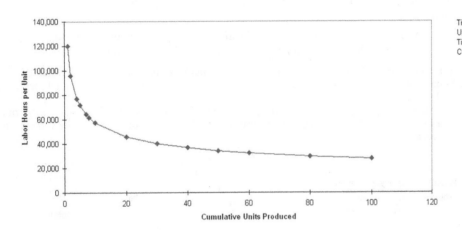

Time for first unit	120,000
Unit number	10
Time for unit 10	57,172
Cumulative average time per unit	75,784

◀ **FIGURE 7**
Learning Curve with 80% Learning Rate Using OM Explorer's *Learning Curves* Solver.

Process Charts

A **process chart** is an organized way of documenting all the activities performed by a person or group of people at a workstation, with a customer, or working with certain materials. It analyzes a process using a table, and provides information about each step in the process. In contrast to flowcharts, swim lane flowcharts, and service blueprints, it requires the time estimates (see work measurement techniques covered in the last section). Often it is used to drill down to the job level for an individual person, a team, or a focused nested process. It can have many formats. Here, we group the type of activities for a typical process into five categories:

process chart

An organized way of documenting all the activities performed by a person or group of people, at a workstation, with a customer, or on materials.

- *Operation.* Changes, creates, or adds something. Drilling a hole or serving a customer are examples of operations.
- *Transportation.* Moves the study's subject from one place to another (sometimes called *materials handling*). The subject can be a person, a material, a tool, or a piece of equipment. A customer walking from one end of a counter to the other, a crane hoisting a steel beam to a location, and a conveyor carrying a partially completed product from one workstation to the next are examples of transportation. It could also be the shipment of a finished product to the customer or a warehouse.
- *Inspection.* Checks or verifies something but does not change it. Getting customer feedback, checking for blemishes on a surface, weighing a product, and taking a temperature reading are examples of inspections.
- *Delay.* Occurs when the subject is held up awaiting further action. Time spent waiting for a server; time spent waiting for materials or equipment; cleanup time; and time that workers, machines, or workstations are idle because they have no work to complete are examples of delays.

- *Storage*. Occurs when something is put away until a later time. Supplies unloaded and placed in a storeroom as inventory, equipment put away after use, and papers put in a file cabinet are examples of storage.

Depending on the situation, other categories can be used. For example, subcontracting for outside services might be a category, temporary storage and permanent storage, or environmental waste might be three separate categories. Choosing the right category for each activity requires taking the perspective of the subject charted. A delay for the equipment could be inspection or transportation for the operator.

To complete a chart for a new process, the analyst must identify each step performed. If the process is an existing one, the analyst can actually observe the steps and categorize each step according to the subject being studied. The analyst then records the distance traveled and the time taken to perform each step. After recording all the activities and steps, the analyst summarizes the steps, times, and distances data. Figure 8 shows a process chart prepared using OM Explorer's *Process Chart* Solver. It is for a patient with a twisted ankle being treated at a hospital. The process begins at the entrance and ends with the patient exiting after picking up the prescription.

After a process is charted, the analyst sometimes estimates the annual cost of the entire process. It becomes a benchmark against which other methods for performing the process can be evaluated. Annual labor cost can be estimated by finding the product of (1) time in hours to perform the process each time, (2) variable costs per hour, and (3) number of times the process is performed each year, or

$$\begin{matrix} \text{Annual} \\ \text{labor cost} \end{matrix} = \begin{pmatrix} \text{Time to perfrom} \\ \text{the process in hours} \end{pmatrix} \begin{pmatrix} \text{Variable costs} \\ \text{per hour} \end{pmatrix} \begin{pmatrix} \text{Number of times process} \\ \text{performed per year} \end{pmatrix}$$

For example, if the average time to serve a customer is 4 hours, the variable cost is $25 per hour, and 40 customers are served per year, then the labor cost is $4,000 per year (or 4 hrs/customer × $25/hr × 40 customers/yr).

In the case of the patient in Figure 8, this conversion would not be necessary, with total patient time being sufficient. What is being tracked is the patient's time, not the time and costs of the service providers.

MyOMLab

Tutor 4.1 in MyOMLab provides a new example to practice creating process charts.

FIGURE 8 ▶
Process Chart for Emergency Room Admission

Process:	Emergency room admission
Subject:	Ankle injury patient
Beginning:	Enter emergency room
Ending:	Leave hospital

Insert Step

Append Step

Remove Step

		Summary		
Activity	Number of Steps	Time (min)	Distance (ft)	
Operation ●	5	23.00		
Transport ➡	9	11.00	815	
Inspect ■	2	8.00		
Delay ◗	3	8.00		
Store ▼	—	—		

Step No.	Time (min)	Distance (ft)	●	➡	■	◗	▼	Step Description
1	0.50	15.0			X			Enter emergency room, approach patient window
2	10.00		X					Sit down and fill out patient history
3	0.75	40.0			X			Nurse escorts patient to ER triage room
4	3.00					X		Nurse inspects injury
5	0.75	40.0		X				Return to waiting room
6	1.00						X	Wait for available bed
7	1.00	60.0		X				Go to ER bed
8	4.00						X	Wait for doctor
9	5.00					X		Doctor inspects injury and questions patient
10	2.00	200.0		X				Nurse takes patient to radiology
11	3.00		X					Technician x-rays patient
12	2.00	200.0		X				Return to bed in ER
13	3.00						X	Wait for doctor to return
14	2.00		X					Doctor provides diagnosis and advice
15	1.00	60.0		X				Return to emergency entrance area
16	4.00		X					Check out
17	2.00	180.0		X				Walk to pharmacy
18	4.00		X					Pick up prescription
19	1.00	20.0		X				Leave the building

You can design your own process chart spreadsheets to bring out issues that are particularly important for the process you are analyzing, such as categories for customer contact, process divergence, and the like. You can also track performance measures other than time and distance traveled, such as error rates. In addition, you can also create a different version of the process chart spreadsheet that examines processes much as done with flowcharts, except now in the form of a table. The columns that categorize the activity type could be replaced by one or more columns reporting different metrics of interest, rather than trying to fit them into a flowchart. Although it might not look as elegant, it could be just as informative—and easier to create.

Evaluating Performance

Metrics and performance information complete the documentation of a process (see step 3 in Figure 1). Metrics can be displayed in various ways. Sometimes, they can be added directly on the flowchart or process chart. When the number of metrics gets unwieldy, another approach is to create a supporting table for the chart. Its rows are the steps in the flowchart, swim lane flowchart, service blueprint, or process chart. The columns are the current performance, goals, and performance gaps for various metrics.

The specific metrics analysts choose depends on the process being analyzed and on the competitive priorities. Good starting points are the per-unit processing time and cost at each step, and the time elapsed from beginning to end of the process. Capacity utilization, environmental issues, and customer (or job) waiting times reveal where in the process delays are most likely to occur. Customer satisfaction measures, error rates, and scrap rates identify possible quality problems.

The leader of a design team presents several charts that document a process in their office that they are analyzing. He is identifying several areas of substandard performance across a range of different metrics. The next step will be to redesign the process. The flipchart on the right will be quite useful in generating rapid fire ideas from the team on how the process might be improved.

Andresr/Shutterstock.com

Data Analysis Tools

Metrics may reveal a performance gap. Various tools are available to help you understand the causes of the problem[1]. Here we present six tools: (1) checklists, (2) histograms and bar charts, (3) Pareto charts, (4) scatter diagrams, (5) cause-and-effect diagrams, and (6) graphs. Many of them were developed initially to analyze quality issues, but they apply equally well to the full range of performance measures.

Checklists   Data collection through the use of a checklist is often the first step in the analysis of a metric. A **checklist** is a form used to record the frequency of occurrence of certain process failures. A **process failure** is any performance shortfall, such as error, delay, environmental waste, rework, and the like. The characteristics may be measurable on a continuous scale (e.g., weight, customer satisfaction on a 1-to-7 scale, unit cost, scrap loss percentage, time, or length) or on a yes-or-no basis (e.g., customer complaint, posting error, paint discoloration, or inattentive servers).

Histograms and Bar Charts   Data from a checklist often can be presented succinctly and clearly with histograms or bar charts. A **histogram** summarizes data measured on a continuous scale, showing the frequency distribution of some process failure (in statistical terms, the central tendency and dispersion of the data). Often the mean of the data is indicated on the histogram. A **bar chart** (see Figure 10) is a series of bars representing the frequency of occurrence of data characteristics measured on a yes-or-no basis. The bar height indicates the number of times a particular process failure was observed.

Pareto Charts   When managers discover several process problems that need to be addressed, they have to decide which should be attacked first. Vilfredo Pareto, a nineteenth-century Italian scientist whose statistical work focused on inequalities in data, proposed that most of an "activity" is caused by relatively few of its factors. In a restaurant quality problem, the activity could be customer complaints and the factor could be "discourteous server." For a manufacturer, the activity could be product defects and the factor could be "missing part." Pareto's concept, called the 80–20 rule, is that 80 percent of the activity is caused by 20 percent of the factors. By concentrating on the 20 percent of the factors (the "vital few"), managers can attack 80 percent of the process failure problems. Of course, the exact percentages vary with each situation, but inevitably relatively few factors cause most of the performance shortfalls.

The few vital factors can be identified with a **Pareto chart**, a bar chart on which the factors are plotted along the horizontal axis in decreasing order of frequency (see Figure 11). The chart has two vertical axes, the one on the left showing frequency (as in a histogram) and the one on the right showing the cumulative percentage of frequency. The cumulative frequency curve identifies the few vital factors that warrant immediate managerial attention.

---

checklist

A form used to record the frequency of occurrence of certain process failures.

process failure

Any performance shortfall, such as error, delay, environmental waste, rework, and the like.

histogram

A summarization of data measured on a continuous scale, showing the frequency distribution of some process failure (in statistical terms, the central tendency and dispersion of the data).

bar chart

A series of bars representing the frequency of occurrence of data characteristics measured on a yes-or-no basis.

Pareto chart

A bar chart on which factors are plotted along the horizontal axis in decreasing order of frequency.

EXAMPLE 2	Pareto Chart for a Restaurant

MyOMLab

Active Model 4.1 in MyOMLab provides additional insights on this Pareto chart example and its extensions.

MyOMLab

Tutor 4.2 in MyOMLab provides a new example on creating Pareto charts.

The manager of a neighborhood restaurant is concerned about the lower numbers of customers patronizing his eatery. Complaints have been rising, and he would like to find out what issues to address and present the findings in a way his employees can understand.

SOLUTION

The manager surveyed his customers over several weeks and collected the following data:

Complaint	Frequency
Discourteous server	12
Slow service	42
Cold dinner	5
Cramped tables	20
Atmosphere	10

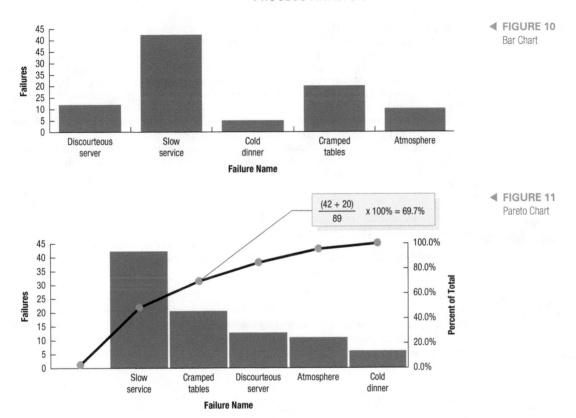

◀ **FIGURE 10**
Bar Chart

◀ **FIGURE 11**
Pareto Chart

Figure 10 is a bar chart and Figure 11 is a Pareto chart, both created with OM Explorer's *Bar, Pareto, and Line Charts* Solver. They present the data in a way that shows which complaints are more prevalent (the vital few). You can reformat these charts for any "yes-or-no" metrics by unprotecting the spreadsheet and then making your revisions. For example, if you are using Microsoft Excel 2010, just click on Home/Format/Protection/Unprotect Sheet. Another approach is to create your own spreadsheets from scratch. More advanced software with point-and-click interfaces include Minitab (**www.minitab.com/index.htm**), SAS (**www.sas.com/rnd/app/qc.html**), and Microsoft Visio (**www.microsoft.com/office/visio**).

DECISION POINT

It was clear to the manager (and all employees) which complaints, if rectified, would cover most of the process failure problems in the restaurant. First, slow service will be addressed by training the existing staff, adding another server, and improving the food preparation process. Removing some decorative furniture from the dining area and spacing the tables better will solve the problem with cramped tables. The Pareto chart shows that these two problems, if rectified, will account for almost 70 percent of the complaints.

Scatter Diagrams Sometimes managers suspect that a certain factor is causing a particular process failure. A **scatter diagram**, which is a plot of two variables showing whether they are related, can be used to verify or negate the suspicion. Each point on the scatter diagram represents one data observation. For example, the manager of a castings shop may suspect that casting defects are a function of the diameter of the casting. A scatter diagram could be constructed by plotting the number of defective castings found for each diameter of casting produced. After the diagram is completed, any relationship between diameter and number of process failures will be clear.

scatter diagram

A plot of two variables showing whether they are related.

Cause-and-Effect Diagrams An important aspect of process analysis is linking each metric to the inputs, methods, and process steps that build a particular attribute into the service or product. One way to identify a design problem is to develop a **cause-and-effect diagram** that relates a key performance problem to its potential causes. First developed by Kaoru Ishikawa, the diagram helps management trace disconnects directly to the operations involved. Processes that have no bearing on a particular problem are not shown on the diagram.

cause-and-effect diagram

A diagram that relates a key performance problem to its potential causes.

The cause-and-effect diagram sometimes is called a *fishbone diagram*. The main performance gap is labeled as the fish's "head," the major categories of potential causes as structural "bones," and the likely specific causes as "ribs." When constructing and using a cause-and-effect diagram, an analyst identifies all the major categories of potential causes for the problem. These might be personnel, machines, materials, and processes. For each major category, the analyst lists all the likely causes of the performance gap. Under personnel might be listed "lack of training," "poor communication," and "absenteeism." Creative thinking helps the analyst identify and properly classify all suspected causes. The analyst then systematically investigates the causes listed on the diagram for each major category, updating the chart as new causes become apparent. The process of constructing a cause-and-effect diagram calls management and worker attention to the primary factors affecting process failures. Example 3 demonstrates the use of a cause-and-effect diagram by an airline.

EXAMPLE 3	**Analysis of Flight Departure Delays**

The operations manager for Checker Board Airlines at Port Columbus International Airport noticed an increase in the number of delayed flight departures.

▼ FIGURE 12
Cause-and-Effect Diagram for Flight Departure Delays
Source: Adopted from D. Daryl Wyckoff, "New Tools for Achieving Service Quality," *The Cornell H.R.A. Quarterly.* Used by permission. All rights reserved.

SOLUTION

To analyze all the possible causes of that problem, the manager constructed a cause-and-effect diagram, shown in Figure 12. The main problem, delayed flight departures, is the "head" of the diagram. He brainstormed all possible causes with his staff, and together they identified several major categories: equipment, personnel, materials, procedures, and "other factors" that are beyond managerial control. Several suspected causes were identified for each major category.

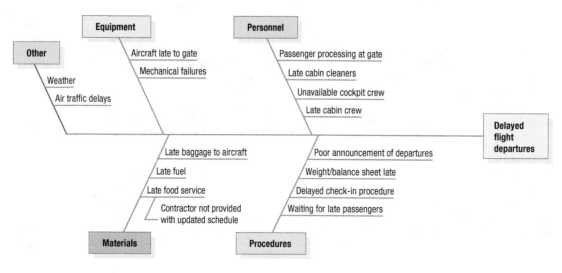

DECISION POINT

The operations manager, having a good understanding of the process, suspected that most of the flight delays were caused by problems with materials. Consequently, he had food service, fueling, and baggage-handling operations examined. He learned that the number of tow trucks for the baggage-transfer operations was insufficient and that planes were delayed waiting for baggage from connecting flights.

---

graphs

Representations of data in a variety of pictorial forms, such as line charts and pie charts.

Graphs Graphs represent data in a variety of pictorial formats, such as line charts and pie charts. *Line charts* represent data sequentially with data points connected by line segments to highlight trends in the data. Line charts are used in control charts and forecasting. Pie charts represent process factors as slices of a pie; the size of each slice is in proportion to the number of occurrences of the factor. Pie charts are useful for showing data from *a group of factors* that can be represented as percentages totaling 100 percent.

Each of the tools for improving quality may be used independently, but their power is greatest when they are used together. In solving a process-related problem, managers often must act as detectives, sifting data to clarify the issues involved and deducing the causes. We call this process *data snooping*. Example 4 demonstrates how the tools for improving quality can be used for data snooping.

A simulation model goes one step further than data analysis tools, because it can show how the process dynamically changes over time. **Process simulation** is the act of reproducing the behavior of a process, using a model that describes each step. Once the process is modeled, the analyst can make changes in the model to measure the impact on certain metrics, such as response time, waiting lines, resource utilization, and the like. To learn more about how simulation works, see MyOMLab Supplement E, "Simulation". A more advanced capability is possible using SimQuick, found in MyOMLab (**www.nd.edu/~dhartvig/simquick/top.html**). Other software packages include Extend (**http://www.extendsim.com//**), SIMPROCESS (**www.caciasl .com**), ProModel (**www.promodel.com**), and Witness (**www.lanner.com**).

process simulation

The act of reproducing the behavior of a process, using a model that describes each step.

MyOMLab

Redesigning the Process

A doctor pinpoints an illness after a thorough examination of the patient, and then the doctor recommends treatments based on the diagnosis; so it is with processes. After a process is documented, metrics data collected, and disconnects identified, the process analyst or design team puts together a set of changes that will make the process better. At this step, people directly involved in the process are brought in to get their ideas and inputs.

Generating Ideas: Questioning and Brainstorming

Sometimes, ideas for reengineering or improving a process become apparent after documenting the process and carefully examining the areas of substandard performance, handoffs between departments, and steps where customer contact is high. Example 4 illustrates how such documentation pointed to a better way of handling the fiber boards through better training. In other cases, the better solution is less evident. Ideas can be uncovered (because there is always a better way) by asking six questions about each step in the process, and about the process as a whole:

1. *What* is being done?
2. *When* is it being done?
3. *Who* is doing it?
4. *Where* is it being done?
5. *How* is it being done?
6. *How* **well** does it do on the various metrics of importance?

Answers to these questions are challenged by asking still another series of questions. *Why* is the process even being done? *Why* is it being done where it is being done? *Why* is it being done when it is being done?

Creativity can also be stimulated by **brainstorming**, letting a group of people knowledgeable about the process propose ideas for change by saying whatever comes to mind. A facilitator records the ideas on a flipchart, so that all can see. Participants are discouraged from evaluating any of the ideas generated during the session. The purpose is to encourage creativity and to get as many ideas as possible, no matter how far-fetched the ideas may seem. The participants of a brainstorming session need not be limited to the design team as long as they have seen or heard the process documentation. A growing number of big companies, such as Sun Life Financial and Georgia-Pacific, are taking advantage of the Internet and specially designed software to run brainstorming sessions that allow people at far-flung locations to "meet" online and hash out solutions to particular problems. The technology lets employees see, and build on, one another's ideas, so that one person's seed of a notion can grow into a practical plan.

brainstorming

Letting a group of people, knowledgeable about the process, propose ideas for change by saying whatever comes to mind.

| **EXAMPLE 4** | **Identifying Causes of Poor Headliner Process Failures** |

The Wellington Fiber Board Company produces headliners, the fiberglass components that form the inner roof of passenger cars. Management wanted to identify which process failures were most prevalent and to find the cause.

Step 1. Checklist

Headliner failures

Process failure	Tally	Total
A. Tears in fabric	IIII	4
B. Discolored fabric	III	3
C. Broken fiber board	HHT HHT HHT HHT HHT HHT HHT I	36
D. Ragged edges	HHT II	7
		Total 50

Step 2. Pareto Chart

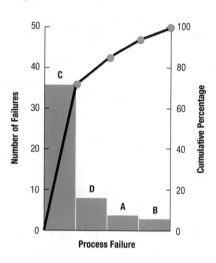

Step 3. Cause-and-Effect Diagram

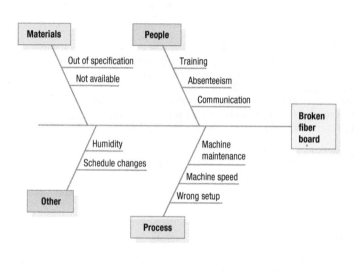

Step 4. Bar Chart

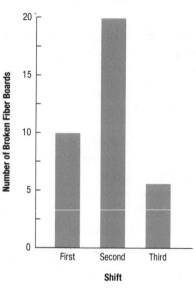

▲ **FIGURE 13**
Application of the Tools
for Improving Quality

SOLUTION

Figure 13 shows the sequential application of several tools for improving quality.

Step 1: A checklist of different types of process failures was constructed from last month's production records.

Step 2: A Pareto chart prepared from the checklist data indicated that broken fiber board accounted for 72 percent of the process failures.

Step 3: A cause-and-effect diagram for broken fiber board identified several potential causes for the problem. The one strongly suspected by the manager was employee training.

Step 4: The manager reorganized the production reports into a bar chart according to shift because the personnel on the three shifts had varied amounts of experience.

DECISION POINT

The bar chart indicated that the second shift, with the least experienced workforce, had most of the process failures. Further investigation revealed that workers were not using proper procedures for stacking the fiber boards after the press operation, which caused cracking and chipping. The manager set up additional training sessions focused on board handling. Although the second shift was not responsible for all the process failures, finding the source of many of the failures enabled the manager to improve the performance of her operations.

After the brainstorming session is over, the design team moves into the "get real" phase: They evaluate the different ideas. The team identifies the changes that give the best payoffs for process redesign. The redesign could involve issues of capacity, layout, technology, or even location.

The redesigned process is documented once again, this time as the "after" view of the process. Expected payoffs are carefully estimated, along with risks. For changes involving investments, the time value of money must be considered (see MyOMLab Supplement F, "Financial Analysis,"). The impact on people (skills, degree of change, training requirements, and resistance to change) must also be factored into the evaluation of the new design.

Managerial Practice 1 describes how Baptist Memorial Hospital analyzed its processes to solve its capacity problem and improve patient satisfaction at the same time without any addition of new resources.

MyOMLab

Benchmarking

Benchmarking can be another valuable source for process redesign. **Benchmarking** is a systematic procedure that measures a firm's processes, services, and products against those of industry leaders. Companies use benchmarking to better understand how outstanding companies do things so that they can improve their own processes.

benchmarking

A systematic procedure that measures a firm's processes, services, and products against those of industry leaders.

MANAGERIAL PRACTICE 1 — Baptist Memorial Hospital

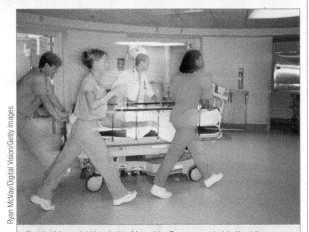

Baptist Memorial Hospital–Memphis is a 760-bed tertiary care hospital. It had a capacity problem, or so it seemed, with occupancy routinely exceeding 90 percent. However, it solved the problem with process improvement, rather than adding staff or bed capacity. Administration, nurses, and physicians centralized bed assignments and added a new bed-tracking system to provide bed information in real time. They then focused on improving processes at the emergency department (ED). An express admission unit (EAU), a 21-bed dedicated area that processes direct and emergency department admissions, was opened to remove responsibility for a particularly time-intensive activity from busy unit nurses. The new processes were less divergent and had more of a line flow. They then began testing process improvement ideas for change on a small scale, altering processes to improve them, and spreading the processes to other areas when they are successful. They began to fax reports from the ED to the receiving unit, shifted more nurses to work during peak periods, began lab and X-ray diagnostic procedures at triage when the EU was at capacity, took patients directly to a room when one became available with bedside registration, and segmented the urgent care population within the ED.

Redesigned processes reduced patient delays. Turnaround time for the overall ED was reduced by 9 percent, even while the ED volume was increasing. Length of stay was reduced by 2 days, the equivalent of building 12 Intensive care unit (ICU) beds. The mortality rate decreased, volume increased by 20 percent, and patient satisfaction improved significantly. What first appeared to be a capacity problem was resolved without adding staff or the number of beds—it was solved with redesigned processes.

Baptist Memorial Hospital in Memphis, Tennessee, holds "huddle meetings" at least three times a day seeking out process improvements. The meetings bring together the hospital's house supervisor, housekeeping supervisor, and key nurses. Improvements have been dramatic. In 2011, the hospital was ranked in the top 5 percent nationally for emergency medicine.

Ryan McVay/Digital Vision/Getty Images

Source: Suzanne S. Horton, "Increasing Capacity While Improving the Bottom Line," *Frontiers of Health Services Management,* vol. 20, no. 4 (Summer 2004), pp. 17–23; Richard S. Zimmerman, "Hospital Capacity, Productivity, and Patient Safety—It All Flows Together," *Frontiers of Health Services Management,* vol. 20, no. 4 (Summer 2004), pp. 33–38, *baptistonline.org,* April, 2011.

Omgeo is a behind-the-scenes company that settles trades between financial services firms. The process used to involve dozens of scribbled faxes, telexes, and telephone calls made for the typical trade costs from $10 to $12. Now, the process costs only 20 cents to $1 per trade—and investment managers essentially got the service free. A key change was using the Internet and new information technology solutions. Information goes into a central database that the broker, investment manager, and custodian banks all have access to in real time. The details of the trades are automatically compared to eliminate errors.

Gerard Vesey/Alamy

Benchmarking focuses on setting quantitative goals for improvement. *Competitive* benchmarking is based on comparisons with a direct industry competitor. *Functional* benchmarking compares areas such as administration, customer service, and sales operations with those of outstanding firms in any industry. For instance, Xerox benchmarked its distribution function against L.L. Bean's because L.L. Bean is renowned as a leading retailer in distribution efficiency and customer service.

Internal benchmarking involves using an organizational unit with superior performance as the benchmark for other units. This form of benchmarking can be advantageous for firms that have several business units or divisions. All forms of benchmarking are best applied in situations where you are looking for a long-term program of continuous improvement.

Typical measures used in benchmarking include cost per unit, service upsets (breakdowns) per customer, processing time per unit, customer retention rates, revenue per unit, return on investment, and customer satisfaction levels.

Benchmarking consists of four basic steps:

Step 1. Planning. Identify the process, service, or product to be benchmarked and the firm(s) to be used for comparison; determine the performance metrics for analysis; collect the data.

Step 2. Analysis. Determine the gap between the firm's current performance and that of the benchmark firm(s); identify the causes of significant performance gaps.

Step 3. Integration. Establish goals and obtain the support of managers who must provide the resources for accomplishing the goals.

Step 4. Action. Develop cross-functional teams of those most affected by the changes; develop action plans and team assignments; implement the plans; monitor progress; recalibrate benchmarks as improvements are made.

Collecting benchmarking data can sometimes be a challenge. Internal benchmarking data is surely the most accessible. One way of benchmarking is always available—tracking the performance of a process over time. Functional benchmarking data are often collected by professional associations or consulting firms. Several corporations and government organizations have agreed to share and standardize performance benchmarks. The American Productivity and Quality Center, a nonprofit organization, created thousands of measures, as Figure 14 illustrates. A full range of metrics can be explored at **www.apqc.org**. Another source is the Supply-Chain Council, which has defined key metrics in its Supply-Chain Operations Reference (SCOR) model.

Managing and Implementing Processes

Failure to manage processes is failure to manage the business. Implementing a beautifully redesigned process is only the beginning to continually monitoring and improving processes. Metrics goals must be continually evaluated and reset to fit changing requirements. Avoid the following seven mistakes when managing processes:[2]

1. *Not Connecting with Strategic Issues.* Is particular attention being paid to core processes, competitive priorities, impact of customer contact and volume, and strategic fit during process analysis?

---

[2]Geary A. Rummler and Alan P. Brache, *Improving Performance,* 2nd ed. (San Francisco: Jossey-Bass, 1995), pp. 126–133.

PROCESS ANALYSIS

Customer Relationship Process

- Total cost of "enter, process, and track orders" per $1,000 revenue
- System costs of process per $100,000 revenue
- Value of sales order line item not fulfilled due to stockouts, as percentage of revenue
- Percentage of finished goods sales value that is returned
- Average time from sales order receipt until manufacturing or logistics is notified
- Average time in direct contact with customer per sales order line item
- Energy consumed in transporting product
- Total distance travelled for products
- Green house gas emissions

Order Fulfillment Process

- Value of plant shipments per employee
- Finished goods inventory turnover
- Reject rate as percentage of total orders processed
- Percentage of orders returned by customers due to quality problems
- Standard customer lead time from order entry to shipment
- Percentage of orders shipped on time
- Use of non-renewable energy sources
- Use of toxic ingredients
- Safe and healthy work environment

New Service/Product Development Process

- Percentage of sales due to services/products launched last year
- Cost of "generate new services/products" process per $1,000 revenue
- Ratio of projects entering the process to projects completing the process
- Time to market for existing service/product improvement project
- Time to market for new service/product project
- Time to profitability for existing service/product improvement project

Supplier Relationship Process

- Cost of "select suppliers and develop/maintain contracts" process per $1,000 revenue
- Number of employees per $1,000 of purchases
- Percentage of purchase orders approved electronically
- Average time to place a purchase order
- Total number of active vendors per $1,000 of purchases
- Percentage of value of purchased material that is supplier certified
- Amount of toxic chemicals used in supplies production process
- Energy consumed in transporting raw materials and parts
- Total distance travelled for raw materials and parts
- Green house gas emissions
- Supplier's use of toxic chemicals in production process
- Percentage of child labor used by supplier

Support Process

- Systems cost of finance function per $1,000 revenue
- Percentage of finance staff devoted to internal audit
- Total cost of payroll processes per $1,000 revenue
- Number of accepted jobs as percentage of job offers
- Total cost of "source, recruit, and select" process per $1,000 revenue
- Average employee turnover rate

◄ **FIGURE 14**
Illustrative Benchmarking
Metrics by Type of Process

---

2. *Not Involving the Right People in the Right Way.* Does process analysis closely involve the people performing the process, or those closely connected to it as internal customers and suppliers?

3. *Not Giving the Design Teams and Process Analysts a Clear Charter, and then Holding Them Accountable.* Does management set expectations for change and maintain pressure for results? Does it allow paralysis in process improvement efforts by requiring excessive analysis?

4. *Not Being Satisfied Unless Fundamental "Reengineering" Changes are Made.* Is the radical change from process reengineering the expectation? If so, the cumulative effect of many small improvements that could be made incrementally could be lost. Process management efforts should not be limited to downsizing or to reorganization only, even though jobs may be eliminated or the structure changed. It should not be limited to big technological innovation projects, even though technological change occurs often.

5. *Not Considering the Impact on People.* Are the changes aligned with the attitudes and skills of the people who must implement the redesigned process? It is crucial to understand and deal with the *people side* of process changes.

6. *Not Giving Attention to Implementation.* Are processes redesigned, but never implemented? A great job of flowcharting and benchmarking is of only academic interest if the proposed changes are not implemented. Sound project management practices are required.

7. *Not Creating an Infrastructure for Continuous Process Improvement.* Is a measurement system in place to monitor key metrics over time? Is anyone checking to see whether anticipated benefits of a redesigned process are actually being realized?

Managers must make sure that their organization spots new performance gaps in the continual search for process improvements. Process redesign efforts need to be part of periodic reviews and even annual plans. A performance tracking system is the basis for feedback and improvement efforts. The essence of a learning organization is the intelligent use of such feedback.

LEARNING GOALS IN REVIEW

1 **Explain a systematic way to analyze processes.** The section "A Systematic Approach" on gives six steps to analysis. Focus on Figure 1 for the sequence of these steps.

2 **Define flowcharts, swim lane flowcharts, and service blueprints.** The "Documenting the Process" section, demonstrates these three techniques for documenting and evaluating processes. More than one flowchart can be used to handle nested processes. Service blueprints show the line of visibility where there is customer contact.

3 **Describe the various work measurement techniques.** The time study method, elemental standard data approach, predetermined data approach, work sampling method, and learning curve analysis are briefly described in the "Work Measurement Techniques" section. For a more complete description, see MyOMLab Supplement H, "Measuring Output Rates"

4 **Identify metrics for process evaluation.** The "Evaluating Performance" section, identifies a variety of performance measures.

5 **Describe Pareto charts, cause-and-effect diagrams, and process simulation.** These techniques, described in the "Data Analysis Tools" section on help you to understand the causes of performance gaps. Process simulation is a more advanced tool and described in more depth in MyOMLab Supplement E.

6 **Create better processes using benchmarking.** "Benchmarking" whether it is functional, internal, or competitive, is a systematic procedure that measures a firm's processes or products against those in other areas. Figure 14 provides an array of metrics that can be used, depending on the process being evaluated.

7 **Identify keys for effective process management.** The "Managing and Implementing Processes" section, gives seven mistakes that can be made. There must be a continual search for process improvements.

MyOMLab helps you develop analytical skills and assesses your progress with multiple problems on process charts, standard times, learning curves, bar charts, scatter diagrams, Pareto charts, and histograms.

MyOMLab Resources	Titles	Link to the Book
Videos	*Process Analysis at Starwood*	Entire chapter
Active Model	4.1 Pareto Chart	Active Model Exercise: 1 Pareto Chart; Evaluating Performance; Example 2; Example 4
OM Explorer Solvers	Process Charts Bar, Pareto, and Line Charts	Documenting the Process; Figure 8 Evaluating the Process; Example 2; Example 4
OM Explorer Tutors	4.1 Process Charts 4.2 Pareto Charts	Process Charts; Figure 8; Solved Problem 2 Evaluating Performance; Example 2; Example 4
OM Explorer Tutor Exercises	4.1 Process Chart of your choosing 4.2 Pareto Chart	Documenting the Process; Figure 8 Evaluating Performance; Example 2; Example 4

MyOMLab Resources	Titles	Link to the Book
Flowchart Tutorials	4.1 Flowcharting in Excel 4.2 Flowcharting in PowerPoint 4.3 Live Flowcharting for Figures 2–3	Documenting the Process Documenting the Process Documenting the Process
SmartDraw	Often used in practice to create flowcharts	Get free trial version online
Virtual Tours	1. Anrosia and Hershey Foods Corporation	Strategic Fit
MyOMLab Supplements	F. Financial Analysis H. Measuring Output Rates I. Learning Curve Analysis	Redesigning the Process Work Measurement Techniques Learning Curve Analysis
Internet Exercises	1. BIC Stationary, BIC Lighters, BIC Shavers 2. Fender Guild Guitars	Documenting the Process Benchmarking
Additional Case	The Facilities Maintenance Problem at Midwest University	Entire chapter
Key Equations		
Image Library		

Key Terms

bar chart	graphs	process failure
benchmarking	histogram	process simulation
brainstorming	learning curve	scatter diagram
cause-and-effect diagram	metrics	service blueprint
checklist	Pareto chart	suggestion system
design team	predetermined data approach	swim lane flowchart
elemental standard data	process analysis	time study
flowchart	process chart	work sampling

Solved Problem 1

Create a flowchart for the following telephone-ordering process at a retail chain that specializes in selling books and music CDs. It provides an ordering system via the telephone to its time-sensitive customers besides its regular store sales.

First, the automated system greets customers and identifies whether they have a tone or pulse phone. Customers choose 1 if they have a tone phone; otherwise, they wait for the first available service representative to process their request. If customers have a tone phone, they complete their request by choosing options on the phone. First, the system checks to see whether customers have an existing account. Customers choose 1 if they have an existing account or choose 2 if they want to open a new account. Customers wait for the service representative to open a new account if they choose 2.

Next, customers choose between the options of making an order, canceling an order, or talking to a customer representative for questions and/or complaints. If customers choose to make an order, then they specify the order type as a book or a music CD, and a specialized customer representative for books or music CDs picks up the phone to get the order details. If customers choose to cancel an order, then they wait for the automated response. By entering the order code via phone, customers can cancel the order. The automated system says the name of the ordered item and asks for the confirmation of the customer. If the customer validates the cancellation of the order, then the system cancels the order; otherwise, the system asks the customer to input the order code again. After responding to the request, the system asks whether the customer has additional requests; if not, the process terminates.

SOLUTION

Figure 15 shows the flowchart.

FIGURE 15 ▶
Flowchart of Telephone Ordering
Process

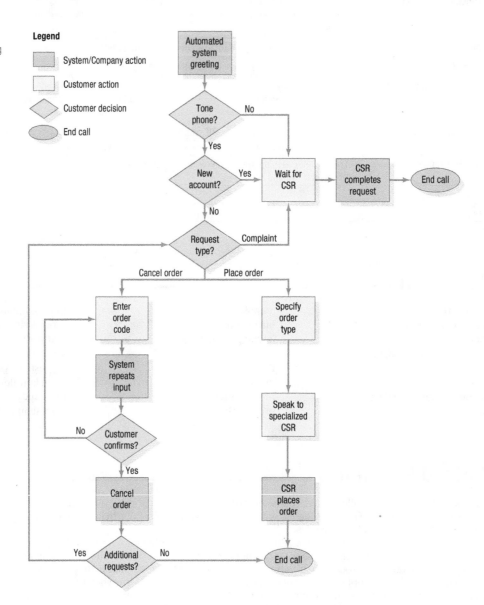

Solved Problem 2

An automobile service is having difficulty providing oil changes in the 29 minutes or less mentioned in its advertising. You are to analyze the process of changing automobile engine oil. The subject of the study is the service mechanic. The process begins when the mechanic directs the customer's arrival and ends when the customer pays for the services.

SOLUTION

Figure 16 shows the completed process chart. The process is broken into 21 steps. A summary of the times and distances traveled is shown in the upper right-hand corner of the process chart.

The times add up to 28 minutes, which does not allow much room for error if the 29-minute guarantee is to be met and the mechanic travels a total of 420 feet.

PROCESS ANALYSIS

Process: Changing engine oil
Subject: Mechanic
Beginning: Direct customer arrival
Ending: Total charges, receive payment

Insert Step

Append Step

Remove Step

◄ FIGURE 16
Process Chart for Changing Engine Oil

Summary

Activity		Number of Steps	Time (min)	Distance (ft)
Operation	●	7	16.50	
Transport	➡	8	5.50	420
Inspect	■	4	5.00	
Delay	▶	1	0.70	
Store	▼	1	0.30	

Step No.	Time (min)	Distance (ft)	●	➡	■	▶	▼	Step Description
1	0.80	50.0		X				Direct customer into service bay
2	1.80		X					Record name and desired service
3	2.30				X			Open hood, verify engine type, inspect hoses, check fluids
4	0.80	30.0		X				Walk to customer in waiting area
5	0.60		X					Recommend additional services
6	0.70					X		Wait for customer decision
7	0.90	70.0		X				Walk to storeroom
8	1.90		X					Look up filter number(s), find filter(s)
9	0.40				X			Check filter number(s)
10	0.60	50.0		X				Carry filter(s) to service pit
11	4.20		X					Perform under-car services
12	0.70	40.0		X				Climb from pit, walk to automobile
13	2.70		X					Fill engine with oil, start engine
14	1.30				X			Inspect for leaks
15	0.50	40.0		X				Walk to pit
16	1.00				X			Inspect for leaks
17	3.00		X					Clean and organize work area
18	0.70	80.0		X				Return to auto, drive from bay
19	0.30						X	Park the car
20	0.50	60.0		X				Walk to customer waiting area
21	2.30		X					Total charges, receive payment

Solved Problem 3

What improvement can you make in the process shown in Figure 16?

SOLUTION

Your analysis should verify the following three ideas for improvement. You may also be able to come up with others.

a. **Move Step 17 to Step 21.** Customers should not have to wait while the mechanic cleans the work area.

b. **Store Small Inventories of Frequently Used Filters in the Pit.** Steps 7 and 10 involve travel to and from the storeroom. If the filters are moved to the pit, a copy of the reference material must also be placed in the pit. The pit will have to be organized and well lighted.

c. **Use Two Mechanics.** Steps 10, 12, 15, and 17 involve running up and down the steps to the pit. Much of this travel could be eliminated. The service time could be shortened by having one mechanic in the pit working simultaneously with another working under the hood.

Solved Problem 4

Vera Johnson and Merris Williams manufacture vanishing cream. Their packaging process has four steps: (1) mix, (2) fill, (3) cap, and (4) label. They have had the reported process failures analyzed, which shows the following:

Process failure		Frequency
Lumps of unmixed product		7
Over- or underfilled jars		18
Jar lids did not seal		6
Labels rumpled or missing		29
	Total	60

Draw a Pareto chart to identify the vital failures.

SOLUTION

Defective labels account for 48.33 percent of the total number of failures:

$$\frac{29}{60} \times 100\% = 48.33\%$$

Improperly filled jars account for 30 percent of the total number of failures:

$$\frac{18}{60} \times 100\% = 30.00\%$$

The cumulative percent for the two most frequent failures is

$$48.33\% + 30.00\% = 78.33\%$$

Lumps represent $\frac{7}{60} \times 100\% = 11.67\%$ of failures; the cumulative percentage is

$$78.33\% + 11.67\% = 90.00\%$$

Defective seals represent $\frac{6}{60} \times 100\% = 10\%$ of failures; the cumulative percentage is

$$10\% + 90\% = 100.00\%$$

The Pareto chart is shown in Figure 17.

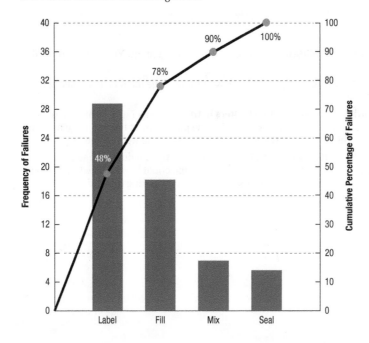

FIGURE 17 ▶
Pareto Chart

Discussion Questions

1. Continuous improvement recognizes that many small improvements add up to sizable benefits. Will continuous improvement take a company at the bottom of an industry to the top? Explain.

2. The Hydro-Electric Company (HEC) has three sources of power. A small amount of hydroelectric power is generated by damming wild and scenic rivers; a second source of power comes from burning coal, with emissions that create acid rain and contribute to global warming; the third source of power comes from nuclear fission. HEC's coal-fired plants use obsolete pollution-control technology, and an investment of several hundred million dollars would be required to update it. Environmentalists urge HEC to promote conservation and purchase power from suppliers that use the cleanest fuels and technology.

   However, HEC is already suffering from declining sales, which have resulted in billions of dollars invested in idle equipment. Its large customers are taking advantage of laws that permit them to buy power from low-cost suppliers. HEC must cover the fixed costs of idle capacity by raising rates charged to its remaining customers or face defaulting on bonds (bankruptcy). The increased rates motivate even more customers to seek low-cost suppliers, the start of a death spiral for HEC. To prevent additional rate increases, HEC implements a cost-cutting program and puts its plans to update pollution controls on hold.

   Form sides and discuss the ethical, environmental, and political issues and trade-offs associated with HEC's strategy.

3. Paul O'Neill, former U.S. Treasury Secretary, estimates that arguably half of the $2 trillion a year that Americans spend on health care is needlessly wasted. Brainstorm up to 10 blue-sky ideas to solve the following problems:

   a. A typical retail pharmacy spends 20 percent of its time playing telephone tag with doctors trying to find out what the intent was for a given prescription.

   b. After the person responsible for filling the prescription determines what they think they are supposed to do, errors can be made even in filling the prescription. For example, administering an adult dose (rather than the dose for a premature baby) of Heparin in a preemie ICU is fatal.

   c. Drugs get distributed at a hospital on a batch basis. For example, carts can be filled on Monday, Wednesday, and Friday. A huge volume of drugs can come back on Monday because they are not consumed on the wards between Friday and Monday, patient conditions changed, or the doctor decided on a different intervention. A technician spends the rest of the day restocking the shelves with the returns and 40 percent of the intravenous materials prepared on Friday morning are poured down the drain.

   d. Sometimes the administration of the drug was not done on the agreed schedule, because the nurses were busy doing something else.

   e. For every bed in an acute care hospital system, someone falls during the year. Most falls occur after 11 P.M. and before 6 A.M. Sometimes a bone is fractured, leading to immobilization and then pneumonia.

   f. One in every 14 people who goes to a U.S. hospital gets an infection they did not bring with them.

Problems

The OM Explorer and POM for Windows software is available to all students using the 10th edition of this text. Go to **www.pearsonhighered.com/krajewski** to download these computer packages. If you purchased MyOMLab, you also have access to Active Models software and significant help in doing the following problems. Check with your instructor on how best to use these resources. In many cases, the instructor wants you to understand how to do the calculations by hand. At the least, the software provides a check on your calculations. When calculations are particularly complex and the goal is interpreting the results in making decisions, the software replaces entirely the manual calculations.

1. Consider the Custom Molds, Inc. case at the end of this chapter." Prepare a flowchart of the mold fabrication process and the parts manufacturing process, showing how they are linked. For a good tutorial on how to create flowcharts, see **http://www.hci.com.au/hcisite5/library/materials/Flowcharting.htm.** Also check out the Flowcharting Tutor in Excel in MyOMLab.

2. Do Problem 1 using a process chart spreadsheet of your own design, one that differs from the *Process Chart* Solver in OM Explorer. It should have one or more columns to record information or metrics that you think are relevant, be it external customer contact, time delays, completion times, percent rework, costs, capacity, and/or demand rates. Your entries should show what information you would collect, even though only part of it is available in the case.

3. Founded in 1970, ABC is one of the world's largest insurance companies with locations in 28 countries. Given the following description, flowchart the new policy setup process as it existed in 1970:

   Individual customers who wanted to set up a new policy would visit one of ABC's 70 branch offices or make contact with an agent. They would then fill out an application and sometimes attach a check. The branch office then sent the application package through company mail to the XYZ division in London. In addition, a customer might also fill out the application at home and send it directly to any number of ABC locations, which would then transfer it to the London operation. Once received, XYZ separated the various parts of the application, then scanned and digitized it. The electronic image was then retrieved from a server and delivered to an associate's desktop client computer. The associate was responsible for entering the information on the form into the appropriate database. If the information supplied on the application was complete, a confirmation notice was automatically printed and sent to the customer. If the information was incomplete, then another associate, trained to deal with customers on the telephone, would call the customer to obtain the additional information. If the customer noticed something wrong on the confirmation notice received, she or he would either call a toll-free number or send in a letter describing the problem. The Customer Problem Resolution division dealt with problems arising at this point. An updated confirmation notice was sent to the customer. If the information was correct, the application transaction was complete.

4. Do Problem 3 using a process chart spreadsheet of your own design, one that differs from the *Process Chart* Solver in OM Explorer. It should have one or more columns to record information or metrics that you think should be collected to analyze the process (see Problem 2).

5. Prepare a flowchart of the field service division process at DEF, as described here. Start from the point where a call is received and end when a technician finishes the job.

DEF was a multibillion dollar company that manufactured and distributed a wide variety of electronic, photographic, and reprographic equipment used in many engineering and medical system applications. The Field Service Division employed 475 field service technicians, who performed maintenance and warranty repairs on the equipment sold by DEF. Customers would call DEF's National Service Center (NSC), which received about 3,000 calls per day. The NSC staffed its call center with about 40 call-takers. A typical incoming service call was received at the NSC and routed to one of the call-takers, who entered information about the machine, the caller's name, and the type of problem into DEF's mainframe computer. In some cases, the call-taker attempted to help the customer fix the problem. However, call-takers were currently only able to avoid about 10 percent of the incoming emergency maintenance service calls. If the service call could not be avoided, the call-taker usually stated the following script: "Depending upon the availability of our technicians, you should expect to see a technician sometime between now and (now 2 X)." ("X" was the target response time based on the model number and the zone.) This information was given to the customer because many customers wanted to know when a tech would arrive on site.

Call-takers entered service call information on DEF's computer system, which then sent the information electronically to the regional dispatch center assigned to that customer location. (DEF had four regional dispatch centers with a total of about 20 dispatchers.) Service call information was printed on a small card at the dispatch center. About every hour, cards were ripped off the printer and given to the dispatcher assigned to that customer location. The dispatcher placed each card on a magnetic board under the name of a tech that the dispatcher believed would be the most likely candidate for the service call, given the location of the machine, the current location of the tech, and the tech's training profile. After completing a service call, techs called the dispatcher in the regional dispatch center, cleared the call, and received a new call assigned by the dispatcher. After getting the service call from a dispatcher, a tech called the customer to give an expected time of arrival, drove to the customer site, diagnosed the problem, repaired the machine if parts were available in the van, and then telephoned the dispatcher for the next call. If the tech did not have the right parts for a repair, the tech informed the NSC and the part was express mailed to the customer; the repair was done the next morning.

6. Big Bob's Burger Barn would like to graphically depict the interaction among its lunch-ordering customers and its three employees. Customers come into the restaurant and eat there, rather than drive through and eat in the car. Using the brief process descriptions below, develop a service blueprint.

Fry Employee: receive customer order from counter employee, retrieve uncooked food, drop food into fry vat, wrap cooked food into special packaging, place wrapped items on service counter.

Grill Employee: receive customer order from counter employee, retrieve uncooked food, place food onto grill, build sandwich with requested condiments, deliver sandwich to Counter Employee.

Counter Employee: take order from customer, transmit appropriate orders to Fry and Grill Employee, transact payment, retrieve drinks, wrap sandwich, package order, and deliver order to customer.

7. After viewing the *Process Choice at the King Soopers Bakery* video in MyOMLab, prepare a flowchart for the three processes at King Soopers. For additional information on the processes, see the *Big Picture* for Chapter 3 in MyOMLab.

8. Your class has volunteered to work for Referendum 13 on the November ballot, which calls for free tuition and books for all college courses except Operations Management. Support for the referendum includes assembling 10,000 yard signs (preprinted water-resistant paper signs to be glued and stapled to a wooden stake) on a fall Saturday. Construct a flowchart and a process chart for yard sign assembly. What inputs in terms of materials, human effort, and equipment are involved? Estimate the amount of volunteers, staples, glue, equipment, lawn and garage space, and pizza required.

9. Suppose you are in charge of a large mailing to the alumni of your college, inviting them to contribute to a scholarship fund. The letters and envelopes have been individually addressed (mailing labels were not used). The letters are to be processed (matched with correct envelope, time estimated to be 0.2 minutes each), folded (0.12 minutes each), and stuffed into the correct envelope (0.10 minutes each). The envelopes are to be sealed (0.05 minutes each), and a large commemorative stamp is to be placed in the upper right-hand corner of each envelope (0.10 minutes each).

a. Make a process chart for this activity, assuming that it is a one-person operation.

b. Estimate how long it will take to stuff, seal, and stamp 2,000 envelopes. Assume that the person doing this work is paid $8 per hour. How much will it cost to process 2,000 letters?

c. Consider each of the following process changes. Which changes would reduce the time and cost of the current process?

■ Each letter has the same greeting "Dear Alumnus or Alumna," instead of the person's name.

■ Mailing labels are used and have to be put on the envelopes (0.10 minutes each).

- Prestamped envelopes are used.
- Envelopes are stamped by a postage meter which can stamp 200 letters per minute.
- Window envelopes are used.
- A preaddressed envelope is included with each letter for contributions (adds 0.05 minutes to stuffing step).

d. Would any of these changes be likely to reduce the effectiveness of the mailing? If so, which ones? Why?

e. Would the changes that increase time and cost be likely to increase the effectiveness of the mailing? Why or why not?

10. Diagrams of two self-service gasoline stations, both located on corners, are shown in Figure 18 (a) and (b). Both have two rows of four pumps and a booth at which an attendant receives payment for the gasoline. At neither station is it necessary for the customer to pay in advance. The exits and entrances are marked on the diagrams. Analyze the flows of cars and people through each station.

a. Which station has the more efficient flows from the standpoint of the customer?

b. Which station is likely to lose more potential customers who cannot gain access to the pumps because another car is headed in the other direction?

c. At which station can a customer pay without getting out of the car?

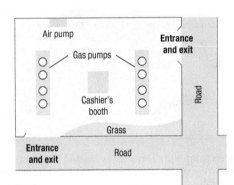

(a)

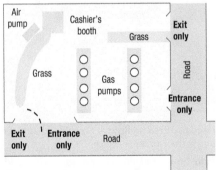

(b)

▲ **FIGURE 18**
Two Self-Service Gasoline Stations

11. The management of the Just Like Home Restaurant has asked you to analyze some of its processes. One of these processes is making a single-scoop ice cream cone. Cones can be ordered by a server (for table service) or by a customer (for takeout).

Figure 19 illustrates the process chart for this operation.

- The ice cream counter server earns $10 per hour (including variable fringe benefits).
- The process is performed 10 times per hour (on average).
- The restaurant is open 363 days a year, 10 hours a day.

a. Complete the Summary (top-right) portion of the chart.

b. What is the total labor cost associated with the process?

c. How can this operation be made more efficient? Make a process chart using OM Explorer's *Process Charts* Solver of the improved process. What are the annual labor savings if this new process is implemented?

12. As a graduate assistant, your duties include grading and keeping records for Operations Management course homework assignments. Five sections for 40 students each are offered each semester. A few graduate students attend sections 3 and 4. Graduate students must complete some extra work to higher standards for each assignment. Every student delivers (or is supposed to deliver) directly to (under) the door of your office one homework assignment every Tuesday. Your job is to correct the homework, record grades, sort the papers by class section, sort by student last name in alphabetical order, and return the homework papers to the appropriate instructors (not necessarily in that order). There are some complications. A fair majority of the students sign their names legibly, others identify work with their correct ID number, and a few do neither. Rarely do students identify their section number or graduate status. Prepare a list of process chart steps and place them in an efficient sequence.

13. At the Department of Motor Vehicles (DMV), the process of getting license plates for your car begins when you enter the facility and take a number. You walk 50 feet to the waiting area. During your wait, you count about 30 customers waiting for service. You notice that many customers become discouraged and leave. When a number is called, if a customer stands, the ticket is checked by a uniformed person, and the customer is directed to the available clerk. If no one stands, several minutes are lost while the same number is called repeatedly. Eventually, the next number is called, and more often than not, that customer has left too. The DMV clerk has now been idle for several minutes but does not seem to mind.

After 4 hours, your number is called and checked by the uniformed person. You walk 60 feet to the clerk, and the process of paying city sales taxes is completed in four minutes. The clerk then directs you to the waiting area for paying state personal property tax, 80 feet away. You take a different number and sit down with some different customers who are just renewing licenses. A 1-hour, 40-minute wait this time, and after a walk of 25 feet you pay property taxes in a process that takes two minutes. Now that you have paid taxes, you are eligible to pay registration and license fees. That department is 50 feet away, beyond the employees' cafeteria.

FIGURE 19 ▶
Process Chart for Making Ice
Cream Cones

Process:	Making one ice cream cone
Subject:	Server at counter
Beginning:	Walk to cone storage area
Ending:	Give it to server or customer

Insert Step

Append Step

Remove Step

Summary

Activity	Number of Steps	Time (min)	Distance (ft)
Operation ●			
Transport ➡			
Inspect ■			
Delay ▶			
Store ▼			

Step No.	Time (min)	Distance (ft)	●	➡	■	▶	▼	Step Description
1	0.20	5.0		X				Walk to cone storage area
2	0.05		X					Remove empty cone
3	0.10	5.0		X				Walk to counter
4	0.05		X					Place cone in holder
5	0.20	8.0		X				Walk to sink area
6	0.50						X	Ask dishwasher to wash scoop
7	0.15	8.0		X				Walk to counter with clean scoop
8	0.05		X					Pick up empty cone
9	0.10	2.5		X				Walk to flavor ordered
10	0.75		X					Scoop ice cream from container
11	0.75		X					Place ice cream in cone
12	0.25				X			Check for stability
13	0.05	2.5		X				Walk to order placement area
14	0.05		X					Give server or customer the cone

The registration and license customers are called in the same order in which personal property taxes were paid. There is only a ten-minute wait and a three-minute process. You receive your license plates, take a minute to abuse the license clerk, and leave exactly six hours after arriving.

Make a process chart using OM Explorer's *Process Charts Solver* to depict this process, and suggest improvements.

14. Refer to the process chart for the automobile oil change in Solved Problem 2. Calculate the annual labor cost if:

   ■ The mechanic earns $40 per hour (including variable fringe benefits).

   ■ The process is performed twice per hour (on average).

   ■ The shop is open 300 days a year, 10 hours a day.

   a. What is the total labor cost associated with the process?

   b. If steps 7, 10, 12, and 15 were eliminated, estimate the annual labor savings associated with implementing this new process.

15. A time study of an employee assembling peanut valves resulted in the following set of observations. What is the standard time, given a performance rating of 95 percent and an allowance of 20 percent of the total normal time?

Average Time (seconds)	Observations
15	14
20	12
25	15

16. An initial time study was done on a process with the following results (in minutes). Based on the data obtained so far, assuming an allowance of 20 percent of the normal

time, what do you estimate for the time per customer served, based on this preliminary sample?

Element	Performance Rating	Obs 1	Obs 2	Obs 3	Obs 4	Obs 5
Element 1	70	4	3	5	4	3
Element 2	110	8	10	9	11	10
Element 3	90	6	8	7	7	6

17. A work sampling study was conducted to determine the proportion of the time a worker is idle. The following information was gathered on a random basis:

Day	Number of Times Worker Idle	Total Number of Observations
Monday	17	44
Tuesday	18	56
Wednesday	14	48
Thursday	16	60

   a. Based on these preliminary results, what percent of the time is the worker working?

   b. If idle time is judged to be excessive, what additional categories might you add to a follow-up work sampling study to identify the root causes?

18. A contractor is preparing a bid to install swimming pools at a new housing addition. The estimated time to build the first pool is 35 hours. The contractor estimates an 85 percent learning rate. Without using the computer:

a. How long do you estimate the time required to install the second pool?

b. How long do you estimate the time required to install the fourth pool?

19. Return to Problem 18. Using OM Explorer's *Learning Curves* Solver, how long do you estimate the time required to install the fifth pool? What is your estimate of the total time for all five pools?

20. The manager of Perrotti's Pizza collects data concerning customer complaints about pizza delivery. Either the pizza arrives late, or the wrong pizza is delivered.

Problem	Frequency
Topping is stuck to box lid	17
Pizza arrives late	35
Wrong topping or combination	9
Wrong style of crust	6
Wrong size	4
Pizza is partially eaten	3
Pizza never arrives	6

a. Use a Pareto chart to identify the "vital few" delivery problems. Comment on potential root causes of these problems and identify any especially egregious quality failures.

b. The manager of Perrotti's Pizza is attempting to understand the root causes of late pizza delivery and has asked each driver to keep a log of specific difficulties that create late deliveries. After one week, the logs included the following entries:

delivery vehicle broke down, couldn't make it across town to deliver second pizza in time, couldn't deliver four pizzas to four different customers in time, kitchen was late in producing order, got lost, order ticket was lost in production, couldn't read address on ticket and went to wrong house.

Organize these causes into a cause-and-effect diagram.

21. Smith, Schroeder, and Torn (SST) is a short-haul household furniture moving company. SST's labor force, selected from the local community college football team, is temporary and part-time. SST is concerned with recent complaints, as tabulated on the following tally sheet:

Complaint	Tally
Broken glass	ⅢⅢ ⅢⅢ Ⅲ
Delivered to wrong address	ⅢⅢ ⅢⅢ
Furniture rubbed together while on truck	ⅢⅢ ⅢⅢ ⅢⅢ ⅢⅢ
Late delivery	ⅢⅢ
Late arrival for pickup	ⅢⅢ ⅢⅢ ⅢⅢ Ⅲ
Missing items	ⅢⅢ ⅢⅢ ⅢⅢ ⅢⅢ ⅢⅢ Ⅰ
Nicks and scratches from rough handling	ⅢⅢ ⅢⅢ
Soiled upholstery	ⅢⅢ Ⅲ

a. Draw a bar chart and a Pareto chart using OM Explorer to identify the most serious moving problems.

b. The manager of Smith, Schroeder, and Torn is attempting to understand the root causes of complaints. He has compiled the following list of issues that occurred during problem deliveries.

truck broke down, ran out of packing boxes, multiple deliveries in one day caused truck to be late, no furniture pads, employee dropped several items, drive got lost on route to address, ramp into truck was bent, no packing tape, new employee doesn't know how to pack, moving dolly has broken wheel, employee late to work

Organize these causes into a cause-and-effect diagram.

22. Rick DeNeefe, manager of the Golden Valley Bank credit authorization department, recently noticed that a major competitor was advertising that applications for equity loans could be approved within two working days. Because fast credit approval was a competitive priority, DeNeefe wanted to see how well his department was doing relative to the competitor's. Golden Valley stamps each application with the date and time it is received and again when a decision is made. A total of 104 applications were received in March. The time required for each decision, rounded to the nearest hour, is shown in the following table. Golden Valley's employees work 8 hours per day.

Decision Process Time (hours)	Frequency
8	8
11	19
14	28
17	10
20	25
23	4
26	10
Total	104

a. Draw a bar chart for these data.

b. Analyze the data. How is Golden Valley Bank doing with regard to this competitive priority?

23. Last year, the manager of the service department at East Woods Ford instituted a customer opinion program to find out how to improve service. One week after service on a vehicle was performed, an assistant would call the customer to find out whether the work had been done satisfactorily and how service could be improved. After one year of gathering data, the assistant discovered that the complaints could be grouped into the following five categories:

Complaint	Frequency
Unfriendly atmosphere	5
Long wait for service	17
Price too high	20
Incorrect bill	8
Needed to return to correct problem	50
Total	100

a. Use OM Explorer to draw a bar chart and a Pareto chart to identify the significant service problems.

b. Categorize the following causes of complaints into a cause-and-effect diagram: tools, scheduling, defective parts, training, billing system, performance measures, diagnostic equipment, and communications.

24. Oregon Fiber Board makes roof liners for the automotive industry. The manufacturing manager is concerned about product quality. She suspects that one particular failure, tears in the fabric, is related to production-run size. An assistant gathers the following data from production records:

Run	Size	Failures (%)	Run	Size	Failures (%)
1	1,000	3.5	11	6,500	1.5
2	4,100	3.8	12	1,000	5.5
3	2,000	5.5	13	7,000	1.0
4	6,000	1.9	14	3,000	4.5
5	6,800	2.0	15	2,200	4.2
6	3,000	3.2	16	1,800	6.0
7	2,000	3.8	17	5,400	2.0
8	1,200	4.2	18	5,800	2.0
9	5,000	3.8	19	1,000	6.2
10	3,800	3.0	20	1,500	7.0

a. Draw a scatter diagram for these data.

b. Does there appear to be a relationship between run size and percent failures? What implications does this data have for Oregon Fiber Board's business?

25. Grindwell, Inc., a manufacturer of grinding tools, is concerned about the durability of its products, which depends on the permeability of the sinter mixtures used in production. Suspecting that the carbon content might be the source of the problem, the plant manager collected the following data:

Carbon Content (%)	Permeability Index
5.5	16
3.0	31
4.5	21
4.8	19
4.2	16
4.7	23
5.1	20
4.4	11
3.6	20

a. Draw a scatter diagram for these data.

b. Is there a relationship between permeability and carbon content?

c. If low permeability is desirable, what does the scatter diagram suggest with regard to the carbon content?

26. The operations manager for Superfast Airlines at Chicago's O'Hare Airport noticed an increase in the number of delayed flight departures. She brainstormed possible causes with her staff:

- Aircraft late to gate
- Acceptance of late passengers
- Passengers arriving late at gate
- Passenger processing delays at gate
- Late baggage to aircraft
- Other late personnel or unavailable items
- Mechanical failures

Draw a cause-and-effect diagram to organize the possible causes of delayed flight departures into the following major categories: equipment, personnel, material, procedures, and "other factors" beyond managerial control. Provide a detailed set of causes for each major cause identified by the operations manager, and incorporate them in your cause-and-effect diagram.

27. Plastomer, Inc. specializes in the manufacture of high-grade plastic film used to wrap food products. Film is rejected and scrapped for a variety of reasons (e.g., opacity, high carbon content, incorrect thickness or gauge, scratches, and so on). During the past month, management collected data on the types of rejects and the amount of scrap generated by each type. The following table presents the results:

Type of Failure	Amount of Scrap (lbs.)
Air bubbles	500
Bubble breaks	19,650
Carbon content	150
Unevenness	3,810
Thickness or gauge	27,600
Opacity	450
Scratches	3,840
Trim	500
Wrinkles	10,650

Draw a Pareto chart to identify which type of failure management should attempt to eliminate first.

28. Management of a shampoo bottling company introduced a new 13.5-ounce pack and used an existing machine, with some modifications, to fill it. To measure filling consistency by the modified machine (set to fill 13.85 ounces), an analyst collected the following data (volume in ounces) for a random sample of 100 bottles:

a. Draw a histogram for these data.

b. Bottles with less than 12.85 ounces or more than 14.85 ounces are considered to be out of specification. Based on the sample data, what percentage of the bottles filled by the machine will be out of specification?

Bottle Volume (ounces)									
13.0	13.3	13.6	13.2	14.0	12.9	14.2	12.9	14.5	13.5
14.1	14.0	13.7	13.4	14.4	14.3	14.8	13.9	13.5	14.3
14.2	14.1	14.0	13.9	13.9	14.0	14.5	13.6	13.3	12.9
12.8	13.1	13.6	14.5	14.6	12.9	13.1	14.4	14.0	14.4
13.1	14.1	14.2	12.9	13.3	14.0	14.1	13.1	13.6	13.7
14.0	13.6	13.2	13.4	13.9	14.5	14.0	14.4	13.9	14.6
12.9	14.3	14.0	12.9	14.2	14.8	14.5	13.1	12.7	13.9
13.6	14.4	13.1	14.5	13.5	13.3	14.0	13.6	13.5	14.3
13.2	13.8	13.7	12.8	13.4	13.8	13.3	13.7	14.1	13.7
13.7	13.8	13.4	13.7	14.1	12.8	13.7	13.8	14.1	14.3

Advanced Problems

29. This problem should be solved as a team exercise:

Shaving is a process that most men perform each morning. Assume that the process begins at the bathroom sink with the shaver walking (say, 5 feet) to the cabinet (where his shaving supplies are stored) to pick up bowl, soap, brush, and razor. He walks back to the sink, runs the water until it gets warm, lathers his face, shaves, and inspects the results. Then, he rinses the razor, dries his face, walks over to the cabinet to return the bowl, soap, brush, and razor, and comes back to the sink to clean it up and complete the process.

a. Develop a process chart for shaving. (Assume suitable values for the time required for the various activities involved in the process.)

b. Brainstorm to generate ideas for improving the shaving process. Having fewer than 20 ideas is unacceptable. (Do not try to evaluate the ideas until the group has compiled as complete a list as possible. Otherwise, judgment will block creativity.)

30. At Conner Company, a custom manufacturer of printed circuit boards, the finished boards are subjected to a final inspection prior to shipment to its customers. As Conner's quality assurance manager, you are responsible for making a presentation to management on quality problems at the beginning of each month. Your assistant has analyzed the reject memos for all the circuit boards that were rejected during the past month. He has given you a summary statement listing the reference number of the circuit board and the reason for rejection from one of the following categories:

A = Poor electrolyte coverage

B = Improper lamination

C = Low copper plating

D = Plating separation

E = Improper etching

For 50 circuit boards that had been rejected last month, the summary statement showed the following:

C B C C D E C C B A D A C C C B C A C D C A C C B

A C A C B C C A C A A C C D A C C C E C C A B A C

a. Prepare a tally sheet (or checklist) of the different reasons for rejection.

b. Develop a Pareto chart to identify the more significant types of rejection.

c. Examine the causes of the most significant type of defect, using a cause-and-effect diagram.

Active Model Exercise

This Active Model appears in MyOMLab. Continuing on with Example 2, it allows you to evaluate the structure of a Pareto chart.

QUESTIONS

1. What percentage of overall complaints does discourteous service account for?

2. What percentage of overall complaints do the three most common complaints account for?

3. How does it affect the chart if we eliminate discourteous service?

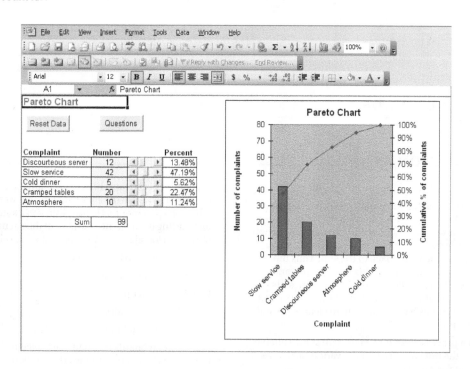

CASE   Custom Molds, Inc.

Custom Molds, Inc., manufactures custom-designed molds for plastic parts and produces custom-made plastic connectors for the electronics industry. Located in Tucson, Arizona, Custom Molds was founded by the father-and-son-team of Tom and Mason Miller in 1987. Tom Miller, a mechanical engineer, had more than 20 years of experience in the connector industry with AMP, Inc., a large multinational producer of electronic connectors. Mason Miller graduated from the Arizona State University in 1986 with joint degrees in chemistry and chemical engineering.

The company was originally formed to provide manufacturers of electronic connectors with a source of high-quality, custom-designed molds for producing plastic parts. The market consisted mainly of the product design and development divisions of those manufacturers. Custom Molds worked closely with each customer to design and develop molds to be used in the customer's product development processes. Thus, virtually every mold had to meet exacting standards and was somewhat unique. Orders for multiple molds would arrive when customers moved from the design and pilot-run stage of development to large-scale production of newly designed parts.

As the years went by, Custom Molds's reputation grew as a designer and fabricator of precision molds. Building on this reputation, the Millers decided to expand into the limited manufacture of plastic parts.

Ingredient-mixing facilities and injection-molding equipment were added, and by the mid-1990s, Custom Molds developed its reputation to include being a supplier of high-quality plastic parts. Because of limited capacity, the company concentrated its sales efforts on supplying parts that were used in limited quantities for research and development efforts and in preproduction pilot runs.

Production Processes

By 2000, operations at Custom Molds involved two distinct processes: one for fabricating molds and one for producing plastic parts. Although different, in many instances these two processes were linked, as when a customer would have Custom Molds both fabricate a mold and produce the necessary parts to support the customer's research and design efforts. All fabrication and production operations were housed in a single facility. The layout was characteristic of a typical job shop, with like processes and similar equipment grouped in various places in the plant. Figure 18 shows a layout of the plant floor. Multiple pieces of various types of high-precision machinery, including milling, turning, cutting, and drilling equipment, were located in the mold-fabrication area.

Fabricating molds is a skill-oriented, craftsman-driven process. When an order is received, a design team, comprising a design engineer and one of 13 master machinists, reviews the design specifications. Working closely with the customer, the team establishes the final specifications for the mold and gives them to the master machinist for fabrication. It is always the same machinist who was assigned to the design team. At the same time, the purchasing department is given a copy of the design specifications, from which it orders the appropriate raw materials and special tooling. The time needed to receive the ordered materials is usually three to four weeks. When the materials are received for a particular mold, the plant master scheduler reviews the workload of the assigned master machinist and schedules the mold for fabrication.

Fabricating a mold takes from two to four weeks, depending on the amount of work the machinist already has scheduled. The fabrication process itself takes only three to five days. Upon completion, the mold is sent to the testing and inspection area, where it is used to produce a small number of parts on one of the injection molding machines. If the parts meet the design specifications established by the design team, the mold is passed on to be cleaned and polished. It is then packed and shipped to the customer. One day is spent inspecting and testing the mold and a second day cleaning, polishing, packing, and shipping it to the customer. If the parts made by the mold do not meet design specifications, the mold is returned to the master machinist for retooling and the process starts over. Currently, Custom Molds has a published lead time of nine weeks for delivery of custom-fabricated molds.

The manufacturing process for plastic parts is somewhat different from that for mold fabrication. An order for parts may be received in conjunction with an order for a mold to be fabricated. In instances where Custom Molds has previously fabricated the mold and maintains it in inventory, an order may be just for parts. If the mold is already available, the order is reviewed by a design engineer, who verifies the part and raw material specifications. If the design engineer has any questions concerning the specifications, the customer is contacted and any revisions to specifications are mutually worked out and agreed upon.

Upon acceptance of the part and raw material specifications, raw material orders are placed and production is scheduled for the order. Chemicals and compounds that support plastic-parts manufacturing are typically ordered and received within one week. Upon receipt, the compounds are first dry-mixed and blended to achieve the correct composition. Then, the mixture is wet-mixed to the desired consistency (called *slurry*) for injection into molding machines. When ready, the slurry is transferred to the injection molding area by an overhead pipeline and deposited in holding tanks adjacent to the injection machines. The entire mixing process takes only one day.

When the slurry is staged and ready, the proper molds are secured—from inventory or from the clean and polish operation if new molds were fabricated for the order—and the parts are manufactured. Although different parts require different temperature and pressure settings, the time to produce a part is relatively constant. Custom Molds has the capacity to produce 5,000 parts per day in the injection-molding department; historically, however, the lead time for handling orders in this department has averaged one week. Upon completion of molding, the parts are taken to the cut and trim operation, where they are disconnected and leftover flashing is removed. After being inspected, the parts may be taken to assembly or transferred to the packing and shipping area for shipment to the customer. If assembly of the final parts is not required, the parts can be on their way to the customer two days after being molded.

▲ FIGURE18
Plant Layout

Sometimes, the final product requires some assembly. Typically, this entails attaching metal leads to plastic connectors. If assembly is necessary, an additional three days are needed before the order can be shipped. Custom Molds is currently quoting a three-week lead time for parts not requiring fabricated molds.

The Changing Environment

In early 2009, Tom and Mason Miller began to realize that the electronics industry they supplied, along with their own business, was changing. Electronics manufacturers had traditionally manufactured their own component parts to reduce costs and ensure a timely supply of parts. By the 1990s, this trend had changed. Manufacturers were developing strategic partnerships with parts suppliers to ensure the timely delivery of high-quality, cost-effective parts. This approach allowed funds to be diverted to other uses that could provide a larger return on investment.

The impact on Custom Molds could be seen in sales figures over the past three years. The sales mix was changing. Although the number of orders per year for mold fabrication remained virtually constant, orders for multiple molds were declining, as shown in the following table:

	NUMBER OF ORDERS		
Order Size	Molds 2006	Molds 2007	Molds 2008
1	80	74	72
2	60	70	75
3	40	51	55
4	5	6	5
5	3	5	4
6	4	8	5
7	2	0	1
8	10	6	4
9	11	8	5
10	15	10	5
Total orders	230	238	231

The reverse was true for plastic parts, for which the number of orders per year had declined, but for which the order sizes were becoming larger, as illustrated in the following table:

Order Size	NUMBER OF ORDERS		
	Parts 2006	Parts 2007	Parts 2008
50	100	93	70
100	70	72	65
150	40	30	35
200	36	34	38
250	25	27	25
500	10	12	14
750	1	3	5
1,000	2	2	8
3,000	1	4	9
5,000	1	3	8
Total orders	286	280	277

During this same period, Custom Molds began having delivery problems. Customers were complaining that parts orders were taking four to five weeks instead of the stated three weeks and that the delays were disrupting production schedules. When asked about the situation, the master scheduler said that determining when a particular order could be promised for delivery was difficult. Bottlenecks were occurring during the production process, but where or when they would occur could not be predicted. The bottlenecks always seemed to be moving from one operation to another.

Tom Miller thought that he had excess labor capacity in the mold-fabrication area. So, to help push through those orders that were behind schedule, he assigned one of the master machinists the job of identifying and expediting those late orders. However, that tactic did not seem to help much. Complaints about late deliveries were still being received. To add to the problems, two orders had been returned recently because of the number of defective parts. The Millers knew that something had to be done. The question was "What?"

QUESTIONS

1. What are the major issues facing Tom and Mason Miller?
2. What are the competitive priorities for Custom Molds's processes and the changing nature of the industry?
3. What alternatives might the Millers pursue? What key factors should they consider as they evaluate these alternatives?

VIDEO CASE · Process Analysis at Starwood

The features and layout of The Phoenician property of Starwood Hotels and Resorts at Scottsdale, Arizona, are shown in the following figure. Starwood Hotels and Resorts is no stranger to process improvement. In fact, the president's letter in a recent annual report stated that through "... benchmarking, Six Sigma, and recognition of excellence, [Starwood is] driving results in a virtual cycle of self-improvement at all levels of the Company." Recognizing that improved processes in one department of a single hotel, if rolled out across the organization, could lead to significant improvements, the company recently created a program called the "Power of Innovation," or POI.

The Power of Innovation program in Starwood seeks to capture best practices that exist throughout hotels across all brands in North America. An internal team with expertise in kitchen preparation and production, laundry, stewarding, front office, and housekeeping works with individual properties to build upon and maximize the existing knowledge of local property management teams. The team usually spends about a week on property entrenched in operations to really see day-to-day activity over an extended period. Of particular interest is scheduling the workforce to meet the demand of each hotel's individual operations while streamlining operations processes.

At the Westin Galleria-Oaks in Houston, Texas, for example, the POI team helped management achieve a 6 percent productivity improvement in the kitchen preparation and production job, with a reduction of 2,404 hours used and $23,320 in annual payroll savings alone. At the same time, other POI projects at the hotel generated an additional $14,400 in annual payroll savings.

The Phoenician in Scottsdale also had a visit from the POI team. One area the team focused on was stewarding. The typical stewarding process includes the following duties: dishwashing, kitchen trash removal, polishing silver, and assisting with banquet meal food prep lines. Stewards support eight kitchens and two bakeries, and work with housekeeping in keeping public areas, such as restrooms and pool cabanas, clean.

A flowchart that diagrams the existing stewarding process that the team documented is shown in the figure. In any given day, a particular steward may provide support to more than one kitchen, and be called upon to do a variety of tasks.

Before the POI team arrived, stewards were dedicated to a particular kitchen or area during their shift. Each kitchen required stewarding coverage as outlined by the executive chef, so more than one steward may be assigned to an area. A certain amount of stewarding work could be forecast

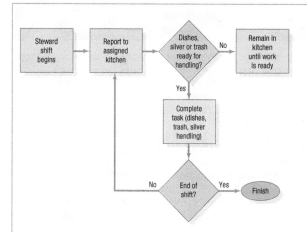

by the food and beverage manager, based on scheduled banquets, afternoon teas, conference buffets, and restaurant reservations. Considerable uncertainty also arose from traffic generated by leisure travelers and local clientele, meaning that stewards assigned to designated areas periodically did not have a steady flow of work.

On a weekly basis, activity levels for the dedicated stewarding staff were determined, based on executive chef input. Other factors considered in the weekly planning included prior year activity, special events and holidays, and number of children. With this information, the executive steward created a summary of all meals, called covers, by location, date, and time of day. Then, an Excel spreadsheet template was used to create the schedule for deployment of stewarding staff throughout the resort's kitchens and restaurants.

In performing its analysis, the POI team examined staff availability, banquet events, restaurants, occupied room counts, and other drivers of business to areas supported by stewards. Time studies were done to determine how far stewards were traveling throughout the property, and how long it

took to perform each stewarding task. Some restaurants and kitchens did not require full-time coverage by a steward, so the steward would be assigned multiple kitchens to fill a work shift. In the case of coverage between the 19th Hole restaurant on one side of the resort, and the Canyon Building on the other side, that steward would walk one-half mile, one way, to take care of duties in both locations because they lacked enough work for a dedicated steward in each location.

Often, stewards had downtime as they waited for banquet dishes to be cleared, or kitchen pots and utensils to be brought in for cleaning. Some restaurants had china with special cleaning requirements, meaning those dishes had to be handwashed instead of being placed in an automated sanitizing dishwasher. This situation required a dedicated steward to perform that task.

Time studies revealed how long it took stewards to move from one kitchen to the next. The studies also helped the POI team understand how long it took to wash dishes in the five-star restaurant versus the casual poolside dining area's kitchen. Additionally, the studies uncovered building design and landscaping limitations that prevented staff from moving between kitchens quickly. In some cases, a maze of corridors added miles to the distances covered each day, and thick privacy hedges barred entry to sidewalk shortcuts.

QUESTIONS

1. How can the management specifically improve the stewarding process at The Phoenician? Using the information provided, create a flowchart illustrating the new process.

2. What are the benefits that the POI program can bring to Starwood? Can these benefits be extended to other processes and properties within the Starwood system?

3. Of the seven mistakes organizations can make when managing processes (see last section of this chapter), which ones might Starwood be most at risk of making? Why?

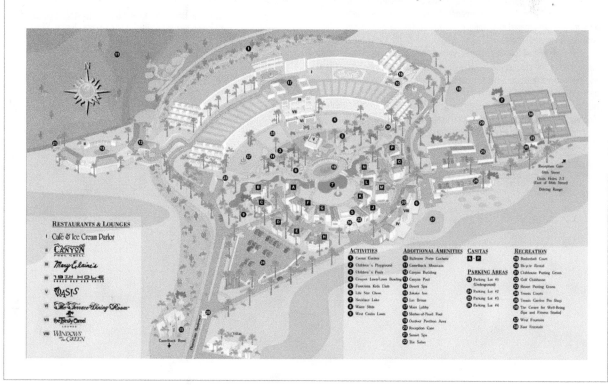

CASE | José's Authentic Mexican Restaurant

"Two bean tacos, a chicken burrito grande, and a side order of Spanish rice, please." Ivan Karetski called his table's order into the kitchen as he prepared the beverage orders. Business was brisk. Karetski liked it that way. Lots of customers meant lots of tips and, as a struggling graduate student, the extra income was greatly appreciated. Lately, however, his tips had been declining.

José's is a small, 58-seat restaurant that offers a reasonably broad range of Mexican food prepared and presented in a traditional Mexican style. It is located in New England in a mature business district on the edge of a large metropolitan area. The site is adjacent to a central artery and offers limited free off-street parking. The restaurant's interior decoration promotes the Mexican theme: The walls appear to be made of adobe and are draped with serapes, the furniture is Spanish–Mexican style, and flamenco guitar and mariachi alternate as background music.

Patrons enter the restaurant through a small vestibule that opens directly into the dining area; there is no separate waiting area. Upon arrival, patrons are greeted by a hostess and either seated directly or apprised of the expected wait. Seating at José's is usually immediate except for Friday and Saturday nights when waits of as long as 45 minutes can be encountered. Because space inside for waiting is very limited, patrons must remain outside until their party is called. José's does not take reservations.

After seating patrons, the hostess distributes menus and fills glasses with water. If standards are being met, the waiter assigned to the table greets the patrons within one minute of their being seated. (Being a traditional Mexican restaurant, its entire wait staff is male.) The waiter introduces himself, announces the daily specials, and takes the beverage orders. After delivering the beverages, the waiter takes the meal orders.

The menu consists of 23 main entrees assembled from eight basic stocks (chicken, beef, beans, rice, corn tortillas, flour tortillas, tomatoes, and lettuce) and a variety of other ingredients (fruits, vegetables, sauces, herbs, and spices). Before the dining hours begin, the cook prepares the basic stocks so that they can be quickly combined and finished off to complete the requested meals. The typical amount of time needed to complete a meal once it has been ordered is 12 minutes. A good portion of this time is for final cooking, so several meals may be in preparation at the same time. As can be imagined, one of the skills a good cook needs is to be able to schedule production of the various meals ordered at a table so that they are ready at approximately the same time. Once all the meals and any side dishes have been completed by the cook, the waiter checks to see that all meals are correct and pleasing to the eye, corrects any mistakes, and adds any finishing touches. When everything is in order, he assembles them on a tray and delivers them to the table. From this point on, the waiter keeps an eye on the table to detect when any additional service or assistance is needed.

When the diners at the table appear to be substantially finished with their main meal, the waiter approaches, asks if he can clear away any dishes, and takes any requests for dessert or coffee. When the entire meal has been completed, the waiter presents the bill and shortly thereafter collects payment. José's accepts cash or major credit card, but no checks.

Karetski feels that his relationship with the cook is important. As the cook largely controls the quality of the food, Karetski wants to stay on good terms with him. He treats the cook with respect, tries to place the items on his order slip in the sequence of longest preparation time, and makes sure to write clearly so that the orders are easy to read. Although it is not his job, he helps out by fetching food stocks from the refrigerator or the storage area when the cook is busy and by doing some of the food preparation himself. The cook has been irritable lately, complaining of the poor quality of some of the ingredients that have been delivered. Last week, for example, he received lettuce that appeared wilted and chicken that was tough and more bone than meat. During peak times, it can take more than 20 minutes to get good meals delivered to the table.

Karetski had been shown the results of a customer survey that management conducted last Friday and Saturday during the evening mealtime. The following table shows a summary of the responses:

Customer Survey Results		
Were you seated promptly?	Yes: 70	No: 13
Was your waiter satisfactory?	Yes: 73	No: 10
Were you served in a reasonable time?	Yes: 58	No: 25
Was your food enjoyable?	Yes: 72	No: 11
Was your dining experience worth the cost?	Yes: 67	No: 16

As Karetski carried the tray of drinks to the table, he wondered whether the recent falloff in tips was due to anything that he could control.

QUESTIONS

1. How should quality be defined at this restaurant?
2. What are the restaurant's costs of process failures?
3. Use some of the tools for process analysis to assess the situation at José's.

Source: This case was prepared by Larry Meile, Boston College, as a basis for classroom discussion. By permission of Larry Meile.

Selected References

Andersen, Bjørn. *Business Process Improvement Toolbox*. 2nd ed. Milwaukee, Wiscconsin: American Society for Quality, 2007.

Ahire, Sanjay L. and Manoj. K. Malhotra. "Scripting a Holistic Rx for Process Improvement at Palmetto Health Imaging Centers." *Journal of Global Business and Organizational Excellence*, vol. 30, no. 2 (January/February 2011), pp. 23–35.

Bhuiyan, Nadjia, Amit Baghel, Jim Wilson. "A Sustainable Continuous Improvement Methodology at an Aerospace Company," *International Journal of Productivity and Performance Management*, vol. 55, no. 8 (2006), pp. 671–687.

Carey, Susan. "Case of the Vanishing Airport Lines." *Wall Street Journal* (August 9, 2007).

Davenport, Thomas H. "The Coming Commoditization of Processes." *Harvard Business Review*, (June 2005), pp. 101–108.

Edmondson, Amy C. "The Competitive Imperative of Learning." *Harvard Business Review*, vol. 86 (July August, 2008), pp. 1–13.

Fisher, Anne. "Get Employees to Brainstorm Online." *Fortune*, vol. 150, no. 11 (November 2004), p. 72.

Fleming, John H., Curt Coffman, and James K. Harter. "Manage Your Human Sigma." *Harvard Business Review*, (July–August 2005), pp. 101–108.

Greasley, A. "Using Process Mapping and Business Process Simulation to Support a Process-Based Approach to Change in a Public Sector Organisation." *Technovation*, 26 (2006), pp. 95–103.

Grosskopf, Alexander, Gero Decker, and Mathias Weske. *The Process: Business Process Modelling Using BPMN*. Tampa, Florida: Meghan-Kiffer Press, 2009.

Hammer, Michael. "The Process Audit." *Harvard Business Review*, vol. 82, no. 4 (April 2007), pp. 111–123.

Hammer, Michael. "What is Business Process Management?" *Handbook on Business Process Management 1*, 2010, pp. 3–16.

Hartvigsen, David. *SimQuick: Process Simulation with Excel*, 2nd ed. Upper Saddle River, NJ: Prentice Hall, 2004.

Jain, Rashmi, Angappa Gunasekaran, and Anithashree Chandrasekaran. "Evolving Role of Process Reengineering: A Perspective of Employers." *Industrial and Commercial Training*, vol. 41, no. 7 (2009), pp. 382–390.

Jeston, John and Johan Nelis. *Management by Process: A Roadmap to Sustainable Business Process Management*, Oxford, UK: Elsevier, 2008.

Karmarkar, Uday. "Will You Survive the Services Revolution?" *Harvard Business Review*, vol. 82, no. 6 (June 2004), pp. 100–107.

Kulpa, Margaret, K. and Kent A. Johnson. *Interpeting the CMMI: A Process Improvement Approach*, 2nd ed. Boca Raton, FL: Auerbach Publications, 2008.

La Ferla, Beverly. "Mapping the Way to Process Improvement." *IEE Engineering Management* (December 2004–January 2005), pp. 16–17.

Lee, Hau L. "The Triple-A Supply Chain." *Harvard Business Review* (October 2004), pp. 102–112.

Rummler, Geary A., and Alan P. Brache. *Improving Performance*, 2nd ed. San Francisco: Jossey-Bass Inc., 1995.

Scott, Bradley, S., Anne E. Wilcock, and Vinay Kanetkar. "A Survey of Structured Continuous Improvement Programs in the Canadian Food Sector." *Food Control*, vol. 20 (2009), 209–217.

A Baseline Engineer for Verizon readies his computer that will control a bank of cell phones making and receiving calls on different networks. He travels through northern Virginia, Washington, DC, and Maryland with a truck outfitted to test the services of Verizon and its competitors to see where faults lie in Verizon's system.

Verizon Wireless

Anyone who owns a cell phone knows the agony of a dropped call. Did you know that the reason for the dropped call may be the phone itself, and not the strength of the signal? Verizon Wireless serves more than 62 million customers in the United States and, along with the other major carriers, it knows that if the phone does not work, the company, and not the manufacturer, will likely take the blame from the customer. Verizon touts the reliability of its services and can ill afford the failure of cell phones due to the quality of manufacture. Verizon expects manufacturers such as Motorola, Samsung, and LG Electronics to provide defect-free phones; however, experience has indicated that extensive testing by Verizon employees is also needed.

In addition to a tear-down analysis that looks for weaknesses in a phone's hardware and components, the device is tested for its ability to withstand temperature extremes, vibration, and stress. Beyond these physical tests, Verizon uses two approaches to assess a phone's capability to receive cellular signals and clearly communicate to the caller. First, Verizon hires 98 test personnel who drive $300,000 specially equipped vans more than 1 million miles a year to measure network performance using prospective new cell phones. They make more than 3 million voice call attempts and 16 million data tests annually. The tests check the coverage of the network as well as the capability of the cell phones to pick up the signals and clearly communicate to the caller. Second, Verizon uses Mr. Head, a robotic mannequin, who has a recorded voice and is electronically equipped with a rubber ear that evaluates how well the phone's mouthpiece transmits certain phonetics. Mr. Head utters what sounds like gibberish; however, it actually covers the range of sounds in normal speech patterns. Other systems monitor the tests and summarize results.

Some phones spend so much time in the test phase that ultimately they never make it to the market. Clearly, in those cases, the cost of poor quality to the manufacturer is very high.

Source: Amol Sharma, "Testing, Testing," *Wall Street Journal* (October 23, 2007); Janet Hefler, "Verizon Tester Checks Vineyard Networks," *The Martha's Vineyard Times* (August 30, 2007); Jon Gales, "Ride Along With a Verizon Wireless Test Man," *Mobile Tracker* (April 4, 2005) **http:// investor.verizon.com** (2007).

LEARNING GOALS *After reading this chapter, you should be able to:*

1. Define the four major costs of quality.
2. Describe the role of ethics in the quality of services and products.
3. Explain the basic principles of TQM programs.
4. Explain the basic principles of Six Sigma programs.
5. Describe how to construct control charts and use them to determine whether a process is out of statistical control.
6. Describe how to determine whether a process is capable of producing a service or product to specifications.

Creating Value through Operation Management

Using Operations to Compete
Project Management

Managing Processes

Process Strategy
Process Analysis
Quality and Performance
Capacity Planning
Constraint Management
Lean Systems

Managing Supply Chains

Supply Chain Inventory Management
Supply Chain Design
Supply Chain Location Decisions
Supply Chain Integration
Supply Chain Sustainability and Humanitarian Logistics
Forecasting
Operations Planning and Scheduling
Resource Planning

The challenge for businesses today is to satisfy their customers through the exceptional performance of their processes. Verizon Wireless is one example of a company that met the challenge by designing and managing processes that provide customers with total satisfaction. Evaluating process performance is important if this is to happen.

Evaluating process performance is also necessary for managing supply chains. For example, at Verizon Wireless, the process of delivering cell phone communications to the customer might be measured on the consistency of service and the sound quality of the voice transmissions. The procurement process, which involves selecting the suppliers for the cell phones and evaluating how they deliver their products, might be measured in terms of the quality of the cell phones delivered to Verizon, the on-time delivery performance of the suppliers, and the cost of the cell phones. Ultimately, the evaluation of the supply chain consisting of these two processes and many others will depend on how well it satisfies the customers of Verizon, who consider the value of the service to be how well it meets or exceeds expectations. The performance of these individual processes must be consistent with the performance measures for the supply chain.

Quality and Performance across the Organization

Quality and performance should be everybody's concern. Take for example QVC, a $7.4 billion televised shopping service. QVC airs 24 hours a day, all year round. QVC sells some 60,000 items ranging from jewelry, tools, cookware, clothing, and gourmet food to computers and annually ships more than 166 million packages worldwide.

QVC's processes, which span all the functional areas, spring into action with a customer order: Order taking and delivery date promising, billing, and order delivery all ensue once an order is placed. QVC operates four call centers that handle 179 million calls annually from customers who want to order something, complain about a problem, or just get product information. The call center representative's demeanor and skill are critical to achieving a successful customer encounter. QVC management keeps track of productivity, quality, and customer satisfaction measures for all processes. When the measures slip, problems are addressed aggressively. Knowing how to assess whether the process is performing well and when to take action are key skills QVC managers must have. In this chapter, we first address the costs of quality and then focus on Total Quality Management and Six Sigma, two philosophies and supporting tools that many companies embrace to evaluate and improve quality and performance.

Costs of Quality

When a process fails to satisfy a customer, the failure is considered a **defect**. For example, according to the California Academy of Family Physicians, defects for the processes in a doctor's practice are defined as "anything that happened in my office that should not have happened, and that I absolutely do not want to happen again." Obviously, this definition covers process failures that the patient sees, such as poor communication and errors in prescription dosages. It also includes failures the patient does not see, such as incorrect charting.

Many companies spend significant time, effort, and expense on systems, training, and organizational changes to improve the quality and performance of their processes. They believe that it is important to be able to gauge current levels of performance so that any process gaps can be determined. Gaps reflect potential dissatisfied customers and additional costs for the firm. Most experts estimate that the costs of quality range from 20 to 30 percent of gross sales. These costs can be broken down into four major categories: (1) prevention, (2) appraisal, (3) internal failure, and (4) external failure.

defect
Any instance when a process fails to satisfy its customer.

Prevention Costs

Prevention costs are associated with preventing defects before they happen. They include the costs of redesigning the process to remove the causes of poor performance, redesigning the service or product to make it simpler to produce, training employees in the methods of continuous improvement, and working with suppliers to increase the quality of purchased items or contracted services. In order to prevent problems from happening, firms must invest additional time, effort, and money.

prevention costs
Costs associated with preventing defects before they happen.

Appraisal Costs

Appraisal costs are incurred when the firm assesses the level of performance of its processes. As the costs of prevention increase and performance improves, appraisal costs decrease because fewer resources are needed for quality inspections and the subsequent search for causes of any problems that are detected.

appraisal costs
Costs incurred when the firm assess the performance level of its processes.

Internal Failure Costs

Internal failure costs result from defects that are discovered during the production of a service or product. Defects fall into two main categories: (1) *rework*, which is incurred if some aspect of a service must be performed again or if a defective item must be rerouted to some previous operation(s) to correct the defect; and (2) *scrap*, which is incurred if a defective item is unfit for further processing. For example, an analysis of the viability of acquiring a company might be sent back to the mergers and acquisitions department if an assessment of the company's history of environmental compliance is missing. The proposal for the purchase of the company may be delayed, which may result in the loss of the purchase opportunity.

internal failure costs
Costs resulting from defects that are discovered during the production of a service or product.

External Failure Costs

External failure costs arise when a defect is discovered after the customer receives the service or product. Dissatisfied customers talk about bad service or products to their friends, who in turn tell others. If the problem is bad enough, consumer protection groups may even alert the media. The potential impact on future profits is difficult to assess, but without doubt external failure costs erode market share and profits. Encountering defects and correcting them after the product is in the customer's hands is costly.

External failure costs also include warranty service and litigation costs. A **warranty** is a written guarantee that the producer will replace or repair defective parts or perform the service to the customer's satisfaction. Usually, a warranty is given for some specified period. For example, television repairs are usually guaranteed for 90 days and new automobiles for 5 years or 50,000 miles, whichever comes first. Warranty costs must be considered in the design of new services or products.

external failure costs
Costs that arise when a defect is discovered after the customer receives the service or product.

warranty
A written guarantee that the producer will replace or repair defective parts or perform the service to the customer's satisfaction.

Ethics and Quality

The costs of quality go beyond the out-of-pocket costs associated with training, appraisal, scrap, rework, warranties, litigation, or the lost sales from dissatisfied customers. There is a greater societal effect that must be factored into decision making involving the production of services or products, which often requires balancing the traditional measures of quality performance and the overall benefits to society. For example, in the health care industry, aiming for zero complications in cardiac surgery might sound good; however, if it comes at the cost of turning down high-risk patients, is society being served in the best way? Or, how much time, energy, and money should go into delivering vaccines or preventing complications? These are questions that often do not have clear answers.

Deceptive business practices are another source of concern for service or product quality. Deceptive business practice involves three elements: (1) the conduct of the provider is intentional and motivated by a desire to exploit the customer; (2) the provider conceals the truth based upon what is actually known to the provider; and (3) the transaction is intended to generate a disproportionate economic benefit to the provider at the expense of the customer. This behavior is unethical, diminishes the quality of the customers' experience, and may impose a substantial cost on society. Quality is all about increasing the satisfaction of customers. When a firm engages in unethical behavior and the customer finds out about it, the customer is unlikely to favorably assess the quality of his or her experience with that firm or to return as a customer.

Firms that produce better quality services or products can expect to earn a premium for that higher quality. They can also expect to grow and prosper over time because of their ability to create true value for customers. Firms that engage in deception, however, undermine the ability and competence of their employees and demean their relationship with external customers. The unfortunate message these firms send to their employees, who are also their internal customers, is that management views them as being less capable of producing quality services or products than their counterparts in ethical firms. Under these conditions employees are also less likely to be motivated to put forth their best effort. The message unethical firms send to their external customers is that their product or service cannot effectively compete with that of others and so they must engage in deception in order to be profitable. Employees of firms that attempt to profit by deceiving customers are less likely to create true value for customers through product or service improvements that can enhance the customers' experience. That erodes a firm's ability to compete now and in the future.

Ethical behavior falls on the shoulders of all employees of an organization. It is not ethical to knowingly deceive customers and pass defective services or products to internal or external customers. The well-being of all stakeholders, such as stockholders, customers, employees, partners, and creditors, should be considered.

The quality costs of prevention, assessment, internal failure, and external failure must be balanced with ethical considerations to arrive at the appropriate processes and approaches to manage them. Nonetheless, developing the cultural environment for ethical behavior is not cost-free. Employees must be educated in how ethics interfaces with their jobs. The firm may organize an ethics task force or an ethics public relations group to provide an interface between the firm and society. Documentation may be required. We now turn to a discussion of Total Quality Management and Six Sigma, two philosophies companies use to evaluate and improve quality and process performance along technical, service, and ethical dimensions.

total quality management (TQM)

A philosophy that stresses three principles for achieving high levels of process performance and quality: (1) customer satisfaction, (2) employee involvement, and (3) continuous improvement in performance.

quality

A term used by customers to describe their general satisfaction with a service or product.

Total Quality Management

Total quality management (TQM) is a philosophy that stresses three principles for achieving high levels of process performance and quality. These principles are related to (1) customer satisfaction, (2) employee involvement, and (3) continuous improvement in performance. As Figure 1 indicates, TQM also involves a number of other important elements. Service/product design and purchasing are covered later in this text. Here, we just focus on the three main principles of TQM.

Customer Satisfaction

Customers, internal or external, are satisfied when their expectations regarding a service or product have been met or exceeded. Often, customers use the general term **quality** to describe their level of satisfaction with a service or product. Quality has multiple dimensions in the mind of the customer. One or more of the following five definitions apply at any one time.

▲ FIGURE 1
TQM Wheel

Conformance to Specifications   Although customers evaluate the service or product they receive, it is the processes that produced the service or product that are really being judged. In this case, a process failure would be the process's inability to meet certain advertised or implied performance standards. Conformance to specifications may relate to consistent quality, on-time delivery, or delivery speed.

Value   Another way customers define quality is through value, or how well the service or product serves its intended purpose at a price customers are willing to pay. The service/product development process plays a role here, as do the firm's competitive priorities relating to top quality versus low-cost operations. The two factors must be balanced to produce value for the customer. How much value a service or product has in the mind of the customer depends on the customer's expectations before purchasing it.

Fitness for Use   When assessing how well a service or product performs its intended purpose, the customer may consider the convenience of a service, the mechanical features of a product, or other aspects such as appearance, style, durability, reliability, craftsmanship, and serviceability. For example, you may define the quality of the entertainment center you purchased on the basis of how easy it was to assemble and its appearance and styling.

Support   Often the service or product support provided by the company is as important to customers as the quality of the service or product itself. Customers get upset with a company if its financial statements are incorrect, responses to its warranty claims are delayed, its advertising is misleading, or its employees are not helpful when problems are incurred. Good support once the sale has been made can reduce the consequences of quality failures.

Psychological Impressions   People often evaluate the quality of a service or product on the basis of psychological impressions: atmosphere, image, or aesthetics. In the provision of services where the customer is in close contact with the provider, the appearance and actions of the provider are especially important. Nicely dressed, courteous, friendly, and sympathetic employees can affect the customer's perception of service quality.

Call centers provide support for a firm's products or services as well as contribute to the psychological impression of the customer regarding the experience. Calls to the center are often monitored to ensure that the customer is satisfied.

Attaining quality in all areas of a business is a difficult task. To make things even more difficult, consumers change their perceptions of quality. In general, a business's success depends on the accuracy of its perceptions of consumer expectations and its ability to bridge the gap between those expectations and operating capabilities. Good quality pays off in higher profits. High-quality services and products can be priced higher and yield a greater return. Poor quality erodes the firm's ability to compete in the marketplace and increases the costs of producing its service or product. Managerial Practice 1 shows how Steinway & Sons balanced consumer expectations for high-end pianos with its capability to meet those expectations.

Employee Involvement

One of the important elements of TQM is employee involvement, as shown in Figure 1. A program in employee involvement includes changing organizational culture and encouraging teamwork.

Cultural Change   One of the main challenges in developing the proper culture for TQM is to define *customer* for each employee. In general, customers are internal or external. *External customers* are the people or firms who buy the service or product. Some employees, especially those having little contact with external customers, may have difficulty seeing how their jobs contribute to the whole effort.

It is helpful to point out to employees that each employee also has one or more *internal customers*—employees in the firm who rely on the output of other employees. All employees must do a good job of serving their internal customers if external customers ultimately are to be satisfied. They will be satisfied only if each internal customer demands value be added that the external customer will recognize and pay for. The notion of internal customers applies to all parts of a firm and enhances cross-functional coordination. For example, accounting must prepare accurate and timely reports for management, and purchasing must provide high-quality materials on time for operations.

MANAGERIAL PRACTICE 1 — Quality and Performance at Steinway & Sons

A specialist adjusts the levers and dampers of a grand concert piano at the Steinway & Sons factory in Hamburg.

Christian Charisius/Reuters/Corbis

The first contestant in the Van Cliburn International Piano Competition is about to play Tchaikovsky Piano Concerto No. 1 before a packed audience in Fort Worth, Texas. The tension mounts as his fingers approach the keyboard of the Steinway & Sons grand concert piano; both the contestant and piano perform admirably much to the relief of the contestant and the operations manager of the concert. Why was the Steinway piano chosen for such a visible event? It is one of the highest-quality grand pianos you can buy. In addition, Steinway has a market share of over 95 percent in concert halls and it is the piano of choice for professional musicians from Van Cliburn to Billy Joel.

Steinway began operations in the 1880s. Today, the company blends the art of hand crafting, which uses methods essentially the same as when the company started, with twenty-first-century manufacturing technology to produce about 3,100 grand pianos a year. Some 12,000 parts are fashioned, mostly in-house, and assembled for each piano; it takes 9 months to a year compared to 20 days for a mass-produced piano. Eight different species of wood go into every grand piano, each selected for its physical properties and aesthetic characteristics. The craft-oriented production process is painstaking to ensure quality at each step. For example, each board for a piano is hand

selected for a given part. In a time-consuming process, craftsmen bend 17 laminations of the piano's hard maple rim into place with clamps. The Alaska Sitka spruce soundboard is hand-planed so it is arched, thicker at its center than its tapered edges, to withstand the 1,000 pounds of pressure from the more than 200 strings. The piano's "action," which contains keys (88 of them), whippens, shanks, and hammers, uses 100 parts, manufactured on numerical control machines, to sound each note and is pieced together at 30 different desks. Quality is checked at each operation to avoid passing defective parts downstream.

There are six characteristics of quality in Steinway pianos:

- **Sound** Tone and pitch contribute to the fullness and roundness of the sound from the piano. In a process called "voicing," minute adjustments are made to the felt pad of each hammer in the piano's action to either mellow the tone or increase its brilliance. Then a tone regulator listens to the piano's pitch and turns the tuning pins to adjust string tension. Steinways are world renowned for their sound; however, because of the natural characteristics of the wood, each piano will have its own personality.

- **Finish** Wood veneers are selected for their beauty. Boards not meeting standards are discarded, creating a large amount of scrap.

- **Feel** Each of the 88 keys must require the same amount of pressure to activate. In a process called "action weigh-off," lead is added to each key so that there is a consistent feel. Action parts are held to tolerances within +/−0.0005 inch.

- **Durability** The piano must have a long life and perform up to expectations throughout.

- **Image** There is a certain mystique associated with the Steinway brand. Some people attribute a cult-like experience to owning a Steinway.

- **Service** Steinway will go out of its way to service a piano that is inoperative, even to the extent of providing a loaner for a major concert.

The six characteristics link to four of our definitions of quality: (1) conformance to specifications (*feel*), (2) fitness for use (*sound, finish, durability*); (3) support (*service*); and (4) psychological impressions (*image*). As for value, our fifth definition of quality, Steinway grand pianos cost anywhere from $47,000 to $165,000 unless you want a nine-foot recreation of the famous Alma-Tadema piano built in 1887, in which case it will cost $675,000. Want to buy one?

Sources: Andy Serwer, "Happy Birthday, Steinway," *Fortune*, vol. 147, no. 5 (March 17, 2003), pp. 94–97; Leo O'Connor, "Engineering on a Grand scale," *Mechanical Engineering*, vol. 116, no. 10 (October, 1994), pp. 52–58; Steinway Musical Instruments, Inc. Annual Report 2006, **www.steinwaymusical.com**; **www.steinway.com/factory/tour.shtml**, 2007.

quality at the source

A philosophy whereby defects are caught and corrected where they were created.

teams

Small groups of people who have a common purpose, set their own performance goals and approaches, and hold themselves accountable for success.

In TQM, everyone in the organization must share the view that quality control is an end in itself. Errors or defects should be caught and corrected at the source, not passed along to an internal or external customer. For example, a consulting team should make sure its billable hours are correct before submitting them to the accounting department. This philosophy is called **quality at the source**. In addition, firms should avoid trying to "inspect quality into the product" by using inspectors to weed out unsatisfactory services or defective products after all operations have been performed. By contrast, in some manufacturing firms, workers have the authority to stop a production line if they spot quality problems.

Teams Employee involvement is a key tactic for improving processes and quality. One way to achieve employee involvement is by the use of **teams**, which are small groups of people who have a common purpose, set their own performance goals and approaches, and hold themselves accountable for success.

The three approaches to teamwork most often used are (1) problem-solving teams, (2) special-purpose teams, and (3) self-managed teams. All three use some amount of **employee empowerment**, which moves responsibility for decisions further down the organizational chart—to the level of the employee actually doing the job.

First introduced in the 1920s, *problem-solving teams*, also called **quality circles**, became popular in the late 1970s after the Japanese used them successfully. Problem-solving teams are small groups of supervisors and employees who meet to identify, analyze, and solve process and quality problems. Employees take more pride and interest in their work if they are allowed to help shape it. Although problem-solving teams can successfully reduce costs and improve quality, they die if management fails to implement many of the suggestions they generate.

An outgrowth of the problem-solving teams, **special-purpose teams** address issues of paramount concern to management, labor, or both. For example, management may form a special-purpose team to design and introduce new work policies or new technologies or to address customer service problems. Essentially, this approach gives workers a voice in high-level decisions. Special-purpose teams first appeared in the United States in the early 1980s.

The **self-managed team** approach takes worker participation to its highest level: A small group of employees work together to produce a major portion, or sometimes all, of a service or product. Members learn all the tasks involved in the operation, rotate from job to job, and take over managerial duties such as work and vacation scheduling, ordering supplies, and hiring. In some cases, team members design the process and have a high degree of latitude as to how it takes shape. Self-managed teams essentially change the way work is organized because employees have control over their jobs. Some self-managed teams have increased productivity by 30 percent or more in their firms.

Process measurement is the key to quality improvement. Here a quality inspector measures the diameter of holes in a machined part.

Continuous Improvement

Continuous improvement, based on a Japanese concept called *kaizen*, is the philosophy of continually seeking ways to improve processes. Continuous improvement involves identifying benchmarks of excellent practice and instilling a sense of employee ownership in the process. The focus of continuous improvement projects is to reduce waste, such as reducing the length of time required to process requests for loans at a bank, the amount of scrap generated at a milling machine, or the number of employee injuries at a construction site. The basis of the continuous improvement philosophy are the beliefs that virtually any aspect of a process can be improved and that the people most closely associated with a process are in the best position to identify the changes that should be made. The idea is not to wait until a massive problem occurs before acting.

Employees should be given problem-solving tools, such as the statistical process control (SPC) methods we discuss later in this chapter, and a sense of ownership of the process to be improved. A sense of operator ownership emerges when employees feel a responsibility for the processes and methods they use and take pride in the quality of the service or product they produce. It comes from participation on work teams and in problem-solving activities, which instill in employees a feeling that they have some control over their workplace and tasks.

Most firms actively engaged in continuous improvement train their work teams to use the **plan-do-study-act cycle** for problem solving. Another name for this approach is the Deming Wheel, named after the renowned statistician W. Edwards Deming who taught quality improvement techniques to the Japanese after World War II. Figure 2 shows this cycle, which lies at the heart of the continuous improvement philosophy. The cycle comprises the following steps:

1. *Plan*. The team selects a process (an activity, method, machine, or policy) that needs improvement. The team then documents the selected process, usually by analyzing related data; sets qualitative goals for improvement; and discusses various ways to achieve the goals. After assessing the benefits and costs of the alternatives, the team develops a plan with quantifiable measures for improvement.

2. *Do*. The team implements the plan and monitors progress. Data are collected continuously to measure the improvements in the process. Any changes in the process are documented, and further revisions are made as needed.

employee empowerment

An approach to teamwork that moves responsibility for decisions further down the organizational chart—to the level of the employee actually doing the job.

quality circles

Another name for problem-solving teams; small groups of supervisors and employees who meet to identify, analyze, and solve process and quality problems.

special-purpose teams

Groups that address issues of paramount concern to management, labor, or both.

self-managed team

A small group of employees who work together to produce a major portion, or sometimes all, of a service or product.

continuous improvement

The philosophy of continually seeking ways to improve processes based on a Japanese concept called *kaizen*.

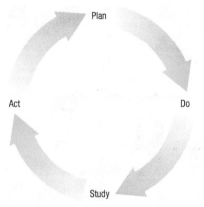

▲ FIGURE 2
Plan-Do-Study-Act Cycle

plan-do-study-act cycle

A cycle, also called the Deming Wheel, used by firms actively engaged in continuous improvement to train their work teams in problem solving.

Six Sigma

A comprehensive and flexible system for achieving, sustaining, and maximizing business success by minimizing defects and variability in processes.

▼ FIGURE 3

Six Sigma Approach Focuses on Reducing Spread and Centering the Process

3. *Study.* The team analyzes the data collected during the *do* step to find out how closely the results correspond to the goals set in the *plan* step. If major shortcomings exist, the team reevaluates the plan or stops the project.

4. *Act.* If the results are successful, the team documents the revised process so that it becomes the standard procedure for all who may use it. The team may then instruct other employees in the use of the revised process.

Problem-solving projects often focus on those aspects of processes that do not add value to the service or product. Value is added in processes such as machining a part or serving a customer through a Web page. No value is added in activities such as inspecting parts for defects or routing requests for loan approvals to several different departments. The idea of continuous improvement is to reduce or eliminate activities that do not add value and, thus, are wasteful.

Six Sigma

Six Sigma, which relies heavily on the principles of TQM, is a comprehensive and flexible system for achieving, sustaining, and maximizing business success by minimizing defects and variability in processes. Six Sigma has a different focus than TQM: It is driven by a close understanding of customer needs; the disciplined use of facts, data, and statistical analysis; and diligent attention to managing, improving, and reinventing business processes. Figure 3 shows how Six Sigma focuses on reducing variation in processes as well as centering processes on their target measures of performance. Either flaw—too much variation or an off-target process—degrades performance of the process. For example, a mortgage loan department of a bank might advertise loan approval decisions in 2 days. If the actual performance ranges from 1 day to 5 days, with an average of 2 days, those customers who had to wait longer than 2 days would be upset. Process variability causes customer dissatisfaction. Similarly, if actual performance consistently produced loan decisions in 3 days, all customers would be dissatisfied. In this case, the process is consistent, but off the target. Six Sigma is a rigorous approach to align processes with their target performance measures with low variability.

The name Six Sigma, originally developed by Motorola for its manufacturing operations, relates to the goal of achieving low rates of defective output by developing processes whose mean output for a performance measure is +/− six standard deviations (sigma) from the limits of the design specifications for the service or product. We will discuss variability and its implications on the capability of a process to perform at acceptable levels when we present the tools of statistical process control.

Although Six Sigma was rooted in an effort to improve manufacturing processes, credit General Electric with popularizing the application of the approach to non-manufacturing processes such as sales, human resources, customer service, and financial services. The concept of eliminating defects is the same, although the definition of "defect" depends on the process involved. For example, a human resource department's failure to meet a hiring target counts as a defect. Six Sigma has been successfully applied to a host of service processes, including financial services, human resource processes, marketing processes, and health care administrative processes.

Six Sigma Improvement Model

Figure 4 shows the Six Sigma Improvement Model, a five-step procedure that leads to improvements in process performance. The model bears a lot of similarity, the Blueprint for Process Analysis, for good reason: Both models strive for process improvement. Either model can be applied to projects involving incremental improvements to processes or to projects requiring major changes, including a redesign of an existing process or the development of a new process. The Six Sigma Improvement Model, however, is heavily reliant on statistical process control. The following steps comprise the model:

- *Define.* Determine the characteristics of the process's output that are critical to customer satisfaction and identify any gaps between these characteristics and the

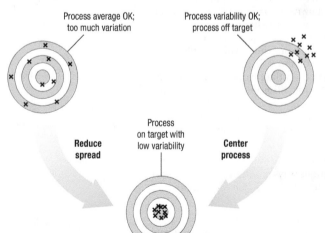

process's capabilities. Get a picture of the current process by documenting it using *flowcharts* and *process charts*.

- *Measure*. Quantify the work the process does that affects the gap. Select what to measure, identify data sources, and prepare a data collection plan.

- *Analyze*. Use the data on measures to perform process analysis, applying tools such as Pareto charts, scatter diagrams, and cause-and-effect diagrams and the statistical process control (SPC) tools in this chapter to determine where improvements are necessary. Whether or not major redesign is necessary, establish procedures to make the desired outcome routine.

- *Improve*. Modify or redesign existing methods to meet the new performance objectives. Implement the changes.

- *Control*. Monitor the process to make sure that high performance levels are maintained. Once again, data analysis tools such as Pareto charts, bar charts, scatter diagrams, as well as the statistical process control tools can be used to control the process.

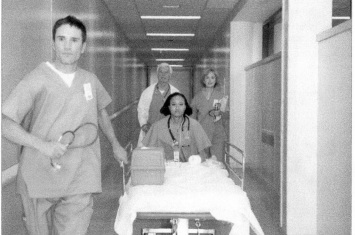

Hospital personnel rush to help a patient in an emergency. Six Sigma can be used to improve service processes in a hospital.

Successful users of Six Sigma have found that it is essential to rigorously follow the steps in the Six Sigma Improvement Model, which is sometimes referred to as the *DMAIC process* (whose name comes from using the first letter of each step in the model). To accomplish the goals of Six Sigma, employees must be trained in the "whys" and the "how-tos" of quality and what it means to customers, both internal and external. Successful firms using Six Sigma develop a cadre of internal teachers who then are responsible for teaching and assisting teams involved in a process improvement project. These teachers have different titles depending on their experience and level of achievement. **Green Belts** devote part of their time to teaching and helping teams with their projects and the rest of their time to their normally assigned duties. **Black Belts** are full-time teachers and leaders of teams involved in Six Sigma projects. Finally, **Master Black Belts** are full-time teachers who review and mentor Black Belts.

Acceptance Sampling

Before any internal process can be evaluated for performance, the inputs to that process must be of good quality. **Acceptance sampling**, which is the application of statistical techniques to determine if a quantity of material from a supplier should be accepted or rejected based on the inspection or test of one or more samples, limits the buyer's risk of rejecting good-quality materials (and unnecessarily delaying the production of goods or services) or accepting bad-quality materials (and incurring downtime due to defective materials or passing bad products to customers). Relative to the specifications for the material the buyer is purchasing, the buyer specifies an **acceptable quality level (AQL)**, which is a statement of the proportion of defective items (outside of specifications) that the buyer will accept in a shipment. These days, that proportion is getting very small, often measured in parts per ten-thousand. The idea of acceptance sampling is to take a sample, rather than testing the entire quantity of material, because that is often less expensive. Therein lies the risk—the sample may not be representative of the entire lot of goods from the supplier. The basic procedure is straightforward.

1. A random sample is taken from a large quantity of items and tested or measured relative to the specifications or quality measures of interest.

2. If the sample passes the test (low number of defects), the entire quantity of items is accepted.

3. If the sample fails the test, either (a) the entire quantity of items is subjected to 100 percent inspection and all defective items repaired or replaced or (b) the entire quantity is returned to the supplier.

In a supply chain, any company can be both a producer of goods purchased by another company and a consumer of goods or raw materials supplied by another company. Figure 5 shows

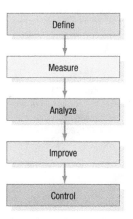

▲ FIGURE 4
Six Sigma Improvement Model

Green Belt

An employee who achieved the first level of training in a Six Sigma program and spends part of his or her time teaching and helping teams with their projects.

Black Belt

An employee who reached the highest level of training in a Six Sigma program and spends all of his or her time teaching and leading teams involved in Six Sigma projects.

Master Black Belt

Full-time teachers and mentors to several Black Belts.

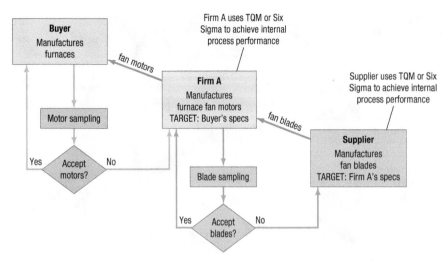

acceptable quality level (AQL)

The quality level desired by the
consumer.

acceptance sampling

The application of statistical
techniques to determine whether
a quantity of material should be
accepted or rejected based on
the inspection or test of a sample.

**statistical process control
(SPC)**

The application of statistical
techniques to determine whether
a process is delivering what the
customer wants.

a flowchart of how acceptance sampling and internal process performance (TQM or Six Sigma) interface in a supply chain. From the perspective of the supply chain, the buyer's specifications for various dimensions of quality become the targets the supplier shoots for in a supply contract. The supplier's internal processes must be up to the task; TQM or Six Sigma can help achieve the desired performance. The buyer's sampling plan will provide a high probability of accepting AQL (or better). MyOMLab Supplement G, "Acceptance Sampling Plans," shows how to design an acceptance sampling plan that meets the level of risk desired.

Statistical Process Control

Regardless of whether a firm is producing a service or a product, it is important to ensure that the firm's processes are providing the quality that customers want. A key element of TQM or Six Sigma is building the capability to monitor the performance of processes so that corrective action can be initiated in a timely fashion. Evaluating the performance of processes requires a variety of data gathering approaches. Think as checklists, histograms and bar charts, Pareto charts, scatter diagrams, cause-and-effect diagrams, and graphs. All of these tools can be used with TQM or Six Sigma. Here. we focus on the powerful statistical tools that can be used to monitor and manage repetitive processes.

Statistical process control (SPC) is the application of statistical techniques to determine whether a process is delivering what customers want. In SPC, tools called control charts are used primarily to detect defective services or products or to indicate that the process has changed and that services or products will deviate from their design specifications, unless something is done to correct the situation. SPC can also be used to inform management of improved process changes. Examples of process changes that can be detected by SPC include the following:

- A decrease in the average number of complaints per day at a hotel
- A sudden increase in the proportion of defective gear boxes
- An increase in the time to process a mortgage application
- A decline in the number of scrapped units at a milling machine
- An increase in the number of claimants receiving late payment from an insurance company

Let us consider the last situation. Suppose that the manager of the accounts payable department of an insurance company notices that the proportion of claimants receiving late payments rose from an average of 0.01 to 0.03. The first question is whether the rise is a cause for alarm or just a random occurrence. Statistical process control can help the manager decide whether further action should be taken. If the rise in the proportion is not just a random occurrence, the manager should seek explanations of the poor performance. Perhaps the number of claims significantly increased, causing an overload on the employees in the department. The decision might be to hire more personnel. Or perhaps the procedures being used are ineffective or the training of employees is inadequate. SPC is an integral part of TQM and Six Sigma.

Variation of Outputs

No two services or products are exactly alike because the processes used to produce them contain many sources of variation, even if the processes are working as intended. Nonetheless, it is important to minimize the variation in outputs because frequently variation is what the customer sees and feels. Suppose a physicians' clinic submits claims on behalf of its patients to a particular insurance company. In this situation, the physicians' clinic is the customer of the insurance company's bill payment process. In some cases, the clinic receives payment in 4 weeks, and in other cases 20 weeks. The time to process a request for payment varies because of the load on the insurance company's processes, the medical history of the patient, and the skills and attitudes of the employees. Meanwhile, the clinic must cover its expenses while it waits for payment. Regardless of whether the process is producing services or products, nothing can be done to eliminate variation in output completely; however, management should investigate the *causes* of the variation in order to minimize it.

Performance Measurements   Performance can be evaluated in two ways. One way is to measure **variables**—that is, service or product characteristics, such as weight, length, volume, or time, that can be *measured*. The advantage of using performance variables is that if a service or product misses its performance specifications, the inspector knows by how much. The disadvantage is that such measurements typically involve special equipment, employee skills, exacting procedures, and time and effort.

Another way to evaluate performance is to measure **attributes**; service or product characteristics that can be quickly *counted* for acceptable performance. This method allows inspectors to make a simple "yes/no" decision about whether a service or product meets the specifications. Attributes often are used when performance specifications are complex and measurement of variables is difficult or costly. Some examples of attributes that can be counted are the number of insurance forms containing errors that cause underpayments or overpayments, the proportion of airline flights arriving within 15 minutes of scheduled times, and the number of stove-top assemblies with spotted paint.

The advantage of counting attributes is that less effort and fewer resources are needed than for measuring variables. The disadvantage is that, even though attribute counts can reveal that process performance has changed, they do not indicate by how much. For example, a count may determine that the proportion of airline flights arriving within 15 minutes of their scheduled times declined, but the result does not show how much beyond the 15-minute allowance the flights are arriving. For that, the actual deviation from the scheduled arrival, a variable, would have to be measured.

Sampling   The most thorough approach to inspection is to inspect each service or product at each stage of the process for quality. This method, called *complete inspection*, is used when the costs of passing defects to an internal or external customer outweigh the inspection costs. Firms often use automated inspection equipment that can record, summarize, and display data. Many companies find that automated inspection equipment can pay for itself in a reasonably short time.

A well-conceived **sampling plan** can approach the same degree of protection as complete inspection. A sampling plan specifies a **sample size**, which is a quantity of randomly selected observations of process outputs, the time between successive samples, and decision rules that determine when action should be taken. Sampling is appropriate when inspection costs are high because of the special knowledge, skills, procedures, and expensive equipment that are required to perform the inspections, or because the tests are destructive.

Sampling Distributions   Relative to a performance measure, a process will produce output that can be described by a *process distribution*, with a mean and variance that will be known only with a complete inspection with 100 percent accuracy. The purpose of sampling, however, is to estimate a variable or attribute measure for the output of the process without doing a complete inspection. That measure is then used to assess the performance of the process itself. For example, the time required to process specimens at an intensive care unit lab in a hospital (a variable measure) will vary. If you measured the time to complete an analysis of a large number of patients and plotted the results, the data would tend to form a pattern that can be described as a process distribution. With sampling, we try to estimate the parameters of the process distribution using statistics such as the sample mean and the sample range or standard deviation.

1.   The *sample mean* is the sum of the observations divided by the total number of observations:

$$\bar{x} = \frac{\sum_{i=1}^{n} x_i}{n}$$

variables

Service or product characteristics, such as weight, length, volume, or time, that can be measured.

attributes

Service or product characteristics that can be quickly counted for acceptable performance.

sampling plan

A plan that specifies a sample size, the time between successive samples, and decision rules that determine when action should be taken.

sample size

A quantity of randomly selected observations of process outputs.

Wine production is an example of a situation where complete inspection is not an option. Here a quality inspector draws a sample of white wine from a stainless steel maturation tank.

where

$x_i =$ observation of a quality characteristic (such as time)

$n =$ total number of observations

$\bar{x} =$ mean

2. The *range* is the difference between the largest observation in a sample and the smallest. The *standard deviation* is the square root of the variance of a distribution. An estimate of the process standard deviation based on a sample is given by

$$\sigma = \sqrt{\frac{\sum_{i=1}^{n}(x_i - \bar{x})^2}{n - 1}} \quad \text{or} \quad \sigma = \sqrt{\frac{\sum_{i=1}^{n}x^2 - \frac{\left(\sum_{i=1}^{n}x_i\right)^2}{n}}{n - 1}}$$

where

$\sigma =$ standard deviation of a sample

$n =$ total number of observations in the sample

$\bar{x} =$ mean

$x_i =$ observation of a quality characteristic

Relatively small values for the range or the standard deviation imply that the observations are clustered near the mean.

These sample statistics have their own distribution, which we call a *sampling distribution*. For example, in the lab analysis process, an important performance variable is the time it takes to get results to the critical care unit. Suppose that management wants results available in an average of 25 minutes. That is, it wants the process distribution to have a mean of 25 minutes. An inspector periodically taking a sample of five analyses and calculating the sample mean could use it to determine how well the process is doing. Suppose that the process is actually producing the analyses with a mean of 25 minutes. Plotting a large number of these sample means would show that they have their own sampling distribution with a mean centered on 25 minutes, as does the process distribution mean, but with much less variability. The reason is that the sample means offset the highs and lows of the individual times in each sample. Figure 6 shows the relationship between the sampling distribution of sample means and the process distribution for the analysis times.

Some sampling distributions (e.g., for means with sample sizes of four or more and proportions with sample sizes of 20 or more) can be approximated by the normal distribution, allowing the use of the normal tables. For example, suppose you wanted to determine the probability that a sample mean will be more than 2.0 standard deviations higher than the process mean. For $z = 2.0$ standard deviations is 0.9772. Consequently, the probability is $1.0000 - 0.9772 = 0.0228$, or 2.28 percent. The probability that the sample mean will be more than 2.0 standard deviations lower than the process mean is also 2.28 percent because the normal distribution is symmetric to the mean. The ability to assign probabilities to sample results is important for the construction and use of control charts.

Common Causes The two basic categories of variation in output include common causes and assignable causes. **Common causes of variation** are the purely random, unidentifiable sources of variation that are unavoidable with the current process. A process distribution can be characterized by its *location*, *spread*, and *shape*. Location is measured by the *mean* of the distribution, while spread is measured by the *range* or *standard deviation*. The shape of process distributions can be characterized as either symmetric or skewed. A *symmetric* distribution has the same number of observations above and below the mean. A *skewed* distribution has a greater number of observations either above or below the mean. If process variability results solely from common causes of variation, a typical assumption is that the distribution is symmetric, with most observations near the center.

Assignable Causes The second category of variation, **assignable causes of variation**, also known as *special causes*, includes any variation-causing factors that can be identified and eliminated. Assignable causes of variation include an employee needing training or a machine needing repair. Let us return to the example of the lab analysis process. Figure 7 shows how assignable causes can change the distribution of output for the analysis process. The **green** curve is

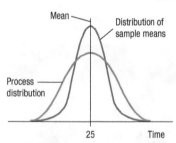

▲ FIGURE 6
Relationship Between the Distribution of Sample Means and the Process Distribution

common causes of variation

The purely random, unidentifiable sources of variation that are unavoidable with the current process.

assignable causes of variation

Any variation-causing factors that can be identified and eliminated.

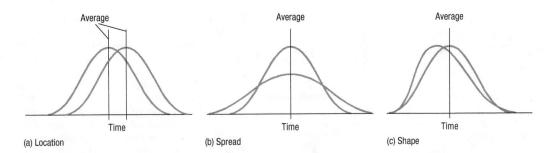

(a) Location   (b) Spread   (c) Shape

the process distribution when only common causes of variation are present. The **purple** curves depict a change in the distribution because of assignable causes. In Figure 7(a), the **purple** curve indicates that the process took more time than planned in many of the cases, thereby increasing the average time of each analysis. In Figure 7(b), an increase in the variability of the time for each case affected the spread of the distribution. Finally, in Figure 7(c), the **purple** curve indicates that the process produced a preponderance of the tests in less than average time. Such a distribution is skewed, or no longer symmetric to the average value. A process is said to be in statistical control when the location, spread, or shape of its distribution does not change over time. After the process is in statistical control, managers use SPC procedures to detect the onset of assignable causes so that they can be addressed.

▲ **FIGURE 7**
Effects of Assignable Causes on the Process Distribution for the Lab Analysis Process

control chart
A time-ordered diagram that is used to determine whether observed variations are abnormal.

Control Charts

To determine whether observed variations are abnormal, we can measure and plot the performance measure taken from the sample on a time-ordered diagram called a **control chart**. A control chart has a nominal value, or central line, which can be the process's historic average or a target that managers would like the process to achieve, and two control limits based on the sampling distribution of the quality measure. The control limits are used to judge whether action is required. The larger value represents the *upper control limit* (UCL), and the smaller value represents the *lower control limit* (LCL). Figure 8 shows how the control limits relate to the sampling distribution. A sample statistic that falls between the UCL and the LCL indicates that the process is exhibiting common causes of variation. A statistic that falls outside the control limits indicates that the process is exhibiting assignable causes of variation.

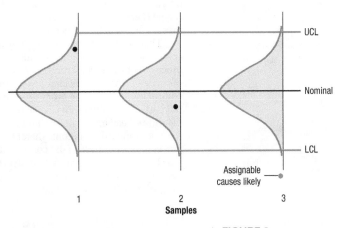

Samples

▲ **FIGURE 8**
How Control Limits Relate to the Sampling Distribution: Observations from Three Samples

Observations falling outside the control limits do not always mean poor quality. For example, in Figure 8 the assignable cause may be a new billing process introduced to reduce the number of incorrect bills sent to customers. If the proportion of incorrect bills, that is, the performance measure from a sample of bills, falls *below* the LCL of the control chart, the new procedure likely changed the billing process for the better, and a new control chart should be constructed.

Managers or employees responsible for evaluating a process can use control charts in the following way:

1. Take a random sample from the process and calculate a variable or attribute performance measure.

2. If the statistic falls outside the chart's control limits or exhibits unusual behavior, look for an assignable cause.

3. Eliminate the cause if it degrades performance; incorporate the cause if it improves performance. Reconstruct the control chart with new data.

4. Repeat the procedure periodically.

Sometimes, problems with a process can be detected even though the control limits have not been exceeded. Figure 9 contains four examples of control charts. Chart (a) shows a process that is in statistical control. No action is needed. However, chart (b) shows a pattern called a *run* or a sequence of observations with a certain characteristic. A typical rule is to take remedial action

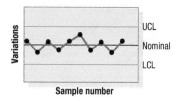

(a) Normal—No action

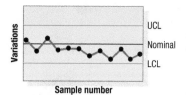

(b) Run—Take action

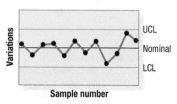

(c) Sudden change—Monitor

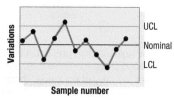

(d) Exceeds control limits—Take action

▲ **FIGURE 9**
Control Chart Examples

type I error

An error that occurs when the employee concludes that the process is out of control based on a sample result that falls outside the control limits, when in fact it was due to pure randomness.

type II error

An error that occurs when the employee concludes that the process is in control and only randomness is present, when actually the process is out of statistical control.

when five or more observations show a downward or upward trend, even if the points have not yet exceeded the control limits. Here, nine sequential observations are below the mean and show a downward trend. The probability is low that such a result could take place by chance.

Chart (c) shows that the process takes a sudden change from its normal pattern. The last four observations are unusual: The first drops close to the LCL, the next two rise toward the UCL, and the fourth remains above the nominal value. Managers or employees should monitor processes with such sudden changes even though the control limits have not been exceeded. Finally, chart (d) indicates that the process went out of control twice because two sample results fell outside the control limits. The probability that the process distribution has changed is high. We discuss more implications of being out of statistical control when we discuss process capability later in this chapter.

Control charts are not perfect tools for detecting shifts in the process distribution because they are based on sampling distributions. Two types of error are possible with the use of control charts. A **type I error** occurs when the conclusion is made that the process is out of control based on a sample result that falls outside the control limits, when in fact it was due to pure randomness. A **type II error** occurs when the conclusion is that the process is in control and only randomness is present, when actually the process is out of statistical control.

These errors can be controlled by the choice of control limits. The choice would depend on the costs of looking for assignable causes when none exist versus the cost of not detecting a shift in the process. For example, setting control limits at +/− three standard deviations from the mean reduces the type I error because chances are only 0.26 percent that a sample result will fall outside of the control limits unless the process is out of statistical control. However, the type II error may be significant; more subtle shifts in the nature of the process distribution will go undetected because of the wide spread in the control limits. Alternatively, the spread in the control limits can be reduced to +/− two standard deviations, thereby increasing the likelihood of sample results from a non-faulty process falling outside of the control limits to 4.56 percent. Now, the type II error is smaller, but the type I error is larger because employees are likely to search for assignable causes when the sample result occurred solely by chance. As a general rule, use wider limits when the cost for searching for assignable causes is large relative to the cost of not detecting a shift in the process distribution.

Statistical Process Control Methods

Statistical process control (SPC) methods are useful for both measuring the current process performance and detecting whether the process has changed in a way that will affect future performance. In this section, we first discuss mean and range charts for variable measures of performance and then consider control charts for attributes measures.

Control Charts for Variables

Control charts for variables are used to monitor the mean and the variability of the process distribution.

R-chart

A chart used to monitor process variability.

R-Chart A range chart, or **R-chart**, is used to monitor process variability. To calculate the range of a set of sample data, the analyst subtracts the smallest from the largest measurement in each sample. If any of the ranges fall outside the control limits, the process variability is not in control.

The control limits for the R-chart are

$$\text{UCL}_R = D_4\bar{R} \quad \text{and} \quad \text{LCL}_R = D_3\bar{R}$$

where

$\bar{R}$ = average of several past R values and the central line of the control chart

D_3, D_4 = constants that provide three standard deviation (three-sigma) limits for a given sample size

Notice that the values for D_3 and D_4 shown in Table 1 change as a function of the sample size. Notice, too, that the spread between the control limits narrows as the sample size increases. This change is a consequence of having more information on which to base an estimate for the process range.

TABLE 1 | FACTORS FOR CALCULATING THREE-SIGMA LIMITS FOR THE $\bar{x}$-CHART AND R-CHART

Size of Sample (n)	Factor for UCL and LCL for $\bar{x}$-Chart (A_2)	Factor for LCL for R-Chart (D_3)	Factor for UCL for R-Chart (D_4)
2	1.880	0	3.267
3	1.023	0	2.575
4	0.729	0	2.282
5	0.577	0	2.115
6	0.483	0	2.004
7	0.419	0.076	1.924
8	0.373	0.136	1.864
9	0.337	0.184	1.816
10	0.308	0.223	1.777

Source: Reprinted with permission from *ASTM Manual on Quality Control of Materials*, copyright © ASTM International, 100 Barr Harbor Drive, West Conshohocken, PA 19428.

$\bar{x}$-Chart An $\bar{x}$-Chart (read "x-bar chart") is used to see whether the process is generating output, on average, consistent with a target value set by management for the process or whether its current performance, with respect to the average of the performance measure, is consistent with its past performance. A target value is useful when a process is completely redesigned and past performance is no longer relevant. When the assignable causes of process variability have been identified and the process variability is in statistical control, the analyst can then construct an $\bar{x}$-chart. The control limits for the $\bar{x}$-chart are

$$\text{UCL}_{\bar{x}} = \bar{\bar{x}} + A_2\bar{R} \quad \text{and} \quad \text{LCL}_{\bar{x}} = \bar{\bar{x}} - A_2\bar{R}$$

where

$\bar{\bar{x}} =$ central line of the chart, which can be either the average of past sample means or a target value set for the process

$A_2 =$ constant to provide three-sigma limits for the sample mean

The values for A_2 are contained in Table 1. Note that the control limits use the value of $\bar{R}$; therefore, the $\bar{x}$-chart must be constructed *after* the process variability is in control.

To develop and use $\bar{x}$- and R-charts, do the following:

Step 1. Collect data on the variable quality measurement (such as time, weight, or diameter) and organize the data by sample number. Preferably, at least 20 samples of size n should be taken for use in constructing a control chart.

Step 2. Compute the range for each sample and the average range, $\bar{R}$, for the set of samples.

Step 3. Use Table 1 to determine the upper and lower control limits of the R-chart.

Step 4. Plot the sample ranges. If all are in control, proceed to step 5. Otherwise, find the assignable causes, correct them, and return to step 1.

Step 5. Calculate $\bar{x}$ for each sample and determine the central line of the chart, $\bar{\bar{x}}$.

Step 6. Use Table 1 to determine the parameters for $\text{UCL}_{\bar{x}}$ and $\text{LCL}_{\bar{x}}$ and construct the $\bar{x}$-chart.

Step 7. Plot the sample means. If all are in control, the process is in statistical control in terms of the process average and process variability. Continue

$\bar{x}$-chart

A chart used to see whether the process is generating output, on average, consistent with a target value set by management for the process or whether its current performance, with respect to the average of the performance measure, is consistent with past performance.

An analyst measures the diameter of a part with a micrometer. After he measures the sample, he plots the range on the control chart.

to take samples and monitor the process. If any are out of control, find the assignable causes, address them, and return to step 1. If no assignable causes are found after a diligent search, assume that the out-of-control points represent common causes of variation and continue to monitor the process.

| EXAMPLE 1 | Using $\bar{x}$- and R-Charts to Monitor a Process |

The management of West Allis Industries is concerned about the production of a special metal screw used by several of the company's largest customers. The diameter of the screw is critical to the customers. Data from five samples appear in the accompanying table. The sample size is 4. Is the process in statistical control?

SOLUTION

Step 1: For simplicity, we use only 5 samples. In practice, more than 20 samples would be desirable. The data are shown in the following table.

DATA FOR THE $\bar{x}$- AND R-CHARTS: OBSERVATIONS OF SCREW DIAMETER (IN.)

Sample Number	Observations				R	$\bar{x}$
	1	2	3	4		
1	0.5014	0.5022	0.5009	0.5027	0.0018	0.5018
2	0.5021	0.5041	0.5024	0.5020	0.0021	0.5027
3	0.5018	0.5026	0.5035	0.5023	0.0017	0.5026
4	0.5008	0.5034	0.5024	0.5015	0.0026	0.5020
5	0.5041	0.5056	0.5034	0.5047	0.0022	0.5045
				Average	0.0021	0.5027

Step 2: Compute the range for each sample by subtracting the lowest value from the highest value. For example, in sample 1 the range is 0.5027 − 0.5009 = 0.0018 in. Similarly, the ranges for samples 2, 3, 4, and 5 are 0.0021, 0.0017, 0.0026, and 0.0022 in., respectively. As shown in the table, $\bar{R} = 0.0021$.

Step 3: To construct the R-chart, select the appropriate constants from Table 1 for a sample size of 4. The control limits are

$$\text{UCL}_R = D_4\bar{R} = 2.282(0.0021) = 0.00479 \text{ in.}$$

$$\text{LCL}_R = D_3\bar{R} = 0(0.0021) = 0 \text{ in.}$$

Step 4: Plot the ranges on the R-chart, as shown in Figure 10. None of the sample ranges falls outside the control limits. Consequently, the process variability is in statistical control. If any of the sample ranges fall outside of the limits, or an unusual pattern appears (see Figure 9), we would search for the causes of the excessive variability, address them, and repeat step 1.

FIGURE 10 ▶
Range Chart from the *OM Explorer* $\bar{x}$- and *R-Chart* Solver, Showing that the Process Variability Is In Control

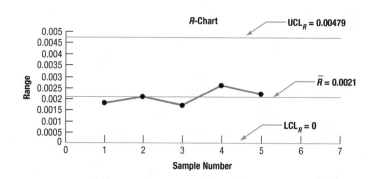

Step 5: Compute the mean for each sample. For example, the mean for sample 1 is

$$\frac{0.5014 + 0.5022 + 0.5009 + 0.5027}{4} = 0.5018 \text{ in.}$$

Similarly, the means of samples 2, 3, 4, and 5 are 0.5027, 0.5026, 0.5020, and 0.5045 in., respectively. As shown in the table, $\bar{\bar{x}} = 0.5027$.

Step 6: Now, construct the $\bar{x}$-chart for the process average. The average screw diameter is 0.5027 in., and the average range is 0.0021 in., so use $\bar{\bar{x}} = 0.5027$, $\bar{R} = 0.0021$, and A_2 from Table 1 for a sample size of 4 to construct the control limits:

$$\text{UCL}_{\bar{x}} = \bar{\bar{x}} + A_2\bar{R} = 0.5027 + 0.729(0.0021) = 0.5042 \text{ in.}$$

$$\text{LCL}_{\bar{x}} = \bar{\bar{x}} - A_2\bar{R} = 0.5027 - 0.729(0.0021) = 0.5012 \text{ in.}$$

Step 7: Plot the sample means on the control chart, as shown in Figure 11.

The mean of sample 5 falls above the UCL, indicating that the process average is out of statistical control and that assignable causes must be explored, perhaps using a cause-and-effect diagram.

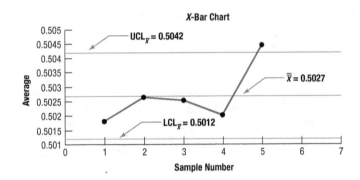

◀ **FIGURE 11**
The x-bar Chart from the *OM Explore $\bar{x}$-* and *R-Chart* Solver for the Metal Screw, Showing that Sample 5 Is Out of Control

DECISION POINT
A new employee operated the lathe machine that makes the screw on the day sample 5 was taken. To solve the problem, management initiated a training session for the employee. Subsequent samples showed that the process was back in statistical control.

If the standard deviation of the process distribution is known, another form of the $\bar{x}$-chart may be used:

$$\text{UCL}_{\bar{x}} = \bar{\bar{x}} + z\sigma_{\bar{x}} \quad \text{and} \quad \text{LCL}_{\bar{x}} = \bar{\bar{x}} - z\sigma_{\bar{x}}$$

where
$\sigma_{\bar{x}} = \sigma/\sqrt{n} = $ standard deviation of sample means

$\sigma = $ standard deviation of the process distribution

$n = $ sample size

$\bar{\bar{x}} = $ central line of the chart, which can be either the average of past sample means or a target value set for the process

$z = $ normal deviate (number of standard deviations from the average)

The analyst can use an R-chart to be sure that the process variability is in control before constructing the $\bar{x}$-chart. The advantage of using this form of the $\bar{x}$-chart is that the analyst can adjust the spread of the control limits by changing the value of z. This approach can be useful for balancing the effects of type I and type II errors.

| EXAMPLE 2 | Designing an $\bar{x}$-Chart Using the Process Standard Deviation |

The Sunny Dale Bank monitors the time required to serve customers at the drive-by window because it is an important quality factor in competing with other banks in the city. After analyzing the data gathered in an extensive study of the window operation, bank management determined that the mean time to process a customer at the peak demand period is 5 minutes, with a standard deviation of 1.5 minutes. Management wants to monitor the mean time to process a customer by periodically using a sample size of six customers. Assume that the process variability is in statistical control. Design an $\bar{x}$-chart that has a type I error of 5 percent. That is, set the control limits so that there is a 2.5 percent chance a sample result will fall below the LCL and a 2.5 percent chance that a sample result will fall above the UCL. After several weeks of sampling, two successive samples came in at 3.70 and 3.68 minutes, respectively. Is the customer service process in statistical control?

SOLUTION

$$\bar{\bar{x}} = 5.0 \text{ minutes}$$

$$\sigma = 1.5 \text{ minutes}$$

$$n = 6 \text{ customers}$$

$$z = 1.96$$

The process variability is in statistical control, so we proceed directly to the $\bar{x}$-chart. The control limits are

$$UCL_{\bar{x}} = \bar{\bar{x}} + z\sigma/\sqrt{n} = 5.0 + 1.96(1.5)/\sqrt{6} = 6.20 \text{ minutes}$$

$$LCL_{\bar{x}} = \bar{\bar{x}} - z\sigma/\sqrt{n} = 5.0 - 1.96(1.5)/\sqrt{6} = 3.80 \text{ minutes}$$

The value for z can be obtained in the following way. The normal distribution table (see Appendix 1) gives the proportion of the total area under the normal curve from $-\infty$ to z. We want a type I error of 5 percent, or 2.5 percent of the curve above the UCL and 2.5 percent below the LCL. Consequently, we need to find the z value in the table that leaves only 2.5 percent in the upper portion of the normal curve (or 0.9750 in the table). The value is 1.96. The two new samples are below the LCL of the chart, implying that the average time to serve a customer has dropped. Assignable causes should be explored to see what caused the improvement.

DECISION POINT

Management studied the time period over which the samples were taken and found that the supervisor of the process was experimenting with some new procedures. Management decided to make the new procedures a permanent part of the customer service process. After all employees were trained in the new procedures, new samples were taken and the control chart reconstructed.

Control Charts for Attributes

Two charts commonly used for performance measures based on attributes measures are the p- and c-chart. The p-chart is used for controlling the proportion of defects generated by the process. The c-chart is used for controlling the number of defects when more than one defect can be present in a service or product.

p-chart

A chart used for controlling the proportion of defective services or products generated by the process.

***p*-Charts**   The **p-chart** is a commonly used control chart for attributes. The performance characteristic is counted rather than measured, and the entire service or item can be declared good or defective. For example, in the banking industry, the attributes counted might be the number of nonendorsed deposits or the number of incorrect financial statements sent to customers. The method involves selecting a random sample, inspecting each item in it, and calculating the sample proportion defective, p, which is the number of defective units divided by the sample size.

Sampling for a p-chart involves a "yes/no" decision: The process output either is or is not defective. The underlying statistical distribution is based on the binomial distribution. However, for large sample sizes, the normal distribution provides a good approximation to it. The standard deviation of the distribution of proportion defectives, σ_p, is

$$\sigma_p = \sqrt{\bar{p}(1 - \bar{p})/n}$$

where

n = sample size
$\bar{p}$ = central line on the chart, which can be either the historical average population proportion defective or a target value

We can use σ_p to arrive at the upper and lower control limits for a p-chart:

$$\text{UCL}_p = \bar{p} + z\sigma_p \quad \text{and} \quad \text{LCL}_p = \bar{p} - z\sigma_p$$

where

z = normal deviate (number of standard deviations from the average)

The chart is used in the following way. Periodically, a random sample of size n is taken, and the number of defective services or products is counted. The number of defectives is divided by the sample size to get a sample proportion defective, p, which is plotted on the chart. When a sample proportion defective falls outside the control limits, the analyst assumes that the proportion defective generated by the process has changed and searches for the assignable cause. Observations falling below the LCL_p indicate that the process may actually have improved. The analyst may find no assignable cause because it is always possible that an out-of-control proportion occurred randomly. However, if the analyst discovers assignable causes, those sample data should not be used to calculate the control limits for the chart.

| **EXAMPLE 3** | **Using a p-Chart to Monitor a Process** |

The operations manager of the booking services department of Hometown Bank is concerned about the number of wrong customer account numbers recorded by Hometown personnel. Each week a random sample of 2,500 deposits is taken, and the number of incorrect account numbers is recorded. The results for the past 12 weeks are shown in the following table. Is the booking process out of statistical control? Use three-sigma control limits, which will provide a Type I error of 0.26 percent.

Sample Number	Wrong Account Numbers	Sample Number	Wrong Account Numbers
1	15	7	24
2	12	8	7
3	19	9	10
4	2	10	17
5	19	11	15
6	4	12	3
			Total 147

SOLUTION

Step 1: Using this sample data to calculate $\bar{p}$

$$\bar{p} = \frac{\text{Total defectives}}{\text{Total number of observations}} = \frac{147}{12(2,500)} = 0.0049$$

$$\sigma_p = \sqrt{\bar{p}(1-\bar{p})/n} = \sqrt{0.0049(1-0.0049)/2,500} = 0.0014$$

$$\text{UCL}_p = \bar{p} + z\sigma_p = 0.0049 + 3(0.0014) = 0.0091$$

$$\text{LCL}_p = \bar{p} - z\sigma_p = 0.0049 - 3(0.0014) = 0.0007$$

Step 2: Calculate each sample proportion defective. For sample 1, the proportion of defectives is $15/2,500 = 0.0060$.

Step 3: Plot each sample proportion defective on the chart, as shown in Figure 12.

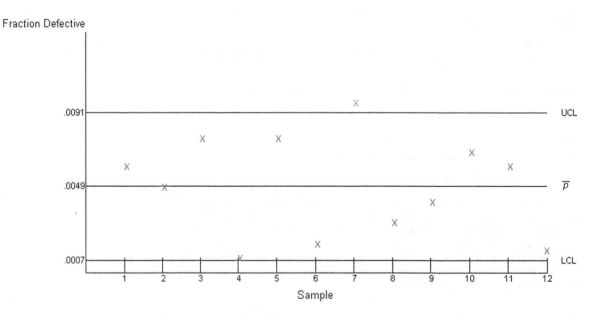

Fraction Defective

.0091 — UCL

.0049 — $\bar{p}$

.0007 — LCL

Sample

▲ **FIGURE 12**
The *p*-Chart from POM
for Windows for Wrong
Account Numbers,
Showing that Sample 7
Is Out of Control

Sample 7 exceeds the UCL; thus, the process is out of control and the reasons for the poor performance that week should be determined.

DECISION POINT

Management explored the circumstances when sample 7 was taken. The encoding machine used to print the account numbers on the checks was defective that week. The following week the machine was repaired; however, the recommended preventive maintenance on the machine was not performed for months prior to the failure. Management reviewed the performance of the maintenance department and instituted changes to the maintenance procedures for the encoding machine. After the problem was corrected, an analyst recalculated the control limits using the data without sample 7. Subsequent weeks were sampled, and the booking process was determined to be in statistical control. Consequently, the *p*-chart provides a tool to indicate when a process needs adjustment.

***c*-chart**

A chart used for controlling the number of defects when more than one defect can be present in a service or product.

***c*-Charts** Sometimes services or products have more than one defect. For example, a roll of carpeting may have several defects, such as tufted or discolored fibers or stains from the production process. Other situations in which more than one defect may occur include accidents at a particular intersection, bubbles in a television picture face panel, and complaints from a patron at a hotel. When management is interested in reducing the number of defects per unit or service encounter, another type of control chart, the ***c*-chart**, is useful.

The underlying sampling distribution for a *c*-chart is the Poisson distribution. The Poisson distribution is based on the assumption that defects occur over a continuous region on the surface of a product or a continuous time interval during the provision of a service. It further assumes that the probability of two or more defects at any one location on the surface or at any instant of time is negligible. The mean of the distribution is $\bar{c}$ and the standard deviation is $\sqrt{\bar{c}}$. A useful tactic is to use the normal approximation to the Poisson so that the central line of the chart is $\bar{c}$ and the control limits are

$$\text{UCL}_c = \bar{c} + z\sqrt{\bar{c}} \quad \text{and} \quad \text{LCL}_c = \bar{c} - z\sqrt{\bar{c}}$$

EXAMPLE 4	Using a *c*-Chart to Monitor Defects per Unit

The Woodland Paper Company produces paper for the newspaper industry. As a final step in the process, the paper passes through a machine that measures various product quality characteristics. When the paper production process is in control, it averages 20 defects per roll.

a. Set up a control chart for the number of defects per roll. For this example, use two-sigma control limits.

b. Five rolls had the following number of defects: 16, 21, 17, 22, and 24, respectively. The sixth roll, using pulp from a different supplier, had 5 defects. Is the paper production process in control?

MyOMLab

Tutor 5.3 in MyOMLab provides a new example to practice the use of the *c*-chart.

SOLUTION

a. The average number of defects per roll is 20. Therefore

$$UCL_c = \bar{c} + z\sqrt{\bar{c}} = 20 + 2(\sqrt{20}) = 28.94$$

$$LCL_c = \bar{c} - z\sqrt{\bar{c}} = 20 - 2(\sqrt{20}) = 11.06$$

The control chart is shown in Figure 13.

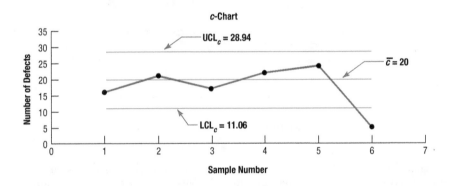

c-Chart

◄ **FIGURE 13**

The *c*-Chart from the *OM Explorer c-Chart* Solver for Defects per Roll of Paper

b. Because the first five rolls had defects that fell within the control limits, the process is still in control. The sixth roll's five defects, however, is below than the LCL, and therefore, the process is technically "out of control." The control chart indicates that something good has happened.

DECISION POINT

The supplier for the first five samples has been used by Woodland Paper for many years. The supplier for the sixth sample is new to the company. Management decided to continue using the new supplier for a while, monitoring the number of defects to see whether it stays low. If the number remains below the LCL for 20 consecutive samples, management will make the switch permanent and recalculate the control chart parameters.

Process Capability

Statistical process control techniques help managers achieve and maintain a process distribution that does not change in terms of its mean and variance. The control limits on the control charts signal when the mean or variability of the process changes. However, a process that is in statistical control may not be producing services or products according to their design specifications because the control limits are based on the mean and variability of the *sampling distribution*, not the design specifications. **Process capability** refers to the ability of the process to meet the design specifications for a service or product. Design specifications often are expressed as a **nominal value**, or target, and a **tolerance**, or allowance above or below the nominal value.

For example, the administrator of an intensive care unit lab might have a nominal value for the turnaround time of results to the attending physicians of 25 minutes and a tolerance of ±5 minutes because of the need for speed under life-threatening conditions. The tolerance gives an *upper specification* of 30 minutes and a *lower specification* of 20 minutes. The lab process must be capable of providing the results of analyses within these specifications; otherwise, it will produce a certain proportion of "defects." The administrator is also interested in detecting occurrences of turnaround times of less than 20 minutes because something might be learned that can be built into the lab process in the future. For the present, the physicians are pleased with results that arrive within 20 to 30 minutes.

nominal value

A target for design specifications.

process capability

The ability of the process to meet the design specifications for a service or product.

tolerance

An allowance above or below the nominal value.

Defining Process Capability

Figure 14 shows the relationship between a process distribution and the upper and lower specifications for the lab process turnaround time under two conditions. In Figure 14(a), the process is capable because the extremes of the process distribution fall within the upper and lower specifications. In Figure 14(b), the process is not capable because the lab process produces too many reports with long turnaround times.

FIGURE 14 ▶
The Relationship Between a Process Distribution and Upper and Lower Specifications

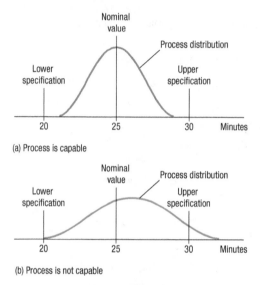

Figure 14 shows clearly why managers are so concerned with reducing process variability. The less variability—represented by lower standard deviations—the less frequently bad output is produced. Figure 15 shows what reducing variability implies for a process distribution that is a normal probability distribution. The firm with two-sigma performance (the specification limits equal the process distribution mean ± 2 standard deviations) produces 4.56 percent defects, or 45,600 defects per million. The firm with four-sigma performance produces only 0.0063 percent defects, or 63 defects per million. Finally, the firm with six-sigma performance produces only 0.0000002 percent defects, or 0.002 defects per million.[1]

How can a manager determine quantitatively whether a process is capable? Two measures commonly are used in practice to assess the capability of a process: the process capability index and the process capability ratio.

FIGURE 15 ▼
Effects of Reducing Variability on Process Capability

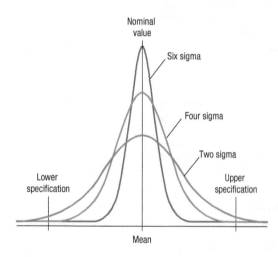

Process Capability Index The **process capability index**, C_{pk}, is defined as

$$C_{pk} = \text{Minimum of} \left[\frac{\bar{\bar{x}} - \text{Lower specification}}{3\sigma}, \frac{\text{Upper specification} - \bar{\bar{x}}}{3\sigma} \right]$$

where

$$\sigma = \text{standard deviation of the process distribution}$$

The process capability index measures how well the process is centered as well as whether the variability is acceptable. As a general rule, most values of any process distribution fall within ± 3 standard deviations of the mean. Consequently, ± 3 standard deviations is used as the benchmark. Because the process capability index is concerned with how well the process distribution is centered relative to the specifications, it checks to see if the process average is at least three standard deviations

---

[1]Our discussion assumes that the process distribution has no assignable causes. Six Sigma programs, however, define defect performance with the assumption that the process average has moved 1.5 standard deviations. In such a case, there would be 3.4 defects per million. See **www.isixsigma.com** for the rationale behind that assumption.

from the upper and lower specifications. We take the minimum of the two ratios because it gives the *worst-case* situation.

The process capability index must be compared to a critical value to judge whether a process is capable. Firms striving to achieve three-sigma performance use a critical value for the ratio of 1.0. A firm targeting four-sigma performance will use 1.33 (or 4/3), a firm targeting five-sigma performance will use 1.67 (or 5/3), and a firm striving for six-sigma performance will use 2.00 (or 6/3). Processes producing services or products with less than three-sigma performance will have C_{pk} values less than 1.0.

If a process passes the process capability index test, we can declare the process is capable. Suppose a firm desires its processes to produce at the level of four-sigma performance. If C_{pk} is greater than or equal to the critical value of 1.33, we can say the process is capable. If C_{pk} is less than the critical value, either the process average is too close to one of the tolerance limits and is generating defective output, or the process variability is too large. To find out whether the variability is the culprit, we need another test.

Process Capability Ratio If a process fails the process capability *index* test, we need a quick test to see if the process variability is causing the problem. If a process is *capable*, it has a process distribution whose extreme values fall within the upper and lower specifications for a service or product. For example, if the process distribution is normal, 99.74 percent of the values fall within ± 3 standard deviations. In other words, the range of values of the quality measure generated by a process is approximately 6 standard deviations of the process distribution. Hence, if a process is capable at the three-sigma level, the difference between the upper and lower specification, called the *tolerance width*, must be greater than 6 standard deviations. The **process capability ratio**, C_p, is defined as

$$C_p = \frac{\text{Upper specification} - \text{Lower specification}}{6\sigma}$$

Suppose management wants four-sigma capability in their processes, and a process just failed the process capability index test at that level. A C_p value of 1.33, say, implies that the variability of the process is at the level of four-sigma quality and that the process is capable of consistently producing outputs within specifications, assuming that the process is centered. Because C_p passed the test, but C_{pk} did not, we can assume that the problem is that the process is not centered adequately.

Using Continuous Improvement to Determine the Capability of a Process

To determine the capability of a process to produce outputs within the tolerances, use the following steps.

Step 1. Collect data on the process output, and calculate the mean and the standard deviation of the process output distribution.

Step 2. Use the data from the process distribution to compute process control charts, such as an $\bar{x}$- and an R-chart.

Step 3. Take a series of at least 20 consecutive random samples of size n from the process and plot the results on the control charts. If the sample statistics are within the control limits of the charts, the process is in statistical control. If the process is not in statistical control, look for assignable causes and eliminate them. Recalculate the mean and standard deviation of the process distribution and the control limits for the charts. Continue until the process is in statistical control.

Step 4. Calculate the process capability *index*. If the results are acceptable, the process is capable and document any changes made to the process; continue to monitor the output by using the control charts. If the results are unacceptable, calculate the process capability *ratio*. If the results are acceptable, the process variability is fine and management should focus on centering the process. If the results of the process capability ratio are unacceptable, management should focus on reducing the variability in the process until it passes the test. As changes are made, recalculate the mean and standard deviation of the process distribution and the control limits for the charts and return to step 3.

Quality Engineering

Successful quality performance is often more than process improvement; it also involves service/product design. Originated by Genichi Taguchi, **quality engineering** is an approach that involves

---

process capability index, C_{pk}

An index that measures the potential for a process to generate defective outputs relative to either upper or lower specifications.

process capability ratio, C_p

The tolerance width divided by six standard deviations.

quality engineering

An approach originated by Genichi Taguchi that involves combining engineering and statistical methods to reduce costs and improve quality by optimizing product design and manufacturing processes.

EXAMPLE 5	Assessing the Process Capability of the Intensive Care Unit Lab

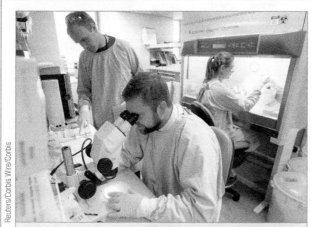

A doctor examines a specimen through his microscope in a lab at St. Vincent's Hospital.

Reuters/Corbis Wire/Corbis

The intensive care unit lab process has an average turnaround time of 26.2 minutes and a standard deviation of 1.35 minutes. The nominal value for this service is 25 minutes with an upper specification limit of 30 minutes and a lower specification limit of 20 minutes. The administrator of the lab wants to have four-sigma performance for her lab. Is the lab process capable of this level of performance?

SOLUTION

The administrator began by taking a quick check to see if the process is capable by applying the process capability index:

$$\text{Lower specification calculation} = \frac{26.2 - 20.0}{3(1.35)} = 1.53$$

$$\text{Upper specification calculation} = \frac{30.0 - 26.2}{3(1.35)} = 0.94$$

$$C_{pk} = \text{Minimum of } [1.53, 0.94] = 0.94$$

Since the target value for four-sigma performance is 1.33, the process capability index told her that the process was not capable. However, she did not know whether the problem was the variability of the process, the centering of the process, or both. The options available to improve the process depended on what is wrong.

She next checked the process variability with the process capability ratio:

$$C_p = \frac{30.0 - 20.0}{6(1.35)} = 1.23$$

The process variability did not meet the four-sigma target of 1.33. Consequently, she initiated a study to see where variability was introduced into the process. Two activities, report preparation and specimen slide preparation, were identified as having inconsistent procedures. These procedures were modified to provide consistent performance. New data were collected and the average turnaround was now 26.1 minutes with a standard deviation of 1.20 minutes. She now had the process variability at the four-sigma level of performance, as indicated by the process capability ratio:

$$C_p = \frac{30.0 - 20.0}{6(1.20)} = 1.39$$

However, the process capability index indicated additional problems to resolve:

$$C_{pk} = \text{Minimum of } \left[\frac{(26.1 - 20.0)}{3(1.20)}, \frac{(30.0 - 26.1)}{3(1.20)} \right] = 1.08$$

DECISION POINT

The lab process was still not at the level of four-sigma performance on turnaround time. The lab administrator searched for the causes of the off-center turnaround time distribution. She discovered periodic backlogs at a key piece of testing equipment. Acquiring a second machine provided the capacity to reduce the turnaround times to four-sigma capability.

MyOMLab

Active Model 5.3 in MyOMLab provides additional insight on the process capability problem at the intensive care unit lab.

MyOMLab

Tutor 5.4 in MyOMLab provides a new example to practice the process capability measures.

quality loss function

The rationale that a service or product that barely conforms to the specifications is more like a defective service or product than a perfect one.

combining engineering and statistical methods to reduce costs and improve quality by optimizing product design and manufacturing processes. Taguchi believes that unwelcome costs are associated with *any* deviation from a quality characteristic's target value. Taguchi's view is that the **quality loss function** is zero when the quality characteristic of the service or product is exactly on the target value, and that the quality loss function value rises exponentially as the quality characteristic gets closer to the specification limits. The rationale is that a service or product that barely conforms to the specifications is more like a defective service or product than a perfect one. Figure 16 shows Taguchi's quality loss function schematically. Taguchi concluded that managers should continually search for ways to reduce *all* variability from the target value in the production process and not be content with merely adhering to specification limits. See **http://elsmar.com/Taguchi.html** for a detailed discussion and animation of the Taguchi Loss Function.

International Quality Documentation Standards

Once a company has gone through the effort of making its processes capable, it must document its level of quality so as to better market its services or products. This documentation of quality is especially important in international trade. However, if each country had its own set of standards, companies selling in international markets would have difficulty complying with quality documentation standards in each country where they did business. To overcome this problem, the International Organization for Standardization devised a family of standards called ISO 9000 for companies doing business in the European Union. Subsequently, ISO 14000 was devised for environmental management systems and ISO 26000 for guidance on social responsibility.

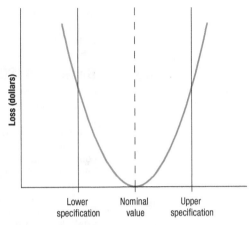

▲ **FIGURE 16**
Taguchi's Quality Loss Function

The ISO 9001:2008 Documentation Standards

ISO 9001:2008 is the latest update of the ISO 9000 standards governing documentation of a quality program. According to the International Organization for Standardization, the ISO 9001:2008 standards address *quality management* by specifying what the firm does to fulfill the customer's quality requirements and applicable regulatory requirements, while aiming to enhance customer satisfaction and achieve continual improvement of its performance in pursuit of these objectives. Companies become certified by proving to a qualified external examiner that they comply with all the requirements. Once certified, companies are listed in a directory so that potential customers can see which companies are certified and to what level. Compliance with ISO 9001:2008 standards says *nothing* about the actual quality of a product. Rather, it indicates to customers that companies can provide documentation to support whatever claims they make about quality. As of 2009, more than 1 million organizations worldwide have been certified in the ISO 9000 family of documentation standards.

ISO 9001:2008

A set of standards governing documentation of a quality program.

ISO 14000:2004 Environmental Management System

The **ISO 14000:2004** standards require documentation of a firm's environmental program. According to the International Organization for Standardization, the ISO 14000:2004 family addresses *environmental management* by specifying what the firm does to minimize harmful effects on the environment caused by its activities, and to achieve continual improvement of its environmental performance. The documentation standards require participating companies to keep track of their raw materials use and their generation, treatment, and disposal of hazardous wastes. Although not specifying what each company is allowed to emit, the standards require companies to prepare a plan for ongoing improvement in their environmental performance. ISO 14000:2004 covers a number of areas, including the following:

ISO 14000:2004

Documentation standards that require participating companies to keep track of their raw materials use and their generation, treatment, and disposal of hazardous wastes.

- *Environmental Management System.* Requires a plan to improve performance in resource use and pollutant output.
- *Environmental Performance Evaluation.* Specifies guidelines for the certification of companies.
- *Environmental Labeling.* Defines terms such as *recyclable, energy efficient,* and *safe for the ozone layer.*
- *Life-Cycle Assessment.* Evaluates the lifetime environmental impact from the manufacture, use, and disposal of a product.

To maintain their certification, companies must be inspected by outside, private auditors on a regular basis. As of 2010, more than 200,000 organizations in 155 countries have been certified for ISO 14000.

ISO 26000:2010 Social Responsibility Guidelines

The **ISO 26000:2010** guidelines, according to the International Organization for Standards, provide harmonized, globally relevant guidance on social responsibility for private and public sector organizations based on international consensus among experts. A firm does not get certified in ISO 26000; the guidelines are voluntary and are intended to promote best practice in ethical behavior in business. The seven core subjects of social responsibility covered in the guidelines are (1) human rights, (2) labor practices, (3) the environment, (4) fair operating practices,

ISO 26000:2010

International guidelines for organizational social responsibility.

(5) consumer issues, (6) community involvement and development, and (7) the organization. In this way the international community is encouraging ethical business behavior between businesses and consumers.

Benefits of ISO Certification

Completing the certification process can take as long as 18 months and involve many hours of management and employee time. The cost of certification can exceed $1 million for large companies. Despite the expense and commitment involved in ISO certification, it bestows significant external and internal benefits. The external benefits come from the potential sales advantage that companies in compliance have. Companies looking for a supplier will more likely select a company that has demonstrated compliance with ISO documentation standards, all other factors being equal. Consequently, more and more firms are seeking certification to gain a competitive advantage.

Internal benefits can be substantial. Registered companies report an average of 48 percent increased profitability and 76 percent improvement in marketing. The British Standards Institute, a leading third-party auditor, estimates that most ISO 9000-registered companies experience a 10 percent reduction in the cost of producing a product because of the quality improvements they make while striving to meet the documentation requirements. Certification in ISO 9001:2008 requires a company to analyze and document its procedures, which is necessary in any event for implementing continuous improvement, employee involvement, and similar programs. The guidelines and requirements of the ISO documentation standards provide companies with a jump-start in pursuing TQM programs.

Baldrige Performance Excellence Program

Baldrige Performance Excellence Program

A program named for the late secretary of commerce, Malcolm Baldrige, who was a strong proponent of enhancing quality as a means of reducing the trade deficit; organizations vie for an award that promotes, recognizes, and publicizes quality strategies and achievements.

Regardless of where a company does business, it is clear that all organizations have to produce high-quality products and services if they are to be competitive. To emphasize that point, in August 1987 the U.S. Congress signed into law the Malcolm Baldrige National Quality Improvement Act, creating the Malcolm Baldrige National Quality Award, which is now entitled the **Baldrige Performance Excellence Program** (www.quality.nist.gov). Named for the late secretary of commerce, who was a strong proponent of enhancing quality as a means of reducing the trade deficit, the award promotes, recognizes, and publicizes quality strategies and achievements.

The application and review process for the Baldrige award is rigorous. However, the act of preparing the application itself is often a major benefit to organizations because it helps firms define what *quality* means for them. According to the U.S. Commerce Department's National Institute of Standards and Technology (NIST), investing in quality principles and performance excellence pays off in increased productivity, satisfied employees and customers, and improved profitability, both for customers and investors. The seven major criteria for the award are the following:

1. *Leadership.* Describes how senior leaders' actions guide and sustain the organization and how they communicate with the workforce and encourage high performance.

2. *Strategic Planning.* Describes how the organization establishes its strategy to address its strategic challenges, leverage its strategic advantages, and summarizes the organization's key strategic objectives and their related goals.

3. *Customer Focus.* Describes how the organization determines its service or product offerings and the mechanisms to support the customers' use of them.

4. *Measurement, Analysis, and Knowledge Management.* Describes how the organization measures, analyzes, reviews, and improves its performance through the use of data and information at all levels of the organization.

5. *Workforce Focus.* Describes how the organization engages, compensates, and rewards its workers and how they are developed to achieve high performance.

6. *Operations Focus.* Describes how the organization designs its work systems and determines its key processes to deliver customer value, prepare for potential emergencies, and achieve organizational success and sustainability.

7. *Results.* Describe the organization's performance and improvement in five categories: products and processes, customer focus, workforce focus, leadership and governance, and financial and market.

Customer satisfaction underpins these seven criteria. Criterion 7, Results, is given the most weight in selecting winners.

LEARNING GOALS IN REVIEW

1 **Define the four major costs of quality.** See the section "Costs of Quality".

2 **Describe the role of ethics in the quality of services and products.** We explain how deceptive business practices can affect a customer's experiences and why the costs of quality should be balanced with ethical considerations in the section "Ethics and Quality".

3 **Explain the basic principles of TQM programs.** See the section "Total Quality Management". Focus on the five customer definitions of quality, Managerial Practice 1, which shows how one company matched processes to the five definitions, the importance of employee involvement, and how continuous improvement works. The key figures are Figures 1 and 2.

4 **Explain the basic principles of Six Sigma Programs.** We have summarized the essence of these important programs in the section "Six Sigma". Be sure to understand Figure 3, which shows the goals of Six Sigma, and Figure 4, which provides the improvement model. Figure 5 shows how TQM or Six Sigma works in a supply chain through the tactic of acceptance sampling.

5 **Describe how to construct control charts and use them to determine whether a process is out of statistical control.** See the section "Statistical Process Control". Understanding Figures 6 and 7 is key to understanding the methods to follow. The section "Statistical Process Control Methods", shows you how to determine if a process is in statistical control. Study Examples 1 to 5 as well as Solved Problems 1 to 3.

6 **Describe how to determine whether a process is capable of producing a service or product to specifications.** The major take-away in the chapter is found in the section "Process Capability". Be sure you understand Figures 4 and 5; study Example 5 and Solved Problem 4.

MyOMLab helps and assesses students with 16 problems on *x*-bar and *R*-bar Charts, *p*-charts, *c*-Charts, and Process Capability.

MyOMLab Resources	Titles	Link to the Book
Video	*Starwood: Process Performance and Quality*	Costs of Quality; Total Quality Management; Six Sigma
	Christchurch Parkroyal TQM	Costs of Quality; Total Quality Management
Active Model	5.1 *x*-bar and *R*-Charts	Control Charts for Variables; Example 1
	5.2 *p*-Chart	Control Charts for Attributes; Example 3
	5.3 Process Capability	Process Capability; Example 5
OM Explorer Solvers	*c*-Charts	Control Charts for Attributes; Example 4; Figure 13; Solved Problem 3
	p-Charts	Control Charts for Attributes; Example 3; Solved Problem 2
	Process Capability	Process Capability; Example 5; Solved Problem 4
	R- and *x*-bar Charts	Control Charts for Variables; Example 1; Figure 10 and Figure 11; Solved Problem 1
OM Explorer Tutors	5.1 *R*- and *x*-bar Charts	Control Charts for Variables; Example 1
	5.2 *p*-Charts	Control Charts for Attributes; Example 3
	5.3 *c*-Charts	Control Charts for Attributes; Example 4
	5.4 Process Capability	Process Capability; Example 5
POM for Windows	*p*-Charts	Control Charts for Attributes; Example 3; Figure 12; Solved Problem 2
	x-bar Charts	Control Charts for Variables; Example 1; Example 2; Solved Problem 1
	c-Charts	Control Charts for Attributes; Example 4; Solved Problem 3
	Process Capability	Process Capability; Example 5; Solved Problem 4
	Acceptance Sampling	Acceptance Sampling
SimQuick Simulation Exercises	Circuit Board Process	Six-Sigma Improvement Model

MyOMLab Resources	Titles	Link to the Book
Tutor Exercises	5.1 x-bar and R-Chart with Target Weight of 7.04 oz.	Control Charts for Variables
	5.2 p-Chart When Changes in Sample Values	Control Charts for Attributes
	5.3 Process Capability with a Change in Process Average and Variability	Process Capability
Virtual Tours	1. Steinway Factory, Verne O. Powell Flutes	Total Quality Management; Six Sigma
	2. Beach Beat Surfboards	Total Quality Management
MyOMLab Supplements	G. Acceptance Sampling Plans	Acceptance Sampling
Internet Exercise	1. National Institute of Standards and Technology, and International Organization for Standardization	Baldrige Performance Excellence Award International Quality Documentation Standards
	2. SAS Scandinavian Airline	Total Quality Management
	3. Jack in the Box	Customer Satisfaction
	4. Maybach	Customer Satisfaction
	5. Bureau of Transportation Statistics	Statistical Process Control
Key Equations		
Image Library		

Key Equations

1. Sample mean: $\bar{x} = \dfrac{\sum\limits_{i=1}^{n} x_i}{n}$

2. Standard deviation of a sample:

$$\sigma = \sqrt{\frac{\sum\limits_{i=1}^{n}(x_i - \bar{x})^2}{n-1}} \quad \text{or} \quad \sigma = \sqrt{\frac{\sum\limits_{i=1}^{n} x_i^2 - \dfrac{(\sum x_i)^2}{n}}{n-1}}$$

3. Control limits for variable process control charts

   a. R-chart, range of sample:

   $$\text{Upper control limit} = \text{UCL}_R = D_4\bar{R}$$
   $$\text{Lower control limit} = \text{LCL}_R = D_3\bar{R}$$

   b. $\bar{x}$-chart, sample mean:

   $$\text{Upper control limit} = \text{UCL}_{\bar{x}} = \bar{\bar{x}} + A_2\bar{R}$$
   $$\text{Lower control limit} = \text{LCL}_{\bar{x}} = \bar{\bar{x}} - A_2\bar{R}$$

   c. When the standard deviation of the process distribution, σ, is known:

   $$\text{Upper control limit} = \text{UCL}_{\bar{x}} = \bar{\bar{x}} + z\sigma_{\bar{x}}$$
   $$\text{Lower control limit} = \text{LCL}_{\bar{x}} = \bar{\bar{x}} - z\sigma_{\bar{x}}$$

   where

   $$\sigma_{\bar{x}} = \frac{\sigma}{\sqrt{n}}$$

4. Control limits for attribute process control charts

   a. p-chart, proportion defective:

   $$\text{Upper control limit} = \text{UCL}_p = \bar{p} + z\sigma_p$$
   $$\text{Lower control limit} = \text{LCL}_p = \bar{p} - z\sigma_p$$

   where

   $$\sigma_p = \sqrt{\bar{p}(1 - \bar{p})/n}$$

   b. c-chart, number of defects:

   $$\text{Upper control limit} = \text{UCL}_c = \bar{c} + z\sqrt{\bar{c}}$$
   $$\text{Lower control limit} = \text{LCL}_c = \bar{c} - z\sqrt{\bar{c}}$$

5. Process capability index:

   $$C_{pk} = \text{Minimum of} \left[\frac{\bar{\bar{x}} - \text{Lower specification}}{3\sigma}, \frac{\text{Upper specification} - \bar{\bar{x}}}{3\sigma} \right]$$

6. Process capability ratio:

   $$C_p = \frac{\text{Upper specification} - \text{Lower specification}}{6\sigma}$$

Key Terms

acceptable quality level (AQL)	internal failure costs	quality loss function
acceptance sampling	ISO 9001:2008	R-chart
appraisal costs	ISO 14000:2004	sample size
assignable causes of variation	ISO 26000:2010	sampling plan
attributes	Master Black Belt	self-managed team
Baldrige Performance Excellence	nominal value	Six Sigma
Program	p-chart	special-purpose teams
Black Belt	plan-do-study-act cycle	statistical process control (SPC)
c-chart	prevention costs	teams
common causes of variation	process capability	tolerance
continuous improvement	process capability index, C_{pk}	total quality management (TQM)
control chart	process capability ratio, C_p	type I error
defect	quality	type II error
employee empowerment	quality at the source	variables
external failure costs	quality circles	warranty 159
Green Belt	quality engineering	$\bar{x}$-chart

Solved Problem 1

The Watson Electric Company produces incandescent lightbulbs. The following data on the number of lumens for 40-watt lightbulbs were collected when the process was in control.

	OBSERVATION			
Sample	1	2	3	4
1	604	612	588	600
2	597	601	607	603
3	581	570	585	592
4	620	605	595	588
5	590	614	608	604

a. Calculate control limits for an R-chart and an $\bar{x}$-chart.

b. Since these data were collected, some new employees were hired. A new sample obtained the following readings: 570, 603, 623, and 583. Is the process still in control?

SOLUTION

a. To calculate $\bar{x}$, compute the mean for each sample. To calculate R, subtract the lowest value in the sample from the highest value in the sample. For example, for sample 1,

$$\bar{x} = \frac{604 + 612 + 588 + 600}{4} = 601$$

$$R = 612 - 588 = 24$$

Sample	$\bar{x}$	R
1	601	24
2	602	10
3	582	22
4	602	32
5	604	24
Total	2,991	112
Average	$\bar{\bar{x}} = 598.2$	$\bar{R} = 22.4$

The R-chart control limits are

$$\text{UCL}_R = D_4 \bar{R} = 2.282(22.4) = 51.12$$
$$\text{LCL}_R = D_3 \bar{R} = 0(22.4) = 0$$

The $\bar{x}$-chart control limits are

$$\text{UCL}_{\bar{x}} = \bar{\bar{x}} + A_2 \bar{R} = 598.2 + 0.729(22.4) = 614.53$$
$$\text{LCL}_{\bar{x}} = \bar{\bar{x}} - A_2 \bar{R} = 598.2 - 0.729(22.4) = 581.87$$

b. First check to see whether the variability is still in control based on the new data. The range is 53 (or 623 – 570), which is outside the UCL for the R-chart. Since the process variability is out of control, it is meaningless to test for the process average using the current estimate for $\bar{R}$. A search for assignable causes inducing excessive variability must be conducted.

Solved Problem 2

The data processing department of the Arizona Bank has five data entry clerks. Each working day their supervisor verifies the accuracy of a random sample of 250 records. A record containing one or more errors is considered defective and must be redone. The results of the last 30 samples are shown in the table. All were checked to make sure that none was out of control.

Sample	Number of Defective Records	Sample	Number of Defective Records	Sample	Number of Defective Records	Sample	Number of Defective Records
1	7	9	6	17	12	24	7
2	5	10	13	18	4	25	13
3	19	11	18	19	6	26	10
4	10	12	5	20	11	27	14
5	11	13	16	21	17	28	6
6	8	14	4	22	12	29	11
7	12	15	11	23	6	30	9
8	9	16	8			Total	300

a. Based on these historical data, set up a *p*-chart using $z = 3$.

b. Samples for the next 4 days showed the following:

Sample	Number of Defective Records
Tues	17
Wed	15
Thurs	22
Fri	21

What is the supervisor's assessment of the data-entry process likely to be?

SOLUTION

a. From the table, the supervisor knows that the total number of defective records is 300 out of a total sample of 7,500 [or 30(250)]. Therefore, the central line of the chart is

$$\bar{p} = \frac{300}{7,500} = 0.04$$

The control limits are

$$\text{UCL}_p = \bar{p} + z\sqrt{\frac{\bar{p}(1 - \bar{p})}{n}} = 0.04 + 3\sqrt{\frac{0.04(0.96)}{250}} = 0.077$$

$$\text{LCL}_p = \bar{p} - z\sqrt{\frac{\bar{p}(1 - \bar{p})}{n}} = 0.04 - 3\sqrt{\frac{0.04(0.96)}{250}} = 0.003$$

b. Samples for the next 4 days showed the following:

Sample	Number of Defective Records	Proportion
Tues	17	0.068
Wed	15	0.060
Thurs	22	0.088
Fri	21	0.084

Samples for Thursday and Friday are out of control. The supervisor should look for the problem and, upon identifying it, take corrective action.

Solved Problem 3

The Minnow County Highway Safety Department monitors accidents at the intersection of Routes 123 and 14. Accidents at the intersection have averaged three per month.

a. Which type of control chart should be used? Construct a control chart with three-sigma control limits.

b. Last month, seven accidents occurred at the intersection. Is this sufficient evidence to justify a claim that something has changed at the intersection?

SOLUTION

a. The safety department cannot determine the number of accidents that did *not* occur, so it has no way to compute a proportion defective at the intersection. Therefore, the administrators must use a *c*-chart for which

$$\text{UCL}_c = \bar{c} + z\sqrt{\bar{c}} = 3 + 3\sqrt{3} = 8.20$$

$$\text{LCL}_c = \bar{c} - z\sqrt{\bar{c}} = 3 - 3\sqrt{3} = -2.196, \text{ adjusted to } 0$$

There cannot be a negative number of accidents, so the LCL in this case is adjusted to zero.

b. The number of accidents last month falls within the UCL and LCL of the chart. We conclude that no assignable causes are present and that the increase in accidents was due to chance.

Solved Problem 4

Pioneer Chicken advertises "lite" chicken with 30 percent fewer calories. (The pieces are 33 percent smaller.) The process average distribution for "lite" chicken breasts is 420 calories, with a standard deviation of the population of 25 calories. Pioneer randomly takes samples of six chicken breasts to measure calorie content.

a. Design an $\bar{x}$-chart using the process standard deviation. Use three-sigma limits.

b. The product design calls for the average chicken breast to contain 400 ± 100 calories. Calculate the process capability index (target = 1.33) and the process capability ratio. Interpret the results.

SOLUTION

a. For the process standard deviation of 25 calories, the standard deviation of the sample mean is

$$\sigma_{\bar{x}} = \frac{\sigma}{\sqrt{n}} = \frac{25}{\sqrt{6}} = 10.2 \text{ calories}$$

$$\text{UCL}_{\bar{x}} = \bar{\bar{x}} + z\sigma_{\bar{x}} = 420 + 3(10.2) = 450.6 \text{ calories}$$

$$\text{LCL}_{\bar{x}} = \bar{\bar{x}} - z\sigma_{\bar{x}} = 420 - 3(10.2) = 389.4 \text{ calories}$$

b. The process capability index is

$$C_{pk} = \text{Minimum of} \left[\frac{\bar{\bar{x}} - \text{Lower specification}}{3\sigma}, \frac{\text{Upper specification} - \bar{\bar{x}}}{3\sigma} \right]$$

$$= \text{Minimum of} \left[\frac{420 - 300}{3(25)} = 1.60, \frac{500 - 420}{3(25)} = 1.07 \right] = 1.07$$

The process capability ratio is

$$C_p = \frac{\text{Upper specification} - \text{Lower specification}}{6\sigma} = \frac{500 \text{ calories} - 300 \text{ calories}}{6(25)} = 1.33$$

Because the process capability ratio is 1.33, the process should be able to produce the product reliably within specifications. However, the process capability index is 1.07, so the current process is not centered properly for four-sigma performance. The mean of the process distribution is too close to the upper specification.

Discussion Questions

1. Consider Managerial Practice 1 and the discussion of Steinway's approach to achieving top quality. To get a better idea of the craft-oriented production process, visit **www.steinway.com/factory/tour.shtml**. However, Steinway also uses automation to produce the action mechanisms, a critical assembly in the grand pianos. Given the overall image of a Steinway piano, a very pricey hand-crafted object of beauty, what do you think of the use of automated equipment? Do you think it is a mistake to use automation in this way?

2. Recently, the Polish General Corporation, well-known for manufacturing appliances and automobile parts, initiated a $13 billion project to produce automobiles. A great deal of learning on the part of management and employees was required. Even though pressure was mounting to get a new product to market in early 2012, the production manager of the newly formed automobile division insisted on almost a year of trial runs before sales started because workers have to do their jobs 60 to 100 times before they can memorize the right sequence. The launch date was set for early 2013. What are the consequences of using this approach to enter the market with a new product?

3. Explain how unethical business practices degrade the quality of the experience a customer has with a service or product. How is the International Organization for Standardization trying to encourage ethical business behavior?

Problems

The OM Explorer and POM for Windows software is available to all students using the 10th edition of this text. Go to **www.pearsonhighered.com/krajewski** to download these computer packages. If you purchased MyOMLab, you also have access to Active Models software and significant help in doing the following problems. Check with your instructor on how best to use these resources. In many cases, the instructor wants you to understand how to do the calculations by hand. At the least, the software provides a check on your calculations. When calculations are particularly complex and the goal is interpreting the results in making decisions, the software replaces entirely the manual calculations. The software also can be a valuable resource well after your course is completed.

1. At Quickie Car Wash, the wash process is advertised to take less than 7 minutes. Consequently, management has set a target average of 390 seconds for the wash process. Suppose the average range for a sample of 9 cars is 10 seconds. Use Table 1 to establish control limits for sample means and ranges for the car wash process.

2. At Isogen Pharmaceuticals, the filling process for its asthma inhaler is set to dispense 150 milliliters (ml) of steroid solution per container. The average range for a sample of 4 containers is 3 ml. Use Table 1 to establish control limits for sample means and ranges for the filling process.

3. Garcia's Garage desires to create some colorful charts and graphs to illustrate how reliably its mechanics "get under the hood and fix the problem." The historic average for the proportion of customers that return for the same repair within the 30-day warranty period is 0.10. Each month, Garcia tracks 100 customers to see whether they return for warranty repairs. The results are plotted as a proportion to report progress toward the goal. If the control limits are to be set at two standard deviations on either side of the goal, determine the control limits for this chart. In March, 8 of the 100 customers in the sample group returned for warranty repairs. Is the repair process in control?

4. The Canine Gourmet Company produces delicious dog treats for canines with discriminating tastes. Management wants the box-filling line to be set so that the process average weight per packet is 45 grams. To make sure that the process is in control, an inspector at the end of the filling line periodically selects a random box of 10 packets and weighs each packet. When the process is in control, the range in the weight of each sample has averaged 6 grams.

   a. Design an R- and an $\bar{x}$-chart for this process.

   b. The results from the last 5 samples of 10 packets are

Sample	$\bar{x}$	R
1	44	9
2	40	2
3	46	5
4	39	8
5	48	3

   Is the process in control? Explain.

5. Aspen Plastics produces plastic bottles to customer order. The quality inspector randomly selects four bottles from the bottle machine and measures the outside diameter of the bottle neck, a critical quality dimension that determines whether the bottle cap will fit properly. The dimensions (in.) from the last six samples are

| Sample | BOTTLE | | | |
	1	2	3	4
1	0.594	0.622	0.598	0.590
2	0.587	0.611	0.597	0.613
3	0.571	0.580	0.595	0.602
4	0.610	0.615	0.585	0.578
5	0.580	0.624	0.618	0.614
6	0.585	0.593	0.607	0.569

   a. Assume that only these six samples are sufficient, and use the data to determine control limits for an R- and an $\bar{x}$-chart.

   b. Suppose that the specification for the bottle neck diameter is 0.600 ± 0.050 and the population standard deviation is 0.013 in. What is the Process Capability Index? The Process Capability Ratio?

   c. If the firm is seeking four-sigma performance, is the process capable of producing the bottle?

6. In an attempt to judge and monitor the quality of instruction, the administration of Mega-Byte Academy devised an examination to test students on the basic concepts that all should have learned. Each year, a random sample of 10 graduating students is selected for the test. The average score is used to track the quality of the educational process. Test results for the past 10 years are shown in Table 2.

   Use these data to estimate the center and standard deviation for this distribution. Then, calculate the two-sigma control limits for the process average. What comments would you make to the administration of the Mega-Byte Academy?

7. As a hospital administrator of a large hospital, you are concerned with the absenteeism among nurses' aides. The issue has been raised by registered nurses, who feel they often have to perform work normally done by their aides. To get the facts, absenteeism data were gathered for the last 3 weeks, which is considered a representative period for future conditions. After taking random samples of 64 personnel files each day, the following data were produced:

TABLE 2 | TEST SCORES ON EXIT EXAM

| | STUDENT | | | | | | | | | | |
Year	1	2	3	4	5	6	7	8	9	10	Average
1	63	57	92	87	70	61	75	58	63	71	69.7
2	90	77	59	88	48	83	63	94	72	70	74.4
3	67	81	93	55	71	71	86	98	60	90	77.2
4	62	67	78	61	89	93	71	59	93	84	75.7
5	85	88	77	69	58	90	97	72	64	60	76.0
6	60	57	79	83	64	94	86	64	92	74	75.3
7	94	85	56	77	89	72	71	61	92	97	79.4
8	97	86	83	88	65	87	76	84	81	71	81.8
9	94	90	76	88	65	93	86	87	94	63	83.6
10	88	91	71	89	97	79	93	87	69	85	84.9

Day	Aides Absent	Day	Aides Absent
1	4	9	7
2	3	10	2
3	2	11	3
4	4	12	2
5	2	13	1
6	5	14	3
7	3	15	4
8	4		

Because your assessment of absenteeism is likely to come under careful scrutiny, you would like a type I error of only 1 percent. You want to be sure to identify any instances of unusual absences. If some are present, you will have to explore them on behalf of the registered nurses.

a. Design a p-chart.

b. Based on your p-chart and the data from the last 3 weeks, what can you conclude about the absenteeism of nurses' aides?

8. A textile manufacturer wants to set up a control chart for irregularities (e.g., oil stains, shop soil, loose threads, and tears) per 100 square yards of carpet. The following data were collected from a sample of twenty 100-square-yard pieces of carpet:

Sample	1	2	3	4	5	6	7	8	9	10
Irregularities	11	8	9	12	4	16	5	8	17	10
Sample	11	12	13	14	15	16	17	18	19	20
Irregularities	11	5	7	12	13	8	19	11	9	10

a. Using these data, set up a c-chart with $z = 3$.

b. Suppose that the next five samples had 15, 18, 12, 22, and 21 irregularities. What do you conclude?

9. The IRS is concerned with improving the accuracy of tax information given by its representatives over the telephone. Previous studies involved asking a set of 25 questions of a large number of IRS telephone representatives to determine the proportion of correct responses. Historically, the average proportion of correct responses has been 72 percent. Recently, IRS representatives have been receiving more training. On April 26, the set of 25 tax questions were again asked of 20 randomly selected IRS telephone representatives. The numbers of correct answers were 18, 16, 19, 21, 20, 16, 21, 16, 17, 10, 25, 18, 25, 16, 20, 15, 23, 19, 21, and 19.

a. What are the upper and lower control limits for the appropriate p-chart for the IRS? Use $z = 3$.

b. Is the tax information process in statistical control?

10. A travel agency is concerned with the accuracy and appearance of itineraries prepared for its clients. Defects can include errors in times, airlines, flight numbers, prices, car rental information, lodging, charge card numbers, and reservation numbers, as well as typographical errors. As the possible number of errors is nearly infinite, the agency measures the number of errors that do occur. The current process results in an average of three errors per itinerary.

a. What are the two-sigma control limits for these defects?

b. A client scheduled a trip to Dallas. Her itinerary contained six errors. Interpret this information.

11. Jim's Outfitters, Inc., makes custom fancy shirts for cowboys. The shirts could be flawed in various ways, including flaws in the weave or color of the fabric, loose buttons or decorations, wrong dimensions, and uneven

stitches. Jim randomly examined 10 shirts, with the following results:

Shirt	Defects
1	8
2	0
3	7
4	12
5	5
6	10
7	2
8	4
9	6
10	6

a. Assuming that 10 observations are adequate for these purposes, determine the three-sigma control limits for defects per shirt.

b. Suppose that the next shirt has 13 flaws. What can you say about the process now?

12. The Big Black Bird Company produces fiberglass camper tops. The process for producing the tops must be controlled so as to keep the number of dimples low. When the process was in control, the following defects were found in 10 randomly selected camper tops over an extended period of time:

Top	Dimples
1	7
2	9
3	14
4	11
5	3
6	12
7	8
8	4
9	7
10	6

a. Assuming 10 observations are adequate for this purpose, determine the three-sigma control limits for dimples per camper top.

b. Suppose that the next camper top has 15 dimples. What can you say about the process now?

13. The production manager at Sunny Soda, Inc., is interested in tracking the quality of the company's 12-ounce bottle filling line. The bottles must be filled within the tolerances set for this product because the dietary information on the label shows 12 ounces as the serving size.

The design standard for the product calls for a fill level of 12.00 ± 0.10 ounces. The manager collected the following sample data (in fluid ounces per bottle) on the production process:

Sample	OBSERVATION			
	1	2	3	4
1	12.00	11.97	12.10	12.08
2	11.91	11.94	12.10	11.96
3	11.89	12.02	11.97	11.99
4	12.10	12.09	12.05	11.95
5	12.08	11.92	12.12	12.05
6	11.94	11.98	12.06	12.08
7	12.09	12.00	12.00	12.03
8	12.01	12.04	11.99	11.95
9	12.00	11.96	11.97	12.03
10	11.92	11.94	12.09	12.00
11	11.91	11.99	12.05	12.10
12	12.01	12.00	12.06	11.97
13	11.98	11.99	12.06	12.03
14	12.02	12.00	12.05	11.95
15	12.00	12.05	12.01	11.97

a. Are the process average and range in statistical control?

b. Is the process capable of meeting the design standard at four-sigma quality? Explain.

14. The Money Pit Mortgage Company is interested in monitoring the performance of the mortgage process. Fifteen samples of 5 completed mortgage transactions each were taken during a period when the process was believed to be in control. The times to complete the transactions were measured. The means and ranges of the mortgage process transaction times, measured in days, are as follows:

Sample	1	2	3	4	5	6	7	8	9	10	11	12	13	14	15
Mean	17	14	8	17	12	13	15	16	13	14	16	9	11	9	12
Range	6	11	4	8	9	14	12	15	10	10	11	6	9	11	13

Subsequently, samples of size 5 were taken from the process every week for the next 10 weeks. The times were measured and the following results obtained:

Sample	16	17	18	19	20	21	22	23	24	25
Mean	11	14	9	15	17	19	13	22	20	18
Range	7	11	6	4	12	14	11	10	8	6

a. Construct the control charts for the mean and the range, using the original 15 samples.

b. On the control charts developed in part (a), plot the values from samples 16 through 25 and comment on whether the process is in control.

c. In part (b), if you concluded that the process was out of control, would you attribute it to a drift in the mean, or an increase in the variability, or both? Explain your answer.

15. The Money Pit Mortgage Company of Problem 14 made some changes to the process and undertook a process capability study. The following data were obtained for 15 samples of size 5. Based on the individual observations, management estimated the process standard deviation to be 4.21 (days) for use in the process capability analysis. The lower and upper specification limits (in days) for the mortgage process times were 5 and 25.

Sample	1	2	3	4	5	6	7	8	9	10	11	12	13	14	15
Mean	11	12	8	16	13	12	17	16	13	14	17	9	15	14	9
Range	9	13	4	11	10	9	8	15	14	11	6	6	12	10	11

a. Calculate the process capability index and the process capability ratio values.

b. Suppose management would be happy with three-sigma performance. What conclusions is management likely to draw from the capability analysis? Can valid conclusions about the process be drawn from the analysis?

c. What remedial actions, if any, do you suggest that management take?

16. Webster Chemical Company produces mastics and caulking for the construction industry. The product is blended in large mixers and then pumped into tubes and capped. Management is concerned about whether the filling process for tubes of caulking is in statistical control. The process should be centered on 8 ounces per tube. Several samples of eight tubes were taken, each tube was weighed, and the weights in Table 3 were obtained.

a. Assume that only six samples are sufficient and develop the control charts for the mean and the range.

b. Plot the observations on the control chart and comment on your findings.

17. Management at Webster, in Problem 16, is now concerned as to whether caulking tubes are being properly capped. If a significant proportion of the tubes are not being sealed, Webster is placing its customers in a messy situation. Tubes are packaged in large boxes of 144. Several boxes are inspected, and the following numbers of leaking tubes are found:

Sample	Tubes	Sample	Tubes	Sample	Tubes
1	3	8	6	15	5
2	5	9	4	16	0
3	3	10	9	17	2
4	4	11	2	18	6
5	2	12	6	19	2
6	4	13	5	20	1
7	2	14	1	Total	72

Calculate p-chart three-sigma control limits to assess whether the capping process is in statistical control.

18. At Webster Chemical Company, lumps in the caulking compound could cause difficulties in dispensing a smooth bead from the tube. Even when the process is in control, an average of four lumps per tube of caulk will remain. Testing for the presence of lumps destroys the product, so an analyst takes random samples. The following results are obtained:

Tube No.	Lumps	Tube No.	Lumps	Tube No.	Lumps
1	6	5	6	9	5
2	5	6	4	10	0
3	0	7	1	11	9
4	4	8	6	12	2

Determine the c-chart two-sigma upper and lower control limits for this process. Is the process in statistical control?

TABLE 3 | OUNCES OF CAULKING PER TUBE

Sample	TUBE NUMBER							
	1	2	3	4	5	6	7	8
1	7.98	8.34	8.02	7.94	8.44	7.68	7.81	8.11
2	8.33	8.22	8.08	8.51	8.41	8.28	8.09	8.16
3	7.89	7.77	7.91	8.04	8.00	7.89	7.93	8.09
4	8.24	8.18	7.83	8.05	7.90	8.16	7.97	8.07
5	7.87	8.13	7.92	7.99	8.10	7.81	8.14	7.88
6	8.13	8.14	8.11	8.13	8.14	8.12	8.13	8.14

19. Janice Sanders, CEO of Pine Crest Medical Clinic, is concerned over the number of times patients must wait more than 30 minutes beyond their scheduled appointments. She asked her assistant to take random samples of 64 patients to see how many in each sample had to wait more than 30 minutes. Each instance is considered a defect in the clinic process. The table below contains the data for 15 samples.

Sample	Number of Defects
1	5
2	2
3	1
4	3
5	1
6	5
7	2
8	3
9	6
10	3
11	9
12	9
13	5
14	2
15	3

a. Assuming Janice Sanders is willing to use three-sigma control limits, construct a *p*-chart.

b. Based on your *p*-chart and the data in the table, what can you conclude about the waiting time of the patients?

20. Representatives of the Patriot Insurance Company take medical information over the telephone from prospective policy applicants prior to a visit to the applicant's place of residence by a registered nurse who takes vital sign measurements. When the telephone interview has incorrect or incomplete information, the entire process of approving the application is unnecessarily delayed and has the potential of causing loss of business. The following data were collected to see how many applications contain errors. Each sample has 200 randomly selected applications.

Sample	Defects	Sample	Defects
1	20	16	15
2	18	17	40
3	29	18	35
4	12	19	21
5	14	20	24
6	11	21	9
7	30	22	20
8	25	23	17
9	27	24	28
10	16	25	10
11	25	26	17
12	18	27	22
13	25	28	14
14	16	29	19
15	20	30	20

a. What are the upper and lower control limits of a *p*-chart for the number of defective applications? Use $z = 3$.

b. Is the process in statistical control?

21. The Digital Guardian Company issues policies that protect clients from downtime costs due to computer system failures. It is very important to process the policies quickly because long cycle times not only put the client at risk, they could also lose business for Digital Guardian. Management is concerned that customer service is degrading because of long cycle times, measured in days. The following table contains the data from five samples, each sample consisting of eight random observations.

Sample	\multicolumn{8}{c}{OBSERVATION (DAYS)}							
	1	**2**	**3**	**4**	**5**	**6**	**7**	**8**
1	13	9	4	8	8	15	8	6
2	7	15	8	10	10	14	10	15
3	8	11	4	11	8	12	9	15
4	12	7	12	9	11	8	12	8
5	8	12	6	12	11	5	12	8

a. What is your estimate of the process average?

b. What is your estimate of the average range?

c. Construct an *R*- and an $\bar{x}$-chart for this process. Are assignable causes present?

22. The Farley Manufacturing Company prides itself on the quality of its products. The company is engaged in competition for a very important project. A key element is a part that ultimately goes into precision testing equipment. The specifications are 8.000 ± 3.000 millimeters.

Management is concerned about the capability of the process to produce that part. The following data (shown below) were randomly collected during test runs of the process:

	OBSERVATION (MILLIMETERS)							
Sample	1	2	3	4	5	6	7	8
1	9.100	8.900	8.800	9.200	8.100	6.900	9.300	9.100
2	7.600	8.000	9.000	10.100	7.900	9.000	8.000	8.800
3	8.200	9.100	8.200	8.700	9.000	7.000	8.800	10.800
4	8.200	8.300	7.900	7.500	8.900	7.800	10.100	7.700
5	10.000	8.100	8.900	9.000	9.300	9.000	8.700	10.000

Assume that the process is in statistical control. Is the process capable of producing the part at the three-sigma level? Explain.

23. A critical dimension of the service quality of a call center is the wait time of a caller to get to a sales representative. Periodically, random samples of three customer calls are measured for time. The results of the last four samples are in the following table:

Sample	Time (Sec)		
1	495	501	498
2	512	508	504
3	505	497	501
4	496	503	492

a. Assuming that management is willing to use three-sigma control limits, and using only the historical information contained in the four samples, show that the call center access time is in statistical control.

b. Suppose that the standard deviation of the process distribution is 5.77. If the specifications for the access time are 500 $\pm$ 18 sec., is the process capable? Why or why not? Assume three-sigma performance is desired.

24. An automatic lathe produces rollers for roller bearings, and the process is monitored by statistical process control charts. The central line of the chart for the sample means is set at 8.50 and for the range at 0.31 mm. The process is in control, as established by samples of size 5. The upper and lower specifications for the diameter of the rollers are $(8.50 + 0.25)$ and $(8.50 - 0.25)$ mm, respectively.

a. Calculate the control limits for the mean and range charts.

b. If the standard deviation of the process distribution is estimated to be 0.13 mm, is the process capable of meeting specifications? Assume four-sigma performance is desired.

c. If the process is not capable, what percent of the output will fall outside the specification limits? (*Hint:* Use the normal distribution.)

Advanced Problems

25. Canine Gourmet Super Breath dog treats are sold in boxes labeled with a net weight of 12 ounces (340 grams) per box. Each box contains 8 individual 1.5-ounce packets. To reduce the chances of shorting the customer, product design specifications call for the packet-filling process average to be set at 43.5 grams so that the average net weight per box of 8 packets will be 348 grams. Tolerances are set for the box to weigh 348 $\pm$ 12 grams. The standard deviation for the *packet-filling* process is 1.01 grams. The target process capability ratio is 1.33. One day, the packet-filling process average weight drifts down to 43.0 grams. Is the packaging process capable? Is an adjustment needed?

26. The Precision Machining Company makes hand-held tools on an assembly line that produces one product every minute. On one of the products, the critical quality dimension is the diameter (measured in thousandths of an inch) of a hole bored in one of the assemblies. Management wants to detect any shift in the process average diameter from 0.015 in. Management considers the variance in the process to be in control. Historically, the average range has been 0.002 in., regardless of the process average. Design an $\bar{x}$-chart to control this process, with a center line at 0.015 in. and the control limits set at three sigmas from the center line.

Management provided the results of 80 minutes of output from the production line, as shown in Table 4. During these 80 minutes, the process average changed once. All measurements are in thousandths of an inch.

a. Set up an $\bar{x}$-chart with $n = 4$. The frequency should be sample four and then skip four. Thus, your first sample would be for minutes $1 - 4$, the second would be for minutes $9 - 12$, and so on. When would you stop the process to check for a change in the process average?

b. Set up an $\bar{x}$-chart with $n = 8$. The frequency should be sample eight and then skip four. When would you stop the process now? What can you say about the desirability of large samples on a frequent sampling interval?

27. Using the data from Problem 26, continue your analysis of sample size and frequency by trying the following plans.

a. Using the $\bar{x}$-chart for $n = 4$, try the frequency sample four, then skip eight. When would you stop the process in this case?

b. Using the $\bar{x}$-chart for $n = 8$, try the frequency sample eight, then skip eight. When would you consider the process to be out of control?

TABLE 4 | SAMPLE DATA FOR PRECISION MACHINING COMPANY

Minutes	Diameter (thousandths of an inch)											
1–12	15	16	18	14	16	17	15	14	14	13	16	17
13–24	15	16	17	16	14	14	13	14	15	16	15	17
25–36	14	13	15	17	18	15	16	15	14	15	16	17
37–48	18	16	15	16	16	14	17	18	19	15	16	15
49–60	12	17	16	14	15	17	14	16	15	17	18	14
61–72	15	16	17	18	13	15	14	14	16	15	17	18
73–80	16	16	17	18	16	15	14	17				

TABLE 5 | SAMPLE DATA FOR DATA TECH CREDIT CARD SERVICE

Samples	Number of Errors in Sample of 250									
1–10	3	8	5	11	7	1	12	9	0	8
11–20	3	5	7	9	11	3	2	9	13	4
21–30	12	10	6	2	1	7	10	5	8	4

c. Using your results from parts (a) and (b), determine what trade-offs you would consider in choosing between them.

28. The manager of the customer service department of Data Tech Credit Card Service Company is concerned about the number of defects produced by the billing process. Every day a random sample of 250 statements was inspected for errors regarding incorrect entries involving account numbers, transactions on the customer's account, interest charges, and penalty charges. Any statement with one or more of these errors was considered a defect. The study lasted 30 days and yielded the data in Table 5.

a. Construct a p-chart for the billing process.

b. Is there any nonrandom behavior in the billing process that would require management attention?

29. Red Baron Airlines serves hundreds of cities each day, but competition is increasing from smaller companies affiliated with major carriers. One of the key competitive priorities is on-time arrivals and departures. Red Baron defines *on time* as any arrival or departure that takes place within 15 minutes of the scheduled time. To stay on top of the market, management set the high standard of 98 percent on-time performance. The operations department was put in charge of monitoring the performance of the airline. Each week, a random sample of 300 flight arrivals and departures was checked for schedule performance. Table 6 contains the numbers of arrivals and departures over the last 30 weeks that did not meet Red Baron's definition of on-time service. What can you tell management about the quality of service? Can you identify any nonrandom behavior in the process? If so, what might cause the behavior?

30. Beaver Brothers, Inc., is conducting a study to assess the capability of its 150-gram bar soap production line. A critical quality measure is the weight of the soap bars after stamping. The lower and upper specification limits are 162 and 170 grams, respectively. As a part of an initial capability study, 25 samples of size 5 were collected by the quality assurance group and the observations in Table 7 were recorded.

After analyzing the data by using statistical control charts, the quality assurance group calculated the process capability ratio, C_p, and the process capability index, C_{pk}. It then decided to improve the stamping process, especially the feeder mechanism. After making all the changes that were deemed necessary, 18 additional samples were collected. The summary data for these samples are

$$\bar{\bar{x}} = 163 \text{ grams}$$

$$\bar{R} = 2.326 \text{ grams}$$

$$\sigma = 1 \text{ gram}$$

All sample observations were within the control chart limits. With the new data, the quality assurance group recalculated the process capability measures. It was pleased with the improved C_p but felt that the process should be centered at 166 grams to ensure that everything was in order. Its decision concluded the study.

a. Draw the control charts for the data obtained in the initial study and verify that the process was in statistical control.

b. What were the values obtained by the group for C_p and C_{pk} for the initial capability study? Comment on your findings and explain why further improvements were necessary.

c. What are the C_p and C_{pk} after the improvements? Comment on your findings, indicating why the group decided to change the centering of the process.

d. What are the C_p and C_{pk} if the process were centered at 166? Comment on your findings.

TABLE 6 | SAMPLE DATA FOR RED BARON AIRLINES

Samples	Number of Late Planes in Sample of 300 Arrivals and Departures									
1–10	3	8	5	11	7	2	12	9	1	8
11–20	3	5	7	9	12	5	4	9	13	4
21–30	12	10	6	2	1	8	4	5	8	2

TABLE 7 | SAMPLE DATA FOR BEAVER BROTHERS, INC.

Sample	OBS.1	OBS.2	OBS.3	OBS.4	OBS.5
1	167.0	159.6	161.6	164.0	165.3
2	156.2	159.5	161.7	164.0	165.3
3	167.0	162.9	162.9	164.0	165.4
4	167.0	159.6	163.7	164.1	165.4
5	156.3	160.0	162.9	164.1	165.5
6	164.0	164.2	163.0	164.2	163.9
7	161.3	163.0	164.2	157.0	160.6
8	163.1	164.2	156.9	160.1	163.1
9	164.3	157.0	161.2	163.2	164.4
10	156.9	161.0	163.2	164.3	157.3
11	161.0	163.3	164.4	157.6	160.6
12	163.3	164.5	158.4	160.1	163.3
13	158.2	161.3	163.5	164.6	158.7
14	161.5	163.5	164.7	158.6	162.5
15	163.6	164.8	158.0	162.4	163.6
16	164.5	158.5	160.3	163.4	164.6
17	164.9	157.9	162.3	163.7	165.1
18	155.0	162.2	163.7	164.8	159.6
19	162.1	163.9	165.1	159.3	162.0
20	165.2	159.1	161.6	163.9	165.2
21	164.9	165.1	159.9	162.0	163.7
22	167.6	165.6	165.6	156.7	165.7
23	167.7	165.8	165.9	156.9	165.9
24	166.0	166.0	165.6	165.6	165.5
25	163.7	163.7	165.6	165.6	166.2

Active Model Exercise

This Active Model appears in MyOMLab. It allows you to see the effects of sample size and z-values on control charts.

QUESTIONS

1. Has the booking process been in statistical control?

2. Suppose we use a 95 percent p-chart. How do the upper and lower control limits change? What are your conclusions about the booking process?

3. Suppose that the sample size is reduced to 2,000 instead of 2,500. How does this affect the chart?

4. What happens to the chart as we reduce the z-value?

5. What happens to the chart as we reduce the confidence level?

p-Chart

Reset Data	Questions

Number of samples	12
Sample size	2500
z value	3.0000
Confidence	99.73%

Total sample size	30000	Upper Control Limit	0.0091
Total defects	147	Center Line	0.0049
Percentage defects	0.0049	Lower Control Limit	0.0007
Std dev of p-bar	0.0014		

	# Defects	Fraction Defective
Sample 1	15	0.0060
Sample 2	12	0.0048
Sample 3	19	0.0076
Sample 4	2	0.0008
Sample 5	19	0.0076
Sample 6	4	0.0016
Sample 7	24	0.0096
Sample 8	7	0.0028
Sample 9	10	0.0040
Sample 10	17	0.0068
Sample 11	15	0.0060
Sample 12	3	0.0012

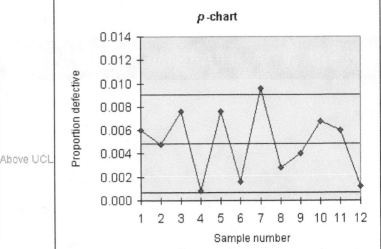

p-Chart Using Data from Example 3

VIDEO CASE — Process Performance and Quality at Starwood Hotels & Resorts

Starwood Hotels & Resorts is no stranger to quality measurement. In the most recent year, Starwood properties around the globe held 51 of approximately 700 spots on Condé Nast's Gold List of the world's best places to stay. Its spa and golf programs have consistently been ranked among the best in the world.

At Starwood, processes and programs are driven by the work of its team of Six Sigma experts, called Black Belts. Developed by Motorola more than 20 years ago, Six Sigma is a comprehensive and flexible system for achieving, sustaining, and maximizing business success by driving out defects and variability in a process. Starwood uses the five-step DMAIC process: (1) define, (2) measure, (3) analyze, (4) improve, and (5) control.

Clearly, understanding customer needs is paramount. To this end, Starwood collects data from customers on its Guest Satisfaction Index survey, called the "Voice of the Customer." The survey covers every department guests may have encountered during their stay, from the front desk and hotel room, to restaurants and concierge. Past surveys indicated that how well

problems were resolved during the guest stay was a key driver in high guest satisfaction scores. To increase its scores for problem resolution, the Sheraton brand of Starwood launched the Sheraton Service Promise program in the United States and Canada. The program was designed to give guests a single point of contact for reporting any problems. It was intended to focus associate (employee) attention on taking care of service issues during the guest's stay within 15 minutes of first receiving notice.

However, although scores did increase, they did not increase by enough. Consequently, Sheraton brought in its Six Sigma team to see what it could do. The team employed the basic Six Sigma model of define-measure-analyze-improve-control to guide its work. To define the problem, the Six Sigma team worked with data collected and analyzed by an independent survey organization, National Family Opinion. The study indicated that three key factors are needed in problem resolution: (1) speed, (2) empathy, and (3) efficiency. All three must be met in order for the guests to be satisfied and the Sheraton Service Promise fulfilled. Then, the team looked at the specific processes that affected performance: telephone operators' handling of requests, procedures for determining who to call, engineering workloads, and so on. The work identified in each area was measured. For example, call logs were established to track speed, empathy of associate handling the call, and efficiency of the staff charged with fixing the problem. The data collected were analyzed to determine why guests' problems were not resolved within the 15-minute standard. Pareto charts and other techniques were used for the analysis.

The final step involved control and monitoring to be sure that the improved processes developed by the Six Sigma team became part of the property's culture, and that they were not abandoned after the team's work was finished. Tracking continues for 12 to 18 months, with monthly feedback to the manager or department head responsible for the improvement of the Sheraton Service Promise program. The improvement effort also receives visibility through the company's intranet so the rest of the organization sees the benefits—including service levels and financial performance—and can use the experience to improve their own operations.

QUESTIONS

1. Implementing Six Sigma programs takes considerable time and commitment from an organization. In terms of top-down commitment, measurement systems to track progress, tough goal setting, education, communication, and customer priorities, evaluate the degree to which Starwood successfully addressed each with the redesign of the Sheraton Service Promise program.

2. How might the new Sheraton Service Promise process help Starwood avoid the four costs of poor process performance and quality (prevention, appraisal, internal failure, and external failure)?

3. Starwood is the first major hotel brand to commit to a dedicated Six Sigma program for improving quality. Why might an organization be reluctant to follow this type of formalized methodology? What other approaches could Starwood or its competitors use?

EXPERIENTIAL LEARNING | Statistical Process Control with a Coin Catapult

Exercise A: Control Charts for Variables

Materials

1 ruler

1 pen or pencil

1 coin (a quarter will do nicely)

1 yardstick

An exercise worksheet

Access to a calculator

Tasks

Divide into teams of two to four. If four people are on a team,

one person holds the yardstick and observes the action,

one person adjusts the catapult and launches the coin,

one person observes the maximum height for each trial, and

one person records the results.

If teams of fewer than four are formed, provide a support for the yardstick and combine the other tasks as appropriate.

Practice

To catapult the coin, put a pen or pencil under the 6-in. mark of the ruler. Put the coin over the 11-in. mark. Press both ends of the ruler down as far as they will go. Let the end that holds the coin snap up, catapulting the coin into the air. The person holding the yardstick should place the stick so that it is adjacent to, but does not interfere with, the trajectory of the coin. To observe the maximum height reached by the coin, the observer should stand back with his or her eye at about the same level as the top of the coin's trajectory. Practice until each person is comfortable with his or her role. The person operating the catapult should be sure that the pen or pencil fulcrum has not moved between shots and that the launch is done as consistently as possible.

Step 1: *Gather data.* Take four samples of five observations (launches) each. Record the maximum height reached by the coin in the first data table on the worksheet. When you have finished, determine the mean and range for each sample, and compute the mean of the means $\bar{\bar{x}}$ and the mean of the ranges $\bar{R}$.

Step 2: *Develop an R-chart.* Using the data gathered and the appropriate D_3 and D_4 values, compute the upper and lower three-sigma control limits for the range. Enter these values and plot the range for each of the four samples on the range chart on the worksheet. Be sure to indicate an appropriate scale for range on the y-axis.

Step 3: *Develop an $\bar{x}$-chart.* Now, using the data gathered and the appropriate value for A_2, compute the upper and lower three-sigma control limits for the sample means. Enter these values and plot the mean for each of the four samples on the $\bar{x}$-chart on the worksheet. Again, indicate an appropriate scale for the y-axis.

Step 4: *Observe the process.* Once a control chart has been established for a process, it is used to monitor the process and to identify when it is not running "normally." Collect two more samples of five trials each, as you did to collect the first set of data. Plot the range and the sample mean on the charts you constructed on the worksheet each time you collect a sample. What have you observed that affects the process? Does the chart indicate that the process is operating the way it did when you first collected data?

Step 5: *Observe a changed process.* Now change something (for instance, move the pencil out to the 8-in. mark). Collect data for samples 7 and 8. Plot the range and the sample mean on the charts you constructed on the worksheet as you complete each sample. Can you detect a change in the process from your control chart? If the process has changed, how sure are you that this change is real and not just due to the particular sample you chose?

Exercise B: Control Charts for Attributes

Materials

1 ruler

1 pen or pencil

1 coin (a quarter will do nicely)

1 paper or plastic cup (with a 4-in. mouth)

An exercise worksheet

Access to a calculator

Tasks

Divide into teams of two or three. If three people are on a team,

one person adjusts the catapult and launches the coin,

one person observes the results and fetches the coin, and

one person records the results.

If teams of two are formed, combine the tasks as appropriate.

Practice

The object is to flip a coin into a cup using a ruler. To catapult the coin, put a pen or pencil under the 6-in. mark of the ruler.

Put a coin over the 11-in. mark and let its weight hold that end of the ruler on the tabletop. Strike the raised end of the ruler with your hand to flip the coin into the air. Position a cup at the place where the coin lands so that on the next flip, the coin will land inside. You will have to practice several times until you find out how hard to hit the ruler and the best position for the cup. Be sure that the pen or pencil fulcrum has not moved between shots and that the launch is done as consistently as possible.

Step 1: *Gather data.* Try to catapult the coin into the cup 10 times for each sample. Record each trial in the data table on the worksheet as a hit (H) when the coin lands inside or a miss (M) when it does not. The proportion of misses will be the number of misses divided by the sample size, *n*, in this case 10. A miss is a "defect," so the proportion of misses is the proportion defective, *p*.

Step 2: *Develop a p-chart.* Compute the upper and lower three-sigma control limits for the average fraction defective. Plot these values and the mean for each of the four samples on the *p*-chart on the worksheet.

Step 3: *Observe the process.* Once a chart has been established for a process, it is used to monitor the process and to identify abnormal behavior. Exchange tasks so that someone else is catapulting the coin. After several practice launches, take four more samples of 10. Plot the proportion defective for this person's output. Is the process still in control? If it is not, how sure are you that it is out of control? Can you determine the control limits for a 95 percent confidence level? With these limits, was your revised process still in control?

Source: The basis for Exercise A was written by J. Christopher Sandvig, Western Washington University, as a variation of the "Catapulting Coins" exercise from *Games and Exercises for Operations Management* by Janelle Heinke and Larry Meile (Prentice Hall, 1995). Given these foundations, Larry Meile of Boston College wrote Exercise A. He also wrote Exercise B as a new extension.

Selected References

Babbar, Sunil. "Service Quality and Business Ethics," *International Journal of Service and Operations Management,* vol. 1, no. 3, 2005, pp. 203–219.

Babbar, Sunil. "Teaching Ethics for Quality as an Innovation in a Core Operations Management Course," *Decision Sciences Journal of Innovative Education,* vol. 8, no. 2, 2010, pp. 361–366.

Besterfield, Dale. *Quality Control,* 8th ed. Upper Saddle River, NJ: Prentice Hall, 2009.

Collier, David A. *The Service Quality Solution.* New York: Irwin Professional Publishing; Milwaukee: ASQC Quality Press, 1994.

Crosby, Philip B. *Quality Is Free: The Art of Making Quality Certain.* New York: McGraw-Hill, 1979.

Deming, W. Edwards. *Out of the Crisis.* Cambridge, MA: Massachusetts Institute of Technology Center for Advanced Engineering Study, 1986.

Duncan, Acheson J. *Quality Control and Industrial Statistics,* 5th ed. Homewood, IL: Irwin, 1986.

Feigenbaum, A.V. *Total Quality Control: Engineering and Management,* 3rd ed. New York: McGraw-Hill, 1983.

Hartvigsen, David. *SimQuick: Process Simulation with Excel,* 2nd ed. Upper Saddle River, NJ: Prentice Hall, 2004.

Hoyle, David. *ISO 9000,* 6th ed. Oxford: Butler-Heinemann, 2009.

Juran, J.M., and Frank Gryna, Jr. *Quality Planning and Analysis,* 2nd ed. New York: McGraw-Hill, 1980.

Kerwin, Kathleen. "When Flawless Isn't Enough." *Business Week* (December 8, 2003), pp. 80–82.

Lucier, Gregory T., and Sridhar Seshadri. "GE Takes Six Sigma Beyond the Bottom Line." *Strategic Finance* (May 2001), pp. 41–46.

Mitra, Amitava. *Fundamentals of Quality Control and Improvement,* 3rd ed. Hoboken, NJ: Wiley & Sons, 2008.

Pande, Peter S., Robert P. Neuman, and Roland R. Cavanagh. *The Six Sigma Way.* New York: McGraw-Hill, 2000.

Russell, J. P., and Dennis Arter. *ISO Lesson Guide to ISO 9001,* 3rd ed. Milwaukee: ASQC Quality Press, 2008.

Schwarz, Anne. "Listening to the Voice of the Customer Is the Key to QVC's Success." *Journal of Organizational Excellence* (Winter 2004), pp. 3–11.

Sester, Dennis. "Motorola: A Tradition of Quality." *Quality* (October 2001), pp. 30–34.

Yannick, Julliard. "Ethics Quality Management," *Techne' Journal,* vol. 8, no. 1 (Fall 2004), pp. 117–135.

Oil containment hard boom collecting foaming sea water at Queen Bess Island near Grand
Isle, Louisiana

British Petroleum Oil Spill in Gulf of Mexico

British Petroleum (BP) is one of the world's leading international oil, gas, and petrochemical products company, with operations in 29 countries, 79,000 employees, and 2010 sales of nearly $30 billion. It operates over 22,000 retail sites. On April 20, 2010, there was an explosion and fire on Transocean Ltd's Deepwater Horizon drilling rig that had been licensed to BP. It sank two days later in 5,000 feet of water, and released as many as 4.9 billion barrels of oil into the Gulf of Mexico before the damaged well was finally capped in mid-July 2010. The resulting oil spill closed down fisheries and threatened the delicate coastline and its fragile ecosystems. Pinnacle Strategies was one of the firms hired by BP to help in boosting the output of spill-fighting equipment like boats, ships, and rigs, as well as supplies of critical resources like containment booms, skimmers, and decontamination suits.

A boom is an inflatable floating device that can be used to trap oil downwind on a body of water. This oil can then be pumped into containers by skimming equipment. Limited production capacities of booms, however, represented a daunting challenge. Prestige Products in Walker, Michigan, could only make 500 feet of boom a day, whereas a single order of the size requested by BP would exceed the combined capacity of every boom manufacturer in the United States. Despite increasing the staff from 5 to 75 and raising production to 12,800 feet daily, the Prestige plant felt that it had reached its limit. That is where Ed Kincer from Pinnacle Strategies stepped in. He noticed that the boom was assembled in a flurry, with little to do in-between for several minutes. Cutters sliced boom by cutting one side, then walking 100 feet to cut the other side. Workers also sat idle while waiting for a welding machine. Waste occurred in the form of excessive walks, waiting for machines, and changing production rhythms. Kincer identified the constraints in the process, found ways to manage them, and more than tripled capacity. Prestige eventually ended up making more than a million feet of boom for BP.

Theory of constraints is the scientific approach that was used by Pinnacle to boost throughput for BP's other key suppliers as well. Kvichak Marine in Seattle quadrupled output of oil skimmers, while Illinois-based Elastec increased production from 4 skimmers a week to 26. Abasco, a Houston-based boom manufacturer, increased production by 20 percent due to rebalancing staff such that the welding operation kept going even during the breaks. At Supply Pro, a Texan manufacturer of absorbent boom, capacity increased several fold by using cellulose instead of scarce polypropylene. In six months, Pinnacle more than doubled the supply of skimmers, booms, and other critical resources by identifying bottlenecks at dozens of factories and working around them. These capacity enhancements throughout BP's supply chain ensured that lack of materials did not end up constraining the clean-up operations in the fight against the oil spill.

Source: Brown, A. "Theory of Constraints Tapped to Accelerate BP's Gulf of Mexico Cleanup." *Industry Week* (March 18, 2011); **http://www.newsweek.com/photo/2010/05/22/oil-spill-timeline.html**; **http://www.bp.com/**, May 5, 2011.

LEARNING GOALS *After reading this chapter, you should be able to:*

1. Explain the theory of constraints.
2. Understand linkage of capacity constraints to financial performance measures.
3. Identify bottlenecks.
4. Apply theory of constraints to product mix decisions.
5. Describe how to manage constraints in an assembly line.

---

constraint

Any factor that limits the performance of a system and restricts its output. In linear programming, a limitation that restricts the permissible choices for the decision variables.

bottleneck

A capacity constraint resource (CCR) whose available capacity limits the organization's ability to meet the product volume, product mix, or demand fluctuation required by the marketplace.

Suppose one of a firm's processes was recently reengineered, and yet results were disappointing. Costs were still high or customer satisfaction still low. What could be wrong? The answer might be constraints that remain in one or more steps in the firm's processes. A **constraint** is any factor that limits the performance of a system and restricts its output, while *capacity* is the maximum rate of output of a process or a system. When constraints exist at any step, as they did at suppliers of BP, capacity can become imbalanced—too high in some departments and too low in others. As a result, the overall performance of the system suffers.

Constraints can occur up or down the supply chain, with either the firm's suppliers or customers, or within one of the firm's processes like service/product development or order fulfillment. Three kinds of constraints can generally be identified: physical (usually machine, labor, or workstation capacity or material shortages, but could be space or quality), market (demand is less than capacity), or managerial (policy, metrics, or mind-sets that create constraints that impede work flow). A **bottleneck**[1] is a special type of a constraint that relates to the capacity shortage of a process, and is defined as any resource whose available capacity limits the organization's ability to meet the service or product volume, product mix, or fluctuating requirements demanded by the marketplace. A business system or a process would have at least one constraint or a bottleneck; otherwise, its output would be limited only by market demand. The experience of BP and other firms in the health care, banking, and manufacturing industries demonstrates how important managing constraints can be to an organization's future.

---

[1]Under certain conditions, a bottleneck is also called a *capacity constrained resource* (CCR). The process with the least capacity is called a bottleneck if its output is less than the market demand, or called a CCR if it is the least capable resource in the system but still has higher capacity than the market demand.

Managing Constraints across the Organization

Firms must manage their constraints and make appropriate capacity choices at the individual-process level, as well as at the organization level. Hence, this process involves inter-functional cooperation. Detailed decisions and choices made within each of these levels affect where resource constraints or bottlenecks show up, both within and across departmental lines. Relieving a bottleneck in one part of an organization might not have the desired effect unless a bottleneck in another part of the organization is also addressed. A bottleneck could be the sales department not getting enough sales or the loan department not processing loans fast enough. The constraint could be a lack of capital or equipment, or it could be planning and scheduling.

Managers throughout the organization must understand how to identify and manage bottlenecks in all types of processes, how to relate the capacity and performance measures of one process to another, and how to use that information to determine the firm's best service or product mix. This chapter explains how managers can best make these decisions.

Traffic bottleneck in Beijing, China.

The Theory of Constraints

The **theory of constraints (TOC)** is a systematic management approach that focuses on actively managing those constraints that impede a firm's progress toward its goal of maximizing profits and effectively using its resources. The theory was developed nearly three decades ago by Eli Goldratt, a well-known business systems analyst. It outlines a deliberate process for identifying and overcoming constraints. The process focuses not just on the efficiency of individual processes, but also on the bottlenecks that constrain the system as a whole. Pinnacle Strategies in the opening vignette followed this theory to improve BP's operations.

TOC methods increase the firm's profits more effectively by focusing on making materials flow rapidly through the entire system. They help firms look at the big picture—how processes can be improved to increase overall work flows, and how inventory and workforce levels can be reduced while still effectively utilizing critical resources. To do this, it is important to understand the relevant performance and capacity measures at the operational level, as well as their relationship to the more broadly understood financial measures at the firm level. These measures and relationships, so critical in successfully applying the principles of the TOC, are defined in Table 1.

theory of constraints (TOC)

A systematic management approach that focuses on actively managing those constraints that impede a firm's progress toward its goal.

> **Creating Value through Operations Management**
>
> Using Operations to Compete
> Project Management
>
> **Managing Processes**
>
> Process Strategy
> Process Analysis
> Quality and Performance
> Capacity Planning
> Constraint Management
> Lean Systems
>
> **Managing Supply Chains**
>
> Supply Chain Inventory Management
> Supply Chain Design
> Supply Chain Location Decisions
> Supply Chain Integration
> Supply Chain Sustainability and Humanitarian Logistics
> Forecasting
> Operations Planning and Scheduling
> Resource Planning

TABLE 1 | HOW THE FIRM'S OPERATIONAL MEASURES RELATE TO ITS FINANCIAL MEASURES

Operational Measures	TOC View	Relationship to Financial Measures
Inventory (I)	All the money invested in a system in purchasing things that it intends to sell	A decrease in I leads to an increase in net profit, ROI, and cash flow.
Throughput (T)	Rate at which a system generates money through sales	An increase in T leads to an increase in net profit, ROI, and cash flows.
Operating Expense (OE)	All the money a system spends to turn inventory into throughput	A decrease in OE leads to an increase in net profit, ROI, and cash flows.
Utilization (U)	The degree to which equipment, space, or workforce is currently being used, and is measured as the ratio of average output rate to maximum capacity, expressed as a percentage	An increase in U at the bottleneck leads to an increase in net profit, ROI, and cash flows.

According to the TOC view, every capital investment in the system, including machines and work-in-process materials, represents inventory because they could all potentially be sold to make money. Producing a product or a service that does not lead to a sale will not increase a firm's throughput, but will increase its inventory and operating expenses. It is always best to manage the system so that utilization at the bottleneck resource is maximized in order to maximize throughput.

Key Principles of the TOC

The chief concept behind the TOC is that the bottlenecks should be scheduled to maximize their throughput of services or products while adhering to promised completion dates. The underlying assumption is that demand is greater or equal to the capacity of the process that produces the service or product, otherwise instead of internal changes, marketing must work towards promoting increasing its demand. For example, manufacturing a garden rake involves attaching a bow to the rake's head. Rake heads must be processed on the blanking press, welded to the bow, cleaned, and attached to the handle to make the rake, which is packaged and finally shipped to Sears, Home Depot, or Walmart, according to a specific delivery schedule. Suppose that the delivery commitments for all styles of rakes for the next month indicate that the welding station is loaded at 105 percent of its capacity, but that the other processes will be used at only 75 percent of their capacities. According to the TOC, the welding station is the bottleneck resource, whereas the blanking, cleaning, handle attaching, packaging, and shipping processes are nonbottleneck resources. Any idle time at the welding station must be eliminated to maximize throughput. Managers should therefore focus on the welding schedule.

Seven key principles of the TOC that revolve around the efficient use and scheduling of bottlenecks and improving flow and throughput are summarized in Table 2.

TABLE 2 | SEVEN KEY PRINCIPLES OF THE THEORY OF CONSTRAINTS

1. The focus should be on balancing flow, not on balancing capacity.

2. Maximizing the output and efficiency of every resource may not maximize the throughput of the entire system.

3. An hour lost at a bottleneck or a constrained resource is an hour lost for the whole system. In contrast, an hour saved at a nonbottleneck resource is a mirage because it does not make the whole system more productive.

4. Inventory is needed only in front of the bottlenecks in order to prevent them from sitting idle, and in front of assembly and shipping points in order to protect customer schedules. Building inventories elsewhere should be avoided.

5. Work, which can be materials, information to be processed, documents, or customers, should be released into the system only as frequently as the bottlenecks need it. Bottleneck flows should be equal to the market demand. Pacing everything to the slowest resource minimizes inventory and operating expenses.

6. Activating a nonbottleneck resource (using it for improved efficiency that does not increase throughput) is not the same as utilizing a bottleneck resource (that does lead to increased throughput). Activation of nonbottleneck resources cannot increase throughput, nor promote better performance on financial measures outlined in Table 1.

7. Every capital investment must be viewed from the perspective of its global impact on overall throughput (T), inventory (I), and operating expense (OE).

Bal Seal Engineering is a designer and manufacturer of custom seals and canted-coil™ springs for aerospace, automotive, transportation, medical and other industries. By applying many modern management principles including the theory of constraints (TOC), the company has been able to grow and improve customer satisfaction.

Practical application of the TOC involves the implementation of the following steps.

1. *Identify the System Bottleneck(s).* For the rake example, the bottleneck is the welding station because it is restricting the firm's ability to meet the shipping schedule and, hence, total value-added funds. Other ways of identifying the bottleneck will be looked at in more detail a little later in this chapter.

2. *Exploit the Bottleneck(s).* Create schedules that maximize the throughput of the bottleneck(s). For the rake example, schedule the welding station to maximize its utilization while meeting the shipping commitments to the extent possible. Also make sure that only good quality parts are passed on to the bottleneck.

3. *Subordinate All Other Decisions to Step 2.* Nonbottleneck resources should be scheduled to support the schedule of the bottleneck and not produce more than the bottleneck can handle. That is, the blanking press should not produce more than the welding station can handle, and the activities of the cleaning and subsequent operations should be based on the output rate of the welding station.

4. *Elevate the Bottleneck(s).* After the scheduling improvements in steps 1–3 have been exhausted and the bottleneck is still a constraint to throughput, management should consider increasing the capacity of the bottleneck. For example, if the welding station is still a constraint after exhausting schedule improvements, consider increasing its capacity by adding another shift or another welding machine. Other mechanisms are also available for increasing bottleneck capacity, and we address them a little later.

5. *Do Not Let Inertia Set In.* Actions taken in steps 3 and 4 will improve the welder throughput and may alter the loads on other processes. Consequently, the system constraint(s) may shift. Then, the practical application of steps 1–4 must be repeated in order to identify and manage the new set of constraints.

Because of its potential for improving performance dramatically, many manufacturers have applied the principles of the theory of constraints. All manufacturers implementing TOC principles can also dramatically change the mind-set of employees and managers. Instead of focusing solely on their own functions, they can see the "big picture" and where other improvements in the system might lie.

Identification and Management of Bottlenecks

Bottlenecks can both be internal or external to the firm, and typically represent a process, a step, or a workstation with the lowest capacity. **Throughput time** is the total elapsed time from the start to the finish of a job or a customer being processed at one or more workcenters. Where a bottleneck lies in a given service or manufacturing process can be identified in two ways. A workstation in a process is a bottleneck if (1) it has the highest total time per unit processed, or (2) it has the highest average utilization and total workload

throughput time

Total elapsed time from the start to the finish of a job or a customer being processed at one or more workcenters.

Managing Bottlenecks in Service Processes

Example 1 illustrates how a bottleneck step or activity can be identified for a loan approval process at a bank.

EXAMPLE 1	Identifying the Bottleneck in a Service Process

Managers at the First Community Bank are attempting to shorten the time it takes customers with approved loan applications to get their paperwork processed. The flowchart for this process, consisting of several different activities, each performed by a different bank employee, is shown in Figure 1. Approved loan applications first arrive at activity or step 1, where they are checked for completeness and put in order. At step 2, the loans are categorized into different classes according to the loan amount and whether they are being requested for personal or commercial reasons. While credit checking commences at step 3, loan application data are entered in parallel into the information system for record-keeping purposes at step 4. Finally, all paperwork for setting up the new loan is finished at step 5. The time taken in minutes is given in parentheses.

Which single step is the bottleneck, assuming that market demand for loan applications exceeds the capacity of the process? The management is also interested in knowing the maximum number of approved loans this system can process in a 5-hour work day.

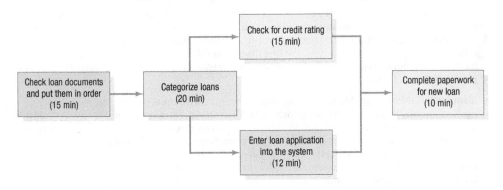

▲ FIGURE 1
Processing Credit Loan Applications at First Community Bank

SOLUTION

We define the bottleneck as step 2, which has the highest time per loan processed. The throughput time to complete an approved loan application is 15 + 20 + max (15, 12) + 10 = **60** minutes. Although we assume no waiting time in front of any step, in practice such a smooth process flow is not always the case. So the actual time taken for completing an approved loan will be longer than 60 minutes due to nonuniform arrival of applications, variations in actual processing times, and the related factors.

The capacity for loan completions is derived by translating the "minutes per customer" at the bottleneck step to "customer per hour." At First Community Bank, it is 3 customers per hour because the bottleneck step 2 can process only 1 customer every 20 minutes (60/3).

DECISION POINT

Step 2 is the bottleneck constraint. The bank will be able to complete a maximum of only 3 loan accounts per hour, or 15 new loan accounts in a 5-hour day. Management can increase the flow of loan applications by increasing the capacity of step 2 up to the point where another step becomes the bottleneck.

Due to constrained resources like doctors, nurses, and equipment, patients wait for medical care in a crowded waiting room at South Central Family Health Center in Los Angeles, California

A front-office process with high customer contact and divergence does not enjoy the simple line flows shown in Example 1. Its operations may serve many different customer types, and the demands on any one operation could vary considerably from one day to the next. However, bottlenecks can still be identified by computing the average utilization of each operation. However, the variability in workload also creates *floating bottlenecks*. One week the mix of work may make operation 1 a bottleneck, and the next week it may make operation 3 the bottleneck. This type of variability increases the complexity of day-to-day scheduling. In this situation, management prefers lower utilization rates, which allow greater slack to absorb unexpected surges in demand.

TOC principles outlined here are fairly broad-based and widely applicable. They can be useful for evaluating individual processes as well as large systems for both manufacturers as well as service providers. Service organizations, such as Delta Airlines, United Airlines, and major hospitals across the United States, including the U.S. Air Force health care system, use the TOC to their advantage.

Managing Bottlenecks in Manufacturing Processes

Bottlenecks can exist in all types of manufacturing processes, including the job process, batch process, line process, and continuous process. Since these processes differ in their design, strategic intent, and allocation of resources identification and management of bottlenecks will also differ accordingly with process type. We first discuss in this section issues surrounding management of bottlenecks in job and batch processes, while relegating constraint management in line processes for a later section.

Identifying Bottlenecks   Manufacturing processes often pose some complexities when identifying bottlenecks. If multiple services or products are involved, extra setup time at a workstation is usually needed to change over from one service or product to the next, which in turn increases the overload at the workstation being changed over. *Setup times* and their associated costs affect the size of the lots traveling through the job or batch processes. Management tries to reduce setup times because they represent unproductive time for workers or machines and thereby allow for smaller, more economic, batches. Nonetheless, whether setup times are significant or not, one way to identify a bottleneck operation is by its utilization. Example 2 illustrates how a bottleneck can be identified in a manufacturing setting where setups are negligible.

| EXAMPLE 2 | Identifying the Bottleneck in a Batch Process |

Diablo Electronics manufactures four unique products (A, B, C, and D) that are fabricated and assembled in five different workstations (V, W, X, Y, and Z) using a small batch process. Each workstation is staffed by a worker who is dedicated to work a single shift per day at an assigned workstation. Batch setup times have been reduced to such an extent that they can be considered negligible. A flowchart denotes the path each product follows through the manufacturing process as shown in Figure 2, where each product's price, demand per week, and processing times per unit are indicated as well. Inverted triangles represent purchased parts and raw materials consumed per unit at different workstations. Diablo can make and sell up to the limit of its demand per week, and no penalties are incurred for not being able to meet all the demand.

Which of the five workstations (V, W, X, Y, or Z) has the highest utilization, and thus serves as the bottleneck for Diablo Electronics?

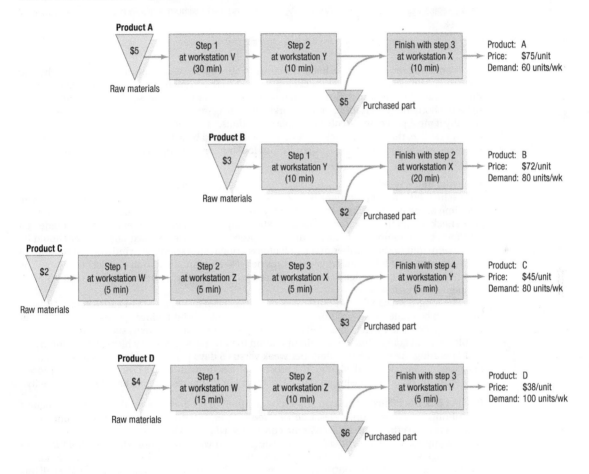

▲ FIGURE 2
Flowchart for Products A, B, C, and D

SOLUTION

Because the denominator in the utilization ratio is the same for every workstation, with one worker per machine at each step in the process, we can simply identify the bottleneck by computing aggregate workloads at each workstation.

The firm wants to satisfy as much of the product demand in a week as it can. Each week consists of 2,400 minutes of available production time. Multiplying the processing time at each station for a given product with the number of units demanded per week yields the workload represented by that product. These loads are summed across all products going through a workstation to arrive at the total load for the workstation, which is then compared with the others and the existing capacity of 2,400 minutes.

Workstation	Load from Product A	Load from Product B	Load from Product C	Load from Product D	Total Load (min)
V	60 × 30 = 1800	0	0	0	1,800
W	0	0	80 × 5 = 400	100 × 15 = 1,500	1,900
X	60 × 10 = 600	80 × 20 = 1,600	80 × 5 = 400	0	2,600
Y	60 × 10 = 600	80 × 10 = 800	80 × 5 = 400	100 × 5 = 500	2,300
Z	0	0	80 × 5 = 400	100 × 10 = 1,000	1,400

DECISION POINT

Workstation X is the bottleneck for Diablo Electronics because the aggregate workload at X is larger than the aggregate workloads of workstations V, W, Y, and Z and the maximum available capacity of 2,400 minutes per week.

Identifying the bottlenecks becomes considerably harder when setup times are lengthy and the degree of divergence in the process is greater than that shown in Example 2. When the setup time is large, the operation with the highest total time per unit processed would typically tend to be the bottleneck. Variability in the workloads will again likely create floating bottlenecks, especially if most processes involve multiple operations, and often their capacities are not identical. In practice, these bottlenecks can also be determined by asking workers and supervisors in the plant where the bottlenecks might lie and looking for piled up material in front of different workstations.

Relieving Bottlenecks   The key to preserving bottleneck capacity is to carefully monitor short-term schedules and keep bottleneck resource as busy as is practical. Managers should minimize idle time at the bottlenecks, caused by delays elsewhere in the system and make sure that the bottleneck has all the resources it needs to stay busy. When a changeover or setup is made at a bottleneck, the number of units or customers processed before the next changeover should be large compared to the number processed at less critical operations. Maximizing the number of units processed per setup means fewer setups per year and, thus, less total time lost to setups. The number of setups also depends on the required product variety; more variety necessitates more frequent changeovers.

The long-term capacity of bottleneck operations can be expanded in various ways. Investments can be made in new equipment and in brick-and-mortar facility expansions. The bottleneck's capacity also can be expanded by operating it more hours per week, such as by hiring more employees and going from a one-shift operation to multiple shifts, or by hiring more employees and operating the plant 6 or 7 days per week versus 5 days per week. Managers also might relieve the bottleneck by redesigning the process, either through *process reengineering* or *process improvement*, or by purchasing additional machines or machines that can handle more capacity.

Product Mix Decisions   Managers might be tempted to produce the products with the highest contribution margins or unit sales. *Contribution margin* is the amount each product contributes to profits and overhead; no fixed costs are considered when making the product mix decision. We call this approach the *traditional method*. The problem with this approach is that the firm's actual throughput and overall profitability depend more upon the contribution margin generated at the bottleneck than by the contribution margin of each individual product produced. We call this latter approach the *bottleneck method*. Example 3 illustrates both of these methods.

EXAMPLE 3	**Determining the Product Mix Using Contribution Margin**

The senior management at Diablo Electronics (see Exercise 2) wants to improve profitability by accepting the right set of orders, and so collected some additional financial data. Variable overhead costs are $8,500 per week. Each worker is paid $18 per hour and is paid for an entire week, regardless of how much the worker is used. Consequently, labor costs are fixed expenses. The plant operates one 8-hour shift per day, or 40 hours each week. Currently, decisions are made using the traditional method, which is to accept as much of the highest contribution margin product as possible (up to the limit of its demand), followed by the next highest contribution margin product, and so on until no more capacity is available. Pedro Rodriguez, the newly hired production supervisor, is knowledgeable about the theory of constraints and bottleneck-based scheduling.

He believes that profitability can indeed be improved if bottleneck resources were exploited to determine the product mix. What is the change in profits if, instead of the traditional method used by Diablo Electronics, the bottleneck method advocated by Pedro is used to select the product mix?

SOLUTION

Decision Rule 1: Traditional Method

Select the best product mix according to the highest overall contribution margin of each product.

Step 1: Calculate the contribution margin per unit of each product as shown here.

	A	B	C	D
Price	$75.00	$72.00	$45.00	$38.00
Raw material and purchased parts	−10.00	−5.00	−5.00	−10.00
= Contribution margin	$65.00	$67.00	$40.00	$28.00

When ordered from highest to lowest, the contribution margin per unit sequence of these products is B, A, C, D.

Step 2: Allocate resources V, W, X, Y, and Z to the products in the order decided in step 1. Satisfy each demand until the bottleneck resource (workstation X) is encountered. Subtract minutes away from 2,400 minutes available for each week at each stage.

Work Center	Minutes at the Start	Minutes Left After Making 80 B	Minutes Left After Making 60 A	Can Only Make 40 C	Can Still Make 100 D
V	2,400	2,400	600	600	600
W	2,400	2,400	2,400	2,200	700
X	2,400	800	200	0	0
Y	2,400	1,600	1,000	800	300
Z	2,400	2,400	2,400	2,200	1,200

The best product mix according to this traditional approach is then 60 A, 80 B, 40 C, and 100 D.

Step 3: Compute profitability for the selected product mix.

Profits		
Revenue	(60 × $75) + (80 × $72) + (40 × $45) + (100 × $38)	= $15,860
Materials	(60 × $10) + (80 × $5) + (40 × $5) + (100 × $10)	= −$2,200
Labor	(5 workers) × (8 hours/day) × (5 days/week) × ($18/hour)	= −$3,600
Overhead		= −$8,500
Profit		= $1,560

Manufacturing the product mix of 60 A, 80 B, 40 C, and 100 D will yield a profit of $1,560 per week.

Decision Rule 2: Bottleneck Method

Select the best product mix according to the dollar contribution margin per minute of processing time at the bottleneck workstation X. This method would take advantage of the principles outlined in the theory of constraints and get the most dollar benefit from the bottleneck.

Step 1: Calculate the contribution margin/minute of processing time at bottleneck workstation X:

	Product A	Product B	Product C	Product D
Contribution margin	$65.00	$67.00	$40.00	$28.00
Time at bottleneck	10 minutes	20 minutes	5 minutes	0 minutes
Contribution margin per minute	$6.50	$3.35	$8.00	Not defined

When ordered from highest to lowest contribution margin/minute at the bottleneck, the manufacturing sequence of these products is D, C, A, B, which is reverse of the earlier order. Product D is scheduled first because it does not consume any resources at the bottleneck.

Step 2: Allocate resources V, W, X, Y, and Z to the products in the order decided in step 1. Satisfy each demand until the bottleneck resource (workstation X) is encountered. Subtract minutes away from 2,400 minutes available for each week at each stage.

Work Center	Minutes at the Start	Minutes Left After Making 100 D	Minutes Left After Making 80 C	Minutes Left After Making 60 A	Can Only Make 70 B
V	2,400	2,400	2,400	600	600
W	2,400	900	500	500	500
X	2,400	2,400	2,000	1,400	0
Y	2,400	1,900	1,500	900	200
Z	2,400	1,400	1,000	1,000	1,000

The best product mix according to this bottleneck-based approach is then 60 A, 70 B, 80 C, and 100 D.

Step 3: Compute profitability for the selected product mix.

	Profits	
Revenue	$(60 \times \$75) + (70 \times \$72) + (80 \times \$45) + (100 \times \$38)$	= $16,940
Materials	$(60 \times \$10) + (70 \times \$5) + (80 \times \$5) + (100 \times \$10)$	= −$2,350
Labor	(5 workers) × (8 hours/day) × (5 days/week) × ($18/hour)	= −$3,600
Overhead		= −$8,500
Profit		= $2,490

Manufacturing the product mix of 60 A, 70 B, 80 C, and 100 D will yield a profit of $2,490 per week.

DECISION POINT
By focusing on the bottleneck resources in accepting customer orders and determining the product mix, the sequence in which products are selected for production is reversed from **B, A, C, D** to **D, C, A, B**. Consequently, the product mix is changed from 60 A, 80 B, 40 C, and 100 D to 60 A, 70 B, 80 C, and 100 D. The increase in profits by using the bottleneck method is $930, ($2,490 − $1,560), or almost 60 percent over the traditional approach.

Linear programming could also be used to find the best product mix in Example 3. It must be noted, however, that the problem in Example 3 did not involve significant setup times. Otherwise, they must be taken into consideration for not only identifying the bottleneck, but also in determining the product mix. The experiential learning exercise of Min-Yo Garment Company at the end of this chapter provides an interesting illustration of how the product mix can be determined when setup times are significant. In this way, the principles behind the theory of constraints can be exploited for making better decisions about a firm's most profitable product mix.

Drum-Buffer-Rope Systems Drum-Buffer-Rope (DBR) is a planning and control system based on the theory of constraints that is often used in manufacturing firms to plan and schedule production. It works by regulating the flow of work-in-process materials at the bottleneck or the capacity constrained resource (CCR). The bottleneck schedule is the *drum* because it sets the beat or the production rate for the entire plant and is linked to the market demand. The *buffer* is a time buffer that plans early flows to the bottleneck and thus protects it from disruption. It also ensures that the bottleneck is never starved for work. A finished-goods inventory buffer can also be placed in front of the shipping point in order to protect customer shipping schedules. Finally, the *rope* represents the tying of material release to the drum beat, which is the rate at which the bottleneck controls the throughput of the entire plant. It is thus a communication device to ensure that raw material is not introduced into the system at a rate faster than what the bottleneck can

drum-buffer-rope (DBR)

A planning and control system that regulates the flow of work-in-process materials at the bottleneck or the capacity constrained resource (CCR) in a productive system.

handle. Completing the loop, *buffer management* constantly monitors the execution of incoming bottleneck work. Working together, the drum, the buffer, and the rope can help managers create a production schedule that reduces lead times and inventories while simultaneously increasing throughput and on-time delivery.

To better understand the drum-buffer-rope system, consider the schematic layout shown in Figure 3. Process B, with a capacity of only 500 units per week, is the bottleneck because the upstream Process A and downstream Process C have capacities of 800 units per week and 700 units per week, respectively, and the market demand is 650 units per week, on average. In this case, because the capacity at process B is less than the market demand, it is the bottleneck. A constraint time buffer, which can be in the form of materials arriving earlier than needed, is placed right in front of the bottleneck (Process B). A shipping buffer, in the form of finished goods inventory, can also be placed prior to the shipping schedule in order to protect customer orders that are firm. Finally, a rope ties the material release schedule to match the schedule, or drum beat, at the bottleneck. The material flow is pulled forward by the drum beat prior to the bottleneck, while it is pushed downstream toward the customer subsequent to the bottleneck.

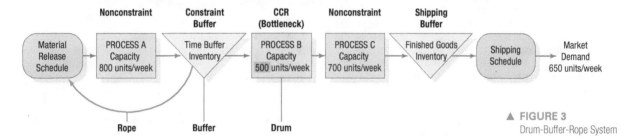

▲ FIGURE 3
Drum-Buffer-Rope System

DBR specifically strives to improve throughput by better utilizing the bottleneck resource and protecting it from disruption through the time buffer and protective buffer capacity elsewhere. So while the process batch in the DBR is any size that minimizes setups and improves utilization at the bottleneck, at nonconstrained resources the process batches are equal to what is needed for production at that time. The material can consequently be released in small batches known as transfer batches at the release point, which then combine at the constraint buffer to make a full process batch at the bottleneck. Transfer batches can be as small as one unit each, to allow a downstream workstation to start work on a batch before it is completely finished at the prior process. Using transfer batches typically facilitates a reduction in overall lead time.

DBR can be an effective system to use when the product the firm produces is relatively simple and the production process has more line flows. Planning is greatly simplified in this case and primarily revolves around scheduling the constrained resource and triggering other points to meet that bottleneck's schedule. Effectively implementing a DBR system requires an understanding of the TOC principles. However, such a system can be utilized in many different kinds of manufacturing and service organizations, either by itself or in conjunction with other planning and control systems. Managerial Practice 2 illustrates how the use of a DBR system improved the performance of the Marine Corps Maintenance Center in Albany, Georgia.

MANAGERIAL PRACTICE 1 — The Drum-Buffer-Rope System at a U.S. Marine Corps Maintenance Center

The U.S. Marine Corps Maintenance Center in Albany, Georgia, overhauls and repairs vehicles used by the corps, such as fuel tankers, trucks, earthmoving equipment, amphibious vehicles, and light armored vehicles. The overhaul process starts with the disassembly of each vehicle to determine the amount and nature of work that needs to be performed. The type and duration of the repair work can vary tremendously for even the same type of vehicle. Faced with such uncertainty, the Center was struggling until four years ago to complete its equipment repairs on time, and it had an increasing backlog to boot. For instance, the Center was able to repair only about 5 MK-48s (heavy-duty haulers) per month, when twice as many MK-48s—10 per month—typically needed repair. Different units of the corps were threatening to divert their orders to the private-sector repair companies.

TOC principles were used to identify the bottlenecks on the shop floor. After the Center's operations were studied in depth, however, contrary to everyone's expectations, it was discovered that more than enough capacity was available to repair and overhaul 10 MK-48s per month. The problem was not capacity; it was the Center's scheduling system. Products were being pushed onto the shop floor without regard for the status of the resources on the floor. Thus, what the Center had was a policy constraint related to the scheduling process, not an actual physical resource constraint.

In order to improve the Center's performance, its managers implemented a simplified form of a drum-buffer-rope system as shown in Figure 3. Since the Marine Corps Maintenance Center was not constrained by any internal resource, the drum in such a simplified system was based on firm orders. As orders came in, a quick check was done to measure the total load the Center's least-capable resource was handling. If the resource was not too heavily loaded, the order was accepted and released onto the shop floor for processing. The rope tied the shipping schedule directly to the material release schedule instead of the bottleneck schedule, and the only buffer maintained was the shipping buffer. Such a simplified DBR system did not require any specialized software. It focused simply on the market demand for repairs.

The Center's results following the change were impressive. Repair cycle times were reduced from an average of 167 days to 58 days, work-in-process levels were reduced from 550 percent of demand to 140 percent, and the cost to repair products went down by 25 to 30 percent due to an increased throughput. The Center's ability to repair MK-48s became much more flexible, too. In fact, it can now repair as many as 23 MK-48s per month. The Center is on schedule for 99 percent of the production lines where the TOC principles have been implemented, and the repair costs have decreased by 25 percent. Carrying out these simple improvements made the Albany Maintenance Center a world-class overhaul and repair operation.

Repairs to assault vehicles can vary tremendously at the U.S. Marine Corps Maintenance Center in Albany, Georgia. The center struggled to keep up with its repairs until managers implemented the simplified form of a drum-buffer-rope system. The result? Repair times fell from 167 days to just 58 days, on average.

Source: Mandyam Srinivasan, Darren Jones, and Alex Miller, "Applying Theory of Constraints Principles and Lean Thinking at the Marine Corps Maintenance Center," *Defense Acquisition Review Journal,* August–November 2004; M. Srinivasan, Darren Jones, and Alex Miller, "Corps Capabilities," *APICS Magazine* (March 2005), pp. 46–50.

Managing Constraints in a Line Process

Products created by a line process include the assembly of computers, automobiles, appliances, and toys. Such assembly lines can exist in providing services as well. For instance, putting together a standardized hamburger with a fixed sequence of steps is akin to operating an assembly line. While the product mix or demand volumes do not change as rapidly for line processes as for job or batch processes, the load can shift between work centers in a line as the end product being assembled is changed or the total output rate of the line is altered. Constraints arising out of such actions can be managed by balancing the workload between different stations in a line, which we explain next in greater detail.

Line Balancing

line balancing

The assignment of work to stations in a line process so as to achieve the desired output rate with the smallest number of workstations.

Line balancing is the assignment of work to stations in a line process so as to achieve the desired output rate with the smallest number of workstations. Normally, one worker is assigned to a station. Thus, the line that produces at the desired pace with the fewest workers is the most efficient one. Achieving this goal is much like the theory of constraints, because both approaches are concerned about bottlenecks. Line balancing differs in how it addresses bottlenecks. Rather than (1) taking on new customer orders to best use bottleneck capacity or (2) scheduling so that bottleneck resources are conserved, line balancing takes a third approach. It (3) creates workstations with workloads as evenly balanced as possible. It seeks to create workstations so that the capacity utilization for the bottleneck is not much higher than for the other workstations in the line. Another difference is that line balancing applies only to line processes that do assembly work, or to work that can be bundled in many ways to create the jobs for each workstation in the line. The latter situation can be found both in manufacturing and service settings.

work elements

The smallest units of work that can be performed independently.

Line balancing must be performed when a line is set up initially, when a line is rebalanced to change its hourly output rate, or when a product or process changes. The goal is to obtain workstations with well-balanced workloads (e.g., every station takes roughly 3 minutes per customer in a cafeteria line with different food stations).

immediate predecessors

Work elements that must be done before the next element can begin.

The analyst begins by separating the work into **work elements**, which are the smallest units of work that can be performed independently. The analyst then obtains the time standard for each element and identifies the work elements, called **immediate predecessors**, which must be done before the next element can begin.

Precedence Diagram Most lines must satisfy some technological precedence requirements; that is, certain work elements must be done before the next can begin. However, most lines also allow for some latitude and more than one sequence of operations. To help you better visualize immediate predecessors, let us run through the construction of a **precedence diagram**.[2] We denote the work elements by circles, with the time required to perform the work shown below each circle. Arrows lead from immediate predecessors to the next work element. Example 4 illustrates a manufacturing process, but a back office line-flow process in a service setting can be approached similarly.

EXAMPLE 4	Constructing a Precedence Diagram

Green Grass, Inc., a manufacturer of lawn and garden equipment, is designing an assembly line to produce a new fertilizer spreader, the Big Broadcaster. Using the following information on the production process, construct a precedence diagram for the Big Broadcaster.

Work Element	Description	Time (sec)	Immediate Predecessor(s)
A	Bolt leg frame to hopper	40	None
B	Insert impeller shaft	30	A
C	Attach axle	50	A
D	Attach agitator	40	B
E	Attach drive wheel	6	B
F	Attach free wheel	25	C
G	Mount lower post	15	C
H	Attach controls	20	D, E
I	Mount nameplate	18	F, G
		Total 244	

SOLUTION

Figure 4 shows the complete diagram. We begin with work element A, which has no immediate predecessors. Next, we add elements B and C, for which element A is the only immediate predecessor. After entering time standards and arrows showing precedence, we add elements D and E, and so on. The diagram simplifies interpretation. Work element F, for example, can be done anywhere on the line after element C is completed. However, element I must await completion of elements F and G.

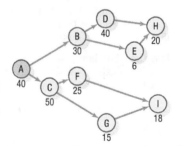

◀ **FIGURE 4**
Precedence Diagram for Assembling the Big Broadcaster

DECISION POINT

Management now has enough information to develop a line-flow layout that clusters work elements to form workstations, with a goal being to balance the workloads and, in the process, minimize the number of workstations required.

Desired Output Rate The goal of line balancing is to match the output rate to the staffing or production plan. For example, if the plan calls for 4,800 units or customers per week and the line operates 80 hours per week, the desired output rate ideally would be 60 units or customers (4,800/80) per hour. Matching output to the plan ensures on-time delivery and prevents buildup of unwanted inventory or customer delays. However, managers should avoid rebalancing a line too frequently because each time a line is rebalanced many workers' jobs on the line must be redesigned, temporarily hurting productivity and sometimes even requiring a new detailed layout for some stations.

---

[2]Precedence relationships and precedence diagrams are also important in the entirely different context of project management.

Cycle Time   After determining the desired output rate for a line, the analyst can calculate the line's cycle time. A line's **cycle time** is the maximum time allowed for work on a unit at each station.[3] If the time required for work elements at a station exceeds the line's cycle time, the station will be a bottleneck, preventing the line from reaching its desired output rate. The target cycle time is the reciprocal of the desired hourly output rate:

$$c = \frac{1}{r}$$

where

$$c = \text{cycle time in hours per unit}$$

$$r = \text{desired output rate in units per hour}$$

For example, if the line's desired output rate is 60 units per hour, the cycle time is $c = 1/60$ hour per unit, or 1 minute.

Theoretical Minimum   To achieve the desired output rate, managers use line balancing to assign every work element to a station, making sure to satisfy all precedence requirements and to minimize the number of stations, n, formed. If each station is operated by a different worker, minimizing n also maximizes worker productivity. Perfect balance is achieved when the sum of the work-element times at each station equals the cycle time, c, and no station has any idle time. For example, if the sum of each station's work-element times is 1 minute, which is also the cycle time, the line achieves perfect balance. Although perfect balance usually is unachievable in practice, owing to the unevenness of work-element times and the inflexibility of precedence requirements, it sets a benchmark, or goal, for the smallest number of stations possible. The **theoretical minimum (TM)** for the number of stations is

$$\text{TM} = \frac{\Sigma t}{c}$$

where

$$\Sigma t = \text{total time required to assemble each unit (the sum of all work-element standard times)}$$

$$c = \text{cycle time}$$

For example, if the sum of the work-element times is 15 minutes and the cycle time is 1 minute, TM = 15/1, or 15 stations. Any fractional values obtained for TM are rounded up because fractional stations are impossible.

Idle Time, Efficiency, and Balance Delay   Minimizing n automatically ensures (1) minimal idle time, (2) maximal efficiency, and (3) minimal balance delay. Idle time is the total unproductive time for all stations in the assembly of each unit:

$$\text{Idle time} = nc - \Sigma t$$

where

$$n = \text{number of stations}$$

$$c = \text{cycle time}$$

$$\Sigma t = \text{total standard time required to assemble each unit}$$

Efficiency is the ratio of productive time to total time, expressed as a percent:

$$\text{Efficiency (\%)} = \frac{\Sigma t}{nc}(100)$$

Balance delay is the amount by which efficiency falls short of 100 percent:

$$\text{Balance delay (\%)} = 100 - \text{Efficiency}$$

As long as c is fixed, we can optimize all three goals by minimizing n.

---

[3]Except in the context of line balancing, *cycle time* has a different meaning. It is the elapsed time between starting and completing a job. Some researchers and practitioners prefer the term *lead time*.

---

cycle time

The maximum time allowed for work on a unit at each station.

theoretical minimum (TM)

A benchmark or goal for the smallest number of stations possible, where the total time required to assemble each unit (the sum of all work-element standard times) is divided by the cycle time.

balance delay

The amount by which efficiency falls short of 100 percent.

Skoda Automotive assembly line in Mlada Boleslav. Since 1991, Skoda has been a part of Volkswagen for over 20 years.

| EXAMPLE 5 | Calculating the Cycle Time, Theoretical Minimum, and Efficiency |

Green Grass's plant manager just received marketing's latest forecasts of Big Broadcaster sales for the next year. She wants its production line to be designed to make 2,400 spreaders per week for at least the next 3 months. The plant will operate 40 hours per week.

a. What should be the line's cycle time?

b. What is the smallest number of workstations that she could hope for in designing the line for this cycle time?

c. Suppose that she finds a solution that requires only five stations. What would be the line's efficiency?

MyOMLab

Tutor 7.1 in MyOMLab provides another example to calculate these line-balancing measures.

SOLUTION

a. First, convert the desired output rate (2,400 units per week) to an hourly rate by dividing the weekly output rate by 40 hours per week to get $r = 60$ units per hour. Then, the cycle time is

$$c = 1/r = 1/60 \text{ (hour/unit)} = 1 \text{ minute/unit} = 60 \text{ seconds/unit}$$

b. Now, calculate the theoretical minimum for the number of stations by dividing the total time, Σt, by the cycle time, $c = 60$ seconds. Assuming perfect balance, we have

$$TM = \frac{\Sigma t}{c} = \frac{244 \text{ seconds}}{60 \text{ seconds}} = 4.067 \text{ or } 5 \text{ stations}$$

c. Now, calculate the efficiency of a five-station solution, assuming for now that one can be found:

$$\text{Efficiency (\%)} = \frac{\Sigma t}{nc}(100) = \frac{244}{5(60)}(100) = 81.3\%$$

DECISION POINT

If the manager finds a solution with five stations that satisfies all precedence constraints, then that is the optimal solution; it has the minimum number of stations possible. However, the efficiency (sometimes called the *theoretical maximum efficiency*) will be only 81.3 percent. Perhaps the line should be operated less than 40 hours per week (thereby adjusting the cycle time) and the employees transferred to other kinds of work when the line does not operate.

Finding a Solution   Often, many assembly-line solutions are possible, even for such simple problems as Green Grass's. The goal is to cluster the work elements into workstations so that (1) the number of workstations required is minimized, and (2) the precedence and cycle-time requirements are not violated. The idea is to assign work elements to workstations subject to the precedence requirements so that the work content for the station is equal (or nearly so, but less than) the cycle time for the line. In this way, the number of workstations will be minimized.

Here we use the trial-and-error method to find a solution, although commercial software packages are also available. Most of these packages use different decision rules in picking which work element to assign next to a workstation being created. The ones used by POM for Windows are described in Table 3. The solutions can be examined for improvement, because there is no guarantee that they are optimal or even feasible. Some work elements cannot be assigned to the same station, some changes can be made to reduce the number of stations, or some shifts can provide better balance between stations.

TABLE 3 | HEURISTIC DECISION RULES IN ASSIGNING THE NEXT WORK ELEMENT TO A WORKSTATION BEING CREATED

Create one station at a time. For the station now being created, identify the unassigned work elements that qualify for assignment: They are candidates if

1. **All of their predecessors have been assigned to this station or stations already created.**

2. **Adding them to the workstation being created will not create a workload that exceeds the cycle time.**

Decision Rule	Logic
Longest work element	Picking the candidate with the longest time to complete is an effort to fit in the most difficult elements first, leaving the ones with short times to "fill out" the station.
Shortest work element	This rule is the opposite of the longest work element rule because it gives preference in workstation assignments to those work elements that are quicker. It can be tried because no single rule guarantees the best solution. It might provide another solution for the planner to consider.
Most followers	When picking the next work element to assign to a station being created, choose the element that has the most *followers* (due to precedence requirements). In Figure 4, item C has three followers (F, G, and I) whereas item D has only one follower (H). This rule seeks to maintain flexibility so that good choices remain for creating the last few workstations at the end of the line.
Fewest followers	Picking the candidate with the fewest followers is the opposite of the most followers rule.

Figure 5 shows a solution that creates just five workstations. We know that five is the minimum possible, because five is the theoretical minimum found in Example 5. All of the precedence and cycle-time requirements are also satisfied. Consequently, the solution is optimal for this problem. Each worker at each station must perform the work elements in the proper sequence. For example, workstation S5 consists of one worker who will perform work elements E, H, and I on each unit that comes along the assembly line. The processing time per unit is 44 seconds (6 + 20 + 18) which does not exceed the cycle time of 60 seconds (see Example 5). Furthermore, the immediate predecessors of these three work elements are assigned to this workstation or upstream workstations, so their precedence requirements are satisfied. The worker at workstation S5 can do element I at any time but will not start element H until element E is finished.

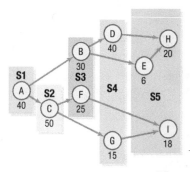

▲ FIGURE 5
Big Broadcaster Precedence
Diagram Solution

pacing

The movement of product from one station to the next as soon as the cycle time has elapsed.

Managerial Considerations

In addition to balancing a line for a given cycle time, managers have four other considerations: (1) pacing, (2) behavioral factors, (3) number of models produced, and (4) different cycle times.

Pacing   The movement of product from one station to the next as soon as the cycle time has elapsed is called **pacing**. Pacing manufacturing processes allows materials handling to be automated and requires less inventory storage area. However, it is less flexible in handling unexpected delays that require either slowing down the entire line or pulling the unfinished work off the line to be completed later.

Behavioral Factors   The most controversial aspect of line-flow layouts is behavioral response. Studies show that installing production lines increases absenteeism, turnover, and grievances.

Paced production and high specialization (say, cycle times of less than 2 minutes) lower job satisfaction. Workers generally favor inventory buffers as a means of avoiding mechanical pacing. One study even showed that productivity increased on unpaced lines.

Number of Models Produced   A line that produces several items belonging to the same family is called a **mixed-model line**. In contrast, a single-model line produces one model with no variations. Mixed-model production enables a plant to achieve both high-volume production *and* product variety. However, it complicates scheduling and increases the need for good communication about the specific parts to be produced at each station.

mixed-model line

A production line that produces several items belonging to the same family.

Cycle Times   A line's cycle time depends on the desired output rate (or sometimes on the maximum number of workstations allowed). In turn, the maximum line efficiency varies considerably with the cycle time selected. Thus, exploring a range of cycle times makes sense. A manager might go with a particularly efficient solution even if it does not match the desired output rate. The manager can compensate for the mismatch by varying the number of hours the line operates through overtime, extending shifts, or adding shifts. Multiple lines might even be the answer.

LEARNING GOALS IN REVIEW

① **Explain the theory of constraints.** Constraints or bottlenecks can exist in the form of internal resources or market demand in both manufacturing and service organizations, and in turn play an important role in determining system performance. See the section on "The Theory of Constraints (TOC)". Review opening vignette on BP Oil Spill clean-up for an application of TOC.

② **Understand linkage of capacity constraints to financial performance measures.** Review and understand Table 1.

③ **Identify bottlenecks.** The TOC provides guidelines on how to identify and manage constraints. The section "Identification and Management of Bottlenecks," shows you how to identify bottlenecks in both service as well as manufacturing firms.

④ **Apply theory of constraints to product mix decisions.** Review Example 3 to understand how using a bottleneck based method for allocating resources and determining the product mix leads to greater profits.

⑤ **Describe how to manage constraints in an assembly line.** Assembly line balancing, as a special form of a constraint in managing a line process within both manufacturing and services, can also be an effective mechanism for matching output to a plan and running such processes more efficiently. The section "Managing Constraints in a Line Process," shows you how to balance assembly lines and create work stations. Review Solved Problem 2 for an application of line balancing principles.

MyOMLab helps you develop analytical skills and assesses your progress with multiple problems on processing time for average customer, bottleneck activity, maximum customers served at bottleneck per hour, average capacity of system, theoretical maximum of stations in an assembly line, longest work element decision rule, line's efficiency, and cycle time.

MyOMLab Resources	Titles	Link to the Book
Video	*Constraint Management at Southwest Airlines*	Managing Constraints Across the Organization; The Theory of Constraints
	1st Bank Villa Italia: Waiting Lines	Identification and Management of Bottlenecks
OM Explorer Solvers	Min-Yo Garment Company Spreadsheet	Estimate Capacity Requirements; Example 1; Managing Bottlenecks in Manufacturing Processes; Example 2
OM Explorer Tutors	7.1 Line Balancing	Line Balancing; Example 5; Solved Problem 2
POM for Windows	Line Balancing	Line Balancing; Example 5; Solved Problem 2
SimQuick Simulation Exercises	Simulating process of making jewelry boxes and making choice on investing in new machine	The Theory of Constraints; Example 1
Internet Exercise	Granite Rock and Chevron	The Theory of Constraints; Identification and Management of Bottlenecks
Key Equations		
Image Library		

Key Equations

1. Cycle time: $c = \dfrac{1}{r}$

2. Theoretical minimum number of workstations: $\text{TM} = \dfrac{\Sigma t}{c}$

3. Idle time: $nc - \Sigma t$

4. Efficiency(%): $\dfrac{\Sigma t}{nc}(100)$

5. Balance delay (%): $100 - \text{Efficiency}$

Key Terms

balance delay
bottleneck
constraint
cycle time
drum-buffer-rope (DBR)

immediate predecessors
line balancing
mixed-model line
pacing
precedence diagram

theoretical minimum (TM)
theory of constraints (TOC)
throughput time
work elements

Solved Problem 1

Bill's Car Wash offers two types of washes: Standard and Deluxe. The process flow for both types of customers is shown in the following chart. Both wash types are first processed through steps A1 and A2. The Standard wash then goes through steps A3 and A4 while the Deluxe is processed through steps A5, A6, and A7. Both offerings finish at the drying station (A8). The numbers in parentheses indicate the minutes it takes for that activity to process a customer.

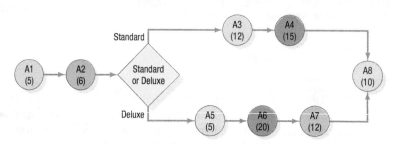

a. Which step is the bottleneck for the Standard car wash process? For the Deluxe car wash process?

b. What is the capacity (measured as customers served per hour) of Bill's Car Wash to process Standard and Deluxe customers? Assume that no customers are waiting at step A1, A2, or A8.

c. If 60 percent of the customers are Standard and 40 percent are Deluxe, what is the average capacity of the car wash in customers per hour?

d. Where would you expect Standard wash customers to experience waiting lines, assuming that new customers are always entering the shop and that no Deluxe customers are in the shop? Where would the Deluxe customers have to wait, assuming no Standard customers?

SOLUTION

a. Step A4 is the bottleneck for the Standard car wash process, and Step A6 is the bottleneck for the Deluxe car wash process, because these steps take the longest time in the flow.

b. The capacity for Standard washes is 4 customers per hour because the bottleneck step A4 can process 1 customer every 15 minutes (60/15). The capacity for Deluxe car washes is 3 customers per hour (60/20). These capacities are derived by translating the "minutes per customer" of each bottleneck activity to "customers per hour."

c. The average capacity of the car wash is $(0.60 \times 4) + (0.40 \times 3) = 3.6$ customers per hour.

d. Standard wash customers would wait before steps A1, A2, A3, and A4 because the activities that immediately precede them have a higher rate of output (i.e., smaller processing times). Deluxe wash customers would experience a wait in front of steps A1, A2, and A6 for the same reasons. A1 is included for both types of washes because the arrival rate of customers could always exceed the capacity of A1.

Solved Problem 2

A company is setting up an assembly line to produce 192 units per 8-hour shift. The following table identifies the work elements, times, and immediate predecessors:

Work Element	Time (Sec)	Immediate Predecessor(s)
A	40	None
B	80	A
C	30	D, E, F
D	25	B
E	20	B
F	15	B
G	120	A
H	145	G
I	130	H
J	115	C, I
	Total 720	

a. What is the desired cycle time (in seconds)?

b. What is the theoretical minimum number of stations?

c. Use trial and error to work out a solution, and show your solution on a precedence diagram.

d. What are the efficiency and balance delay of the solution found?

SOLUTION

a. Substituting in the cycle-time formula, we get

$$c = \frac{1}{r} = \frac{8\ \text{hours}}{192\ \text{units}}(3{,}600\ \text{seconds/hour}) = 150\ \text{seconds/unit}$$

b. The sum of the work-element times is 720 seconds, so

$$TM = \frac{\Sigma t}{c} = \frac{720\ \text{seconds/unit}}{150\ \text{seconds/unit-station}} = 4.8\ \text{or 5 stations}$$

which may not be achievable.

c. The precedence diagram is shown in Figure 6. Each row in the following table shows work elements assigned to each of the five workstations in the proposed solution.

d. Calculating the efficiency, we get

$$\text{Efficiency} = \frac{\Sigma t}{nc}(100) = \frac{720\ \text{seconds/unit}}{5[150\ \text{seconds/unit}]} = 96\%$$

Thus, the balance delay is only 4 percent (100–96).

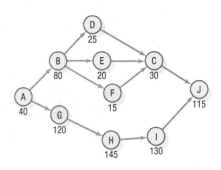

▲ FIGURE 6
Precedence Diagram

Station	Candidate(s)	Choice	Work-Element Time (Sec)	Cumulative Time (Sec)	Idle Time (c = 150 Sec)
S1	A	A	40	40	110
	B	B	80	120	30
	D, E, F	D	25	145	5
S2	E, F, G	G	120	120	30
	E, F	E	20	140	10
S3	F, H	H	145	145	5
S4	F, I	I	130	130	20
	F	F	15	145	5
S5	C	C	30	30	120
	J	J	115	145	5

Discussion Questions

1. Take a process that you encounter on a daily basis, such as the lunch cafeteria or the journey from your home to school/work, and identify the bottlenecks that limit the throughput of this process.

2. Using the same process as in question 1, identify conditions that would lead to the bottlenecks changing or shifting away from the existing bottleneck.

3. How could the efficiency of the redesigned process be improved further?

Problems

The OM Explorer and POM for Windows software is available to all students using the 10th edition of this text. Go to **www.pearsonhighered.com/krajewski** to download these computer packages. If you purchased MyOMLab, you also have access to Active Models software and significant help in doing the following problems. Check with your instructor on how best to use these resources. In many cases, the instructor wants you to understand how to do the calculations by hand. At the least, the software provides a check on your calculations. When calculations are particularly complex and the goal is interpreting the results in making decision, the software entirely replaces the manual calculations.

1. Bill's Barbershop has two barbers available to cut customers' hair. Both barbers provide roughly the same experience and skill, but one is just a little bit slower than the other. The process flow in Figure 7 shows that all customers go through steps B1 and B2 and then can be served at either of the two barbers at step B3. The process ends for all customers at step B4. The numbers in parentheses indicate the minutes it takes that activity to process a customer.

a. How long does it take the average customer to complete this process?

b. What single activity is the bottleneck for the entire process?

c. How many customers can this process serve in an hour?

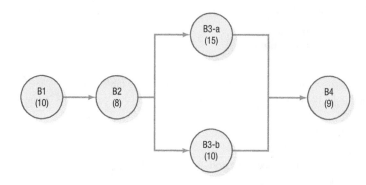

▲ FIGURE 7
Process Flow for Bill's Barbershop

2. Figure 8 details the process flow for two types of customers who enter Barbara's Boutique shop for customized dress alterations. After step T1, Type A customers proceed to step T2 and then to any of the three workstations at T3, followed by steps T4 and T7. After step T1, Type B customers proceed to step T5 and then steps T6 and T7. The numbers in parentheses are the minutes it takes to process a customer.

   a. What is the capacity of Barbara's shop in terms of the numbers of Type A customers who can be served

   in an hour? Assume no customers are waiting at steps T1 or T7.

   b. If 30 percent of the customers are Type A customers and 70 percent are Type B customers, what is the average capacity of Barbara's shop in customers per hour?

   c. Assuming that the arrival rate is greater than five customers per hour, when would you expect Type A customers to experience waiting lines, assuming no Type B customers in the shop? Where would the Type B customers have to wait, assuming no Type A customers?

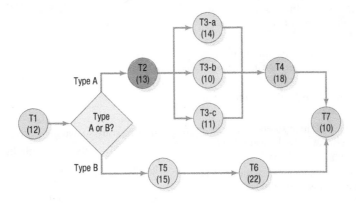

▲ FIGURE 8
Process Flow for Barbara's Boutique Customers

3. Canine Kernels Company (CKC) manufactures two different types of dog chew toys (A and B, sold in 1,000-count boxes) that are manufactured and assembled on three different workstations (W, X, and Y) using a small-batch process (see Figure 9). Batch setup times are negligible. The flowchart denotes the path each product follows through the manufacturing process, and each product's price, demand per week, and processing times per unit are indicated as well. Purchased parts and raw materials consumed during production are represented by inverted triangles. CKC can make and sell up to the limit of its demand per week; no penalties are incurred for not being able to meet all the demand. Each workstation is staffed by a worker who is dedicated to work on that workstation alone and is paid $6 per hour. Total labor costs per week are fixed. Variable overhead costs are $3,500/week. The plant operates one 8-hour shift per day, or 40 hours/week. Which of the three workstations, W, X, or Y, has the highest aggregate workload, and thus serves as the bottleneck for CKC?

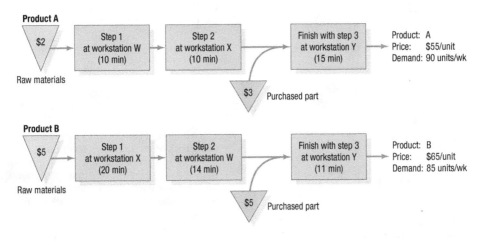

▲ FIGURE 9
Flowchart for Canine Kernels Company (CKC)

4. The senior management at Canine Kernels Company (CKC) is concerned with the existing capacity limitation, so they want to accept the mix of orders that maximizes the company's profits. Traditionally, CKC has utilized a method whereby decisions are made to produce as much of the product with the highest contribution margin as possible (up to the limit of its demand), followed by the next highest contribution margin product, and so on until no more capacity is available. Because capacity is limited, choosing the proper product mix is crucial. Troy Hendrix, the newly hired production supervisor, is an avid follower of the theory of constraints philosophy and the bottleneck method for scheduling. He believes that profitability can indeed be approved if bottleneck resources are exploited to determine the product mix.

   a. What is the profit if the traditional contribution margin method is used for determining CKC's product mix?

   b. What is the profit if the bottleneck method advocated by Troy is used for selecting the product mix?

   c. Calculate the profit gain, both in absolute dollars as well as in terms of percentage gains, by using TOC principles for determining product mix.

5. Use the longest work element rule to balance the assembly line described in the following table and Figure 10 so that it will produce 40 units per hour.

   a. What is the cycle time?

   b. What is the theoretical minimum number of workstations?

   c. Which work elements are assigned to each workstation?

   d. What are the resulting efficiency and balance delay percentages?

   e. Use the shortest work element rule to balance the assembly line. Do you note any changes in solution?

Work Element	Time (Sec)	Immediate Predecessor(s)
A	40	None
B	80	A
C	30	A
D	25	B
E	20	C
F	15	B
G	60	B
H	45	D
I	10	E, G
J	75	F
K	15	H, I, J
	Total 415	

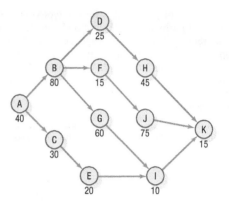

▲ FIGURE 10
Precedence Diagram

6. Johnson Cogs wants to set up a line to serve 60 customers per hour. The work elements and their precedence relationships are shown in the following table.

   a. What is the theoretical minimum number of stations?

   b. How many stations are required using the longest work element decision rule?

   c. Suppose that a solution requiring five stations is obtained. What is its efficiency?

Work Element	Time (Sec)	Immediate Predecessor(s)
A	40	None
B	30	A
C	50	A
D	40	B
E	6	B
F	25	C
G	15	C
H	20	D, E
I	18	F, G
J	30	H, I
	Total 274	

7. The *trim line* at PW is a small subassembly line that, along with other such lines, feeds into the final chassis line. The entire assembly line, which consists of more than 900 workstations, is to make PW's new E cars. The trim line itself involves only 13 work elements and must handle 20 cars per hour. Work-element data are as follows:

Work Element	Time (Sec)	Immediate Predecessor(s)
A	1.8	None
B	0.4	None
C	1.6	None
D	1.5	A
E	0.7	A
F	0.5	E
G	0.8	B
H	1.4	C
I	1.4	D
J	1.4	F, G
K	0.5	H
L	1.0	J
M	0.8	I, K, L

a. Draw a precedence diagram.

b. What cycle time (in minutes) results in the desired output rate?

c. What is the theoretical minimum number of stations?

d. Use the longest work element decision rule to balance the line and calculate the efficiency of your solution.

e. Use the most followers work element decision rule to balance the line and calculate the efficiency of your solution.

8. In order to meet holiday demand, Penny's Pie Shop requires a production line that is capable of producing 50 pecan pies per week, while operating only 40 hours per week. There are only 4 steps required to produce a single pecan pie with respective processing times of 5 min, 5 min, 45 min, and 15 min.

a. What should be the line's cycle time?

b. What is the smallest number of workstations Penny could hope for in designing the line considering this cycle time?

c. Suppose that Penny finds a solution that requires only four stations. What would be the efficiency of this line?

Advanced Problems

9. Melissa's Photo Studio offers both individual and group portrait options. The process flow diagram in Figure 11 shows that all customers must first register and then pay at one of two cashiers. Then, depending on whether they want a single or group portrait they go to different rooms. Finally, everyone picks up their own finished portrait.

a. How long does it take to complete the entire process for a group portrait?

b. What single activity is the bottleneck for the entire process, assuming the process receives equal amounts of both groups and individuals?

c. What is the capacity of the bottleneck for both groups and individuals?

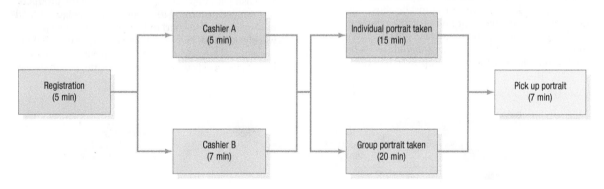

▲ FIGURE 11
Melissa's Photo Studio

10. Yost-Perry Industries (YPI) manufactures a mix of affordable guitars (A, B, C) that are fabricated and assembled at four different processing stations (W, X, Y, Z). The operation is a batch process with small setup times that can be considered negligible. The product information (price, weekly demand, and processing times) and process sequences are shown in Figure 12. Raw materials and purchased parts (shown as a per-unit consumption rate) are represented by inverted triangles. YPI is able to make and sell up to the limit of its demand per week with no penalties incurred for not meeting the full demand. Each workstation is staffed by one highly skilled worker who is dedicated to work on that workstation alone and is paid $15 per hour. The plant operates one 8-hour shift per day and operates on a 5-day work week (i.e., 40 hours of production per person per week). Overhead costs are $9,000/week. Which of the four workstations, W, X, Y, or Z, has the highest aggregate workload, and thus serves as the bottleneck for YPI?

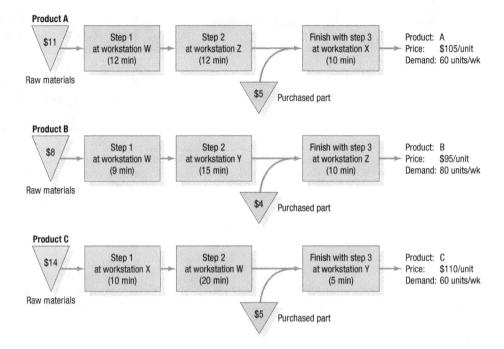

► FIGURE 12
Flowchart for Yost-Perry
Industries (YPI)

11. Yost-Perry Industries' (YPI) senior management team wants to improve the profitability of the firm by accepting the right set of orders. Currently, decisions are made using the traditional method, which is to accept as much of the highest contribution margin product as possible (up to the limit of its demand), followed by the next highest contribution margin product, and so on until all available capacity is utilized. Because the firm cannot satisfy all the demand, the product mix must be chosen carefully. Jay Perry, the newly promoted production supervisor, is knowledgeable about the theory of constraints and the bottleneck-based method for scheduling. He believes that profitability can indeed be improved if bottleneck resources are exploited to determine the product mix. What is the change in profits if, instead of the traditional method that YPI has used thus far, the bottleneck method advocated by Jay is used for selecting the product mix?

12. A.J.'s Wildlife Emporium manufactures two unique bird-feeders (Deluxe and Super Duper) that are manufactured and assembled in up to three different workstations (X, Y, Z) using a small batch process. Each of the products is produced according to the flowchart in Figure 13. Additionally, the flowchart indicates each product's price, weekly demand, and processing times per unit. Batch setup times are negligible. A.J. can make and sell up to the limit of its weekly demand and there are no penalties for

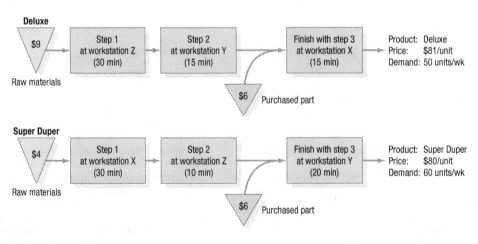

▲ FIGURE 13
A.J.'s Wildlife Emporium Flowchart

not being able to meet all of the demand. Each workstation is staffed by a worker who is dedicated to work on that workstation alone and is paid $16 per hour. The plant operates 40 hours per week, with no overtime. Overhead costs are $2,000 per week. Based on the information provided, as well as the information contained in the flowchart, answer the following questions.

a. Using the traditional method, which bases decisions solely on a product's contribution to profits and overhead, what is the optimal product mix and what is the overall profitability?

b. Using the bottleneck-based method, what is the optimal product mix and what is the overall profitability?

13. Cooper River Glass Works (CRGW) produces four different models of desk lamps as shown in Figure 14. The operations manager knows that total monthly demand exceeds the capacity available for production. Thus, she is interested in determining the product mix which will maximize profits. Each model's price, routing, processing times, and material cost is provided in Figure 14. Demand next month is estimated to be 200 units of model Alpha, 250 units of model Bravo, 150 units of model Charlie, and 225 units of model Delta. CRGW operates only one 8-hour shift per day and is scheduled to work 20 days next month (no overtime). Further, each station requires a 10 percent capacity cushion.

a. Which station is the bottleneck?

b. Using the traditional method, which bases decisions solely on a product's contribution to profits and overhead, what is the optimal product mix and what is the overall profitability?

c. Using the bottleneck-based method, what is the optimal product mix and what is the overall profitability?

14. The senior management at Davis Watercraft would like to determine if it is possible to improve firm profitability by changing their existing product mix. Currently, the product mix is determined by giving resource priority to the highest contribution margin watercraft. Davis Watercraft always has a contingent of 10 workers on hand; each worker is paid $25 per hour. Overhead costs are $35,000 per week. The plant operates 18 hours per day and 6 days per week. Labor is considered a fixed expense because workers are paid for their time regardless of their utilization. The production manager has determined that workstation 1 is the bottleneck. Detailed production information is provided below.

	Model		
	A	B	C
Price	$450	$400	$500
Material Cost	$50	$40	$110
Weekly Demand	100	75	40
Processing Time Station 1	60 min	0 min	30 min
Processing Time Station 2	0 min	0 min	60 min
Processing Time Station 3	10 min	60 min	0 min
Processing Time Station 4	20 min	30 min	40 min

a. Using the traditional method, which bases decisions solely on a product's contribution to profits and overhead, what is the product mix that yields the highest total profit? What is the resulting profit?

b. Using the bottleneck-based method, what is the product mix that yields the highest total profit? What is the resulting profit?

▶ FIGURE 14

Cooper River Glass Works Flowchart

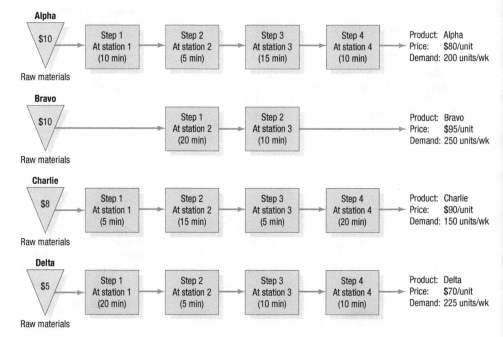

15. A paced assembly line has been devised to manufacture calculators, as the following data show:

Station	Work Element Assigned	Work Element Time (min)
S1	A	2.7
S2	D, E	0.6, 0.9
S3	C	3.0
S4	B, F, G	0.7, 0.7, 0.9
S5	H, I, J	0.7, 0.3, 1.2
S6	K	2.4

    a. What is the maximum hourly output rate from this line? (*Hint*: The line can go only as fast as its slowest workstation.)

    b. What cycle time corresponds to this maximum output rate?

    c. If a worker is at each station and the line operates at this maximum output rate, how much idle time is lost during each 10-hour shift?

    d. What is the line's efficiency?

16. Jane produces custom greeting cards using six distinct work elements. She would like to produce 10 cards in each 8-hour card-making session. Figure 15 details each work element and its associated durations in minutes as well as their precedence relationships.

    a. What cycle time is required to satisfy the required output rate?

    b. What is the theoretical minimum number of workstations required?

    c. If Jane identifies a five-station solution, what is the associated efficiency and balance delay?

    d. If the cycle time increased by 100 percent, would the theoretical minimum number of workstations also increase by 100 percent?

17. Greg Davis, a business major at the University of South Carolina (USC), has opened Six Points Saco (SPS), a specialty subs–taco restaurant, at the rim of the USC campus. SPS has grown in popularity over the one year that it has been in operation, and Greg is trying to perfect the business model before making it into a franchise. He wants to maximize the productivity of his staff, as well as serve customers well in a timely fashion. One area of concern is the drive-thru operation during the 11:30 A.M. to 12:30 P.M. lunch hour.

The process of fulfilling an order involves fulfilling the tasks listed below.

Greg is interested in getting a better understanding of the staffing patterns that will be needed in order to operate his restaurant. After taking a course in operations management at the university, he knows that fulfilling a customer order at SPS is very similar to operating an assembly line. He has also used the POM for Windows software before, and wants to apply it for examining different demand scenarios for serving his customers.

    a. If all the seven tasks are handled by one employee, how many customers could be served per hour?

    b. If Greg wants to process 45 customers per hour, how many employees will he need during the peak period?

    c. With the number of employees determined in part b, what is the maximum number of customers who could be served every hour (i.e., what is the maximum output capacity)?

    d. Assuming that no task is assigned to more than one employee, what is the "maximum output capacity" from this assembly line? How many employees will be needed to actually accomplish this maximum output capacity?

    e. Beyond the output accomplished in part d, if Greg decides to add one additional worker to help out with a bottleneck task, where should he add that worker? With that addition, would he be able to process more customers per hour? If so, what is the new maximum output capacity for the drive-thru?

	Task	Time (Seconds)	Immediate Predecessors
A.	Take an order at the booth. Most orders are for a taco and a sub.	25	
B.	Collect money at the window.	20	A
C.	Gather drinks.	35	B
D.	Assemble taco order.	32	B
E.	Assemble sub order.	30	B
F.	Put drinks, taco, and sub in a bag.	25	C, D, E
G.	Give the bag to the customer.	10	F

18. Refer back to problem 7. Suppose that in addition to the usual precedence constraints, there are two zoning constraints within the trim line. First, work elements K and L should be assigned to the same station; both use a common component, and assigning them to the same station conserves storage space. Second, work elements H and J cannot be performed at the same station.

    a. Using trial and error, balance the line as best you can.

    b. What is the efficiency of your solution?

FIGURE 15 ▶
Precedence Diagram for
Custom Greeting Cards

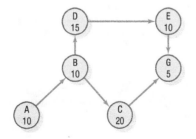

EXPERIENTIAL LEARNING | Min-Yo Garment Company

The Min-Yo Garment Company is a small firm in Taiwan that produces sportswear for sale in the wholesale and retail markets. Min-Yo's garments are unique because they offer fine embroidery and fabrics with a variety of striped and solid patterns. Over the 20 years of its existence, the Min-Yo Garment Company has become known as a quality producer of sports shirts with dependable deliveries. However, during that same period, the nature of the apparel industry has undergone change. In the past, firms could be successful producing standardized shirts in high volumes with few pattern or color choices and long production lead times. Currently, with the advent of regionalized merchandising and intense competition at the retail level, buyers of the shirts are looking for shorter lead times and much more variety in patterns and colors. Consequently, many more business opportunities are available today than ever before to a respected company such as Min-Yo.

Even though the opportunity for business success seemed bright, the management meeting last week was gloomy. Min-Yo Lee, president and owner of Min-Yo Garment, expressed concerns over the performance of the company: "We are facing strong competition for our products. Large apparel firms are driving prices down on high-volume licensed brands. Each day more firms enter the customized shirt business. Our profits are lower than expected, and delivery performance is deteriorating. We must reexamine our capabilities and decide what we can do best."

Products

Min-Yo has divided its product line into three categories: licensed brands, subcontracted brands, and special garments.

Licensed Brands

Licensed brands are brands that are owned by one company but, through a licensing agreement, are produced by another firm that also markets the brand in a specific geographic region. The licenser may have licensees all over the world. The licensee pays the licenser a fee for the privilege of marketing the brand in its region, and the licenser agrees to provide some advertising for the product, typically through media outlets that have international exposure. A key aspect of the licensing agreement is that the licensee must agree to provide sufficient quantities of product at the retail level. Running out of stock hurts the image of the brand name.

Currently, only one licensed brand is manufactured by Min-Yo. The brand, called the Muscle Shirt, is owned by a large "virtual corporation" in Italy that has no manufacturing facilities of its own. Min-Yo has been licensed to manufacture Muscle Shirts and sell them to large retail chains in Taiwan. The retail chains require prompt shipments at the end of each week. Because of competitive pressures from other licensed brands, low prices are important. Min-Yo sells each Muscle Shirt to retail chains for $6.

The demand for Muscle Shirts averages 900 shirts per week. The following demand for Muscle Shirts has been forecasted for the next 12 weeks.

Min-Yo's forecasts of Muscle Shirts are typically accurate to within ±200 shirts per week. If demand exceeds supply in any week, the excess demand is lost. No backorders are taken, and Min-Yo incurs no cost penalty for lost sales.

Subcontracted Brands

Manufacturers in the apparel industry often face uncertain demand. To maintain level production at their plants, many manufacturers seek subcontractors to produce their brands. Min-Yo is often considered a subcontractor because of its reputation in the industry. Although price is a consideration, the owners of subcontracted brands emphasize dependable delivery and the ability of the subcontractor to adjust order quantities on short notice.

Week	Demand	Week	Demand
1*	700	7	1,100
2	800	8	1,100
3	900	9	900
4	900	10	900
5	1,000	11	800
6	1,100	12	700

*In other words, the company expects to sell 700 Muscle Shirts at the end of week 1.

Currently, Min-Yo manufactures only one subcontracted brand, called the Thunder Shirt because of its bright colors. Thunder Shirts are manufactured to order for a company in Singapore. Min-Yo's price to this company is $7 per shirt. When orders are placed, usually twice a month, the customer specifies the delivery of certain quantities in each of the next 2 weeks. The last order the customer placed is overdue, forcing Min-Yo to pay a penalty charge. To avoid another penalty, 200 shirts must be shipped in week 1. The Singapore company is expected to specify the quantities it requires for weeks 2 and 3 at the beginning of week 1. The delivery schedule containing the orders for weeks 4 and 5 is expected to arrive at the beginning of week 3, and so on. The customer has estimated its average weekly needs for the year to be 200 shirts per week, although its estimates are frequently inaccurate.

Because of the importance of this large customer to Min-Yo and the lengthy negotiations of the sales department to get the business, management always tries to satisfy its needs. Management believes that if Min-Yo Garment ever refuses to accept an order from this customer, Min-Yo will lose the Thunder Shirt business. Under the terms of the sales contract, Min-Yo agreed to pay this customer $1 for every shirt not shipped on time for each week the shipment of the shirt is delinquent. Delinquent shipments must be made up.

Special Garments

Special garments are made only to customer order because of their low volume and specialized nature. Customers come to Min-Yo Garment to manufacture shirts for special promotions or special company occasions. Min-Yo's special garments are known as Dragon Shirts because of the elaborate embroidery and oriental flair of the designs. Because each shirt is made to a particular customer's specifications and requires a separate setup, special garments cannot be produced in advance of a firm customer order.

Although price is not a major concern for the customers of special garments, Min-Yo sells Dragon Shirts for $8 a shirt to ward off other companies seeking to enter the custom shirt market. Its customers come to Min-Yo because the company can produce almost any design with high quality and deliver an entire order on time. When placing an order for a Dragon Shirt, a customer specifies the design of the shirt (or chooses from Min-Yo's catalog), supplies specific designs for logos, and specifies the quantity of the order and the delivery date. In the past, management checked to see whether such an order would fit into the schedule, and then either accepted or rejected it on that basis. If Min-Yo accepts an order for delivery at the *end* of a certain week and fails to meet this commitment, it pays a penalty of $2 per shirt for each week delivery is delayed. This penalty is incurred weekly until the delinquent order is delivered. The company tried to forecast demand for specific designs of Dragon Shirts but has given up. Last week, Min-Yo had four Dragon Shirt opportunities of 50, 75, 200, and 60 units but chose not to accept any of the orders. Dragon Shirt orders in the past ranged from 50 units to 300 units with varying lead times.

Figure 16, Min-Yo's current open-order file, shows that in some prior week Min-Yo accepted an order of 400 Thunder Shirts for delivery last week. The open-order file is important because it contains the commitment management made to customers. Commitments are for a certain quantity and a date of delivery. As customer orders are accepted, management enters the quantity in the green cell representing the week that they are due. Because Dragon Shirts are unique unto themselves, they each have their own order number for future use. No Dragon Shirt orders appear in the open-order file because Min-Yo has not committed to any in the past several weeks.

Manufacturing

Process

The Min-Yo Garment Company has the latest process technology in the industry—a machine, called a garment maker, that is run by one operator on each of three shifts. This single machine process can make every garment Min-Yo produces; however, the changeover times consume a substantial amount of capacity. Company policy is to run the machine three shifts a day, five days a week. If business is insufficient to keep the machine busy, the workers are idle because Min-Yo is committed to never fire or lay off a worker. By the same token, the firm has a policy of never working on weekends. Thus, the capacity of the process is 5 days × 24 hours = 120 hours per week. The hourly wage is $10 per hour, so the firm is committed to a fixed labor cost of $10 × 120 = $1,200 per week. Once the machine has been set up to make a particular type of garment, it can produce

that garment at the rate of 10 garments per hour, regardless of type. The cost of the material in each garment, regardless of type, is $4. Raw materials are never a problem and can be obtained overnight.

Scheduling the Garment Maker

Scheduling at Min-Yo is done once each week, after production for the week has been completed and shipped, after new orders from customers have arrived, and before production for the next week has started. Scheduling results in two documents.

The first is a production schedule, shown in Figure 17. The schedule shows what management wants the garment maker process to produce in a given week. Two spreadsheet entries are required for each product that is to be produced in a given week. They are in the green shaded cells. The first is the production quantity. In Figure 17, the schedule shows that Min-Yo produced quantities of 800 units for Muscle and 200 units for Thunder last week. The second input is a "1" if the machine is to be set up for a given product or a "blank" if no changeover is required. Figure 17 shows that last week changeovers were required for the Muscle and Thunder production runs. The changeover information is important because, at the end of a week, the garment maker process will be set up for the last product produced. If the same product is to be produced first the following week, no new changeover will be required. Management must keep track of the sequence of production each week to take advantage of this savings. The only exception to this rule is Dragon Shirts, which are unique orders that always require a changeover. In week 0, Min-Yo did not produce any Dragon Shirts; however, it did produce 800 Muscle Shirts, followed by 200 Thunder Shirts. Finally, the spreadsheet calculates the hours required for the proposed

MIN-YO GARMENT COMPANY

Open Order File (Record of commitments)

Product	\multicolumn{10}{c}{Week Order is Due}
	1	2	3	4	5	6	7	8	9	10
Thunder Orders	400									
Dragon Order 1										
Dragon Order 2										
Dragon Order 3										
Dragon Order 4										
Dragon Order 5										
Dragon Order 6										
Dragon Order 7										
Dragon Order 8										
Dragon Order 9										
Dragon Order 10										
Dragon Order 11										
Dragon Order 12										
Dragon Order 13										
Dragon Order 14										
Dragon Order 15										

▶ ▶│ Intro / Open Order File / Week 1 / Week 2 / Week 3 / Week 4 / Week 5 / Week 6 / Week 7 / Week 8 / Week 9 / Week 10 / S│◀│

▲ **FIGURE 16**

Min-Yo's Open Order File

Note: All orders are to be delivered at the end of the week indicated, after production for the week has been completed and before next week's production is started.

MIN-YO GARMENT COMPANY

PRODUCTION SCHEDULE

The two inputs to the Production Schedule table are:
1. The quantity you decide to produce this time period
2. Whether there is a setup/changover required (1 or 0)

PRODUCT	Changeover	Quantity
Muscle	1	800
Hours		88
Thunder	1	200
Hours		30

	Changeover	Quantity		Changeover	Quantity		Changeover	Quantity
Dragon Order 1			Dragon Order 11			Dragon Order 21		
Dragon Order 2			Dragon Order 12			Dragon Order 22		
Dragon Order 3			Dragon Order 13			Dragon Order 23		
Dragon Order 4			Dragon Order 14			Dragon Order 24		
Dragon Order 5			Dragon Order 15			Dragon Order 25		
Dragon Order 6			Dragon Order 16			Dragon Order 26		
Dragon Order 7			Dragon Order 17			Dragon Order 27		
Dragon Order 8			Dragon Order 18			Dragon Order 28		
Dragon Order 9			Dragon Order 19			Dragon Order 29		
Dragon Order 10			Dragon Order 20			Dragon Order 30		
Total Dragon Hours		0						
Total Dragon Production		0						
Total Hours scheduled		118						

Is production within capacity?   Yes

▲ FIGURE 17
Min-Yo's Production Schedule

schedule. Changeover times for Muscle, Thunder, and Dragon Shirts are 8, 10, and 25 hours respectively. Because the garment maker process produces 10 garments per hour regardless of type, the production hours required for Muscle Shirts is 8 + 800/10 = 88 hours, and the production hours for Thunder Shirts is 10 + 200/10 = 30 hours, as shown in Figure 17. The total time spent on the garment maker process on all products in a week cannot exceed 120 hours. The spreadsheet will not allow you to proceed if this constraint is violated.

The second document is a weekly profit and loss (P&L) statement that factors in sales and production costs, including penalty charges and inventory carrying costs, as shown in Figure 18. The inventory carrying cost for *any type of product* is $0.10 per shirt per week left in inventory after shipments for the week have been made. The spreadsheet automatically calculates the P&L statement, which links to the open-order file and the production schedule, after the demand for Muscle Shirts is known. Figure 18 shows that the actual demand for Muscle Shirts last week was 750 shirts.

P&L STATEMENT

Product	Price	Beg Inv	Production	Available	Demand	Sales	End Inv	Inv/Past due costs
Muscle	$6	550	800	1350	750	4500	600	60
Thunder	$7		200	200	400	1400	-200	200
Dragon Orders	$8		0	0	0	0	0	0
Totals			1000			5900		260

		Current	Cumulative
Sales Total		$5,900	$5,900
Labor	$1,200		
Materials	$4,000		
Inv/Past due	$260		
Total Cost		$5,460	
Profit Contribution		$440	$440

▲ FIGURE 18
Min-Yo's P&L Schedule

- The past due quantity of shirts are those shirts not shipped as promised, and appear as a negative number in the "End Inv" column.

- Available = Beginning inventory + Production

- Sales = Demand × Price when demand < available; Available × Price, otherwise

- Inventory cost = $0.10 times number of shirts in inventory. Past due cost equals past due quantity times the penalty ($1 for Thunder Shirts; $2 for Dragon Shirts). These costs are combined in the "Inv/Past Due Costs" column.

The Simulation

At Min-Yo Garment Company, the executive committee meets weekly to discuss the new order possibilities and the load on the garment maker process. The executive committee consists of top management representatives from finance, marketing, and operations. You will be asked to participate on a team and play the role of a member of the executive committee in class. During this exercise, you must decide how far into the future to plan. Some decisions, such as the markets you want to exploit, are long-term in nature. Before class, you may want to think about the markets and their implications for manufacturing. Other decisions are short-term and have an impact on the firm's ability to meet its commitments. In class, the simulation will proceed as follows.

1. Use the Min-Yo Tables spreadsheet in OM Explorer in MyOMLab. It is found in the Solver menu, under Constraint Management. You will start by specifying the production schedule for week 1, based on the forecasts for week 1 in the case narrative for Muscle Shirts and additional information on new and existing orders for the customized shirts from your instructor. *You may assume that your managerial predecessors left the garment machine set up for Thunder Shirts.* The production schedule decision is to be made in collaboration with your executive committee colleagues in class.

2. When all the teams have finalized their production plans for week 1, the instructor will supply the actual demands for Muscle Shirts in week 1. Enter that quantity in the P&L statement in the spreadsheet for week 1.

3. After the P&L statement for week 1 is completed, the instructor will announce the new order requests for Thunder Shirts and Dragon Shirts to be shipped in week 2 and the weeks beyond.

4. You should look at your order requests, accept those that you want, and reject the rest. Add those that you accept for delivery in future periods to your open-order file. Enter the quantity in the cell representing the week the order is due. You are then irrevocably committed to them and their consequences.

5. You should then make out a new production schedule, specifying what you want your garment-maker process to do in the next week (it will be for week 2 at that time).

6. The instructor will impose a time limit for each period of the simulation. When the time limit for one period has been reached, the simulation will proceed to the next week. Each week the spreadsheet will automatically update your production and financial information in the Summary Sheet.

VIDEO CASE | Constraint Management at Southwest Airlines

What if you could take a commercial airline flight any time, and anywhere you wanted to go? Just show up at the airport without the need to consider time schedules or layovers. Aside from the potentially cost-prohibitive nature of such travel, there are also constraints in the airline system that preclude this kind of operation. From the lobby check-in process through to boarding at the gate and processing plane turnaround, the process of operating the airline is filled with constraints that must be managed in order for them to be successful and profitable. Flight schedules are tightly orchestrated and controlled, departure and arrival gates at airports are limited, and individual aircraft have seating capacities in each section of the plane, to name a few.

Southwest Airlines is one company that has figured out how to manage its constraints and generate positive customer experiences in the process. No other airline can claim the same level of profitability and customer satisfaction Southwest regularly achieves. What is its secret?

Talk to any loyal Southwest customer and you will hear rave reviews about its low fares, great customer service, and lack of assigned seating that gives customers a chance to choose who they sit next to onboard. From an operations perspective, it is much more than what the customer sees. Behind the scenes, operations managers carefully manage and execute—3,400 times a day in over 60 cities in the United States—a process designed to manage all potential bottleneck areas.

Southwest's famous rapid gate-turnaround of 25 minutes or less demonstrates how attention to the activities that ground operations must complete to clean, fuel, and prepare a plane for flight can become bottlenecks if not properly scheduled. In the terminal at the gate, passenger boarding also can be a bottleneck if the boarding process itself is not carefully managed. Since the individual mix of passengers present a different set of issues with each flight that often are not evident until the passengers actually arrive

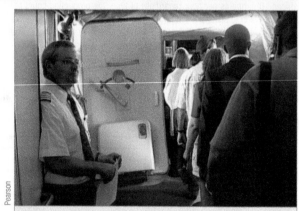

Passengers boarding a Southwest Airlines flight.

at the gate, ranging from families with kids and strollers to large quantities of carry-on bags and passengers needing wheelchair assistance, operations managers must be ready for any and all situations to avoid a boarding bottleneck while also assuring a pleasant and stress-free gate experience for all passengers.

In 2007, as part of the company's continuous improvement activities, Southwest focused its attention on the passenger boarding process to determine whether there was a better way to board. Its existing process consisted of three groups, A, B, C, with no assigned seating. Depending on passenger check-in and arrival time, passengers were given a spot in a group.

Those first to check-in received choice places in the A group. Last to check-in ended up in the C group, and usually had a choice of only middle seats in the back of the plane upon boarding. As passengers arrived at the gate, they queued up in their respective boarding group areas to await the boarding call.

Seven different alternate boarding scenarios were designed and tested. They included

- New family pre-boarding behind the "A" group of first-to-board passengers
- Family pre-boarding before anyone else, but seating choices limited on-board to behind the wing
- Six boarding groups (within A-B-C groups) instead of the original three A-B-C groups
- Assigned boarding gate line positions based on both boarding group and gate arrival time
- Single boarding chute at the gate, but up to nine groups all in one queue
- Boarding with a countdown clock to give customers an incentive to get in line and board quickly; incentives given out if everyone was on time
- Educational boarding video to make the boarding process fun, inform passengers how to board efficiently, and provide the company another way to promote its brand.

QUESTIONS

1. Analyze Southwest's passenger boarding process using the Theory of Constraints.
2. Which boarding scenario among the different ones proposed would you recommend for implementation? Why?
3. How should Southwest evaluate the gate boarding and plane turnaround process?
4. How will Southwest know that the bottleneck had indeed been eliminated after the change in the boarding process?

Selected References

Brown, A. "Theory of Constraints Tapped to Accelerate BP's Gulf of Mexico Cleanup." *Industry Week* (March 18, 2011).

Corominas, Albert, Rafael Pastor, and Joan Plans. "Balancing Assembly Line with Skilled and Unskilled Workers." *Omega*, vol. 36, no. 6 (2008), pp. 1126–1132.

Goldratt, E.M., and J. Cox. *The Goal*, 3rd rev. ed. New York: North River Press, 2004.

McClain, John O., and L. Joseph Thomas. "Overcoming the Dark Side of Worker Flexibility." *Journal of Operations Management*, vol. 21, (2003), pp. 81–92.

Srikanth, Mokshagundam L., and Michael Umble. *Synchronous Management: Profit-Based Manufacturing for the 21st Century*, vol. 1. Guilford, CT: Spectrum Publishing Company, 1997.

Srinivasan, Mandyam, Darren Jones, and Alex Miller. 2004. "Applying Theory of Constraints Principles and Lean Thinking at the Marine Corps Maintenance Center." *Defense Acquisition Rev. Quart.* (August–November 2004), pp. 134–145.

Srinivasan, Mandyam, Darren Jones, and Alex Miller. "Corps Capabilities." *APICS Magazine* (March 2005), pp. 46–50.

Steele, Daniel C., Patrick R. Philipoom, Manoj K. Malhotra, and Timothy D. Fry. "Comparisons Between Drum-Buffer-Rope and Material Requirements Planning: A Case Study." *International Journal of Production Research*, vol. 43, no. 15 (2005), pp. 3181–3208.

Umble, M., E. Umble, and S. Murakami. "Implementing Theory of Constraints in a Traditional Japanese Manufacturing Environment: The Case of Hitachi Tool Engineering." *International Journal of Production Research*, vol. 44, no. 15 (2006), pp. 1863–1880.

FORECASTING

A Motorola Droid phone displayed Google's homepage in Washington, D.C. on August 15, 2011. Google Inc. bought the phone manufacturer Motorola Mobility for $12.5 billion. Motorola considerably improved its demand forecasting process, with payoffs in how it managed its supply chain.

Motorola Mobility

Motorola Mobility makes mobile phone handsets, smartphones, tablets, and cable set-top box assets. In the early 2000s, Motorola's leadership and market share were eroding. Motorola realized that it must transform its supply chain, and embarked on a major initiative to tighten communications and collaboration along its supply chain. It put collaborative planning, forecasting, and replenishment (*CPFR*) into action in 2002. The payoff has been significant.

Motorola sells over 120 handset models globally. Forecasting how many of which models to make and sell is difficult, and accurate replenishment of retailers' shelves is critical. If a customer's favorite handset is not in stock, there is a real risk that Motorola loses that customer for life, and not just for the next service contract. Approximately one half of all stockouts result in lost sales. To make matters worse, a phone model can have multiple SKUs, life cycles average little more than a year, and new product introductions are rapid.

Prior to adopting CPFR, Motorola Mobile's sales were highly variable and were not synchronized with customer demand. Motorola had visibility only for its shipments to retailers' distribution centers, but not for shipments from the retailers' distribution centers to the stores. Knowing what retailers are selling is much more valuable information in forecasting future demand than knowing what retailers are buying. Without this information, forecast errors were very high, resulting in excessive stockouts. CPFR enabled Motorola to collaborate with

From Chapter 14 of *Operations Management: Processes and Supply Chains*, Tenth Edition. Lee J. Krajewski, Larry P. Ritzman, Manoj K. Malhotra. Copyright © 2013 by Pearson Education, Inc. All rights reserved.

its retailers' distribution centers' customers and increase its ability to forecast effectively. Motorola launched an organization-wide shift to customer-focused operations teams. They shared with their retailers their real-time data and plans, including forecasts, inventories, sales to retailers' shelves, promotions, product plans, and exceptions. Traditionally, suppliers and buyers in most supply chains prepare independent demand forecasts.

Before CPFR, the retailers' forecasts were developed at the end of the second week of each month while Motorola's assembled its sales and operations plan earlier in the second week. Motorola convinced the retailer to move up its planning cycle by just two or three days, which eliminated a seven-week forecast lag resulting from the forecast not being incorporated until the next month's planning cycle. Now, the retailer loads its forecasts for the next month on Monday. On Tuesday, Motorola loads its forecast. During the weekly call on Wednesday, the two teams jointly resolve discrepancies line-by-line. The inclusion of a forecasting analyst means they can immediately resolve issues arising from the discrepancies.

The real key to a successful implementation of CPFR is the forging of a cultural alliance that involves peer-to peer relations and cross-functional teams. Prior to CPFR, retailers sometimes gave Motorola "C," "D," and "F" rating on metrics such as on-time delivery, ease of doing business, and stockouts. After CPFR, they give Motorola "A" ratings. Motorola's CPFR initiative reduced forecast error to a fraction of its previous level, allowed quick reductions in safety stock, cut transportation costs in half because of fewer less-than-truckload shipments, and cut stockouts to less than a third of previous levels. Such success is one reason Google paid big ($12.5 billion) to buy Motorola's cellphone business in August 2011.

Source: Jerold P. Cederlund, Rajiv Kohli, Susan A. Sherer, and Yuliang Yao, "How Motorola Put CPFR into Action," *Supply Chain Management Review* (October 2007), pp. 28–35; Sharyn Leaver, Patrick Connaughton, and Elisse Gaynor, "Case Study: Motorola's Quest for Supply Chain Excellence," *Forrester Research, Inc.* (October, 2006), pp. 1–12, **www.motorola.com**, April 29, 2011; Amir Efrati and Spencer A. Ante, "Google's $12.5 Billion Gamble," *The Wall Street Journal*, August 12, 2011.

LEARNING GOALS *After reading this chapter, you should be able to:*

1. Identify the five basic patterns of most demand time series.
2. Identify the various measures of forecast errors.
3. Use regression to make forecasts with one or more independent variables.
4. Make forecasts using the most common approaches for time-series analysis.
5. Make forecasts using trend projection with regression.
6. Describe a typical forecasting process used by businesses.
7. Explain collaborative planning, forecasting, and replenishment (CPFR).

---

forecast

A prediction of future events used for planning purposes.

Balancing supply and demand begins with making accurate forecasts, and then reconciling them across the supply chain as shown by Motorola Mobility. A **forecast** is a prediction of future events used for planning purposes. Planning, on the other hand, is the process of making management decisions on how to deploy resources to best respond to the demand forecasts. Forecasting methods may be based on mathematical models that use available historical data, or on qualitative methods that draw on managerial experience and judgments, or on a combination of both.

In this chapter, our focus is on demand forecasts. We begin with different types of demand patterns. We examine forecasting methods in three basic categories: (1) judgment, (2) causal, and (3) time-series methods. Forecast errors are defined, providing important clues for making better forecasts. We next consider the forecasting techniques themselves, and then how they can be combined to bring together insights from several sources. We conclude with overall processes for making forecasts and designing the forecasting system.

Forecasts are useful for both managing processes and managing supply chains. At the supply chain level, a firm needs forecasts to coordinate with its customers and suppliers. At the process level, output forecasts are needed to design the various processes throughout the organization, including identifying and dealing with in-house bottlenecks.

Forecasting across the Organization

The organization-wide forecasting process cuts across functional areas. Forecasting overall demand typically originates with marketing, but internal customers throughout the organization depend on forecasts to formulate and execute their plans as well. Forecasts are critical inputs to business plans, annual plans, and budgets. Finance needs forecasts to project cash flows and capital requirements. Human resources uses forecasts to anticipate hiring and training needs. Marketing is an important source for sales forecast information because it is closest to external customers. Operations and supply chain managers need forecasts to plan output levels, purchases of services and materials, workforce and output schedules, inventories, and long-term capacities.

Managers throughout the organization make forecasts on many variables other than future demand, such as competitor strategies, regulatory changes, technological changes, processing times, supplier lead times, and quality losses. Tools for making these forecasts are basically the same tools covered here for demand forecasting: judgment, opinions of knowledgeable people, averages of experience, regression, and time-series techniques. Using these tools, forecasting can be improved. Still, forecasts are rarely perfect. As Samuel Clemens (Mark Twain) said in *Following the Equator*, "Prophesy is a good line of business, but it is full of risks." Smart managers recognize this reality and find ways to update their plans when the inevitable forecast error or unexpected event occurs.

Demand Patterns

Forecasting customer demand is a difficult task because the demand for services and goods can vary greatly. For example, demand for lawn fertilizer predictably increases in the spring and summer months; however, the particular weekends when demand is heaviest may depend on uncontrollable factors such as the weather. Sometimes, patterns are more predictable. Thus, the peak hours of the day for a large bank's call center are from 9:00 A.M. to 12:00 P.M., and the peak day of the week is Monday. For its statement-rendering processes, the peak months are January, April, July, and October, which is when the quarterly statements are sent out. Forecasting demand in such situations requires uncovering the underlying patterns from available information. In this section, we discuss the basic patterns of demand.

The repeated observations of demand for a service or product in their order of occurrence form a pattern known as a **time series**. There are five basic patterns of most demand time series:

1. *Horizontal.* The fluctuation of data around a constant mean.

2. *Trend.* The systematic increase or decrease in the mean of the series over time.

3. *Seasonal.* A repeatable pattern of increases or decreases in demand, depending on the time of day, week, month, or season.

4. *Cyclical.* The less predictable gradual increases or decreases in demand over longer periods of time (years or decades).

5. *Random.* The unforecastable variation in demand.

Cyclical patterns arise from two influences. The first is the business cycle, which includes factors that cause the economy to go from recession to expansion over a number of years. The other influence is the service or product life cycle, which reflects the stages of demand from development through decline. Business cycle demand is difficult to predict because it is affected by national or international events.

The four patterns of demand—horizontal, trend, seasonal, and cyclical—combine in varying degrees to define the underlying time pattern of demand for a service or product. The fifth pattern, random variation, results from chance causes and thus, cannot be predicted. Random variation is an aspect of demand that makes every forecast ultimately inaccurate. Figure 1 shows the first four patterns of a demand time series, all of which contain random variations.

Creating Value through Operations Management

Using Operations to Compete
Project Management

Managing Processes

Process Strategy
Process Analysis
Quality and Performance
Capacity Planning
Constraint Management
Lean Systems

Managing Supply Chains

Supply Chain Inventory Management
Supply Chain Design
Supply Chain Location Decisions
Supply Chain Integration
Supply Chain Sustainability and Humanitarian Logistics
Forecasting
Operations Planning and Scheduling
Resource Planning

time series

The repeated observations of demand for a service or product in their order of occurrence.

FIGURE 1 ▶
Patterns of Demand

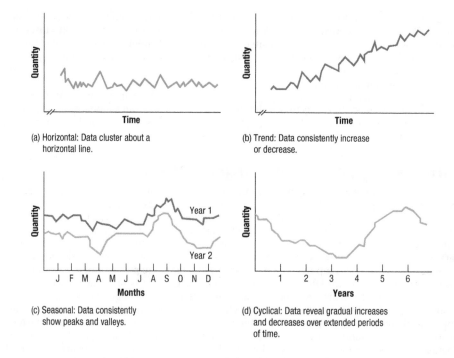

(a) Horizontal: Data cluster about a horizontal line.

(b) Trend: Data consistently increase or decrease.

(c) Seasonal: Data consistently show peaks and valleys.

(d) Cyclical: Data reveal gradual increases and decreases over extended periods of time.

Key Decisions on Making Forecasts

Before using forecasting techniques, a manager must make two decisions: (1) what to forecast, and (2) what type of forecasting technique to select for different items.

Deciding What to Forecast

Although some sort of demand estimate is needed for the individual services or goods produced by a company, forecasting total demand for groups or clusters and then deriving individual service or product forecasts may be easiest. Also, selecting the correct unit of measurement (e.g., service or product units or machine-hours) for forecasting may be as important as choosing the best method.

Level of Aggregation   Few companies err by more than 5 percent when forecasting the annual total demand for all their services or products. However, errors in forecasts for individual items and shorter time periods may be much higher. Recognizing this reality, many companies use a two-tier forecasting system. They first cluster (or "roll up") several similar services or products in a process called **aggregation**, making forecasts for families of services or goods that have similar demand requirements and common processing, labor, and materials requirements. Next, they derive forecasts for individual items, which are sometimes called stock-keeping units. A *stock-keeping unit (SKU)* is an individual item or product that has an identifying code and is held in inventory somewhere along the supply chain, such as in a distribution center.

Units of Measurement   Rather than using dollars as the initial unit of measurement, forecasts often begin with service or product units, such as SKUs, express packages to deliver, or customers needing maintenance service or repairs for their cars. Forecasted units can then be translated to dollars by multiplying them by the unit price. If accurately forecasting demand for a service or product is not possible in terms of number of units, forecast the standard labor or machine-hours required of each of the critical resources.

Choosing the Type of Forecasting Technique

Forecasting systems offer a variety of techniques, and no one of them is best for all items and situations. The forecaster's objective is to develop a useful forecast from the information at hand with the technique that is appropriate for the different patterns of demand. Two general types of forecasting techniques are used: judgment methods and quantitative methods. **Judgment methods** translate the opinions of managers, expert opinions, consumer surveys, and salesforce estimates

aggregation

The act of clustering several similar services or products so that forecasts and plans can be made for whole families.

judgment methods

A forecasting method that translates the opinions of managers, expert opinions, consumer surveys, and salesforce estimates into quantitative estimates.

into quantitative estimates. Quantitative methods include causal methods, time-series analysis, and trend projection with regression. **Causal methods** use historical data on independent variables, such as promotional campaigns, economic conditions, and competitors' actions, to predict demand. **Time-series analysis** is a statistical approach that relies heavily on historical demand data to project the future size of demand and recognizes trends and seasonal patterns. **Trend projection using regression** is a hybrid between a time-series technique and the causal method.

Forecast Error

For any forecasting technique, it is important to measure the accuracy of its forecasts. Forecasts almost always contain errors. Random error results from unpredictable factors that cause the forecast to deviate from the actual demand. Forecasting analysts try to minimize forecast errors by selecting appropriate forecasting models, but eliminating all forms of errors is impossible.

Forecast error for a given period t is simply the difference found by subtracting the forecast from actual demand, or

$$E_t = D_t - F_t$$

where

$$E_t = \text{forecast error for period } t$$
$$D_t = \text{actual demand for period } t$$
$$F_t = \text{forecast for period } t$$

This equation (notice the alphabetical order with D_t coming before F_t) is the starting point for creating several measures of forecast error that cover longer periods of time. Figure 2 shows the output from the *Error Analysis* routine in Forecasting's dropdown menu of POM for Windows. Part (a) gives a big picture view of how well the forecast has been tracking the actual demand. Part (b) shows the detailed calculations needed to obtain the summary error terms. Finally, Part (c) gives the summary error measures summarized across all 10 time periods, as derived from Part (b).

The **cumulative sum of forecast errors (CFE)** measures the total forecast error:

$$\text{CFE} = \sum E_t$$

CFE is a cumulative sum. Figure 3(b) shows that it is the sum of the errors for all 10 periods. For any given period, it would be the sum of errors up through that period. For example, it would be −8 (or −2 −6) for period 2. CFE is also called the *bias error* and results from consistent mistakes—the forecast is always too high or too low. This type of error typically causes the greatest disruption to planning efforts. For example, if a forecast is consistently lower than actual demand, the value of CFE will gradually get larger and larger. This increasingly large error indicates some systematic deficiency in the forecasting approach. The average forecast error, sometimes called the *mean bias*, is simply

$$\bar{E} = \frac{\text{CFE}}{n}$$

causal methods

A quantitative forecasting method that uses historical data on independent variables, such as promotional campaigns, economic conditions, and competitors' actions, to predict demand.

time-series analysis

A statistical approach that relies heavily on historical demand data to project the future size of demand and recognizes trends and seasonal patterns.

trend projection with regression

A forecasting model that is a hybrid between a time-series technique and the causal method.

forecast error

The difference found by subtracting the forecast from actual demand for a given period.

cumulative sum of forecast errors (CFE)

A measurement of the total forecast error that assesses the bias in a forecast.

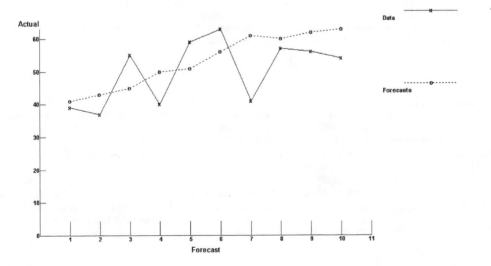

◀ FIGURE 2(a)
Graph of Actual and Forecast Demand Using *Error Analysis* of Forecasting in POM for Windows

▶ **FIGURE 2(b)**
Detailed Calculations of
Forecast Errors

		Forecast	Error	|Error|	Error^2	|Pct Error|
Past period 1	39	41	-2	2	4	5.128%
Past period 2	37	43	-6	6	36	16.216%
Past period 3	55	45	10	10	100	18.182%
Past period 4	40	50	-10	10	100	25%
Past period 5	59	51	8	8	64	13.559%
Past period 6	63	56	7	7	49	11.111%
Past period 7	41	61	-20	20	400	48.78%
Past period 8	57	60	-3	3	9	5.263%
Past period 9	56	62	-6	6	36	10.714%
Past period 10	54	63	-9	9	81	16.667%
TOTALS	501		-31	81	879	170.621%
AVERAGE	50.1		-3.1	8.1	87.9	17.062%
			(Bias)	(MAD)	(MSE)	(MAPE)
				Std dev	29.648	

mean squared error (MSE)

A measurement of the dispersion of forecast errors.

standard deviation (σ)

A measurement of the dispersion of forecast errors.

mean absolute deviation (MAD)

A measurement of the dispersion of forecast errors.

The **mean squared error (MSE), standard deviation of the errors** (σ), and **mean absolute deviation (MAD)** measure the dispersion of forecast errors attributed to trend, seasonal, cyclical, or random effects:

$$\text{MSE} = \frac{\sum E_t^2}{n}$$

$$\sigma = \sqrt{\frac{\sum (E_t - \overline{E})^2}{n - 1}}$$

$$\text{MAD} = \frac{\sum |E_t|}{n}$$

Figure 2(b) shows the squared error in period 1 is 4, and MSE is 87.9 for the whole sample. The standard deviation of the errors is calculated using one of the functions available in Excel and is not shown in Figure 2(b). The absolute value of the error in period 2 is 6, and MAD is 8.1 across the whole sample.

The mathematical symbol $|\ |$ is used to indicate the absolute value—that is, it tells you to disregard positive or negative signs. If MSE, σ, or MAD is small, the forecast is typically close to actual demand; by contrast, a large value indicates the possibility of large forecast errors. The measures do differ in the way they emphasize errors. Large errors get far more weight in MSE and σ because the errors are squared. MAD is a widely used measure of forecast error and is easily understood; it is merely the mean of the absolute forecast errors over a series of time periods, without regard to whether the error was an overestimate or an underestimate.

mean absolute percent error (MAPE)

A measurement that relates the forecast error to the level of demand and is useful for putting forecast performance in the proper perspective.

The **mean absolute percent error (MAPE)** relates the forecast error to the level of demand and is useful for putting forecast performance in the proper perspective:

$$\text{MAPE} = \frac{(\sum |E_t|/D_t)(100)}{n} \text{ (expressed as a percentage)}$$

▼ **FIGURE 2(c)**
Error Measures

Measure	Value
Error Measures	
CFE (Cumulative Forecast Error)	-31
MAD (Mean Absolute Deviation)	8.1
MSE (Mean Squared Error)	87.9
Standard Deviation of Errors	29.648
MAPE (Mean Absolute Percent	17.062%

For example, an absolute forecast error of 100 results in a larger percentage error when the demand is 200 units than when the demand is 10,000 units. MAPE is the best error measure to use when making comparisons between time series for different SKUs. Looking again at Figure 2(b), the percent error in period 2 is 16.22 percent, and MAPE, the average over all 10 periods, is 17.06 percent.

Finally, Figure 2(c) summarizes the key error terms across all 10 time periods. They are actually found in selected portions of Figure 2(b). For example, CFE is -31, which is in the error column of Figure 2(b) in the TOTALS row. MAD is 8.1, found in the $|$Error$|$ column and AVERAGE row. Finally, $|\ |$ is 17.06%, which is in the $|$Pct Error$|$ column and AVERAGE row.

EXAMPLE 1	Calculating Forecast Error Measures

The following table shows the actual sales of upholstered chairs for a furniture manufacturer and the forecasts made for each of the last 8 months. Calculate CFE, MSE, σ, MAD, and MAPE for this product.

Month, t	Demand, D_t	Forecast, F_t	Error, E_t	Error, Squared, E_t^2	Absolute Error $|E_t|$	Absolute Percent Error, $(|E_t|/D_t)(100)$
1	200	225	−25	625	25	12.5%
2	240	220	20	400	20	8.3
3	300	285	15	225	15	5.0
4	270	290	−20	400	20	7.4
5	230	250	−20	400	20	8.7
6	260	240	20	400	20	7.7
7	210	250	−40	1,600	40	19.0
8	275	240	35	1,225	35	12.7
		Total	−15	5,275	195	81.3%

SOLUTION

Using the formulas for the measures, we get

Cumulative forecast error (bias):

CFE = −15 (the bias, or the sum of the errors for all time periods in the time series)

Average forecast error (mean bias):

$$\bar{E} = \frac{CFE}{n} = \frac{-15}{8} = -1.875$$

Mean squared error:

$$MSE = \frac{\sum E_t^2}{n} = \frac{5,275}{8} = 659.4$$

Standard deviation of the errors:

$$\sigma = \sqrt{\frac{\sum [E_t - (-1.875)]^2}{7}} = 27.4$$

Mean absolute deviation:

$$MAD = \frac{\sum |E_t|}{n} = \frac{195}{8} = 24.4$$

Mean absolute percent error:

$$MAPE = \frac{[\sum |E_t|/D_t]100}{n} = \frac{81.3\%}{8} = 10.2\%$$

A CFE of −15 indicates that the forecast has a slight bias to overestimate demand. The MSE, σ, and MAD statistics provide measures of forecast error variability. A MAD of 24.4 means that the average forecast error was 24.4 units in absolute value. The value of σ, 27.4, indicates that the sample distribution of forecast errors has a standard deviation of 27.4 units. A MAPE of 10.2 percent implies that, on average, the forecast error was about 10 percent of actual demand. These measures become more reliable as the number of periods of data increases.

DECISION POINT

Although reasonably satisfied with these forecast performance results, the analyst decided to test out a few more forecasting methods before reaching a final forecasting method to use for the future.

Computer Support

Computer support, such as from OM Explorer or POM for Windows, makes error calculations easy when evaluating how well forecasting models fit with past data. Errors are measured across past data, often called the *history file* in practice. They show the various error measures across the entire history file for each forecasting method evaluated. They also make forecasts into the future, based on the method selected.

Judgment Methods

Forecasts from quantitative methods are possible only when there is adequate historical data, (i.e., the *history file*). However, the history file may be nonexistent when a new product is introduced or when technology is expected to change. The history file might exist but be less useful when certain events (such as rollouts or special packages) are reflected in the past data, or when certain events are expected to occur in the future. In some cases, judgment methods are the only practical way to make a forecast. In other cases, judgment methods can also be used to modify forecasts that are generated by quantitative methods. They may recognize that one or two quantitative models have been performing particularly well in recent periods. Adjustments certainly would be called for if the forecaster has important contextual knowledge. *Contextual knowledge* is knowledge that practitioners gain through experience, such as cause-and-effect relationships, environmental cues, and organizational information that may have an effect on the variable being forecast. Adjustments also could account for unusual circumstances, such as a new sales promotion or unexpected international events. They could also have been used to remove the effect of special one-time events in the history file before quantitative methods are applied. Four of the more successful judgment methods are as follows: (1) salesforce estimates, (2) executive opinion, (3) market research, and (4) the Delphi method.

Salesforce estimates are forecasts compiled from estimates made periodically by members of a company's salesforce. The salesforce is the group most likely to know which services or products customers will be buying in the near future and in what quantities. Forecasts of individual salesforce members can be combined easily to get regional or national sales estimates. However, individual biases of the salespeople may taint the forecast. For example, some people are naturally optimistic, whereas others are more cautious. Adjustments in forecasts may need to be made to account for these individual biases.

Executive opinion is a forecasting method in which the opinions, experience, and technical knowledge of one or more managers or customers are summarized to arrive at a single forecast. All of the factors going into judgmental forecasts would fall into the category of executive opinion. Executive opinion can also be used for **technological forecasting**. The quick pace of technological change makes keeping abreast of the latest advances difficult.

Market research is a systematic approach to determine external consumer interest in a service or product by creating and testing hypotheses through data-gathering surveys. Conducting a market research study includes designing a questionnaire, deciding how to administer it, selecting a representative sample, and analyzing the information using judgment and statistical tools to interpret the responses. Although market research yields important information, it typically includes numerous qualifications and hedges in the findings.

The **Delphi method** is a process of gaining consensus from a group of experts while maintaining their anonymity. This form of forecasting is useful when no historical data are available from which to develop statistical models and when managers inside the firm have no experience on which to base informed projections. A coordinator sends questions to each member of the group of outside experts, who may not even know who else is participating. The coordinator prepares a statistical summary of the responses along with a summary of arguments for particular responses. The report is sent to the same group for another round, and the participants may choose to modify their previous responses. These rounds continue until consensus is obtained.

In the remainder of this chapter, we turn to the commonly used quantitative forecasting approaches.

Causal Methods: Linear Regression

Causal methods are used when historical data are available and the relationship between the factor to be forecasted and other external or internal factors (e.g., government actions or advertising promotions) can be identified. These relationships are expressed in mathematical terms and can be complex. Causal methods are good for predicting turning points in demand and for preparing long-range forecasts. We focus on linear regression, one of the best known and most commonly used causal methods.

In **linear regression**, one variable, called a dependent variable, is related to one or more independent variables by a linear equation. The **dependent variable** (such as demand for door hinges) is the one the manager wants to forecast. The **independent variables** (such as advertising expenditures and new housing starts) are assumed to affect the dependent variable and thereby "cause" the results observed in the past. Figure 3 shows how a linear regression line relates to the data. In technical terms, the regression line minimizes the squared deviations from the actual data.

In the simplest linear regression models, the dependent variable is a function of only one independent variable and, therefore, the theoretical relationship is a straight line:

$$Y = a + bX$$

where

$Y =$ dependent variable

$X =$ independent variable

$a = Y$-intercept of the line

$b =$ slope of the line

The objective of linear regression analysis is to find values of a and b that minimize the sum of the squared deviations of the actual data points from the graphed line. Computer programs are used for this purpose. For any set of matched observations for Y and X, the program computes the values of a and b and provides measures of forecast accuracy. Three measures commonly reported are (1) the sample correlation coefficient, (2) the sample coefficient of determination, and (3) the standard error of the estimate.

The *sample correlation coefficient, r,* measures the direction and strength of the relationship between the independent variable and the dependent variable. The value of r can range from -1.00 to $+1.00$. A correlation coefficient of $+1.00$ implies that period-by-period changes in direction (increases or decreases) of the independent variable are always accompanied by changes in the same direction by the dependent variable. An r of -1.00 means that decreases in the independent variable are always accompanied by increases in the dependent variable, and vice versa. A zero value of r means no linear relationship exists between the variables. The closer the value of r is to ± 1.00, the better the regression line fits the points.

The *sample coefficient of determination* measures the amount of variation in the dependent variable about its mean that is explained by the regression line. The coefficient of determination is the square of the correlation coefficient, or r^2. The value of r^2 ranges from 0.00 to 1.00. Regression equations with a value of r^2 close to 1.00 mean a close fit.

The *standard error of the estimate, s_{xy},* measures how closely the data on the dependent variable cluster around the regression line. Although it is similar to the sample standard deviation, it measures the error from the dependent variable, Y, to the regression line, rather than to the mean. Thus, it is the standard deviation of the difference between the actual demand and the estimate provided by the regression equation.

independent variables

Variables that are assumed to affect the dependent variable and thereby "cause" the results observed in the past.

FIGURE 3 ▲
Linear Regression Line Relative to Actual Demand

EXAMPLE 2	Using Linear Regression to Forecast Product Demand

The supply chain manager seeks a better way to forecast the demand for door hinges and believes that the demand is related to advertising expenditures. The following are sales and advertising data for the past 5 months:

Month	Sales (Thousands of Units)	Advertising (Thousands of $)
1	264	2.5
2	116	1.3
3	165	1.4
4	101	1.0
5	209	2.0

MyOMLab
Active Model 14.1 in MyOMLab provides insight on varying the intercept and slope of the model.

The company will spend $1,750 next month on advertising for the product. Use linear regression to develop an equation and a forecast for this product.

SOLUTION

We used POM for Windows to determine the best values of a, b, the correlation coefficient, the coefficient of determination, and the standard error of the estimate.

$$a = -8.135$$
$$b = 109.229X$$
$$r = 0.980$$
$$r^2 = 0.960$$
$$s_{yx} = 15.603$$

The regression equation is

$$Y = -8.135 + 109.229X$$

and the regression line is shown in Figure 4. The sample correlation coefficient, r, is 0.98, which is unusually close to 1.00 and suggests an unusually strong positive relationship exists between sales and advertising expenditures. The sample coefficient of determination, r^2, implies that 96 percent of the variation in sales is explained by advertising expenditures.

FIGURE 4 ▶
Linear Regression Line for the Sales and Advertising Data Using POM for Windows

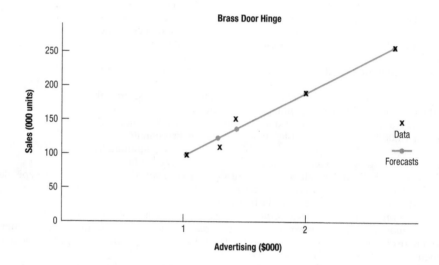

DECISION POINT

The supply chain manager decided to use the regression model as input to planning production levels for month 6. As the advertising expenditure will be \$1,750, the forecast for month 6 is $Y = -8.135 + 109.229(1.75) = 183.016$, or 183,016 units.

Often several independent variables may affect the dependent variable. For example, advertising expenditures, new corporation start-ups, and residential building contracts all may be important for estimating the demand for door hinges. In such cases, *multiple regression analysis* is helpful in determining a forecasting equation for the dependent variable as a function of several independent variables. Such models can be analyzed with POM for Windows or OM Explorer and can be quite useful for predicting turning points and solving many planning problems.

Time-Series Methods

Rather than using independent variables for the forecast as regression models do, time-series methods use historical information regarding only the dependent variable. These methods are based on the assumption that the dependent variable's past pattern will continue in the future. Time-series analysis identifies the underlying patterns of demand that combine to produce an observed historical pattern of the dependent variable and then develops a model to replicate it. In this section, we focus on time-series methods that address the horizontal, trend, and seasonal patterns of demand. Before we discuss statistical methods, let us take a look at the simplest time-series method for addressing all patterns of demand—the naïve forecast.

Naïve Forecast

A method often used in practice is the **naïve forecast**, whereby the forecast for the next period (F_{t+1}) equals the demand for the current period (D_t). So if the actual demand for Wednesday is 35 customers, the forecasted demand for Thursday is 35 customers. Despite its name, the naïve forecast can perform well.

The naïve forecast method may be adapted to take into account a demand trend. The increase (or decrease) in demand observed between the last two periods is used to adjust the current demand to arrive at a forecast. Suppose that last week the demand was 120 units and the week before it was 108 units. Demand increased 12 units in 1 week, so the forecast for next week would be 120 + 12 = 132 units. The naïve forecast method also may be used to account for seasonal patterns. If the demand last July was 50,000 units, and assuming no underlying trend from one year to the next, the forecast for this July would be 50,000 units. The method works best when the horizontal, trend, or seasonal patterns are stable and random variation is small.

naïve forecast

A time-series method whereby the forecast for the next period equals the demand for the current period, or Forecast = D_t.

Estimating the Average

We begin our discussion of statistical methods of time-series forecasting with demand that has no apparent trend, seasonal, or cyclical patterns. The horizontal pattern in a time series is based on the mean of the demands, so we focus on forecasting methods that estimate the average of a time series of data. The forecast of demand for *any* period in the future is the average of the time series computed in the current period. For example, if the average of past demand calculated on Tuesday is 65 customers, the forecasts for Wednesday, Thursday, and Friday are 65 customers each day.

Consider Figure 5, which shows patient arrivals at a medical clinic over the past 28 weeks. Assuming that the time series has only a horizontal and random pattern, one approach is simply to calculate the average of the data. However, this approach has no adaptive quality if there is a trend, seasonal, or cyclical pattern. The statistical techniques that do have an adaptive quality in estimating the average in a time series are (1) simple moving averages, (2) weighted moving averages, and (3) exponential smoothing. Another option is the simple average, but it has no adaptive capability.

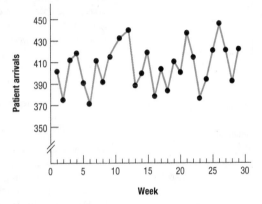

FIGURE 5 ▲
Weekly Patient Arrivals at a Medical Clinic

Simple Moving Averages The **simple moving average method** simply involves calculating the average demand for the n most recent time periods and using it as the forecast for future time periods. For the next period, after the demand is known, the oldest demand from the previous average is replaced with the most recent demand and the average is recalculated. In this way, the n most recent demands are used, and the average "moves" from period to period.

Specifically, the forecast for period $t + 1$ can be calculated at the end of period t (after the actual demand for period t is known) as

simple moving average method

A time-series method used to estimate the average of a demand time series by averaging the demand for the n most recent time periods.

$$F_{t+1} = \frac{\text{Sum of last } n \text{ demands}}{n} = \frac{D_t + D_{t-1} + D_{t-2} + \cdots + D_{t-n+1}}{n}$$

where

$$D_t = \text{actual demand in period } t$$

$$n = \text{total number of periods in the average}$$

$$F_{t+1} = \text{forecast for period } t + 1$$

EXAMPLE 3	Using the Moving Average Method to Estimate Average Demand

a. Compute a *three-week* moving average forecast for the arrival of medical clinic patients in week 4. The numbers of arrivals for the past 3 weeks were as follows:

Week	Patient Arrivals
1	400
2	380
3	411

b. If the actual number of patient arrivals in week 4 is 415, what is the forecast error for week 4?

c. What is the forecast for week 5?

MyOMLab

Active Model 14.2 in MyOMLab provides insight on the impact of varying n using the example in Figure 5.

MyOMLab

Tutor 14.1 in MyOMLab provides another example to practice making forecasts with the moving average method.

SOLUTION

a. The moving average forecast at the end of week 3 is

$$F_4 = \frac{411 + 380 + 400}{3} = 397.0$$

b. The forecast error for week 4 is

$$E_4 = D_4 - F_4 = 415 - 397 = 18$$

c. The forecast for week 5 requires the actual arrivals from weeks 2 through 4, the 3 most recent weeks of data.

$$F_5 = \frac{415 + 411 + 380}{3} = 402.0$$

DECISION POINT

Thus, the forecast at the end of week 3 would have been 397 patients for week 4, which fell short of actual demand by 18 patients. The forecast for week 5, made at the end of week 4, would be 402 patients. If a forecast is needed now for week 6 and beyond, it would also be for 402 patients.

The moving average method may involve the use of as many periods of past demand as desired. Large values of n should be used for demand series that are stable, and small values of n should be used for those that are susceptible to changes in the underlying average. If n is set to its lowest level (i.e., 1), it becomes the naïve method.

weighted moving average method

A time-series method in which each historical demand in the average can have its own weight; the sum of the weights equals 1.0.

Weighted Moving Averages In the simple moving average method, each demand has the same weight in the average—namely, $1/n$. In the **weighted moving average method**, each historical demand in the average can have its own weight. The sum of the weights equals 1.0. For example, in a *three-period* weighted moving average model, the most recent period might be assigned a weight of 0.50, the second most recent might be weighted 0.30, and the third most recent might be weighted 0.20. The average is obtained by multiplying the weight of each period by the value for that period and adding the products together:

$$F_{t+1} = 0.50D_t + 0.30D_{t-1} + 0.20D_{t-2}$$

For a numerical example of using the weighted moving average method to estimate average demand, see Solved Problem 2 and Tutor 14.2 of OM Explorer in MyOMLab.

The advantage of a weighted moving average method is that it allows you to emphasize recent demand over earlier demand. (It can even handle seasonal effects by putting higher weights on prior years in the same season.) The forecast will be more responsive to changes in the underlying average of the demand series than the simple moving average forecast.

exponential smoothing method

A weighted moving average method that calculates the average of a time series by implicitly giving recent demands more weight than earlier demands.

Exponential Smoothing The **exponential smoothing method** is a sophisticated weighted moving average method that calculates the average of a time series by implicitly giving recent demands more weight than earlier demands, all the way back to the first period in the history file. It is the most frequently used formal forecasting method because of its simplicity and the small amount of data needed to support it. Unlike the weighted moving average method, which requires n periods of past demand and n weights, exponential smoothing requires only three items of data: (1) the last period's forecast; (2) the actual demand for this period; and (3) a smoothing parameter, alpha (α), which has a value between 0 and 1.0. The equation for the exponentially smoothed forecast for period $t + 1$ is calculated

$$F_{t+1} = \alpha D_t + (1 - \alpha)F_t$$

Unilever—the purveyor of Lipton Tea, Dove, Hellmann's, and hundreds of other brands, must forecast demand around the world. It has a state-of-the-art forecasting system. Using software from Manugistics, the system blends forecasts from time series techniques with judgmental adjustments for planned promotions from its sales teams. Unilever compares point-of-sales data with its own forecasts. The forecasts are reviewed and judgmentally adjusted as needed.

The emphasis given to the most recent demand levels can be adjusted by changing the smoothing parameter. Larger α values emphasize recent levels of demand and result in forecasts more responsive to changes in the underlying average. Smaller α values treat past demand more uniformly and result in more stable forecasts. Smaller α values are analogous to increasing the value of n in the moving average method and giving greater weight to past demand. In practice, various values of α are tried and the one producing the best forecasts is chosen.

Exponential smoothing requires an initial forecast to get started. There are several ways to get this initial forecast. OM Explorer and POM for Windows use as a default setting the actual demand in the first period, which becomes the forecast for the second period. Forecasts and forecast errors then are calculated beginning with period 2. If some historical data are available, the initial forecast can be found by calculating the average of several recent periods of demand. The effect of the initial estimate of the average on successive estimates of the average diminishes over time.

EXAMPLE 4	**Using Exponential Smoothing to Estimate Average Demand**

a. Reconsider the patient arrival data in Example 3. It is now the end of week 3, so the actual number of arrivals is known to be 411 patients. Using $\alpha = 0.10$, calculate the exponential smoothing forecast for week 4.

b. What was the forecast error for week 4 if the actual demand turned out to be 415?

c. What is the forecast for week 5?

SOLUTION

a. The exponential smoothing method requires an initial forecast. Suppose that we take the demand data for the first 2 weeks and average them, obtaining $(400 + 380)/2 = 390$ as an initial forecast. (POM for Windows and OM Explorer simply use the actual demand for the first week as a default setting for the initial forecast for period 1, and do not begin tracking forecast errors until the second period). To obtain the forecast for week 4, using exponential smoothing with $D_3 = 411$, $\alpha = 0.10$, and $F_3 = 390$, we calculate the forecast for week 4 as

$$F_4 = 0.10(411) + 0.90(390) = 392.1$$

Thus, the forecast for week 4 would be 392 patients.

b. The forecast error for week 4 is

$$E_4 = 415 - 392 = 23$$

c. The new forecast for week 5 would be

$$F_5 = 0.10(415) + 0.90(392.1) = 394.4$$

or 394 patients. Note that we used F_4, not the integer-value forecast for week 4, in the computation for F_5. In general, we round off (when it is appropriate) only the final result to maintain as much accuracy as possible in the calculations.

DECISION POINT

Using this exponential smoothing model, the analyst's forecasts would have been 392 patients for week 4 and then 394 patients for week 5 and beyond. As soon as the actual demand for week 5 is known, then the forecast for week 6 will be updated.

MyOMLab

Active Model 14.3 in MyOMLab provides insight on the impact of varying α in Figure 5.

MyOMLab

Tutor 14.3 in MyOMLab provides a new practice example of how to make forecasts with the exponential smoothing method.

Because exponential smoothing is simple and requires minimal data, it is inexpensive and attractive to firms that make thousands of forecasts for each time period. However, its simplicity also is a disadvantage when the underlying average is changing, as in the case of a demand series with a trend. Like any method geared solely to the assumption of a stable average, exponential smoothing results will lag behind changes in the underlying average of demand. Higher α values may help reduce forecast errors when there is a change in the average; however, the lags will still occur if the average is changing systematically. Typically, if large α values (e.g., > 0.50) are required for an exponential smoothing application, chances are good that another model is needed because of a significant trend or seasonal influence in the demand series.

Trend Projection with Regression

Let us now consider a demand time series that has a trend. A *trend* in a time series is a systematic increase or decrease in the average of the series over time. Where a significant trend is present, forecasts from naïve, moving average, and exponential smoothing approaches are adaptive, but still lag behind actual demand and tend to be below or above the actual demand.

Trend projection with regression is a forecasting model that accounts for the trend with simple regression analysis. To develop a regression model for forecasting the trend, let the dependent variable, *Y*, be a period's demand and the independent variable, *t*, be the time period. For the first period, let $t = 1$; for the second period, let $t = 2$; and so on. The regression equation is

$$F_t = a + bt$$

One advantage of the trend projection with regression model is that it can forecast demand well into the future. The previous models project demand just one period ahead, and assume that demand beyond that will remain at that same level. Of course, all of the models (including the trend projection with regression model) can be updated each period to stay current. One *apparent* disadvantage of the trend with regression model is that it is not adaptive. The solution to this problem comes when you answer the following question. If you had the past sales of Ford automobiles since 1920, would you include each year in your regression analysis, giving equal weight to each year's sales, or include just the sales for more recent years? You most likely would decide to include just the more recent years, making your regression model more adaptive. The trend projection with regression model can thus be made more or less adaptive by the selection of historical data periods to include in the same way that moving average (changing *n*) or exponential smoothing (changing α) models do.

The trend projection with regression model can be solved with either the *Trend Projection with Regression* Solver or the *Time Series Forecasting* Solver in OM Explorer. Both solvers provide the regression coefficients, coefficient of determination r^2, error measures, and forecasts into the future. POM for Windows has an alternative model (description provided in MyOMLab) that includes the trend, called the *Trend-Adjusted Smoothing* model.

The *Trend Projection with Regression* Solver focuses exclusively on trend analysis. Its graph gives a big-picture view of how well the model fits the actual demand. Its sliders allow you to control when the regression begins, how many periods are included in the regression analysis, and how many periods you want forecasted into the future. The *Time Series Forecasting* Solver, on the other hand, covers all time series models, including the trend projection with regression. It also computes a combination forecast, which we cover in a subsequent section on using multiple techniques.

MyOMLab

EXAMPLE 5 | **Using Trend Projection with Regression to Forecast a Demand Series with a Trend**

MyOMLab

Active Model 14.4 in MyOMLab provides insight on the behavior of the Trend Projetion with Regression model on the Medanalysis data.

Medanalysis, Inc., provides medical laboratory services to patients of Health Providers, a group of 10 family-practice doctors associated with a new health maintenance program. Managers are interested in forecasting the number of blood analysis requests per week. Recent publicity about the damaging effects of cholesterol on the heart has caused a national increase in requests for standard blood tests. The arrivals over the last 16 weeks are given in Table 1. What is the forecasted demand for the next three periods?

TABLE 1 ARRIVALS AT MEDANALYSIS FOR LAST 16 WEEKS

Week	Arrivals	Week	Arrivals
1	28	9	61
2	27	10	39
3	44	11	55
4	37	12	54
5	35	13	52
6	53	14	60
7	38	15	60
8	57	16	75

SOLUTION

Figure 6(a) shows the results using the *Trend Projection with Regression* Solver when all 16 weeks are included in the regression analysis, with Figure 6(b) showing the worksheet that goes with it.

Solver - Trend Projection with Regression

Regression begins in period	1 ◄ ►
Error analysis begins in period	1 ◄ ►
Number of future forecasts	3 ◄ ►

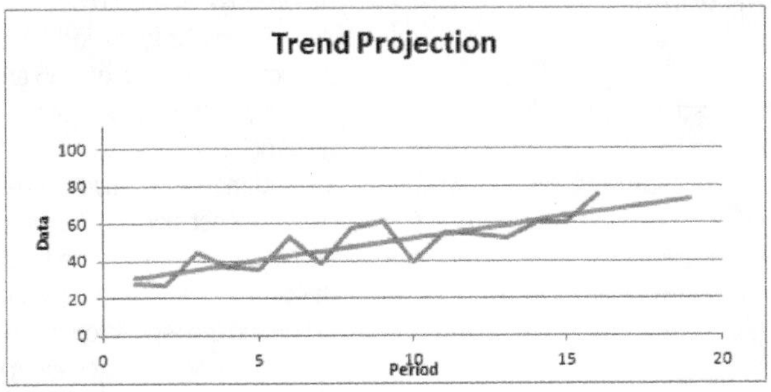

▼ **FIGURE 6(a)**
First Model

Trend Projection

a (Y intercept)	28.50
b (slope or trend)	2.35
r2	0.69

CFE	0.00
MAD	6.21
MSE	52.96
MAPE	13.53%

Forecast for period 17	68.375
Forecast for period 18	70.72059
Forecast for period 19	73.06618

▼ **FIGURE 6(b)**
Detailed Calculations of Forecast Errors for First Model

					Averages		
				CFE	MSE	MAD	MAPE
				0.000	52.958	6.210	13.53%
	Actual				Error	Absolute	Abs %
Period #	Demand	Forecast	Error	Running CFE	Squared	Error	error
1	28	31	-2.846	-2.846	8.097	2.846	10.16%
2	27	33	-6.191	-9.037	38.331	6.191	22.93%
3	44	36	8.463	-0.574	71.626	8.463	19.23%
4	37	38	-0.882	-1.456	0.779	0.882	2.38%
5	35	40	-5.228	-6.684	27.331	5.228	14.94%
6	53	43	10.426	3.743	108.711	10.426	19.67%
7	38	45	-6.919	-3.176	47.874	6.919	18.21%
8	57	47	9.735	6.559	94.776	9.735	17.08%
9	61	50	11.390	17.949	129.725	11.390	18.67%
10	39	52	-12.956	4.993	167.855	12.956	33.22%
11	55	54	0.699	5.691	0.488	0.699	1.27%
12	54	57	-2.647	3.044	7.007	2.647	4.90%
13	52	59	-6.993	-3.949	48.897	6.993	13.45%
14	60	61	-1.338	-5.287	1.791	1.338	2.23%
15	60	64	-3.684	-8.971	13.571	3.684	6.14%
16	75	66	8.971	0.000	80.471	8.971	11.96%

▼ **FIGURE 6(c)**
Second Model

Solver - Trend Projection with Regression

Regression begins in period 9
Error analysis begins in period 9
Number of future forecasts 3

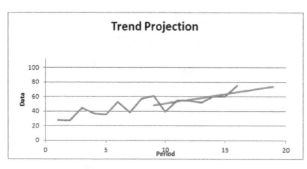

Trend Projection

a (Y intercept)	24.86
b (slope or trend)	2.57
r2	0.39
CFE	0.00
MAD	5.96
MSE	55.29
MAPE	11.10%
Forecast for period 17	68.57143
Forecast for period 18	71.14286
Forecast for period 19	73.71429

Looking at the Results sheet of Figure 6(a), we see that the Y intercept of the trend line (*a*) is 28.50 and the slope of the line (*b*) is 2.35. Thus, the trend equation is $F_t = a + bt$, where *t* is the time period for which you are forecasting. The forecast for period 19 is 28.5 + 2.35 (19) = 73. The error terms are CFE = 0 (which is to be expected when the regression begins at the same time that error analysis begins), MAD = 6.21, MSE = 52.96, and MAPE = 13.53 percent. The coefficient of determination r^2 is decent at 0.69. The trend line is rising gently and reaches 73 for period 19. Each period the forecast predicts an increase of 2.35 arrivals per week.

When the number of periods included in the regression analysis is reduced to 9, Figure 6(c) shows this second model produces mixed results. The trend line has a steeper slope. MAD and MAPE are better, but r^2 and MSE are worse. The third model in Figure 6(d) is the extreme, where only the last four periods are used in building the regression model. It has the best r^2, and all of the error measures are much better than the first two models. Its forecast for period 19 is 93 arrivals. However, this model is based only on the last 4 weeks of data, ignoring all previous data in the history file. For that reason, management decided to split the difference with a forecast of 83 arrivals. It is halfway between the more conservative forecast of 73 in Figure 6(a) and Figure 6(c), and the optimistic forecast of 93 in Figure 6(d).

Solver - Trend Projection with Regression

Regression begins in period 13
Error analysis begins in period 13
Number of future forecasts 3

FIGURE 6(d) ▶
Third Model

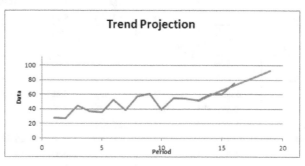

Trend Projection

a (Y intercept)	-38.30
b (slope or trend)	6.90
r2	0.86
CFE	0.00
MAD	2.60
MSE	9.67
MAPE	4.13%
Forecast for period 17	79
Forecast for period 18	85.9
Forecast for period 19	92.8

Seasonal Patterns

Seasonal patterns are regularly repeating upward or downward movements in demand measured in periods of less than one year (hours, days, weeks, months, or quarters). In this context, the time periods are called *seasons*. For example, customer arrivals at a fast-food shop on any day may peak between 11 A.M. and 1 P.M. and again from 5 P.M. to 7 P.M.

An easy way to account for seasonal effects is to use one of the techniques already described, but to limit the data in the time series to those time periods in the same season. For example, for a day-of-the-week seasonal effect, one time series would be for Mondays, one for Tuesdays, and so on. Such an approach accounts for seasonal effects, but has the disadvantage of discarding considerable information on past demand.

Other methods are available that analyze all past data, using one model to forecast demand for all of the seasons. We describe only the **multiplicative seasonal method**, whereby an estimate of average demand is multiplied by seasonal factors to arrive at a seasonal forecast. The four-step procedure presented here involves the use of simple averages of past demand, although more sophisticated methods for calculating averages, such as a moving average or exponential smoothing approach, could be used. The following description is based on a seasonal pattern lasting one year and seasons of one month, although the procedure can be used for any seasonal pattern and season of any length.

multiplicative seasonal method

A method whereby seasonal factors are multiplied by an estimate of average demand to arrive at a seasonal forecast.

1. For each year, calculate the average demand per season by dividing annual demand by the number of seasons per year.

2. For each year, divide the actual demand for a season by the average demand per season. The result is a *seasonal index* for each season in the year, which indicates the level of demand relative to the average demand. For example, a seasonal index of 1.14 calculated for April implies that April's demand is 14 percent greater than the average demand per month.

3. Calculate the average seasonal index for each season, using the results from step 2. Add the seasonal indices for a season and divide by the number of years of data.

4. Calculate each season's forecast for next year. Begin by forecasting next year's annual demand using the naïve method, moving averages, exponential smoothing, or trend projection with regression. Then, divide annual demand by the number of seasons per year to get the average demand per season. Finally, make the seasonal forecast by multiplying the average demand per season by the appropriate seasonal index found in step 3.

EXAMPLE 6	Using the Multiplicative Seasonal Method to Forecast the Number of Customers

The manager of the Stanley Steemer carpet cleaning company needs a quarterly forecast of the number of customers expected next year. The carpet cleaning business is seasonal, with a peak in the third quarter and a trough in the first quarter. The manager wants to forecast customer demand for each quarter of year 5, based on an estimate of total year 5 demand of 2,600 customers.

SOLUTION

The following table calculates the seasonal factor for each week.

It shows the quarterly demand data from the past 4 years, as well as the calculations performed to get the average seasonal factor for each quarter.

	YEAR 1		YEAR 2		YEAR 3		YEAR 4		Average Seasonal Factor [(1+2+3+4+)/4]
Quarter	Demand	Seasonal Factor (1)	Demand	Seasonal Factor (2)	Demand	Seasonal Factor (3)	Demand	Seasonal Factor (4)	
1	45	45/250 = 0.18	70	70/300 = 0.23333	100	100/450 = 0.22222	100	100/550 = 0.18182	0.2043
2	335	335/250 = 1.34	370	370/300 = 1.23333	585	585/450 = 1.30	725	725/550 = 1.31818	1.2979
3	520	520/250 = 2.08	590	590/300 = 1.96667	830	830/450 = 1.84444	1160	1160/550 = 2.10909	2.0001
4	100	100/250 = 0.40	170	170/300 = 0.56667	285	285/450 = 0.63333	215	215/550 = 0.39091	0.4977
Total	1,000		1,200		1,800		2,200		
Average	1,000/4 = 250		1,200/4 = 300		1,800 = 450		2,200/4 = 550		

For example, the seasonal factor for quarter 1 in year 1 is calculated by dividing the actual demand (45) by the average demand for the whole year (1000/4 = 250). When this is done for all 4 years, we then can average the seasonal factors for quarter 1 over all 4 years. The result is a seasonal factor of 0.2043 for quarter 1.

Once seasonal factors are calculated for all four seasons (see last column in the table on the previous page), we then turn to making the forecasts for year 5. The manager suggests a forecast of 2,600 customers for the whole year, which seems reasonable given that the annual demand has been increasing by an average of 400 customers each year (from 1,000 in year 1 to 2,200 in year 4, or 1,200/3 = 400. The computed forecast demand is found by extending that trend, and projecting an annual demand in year 5 of 2,200 + 400 = 2,600 customers. (This same result is confirmed using the *Trend Projection with Regression* Solver of OM Explorer.) The quarterly forecasts are straight-forward. First, find the average demand forecast for year 5, which is 2,600/4 = 650. Then multiple this average demand by the average seasonal index, giving us

Quarter	Forecast
1	$650 \times 0.2043 = 132.795$
2	$650 \times 1.2979 = 843.635$
3	$650 \times 2.0001 = 1{,}300.065$
4	$650 \times 0.4977 = 323.505$

Figure 7 shows the computer solution using the *Seasonal Forecasting* Solver in OM Explorer. Figure 7(b) confirms all of the calculations made above. Notice in Figure 7(a) that a computer demand forecast is provided as a default for year 5. However, there is an option for user-supplied demand forecast that overrides the computer-supplied forecast if the manager wishes to make a judgmental forecast based on additional information.

FIGURE 7 ▶
Demand Forecasts Using the
Seasonal Forecasting Solver
of *OM Explorer*

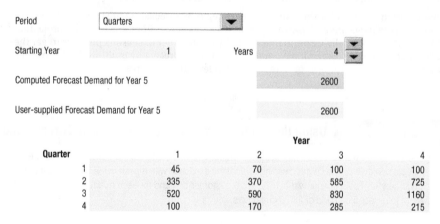

Period	Quarters ▼			
Starting Year	1	Years	4	
Computed Forecast Demand for Year 5			2600	
User-supplied Forecast Demand for Year 5			2600	

			Year		
Quarter		1	2	3	4
1		45	70	100	100
2		335	370	585	725
3		520	590	830	1160
4		100	170	285	215

(a) Inputs sheet

	Seasonal	
Quarter	Index	Forecast
1	0.2043	132.795
2	1.2979	843.635
3	2.0001	1300.065
4	0.4977	323.505

(b) Results

DECISION POINT
Using this seasonal method, the analyst makes a demand forecast as low as 133 customers in the first quarter and as high as 1,300 customers in the third quarter. The season of the year clearly makes a difference.

An alternative to the multiplicative seasonal method is the **additive seasonal method**, whereby seasonal forecasts are generated by adding or subtracting a seasonal constant (say, 50 units) to the estimate of average demand per season. This approach is based on the assumption that the seasonal pattern is constant, regardless of average demand. The amplitude of the seasonal adjustment remains the same regardless of the level of demand.

additive seasonal method

A method in which seasonal forecasts are generated by adding a constant to the estimate of average demand per season.

Choosing a Quantitative Forecasting Method

Criteria for Selecting Time-Series Methods

Forecast error measures provide important information for choosing the best forecasting method for a service or product. They also guide managers in selecting the best values for the parameters needed for the method: n for the moving average method, the weights for the weighted moving average method, α for the exponential smoothing method, and when regression data begins for the trend projection with regression method. The criteria to use in making forecast method and parameter choices include (1) minimizing bias (CFE); (2) minimizing MAPE, MAD, or MSE; (3) maximizing r^2; (4) meeting managerial expectations of changes in the components of demand; and (5) minimizing the forecast errors in recent periods. The first three criteria relate to statistical measures based on historical performance, the fourth reflects expectations of the future that may not be rooted in the past, and the fifth is a way to use whatever method seems to be working best at the time a forecast must be made.

Using Statistical Criteria   Statistical performance measures can be used in the selection of which forecasting method to use. The following guidelines will help when searching for the best time-series models:

1. For projections of more stable demand patterns, use lower α values or larger n values to emphasize historical experience.

2. For projections of more dynamic demand patterns using the models covered in this chapter, try higher α values or smaller n values. When historical demand patterns are changing, recent history should be emphasized.

Often, the forecaster must make trade-offs between bias (CFE) and the measures of forecast error dispersion (MAPE, MAD, and MSE). Managers also must recognize that the best technique in explaining the past data is not necessarily the best technique to predict the future, and that "overfitting" past data can be deceptive. Such was the case in Example 5. All of the forecast error measures suggested that the regression model in Figure 5(d) was best, but management was hesitant because it used so little of the time series. A forecasting method may have small errors relative to the history file, but may generate high errors for future time periods. For this reason, some analysts prefer to use a **holdout sample** as a final test (see the two Experiential Learning Exercises at the end of this chapter). To do so, they set aside some of the more recent periods from the time series and use only the earlier time periods to develop and test different models. Once the final models have been selected in the first phase, they are tested again with the holdout sample. Performance measures, such as MAD and CFE, would still be used but they would be applied to the holdout sample. Whether this idea is used or not, managers should monitor future forecast errors, and modify their forecasting approaches as needed. Maintaining data on forecast performance is the ultimate test of forecasting power—rather than how well a model fits past data or holdout samples.

holdout sample

Actual demands from the more recent time periods in the time series that are set aside to test different models developed from the earlier time periods.

Tracking Signals

A **tracking signal** is a measure that indicates whether a method of forecasting is accurately predicting actual changes in demand. The tracking signal measures the number of MADs represented by the cumulative sum of forecast errors, the CFE. The CFE tends to be close to 0 when a correct forecasting system is being used. At any time, however, random errors can cause the CFE to be a nonzero number. The tracking signal formula is

tracking signal

A measure that indicates whether a method of forecasting is accurately predicting actual changes in demand.

$$\text{Tracking signal} = \frac{\text{CFE}}{\text{MAD}} \ \text{ or } \ \frac{\text{CFE}}{\text{MAD}_t}$$

Each period, the CFE and MAD are updated to reflect current error, and the tracking signal is compared to some predetermined limits. The MAD can be calculated in one of two ways: (1) as the simple average of all absolute errors (as demonstrated in Example 1) or (2) as a weighted average determined by the exponential smoothing method:

$$\text{MAD}_t = \alpha |E_t| + (1 - \alpha)\text{MAD}_{t-1}$$

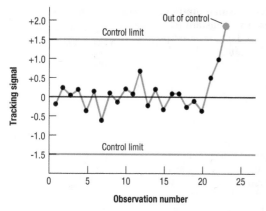

FIGURE 8 ▲
Tracking Signal

If forecast errors are normally distributed with a mean of 0, the relationship between σ and MAD is simple:

$$\sigma = (\sqrt{\pi/2})(\text{MAD}) \cong 1.25(\text{MAD})$$

$$\text{MAD} = 0.7978\sigma \cong 0.8\sigma$$

where

$$\pi = 3.1416$$

This relationship allows use of the normal probability tables to specify limits for the tracking signal. If the tracking signal falls outside those limits, the forecasting model no longer is tracking demand adequately. A tracking system is useful when forecasting systems are computerized because it alerts analysts when forecasts are getting far from desirable limits. Figure 8 shows tracking signal results for 23 periods plotted on a *control chart*. The control chart is useful for determining whether any action needs to be taken to improve the forecasting model. In the example, the first 20 points cluster around 0, as we would expect if the forecasts are not biased. The CFE will tend toward 0. When the underlying characteristics of demand change but the forecasting model does not, the tracking signal eventually goes out of control. The steady increase after the 20th point in Figure 8 indicates that the process is going out of control. The 21st and 22nd points are acceptable, but the 23rd point is not.

Using Multiple Techniques

We described several individual forecasting methods and showed how to assess their forecast performance. However, we need not rely on a single forecasting method. Several different forecasts can be used to arrive at a final forecast. Initial statistical forecasts using several time-series methods and regression are distributed to knowledgeable individuals, such as marketing directors and sales teams, (and sometimes even suppliers and customers) for their adjustments. They can account for current market and customer conditions that are not necessarily reflected in past data. Multiple forecasts may come from different sales teams, and some teams may have a better record on forecast errors than others.

Research during the last two decades suggests that combining forecasts from multiple sources often produces more accurate forecasts. **Combination forecasts** are forecasts that are produced by averaging independent forecasts based on different methods, different sources, or different data. It is intriguing that combination forecasts often perform better over time than even the *best* single forecasting procedure. For example, suppose that the forecast for the next period is 100 units from technique 1 and 120 units from technique 2 and that technique 1 has provided more accurate forecasts to date. The combination forecast for next period, giving equal weight to each technique, is 110 units (or $0.5 \times 100 + 0.5 \times 120$). When this averaging technique is used consistently into the future, its combination forecasts often will be much more accurate than those of any single best forecasting technique (in this example, technique 1). Combining is most effective when the individual forecasts bring different kinds of information into the forecasting process. Forecasters have achieved excellent results by weighting forecasts equally, and this is a good starting point. However, unequal weights may provide better results under some conditions.

OM Explorer and POM for Windows allow you to evaluate several forecasting models, and then you can create combination forecasts from them. In fact, the *Time-Series Forecasting* Solver of OM Explorer automatically computes a combination forecast as a weighted average, using the weights that you supply for the various models that it evaluates. The models include the naïve, moving average, exponential smoothing, and regression projector methods. Alternately, you can create a simple Excel spreadsheet that combines forecasts generated by POM for Windows to create combination forecasts. The *Time Series Forecasting* Solver also allows you evaluate your forecasting process with a holdout sample. The forecaster makes a forecast just one period ahead, and learns of given actual demand. Next the solver computes forecasts and forecast errors for the period. The process continues to the next period in the holdout sample with the forecaster committing to a forecast for the next period. To be informed, the forecaster should also be aware of how the other forecasting methods have been performing, particularly in the recent past.

combination forecasts

Forecasts that are produced by averaging independent forecasts based on different methods, different sources, or different data.

| **Combination Forecasts and the Forecasting Process**

Fiskars Brands, Inc., totally overhauled its forecasting process. It serves 2,000 customers ranging from large discounters to local craft stores providing about 2,300 finished SKUs. Its parent company, Fiskars Corporation, is the second oldest incorporated entity in the world and produces a variety of high-quality products such as garden shears, pruners, hand tools, scissors for preschoolers, ratchet tools, screwdrivers, and the like. Business is highly seasonal and prices quite variable. About 10 percent to 15 percent of the annual revenue comes from one-time promotions, and 25 percent to 35 percent of its products are new every year.

It introduced a statistical-based analysis along with a Web-based business intelligence tool for reporting. It put much more emphasis on combination forecasts. Instead of asking members of the sales staff to provide their own forecasts, forecasts were sent to them, and they were asked for their validation and refinement. Their inputs are most useful relative to additions, deletions, and promotions. Converting multiple forecasts into one number (forecasts from time-series techniques, sales input, and customer input) creates more accurate forecasts by SKU. Fiskars's software has the ability to weigh each input. It gives more weight to a statistical forecast for in-line items, and inputs from the sales staff get much more weight for promoted products and new items.

It also segments SKUs by value and forecastability so as to focus forecasting efforts on SKUs that have the biggest impact on the business. High-value items that also have high forecastability (stable demand with low forecast errors to date) tend to do well with the time-series techniques, and **judgmental adjustments** are made with caution. High-value items with low forecastability get top priority in the forecasting effort, such as with CPFR. Much less attention is given to improving forecasts for "C" items for which there is some history and fairly steady demand.

Finally, Fiskars instituted a Web-based program that gives the entire company visibility to forecast information in whatever form it needs. For example, Finance wants monthly, quarterly, and yearly projections in dollars, whereas Operations wants projections in units as well as accuracy measures. Everybody can track updated forecast information by customer, brand, and SKU.

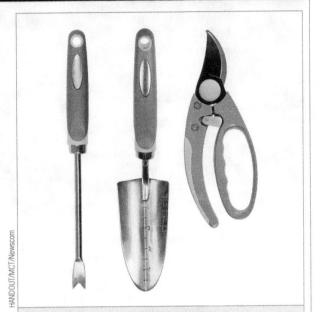

HANDOUT/MCT/Newscom

Fiskars Brands, Inc., totally overhauled its forecasting process. Its products include garden shears, pruners, hand tools, scissors, ratchet tools, and the like. It introduced time-series tools, with much emphasis placed on combination forecasts. Instead of asking members of the sales staff to provide their own forecasts, forecasts were sent to them, and they were asked for validation and refinement. Their judgmental inputs provide valuable information relative to additions, deletions, and promotions. Combining multiple forecasts (forecasts from several time-series techniques and judgment inputs) into one number creates more accurate forecasts by SKU.

Source: David Montgomery, "Flashpoints for Changing Your Forecasting Process," *The Journal of Business Forecasting,* (Winter 2006–2007), pp. 35–37; **http://www.fiskars.com**, May 21, 2011.

Another way to take advantage of multiple techniques is **focus forecasting**, which selects the best forecast (based on past error measures) from a group of forecasts generated by individual techniques. Every period, all techniques are used to make forecasts for each item. The forecasts are made with a computer because there can be 100,000 SKUs at a company, each needing to be forecast. Using the history file as the starting point for each method, the computer generates forecasts for the current period. The forecasts are compared to actual demand, and the method that produces the forecast with the least error is used to make the forecast for the next period. The method used for each item may change from period to period.

Putting It All Together: Forecasting as a Process

Often companies must prepare forecasts for hundreds or even thousands of services or products repeatedly. For example, a large network of health care facilities must calculate demand forecasts for each of its services for every department. This undertaking involves voluminous data that must be manipulated frequently. However, software such as Motorola Mobility's system can ease the burden of making these forecasts and coordinating the forecasts between customers

judgmental adjustment

An adjustment made to forecasts from one or more quantitative models that accounts for recognizing which models are performing particularly well in recent past, or take into account contextual information.

focus forecasting

A method of forecasting that selects the best forecast from a group of forecasts generated by individual techniques.

West Marine acquired its East Coast competitor, E&B Marine, in 1997. The consequences were quickly apparent. Peak-season out-of-stock levels rose more than 12 percent compared to the prior year. After six years of steady growth, net income dropped from $15 million in 1997 to not much more than $1 million the next year. Fast-forward six years. They had no supply problems in any of their warehouses or stores. What changed? Two words: supply chain. Managers recognized that they needed to make a significant shift in managing its supply chain. A crucial element was greater collaboration with their suppliers. It is not enough to coordinate the supply chain within the boundaries of a single organization.

and suppliers. Many forecasting software packages are available, including Manugistics, Forecast Pro, and SAS. The forecasting routines in OM Explorer and POM for Windows give some hint of their capabilities. Forecasting is not just a set of techniques, but instead a process that must be designed and managed. While there is no one process that works for everyone, here we describe two comprehensive processes that can be quite effective in managing operations and the supply chain.

A Typical Forecasting Process

Many *inputs* to the forecasting process are informational, beginning with the *history file* on past demand. The history file is kept up-to-date with the actual demands. Clarifying notes and adjustments are made to the database to explain unusual demand behavior, such as the impact of special promotions and closeouts. Often the database is separated into two parts: *base* data and *nonbase* data. The second category reflects irregular demands. Final forecasts just made at the end of the prior cycle are entered in the history file, so as to track forecast errors. Other information sources are from salesforce estimates, outstanding bids on new orders, booked orders, market research studies, competitor behavior, economic outlook, new product introductions, pricing, and promotions. If CPFR is used, as is done by Motorola Mobility in our opening vignette, then considerable information sharing will take place with customers and suppliers. For new products, a history database is fabricated based on the firm's experience with prior products and the judgment of personnel.

Outputs of the process are forecasts for multiple time periods into the future. Typically, they are on a monthly basis and are projected out from six months to two years. Most software packages have the ability to "roll up" or "aggregate" forecasts for individual stock-keeping units (SKUs) into forecasts for whole product families. Forecasts can also be "blown down" or "disaggregated" into smaller pieces. In a make-to-stock environment, forecasts tend to be more detailed and can get down to specific individual products. In a make-to-order environment, the forecasts tend to be for groups of products. Similarly, if the lead times to buy raw materials and manufacture a product or provide a service are long, the forecasts go farther out into the future.

The forecast process itself, typically done on a monthly basis, consists of structured steps. These steps often are facilitated by someone who might be called a demand manager, forecast analyst, or demand/supply planner. However, many other people are typically involved before the plan for the month is authorized.

Step 1. The cycle begins mid-month just after the forecasts have been finalized and communicated to the stakeholders. Now is the time to update the history file and review forecast accuracy. At the end of the month, enter actual demand and review forecast accuracy.

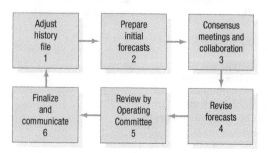

Step 2. Prepare initial forecasts using some forecasting software package and judgment. Adjust the parameters of the software to find models that fit the past demand well and yet reflect the demand manager's judgment on irregular events and information about future sales pulled from various sources and business units.

Step 3. Hold consensus meetings with the stakeholders, such as marketing, sales, supply chain planners, and finance. Make it easy for business unit and field sales personnel to make inputs. Use the Internet to get collaborative information from key customers and suppliers. The goal is to arrive at consensus forecasts from all of the important players.

Step 4. Revise the forecasts using judgment, considering the inputs from the consensus meetings and collaborative sources.

Step 5. Present the forecasts to the operating committee for review and to reach a final set of forecasts. It is important to have a set of forecasts that everybody agrees upon and will work to support.

Step 6. Finalize the forecasts based on the decisions of the operating committee and communicate them to the important stakeholders. Supply chain planners are usually the biggest users.

As with all work activity, forecasting is a process and should be continually reviewed for improvements. A better process will foster better relationships between departments such as marketing, sales, and operations. It will also produce better forecasts. This principle is the first one in Table 2 to guide process improvements.

Adding Collaboration to the System

This process is similar to the first one, except that it adds considerable collaboration with the company's customers and suppliers, particularly in step 3. **Collaborative planning, forecasting, and replenishment (CPFR)** is a specific nine-step process for supply chain integration that allows a supplier and its customers to collaborate on making the forecast by using the Internet. Many other firms, including Motorola as described in the opening vignette, are turning to CPFR to coordinate up and down the supply chain.

Forecasting as a Nested Process

Forecasting is not a stand-alone activity, but instead part of a larger process. After all, demand is only half of the equation—the other half is supply. Future plans must be developed to supply the resources needed to meet the forecasted demand. Resources include the workforce, materials, inventories, dollars, and equipment capacity.

Mark Peterson/CORBIS

Walmart has long been known for its careful analysis of cash register receipts and for working with suppliers to reduce inventories. In the past, like many other retailers, Walmart did not share its forecasts with its suppliers. The result was forecast errors as much as 60 percent of actual demand. Retailers ordered more than they needed, and suppliers produced more than they could sell. To combat the ill effects of forecast errors on inventories, Benchmarking Partners, Inc., was funded in the mid-1990s by Walmart, IBM, SAP, and Manugistics to develop a software package. Walmart initiated this new approach with Listerine, a primary product of Warner-Lambert (now produced and distributed by Johnson & Johnson). The system worked in the following way during this pilot period. Walmart and Warner-Lambert independently calculated the demand they expected for Listerine six months into the future, taking into consideration factors such as past sales trends and promotion plans. They then exchanged their forecasts over the Internet. If the forecasts differed by more than a predetermined percentage, the retailer and the manufacturer used the Internet to exchange written comments and supporting data. The parties went through as many cycles as needed to converge on an acceptable forecast. They passed the pilot period in flying colors. Benefits to Walmart included a reduction in stockouts from 15 percent to 2 percent as well as significant increases in sales and reductions in inventory costs. Likewise, Warner-Lambert benefited by having a smoother production plan and lower average costs. This system was later generalized and dubbed CPFR, which stands for collaborative planning, forecasting, and replenishment.

TABLE 2 │ SOME PRINCIPLES FOR THE FORECASTING PROCESS

- Better processes yield better forecasts.
- Demand forecasting is being done in virtually every company, either formally or informally. The challenge is to do it well—better than the competition.
- Better forecasts result in better customer service and lower costs, as well as better relationships with suppliers and customers.
- The forecast can and must make sense based on the big picture, economic outlook, market share, and so on.
- The best way to improve forecast accuracy is to focus on reducing forecast error.
- Bias is the worst kind of forecast error; strive for zero bias.
- Whenever possible, forecast at more aggregate levels. Forecast in detail only where necessary.
- Far more can be gained by people collaborating and communicating well than by using the most advanced forecasting technique or model.

Source: Based on Thomas F. Wallace and Robert A. Stahl, *Sales Forecasting: A New Approach* (Cincinnati, OH: T. E. Wallace & Company, 2002), p. 112. Copyright © 2002 T.E. Wallace & Company. Used with permission.

collaborative planning, forecasting, and replenishment (CPFR)

A nine-step process for supply chain integration that allows a supplier and its customers to collaborate on making the forecast by using the Internet.

LEARNING GOALS IN REVIEW

1 **Identify the various forecasting methods available to forecasting systems.** The section "Choosing the Type of Forecasting Technique," gives a quick introduction to the four groups of forecasting techniques. Each is described fully in subsequent sections.

2 **Identify the various measures of forecast errors.** Review the "Forecast Error," and "Choosing a Quantitative Forecasting Method," to understand CFE, MSE, σ, MAD, MAPE, and the tracking signals.

3 **Use regression to make forecasts with one or more independent variables.** The "Causal Methods: Linear Regression" section and Example 2, describe how linear regression, when historical data is available, can express demand as a linear function of one or more independent variables. Example 2 and Solved Problem 1 illustrate the computer output, including the various statistics on how well the regression equation fits the data.

4 **Make forecasts using the most common approaches for time-series analysis.** The "Time-Series Methods" explain the naïve method, simple moving average, weighted moving average, and exponential smoothing techniques that are used. Examples 3 and 4 demonstrate some of the methods, as do Solved Problems 2 and 3.

5 **Make forecasts using Trend Projection with Regression.** We cover this technique with four figures illustrating the computer output and how varying number of periods included in the regression analysis can impact the results.

6 **Describe a typical forecasting process used by businesses.** See the section "A Typical Forecasting Process," and the six steps involved. There is much more complexity when you realize the number of SKUs involved and the need to update the history file.

7 **Explain collaborative planning, forecasting, and replenishment (CPFR).** The "Adding Collaboration to the System" section, is a big step in increasing the coordination up and down the supply chain. In the chapter opener, we see what Motorola Mobility has done with its customers to improve its demand forecasts.

MyOMLab helps you develop analytical skills and assesses your progress with multiple problems on moving average, mean absolute deviation, mean absolute percent error, mean squared error (MSE), exponential smoothing, MAD, MAPE, multiplicative seasonal method, least squares regression model, and trend projection with regression.

MyOMLab Resources	Titles	Link to the Book
Video	*Forecasting and Supply Chain Management at Deckers Outdoor Corporation*	Using Multiple Techniques; Putting It All Together: Forecasting as a Process
Active Model Exercises	14.1 Linear Regression 14.2 Simple Moving Averages 14.3 Exponential Smoothing	Casual Methods: Linear Regression; Example 2; Solved Problem 1 Estimating the Average; Example 3; Solved Problem 2 Exponential Smoothing; Example 4; Solved Problem 3
OM Explorer Solvers	Regression Analysis Seasonal Forecasting Time Series Forecasting Trend Projection with Regression	Casual Methods: Linear Regression; Example 2; Solved Problem 1 Seasonal Patterns; Example 6; Solved Problem 4 Time Series Methods Examples 3 – 5 Trend Projection with Regression; Example 5
OM Explorer Tutors	14.1 Moving Average Method 14.2 Weighted Moving Average Method 14.3 Exponential Smoothing	Estimating the Average; Example 3; Solved Problem 2 Weighted Moving Average and Solved Problem 2 Exponential Smoothing; Example 4; Solved Problem 3
Virtual Tours	Ferrara Pan Cape Cod Chips	Key Decisions on Making Forecasts Demand Patterns; Judgment Methods
POM for Windows	Time Series Analysis Regression Projector Least Squares – Simple and Multiple Regression Error Analysis	Time Series Methods; Examples 3 – 5; Seasonal Patterns; Example 6; Solved Problem 4 Casual Methods: Linear Regression; Example 2; Solved Problem 1 Casual Methods: Linear Regression; Example 2; Solved Problem 1 Judgment Methods; Forecast Error, Example 1, Choosing a Quantitative Forecasting Method; Solved Problem 3

MyOMLab Resources	Titles	Link to the Book
Student Data File	Experiential Exercise Two	Time-Series Methods; Choosing a Time-Series Method; Using Multiple Techniques
Tutorial	Trend-Adjusted Exponential Smoothing	Trend Projection with Regression
Internet Exercise	National Climate Data Center	Casual Methods: Linear Regression; Example 2; Trend Projection with Regression; Example 5
Key Equations		
Image Library		

Key Equations

1. Forecast error:

$$E_t = D_t - F_t$$

$$\text{CFE} = \sum E_t$$

$$\bar{E} = \frac{\text{CFE}}{n}$$

$$\text{MSE} = \frac{\sum E_t^2}{n}$$

$$\sigma = \sqrt{\frac{\sum (E_t - \bar{E})^2}{n - 1}}$$

$$\text{MAD} = \frac{\sum |E_t|}{n}$$

$$\text{MAPE} = \frac{(\sum |E_t|/D_t)(100\%)}{n}$$

2. Linear regression:

$$Y = a + bX$$

3. Naïve forecasting:

$$\text{Forecast} = D_t$$

4. Simple moving average:

$$F_{t+1} = \frac{D_t + D_{t-1} + D_{t-2} + \cdots + D_{t-n+1}}{n}$$

5. Weighted moving average:

$$F_{t+1} = \text{Weight}_1(D_t) + \text{Weight}_2(D_{t-1}) + \text{Weight}_3(D_{t-2}) + \cdots + \text{Weight}_n(D_{t-n+1})$$

6. Exponential smoothing:

$$F_{t+1} = \alpha D_t + (1 - \alpha)F_t$$

7. Trend Projection using Regression

$$F_t = a + bt$$

8. Tracking signal:

$$\frac{\text{CFE}}{\text{MAD}} \quad \text{or} \quad \frac{\text{CFE}}{\text{MAD}_t}$$

9. Exponentially smoothed error:

$$\text{MAD}_t = \alpha |E_t| + (1 - \alpha)\text{MAD}_{t-1}$$

Key Terms

additive seasonal method
aggregation
causal methods
collaborative planning, forecasting,
    and replenishment (CPFR)
combination forecasts
cumulative sum of forecast errors
    (CFE)
dependent variable
Delphi method
executive opinion
exponential smoothing method

focus forecasting
forecast
forecast error
holdout sample
independent variables
judgment methods
judgmental adjustment
linear regression
market research
mean absolute deviation (MAD)
mean absolute percent error
    (MAPE)

mean squared error (MSE)
multiplicative seasonal method
naïve forecast
salesforce estimates
simple moving average method
standard deviation (σ)
technological forecasting
time series
time-series analysis
tracking signal
trend projection with regression
weighted moving average method

Solved Problem 1

Chicken Palace periodically offers carryout five-piece chicken dinners at special prices. Let Y be the number of dinners sold and X be the price. Based on the historical observations and calculations in the following table, determine the regression equation, correlation coefficient, and coefficient of determination. How many dinners can Chicken Palace expect to sell at $3.00 each?

Observation	Price (X)	Dinners Sold (Y)
1	$ 2.70	760
2	$ 3.50	510
3	$ 2.00	980
4	$ 4.20	250
5	$ 3.10	320
6	$ 4.05	480
Total	$19.55	3,300
Average	$ 3.258	550

SOLUTION

We use the computer (*Regression Analysis* Solver of OM Explorer or *Regression Projector* module of POM for Windows) to calculate the best values of a, b, the correlation coefficient, and the coefficient of determination.

$$a = 1{,}454.60$$
$$b = -277.63$$
$$r = -0.84$$
$$r^2 = 0.71$$

The regression line is

$$Y = a + bX = 1{,}454.60 - 277.63X$$

The correlation coefficient ($r = -0.84$) shows a negative correlation between the variables. The coefficient of determination ($r^2 = 0.71$) is not too large, which suggests that other variables (in addition to price) might appreciably affect sales.

  If the regression equation is satisfactory to the manager, estimated sales at a price of $3.00 per dinner may be calculated as follows:

$$Y = a + bX = 1{,}454.60 - 277.63(3.00)$$
$$= 621.71 \text{ or } 622 \text{ dinners}$$

Solved Problem 2

The Polish General's Pizza Parlor is a small restaurant catering to patrons with a taste for European pizza. One of its specialties is Polish Prize pizza. The manager must forecast weekly demand for these special pizzas so that he can order pizza shells weekly. Recently, demand has been as follows:

Week	Pizzas	Week	Pizzas
June 2	50	June 23	56
June 9	65	June 30	55
June 16	52	July 7	60

a. Forecast the demand for pizza for June 23 to July 14 by using the simple moving average method with $n = 3$. Then, repeat the forecast by using the weighted moving average method with $n = 3$ and weights of 0.50, 0.30, and 0.20, with 0.50 applying to the most recent demand.

b. Calculate the MAD for each method.

SOLUTION

a. The simple moving average method and the weighted moving average method give the following results:

Current Week	Simple Moving Average Forecast for Next Week	Weighted Moving Average Forecast for Next Week
June 16	$\dfrac{52 + 65 + 50}{3} = 55.7$ or 56	$[(0.5 \times 52) + (0.3 \times 65) + (0.2 \times 50)] = 55.5$ or 56
June 23	$\dfrac{56 + 52 + 65}{3} = 55.7$ or 58	$[(0.5 \times 56) + (0.3 \times 52) + (0.2 \times 65)] = 56.6$ or 57
June 30	$\dfrac{55 + 56 + 52}{3} = 54.3$ or 54	$[(0.5 \times 55) + (0.3 \times 56) + (0.2 \times 52)] = 54.7$ or 55
July 7	$\dfrac{60 + 55 + 56}{3} = 57.0$ or 57	$[(0.5 \times 60) + (0.3 \times 55) + (0.2 \times 56)] = 57.7$ or 58

Forecasts in each row are for the next week's demand. For example, the simple moving average and weighted moving average forecasts (both are 56 units) calculated after learning the demand on June 16 apply to June 23's demand forecast.

b. The mean absolute deviation is calculated as follows:

		SIMPLE MOVING AVERAGE		WEIGHTED MOVING AVERAGE	
Week	Actual Demand	Forecast for This Week	Absolute Errors $\lvert E_t \rvert$	Forecast for This Week	Absolute Errors $\lvert E_t \rvert$
June 23	56	56	$\lvert 56 - 56 \rvert = 0$	56	$\lvert 56 - 56 \rvert = 0$
June 30	55	58	$\lvert 55 - 58 \rvert = 3$	57	$\lvert 55 - 57 \rvert = 2$
July 7	60	54	$\lvert 60 - 54 \rvert = 6$	55	$\lvert 60 - 55 \rvert = 5$
			MAD $= \dfrac{0 + 3 + 6}{3} = 3.0$		MAD $= \dfrac{0 + 2 + 5}{3} = 2.3$

For this limited set of data, the weighted moving average method resulted in a slightly lower mean absolute deviation. However, final conclusions can be made only after analyzing much more data.

Solved Problem 3

The monthly demand for units manufactured by the Acme Rocket Company has been as follows:

Month	Units	Month	Units
May	100	September	105
June	80	October	110
July	110	November	125
August	115	December	120

a. Use the exponential smoothing method to forecast the number of units for June to January. The initial forecast for May was 105 units; $\alpha = 0.2$.

b. Calculate the absolute percentage error for each month from June through December and the MAD and MAPE of forecast error as of the end of December.

c. Calculate the tracking signal as of the end of December. What can you say about the performance of your forecasting method?

SOLUTION

a.

Current Month, t	Calculating Forecast for Next Month $F_{t+1} = \alpha D_t + (1 - \alpha)F_t$	Forecast for Month $t + 1$
May	$0.2(100) + 0.8(105) = 104.0$ or 104	June
June	$0.2(80) + 0.8(104.0) = 99.2$ or 99	July
July	$0.2(110) + 0.8(99.2) = 101.4$ or 101	August
August	$0.2(115) + 0.8(101.4) = 104.1$ or 104	September
September	$0.2(105) + 0.8(104.1) = 104.3$ or 104	October
October	$0.2(110) + 0.8(104.3) = 105.4$ or 105	November
November	$0.2(125) + 0.8(105.4) = 109.3$ or 109	December
December	$0.2(120) + 0.8(109.3) = 111.4$ or 111	January

b.

Month, t	Actual Demand, D_t	Forecast, F_t	Error, $E_t = D_t - F_t$	Absolute Error, $\lvert E_t \rvert$	Absolute Percentage Error,$(\lvert E_t \rvert/D_t)(100\%)$
June	80	104	−24	24	30.0%
July	110	99	11	11	10.0
August	115	101	14	14	12.0
September	105	104	1	1	1.0
October	110	104	6	6	5.5
November	125	105	20	0	16.0
December	120	109	11	11	9.2
Total	765		39	87	83.7%

$$\text{MAD} = \frac{\Sigma \lvert E_t \rvert}{n} = \frac{87}{7} = 12.4 \text{ and MAPE} = \frac{(\Sigma \lvert E_t \rvert/D_t)(100)}{n} = \frac{83.7\%}{7} = 11.96\%$$

c. As of the end of December, the cumulative sum of forecast errors (CFE) is 39. Using the mean absolute deviation calculated in part (b), we calculate the tracking signal:

$$\text{Tracking signal} = \frac{\text{CFE}}{\text{MAD}} = \frac{39}{12.4} = 3.14$$

The probability that a tracking signal value of 3.14 could be generated completely by chance is small. Consequently, we should revise our approach. The long string of forecasts lower than actual demand suggests use of a trend method.

Solved Problem 4

The Northville Post Office experiences a seasonal pattern of daily mail volume every week. The following data for two representative weeks are expressed in thousands of pieces of mail:

Day	Week 1	Week 2
Sunday	5	8
Monday	20	15
Tuesday	30	32
Wednesday	35	30
Thursday	49	45
Friday	70	70
Saturday	15	10
Total	224	210

a. Calculate a seasonal factor for each day of the week.
b. If the postmaster estimates 230,000 pieces of mail to be sorted next week, forecast the volume for each day of the week.

SOLUTION

a. Calculate the average daily mail volume for each week. Then, for each day of the week, divide the mail volume by the week's average to get the seasonal factor. Finally, for each day, add the two seasonal factors and divide by 2 to obtain the average seasonal factor to use in the forecast (see part [b]).

Day	WEEK 1		WEEK 2		Average Seasonal Factor [(1) + (2)]/2
	Mail Volume	Seasonal Factor (1)	Mail Volume	Seasonal Factor (2)	
Sunday	5	5/32 = 0.15625	8	8/30 = 0.26667	0.21146
Monday	20	20/32 = 0.62500	15	15/30 = 0.50000	0.56250
Tuesday	30	30/32 = 0.93750	32	32/30 = 1.06667	1.00209
Wednesday	35	35/32 = 1.09375	30	30/30 = 1.00000	1.04688
Thursday	49	49/32 = 1.53125	45	45/30 = 1.50000	1.51563
Friday	70	70/32 = 2.18750	70	70/30 = 2.33333	2.26042
Saturday	15	15/32 = 0.46875	10	10/30 = 0.33333	0.40104
Total	224		210		
Average	224/7 = 32		210/7 = 30		

b. The average daily mail volume is expected to be $230{,}000/7 = 32{,}857$ pieces of mail. Using the average seasonal factors calculated in part (a), we obtain the following forecasts:

Day	Calculation		Forecast
Sunday	0.21146(32,857) =		6,948
Monday	0.56250(32,857) =		18,482
Tuesday	1.00209(32,857) =		32,926
Wednesday	1.04688(32,857) =		34,397
Thursday	1.51563(32,857) =		49,799
Friday	2.26042(32,857) =		74,271
Saturday	0.40104(32,857) =		13,177
		Total	230,000

Discussion Questions

1. Figure 9 shows summer air visibility measurements for Denver, Colorado. The acceptable visibility standard is 100, with readings above 100 indicating clean air and good visibility, and readings below 100 indicating temperature inversions caused by forest fires, volcanic eruptions, or collisions with comets.

   a. Is a trend evident in the data? Which time-series techniques might be appropriate for estimating the average of these data?

   b. A medical center for asthma and respiratory diseases located in Denver has great demand for its services when air quality is poor. If you were in charge of developing a short-term (say, 3-day) forecast of visibility, which causal factor(s) would you analyze? In other words, which external factors hold the potential to significantly affect visibility in the *short term*?

   c. Tourism, an important factor in Denver's economy, is affected by the city's image. Air quality, as measured by visibility, affects the city's image. If you were responsible for development of tourism, which causal factor(s) would you analyze to forecast visibility for the *medium term* (say, the next two summers)?

   d. The federal government threatens to withhold several hundred million dollars in Department of Transportation funds unless Denver meets visibility standards within 8 years. How would you proceed to generate a *long-term* judgment forecast of technologies that will be available to improve visibility in the next 10 years?

2. Kay and Michael Passe publish *What's Happening?*—a biweekly newspaper to publicize local events. *What's Happening?* has few subscribers; it typically is sold at checkout stands. Much of the revenue comes from advertisers of garage sales and supermarket specials. In an effort to reduce costs associated with printing too many papers or delivering them to the wrong location, Michael implemented a computerized system to collect sales data. Sales-counter scanners accurately record sales data for each location. Since the system was implemented, total sales volume has steadily declined. Selling advertising space and maintaining shelf space at supermarkets are getting more difficult.

   Reduced revenue makes controlling costs all the more important. For each issue, Michael carefully makes a forecast based on sales data collected at each location. Then, he orders papers to be printed and distributed in quantities matching the forecast. Michael's forecast reflects a downward trend, which *is* present in the sales data. Now only a few papers are left over at only a few locations. Although the sales forecast accurately predicts the actual sales at most locations, *What's Happening?* is spiraling toward oblivion. Kay suspects that Michael is doing something wrong in preparing the forecast but can find no mathematical errors. Tell her what is happening.

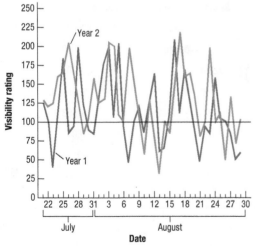

▲ FIGURE 9
Summer Air Visibility Measurements

Problems

The OM Explorer and POM for Windows software is available to all students using the 10th edition of this text. Go to **www.pearsonhighered.com/krajewski** to download these computer packages. If you purchased MyOMLab, you also have access to Active Models software and significant help in doing the following problems. Check with your instructor on how best to use these resources. In many cases, the instructor wants you to understand how to do the calculations by hand. At the least, the software provides a check on your calculations. When calculations are particularly complex and the goal is interpreting the results in making decisions, the software entirely replaces the manual calculations.

1. The owner of a computer store rents printers to some of her preferred customers. She is interested in arriving at a forecast of rentals so that she can order the correct quantities of supplies that go with the printers. Data for the last 10 weeks are shown here.

Week	Rentals	Week	Rentals
1	23	6	28
2	24	7	32
3	32	8	35
4	26	9	26
5	31	10	24

   a. Prepare a forecast for weeks 6 through 10 by using a 5-week moving average. What is the forecast for week 11?

   b. Calculate the mean absolute deviation as of the end of week 10.

2. Sales for the past 12 months at Dalworth Company are given here.

Month	Sales ($ millions)	Month	Sales ($ millions)
January	20	July	53
February	24	August	62
March	27	September	54
April	31	October	36
May	37	November	32
June	47	December	29

   a. Use a three-month moving average to forecast the sales for the months May through December.

   b. Use a four-month moving average to forecast the sales for the months May through December.

   c. Compare the performance of the two methods by using the mean absolute deviation as the performance criterion. Which method would you recommend?

   d. Compare the performance of the two methods by using the mean absolute percent error as the performance criterion. Which method would you recommend?

   e. Compare the performance of the two methods by using the mean squared error as the performance criterion. Which method would you recommend?

3. Karl's Copiers sells and repairs photocopy machines. The manager needs weekly forecasts of service calls so that he can schedule service personnel. Use the actual demand in the first period for the forecast for the first week so error measurement begins in the second week. The manager uses exponential smoothing with $\alpha = 0.20$. Forecast the number of calls for week 6, which is next week.

Week	Actual Service Calls
1	24
2	32
3	36
4	23
5	25

4. Consider the sales data for Dalworth Company given in Problem 2.

   a. Use a 3-month weighted moving average to forecast the sales for the months April through December. Use weights of (3/6), (2/6), and (1/6), giving more weight to more recent data.

   b. Use exponential smoothing with $\alpha = 0.6$ to forecast the sales for the months April through December. Assume that the initial forecast for January was $22 million. Start error measurement in April.

   c. Compare the performance of the two methods by using the mean absolute deviation as the performance criterion, with error measurement beginning in April. Which method would you recommend?

   d. Compare the performance of the two methods by using the mean absolute percent error as the performance criterion, with error measurement beginning in April. Which method would you recommend?

   e. Compare the performance of the two methods by using the mean squared error as the performance criterion, with error measurement beginning in April. Which method would you recommend?

5. A convenience store recently started to carry a new brand of soft drink. Management is interested in estimating future sales volume to determine whether it should continue to carry the new brand or replace it with another brand. The table at the top of the next page provides the number of cans sold per week. Use both the trend projection with regression and the exponential smoothing (let $\alpha = 0.4$ with an initial forecast for week 1 of 617) methods to forecast demand for week 13. Compare these methods by using the mean absolute deviation and mean absolute percent error performance criteria. Does your analysis suggest that sales are trending and if so, by how much?

Week	1	2	3	4	5	6	7	8	9	10	11	12
Sales	617	617	648	739	659	623	742	704	724	715	668	740

6. Community Federal Bank in Dothan, Alabama, recently increased its fees to customers who use employees as tellers. Management is interested in whether its new fee policy has increased the number of customers now using its automatic teller machines to that point that more machines are required. The following table provides the number of automatic teller transactions by week. Use trend projection with regression to forecast usage for weeks 13–16.

Week	1	2	3	4	5	6	7	8	9	10	11	12
Transactions	716	721	833	639	689	736	779	711	723	835	829	667

7. The number of heart surgeries performed at Heartville General Hospital has increased steadily over the past several years. The hospital's administration is seeking the best method to forecast the demand for such surgeries in year 6. The data for the past 5 years are shown.

Year	Demand
1	45
2	50
3	52
4	56
5	58

The hospital's administration is considering the following forecasting methods. Begin error measurement in year 3, so all methods are compared for the same years.

i. Exponential smoothing, with $\alpha = 0.6$. Let the initial forecast for year 1 be 45, the same as the actual demand.

ii. Exponential smoothing, with $\alpha = 0.9$. Let the initial forecast for year 1 be 45, the same as the actual demand.

iii. Trend projection with regression.

iv. Two-year moving average.

v. Two-year weighted moving average, using weights 0.6 and 0.4, with more recent data given more weight.

vi. If MAD is the performance criterion chosen by the administration, which forecasting method should it choose?

vii. If MSE is the performance criterion chosen by the administration, which forecasting method should it choose?

viii. If MAPE is the performance criterion chosen by the administration, which forecasting method should it choose?

8. The following data are for calculator sales in units at an electronics store over the past 9 weeks:

Week	Sales	Week	Sales
1	46	6	58
2	49	7	62
3	43	8	56
4	50	9	63
5	53		

Use trend projection with regression to forecast sales for weeks 10–13. What are the error measures (CFE, MSE, σ, MAD, and MAPE) for this forecasting procedure? How about r^2?

9. The demand for Krispee Crunchies, a favorite breakfast cereal of people born in the 1940s, is experiencing a decline. The company wants to monitor demand for this product closely as it nears the end of its life cycle. The following table shows the actual sales history for January–October. Generate forecasts for November–December, using the trend projection by regression method. Looking at the accuracy of its forecasts over the history file, as well as the other statistics provided, how confident are you in these forecasts for November–December?

Month	Sales	Month	Sales
January	890,000	July	710,000
February	800,000	August	730,000
March	825,000	September	680,000
April	840,000	October	670,000
May	730,000	November	
June	780,000	December	

10. Forrest and Dan make boxes of chocolates for which the demand is uncertain. Forrest says, "That's life." On the other hand, Dan believes that some demand patterns exist that could be useful for planning the purchase of sugar, chocolate, and shrimp. Forrest insists on placing a surprise chocolate-covered shrimp in some boxes so that "You never know what you'll get." Quarterly demand (in boxes of chocolates) for the last 3 years follows:

Quarter	Year 1	Year 2	Year 3
1	3,000	3,300	3,502
2	1,700	2,100	2,448
3	900	1,500	1,768
4	4,400	5,100	5,882
Total	10,000	12,000	13,600

a. Use intuition and judgment to estimate quarterly demand for the fourth year.

b. If the expected sales for chocolates are 14,800 cases for year 4, use the multiplicative seasonal method to prepare a forecast for each quarter of the year. Are any of the quarterly forecasts different from what you thought you would get in part (a)?

11. The manager of Snyder's Garden Center must make the annual purchasing plans for rakes, gloves, and other gardening items. One of the items the company stocks is Fast-Grow, a liquid fertilizer. The sales of this item are seasonal, with peaks in the spring, summer, and fall months. Quarterly demand (in cases) for the past 2 years follows:

Quarter	Year 1	Year 2
1	40	60
2	350	440
3	290	320
4	210	280
Total	890	1,100

If the expected sales for Fast-Grow are 1,150 cases for year 3, use the multiplicative seasonal method to prepare a forecast for each quarter of the year.

12. The manager of a utility company in the Texas panhandle wants to develop quarterly forecasts of power loads for the next year. The power loads are seasonal, and the data on the quarterly loads in megawatts (MW) for the last 4 years are as follows:

Quarter	Year 1	Year 2	Year 3	Year 4
1	103.5	94.7	118.6	109.3
2	126.1	116.0	141.2	131.6
3	144.5	137.1	159.0	149.5
4	166.1	152.5	178.2	169.0

The manager estimates the total demand for the next year at 600 MW. Use the multiplicative seasonal method to develop the forecast for each quarter.

13. Demand for oil changes at Garcia's Garage has been as follows:

Month	Number of Oil Changes
January	41
February	46
March	57
April	52
May	59
June	51
July	60
August	62

a. Use simple linear regression analysis to develop a forecasting model for monthly demand. In this application, the dependent variable, Y, is monthly demand and the independent variable, X, is the month. For January, let $X = 1$; for February, let $X = 2$; and so on.

b. Use the model to forecast demand for September, October, and November. Here, $X = 9$, 10, and 11, respectively.

14. At a hydrocarbon processing factory, process control involves periodic analysis of samples for a certain process quality parameter. The analytic procedure currently used is costly and time consuming. A faster and more economical alternative procedure has been proposed. However, the numbers for the quality parameter given by the alternative procedure are somewhat different from those given by the current procedure, not because of any inherent errors but because of changes in the nature of the chemical analysis.

Management believes that if the numbers from the new procedure can be used to forecast reliably the corresponding numbers from the current procedure, switching to the new procedure would be reasonable and cost effective. The following data were obtained for the quality parameter by analyzing samples using both procedures:

Current (Y)	Proposed (X)	Current (Y)	Proposed (X)
3.0	3.1	3.1	3.1
3.1	3.9	2.7	2.9
3.0	3.4	3.3	3.6
3.6	4.0	3.2	4.1
3.8	3.6	2.1	2.6
2.7	3.6	3.0	3.1
2.7	3.6	2.6	2.8

a. Use linear regression to find a relation to forecast Y, which is the quality parameter from the current procedure, using the values from the proposed procedure, X.

b. Is there a strong relationship between Y and X? Explain.

15. Ohio Swiss Milk Products manufactures and distributes ice cream in Ohio, Kentucky, and West Virginia. The company wants to expand operations by locating another plant in northern Ohio. The size of the new plant will be a function of the expected demand for ice cream within the area served by the plant. A market survey is currently under way to determine that demand.

Ohio Swiss wants to estimate the relationship between the manufacturing cost per gallon and the number of gallons sold in a year to determine the demand for ice cream and, thus, the size of the new plant. The following data have been collected:

a. Develop a regression equation to forecast the cost per gallon as a function of the number of gallons produced.

Plant	Cost per Thousand Gallons (Y)	Thousands of Gallons Sold (X)
1	$ 1,015	416.9
2	973	472.5
3	1,046	250.0
4	1,006	372.1
5	1,058	238.1
6	1,068	258.6
7	967	597.0
8	997	414.0
9	1,044	263.2
10	1,008	372.0
Total	$10,182	3,654.4

b. What are the correlation coefficient and the coefficient of determination? Comment on your regression equation in light of these measures.

c. Suppose that the market survey indicates a demand of 325,000 gallons in the Bucyrus, Ohio, area. Estimate the manufacturing cost per gallon for a plant producing 325,000 gallons per year.

Advanced Problems

16. Franklin Tooling, Inc., manufactures specialty tooling for firms in the paper-making industry. All of their products are engineer-to-order and so the company never knows exactly what components to purchase for a tool until a customer places an order. However, the company believes that weekly demand for a few components is fairly stable. Component 135.AG is one such item. The last 26 weeks of historical use of component 135.AG is recorded below.

Week	Demand	Week	Demand
1	137	14	131
2	136	15	132
3	143	16	124
4	136	17	121
5	141	18	127
6	128	19	118
7	149	20	120
8	136	21	115
9	134	22	106
10	142	23	120
11	125	24	113
12	134	25	121
13	118	26	119

Use OM Explorer's *Time Series Forecasting* Solver to evaluate the following forecasting methods. Start error measurement in the fifth week, so all methods are evaluated over the same time interval. Use the default settings for initial forecasts.

i. Naïve (1-Period Moving Average)

ii. 3-Period Moving Average

iii. Exponential Smoothing, with $\alpha = .28$

iv. Trend Projection with Regression

v. Which forecasting method should management use, if the performance criterion it chooses is:

- CFE?
- MSE?
- MAD?
- MAPE?

17. Create an Excel spreadsheet on your own that can create combination forecasts for Problem 16. Create a combination forecast using all four techniques from problem 16. Give each technique an equal weight. Create a second combination forecast by using the three techniques that seem best based on MAD. Give equal weight to each technique. Finally, create a third forecast by equally weighting the two best techniques. Calculate CFE, MAD, MSE, and MAPE for the combination forecast. Are these forecasts better or worse than the forecasting techniques identified in Problem 16?

18. The director of a large public library must schedule employees to reshelf books and periodicals checked out of the library. The number of items checked out will determine the labor requirements. The following data reflect the number of items checked out of the library for the past 3 years:

Month	Year 1	Year 2	Year 3
January	1,847	2,045	1,986
February	2,669	2,321	2,564
March	2,467	2,419	2,635
April	2,432	2,088	2,150
May	2,464	2,667	2,201
June	2,378	2,122	2,663
July	2,217	2,206	2,055
August	2,445	1,869	1,678
September	1,894	2,441	1,845
October	1,922	2,291	2,065
November	2,431	2,364	2,147
December	2,274	2,189	2,451

The director needs a time-series method for forecasting the number of items to be checked out during the next month. Find the best simple moving average forecast you can. Decide what is meant by "best" and justify your decision.

19. Using the data in Problem 18, find the best exponential smoothing solution you can. Justify your choice.

20. Using the data in Problem 18, find the best trend projection with regression solution you can. Compare the performance of this method with those of the best moving average method (from Problem 18) and the exponential smoothing method (from Problem 19). Which of these three methods would you choose?

21. Cannister, Inc., specializes in the manufacture of plastic containers. The data on the monthly sales of 10-ounce shampoo bottles for the past 5 years are as follows:

Year	1	2	3	4	5
January	742	741	896	951	1,030
February	697	700	793	861	1,032
March	776	774	885	938	1,126
April	898	932	1,055	1,109	1,285
May	1,030	1,099	1,204	1,274	1,468
June	1,107	1,223	1,326	1,422	1,637
July	1,165	1,290	1,303	1,486	1,611
August	1,216	1,349	1,436	1,555	1,608
September	1,208	1,341	1,473	1,604	1,528
October	1,131	1,296	1,453	1,600	1,420
November	971	1,066	1,170	1,403	1,119
December	783	901	1,023	1,209	1,013

a. Using the multiplicative seasonal method, calculate the monthly seasonal indices.

b. Develop a simple linear regression equation to forecast annual sales. For this regression, the dependent variable, Y, is the demand in each year and the independent variable, X, is the index for the year (i.e., $X = 1$ for year 1, $X = 2$ for year 2, and so on until $X = 5$ for year 5).

c. Forecast the annual sales for year 6 by using the regression model you developed in part (b).

d. Prepare the seasonal forecast for each month by using the monthly seasonal indices calculated in part (a).

22. The Midwest Computer Company serves a large number of businesses in the Great Lakes region. The company sells supplies and replacements and performs service on all computers sold through seven sales offices. Many items are stocked, so close inventory control is necessary to assure customers of efficient service. Recently, business has been increasing, and management is concerned about stockouts. A forecasting method is needed to estimate requirements several months in advance so that adequate replenishment quantities can be purchased. An example of the sales growth experienced during the last 50 months is the growth in demand for item EP-37, a laser printer cartridge, shown in Table 3.

a. Develop a trend projection with regression solution using OM Explorer. Forecast demand for month 51.

b. A consultant to Midwest's management suggested that new office building leases would be a good leading indicator for company sales. The consultant quoted a recent university study finding that new office building leases precede office equipment and supply sales by 3 months. According to the study findings, leases in month 1 would affect sales in month 4, leases in month 2 would affect sales in month 5, and so on. Use POM for Windows' linear regression module to develop a forecasting model for sales, with leases as the independent variable. Forecast sales for month 51.

c. Which of the two models provides better forecasts? Explain.

23. A certain food item at P&Q Supermarkets has the demand pattern shown in the table at the bottom of the next page. There are 5 periods per cycle. Find the "best" forecast you can for month 25 and justify your methodology. If you wish to explore the Seasonal Forecasting method as one of the techniques tested, you will find that OM Explorer's *Seasonal Forecasting* Solver does not cover the case where there are 5 periods in a cycle (or seasons in a year). You must do some manual calculations or write an Excel spreadsheet on your own.

TABLE 3 | EP-37 SALES AND LEASE DATA

Month	EP-37 Sales	Leases	Month	EP-37 Sales	Leases
1	80	32	26	1,296	281
2	132	29	27	1,199	298
3	143	32	28	1,267	314
4	180	54	29	1,300	323
5	200	53	30	1,370	309
6	168	89	31	1,489	343
7	212	74	32	1,499	357
8	254	93	33	1,669	353
9	397	120	34	1,716	360
10	385	113	35	1,603	370
11	472	147	36	1,812	386
12	397	126	37	1,817	389
13	476	138	38	1,798	399
14	699	145	39	1,873	409
15	545	160	40	1,923	410
16	837	196	41	2,028	413
17	743	180	42	2,049	439
18	722	197	43	2,084	454
19	735	203	44	2,083	441
20	838	223	45	2,121	470
21	1,057	247	46	2,072	469
22	930	242	47	2,262	490
23	1,085	234	48	2,371	496
24	1,090	254	49	2,309	509
25	1,218	271	50	2,422	522

Period	Demand	Period	Demand
1	33	13	37
2	37	14	43
3	31	15	56
4	39	16	41
5	54	17	36
6	38	18	39
7	42	19	41
8	40	20	58
9	41	21	42
10	54	22	45
11	43	23	41
12	39	24	38

24. The data for the visibility chart in Discussion Question 1 are shown in Table 4. The visibility standard is set at 100. Readings below 100 indicate that air pollution has reduced visibility, and readings above 100 indicate that the air is clearer.

   a. Use several methods to generate a visibility forecast for August 31 of the second year. Which method seems to produce the best forecast?

   b. Use several methods to forecast the visibility index for the summer of the third year. Which method seems to produce the best forecast? Support your choice.

25. Tom Glass forecasts electrical demand for the Flatlands Public Power District (FPPD). The FPPD wants to take its Comstock power plant out of service for maintenance when demand is expected to be low. After shutdown, performing maintenance and getting the plant back on line takes two weeks. The utility has enough other generating capacity to satisfy 1,550 megawatts (MW) of demand while Comstock is out of service. Table 5 at the end of

TABLE 4 | VISIBILITY DATA

Date	Year 1	Year 2	Date	Year 1	Year 2	Date	Year 1	Year 2
July 22	125	130	Aug 5	105	200	Aug 19	170	160
23	100	120	6	205	110	20	125	165
24	40	125	7	90	100	21	85	135
25	100	160	8	45	200	22	45	80
26	185	165	9	100	160	23	95	100
27	85	205	10	120	100	24	85	200
28	95	165	11	85	55	25	160	100
29	200	125	12	125	130	26	105	110
30	125	85	13	165	75	27	100	50
31	90	105	14	60	30	28	95	135
Aug 1	85	160	15	65	100	29	50	70
2	135	125	16	110	85	30	60	105
3	175	130	17	210	150			
4	200	205	18	110	220			

the Advanced Problems shows weekly peak demands (in MW) for the past several autumns. When next fall should the Comstock plant be scheduled for maintenance?

26. A manufacturing firm seeks to develop a better forecast for an important product, and believes that there is a trend to the data. OM Explorer's *Trend Projection with Regression* Solver has been set up with the 47 demands in the history file. Note the "Load Problem 26 Data" button in the *Trend Projection with Regression* Solver that when clicked will automatically input the demand data. Otherwise, you can enter the demand data directly into the Inputs sheet.

Yr	1	2	3	4
Jan	4507	4589	4084	4535
Feb	4400	4688	4158	4477
Mar	4099	4566	4174	4601
Apr	4064	4485	4225	4648
May	4002	4385	4324	4860
Jun	3963	4377	4220	4998
Jul	4037	4309	4267	5003
Aug	4162	4276	4187	4960
Sep	4312	4280	4239	4943
Oct	4395	4144	4352	5052
Nov	4540	4219	4331	5107
Dec	4471	4052	4371	

a. What is your forecast for December of Year 4, making period 1 as the starting period for the regression?

b. The actual demand for period 48 was just learned to be 5,100. Add this demand to the Inputs file and change the starting period for the regression to period 2 so that the number of periods in the regression remains unchanged. How much or little does the forecast for period 49 change from the one for period 48? The error measures? Are you surprised?

c. Now change the time when the regression starts to period 25 and repeat the process. What differences do you note now? What forecast will you make for period 49?

27. A manufacturing firm has developed a skills test, the scores from which can be used to predict workers' production rating factors. Data on the test scores of various workers and their subsequent production ratings are shown.

Worker	Test Score	Production Rating	Worker	Test Score	Production Rating
A	53	45	K	54	59
B	36	43	L	73	77
C	88	89	M	65	56
D	84	79	N	29	28
E	86	84	O	52	51
F	64	66	P	22	27
G	45	49	Q	76	76
H	48	48	R	32	34
I	39	43	S	51	60
J	67	76	T	37	32

a. Using POM for Windows' least squares-linear regression module, develop a relationship to forecast production ratings from test scores.

b. If a worker's test score was 80, what would be your forecast of the worker's production rating?

c. Comment on the strength of the relationship between the test scores and production ratings.

28. The materials handling manager of a manufacturing company is trying to forecast the cost of maintenance for the company's fleet of over-the-road tractors. The manager believes that the cost of maintaining the tractors increases with their age. The following data was collected:

Age (years)	Yearly Maintenance Cost ($)	Age (years)	Yearly Maintenance Cost ($)
4.5	619	5.0	1,194
4.5	1,049	0.5	163
4.5	1,033	0.5	182
4.0	495	6.0	764
4.0	723	6.0	1,373
4.0	681	1.0	978
5.0	890	1.0	466
5.0	1,522	1.0	549
5.5	987		

a. Use POM for Windows' least squares-linear regression module to develop a relationship to forecast the yearly maintenance cost based on the age of a tractor.

b. If a section has 20 three-year-old tractors, what is the forecast for the annual maintenance cost?

TABLE 5 | WEEKLY PEAK POWER DEMANDS

	AUGUST			SEPTEMBER				OCTOBER				NOVEMBER	
Year	1	2	3	4	5	6	7	8	9	10	11	12	13
1	2,050	1,925	1,825	1,525	1,050	1,300	1,200	1,175	1,350	1,525	1,725	1,575	1,925
2	2,000	2,075	2,225	1,800	1,175	1,050	1,250	1,025	1,300	1,425	1,625	1,950	1,950
3	1,950	1,800	2,150	1,725	1,575	1,275	1,325	1,100	1,500	1,550	1,375	1,825	2,000
4	2,100	2,400	1,975	1,675	1,350	1,525	1,500	1,150	1,350	1,225	1,225	1,475	1,850
5	2,275	2,300	2,150	1,525	1,350	1,475	1,475	1,175	1,375	1,400	1,425	1,550	1,900

VIDEO CASE | Forecasting and Supply Chain Management at Deckers Outdoor Corporation

Deckers Outdoor Corporation's footwear products are among some of the most well-known brands in the world. From UGG sheepskin boots and Teva sport sandals to Simple shoes, Deckers flip-flops, and Tsubo footwear, Deckers is committed to building niche footwear brands into global brands with market leadership positions. Net sales for fiscal year 2007 were close to $449 million. In addition to traditional retail store outlets for Deckers' footwear styles, the company maintains an active and growing "direct to consumer" e-commerce business. Since most retail stores cannot carry every style in every color and size, the company offers the full line for each of its brands directly to consumers through the brands' individual Web sites. Online sales at its virtual store are handled by its e-commerce group. Customers who want a pair of shoes not available at the retail store can always buy from the virtual store.

Founded in 1973, the company manufactured a single line of sandals in a small factory in Southern California. The challenges of managing the raw materials and finished goods inventories were small compared to today's global sourcing and sales challenges for the company's various brands. Today, each brand has its own development team and brand managers who generate, develop, and test-market the seasonal styles that appear on the shelves of retailers such as Nordstrom, Lord & Taylor, REI, the Walking Company, and the company's own UGG brand retail stores in the United States and Japan.

At Deckers, forecasting is the starting point for inventory management, sales and operations planning, resource planning, and scheduling—in short, managing its supply chain. It carries a considerable amount of seasonal stock. Shoes with seasonal demand that are left over at the end of their season must be sold at heavily discounted prices. Its products fall into three categories: (1) carry-over items that were sold in prior years, (2) new items that look similar to past models, and (3) completely new designs that are fashionable with no past history.

Pearson

Twice a year, the brand development teams work on the fall and spring product lines. They come up with new designs about one year in advance of each season. Each brand (UGG, Teva, Simple, Tsubo, and Deckers) contains numerous products, called stock keeping units (SKUs). The materials for new designs are selected and tested in prototypes. Approved designs are put into the seasonal line-up. Forecasts must be made at both the SKU and aggregate levels months before the season begins. "Bottoms-up" forecasts for each SKU begin by analyzing any available history files of past demand. Judgment forecasts are also important inputs, particularly for the second and third categories of shoes that are not carry-overs. For example, Char Nicanor-Kimball is an expert in spotting trends in shoe sales and makes forecasts for the virtual store. For new designs, historical sales on similar items are used to make a best guess on demand for those items. This process is facilitated by a forecasting and inventory system on the company's Intranet. At the same time, the sales teams for each brand call on their retail accounts and secure customer orders of approved designs for the coming season. Then, the virtual store forecasts are merged with orders from the retail store orders to get the total seasonal demand forecasted by SKU. Next, the SKU forecasts are "rolled up" by category and "top down" forecasts are also made.

These forecasts then go to top management where some adjustments may be made to account for financial market conditions, consumer credit, weather, demographic factors, and customer confidence. The impact of public relations and advertising must also be considered.

Actually, forecasting continues on throughout the year on a daily and weekly basis to "get a handle" on demand. Comparing actual demand with what was forecasted for different parts of the season also helps the forecasters make better forecasts for the future and better control inventories.

Based on initial demand forecasts, the company must begin sourcing the materials needed to produce the footwear. The company makes most of its products in China and sources many of the raw materials there as well. For UGG products sheepskin sourcing occurs in Australia with top grade producers, but the rawhide tanning still takes places in China. With potential suppliers identified and assurance from internal engineering that the footwear can be successfully made, the engineering and material data are handed over to the manufacturing department to determine how best to make the footwear in mass quantities. At this point, Deckers places a seasonal "buy" with its suppliers.

The orders for each SKU are fed into the manufacturing schedules at the Chinese factories. All the SKUs for a given brand are manufactured at the same factory. While Deckers agents negotiate the raw materials contracts early in the development process, the factories only place the orders for the raw materials when the company sends in the actual orders for the finished goods. No footwear is made by the factories until orders are received.

At the factories, finished goods footwear is inspected and packaged for the month-long ocean voyage from Hong Kong to ports in the United States. Deckers ships fifty containers a week from its Chinese manufacturing sources, each holding approximately 5,000 pairs of shoes. Ownership of the finished goods transfers from the factories to Deckers in Hong Kong.

When the shipping containers arrive in the United States, the footwear is transferred to Deckers' distribution centers in Southern California. Teva products are warehoused in Ventura, California; all other products are handled by the company's state-of-the-art facility in Camarillo, California. Typically, Deckers brings product into the distribution centers two to three months in advance of expected needs so that the production at the suppliers' factories and the labor activities at the distribution centers are leveled. There are definitive spikes in the demand for footwear, with Teva spiking in Quarter 1 and UGG spiking in Quarter 4. The leveling approach works to keep costs low in the supply chain. However, it also means that Deckers must maintain sizeable inventories. Most shipments from suppliers come in to the distribution centers and are stored in inventory for one to two months awaiting a customer order. By the time the footwear is stocked in the distribution center, the company knows which retail customers will be getting the various products, based on the orders booked months earlier. Then, according to delivery schedules negotiated with the customers, the company begins filling orders and shipping products to retail locations. The warehouse tracks incoming shipments, goods placed on the shelves for customers, and outgoing orders. The inventory system helps manage the customer order filling process.

Because the booked orders are a relatively large proportion of the total orders from retailers, and the number of unanticipated orders is very small, only small safety stocks are needed to service the retailers. Occasionally, the purchase order from Deckers to one of its suppliers matches the sales order from the customer. In such a case, Deckers uses a "cross-dock" system. When the shipment is received at the distribution center, it is immediately checked in and loaded on another truck for delivery to customers. Cross docking reduces the need to store vast quantities of product for long periods of time and cuts down on warehousing expenses for Deckers. The company has been successful in turning its inventory over about four times a year, which is in line with footwear industry standards.

The online sales traffic is all managed centrally. In fact, for ordering and inventory management purposes, the online side of the business is treated just like another major retail store account. As forecasted seasonal orders are generated by each brand's sales team, a manufacturing order for the online business is placed by the e-commerce sales team at the same time. However, unlike the retail outlets that take delivery of products on a regular schedule, the inventory pledged to the online business is held in the distribution center until a Web site order is received. Only then is it shipped directly to the consumer who placed the online order. If actual demand exceeds expected demand, Char Nicanor-Kimball checks if more inventory can be secured from other customer orders that have scaled back.

The forecasting and supply chain management challenges now facing Deckers are two-fold. First, the company plans to grow the brands that have enjoyed seasonal sales activity into year-round footwear options for consumers by expanding the number of SKUs for those brands. For example, most sales for UGG footwear occur in the fall/winter season. Sales for Teva historically have been in the spring and summer. Product managers are now working to develop styles that will allow the brands to cross over the seasons. Second, the company plans to expand internationally, and will have retail outlets in Europe, China, and other Asian locations in the very near future. Company managers are well aware of the challenges and opportunities such global growth will bring, and are taking steps now to assure that the entire supply chain is prepared to forecast and handle the demand when the time comes.

QUESTIONS

1. How much does the forecasting process at Deckers correspond with the "typical forecasting process" described at the end of this chapter?

2. Based on what you see in the video, what kinds of information technology are used to make forecasts, maintain accurate inventory records, and project future inventory levels?

3. What factors make forecasting at Deckers particularly challenging? How can forecasts be made for seasonal, fashionable products for which there is no history file? What are the costs of over-forecasting demand for such items? Under-forecasting?

4. How does the concept of *postponement* get implemented at Deckers by having online sales and positioning inventory at the DCs for every model, color, and size?

5. Where in the supply chain are cycle, pipeline, safety stock, and anticipation inventories being created?

6. What are the benefits of leveling aggregate demand by having a portfolio of SKUs that create 365-day demand?

7. Deckers plans to expand internationally, thereby increasing the volume of shoes it must manage in the supply chain and the pattern of material flows. What implications does this strategy have on forecasting, order quantities, logistics, and relationships with its suppliers and customers?

CASE | Yankee Fork and Hoe Company

The Yankee Fork and Hoe Company is a leading producer of garden tools ranging from wheelbarrows, mortar pans, and hand trucks to shovels, rakes, and trowels. The tools are sold in four different product lines ranging from the top-of-the-line Hercules products, which are rugged tools for the toughest jobs, to the Garden Helper products, which are economy tools for the occasional user. The market for garden tools is extremely competitive because of the simple design of the products and the large number of competing producers. In addition, more people are using power tools, such as lawn edgers, hedge trimmers, and thatchers, reducing demand for their manual counterparts. These factors compel Yankee to maintain low prices while retaining high quality and dependable delivery.

Garden tools represent a mature industry. Unless new manual products can be developed or a sudden resurgence occurs in home gardening, the prospects for large increases in sales are not bright. Keeping ahead of the competition is a constant battle. No one knows this better than Alan Roberts, president of Yankee.

The types of tools sold today are, by and large, the same ones sold 30 years ago. The only way to generate new sales and retain old customers is to provide superior customer service and produce a product with high customer value. This approach puts pressure on the manufacturing system, which has been having difficulties lately. Recently, Roberts has been receiving calls from long-time customers, such as Sears and True Value Hardware Stores, complaining about late shipments. These customers advertise promotions for garden tools and require on-time delivery.

Roberts knows that losing customers like Sears and True Value would be disastrous. He decides to ask consultant Sharon Place to look into the matter and report to him in one week. Roberts suggests that she focus on the bow rake as a case in point because it is a high-volume product and has been a major source of customer complaints of late.

Planning Bow Rake Production

A bow rake consists of a head with 12 teeth spaced 1 inch apart, a hardwood handle, a bow that attaches the head to the handle, and a metal ferrule that reinforces the area where the bow inserts into the handle. The bow is a metal strip that is welded to the ends of the rake head and bent in the middle to form a flat tab for insertion into the handle. The rake is about 64 inches long.

Place decides to find out how Yankee plans bow rake production. She goes straight to Phil Stanton, who gives the following account:

Planning is informal around here. To begin, marketing determines the forecast for bow rakes by month for the next year. Then they pass it along to me. Quite frankly, the forecasts are usually inflated—must be their big egos over there. I have to be careful because we enter into long-term purchasing agreements for steel, and having it just sitting around is expensive. So I usually reduce the forecast by 10 percent or so. I use the modified forecast to generate a monthly final-assembly schedule, which determines what I need to have from the forging and woodworking areas. The system works well if the forecasts are good. But when marketing comes to me and says they are behind on customer orders, as they often do near the end of the year, it wreaks havoc with the schedules. Forging gets hit the hardest. For example, the presses that stamp the rake heads from blanks of steel can handle only 7,000 heads per day, and the bow rolling machine can do only 5,000 per day. Both operations are also required for many other products.

Because the marketing department provides crucial information to Stanton, Place decides to see the marketing manager, Ron Adams. Adams explains how he arrives at the bow rake forecasts.

Things do not change much from year to year. Sure, sometimes we put on a sales promotion of some kind, but we try to give Phil enough warning before the demand kicks in—usually a month or so. I meet with several managers from the various sales regions to go over shipping data from last year and discuss anticipated promotions, changes in the economy, and shortages we experienced last year. Based on these meetings, I generate a monthly forecast for the next year. Even though we take a lot of time getting the forecast, it never seems to help us avoid customer problems.

The Problem

Place ponders the comments from Stanton and Adams. She understands Stanton's concerns about costs and keeping inventory low and Adams's concern about having enough rakes on hand to make timely shipments. Both are also somewhat concerned about capacity. Yet she decides to check actual customer demand for the bow rake over the past 4 years (in Table 6) before making her final report to Roberts.

QUESTIONS

1. Comment on the forecasting system being used by Yankee. Suggest changes or improvements that you believe are justified.

2. Develop your own forecast for bow rakes for each month of the next year (year 5). Justify your forecast and the method you used.

TABLE 6 | FOUR-YEAR DEMAND HISTORY FOR THE BOW RAKE

Month	DEMAND			
	Year 1	Year 2	Year 3	Year 4
1	55,220	39,875	32,180	62,377
2	57,350	64,128	38,600	66,501
3	15,445	47,653	25,020	31,404
4	27,776	43,050	51,300	36,504
5	21,408	39,359	31,790	16,888
6	17,118	10,317	32,100	18,909
7	18,028	45,194	59,832	35,500
8	19,883	46,530	30,740	51,250
9	15,796	22,105	47,800	34,443
10	53,665	41,350	73,890	68,088
11	83,269	46,024	60,202	68,175
12	72,991	41,856	55,200	61,100

Note: The demand figures shown in the table are the number of units promised for delivery each month. Actual delivery quantities differed because of capacity or shortages of materials.

EXPERIENTIAL LEARNING 1 | Forecasting with Holdout Sample

A company's history file, as shown in the following table, gives monthly sales in thousands of dollars "rolled up" into aggregated totals for one of its major product lines.

Your team should use the *Time Series Forecasting* Solver to make forecasts into the future. Note the "Load EL1 Data" button in this solver when clicked will automatically input the demand data. Otherwise, you can enter the demand data directly into the Inputs sheet. Seek out which models you wish to use in making in-class forecasts of monthly sales for the last two months of year 8 and several months into year 9. Perhaps you might want to know the forecasts of all of them, or alternately focus on just two or three of them. If one of the models is the combination forecast, you must decide on the weights to give the models going into its forecast. The weights should add up to 1.0.

Bring to class a one-page document that

- characterizes the monthly sales of the product line in terms of its forecastability.
- identifies the relative importance of four demand patterns: horizontal, trend, seasonal, and cyclical.
- identifies the forecasting models that you will use to make the forecasts for the last of year 8, and future months into year 9, and the extent that judgmental adjustments might be used during the holdout sample exercise. Explain why you made this selection, given that MAD will be used as your error measure.
- makes the November forecast for year 8.

At the start of the in-class portion of the experiential exercise, hand in your one-page document and open the final *Time Series Forecasting* Solver file that you used in modeling the history file. Do not change any of the final parameters chosen for your various forecasting models using the history file

(n for moving average, weights for weighted moving average, α for exponential smoothing, and weights for combination).

To start the Holdout Sample session, click on the Worksheet tab and set the time when error analysis begins to be period 95 (November, Year 8). In doing so, error analysis will be tracked only for the holdout periods. Now click on the "Holdout Sample" tab to begin the session. You will initially be presented with the November forecasts for all of the techniques used during your analysis of the history file (including the combination model if you used it). Your next step is to input your team's forecast for November. It can be the forecast from any of the techniques shown, or one of your own if you believe that judgmental adjustment is appropriate. You have no contextual information, but may observe that one model has been performing particularly well in the last few months. You team might have different opinions, but you must reach a consensus. Your instructor will then provide November's actual sales from the holdout sample. After you input that additional information, forecast errors are computed for each model and for your team's November forecast. In addition, computer forecasts (naïve, moving average, weighted moving average, exponential smoothing, trend projection, and combination) are posted for December.

Begin December by inputting your team's forecast. The instructor then provides December's actual sales, and so forth. Continue this process until all errors are calculated for the last period in the holdout sample, which will be announced by your instructor. At the end of this exercise, create a second one-page document that reports your forecasts for the holdout sample, the corresponding average MAD, and CFE whether (and how) you modified your forecasting process as the exercise progressed, and what you learned from this exercise. You will need to write an Excel spreadsheet to calculate the MAD and CFE statistics for the holdout sample. Its output can be attached to your second one-page document. Submit your report to your instructor at the end of the class session.

Your grade on this exercise will be based on (1) the insights provided in the two documents (50 percent of grade) (2) the average MAD for the history file (25 percent of grade), and (3) the average MAD for the holdout sample (25 percent of grade).

Yr	Jan	Feb	Mar	Apr	May	Jun	Jul	Aug	Sep	Oct	Nov	Dec
1	3,255	3,420	3,482	3,740	3,713	3,785	3,817	3,900	3,878	3,949	4,004	4,035
2	3,892	3,730	4,115	4,054	4,184	4,321	4,307	4,481	4,411	4,443	4,395	4,403
3	4,507	4,400	4,099	4,064	4,002	3,963	4,037	4,162	4,312	4,395	4,540	4,471
4	4,589	4,688	4,566	4,485	4,385	4,377	4,309	4,276	4,280	4,144	4,219	4,052
5	4,084	4,158	4,174	4,225	4,324	4,220	4,267	4,187	4,239	4,352	4,331	4,371
6	4,535	4,477	4,601	4,648	4,860	4,998	5,003	4,960	4,943	5,052	5,107	5,100
7	5,303	5,550	5,348	5,391	5,519	5,602	5,557	5,608	5,663	5,497	5,719	5,679
8	5,688	5,604	5,703	5,899	5,816	5,745	5,921	5,900	5,911	5,987		

Sources: This experiential exercise was adapted from an in-class exercise prepared by Dr. Richard J. Penlesky, Carroll University, as a basis for classroom discussion. By permission of Richard J. Penlesky.

EXPERIENTIAL LEARNING 2 | Forecasting a Vital Energy Statistic

The following time series data captures the weekly average of East Coast crude oil imports in thousands of barrels per day.

QUARTER 2 2010		QUARTER 3 2010		QUARTER 4 2010		QUARTER 1 2011	
Time Period	Data	Time Period	Data	Time Period	Data	Time Period	Data
Apr 02, 2010	1,160	Jul 02, 2010	1,116	Oct 01, 2010	1,073	Dec 31, 2010	994
Apr 09, 2010	779	Jul 09, 2010	1,328	Oct 08, 2010	857	Jan 07, 2011	1,307
Apr 16, 2010	1,134	Jul 16, 2010	1,183	Oct 15, 2010	1,197	Jan 14, 2011	997
Apr 23, 2010	1,275	Jul 23, 2010	1,219	Oct 22, 2010	718	Jan 21, 2011	1,082
Apr 30, 2010	1,355	Jul 30, 2010	1,132	Oct 29, 2010	817	Jan 28, 2011	887
May 07, 2010	1,513	Aug 06, 2010	1,094	Nov 05, 2010	946	Feb 04, 2011	1,067
May 14, 2010	1,394	Aug 13, 2010	1,040	Nov 12, 2010	725	Feb 11, 2011	890
May 21, 2010	1,097	Aug 20, 2010	1,053	Nov 19, 2010	748	Feb 18, 2011	865
May 28, 2010	1,206	Aug 27, 2010	1,232	Nov 26, 2010	1,031	Feb 25, 2011	858
Jun 04, 2010	1,264	Sep 03, 2010	1,073	Dec 03, 2010	1,061	Mar 04, 2011	814
Jun 11, 2010	1,153	Sep 10, 2010	1,329	Dec 10, 2010	1,074	Mar 11, 2011	871
Jun 18, 2010	1,424	Sep 17, 2010	1,096	Dec 17, 2010	941	Mar 18, 2011	1,255
Jun 25, 2010	1,274	Sep 24, 2010	1,125	Dec 24, 2010	994	Mar 25, 2011	980

Your instructor has a "holdout" sample representing the values for April 1, 2011 and beyond. Your task is to use the POM for Windows *Time Series Forecasting* module and the history file to project this statistic into the future. If you have MyOMLab, the demand data is available in the *Exercise 2* Excel file. It can be pasted into the Data Table of the *Time Series Forecasting*

module. Otherwise, you can enter the demand data directly into the Data Table. Prior to your next class meeting:

a. Use the POM for Windows *Time Series Forecasting* module to locate the best naïve, moving average, weighted moving average, and trend projection with regression models that you think will most accurately forecast demand during the holdout sample. *Begin your error calculations with period 5 (April 30, 2010).*

b. Create an Excel spreadsheet that begins with inputs of the four forecasts from the *Time Series Forecasting* module. Its purpose is to develop a combination forecast that will serve as your team's forecasts for each period. Assign a weight to each forecast model (the sum of all four forecast weights for one period should equal 1.0) and develop a "combination forecast" by multiplying each forecast by its weight. Keep the weights constant for the whole history file as you search for the best set of weights. If you do not like a particular model, give it a weight of 0. Calculate appropriate forecast error measures for your combination forecast in your Excel spreadsheet.

c. Create a management report that shows your period-by-period forecasts and their overall historical CFE and MAPE performance for each model and your combination forecast.

In-Class Exercise—Part 1

a. Input into your Excel spreadsheet the forecasts from the POM for Windows *Time Series Forecasting* module to get the combination forecast for the first period (the week of April 1, 2011) in the holdout sample. The combination forecast is considered your team's forecast.

b. Enter the actual data announced by your instructor, and have Excel compute appropriate forecast error measures for your four models and the combination forecast. Decide on any revisions of weights for the combination forecast.

c. Update the POM for Windows *Time Series Forecasting* module with the actual demand for the new period and get the new forecasts.

In-Class Exercise—Part 2

a. Input the forecasts from the POM for Windows *Time Series Forecasting* module into your Excel spreadsheet to get the final combination forecast for the next period (the week of April 8, 2011). At this point, you may change this period's weights on each forecasting technique going into the combination forecast. You have no contextual information, but may observe that one model has been performing particularly well in the last few periods. Your team might have different opinions, but you must reach a consensus.

b. Enter the actual data announced by your instructor, with Excel computing appropriate forecast error measures for your four models and the combination forecast.

c. Update the POM for Windows *Time Series Forecasting* module with the actual demand for the new period and get the new forecasts.

In-Class Exercise—Parts 3 and beyond

Continue in the fashion of Parts 1 and 2 to produce forecasts as directed by your instructor. At the end of the exercise, create a second management report that shows for the holdout sample your period-by-period forecasts, their individual forecast errors and percent deviations for each model and your combination forecast. Explain your logic regarding any changes made to your combination forecast weights over the holdout period.

Source: This experiential exercise was prepared as an in-class exercise prepared by Dr. John Jensen, University of South Carolina, as a basis for classroom discussion. By permission of John B. Jensen.

Selected References

Armstrong, J. Scott. "Findings from Evidence-based Forecasting: Methods for Reducing Forecast Error." *International Journal of Forecasting,* vol. 22, no. 3 (2006), pp. 583–598.

Attaran, Mohsen, and Sharmin Attaran. "Collaborative Supply Chain Management." *Business Process Management Journal Management Journal,* vol. 13, no. 13 (June 2007), pp. 390–404.

Cederlund, Jerold P., Rajiv Kohli, Susan A. Sherer, and Yuliang Yao. "How Motorola Put CPFR into Action." *Supply Chain Management Review* (October 2007), pp. 28–35.

Daugherty, Patricia J., R. Glenn Richey, Anthony S. Roath, Soonhong Min, Haozhe Chen, Aaron D. Arndt, and Stefan E. Genchev. "Is Collaboration Paying Off for Firms?" *Business Horizons* (2006), pp. 61–70.

Fildes, Robert, Paul Goodwin, Michael Lawrence, and Konstantinos Nikolopoulos. "Effective Forecasting and Judgmental Adjustments: An Empirical Evaluation and Strategies for Improvement in Supply-Chain Planning." *International Journal of Forecasting,* vol. 25, no. 1 (2009), pp. 3–23.

Lawrence, Michael, Paul Goodwin, Marcus O'Connor, and Dilek Onkal. "Judgmental Forecasting: A Review of Progress over the Last 25 Years." *International Journal of Forecasting* (June 2006), pp. 493–518.

McCarthy, Teresa, Donna F. Davis, Susan L. Golicic, and John T. Mentzer. "The Evolution of Sales Forecasting Management: A 20-Year Longitudinal Study of Forecasting Practices." *Journal of Forecasting,* vol. 25 (2006), pp. 303–324.

Min, Hokey, and Wen-Bin Vincent Yu. "Collaborative Planning, Forecasting and Replenishment: Demand Planning in Supply Chain Management." *International Journal of Information Technology and Management,* vol. 7, no. 1 (2008), pp. 4–20.

Montgomery, David. "Flashpoints for Changing Your Forecasting Process." *The Journal of Business Forecasting* (Winter 2006–2007), pp. 35–42.

Principles of Forecasting: A Handbook for Researchers and Practitioners. J. Scott Armstrong (ed.). Norwell, MA: Kluwer Academic Publishers, 2001. Also visit **http://www.forecastingprinciples.com** for valuable information on forecasting, including frequently asked questions, a forecasting methodology tree, and a dictionary.

Saffo, Paul. "Six Rules for Effective Forecasting." *Harvard Business Review* (July–August 2007), pp. 1–30.

Smaros, Johanna. "Forecasting Collaboration in the European Grocery Sector: Observations from a Case Study." *Journal of Operations Management,* vol. 25, no. 3 (April 2007), pp. 702–716.

Smith, Larry. "West Marine: A CPFR Success Story." *Supply Chain Management Review* (March 2006), pp. 29–36.

Syntetos, Aris Konstantinos Nikolopoulos, John Boylan, Robert Fildes, and Paul Goodwin. "The Effects of Integrating Management Judgement into Intermittent Demand Forecasts." *International Journal of Production Economics,* vol. 118, no. 1 (March, 2009), pp. 72–81.

Wikipedia, "Collaborative Planning, Forecasting, and Replenishment," http:en.wikipedia.org/wiki/Collaborative Planning Forecasting and Replenishment, (April, 2011).

DECISION MAKING

Operations managers make many decisions as they manage processes and supply chains. Although the specifics of each situation vary, decision making generally involves the same basic steps: (1) recognize and clearly define the problem, (2) collect the information needed to analyze possible alternatives, and (3) choose and implement the most feasible alternative.

Sometimes, hard thinking in a quiet room is sufficient. At other times, interacting with others or using more formal procedures are needed. Here, we present four such formal procedures: break-even analysis, the preference matrix, decision theory, and the decision tree.

- Break-even analysis helps the manager identify how much change in volume or demand is necessary before a second alternative becomes better than the first alternative.
- The preference matrix helps a manager deal with multiple criteria that cannot be evaluated with a single measure of merit, such as total profit or cost.
- Decision theory helps the manager choose the best alternative when outcomes are uncertain.
- A decision tree helps the manager when decisions are made sequentially—when today's best decision depends on tomorrow's decisions and events.

Break-Even Analysis

To evaluate an idea for a new service or product, or to assess the performance of an existing one, determining the volume of sales at which the service or product breaks even is useful. The **break-even quantity** is the volume at which total revenues equal total costs. Use of this technique is known as **break-even analysis**. Break-even analysis can also be used to compare processes by finding the volume at which two different processes have equal total costs.

break-even quantity

The volume at which total revenues equal total costs.

break-even analysis

The use of the break-even quantity; it can be used to compare processes by finding the volume at which two different processes have equal total costs.

LEARNING GOALS *After reading this supplement, you should be able to:*

1. Explain break-even analysis, using both the graphic and algebraic approaches.

2. Define a preference matrix.

3. Explain how to construct a payoff table.

4. Identify the maximin, maximax, Laplace, minimax regret, and expected value decision rules.

5. Describe how to draw and analyze a decision tree.

A manager is doing some hard thinking and analysis on his computer before reaching a final decision.

Evaluating Services or Products

We begin with the first purpose: to evaluate the profit potential of a new or existing service or product. This technique helps the manager answer questions, such as the following:

- Is the predicted sales volume of the service or product sufficient to break even (neither earning a profit nor sustaining a loss)?

- How low must the variable cost per unit be to break even, based on current prices and sales forecasts?

- How low must the fixed cost be to break even?

- How do price levels affect the break-even volume?

Break-even analysis is based on the assumption that all costs related to the production of a specific service or product can be divided into two categories: (1) variable costs and (2) fixed costs.

variable cost

The portion of the total cost that varies directly with volume of output.

fixed cost

The portion of the total cost that remains constant regardless of changes in levels of output.

The **variable cost**, c, is the portion of the total cost that varies directly with volume of output: costs per unit for materials, labor, and usually some fraction of overhead. If we let Q equal the number of customers served or units produced per year, total variable cost = cQ. The **fixed cost**, F, is the portion of the total cost that remains constant regardless of changes in levels of output: the annual cost of renting or buying new equipment and facilities (including depreciation, interest, taxes, and insurance); salaries; utilities; and portions of the sales or advertising budget. Thus, the total cost of producing a service or good equals fixed costs plus variable costs multiplied by volume, or

$$\text{Total cost} = F + cQ$$

The variable cost per unit is assumed to be the same no matter how small or large Q is, and thus, total cost is linear. If we assume that all units produced are sold, total annual revenues equal revenue per unit sold, p, multiplied by the quantity sold, or

$$\text{Total revenue} = pQ$$

If we set total revenue equal to total cost, we get the break-even quantity point as

$$pQ = F + cQ$$
$$(p - c)Q = F$$
$$Q = \frac{F}{p - c}$$

We can also find this break-even quantity graphically. Because both costs and revenues are linear relationships, the break-even quantity is where the total revenue line crosses the total cost line.

| EXAMPLE 1 | Finding the Break-Even Quantity |

MyOMLab

Active Model A.1 in MyOMLab provides additional insight on this break-even example and its extensions with four "what-if" questions.

A hospital is considering a new procedure to be offered at $200 per patient. The fixed cost per year would be $100,000, with total variable costs of $100 per patient. What is the break-even quantity for this service? Use both algebraic and graphic approaches to get the answer.

SOLUTION

The formula for the break-even quantity yields

$$Q = \frac{F}{p - c} = \frac{100,000}{200 - 100} = 1,000 \text{ patients}$$

MyOMLab

Tutor A.1 in MyOMLab provides a new example to practice break-even analysis.

To solve graphically we plot two lines: one for costs and one for revenues. Two points determine a line, so we begin by calculating costs and revenues for two different output levels. The following table shows the results for $Q = 0$ and $Q = 2,000$. We selected zero as the first point because of the ease of plotting total revenue (0) and total cost (F). However, we could have used any two reasonably spaced output levels.

Quantity (patients) (Q)	Total Annual Cost ($) (100,000 + 100Q)	Total Annual Revenue ($) (200Q)
0	100,000	0
2,000	300,000	400,000

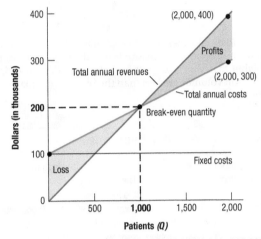

◀ **FIGURE 1**
Graphic Approach to Break-Even Analysis

We can now draw the cost line through points (0, 100,000) and (2,000, 300,000). The revenue line goes between (0, 0) and (2,000, 400,000). As Figure 1 indicates, these two lines intersect at 1,000 patients, the break-even quantity.

DECISION POINT
Management expects the number of patients needing the new procedure will exceed the 1,000-patient break-even quantity but first wants to learn how sensitive the decision is to demand levels before making a final choice.

Break-even analysis cannot tell a manager whether to pursue a new service or product idea or drop an existing line. The technique can only show what is likely to happen for various forecasts of costs and sales volumes. To evaluate a variety of "what-if" questions, we use an approach called **sensitivity analysis**, a technique for systematically changing parameters in a model to determine the effects of such changes. The concept can be applied later to other techniques, such as linear programming. Here we assess the sensitivity of total profit to different pricing strategies, sales volume forecasts, or cost estimates.

sensitivity analysis

A technique for systematically changing parameters in a model to determine the effects of such changes.

EXAMPLE 2	**Sensitivity Analysis of Sales Forecasts**

If the most pessimistic sales forecast for the proposed service in Figure 1 were 1,500 patients, what would be the procedure's total contribution to profit and overhead per year?

SOLUTION
The graph shows that even the pessimistic forecast lies above the break-even volume, which is encouraging. The procedure's total contribution, found by subtracting total costs from total revenues, is

$$pQ - (F + cQ) = 200(1,500) - [100,000 + 100(1,500)]$$
$$= \$50,000$$

DECISION POINT
Even with the pessimistic forecast, the new procedure contributes $50,000 per year. After evaluating the proposal with present value method (see MyOMLab Supplement F), management added the new procedure to the hospital's services.

MyOMLab

Evaluating Processes

Often, choices must be made between two processes or between an internal process and buying services or materials on the outside. In such cases, we assume that the decision does not affect revenues. The manager must study all the costs and advantages of each approach. Rather than find the quantity at which total costs equal total revenues, the analyst finds the quantity for which the total costs for two alternatives are equal. For the make-or-buy decision, it is the quantity for which the total "buy" cost equals the total "make" cost. Let F_b equal the fixed cost (per year) of the buy option, F_m equal the fixed cost of the make option, c_b equal the variable cost (per unit) of the buy option, and c_m equal the variable cost of the make option. Thus, the total cost to buy is $F_b + c_bQ$ and the total cost to make is $F_m + c_mQ$. To find the break-even quantity, we set the two cost functions equal and solve for Q:

$$F_b + c_bQ = F_m + c_mQ$$

$$Q = \frac{F_m - F_b}{c_b - c_m}$$

The make option should be considered, ignoring qualitative factors, only if its variable costs are lower than those of the buy option. The reason is that the fixed costs for making the service or product are typically higher than the fixed costs for buying. Under these circumstances, the buy option is better if production volumes are less than the break-even quantity. Beyond that quantity, the make option becomes better.

| EXAMPLE 3 | Break-Even Analysis for Make-or-Buy Decisions |

MyOMLab

Active Model A.2 in MyOMLab provides additional insight on this make-or-buy example and its extensions.

MyOMLab

Tutor A.2 in MyOMLab provides a new example to practice break-even analysis on make-or-buy decisions.

The manager of a fast-food restaurant featuring hamburgers is adding salads to the menu. For each of the two new options, the price to the customer will be the same. The make option is to install a salad bar stocked with vegetables, fruits, and toppings and let the customer assemble the salad. The salad bar would have to be leased and a part-time employee hired. The manager estimates the fixed costs at $12,000 and variable costs totaling $1.50 per salad. The buy option is to have preassembled salads available for sale. They would be purchased from a local supplier at $2.00 per salad. Offering preassembled salads would require installation and operation of additional refrigeration, with an annual fixed cost of $2,400. The manager expects to sell 25,000 salads per year.

What is the make-or-buy quantity?

SOLUTION

The formula for the break-even quantity yields the following:

$$Q = \frac{F_m - F_b}{c_b - c_m}$$
$$= \frac{12,000 - 2,400}{2.0 - 1.5} = 19,200 \text{ salads}$$

FIGURE 2 ▶
Break-Even Analysis Solver of OM Explorer for Example A.3

	Process 1	Process 2
Fixed costs (F)	$12,000	$2,400
Variable costs (c)	$1.50	$2.00
Expected demand	25,000	
Break-even quantity	19,200.0	

Decision: Process 1

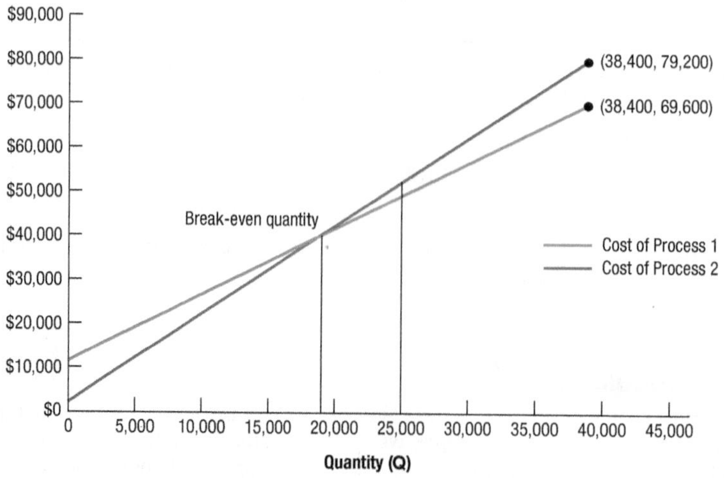

Figure 2 shows the solution from OM Explorer's *Break-Even Analysis* Solver. The break-even quantity is 19,200 salads. As the 25,000-salad sales forecast exceeds this amount, the make option is preferred. Only if the restaurant expected to sell fewer than 19,200 salads would the buy option be better.

DECISION POINT

Management chose the make option after considering other qualitative factors, such as customer preferences and demand uncertainty. A deciding factor was that the 25,000-salad sales forecast is well above the 19,200-salad break-even quantity.

Preference Matrix

Decisions often must be made in situations where multiple criteria cannot be naturally merged into a single measure (such as dollars). For example, a manager deciding in which of two cities to locate a new plant would have to consider such unquantifiable factors as quality of life, worker attitudes toward work, and community reception in the two cities. These important factors cannot be ignored. A **preference matrix** is a table that allows the manager to rate an alternative according to several performance criteria. The criteria can be scored on any scale, such as from 1 (worst possible) to 10 (best possible) or from 0 to 1, as long as the same scale is applied to all the alternatives being compared. Each score is weighted according to its perceived importance, with the total of these weights typically equaling 100. The total score is the sum of the weighted scores (weight × score) for all the criteria. The manager can compare the scores for alternatives against one another or against a predetermined threshold.

preference matrix

A table that allows the manager to rate an alternative according to several performance criteria.

EXAMPLE 4	Evaluating an Alternative with a Preference Matrix

The following table shows the performance criteria, weights, and scores (1 = worst, 10 = best) for a new product: a thermal storage air conditioner. If management wants to introduce just one new product and the highest total score of any of the other product ideas is 800, should the firm pursue making the air conditioner?

MyOMLab

Tutor A.3 in MyOMLab provides a new example to practice with preference matrixes.

Performance Criterion	Weight *(A)*	Score *(B)*	Weighted Score *(A × B)*
Market potential	30	8	240
Unit profit margin	20	10	200
Operations compatibility	20	6	120
Competitive advantage	15	10	150
Investment requirement	10	2	20
Project risk	5	4	20
			Weighted score = 750

SOLUTION

Because the sum of the weighted scores is 750, it falls short of the score of 800 for another product. This result is confirmed by the output from OM Explorer's *Preference Matrix* Solver in Figure 3.

◀ **FIGURE 3**
Preference Matrix Solver for Example 4

Insert a Criterion	Add a Criterion	Remove a Criterion

	Weight (A)	Score (B)	Weighted Score (A x B)
Market potential	30	8	240
Unit profit margin	20	10	200
Operations compatability	20	6	120
Competitive advantage	15	10	150
Investment requirement	10	2	20
Project risk	5	4	20
	Final Weighted Score		750

Not all managers are comfortable with the preference matrix technique. It requires the manager to state criteria weights before examining the alternatives, although the proper weights may not be readily apparent. Perhaps, only after seeing the scores for several alternatives can the manager decide what is important and what is not. Because a low score on one criterion can be compensated for or overridden by high scores on others, the preference matrix method also may cause managers to ignore important signals. In Example 4, the investment required for the thermal storage air conditioner might exceed the firm's financial capability. In that case, the manager should not even be considering the alternative, no matter how high its score.

Decision Theory

decision theory

A general approach to decision making when the outcomes associated with alternatives are often in doubt.

Decision theory is a general approach to decision making when the outcomes associated with alternatives are often in doubt. It helps operations managers with decisions on process, capacity, location, and inventory because such decisions are about an uncertain future. Decision theory can also be used by managers in other functional areas. With decision theory, a manager makes choices using the following process:

1. List the feasible *alternatives*. One alternative that should always be considered as a basis for reference is to do nothing. A basic assumption is that the number of alternatives is finite. For example, in deciding where to locate a new retail store in a certain part of the city, a manager could theoretically consider every grid coordinate on the city's map. Realistically, however, the manager must narrow the number of choices to a reasonable number.

2. List the *events* (sometimes called *chance events* or *states of nature*) that have an impact on the outcome of the choice but are not under the manager's control. For example, the demand experienced by the new facility could be low or high, depending not only on whether the location is convenient to many customers, but also on what the competition does and general retail trends. Then, group events into reasonable categories. For example, suppose that the average number of sales per day could be anywhere from 1 to 500. Rather than have 500 events, the manager could represent demand with just 3 events: 100 sales/day, 300 sales/day, or 500 sales/day. The events must be mutually exclusive and collectively exhaustive, meaning that they do not overlap and that they cover all eventualities.

payoff table

A table that shows the amount for each alternative if each possible event occurs.

3. Calculate the *payoff* for each alternative in each event. Typically, the payoff is total profit or total cost. These payoffs can be entered into a **payoff table**, which shows the amount for each alternative if each possible event occurs. For 3 alternatives and 4 events, the table would have 12 payoffs (3 × 4). If significant distortions will occur if the time value of money is not recognized, the payoffs should be expressed as present values or internal rates of return (see MyOMLab Supplement F.) For multiple criteria with important qualitative factors, use the weighted scores of a preference matrix approach as the payoffs.

MyOMLab

4. Estimate the likelihood of each event, using past data, executive opinion, or other forecasting methods. Express it as a *probability*, making sure that the probabilities sum to 1.0. Develop probability estimates from past data if the past is considered a good indicator of the future.

5. Select a *decision rule* to evaluate the alternatives, such as choosing the alternative with the lowest expected cost. The rule chosen depends on the amount of information the manager has on the event probabilities and the manager's attitudes toward risk.

Using this process, we examine decisions under three different situations: certainty, uncertainty, and risk.

Decision Making under Certainty

The simplest situation is when the manager knows which event will occur. Here the decision rule is to pick the alternative with the best payoff for the known event. The best alternative is the highest payoff if the payoffs are expressed as profits. If the payoffs are expressed as costs, the best alternative is the lowest payoff.

EXAMPLE 5	Decisions under Certainty

A manager is deciding whether to build a small or a large facility. Much depends on the future demand that the facility must serve, and demand may be small or large. The manager knows with certainty the payoffs that will result under each alternative, shown in the following payoff table. The payoffs (in $000) are the present values of future revenues minus costs for each alternative in each event.

	POSSIBLE FUTURE DEMAND	
Alternative	**Low**	**High**
Small facility	200	270
Large facility	160	800
Do nothing	0	0

What is the best choice if future demand will be low?

SOLUTION

In this example, the best choice is the one with the highest payoff. If the manager knows that future demand will be low, the company should build a small facility and enjoy a payoff of $200,000. The larger facility has a payoff of only $160,000. The "do nothing" alternative is dominated by the other alternatives; that is, the outcome of one alternative is no better than the outcome of another alternative for each event. Because the "do nothing" alternative is dominated, the manager does not consider it further.

DECISION POINT

If management really knows future demand, it would build the small facility if demand will be low and the large facility if demand will be high. If demand is uncertain, it should consider other decision rules.

Decision Making under Uncertainty

Here, we assume that the manager can list the possible events but cannot estimate their probabilities. Perhaps, a lack of prior experience makes it difficult for the firm to estimate probabilities. In such a situation, the manager can use one of four decision rules:

1. *Maximin*. Choose the alternative that is the "best of the worst." This rule is for the *pessimist*, who anticipates the "worst case" for each alternative.

2. *Maximax*. Choose the alternative that is the "best of the best." This rule is for the *optimist* who has high expectations and prefers to "go for broke."

3. *Laplace*. Choose the alternative with the best *weighted payoff*. To find the weighted payoff, give equal importance (or, alternatively, equal probability) to each event. If there are n events, the importance (or probability) of each is $1/n$, so they add up to 1.0. This rule is for the *realist*.

4. *Minimax Regret*. Choose the alternative with the best "worst regret." Calculate a table of regrets (or opportunity losses), in which the rows represent the alternatives and the columns represent the events. A regret is the difference between a given payoff and the best payoff in the same column. For an event, it shows how much is lost by picking an alternative to the one that is best for this event. The regret can be lost profit or increased cost, depending on the situation.

EXAMPLE 6	Decisions under Uncertainty

Reconsider the payoff matrix in Example 5. What is the best alternative for each decision rule?

SOLUTION

a. *Maximin*. An alternative's worst payoff is the *lowest* number in its row of the payoff matrix, because the payoffs are profits. The worst payoffs ($000) are

Alternative	**Worst Payoff**
Small facility	200
Large facility	160

The best of these worst numbers is $200,000, so the pessimist would build a small facility.

MyOMLab

Tutor A.4 in MyOMLab provides a new example to make decisions under uncertainty.

b. *Maximax.* An alternative's best payoff ($000) is the *highest* number in its row of the payoff matrix, or

Alternative	Best Payoff
Small facility	270
Large facility	800

The best of these best numbers is $800,000, so the optimist would build a large facility.

c. *Laplace.* With two events, we assign each a probability of 0.5. Thus, the weighted payoffs ($000) are

Alternative	Weighted Payoff
Small facility	0.5(200) + 0.5(270) = **235**
Large facility	0.5(160) + 0.5(800) = **480**

The best of these weighted payoffs is $480,000, so the realist would build a large facility.

d. *Minimax Regret.* If demand turns out to be low, the best alternative is a small facility and its regret is 0 (or 200 − 200). If a large facility is built when demand turns out to be low, the regret is 40 (or 200 − 160).

Alternative	REGRET		Maximum Regret
	Low Demand	High Demand	
Small facility	200 − 200 = **0**	800 − 270 = **530**	530
Large facility	200 − 160 = **40**	800 − 800 = **0**	40

The column on the right shows the worst regret for each alternative. To minimize the maximum regret, pick a large facility. The biggest regret is associated with having only a small facility and high demand.

DECISION POINT
The pessimist would choose the small facility. The realist, optimist, and manager choosing to minimize the maximum regret would build the large facility.

Decision Making under Risk

Here we assume that the manager can list the events and estimate their probabilities. The manager has less information than with decision making under certainty, but more information than with decision making under uncertainty. For this intermediate situation, the *expected value* decision rule is widely used (both in practice and in this text). The expected value for an alternative is found by weighting each payoff with its associated probability and then adding the weighted payoff scores. The alternative with the best expected value (highest for profits and lowest for costs) is chosen.

This rule is much like the Laplace decision rule, except that the events are no longer assumed to be equally likely (or equally important). The expected value is what the *average* payoff would be if the decision could be repeated time after time. Of course, the expected value decision rule can result in a bad outcome if the wrong event occurs. However, it gives the best results if applied consistently over a long period of time. The rule should not be used if the manager is inclined to avoid risk.

EXAMPLE 7	Decisions under Risk

Reconsider the payoff matrix in Example 5. For the expected value decision rule, which is the best alternative if the probability of small demand is estimated to be 0.4 and the probability of large demand is estimated to be 0.6?

MyOMLab

Tutor A.5 in MyOMLab provides a new example to make decisions under risk.

SOLUTION
The expected value for each alternative is as follows:

Alternative	Expected Value
Small facility	$0.4(200) + 0.6(270) = \mathbf{242}$
Large facility	$0.4(160) + 0.6(800) = \mathbf{544}$

DECISION POINT
Management would choose a large facility if it used this expected value decision rule, because it provides the best long-term results if consistently applied over time.

Decision Trees

The decision tree method is a general approach to a wide range of processes and supply chain decisions, such as product planning, process analysis, process capacity, and location. It is particularly valuable for evaluating different capacity expansion alternatives when demand is uncertain and sequential decisions are involved. For example, a company may expand a facility in 2013 only to discover in 2016 that demand is much higher than forecasted. In that case, a second decision may be necessary to determine whether to expand again or build a second facility.

A **decision tree** is a schematic model of alternatives available to the decision maker, along with their possible consequences. The name derives from the tree-like appearance of the model. It consists of a number of square *nodes*, representing decision points, which are left by *branches* (which should be read from left to right), representing the alternatives. Branches leaving circular, or chance, nodes represent the events. The probability of each chance event, *P(E)*, is shown above each branch. The probabilities for all branches leaving a chance node must sum to 1.0. The conditional payoff, which is the payoff for each possible alternative-event combination, is shown at the end of each combination. Payoffs are given only at the outset, before the analysis begins, for the end points of each alternative-event combination. In Figure 4, for example, payoff 1 is the financial outcome the manager expects if alternative 1 is chosen and then chance event 1 occurs.

No payoff can be associated yet with any branches farther to the left, such as alternative 1 as a whole, because it is followed by a chance event and is not an end point. Payoffs often are

decision tree

A schematic model of alternatives available to the decision maker, along with their possible consequences.

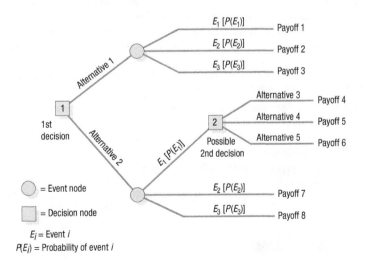

◄ **FIGURE 4**
A Decision Tree Model

expressed as the present value of net profits. If revenues are not affected by the decision, the payoff is expressed as net costs.

After drawing a decision tree, we solve it by working from right to left, calculating the *expected payoff* for each node as follows:

1. For an event node, we multiply the payoff of each event branch by the event's probability. We add these products to get the event node's expected payoff.

2. For a decision node, we pick the alternative that has the best expected payoff. If an alternative leads to an event node, its payoff is equal to that node's expected payoff (already calculated). We "saw off," or "prune," the other branches not chosen by marking two short lines through them. The decision node's expected payoff is the one associated with the single remaining unpruned branch. We continue this process until the leftmost decision node is reached. The unpruned branch extending from it is the best alternative to pursue. If multistage decisions are involved, we must await subsequent events before deciding what to do next. If new probability or payoff estimates are obtained, we repeat the process.

Various software is available for drawing decision trees. PowerPoint can be used to draw decision trees, although it does not have the capability to analyze the decision tree. More extensive capabilities, in addition to POM for Windows, are found with SmartDraw (**www.smartdraw.com**), PrecisionTree decision analysis from Palisade Corporation (**www.palisade.com**), and TreePlan (**www.treeplan.com/treeplan.htm**).

| **EXAMPLE 8** | **Analyzing a Decision Tree** |

MyOMLab

Active Model A.3 in MyOMLab provides additional insight on this decision tree example and its extensions.

A retailer must decide whether to build a small or a large facility at a new location. Demand at the location can be either low or high, with probabilities estimated to be 0.4 and 0.6, respectively. If a small facility is built and demand proves to be high, the manager may choose not to expand (payoff = $223,000) or to expand (payoff = $270,000). If a small facility is built and demand is low, there is no reason to expand and the payoff is $200,000. If a large facility is built and demand proves to be low, the choice is to do nothing ($40,000) or to stimulate demand through local advertising. The response to advertising may be either modest or sizable, with their probabilities estimated to be 0.3 and 0.7, respectively. If it is modest, the payoff is estimated to be only $20,000; the payoff grows to $220,000 if the response is sizable. Finally, if a large facility is built and demand turns out to be high, the payoff is $800,000.

Draw a decision tree. Then analyze it to determine the expected payoff for each decision and event node. Which alternative—building a small facility or building a large facility—has the higher expected payoff?

SOLUTION

The decision tree in Figure 5 shows the event probability and the payoff for each of the seven alternative-event combinations. The first decision is whether to build a small or a large facility. Its node is shown first, to the left, because it is the decision the retailer must make now. The second decision node—whether to expand at a later date—is reached only if a small facility is built and demand turns out to be high. Finally, the third decision point—whether to advertise—is reached only if the retailer builds a large facility and demand turns out to be low.

Analysis of the decision tree begins with calculation of the expected payoffs from right to left, shown on Figure 5 beneath the appropriate event and decision nodes.

1. For the event node dealing with advertising, the expected payoff is 160, or the sum of each event's payoff weighted by its probability [0.3(20) + 0.7(220)].

2. The expected payoff for decision node 3 is 160 because *Advertise* (160) is better than *Do nothing* (40). Prune the *Do nothing* alternative.

3. The payoff for decision node 2 is 270 because *Expand* (270) is better than *Do not expand* (223). Prune *Do not expand*.

4. The expected payoff for the event node dealing with demand, assuming that a small facility is built, is 242 [or 0.4(200) + 0.6(270)].

5. The expected payoff for the event node dealing with demand, assuming that a large facility is built, is 544 [or 0.4(160) + 0.6(800)].

6. The expected payoff for decision node 1 is 544 because the large facility's expected payoff is largest. Prune *Small facility*.

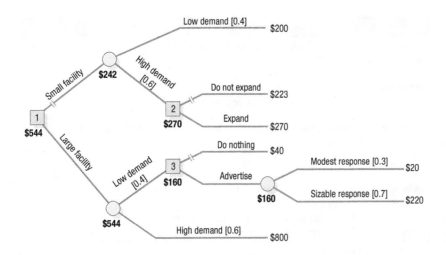

◀ **FIGURE 5**
Decision Tree for Retailer
(in $000)

DECISION POINT

The retailer should build the large facility. This initial decision is the only one made now. Subsequent decisions are made after learning whether demand actually is low or high.

LEARNING GOALS IN REVIEW

① **Explain break-even analysis, using both the graphic and algebraic approaches.** The section "Evaluating Services and Products," covers this analysis. Example 1 and Solved Problem 1 demonstrate both approaches. Example 3 shows its use in evaluating different processes.

② **Define a preference matrix.** See the section "Preference Matrix," for making decisions involving unquantifiable factors, where some factors are rated more important than others. Example 4 and Solved Problem 2 demonstrate the calculations.

③ **Explain how to construct a payoff table.** The section "Decision Theory," begins with the construction of a payoff table that shows the payoff for each feasible alternative and each event. See the table in Example 5.

④ **Identify the maximin, maximax, Laplace, minimax regret, and expected value decision rules.** The sections "Decision Making under Uncertainty" and "Decision Making under Risk," cover these decision rules for when the outcomes associated with alternatives are in doubt. Examples 6 and 7 demonstrate how these rules work, and so does Solved Problem 3.

⑤ **Describe how to draw and analyze a decision tree.** The section "Decision Trees," show how to draw and analyze decision trees where several alternatives are available over time. Example 8 and Solved Problem 4 shows how to work back from right to left, pruning as you go, until the best alternate is found for decision node 1.

MyOMLab helps you develop analytical skills and assess your progress with multiple problems on break-even analysis, sensitivity analysis, make-or-buy, the preference matrix, decisions under uncertainty, decisions under risks, and decision trees.

MyOMLab Resources	Titles	Link to the Book
Active Model Exercise	A.1 Break-Even Analysis A.3 Make-or-Buy Decision A.3 Decision Tree	Evaluating Services or Products; Examples 1–2; Solved Problem 1 Evaluating Processes; Example 3 Decision Trees; Example 8
OM Explorer Solvers	Break-Even Analysis Decision Theory Preference Matrix	Break-Even Analysis; Examples 1–3 Decision Theory; Example 5–7 Preference Matrix; Examples 4–6; Solved Problem 2

MyOMLab Resources	Titles	Link to the Book
OM Explorer Tutors	A.1 Break-Even, Evaluating Services and Products	Evaluating Services or Products; Example 1–2; Solved Problem 1
	A.2 Evaluating Processes	Evaluating Processes; Example 3
	A.3 Preferences Matrix	Preference Matrix; Example 4
	A.4 Decisions under Uncertainty	Decisions under Uncertainty; Example 6
	A.5 Decisions under Risk	Decision Making under Risk; Solved Problem 7; Solved Problem 3
	A.6 Location Decisions under Uncertainty	Tutor A.6
POM for Windows	Decision Tables	Decision Theory
	Decision Trees (graphical)	Decision Trees (Graphical); Example 8; Solved Problem 4
	Cost-Volume Analysis	Evaluating Processes
	Preference Matrix	Preference Matrix; Example 4; Solved Problem 2
	Break-Even Analysis	Break-Even Analysis; Example 1–3; Solved Problem 1
Virtual Tours	Flir infrared cameras	Decision Theory
	E* Trade investment services	Decision Theory
MyOMLab Supplements	F. Financial Analysis	MyOMLab Supplement F
Internet Exercises	Florida Small Business	Break–Even Analysis
Key Equations		
Image Library		

Key Equations

1. Break-even quantity: $Q = \dfrac{F}{p - c}$

2. Evaluating processes, make-or-buy indifference quantity: $Q = \dfrac{F_m - F_b}{c_b - c_m}$

Key Terms

break-even analysis
break-even quantity
decision theory

decision tree
fixed cost
payoff table

preference matrix
sensitivity analysis
variable cost

Solved Problem 1

The owner of a small manufacturing business has patented a new device for washing dishes and cleaning dirty kitchen sinks. Before trying to commercialize the device and add it to his or her existing product line, the owner wants reasonable assurance of success. Variable costs are estimated at $7 per unit produced and sold. Fixed costs are about $56,000 per year.

a. If the selling price is set at $25, how many units must be produced and sold to break even? Use both algebraic and graphic approaches.

b. Forecasted sales for the first year are 10,000 units if the price is reduced to $15. With this pricing strategy, what would be the product's total contribution to profits in the first year?

SOLUTION

a. Beginning with the algebraic approach, we get

$$Q = \frac{F}{p - c} = \frac{56,000}{25 - 7}$$
$$= 3,111 \text{ units}$$

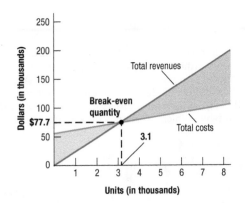

Using the graphic approach, shown in Figure 6, we first draw two lines:

$$\text{Total revenue} = 25Q$$
$$\text{Total cost} = 56{,}000 + 7Q$$

The two lines intersect at $Q = 3{,}111$ units, the break-even quantity.

b. Total profit contribution = Total revenue – Total cost

$$= pQ - (F + cQ)$$
$$= 15(10{,}000) - [56{,}000 + 7(10{,}000)]$$
$$= \$24{,}000$$

Solved Problem 2

Herron Company is screening three new product ideas: A, B, and C. Resource constraints allow only one of them to be commercialized. The performance criteria and ratings, on a scale of 1 (worst) to 10 (best), are shown in the following table. The Herron managers give equal weights to the performance criteria. Which is the best alternative, as indicated by the preference matrix method?

	RATING		
Performance Criterion	Product A	Product B	Product C
1. Demand uncertainty and project risk	3	9	2
2. Similarity to present products	7	8	6
3. Expected return on investment (ROI)	10	4	8
4. Compatibility with current manufacturing process	4	7	6
5. Competitive advantage	4	6	5

SOLUTION
Each of the five criteria receives a weight of 1/5 or 0.20.

Product	Calculation	Total Score
A	$(0.20 \times 3) + (0.20 \times 7) + (0.20 \times 10) + (0.20 \times 4) + (0.20 \times 4)$	= 5.6
B	$(0.20 \times 9) + (0.20 \times 8) + (0.20 \times 4) + (0.20 \times 7) + (0.20 \times 6)$	= 6.8
C	$(0.20 \times 2) + (0.20 \times 6) + (0.20 \times 8) + (0.20 \times 6) + (0.20 \times 5)$	= 5.4

The best choice is product B. Products A and C are well behind in terms of total weighted score.

Solved Problem 3

MyOMLab

Tutor A.6 in MyOMLab
examines decisions under
uncertainty for a location
example.

Adele Weiss manages the campus flower shop. Flowers must be ordered three days in advance from her supplier in Mexico. Although Valentine's Day is fast approaching, sales are almost entirely last-minute, impulse purchases. Advance sales are so small that Weiss has no way to estimate the probability of low (25 dozen), medium (60 dozen), or high (130 dozen) demand for red roses on the big day. She buys roses for $15 per dozen and sells them for $40 per dozen. Construct a payoff table. Which decision is indicated by each of the following decision criteria?

a. Maximin

b. Maximax

c. Laplace

d. Minimax regret

SOLUTION

The payoff table for this problem is

Alternative	DEMAND FOR RED ROSES		
	Low (25 dozen)	Medium (60 dozen)	High (130 dozen)
Order 25 dozen	$625	$625	$625
Order 60 dozen	$100	$1,500	$1,500
Order 130 dozen	($950)	$450	$3,250
Do nothing	$0	$0	$0

a. Under the maximin criteria, Weiss should order 25 dozen, because if demand is low, Weiss's profits are $625, the best of the worst payoffs.

b. Under the maximax criteria, Weiss should order 130 dozen. The greatest possible payoff, $3,250, is associated with the largest order.

c. Under the Laplace criteria, Weiss should order 60 dozen. Equally weighted payoffs for ordering 25, 60, and 130 dozen are about $625, $1,033, and $917, respectively.

d. Under the minimax regret criteria, Weiss should order 130 dozen. The maximum regret of ordering 25 dozen occurs if demand is high: $3,250 − $625 = $2,625. The maximum regret of ordering 60 dozen occurs if demand is high: $3,250 − $1,500 = $1,750. The maximum regret of ordering 130 dozen occurs if demand is low: $625 − (−$950) = $1,575.

Solved Problem 4

White Valley Ski Resort is planning the ski lift operation for its new ski resort. Management is trying to determine whether one or two lifts will be necessary; each lift can accommodate 250 people per day. Skiing normally occurs in the 14-week period from December to April, during which the lift will operate 7 days per week. The first lift will operate at 90 percent capacity if economic conditions are bad, the probability of which is believed to be about a 0.3. During normal times the first lift will be utilized at 100 percent capacity, and the excess crowd will provide 50 percent utilization of the second lift. The probability of normal times is 0.5. Finally, if times are really good, the probability of which is 0.2, the utilization of the second lift will increase to 90 percent. The equivalent annual cost of installing a new lift, recognizing the time value of money and the lift's economic life, is $50,000. The annual cost of installing two lifts is only $90,000 if both are purchased at the same time. If used at all, each lift costs $200,000 to operate, no matter how low or high its utilization rate. Lift tickets cost $20 per customer per day.

Should the resort purchase one lift or two?

SOLUTION

The decision tree is shown in Figure 7. The payoff ($000) for each alternative-event branch is shown in the following table. The total revenues from one lift operating at 100 percent capacity are $490,000 (or 250 customers × 98 days × $20/customer-day).

Alternative	Economic Condition	Payoff Calculation (Revenue – Cost)
One lift	Bad times	$0.9(490) - (50 + 200) = 191$
	Normal times	$1.0(490) - (50 + 200) = 240$
	Good times	$1.0(490) - (50 + 200) = 240$
Two lifts	Bad times	$0.9(490) - (90 + 200) = 151$
	Normal times	$1.5(490) - (90 + 400) = 245$
	Good times	$1.9(490) - (90 + 400) = 441$

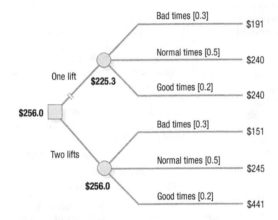

◄ FIGURE 7

Problems

The OM Explorer and POM for Windows software is available to all students using the 10th edition of this text. Go to **www.pearsonhighered.com/krajewski** to download these computer packages. If you purchased MyOMLab, you also have access to Active Models software and significant help in doing the following problems. Check with your instructor on how best to use these resources. In many cases, the instructor wants you to understand how to do the calculations by hand. At the least, the software provides a check on your calculations. When calculations are particularly complex and the goal is interpreting the results in making decisions, the software entirely replaces the manual calculations.

BREAK-EVEN ANALYSIS

1. Mary Williams, owner of Williams Products, is evaluating whether to introduce a new product line. After thinking through the production process and the costs of raw materials and new equipment, Williams estimates the variable costs of each unit produced and sold at $6 and the fixed costs per year at $60,000.

   a. If the selling price is set at $18 each, how many units must be produced and sold for Williams to break even? Use both graphic and algebraic approaches to get your answer.

   b. Williams forecasts sales of 10,000 units for the first year if the selling price is set at $14 each. What would be the total contribution to profits from this new product during the first year?

   c. If the selling price is set at $12.50, Williams forecasts that first-year sales would increase to 15,000 units. Which pricing strategy ($14.00 or $12.50) would result in the greater total contribution to profits?

   d. What other considerations would be crucial to the final decision about making and marketing the new product?

2. A product at the Jennings Company enjoyed reasonable sales volumes, but its contributions to profits were disappointing. Last year, 17,500 units were produced and sold. The selling price is $22 per unit, the variable cost is $18 per unit, and the fixed cost is $80,000.

   a. What is the break-even quantity for this product? Use both graphic and algebraic approaches to get your answer.

   b. If sales were not expected to increase, by how much would Jennings have to reduce their variable cost to break even?

c. Jennings believes that a $1 reduction in price will increase sales by 50 percent. Is this enough for Jennings to break even? If not, by how much would sales have to increase?

d. Jennings is considering ways to either stimulate sales volume or decrease variable cost. Management believes that either sales can be increased by 30 percent or that variable cost can be reduced to 85 percent of its current level. Which alternative leads to higher contributions to profits, assuming that each is equally costly to implement? (Hint: Calculate profits for both alternatives and identify the one having the greatest profits.)

e. What is the percent change in the per-unit profit contribution generated by each alternative in part (d)?

3. An interactive television service that costs $10 per *month* to provide can be sold on the information highway for $15 per client per *month*. If a service area includes a potential of 15,000 customers, what is the most a company could spend on *annual* fixed costs to acquire and maintain the equipment?

4. A restaurant is considering adding fresh brook trout to its menu. Customers would have the choice of catching their own trout from a simulated mountain stream or simply asking the waiter to net the trout for them. Operating the stream would require $10,600 in fixed costs per year. Variable costs are estimated to be $6.70 per trout. The firm wants to break even if 800 trout dinners are sold per year. What should be the price of the new item?

5. Spartan Castings must implement a manufacturing process that reduces the amount of particulates emitted into the atmosphere. Two processes have been identified that provide the same level of particulate reduction. The first process is expected to incur $350,000 of fixed cost and add $50 of variable cost to each casting Spartan produces. The second process has fixed costs of $150,000 and adds $90 of variable cost per casting.

a. What is the break-even quantity beyond which the first process is more attractive?

b. What is the difference in total cost if the quantity produced is 10,000?

6. A news clipping service is considering modernization. Rather than manually clipping and photocopying articles of interest and mailing them to its clients, employees electronically input stories from most widely circulated publications into a database. Each new issue is searched for key words, such as a client's company name, competitors' names, type of business, and the company's products, services, and officers. When matches occur, affected clients are instantly notified via an online network. If the story is of interest, it is electronically transmitted, so the client often has the story and can prepare comments for follow-up interviews before the publication hits the street. The manual process has fixed costs of $400,000 per year and variable costs of $6.20 per clipping mailed. The price charged the client is $8.00 per clipping. The computerized process has fixed costs of $1,300,000 per year and variable costs of $2.25 per story electronically transmitted to the client.

a. If the same price is charged for either process, what is the annual volume beyond which the automated process is more attractive?

b. The present volume of business is 225,000 clippings per year. Many of the clippings sent with the current process are not of interest to the client or are multiple copies of the same story appearing in several publications. The news clipping service believes that by improving service and by lowering the price to $4.00 per story, modernization will increase volume to 900,000 stories transmitted per year. Should the clipping service modernize?

c. If the forecasted increase in business is too optimistic, at what volume will the new process (with the $4.00 price) break even?

7. Hahn Manufacturing purchases a key component of one of its products from a local supplier. The current purchase price is $1,500 per unit. Efforts to standardize parts succeeded to the point that this same component can now be used in five different products. Annual component usage should increase from 150 to 750 units. Management wonders whether it is time to make the component in-house, rather than to continue buying it from the supplier. Fixed costs would increase by about $40,000 per year for the new equipment and tooling needed. The cost of raw materials and variable overhead would be about $1,100 per unit, and labor costs would be $300 per unit produced.

a. Should Hahn make rather than buy?

b. What is the break-even quantity?

c. What other considerations might be important?

8. Techno Corporation is currently manufacturing an item at variable costs of $5 per unit. Annual fixed costs of manufacturing this item are $140,000. The current selling price of the item is $10 per unit, and the annual sales volume is 30,000 units.

a. Techno can substantially improve the item's quality by installing new equipment at additional annual fixed costs of $60,000. Variable costs per unit would increase by $1, but, as more of the better-quality product could be sold, the annual volume would increase to 50,000 units. Should Techno buy the new equipment and maintain the current price of the item? Why or why not?

b. Alternatively, Techno could increase the selling price to $11 per unit. However, the annual sales volume would be limited to 45,000 units. Should Techno buy the new equipment and raise the price of the item? Why or why not?

9. The Tri-County Generation and Transmission Association is a nonprofit cooperative organization that provides electrical service to rural customers. Based on a faulty long-range demand forecast, Tri-County overbuilt its generation and distribution system. Tri-County now has much more capacity than it needs to serve its customers. Fixed costs, mostly debt service on investment in plant and equipment, are $82.5 million per year. Variable costs, mostly fossil fuel costs, are $25 per megawatt-hour (MWh, or million watts of power used for one hour). The new person in charge of demand forecasting prepared a short-range forecast for use in next year's budgeting process. That forecast calls for Tri-County customers to consume 1 million MWh of energy next year.

a. How much will Tri-County need to charge its customers per MWh to break even next year?

b. The Tri-County customers balk at that price and conserve electrical energy. Only 95 percent of forecasted demand materializes. What is the resulting surplus or loss for this nonprofit organization?

10. Earthquake, drought, fire, economic famine, flood, and a pestilence of TV court reporters have caused an exodus from the City of Angels to Boulder, Colorado. The sudden increase in demand is straining the capacity of Boulder's electrical system. Boulder's alternatives have been reduced to buying 150,000 MWh of electric power from Tri-County G&T at a price of $75 per MWh, or refurbishing and recommissioning the abandoned Pearl Street Power Station in downtown Boulder. Fixed costs of that project are $10 million per year, and variable costs would be $35 per MWh. Should Boulder build or buy?

11. Tri-County G&T sells 150,000 MWh per year of electrical power to Boulder at $75 per MWh, has fixed costs of $82.5 million per year, and has variable costs of $25 per MWh. If Tri-County has 1,000,000 MWh of demand from its customers (other than Boulder), what will Tri-County have to charge to break even?

PREFERENCE MATRIX

12. The Forsite Company is screening three ideas for new services. Resource constraints allow only one idea to be commercialized at the present time. The following estimates have been made for the five performance criteria that management believes to be most important:

Performance Criterion	RATING		
	Service A	Service B	Service C
Capital equipment investment required	0.6	0.8	0.3
Expected return on investment (ROI)	0.7	0.3	0.9
Compatibility with current workforce skills	0.4	0.7	0.5
Competitive advantage	1.0	0.4	0.6
Compatibility with EPA requirements	0.2	1.0	0.5

a. Calculate a total weighted score for each alternative. Use a preference matrix and assume equal weights for each performance criterion. Which alternative is best? Worst?

b. Suppose that the expected ROI is given twice the weight assigned to each of the remaining criteria. (The sum of weights should remain the same as in part (a).) Does this modification affect the ranking of the three potential services?

13. You are in charge of analyzing five new suppliers of an important raw material and have been given the information shown below (1 = worst, 10 = best). Management has decided that criteria 2 and 3 are equally important and that criteria 1 and 4 are each four times as important as criterion 2. No more than 2 new suppliers are required but each new vendor must exceed a total score of 70 percent of the maximum total points to be considered.

Performance Criterion	RATING				
	Vendor A	Vendor B	Vendor C	Vendor D	Vendor E
Quality of raw material	8	7	3	6	9
Environmental impact	3	8	4	7	7
Responsiveness to order changes	9	5	7	6	5
Cost of raw material	7	6	9	2	7

a. Which new vendors do you recommend?

b. Would your decision change if the criteria were considered equally important?

14. Accel Express, Inc., collected the following information on where to locate a warehouse (1 = poor, 10 = excellent):

Location Factor	Factor Weight	LOCATION SCORE	
		A	B
Construction costs	10	8	5
Utilities available	10	7	7
Business services	10	4	7
Real estate cost	20	7	4
Quality of life	20	4	8
Transportation	30	7	6

a. Which location, A or B, should be chosen on the basis of the total weighted score?

b. If the factors were weighted equally, would the choice change?

DECISION THEORY AND DECISION TREE

15. Build-Rite Construction has received favorable publicity from guest appearances on a public TV home improvement program. Public TV programming decisions seem to be unpredictable, so Build-Rite cannot estimate the probability of continued benefits from its relationship with the show. Demand for home improvements next year may be either low or high. But Build-Rite must decide now whether to hire more employees, do nothing, or develop

subcontracts with other home improvement contractors. Build-Rite has developed the following payoff table:

	DEMAND FOR HOME IMPROVEMENTS		
Alternative	Low	Moderate	High
Hire	($250,000)	$100,000	$625,000
Subcontract	$100,000	$150,000	$415,000
Do nothing	$50,000	$80,000	$300,000

Which alternative is best, according to each of the following decision criteria?

a. Maximin

b. Maximax

c. Laplace

d. Minimax regret

16. Analyze the decision tree in the following figure. What is the expected payoff for the best alternative? First, be sure to infer the missing probabilities.

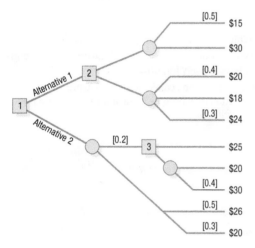

17. A manager is trying to decide whether to buy one machine or two. If only one is purchased and demand proves to be excessive, the second machine can be purchased later. Some sales will be lost, however, because the lead time for producing this type of machine is six months. In addition, the cost per machine will be lower if both are purchased at the same time. The probability of low demand is estimated to be 0.20. The after-tax net present value of the benefits from purchasing the two machines together is $90,000 if demand is low and $180,000 if demand is high.

If one machine is purchased and demand is low, the net present value is $120,000. If demand is high, the manager has three options. Doing nothing has a net present value of $120,000; subcontracting, $160,000; and buying the second machine, $140,000.

a. Draw a decision tree for this problem.

b. How many machines should the company buy initially? What is the expected payoff for this alternative?

18. A manager is trying to decide whether to build a small, medium, or large facility. Demand can be low, average, or high, with the estimated probabilities being 0.25, 0.40, and 0.35, respectively.

A small facility is expected to earn an after-tax net present value of just $18,000 if demand is low. If demand is average, the small facility is expected to earn $75,000; it can be increased to medium size to earn a net present value of $60,000. If demand is high, the small facility is expected to earn $75,000 and can be expanded to medium size to earn $60,000 or to large size to earn $125,000.

A medium-sized facility is expected to lose an estimated $25,000 if demand is low and earn $140,000 if demand is average. If demand is high, the medium-sized facility is expected to earn a net present value of $150,000; it can be expanded to a large size for a net payoff of $145,000.

If a large facility is built and demand is high, earnings are expected to be $220,000. If demand is average for the large facility, the present value is expected to be $125,000; if demand is low, the facility is expected to lose $60,000.

a. Draw a decision tree for this problem.

b. What should management do to achieve the highest expected payoff?

c. Which alternative is best, according to each of the following decision criterion?

Maximin

Maximax

Minimax regret

19. A manufacturing plant has reached full capacity. The company must build a second plant—either small or large—at a nearby location. The demand is likely to be high or low. The probability of low demand is 0.3. If demand is low, the large plant has a present value of $5 million and the small plant, a present value of $8 million. If demand is high, the large plant pays off with a present value of $18 million and the small plant with a present value of only $10 million. However, the small plant can be expanded later if demand proves to be high, for a present value of $14 million.

a. Draw a decision tree for this problem.

b. What should management do to achieve the highest expected payoff?

20. Benjamin Moses, chief engineer of Offshore Chemicals, Inc., must decide whether to build a new processing facility based on an experimental technology. If the new facility works, the company will realize a net profit of $20 million. If the new facility fails, the company will lose $10 million. Benjamin's best guess is that there is a 40 percent chance that the new facility will work.

What decision should Benjamin Moses make?

Selected References

Clemen, Robert T., and Terence Reilly. *Making Hard Decisions with Decision Tools Suite*. Cincinnati, OH: South-Western, 2004.

Ragsdale, Cliff. *Spreadsheet Modeling & Decision Analysis: A Practical Introduction to Management Science*, 6th ed. Cincinnati, OH: South-Western, 2011.

WAITING LINES

Anyone who has ever waited at a stoplight, at McDonald's, or at the registrar's office has experienced the dynamics of waiting lines. Perhaps one of the best examples of effective management of waiting lines is that of Walt Disney World. One day the park may have only 25,000 customers, but on another day the numbers may top 90,000. Careful analysis of process flows, technology for people-mover (materials handling) equipment, capacity, and layout keeps the waiting times for attractions to acceptable levels.

The analysis of waiting lines is of concern to managers because it affects process design, capacity planning, process performance, and ultimately, supply chain performance. In this supplement we discuss why waiting lines form, the uses of waiting-line models in operations management, and the structure of waiting-line models. We also discuss the decisions managers address with the models. Waiting lines can also be analyzed using computer simulation. Software such as SimQuick, a simulation package included in MyOMLab, or Excel spreadsheets can be used to analyze the problems in this supplement.

MyOMLab

Why Waiting Lines Form

A **waiting line** is one or more "customers" waiting for service. The customers can be people or inanimate objects, such as machines requiring maintenance, sales orders waiting for shipping, or inventory items waiting to be used. A waiting line forms because of a temporary imbalance between the demand for service and the capacity of the system to provide the service. In most real-life waiting-line problems, the demand rate varies; that is, customers arrive at unpredictable intervals. Most often, the rate of producing the service also varies, depending on customer needs. Suppose that bank customers arrive at an average rate of 15 per hour throughout the day and that

waiting line
One or more "customers" waiting for service.

LEARNING GOALS *After reading this supplement, you should be able to:*

1. Identify the elements of a waiting-line problem in a real situation.

2. Describe the single-server, multiple-server, and finite-source models.

3. Explain how to use waiting-line models to estimate the operating characteristics of a process.

4. Describe the situations where simulation should be used for waiting line analysis and the nature of the information that can be obtained.

5. Explain how waiting-line models can be used to make managerial decisions.

From Supplement B of *Operations Management: Processes and Supply Chains,* Tenth Edition. Lee J. Krajewski, Larry P. Ritzman, Manoj K. Malhotra. Copyright © 2013 by Pearson Education, Inc. All rights reserved.

the bank can process an average of 20 customers per hour. Why would a waiting line ever develop? The answers are that the customer arrival rate varies throughout the day and the time required to process a customer can vary. During the noon hour, 30 customers may arrive at the bank. Some of them may have complicated transactions requiring above-average process times. The waiting line may grow to 15 customers for a period of time before it eventually disappears. Even though the bank manager provided for more than enough capacity on average, waiting lines can still develop.

Waiting lines can develop even if the time to process a customer is constant. For example, a subway train is computer controlled to arrive at stations along its route. Each train is programmed to arrive at a station, say, every 15 minutes. Even with the constant service time, waiting lines develop while riders wait for the next train or cannot get on a train because of the size of the crowd at a busy time of the day. Consequently, variability in the rate of demand determines the sizes of the waiting lines in this case. In general, if no variability in the demand or service rate occurs and enough capacity is provided, no waiting lines form.

Uses of Waiting-Line Theory

Waiting-line theory applies to service as well as manufacturing firms, relating customer arrival and service-system processing characteristics to service-system output characteristics. In our discussion, we use the term *service* broadly—the act of doing work for a customer. The service system might be hair cutting at a hair salon, satisfying customer complaints, or processing a production order of parts on a certain machine. Other examples of customers and services include lines of theatergoers waiting to purchase tickets, trucks waiting to be unloaded at a warehouse, machines waiting to be repaired by a maintenance crew, and patients waiting to be examined by a physician. Regardless of the situation, waiting-line problems have several common elements.

Structure of Waiting-Line Problems

Analyzing waiting-line problems begins with a description of the situation's basic elements. Each specific situation will have different characteristics, but four elements are common to all situations:

1. An input, or **customer population**, that generates potential customers

2. A waiting line of customers

3. The **service facility**, consisting of a person (or crew), a machine (or group of machines), or both necessary to perform the service for the customer

4. A **priority rule**, which selects the next customer to be served by the service facility

Figure 1 shows these basic elements. The triangles, circles, and squares are intended to show a diversity of customers with different needs. The **service system** describes the number of lines and the arrangement of the facilities. After the service has been performed, the served customers leave the system.

Customer Population

A customer population is the source of input to the service system. If the potential number of new customers for the service system is appreciably affected by the number of customers already in the system, the input source is said to be *finite*. For example, suppose that a maintenance crew is assigned responsibility for the repair of 10 machines. The customer population for the

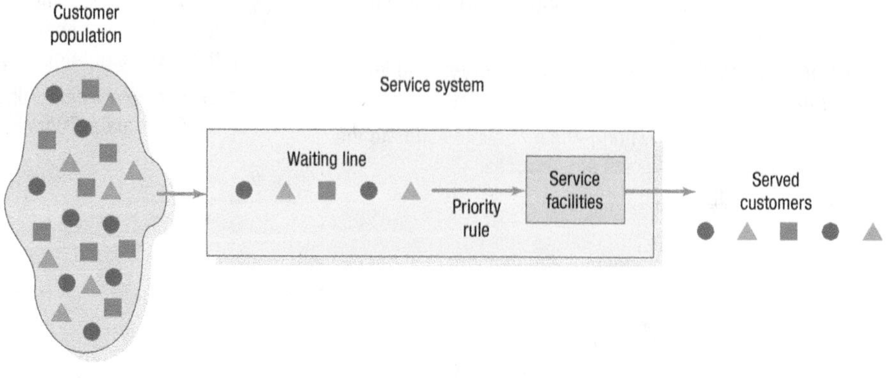

customer population

An input that generates potential customers.

service facility

A person (or crew), a machine (or group of machines), or both necessary to perform the service for the customer.

priority rule

A rule that selects the next customer to be served by the service facility.

service system

The number of lines and the arrangement of the facilities.

FIGURE 1 ▶

Basic Elements of Waiting-Line Models

maintenance crew is 10 machines in working order. The population generates customers for the maintenance crew as a function of the failure rates for the machines. As more machines fail and enter the service system, either waiting for service or being repaired, the customer population becomes smaller and the rate at which it can generate another customer falls. Consequently, the customer population is said to be finite.

Alternatively, an *infinite* customer population is one in which the number of customers in the system does not affect the rate at which the population generates new customers. For example, consider a mail-order operation for which the customer population consists of shoppers who have received a catalog of products sold by the company. Because the customer population is so large and only a small fraction of the shoppers place orders at any one time, the number of new orders it generates is not appreciably affected by the number of orders waiting for service or being processed by the service system. In this case, the customer population is said to be infinite.

Customers in waiting lines may be *patient* or *impatient*, which has nothing to do with the colorful language a customer may use while waiting in line for a long time on a hot day. In the context of waiting-line problems, a patient customer is one who enters the system and remains there until being served; an impatient customer is one who either decides not to enter the system (balks) or leaves the system before being served (reneges). For the methods used in this supplement, we make the simplifying assumption that all customers are patient.

The Service System

The service system may be described by the number of lines and the arrangement of facilities.

Number of Lines Waiting lines may be designed to be a *single line* or *multiple lines*. Figure 2 shows an example of each arrangement. Generally, single lines are utilized at airline counters, inside banks, and at some fast-food restaurants; whereas multiple lines are utilized in grocery stores, at drive-in bank operations, and in discount stores. When multiple servers are available and each one can handle general transactions, the single-line arrangement keeps servers uniformly busy and gives customers a sense of fairness. Customers believe that they are being served on the basis of when they arrived, and not on how well they guessed their waiting time when selecting a particular line. The multiple-line design is best when some of the servers provide a limited set of services. In this arrangement, customers select the services they need and wait in the line where that service is provided, such as at a grocery store that provides special lines for customers paying with cash or having fewer than 10 items.

Sometimes customers are not organized neatly into "lines." Machines that need repair on the production floor of a factory may be left in place, and the maintenance crew comes to them. Nonetheless, we can think of such machines as forming a single line or multiple lines, depending on the number of repair crews and their specialties. Likewise, passengers who telephone for a taxi also form a line even though they may wait at different locations.

Arrangement of Service Facilities Service facilities consist of the personnel and equipment necessary to perform the service for the customer. Service facility arrangement is described by the number of channels and phases. A **channel** is one or more facilities required to perform a given service. A **phase** is a single step in providing the service. Some services require a single phase, while others require a sequence of phases. Consequently, a service facility uses some combination

Sometimes customers are not organized neatly into lines. Here ships wait to use the port facilities in Victoria Harbor, West Kowloon, Hong Kong.

Islemount Images/Alamy

channel
One or more facilities required to perform a given service.

phase
A single step in providing a service.

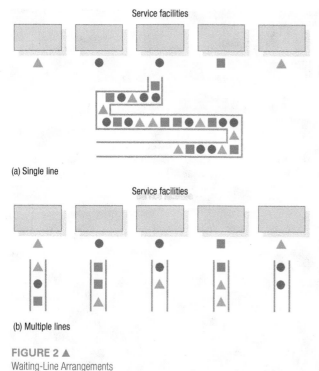

Service facilities

(a) Single line

Service facilities

(b) Multiple lines

FIGURE 2 ▲
Waiting-Line Arrangements

of channels and phases. Managers should choose an arrangement based on customer volume and the nature of services provided. Figure 3 shows examples of the five basic types of service facility arrangements.

In the *single-channel, single-phase* system, all services demanded by a customer can be performed by a single-server facility. Customers form a single line and go through the service facility one at a time. Examples are a drive-through car wash and a machine that must process several batches of parts.

The *single-channel, multiple-phase* arrangement is used when the services are best performed in sequence by more than one facility, yet customer volume or other constraints limit the design to one channel. Customers form a single line and proceed sequentially from one service facility to the next. An example of this arrangement is a McDonald's drive-through, where the first facility takes the order, the second takes the money, and the third provides the food.

The *multiple-channel, single-phase* arrangement is used when demand is large enough to warrant providing the same service at more than one facility or when the services offered by the facilities are different. Customers form one or more lines, depending on the design. In the single-line design, customers are served by the first available server, as in the lobby of a bank. If each channel has its own waiting line, customers wait until the server for their line can serve them, as at a bank's drive-through facilities.

The *multiple-channel, multiple-phase* arrangement occurs when customers can be served by one of the first-phase facilities but then require service from a second-phase facility, and so on. In some cases, customers cannot switch channels after service has begun; in others they can. An example of this arrangement is a laundromat. Washing machines are the first-phase facilities, and dryers are the second-phase facilities. Some of the washing machines and dryers may be designed for extra-large loads, thereby providing the customer a choice of channels.

The most complex waiting-line problem involves customers who have unique sequences of required services; consequently, service cannot be described neatly in phases. A *mixed* arrangement is used in such a case. In the mixed arrangement, waiting lines can develop in front of each facility, as in a medical center, where a patient goes to an exam room for a nurse to take his or her blood pressure and weight, goes back to the waiting room until the doctor can see him or her, and

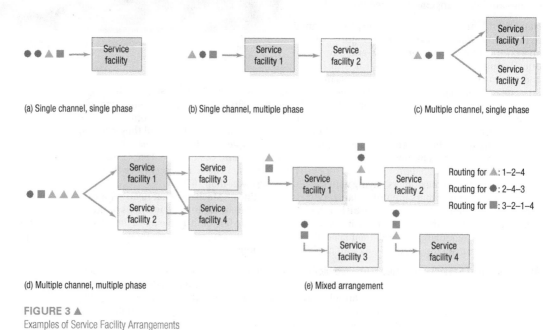

(a) Single channel, single phase

(b) Single channel, multiple phase

(c) Multiple channel, single phase

(d) Multiple channel, multiple phase

(e) Mixed arrangement

Routing for ▲: 1–2–4
Routing for ●: 2–4–3
Routing for ■: 3–2–1–4

FIGURE 3 ▲
Examples of Service Facility Arrangements

after consultation proceeds to the laboratory to give a blood sample, radiology to have an X–ray taken, or the pharmacy for prescribed drugs, depending on specific needs.

Priority Rule

The priority rule determines which customer to serve next. Most service systems that you encounter use the first-come, first-served (FCFS) rule. The customer at the head of the waiting line has the highest priority, and the customer who arrived last has the lowest priority. Other priority disciplines might take the customer with the earliest promised due date (EDD) or the customer with the shortest expected processing time (SPT).[1]

A **preemptive discipline** is a rule that allows a customer of higher priority to interrupt the service of another customer. For example, in a hospital emergency room, patients with the most life-threatening injuries receive treatment first, regardless of their order of arrival. Modeling of systems having complex priority disciplines is usually done using computer simulation.

preemptive discipline

A rule that allows a customer of higher priority to interrupt the service of another customer.

Probability Distributions

The sources of variation in waiting-line problems come from the random arrivals of customers and the variations in service times. Each of these sources can be described with a probability distribution.

Arrival Distribution

Customers arrive at service facilities randomly. The variability of customer arrivals often can be described by a Poisson distribution, which specifies the probability that n customers will arrive in T time periods:

$$P_n = \frac{(\lambda T)^n}{n!} e^{-\lambda T} \text{ for } n = 0,1,2,\dots$$

where

P_n = probability of n arrivals in T time periods

λ = average number of customer arrivals per period

e = 2.7183

The mean of the Poisson distribution is λT, and the variance also is λT. The Poisson distribution is a discrete distribution; that is, the probabilities are for a specific number of arrivals per unit of time.

EXAMPLE 1	Calculating the Probability of Customer Arrivals

Management is redesigning the customer service process in a large department store. Accommodating four customers is important. Customers arrive at the desk at the rate of two customers per hour. What is the probability that four customers will arrive during any hour?

SOLUTION

In this case $\lambda = 2$ customers per hour, $T = 1$ hour, and $n = 4$ customers. The probability that four customers will arrive in any hour is

$$P_4 = \frac{[2(1)]^4}{4!} e^{-2(1)} = \frac{16}{24} e^{-2} = 0.090$$

DECISION POINT

The manager of the customer service desk can use this information to determine the space requirements for the desk and waiting area. There is a relatively small probability that four customers will arrive in any hour. Consequently, seating capacity for two or three customers should be more than adequate unless the time to service each customer is lengthy. Further analysis on service times is warranted.

---

[1]We focus on FCFS in this supplement. See Supplement J, "Operations Scheduling," for SPT and additional rules.

Another way to specify the arrival distribution is to do it in terms of customer **interarrival times**—that is, the time between customer arrivals. If the customer population generates customers according to a Poisson distribution, the *exponential distribution* describes the probability that the next customer will arrive in the next T time periods. As the exponential distribution also describes service times, we discuss the details of this distribution in the next section.

Service Time Distribution

The exponential distribution describes the probability that the service time of the customer at a particular facility will be no more than T time periods. The probability can be calculated by using the formula

$$P(t \leq T) = 1 - e^{-\mu T}$$

where

$\mu =$ average number of customers completing service per period

$t =$ service time of the customer

$T =$ target service time

The mean of the service time distribution is $1/\mu$, and the variance is $(1/\mu)^2$. As T increases, the probability that the customer's service time will be less than T approaches 1.0.

For simplicity, let us look at a single-channel, single-phase arrangement.

EXAMPLE 2	Calculating the Service Time Probability

The management of the large department store in Example 1 must determine whether more training is needed for the customer service clerk. The clerk at the customer service desk can serve an average of three customers per hour. What is the probability that a customer will require less than 10 minutes of service?

SOLUTION

We must have all the data in the same time units. Because $\mu = 3$ customers per hour, we convert minutes of time to hours, or $T = 10$ minutes $= 10/60$ hour $= 0.167$ hour. Then

$$P(t \leq T) = 1 - e^{-\mu T}$$

$$P(t \leq 0.167 \text{ hour}) = 1 - e^{-3(0.167)} = 1 - 0.61 = 0.39$$

DECISION POINT

The probability that the customer will require only 10 minutes or fewer is not high, which leaves the possibility that customers may experience lengthy delays. Management should consider additional training for the clerk so as to reduce the time it takes to process a customer request.

Some characteristics of the exponential distribution do not always conform to an actual situation. The exponential distribution model is based on the assumption that each service time is independent of those that preceded it. In real life, however, productivity may improve as human servers learn about the work. Another assumption underlying the model is that very small, as well as very large, service times are possible. However, real-life situations often require a fixed-length start-up time, some cutoff on total service time, or nearly constant service time.

Using Waiting-Line Models to Analyze Operations

Operations managers can use waiting-line models to balance the gains that might be made by increasing the efficiency of the service system against the costs of doing so. In addition, managers should consider the costs of *not* making improvements to the system: Long waiting lines or long waiting times may cause customers to balk or renege. Managers should therefore be concerned about the following operating characteristics of the system.

1. *Line Length.* The number of customers in the waiting line reflects one of two conditions. Short lines could mean either good customer service or too much capacity. Similarly, long lines could indicate either low server efficiency or the need to increase capacity.

2. *Number of Customers in System.* The number of customers in line and being served also relates to service efficiency and capacity. A large number of customers in the system causes congestion and may result in customer dissatisfaction, unless more capacity is added.

3. *Waiting Time in Line.* Long lines do not always mean long waiting times. If the service rate is fast, a long line can be served efficiently. However, when waiting time seems long, customers perceive the quality of service to be poor. Managers may try to change the arrival rate of customers or design the system to make long wait times seem shorter than they really are. For example, at Walt Disney World, customers in line for an attraction are entertained by videos and also are informed about expected waiting times, which seems to help them endure the wait.

4. *Total Time in System.* The total elapsed time from entry into the system until exit from the system may indicate problems with customers, server efficiency, or capacity. If some customers are spending too much time in the service system, it may be necessary to change the priority discipline, increase productivity, or adjust capacity in some way.

5. *Service Facility Utilization.* The collective utilization of service facilities reflects the percentage of time that they are busy. Management's goal is to maintain high utilization and profitability without adversely affecting the other operating characteristics.

The best method for analyzing a waiting-line problem is to relate the five operating characteristics and their alternatives to dollars. However, placing a dollar figure on certain characteristics (such as the waiting time of a shopper in a grocery store) is difficult. In such cases, an analyst must weigh the cost of implementing the alternative under consideration against a subjective assessment of the cost of *not* making the change.

We now present three models and some examples showing how waiting-line models can help operations managers make decisions. We analyze problems requiring the single-server, multiple-server, and finite-source models, all of which are single phase. References to more advanced models are cited at the end of this supplement.

Single-Server Model

The simplest waiting-line model involves a single server and a single line of customers. To further specify the model, we make the following assumptions:

1. The customer population is infinite and all customers are patient.

2. The customers arrive according to a Poisson distribution, with a mean arrival rate of λ.

3. The service distribution is exponential, with a mean service rate of μ.

4. The mean service rate exceeds the mean arrival rate.

5. Customers are served on a first-come, first-served basis.

6. The length of the waiting line is unlimited.

With these assumptions, we can apply various formulas to describe the operating characteristics of the system:

Visitors to Disney MGM Studios, Disney World, Orlando, Florida patiently wait in line for the Aerosmith Rock N Roller Coaster ride, which is an example of a single-channel, single-phase system.

Melvyn Longhurst/Alamy

$$\rho = \text{Average utilization of the system}$$
$$= \frac{\lambda}{\mu}$$

$$P_n = \text{Probability that } n \text{ customers are in the system}$$
$$= (1 - \rho)\rho^n$$

$$L = \text{Average number of customers in the service system}$$
$$= \frac{\lambda}{\mu - \lambda}$$

$$L_q = \text{Average number of customers in the waiting line}$$
$$= \rho L$$

$$W = \text{Average time spent in the system, including service}$$
$$= \frac{1}{\mu - \lambda}$$

$$W_q = \text{Average waiting time in line}$$
$$= \rho W$$

EXAMPLE 3	Calculating the Operating Characteristics of a Single-Channel, Single-Phase System

The manager of a grocery store in the retirement community of Sunnyville is interested in providing good service to the senior citizens who shop in her store. Currently, the store has a separate checkout counter for senior citizens. On average, 30 senior citizens per hour arrive at the counter, according to a Poisson distribution, and are served at an average rate of 35 customers per hour, with exponential service times. Find the following operating characteristics:

a. Probability of zero customers in the system

b. Average utilization of the checkout clerk

c. Average number of customers in the system

d. Average number of customers in line

e. Average time spent in the system

f. Average waiting time in line

SOLUTION

The checkout counter can be modeled as a single-channel, single-phase system. Figure 4 shows the results from the *Waiting-Lines* Solver from OM Explorer. Manual calculations of the equations for the *single-server model* are demonstrated in the Solved Problem at the end of the supplement.

FIGURE 4 ▶

Waiting-Lines Solver for Single-Channel, Single-Phase System

Servers		(Number of servers s assumed to be 1 in single-serve model)
Arrival Rate (λ)	30	
Service Rate (μ)	35	

Probability of zero customers in the system (P_0)	0.1429
Probability of exactly ▾ 0 customers in the system	0.1429
Average utilization of the server (ρ)	0.8571
Average number of customers in the system (L)	6.0000
Average number of customers in line (L_q)	5.1429
Average waiting/service time in the system (W)	0.2000
Average waiting time in line (W_q)	0.1714

Both the average waiting time in the system (W) and the average time spent waiting in line (W_q) are expressed in hours. To convert the results to minutes, simply multiply by 60 minutes/hour. For example, $W = 0.20(60) = 12.00$ minutes, and $W_q = 0.1714(60) = 10.28$ minutes.

EXAMPLE 4	Analyzing Service Rates with the Single-Server Model

The manager of the Sunnyville grocery in Example 3 wants answers to the following questions:

a. What service rate would be required so that customers averaged only 8 minutes in the system?

b. For that service rate, what is the probability of having more than four customers in the system?

c. What service rate would be required to have only a 10 percent chance of exceeding four customers in the system?

SOLUTION

The *Waiting-Lines* Solver from OM Explorer could be used iteratively to answer the questions. Here we show how to solve the problem manually.

a. We use the equation for the average time in the system and solve for μ.

$$W = \frac{1}{\mu - \lambda}$$

$$8 \text{ minutes} = 0.133 \text{ hour} = \frac{1}{\mu - 30}$$

$$0.133\mu - 0.133(30) = 1$$

$$\mu = 37.52 \text{ customers/hour}$$

b. The probability of more than four customers in the system equals 1 minus the probability of four or fewer customers in the system.

$$P = 1 - \sum_{n=0}^{4} P_n$$

$$= 1 - \sum_{n=0}^{4} (1 - \rho)\rho^n$$

and

$$\rho = \frac{30}{37.52} = 0.80$$

Then,

$$P = 1 - 0.2(1 + 0.8 + 0.8^2 + 0.8^3 + 0.8^4)$$

$$= 1 - 0.672 = 0.328$$

Therefore, there is a nearly 33 percent chance that more than four customers will be in the system.

c. We use the same logic as in part (b), except that μ is now a decision variable. The easiest way to proceed is to find the correct average utilization first, and then solve for the service rate.

$$P = 1 - (1 - \rho)(1 + \rho + \rho^2 + \rho^3 + \rho^4)$$

$$= 1 - (1 + \rho + \rho^2 + \rho^3 + \rho^4) + \rho(1 + \rho + \rho^2 + \rho^3 + \rho^4)$$

$$= 1 - 1 - \rho - \rho^2 - \rho^3 - \rho^4 + \rho + \rho^2 + \rho^3 + \rho^4 + \rho^5$$

$$= \rho^5$$

or

$$\rho = P^{1/5}$$

If $P = 0.10$,

$$\rho = (0.10)^{1/5} = 0.63$$

Therefore, for a utilization rate of 63 percent, the probability of more than four customers in the system is 10 percent. For $\lambda = 30$, the mean service rate must be

$$\frac{30}{\mu} = 0.63$$

$$\mu = 47.62 \text{ customers/hour}$$

DECISION POINT

The service rate would only have to increase modestly to achieve the 8-minute target. However, the probability of having more than four customers in the system is too high. The manager must now find a way to increase the service rate from 35 per hour to approximately 48 per hour. She can increase the service rate in several different ways, ranging from employing a high school student to help bag the groceries to installing self checkout stations.

Multiple-Server Model

With the multiple-server model, customers form a single line and choose one of s servers when one is available. The service system has only one phase. We make the following assumptions in addition to those for the single-server model: There are s identical servers, and the service distribution for each server is exponential, with a mean service time of $1/\mu$. It should always be the case that $s\mu$ exceeds λ.

| **EXAMPLE 5** | **Estimating Idle Time and Hourly Operating Costs with the Multiple-Server Model** |

The management of the American Parcel Service terminal in Verona, Wisconsin, is concerned about the amount of time the company's trucks are idle (not delivering on the road), which the company defines as waiting to be unloaded and being unloaded at the terminal. The terminal operates with four unloading bays. Each bay requires a crew of two employees, and each crew costs $30 per hour. The estimated cost of an idle truck is $50 per hour. Trucks arrive at an average rate of three per hour, according to a Poisson distribution. On average, a crew can unload a semitrailer rig in one hour, with exponential service times. What is the total hourly cost of operating the system?

MyOMLab

Tutor B.2 in MyOMLab provides a new example to practice the multiple-server model.

MyOMLab

Active Model B.2 in
MyOMLab provides
additional insight on the
multiple-server model and
its uses for this problem.

SOLUTION

The *multiple-server model* for $s = 4$, $\mu = 1$, and $\lambda = 3$ is appropriate. To find the total cost of labor and idle trucks, we must calculate the average number of trucks in the system at all times.

Figure 5 shows the results for the American Parcel Service problem using the *Waiting-Lines* Solver from OM Explorer. The results show that the four-bay design will be utilized 75 percent of the time and that the average number of trucks either being serviced or waiting in line is 4.53 trucks. That is, on average at any point in time, we have 4.53 idle trucks. We can now calculate the hourly costs of labor and idle trucks:

Labor cost:	$30(s) = $30(4) = $120.00
Idle truck cost:	$50(L) = $50(4.53) = $226.50
	Total hourly cost = $346.50

FIGURE 5 ▶

Waiting-Lines Solver for
Multiple-Server Model

Servers	4
Arrival Rate (λ)	3
Service Rate (μ)	1

Probability of zero customers in the system (P_0)	0.0377
Probability of exactly ▼ 0 customers in the system	0.0377
Average utilization of the servers (p)	0.7500
Average number of customers in the system (L)	4.5283
Average number of customers in line (L_q)	1.5283
Average waiting/service time in the system (W)	1.5094
Average waiting time in line (W_q)	0.5094

DECISION POINT

Management must now assess whether $346.50 per day for this operation is acceptable. Attempting to reduce costs by eliminating crews will only increase the waiting time of the trucks, which is more expensive per hour than the crews. However, the service rate can be increased through better work methods; for example, L can be reduced and daily operating costs will be less.

Little's Law

Little's law

A fundamental law that relates
the number of customers in a
waiting-line system to the arrival
rate and waiting time of
customers.

One of the most practical and fundamental laws in waiting-line theory is **Little's law**, which relates the number of customers in a waiting-line system to the arrival rate and the waiting time of customers. Using the same notation we used for the single-server model, Little's law can be expressed as $L = \lambda W$ or $L_q = \lambda W_q$. However, this relationship holds for a wide variety of arrival processes, service-time distributions, and numbers of servers. The practical advantage of Little's law is that you only need to know two of the parameters to estimate the third. For example, consider the manager of a motor vehicle licensing facility who receives many complaints about the time people must spend either having their licenses renewed or getting new license plates. It would be difficult to obtain data on the times individual customers spend at the facility. However, the manager can have an assistant monitor the number of people who arrive at the facility each hour and compute the average (λ). The manager also could periodically count the number of people in the sitting area and at the stations being served and compute the average (L). Using Little's law, the manager can then estimate W, the average time each customer spent in the facility. For example, if 40 customers arrive per hour and the average number of customers being served or waiting is 30, the average time each customer spends in the facility can be computed as

$$\text{Average time in the facility} = W = \frac{L \text{ customers}}{\lambda \text{ customers/hour}} = \frac{30}{40} = 0.75 \text{ hours, or 45 minutes}$$

If the time a customer spends at the facility is unreasonable, the manager can focus on either adding capacity or improving the work methods to reduce the time spent serving the customers.

Likewise, Little's law can be used for manufacturing processes. Suppose that a production manager knows the average time a unit of product spends at a manufacturing process (W) and the average number of units per hour that arrive at the process (λ). The production manager can then estimate the average work-in-process (L) using Little's law. *Work-in-process* (WIP) consists of items, such as components or assemblies, needed to produce a final product in manufacturing.

Cars line up at the Triborough Bridge toll, New York City. This is an example of a multiple-channel, single-phase system, where some channels are devoted to special services.

For example, if the average time a gear case used for an outboard marine motor spends at a machine center is 3 hours, and an average of five gear cases arrive at the machine center per hour, the average number of gear cases waiting and being processed (or work-in-process) at the machine center can be calculated as

$$\text{Work-in-process} = L = \lambda W = 5 \text{ gear cases/hour (3 hours)} = 15 \text{ gear cases}$$

Knowing the relationship between the arrival rate, the lead time, and the work-in-process, the manager has a basis for measuring the effects of process improvements on the work-in-process at the facility. For example, adding some capacity to a bottleneck in the process can reduce the average lead time of the product at the process, thereby reducing the work-in-process inventory.

Even though Little's law is applicable in many situations in both service and manufacturing environments, it is not applicable in situations where the customer population is finite, which we address next.

Finite-Source Model

We now consider a situation in which all but one of the assumptions of the single-server model are appropriate. In this case, the customer population is finite, having only N potential customers. If N is greater than 30 customers, the single-server model with the assumption of an infinite customer population is adequate. Otherwise, the finite-source model is the one to use.

EXAMPLE 6	Analyzing Maintenance Costs with the Finite-Source Model

The Worthington Gear Company installed a bank of 10 robots about 3 years ago. The robots greatly increased the firm's labor productivity, but recently attention has focused on maintenance. The firm does no preventive maintenance on the robots because of the variability in the breakdown distribution. Each machine has an exponential breakdown (or interarrival) distribution with an average time between failures of 200 hours. Each machine hour lost to downtime costs $30, which means that the firm has to react quickly to machine failure. The firm employs one maintenance person, who needs 10 hours on average to fix a robot. Actual maintenance times are exponentially distributed. The wage rate is $10 per hour for the maintenance person, who can be put to work productively elsewhere when not fixing robots. Determine the daily cost of labor and robot downtime.

SOLUTION

The *finite-source model* is appropriate for this analysis because the customer population consists of only 10 machines and the other assumptions are satisfied. Here, $\lambda = 1/200$, or 0.005 break-down per hour, and $\mu = 1/10 = 0.10$ robot per hour. To calculate the cost of labor and robot downtime, we need to estimate the average utilization of the maintenance person and L, the average number of robots in the maintenance system at any time. Either OM Explorer or POM for Windows can be used to help with the calculations. Figure 6 shows

MyOMLab
Tutor B.3 in MyOMLab provides a new example to practice the finite-source model.

MyOMLab
Active Model B.3 in MyOMLab provides additional insight on the finite-source model and its uses for this problem.

the results for the Worthington Gear Problem using the *Waiting-Lines* Solver from OM Explorer. The results show that the maintenance person is utilized only 46.2 percent of the time, and the average number of robots waiting in line or being repaired is 0.76 robot. However, a failed robot will spend an average of 16.43 hours in the repair system, of which 6.43 hours of that time is spent waiting for service. While an individual robot may spend more than 2 days with the maintenance person, the maintenance person has a lot of idle time with a utilization rate of only 42.6 percent. That is why there is only an average of 0.76 robot being maintained at any point of time.

FIGURE 6 ▶
Waiting-Lines Solver for Finite-Source Model

Customers	10
Arrival Rate (λ)	0.005
Service Rate (μ)	0.1

Probability of zero customers in the system (P_0)	0.5380
Probability of fewer than ▼ 0 customers in the system	#N/A
Average utilization of the server (p)	0.4620
Average number of customers in the system (L)	0.7593
Average number of customers in line (L_q)	0.2972
Average waiting/service time in the system (W)	16.4330
Average waiting time in line (W_q)	6.4330

The daily cost of labor and robot downtime is

Labor cost:	($10/hour)(8 hours/day)(0.462 utilization)	=	$ 36.96
Idle robot cost:	(0.76 robot)($30/robot hour)(8 hours/day)	=	182.40
	Total daily cost	=	$219.36

DECISION POINT

The labor cost for robot repair is only 20 percent of the idle cost of the robots. Management might consider having a second repair person on call in the event two or more robots are waiting for repair at the same time.

Waiting Lines and Simulation

For each of the problems we analyzed with the waiting-line models, the arrivals had a Poisson distribution (or exponential interarrival times), the service times had an exponential distribution, the service facilities had a simple arrangement, the waiting line was unlimited, and the priority discipline was first-come, first-served. Waiting-line theory has been used to develop other models in which these criteria are not met, but these models are complex. For example, POM for Windows includes a finite system-size model in which limits can be placed on the size of the system (waiting line and server capacity). It also has several models that relax assumptions on the service time distribution. Nonetheless, many times the nature of the customer population, the constraints on the line, the priority rule, the service-time distribution, and the arrangement of the facilities are such that waiting-line theory is no longer useful. In these cases, simulation often is used. MyOMLab Supplement E, "Simulation," discusses simulation programming languages and powerful PC-based packages. Here we illustrate process simulation with the SimQuick software (also provided in MyOMLab).

SimQuick SimQuick is an easy-to-use package that is simply an Excel spreadsheet with some macros. Models can be created for a variety of simple processes, such as waiting lines, inventory control, and projects. Here, we consider the passenger security process at one terminal of a medium-sized airport between the hours of 8 A.M. and 10 A.M. The process works as follows. Passengers arriving at the security area immediately enter a single line. After waiting in line, each passenger goes through one of two inspection stations, which involves walking through a metal detector and running any carry-on baggage through a scanner. After completing this inspection, 10 percent of the passengers are randomly selected for an additional inspection, which involves a pat-down and a more thorough search of the person's

A passenger, randomly selected for additional screening, helps LA International Airport security personnel examine his luggage. The airport security process is a multiple-channel, multiple-phase system.

carry-on baggage. Two stations handle this additional inspection, and selected passengers go through only one of them. Management is interested in examining the effect of increasing the percentage of passengers who undergo the second inspection. In particular, they want to compare the waiting times for the second inspection when 10 percent, then 15 percent, and then 20 percent of the passengers are randomly selected for this inspection. Management also wants to know how opening a third station for the second inspection would affect these waiting times.

A first step in simulating this process with SimQuick is to draw a flowchart of the process using SimQuick's building blocks. SimQuick has five building blocks that can be combined in a wide variety of ways. Four of these types are used to model this process. An *entrance* is used to model the arrival of passengers at the security process. A *buffer* is used to model each of the two waiting lines, one before each type of inspection, as well as the passengers that have finished the process. Each of the four inspection stations is modeled with a *workstation*. Finally, the random selection of passengers for the second inspection is modeled with a *decision point*. Figure 7 shows the flowchart.

Information describing each building block is entered into SimQuick tables. In this model, three key types of information are entered: (1) when people arrive at the entrance, (2) how long inspections take at the four stations, and (3) what percentage of passengers are randomly selected for the additional inspection. All of this information must be entered into SimQuick in the form of statistical distributions. The first two types of information are determined by observing the real process from 8 A.M. and 10 A.M. The third type of information is a policy decision (10 percent, 15 percent, or 20 percent).

The original model is run 30 times, simulating the arrival of passengers during the hours from 8 A.M. to 10 A.M. Statistics are collected by SimQuick and summarized. Figure 8 provides some key results for the model of the present process as output by SimQuick (many other statistics are collected, but not displayed here).

The numbers shown are averages across the 30 simulations. The number 237.23 is the average number of passengers that enter line 1 during the simulated two hours. The two mean inventory statistics tell us, on average, 5.97 simulated passengers were standing in line 1 and 0.10 standing in line 2. The two statistics on *cycle time*, interpreted here as the time a passenger spends in one or more SimQuick building blocks, tell us that the simulated passengers in line 1 waited an average of 3.12 minutes, while those in line 2 waited 0.53 minutes. The final inventory statistic tells us that, on average, 224.57 simulated passengers passed through the security process in the simulated two hours. The next step is to change the percentage of simulated passengers selected for the second inspection to 15 percent, and then to 20 percent, and rerun the model. Of course, these process changes will increase the average waiting time for the second inspection, but by how much? The final step is to rerun these simulations with one more workstation and see its effect on the waiting time for the second inspection. All the details for this model (as well as many others) appear in the book *SimQuick: Process Simulation with Excel*, which is included, along with the SimQuick software, in MyOMLab.

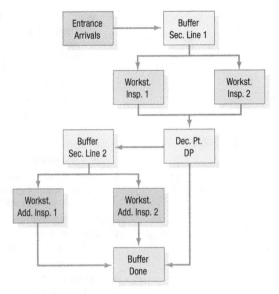

FIGURE 7 ▲
Flowchart of Passenger Security Process

Element Types	Element Names	Statistics	Overall Means
Entrance(s)	Door	Objects entering process	237.23
Buffer(s)	Line 1	Mean inventory	5.97
		Mean cycle time	3.12
	Line 2	Mean inventory	0.10
		Mean cycle time	0.53
	Done	Final inventory	224.57

FIGURE 8 ▲
Simulation Results of Passenger Security Process

MyOMLab

Decision Areas for Management

After analyzing a waiting-line problem, management can improve the service system by making changes in one or more of the following areas.

1. *Arrival Rates.* Management often can affect the rate of customer arrivals, λ, through advertising, special promotions, or differential pricing. For example, hotels in the Caribbean will reduce their room rates during the hot, rainy season to attract more customers and increase their utilization.

2. *Number of Service Facilities.* By increasing the number of service facilities, such as tool cribs, toll booths, or bank tellers, or by dedicating some facilities in a phase to a unique set of services, management can increase system capacity.

3. *Number of Phases.* Managers can decide to allocate service tasks to sequential phases if they determine that two sequential service facilities may be more efficient than one. For instance, in assembly lines a decision concerns the number of phases or workers needed along the assembly line. Determining the number of workers needed on the line also involves assigning a certain set of work elements to each one. Changing the facility arrangement can increase the service rate, μ, of each facility and the capacity of the system.

4. *Number of Servers per Facility.* Managers can influence the service rate by assigning more than one person to a service facility.

5. *Server Efficiency.* By adjusting the capital-to-labor ratio, devising improved work methods, or instituting incentive programs, management can increase the efficiency of servers assigned to a service facility. Such changes are reflected in μ.

6. *Priority Rule.* Managers set the priority rule to be used, decide whether to have a different priority rule for each service facility, and decide whether to allow preemption (and, if so, under what conditions). Such decisions affect the waiting times of the customers and the utilization of the servers.

7. *Line Arrangement.* Managers can influence customer waiting times and server utilization by deciding whether to have a single line or a line for each facility in a given phase of service.

Obviously, these factors are interrelated. An adjustment in the customer arrival rate might have to be accompanied by an increase in the service rate, λ, in some way. Decisions about the number of facilities, the number of phases, and waiting-line arrangements also are related.

LEARNING GOALS IN REVIEW

1 **Identify the elements of a waiting-line problem in a real situation.** The section "Structure of Waiting-Line Problems," defines the four elements of every waiting-line problem. Figures 1, 2, and 3 depict these elements and various service facility arrangements.

2 **Describe the single-server, multiple-server, and finite-source models.** See the section "Using Waiting-Line Models to Analyze Operations," for a description and demonstration of these three models. Examples 3, 4 and the Solved Problem at the end of the supplement apply the single-server model. Example 5 shows the multiple-server model and Example 6 applies the finite-source model.

3 **Explain how to use waiting-line models to estimate the operating characteristics of a process.** Examples 3 through 6

show how to obtain estimates for the important operating characteristics of processes using waiting-line models.

4 **Describe the situations where simulation should be used for waiting line analysis and the nature of the information that can be obtained.** The section "Waiting Lines and Simulation," explains when simulation must be used and discusses an example that demonstrates the nature of the managerial information that can be obtained from that analysis.

5 **Explain how waiting-line models can be used to make managerial decisions.** The section "Decision Areas for Management," describes seven decision areas that can be analyzed with waiting-line models.

MyOMLab helps you develop analytical skills and assesses your progress with multiple problems on utilization rate, probability of more than *n* customers in the system, number of customers waiting, probability of no customers in the system, average number of customers in the system, and service rate to keep average number of customers to a certain level.

MyOMLab Resources	Titles	Link to the Book
Video	*1st Bank Villa Italia: Waiting Lines*	Entire supplement
Active Model Exercise	B.1 Single-Server Model B.2 Multiple-Server Model with Costs B.3 Finite-Source Model with Costs	Single-Server Model; Example 3 Multiple-Server Model; Example 5 Finite-Source Model; Example 6
OM Explorer Solvers	Single-Server Model Multiple-Server Model Finite-Source Model	Single-Server Model; Example 3; Figure 4 Multiple-Server Model; Example 5; Figure 5 Finite-Source Model; Example 6; Figure 6

MyOMLab Resources	Titles	Link to the Book
OM Explorer Tutors	B.1 Single-Server Waiting-Line Model B.2 Multi-Server Model B.3 Finite Source	Single-Server Model; Example 3 Multiple-Server Model; Example 5 Finite-Source Model; Example 6
POM for Windows	B.1 Single-Server Model B.2 Multiple-Server Model with Costs B.3 Finite-Source Model with Costs B.4 Finite System-Size Model	Single-Server Model; Example 3 Multiple-Server Model; Example 5 Finite-Source Model; Example 6 Using Waiting-Line Models to Analyze Operations
Virtual Tours	New York City Fire Department	Entire supplement
Internet Exercise	Surfing the net on Google	Structure of Waiting Lines
Online Text	SimQuick: Process Simulation with Excel, 2e	Waiting Lines and Simulation; Figure 7; Figure 8
Key Equations		
Image Library		

Key Equations

1. Customer arrival Poisson distribution:

$$P_n = \frac{(\lambda T)^n}{n!} e^{-\lambda T}$$

2. Service time exponential distribution:

$$P(t \leq T) = 1 - e^{-\mu T}$$

3. Average utilization of the system:

$$\rho = \frac{\lambda}{\mu}$$

4. Probability that n customers are in the system:

$$P_n = (1 - \rho)\rho^n$$

5. Probability that zero customers are in the system:

$$P_0 = 1 - \rho$$

6. Average number of customers in the service system:

$$L = \frac{\lambda}{\mu - \lambda}$$

7. Average number of customers in the waiting line:

$$L_q = \rho L$$

8. Average time spent in the system, including service:

$$W = \frac{1}{\mu - \lambda}$$

9. Average waiting time in line:

$$W_q = \rho W$$

10. Little's Law

$$L = \lambda W$$

Key Terms

channel
customer population
interarrival times
Little's law

phase
preemptive discipline
priority rule
service facility

service system
waiting line

Solved Problem

A photographer takes passport pictures at an average rate of 20 pictures per hour. The photographer must wait until the customer smiles, so the time to take a picture is exponentially distributed. Customers arrive at a Poisson-distributed average rate of 19 customers per hour.

a. What is the utilization of the photographer?

b. How much time will the average customer spend with the photographer?

SOLUTION

a. The assumptions in the problem statement are consistent with a single-server model. Utilization is

$$\rho = \frac{\lambda}{\mu} = \frac{19}{20} = 0.95$$

b. The average customer time spent with the photographer is

$$W = \frac{1}{\mu - \lambda} = \frac{1}{20 - 19} = 1 \text{ hour}$$

Problems

The OM Explorer and POM for Windows software is available to all students using the 10th edition of this textbook. Go to **www.pearsonhighered.com/krajewski** to download these computer packages. If you purchased MyOMLab, you also have access to Active Models software and significant help in doing the following problems. Check with your instructor on how best to use these resources. In many cases, the instructor wants you to understand how to do the calculations by hand. At the least, the software provides a check on your calculations. When calculations are particularly complex and the goal is interpreting the results in making decisions, the software entirely replaces the manual calculations.

1. The Solomon, Smith, and Samson law firm produces many legal documents that must be word processed for clients and the firm. Requests average eight pages of documents per hour, and they arrive according to a Poisson distribution. The secretary can word process 10 pages per hour on average according to an exponential distribution.

   a. What is the average utilization rate of the secretary?

   b. What is the probability that more than four pages are waiting or being word processed?

   c. What is the average number of pages waiting to be word processed?

2. Benny's Arcade has six video game machines. The average time between machine failures is 50 hours. Jimmy, the maintenance engineer, can repair a machine in 15 hours on average. The machines have an exponential failure distribution, and Jimmy has an exponential service-time distribution.

   a. What is Jimmy's utilization?

   b. What is the average number of machines out of service, that is, waiting to be repaired or being repaired?

   c. What is the average time a machine is out of service?

3. Moore, Aiken, and Payne is a critical care dental clinic serving the emergency needs of the general public on a first-come, first-served basis. The clinic has five dental chairs, three of which are currently staffed by a dentist. Patients in distress arrive at the rate of five per hour, according to a Poisson distribution, and do not balk or renege. The average time required for an emergency treatment is 30 minutes, according to an exponential distribution. Use POM for Windows or OM Explorer to answer the following questions:

   a. If the clinic manager would like to ensure that patients do not spend more than 15 minutes on average waiting to see the dentist, are three dentists on staff adequate? If not, how many more dentists are required?

   b. From the current state of three dentists on staff, what is the change in each of the following operating characteristics when a fourth dentist is placed on staff:

   ■ Average utilization
   ■ Average number of customers in line
   ■ Average number of customers in the system

   c. From the current state of three dentists on staff, what is the change in each of the following operating characteristics when a fifth dentist is placed on staff:

- Average utilization
- Average number of customers in line
- Average number of customers in the system

4. Fantastic Styling Salon is run by three stylists, Jenny Perez, Jill Sloan, and Jerry Tiller, each capable of serving four customers per hour, on average. Use POM for Windows or OM Explorer to answer the following questions:

   During busy periods of the day, when nine customers on average arrive per hour, all three stylists are on staff.

   a. If all customers wait in a common line for the next available stylist, how long would a customer wait in line, on average, before being served?

   b. Suppose that each customer wants to be served by a specific stylist, 1/3 want Perez, 1/3 want Sloan, 1/3 want Tiller. How long would a customer wait in line, on average, before being served?

   During less busy periods of the day, when six customers on average arrive per hour, only Perez and Sloan are on staff.

   c. If all customers wait in a common line for the next available stylist, how long would a customer wait in line, on average, before being served?

   d. Suppose that each customer wants to be served by a specific stylist, 60 percent want Perez and 40 percent want Sloan. How long would a customer wait in line, on average, before being served by Perez? By Sloan? Overall?

5. You are the manager of a local bank where three tellers provide services to customers. On average, each teller takes 3 minutes to serve a customer. Customers arrive, on average, at a rate of 50 per hour. Having recently received complaints from some customers that they waited a long time before being served, your boss asks you to evaluate the service system. Specifically, you must provide answers to the following questions:

   a. What is the average utilization of the three-teller service system?

   b. What is the probability that no customers are being served by a teller or are waiting in line?

   c. What is the average number of customers waiting in line?

   d. On average, how long does a customer wait in line before being served?

   e. On average, how many customers would be at a teller's station and in line?

6. Pasquist Water Company (PWC) operates a 24-hour facility designed to efficiently fill water-hauling tanker trucks. Trucks arrive randomly to the facility and wait in line to access a wellhead pump. Since trucks vary in size and the filling operation is manually performed by the truck driver, the time to fill a truck is also random.

   a. If the manager of PWC uses the "multiple-server model" to calculate the operating characteristics of the facility's waiting line, list three assumptions she must make regarding the behavior of waiting trucks and the truck arrival process.

   b. Suppose an average of 336 trucks arrive each day, there are four wellhead pumps, and each pump can serve an average of four trucks per hour.

- What is the probability that exactly 10 trucks will arrive between 1:00 P.M. and 2:00 P.M. on any given day?
- How likely is it that once a truck is in position at a wellhead, the filling time will be less than 15 minutes?

   c. Contrast and comment on the performance differences between:

- One waiting line feeding all four stations.
- One waiting line feeding two wellhead pumps and a second waiting line feeding two other wellhead pumps. Assume that drivers cannot see each line and must choose randomly between them. Further, assume that once a choice is made, the driver cannot back out of the line.

7. The supervisor at the Precision Machine Shop wants to determine the staffing policy that minimizes total operating costs. The average arrival rate at the tool crib, where tools are dispensed to the workers, is eight machinists per hour. Each machinist's pay is $20 per hour. The supervisor can staff the crib either with a junior attendant who is paid $5 per hour and can process 10 arrivals per hour or with a senior attendant who is paid $12 per hour and can process 16 arrivals per hour. Which attendant should be selected, and what would be the total estimated hourly cost?

8. The daughter of the owner of a local hamburger restaurant is preparing to open a new fast-food restaurant called Hasty Burgers. Based on the arrival rates at her father's outlets, she expects customers to arrive at the drive-up window according to a Poisson distribution, with a mean of 20 customers per hour. The service rate is flexible; however, the service times are expected to follow an exponential distribution. The drive-in window is a single-server operation.

   a. What service rate is needed to keep the average number of customers in the service system (waiting line and being served) to four?

   b. For the service rate in part (a), what is the probability that more than four customers are in line and being served?

   c. For the service rate in part (a), what is the average waiting time in line for each customer? Does this average seem satisfactory for a fast-food business?

9. The manager of a branch office of Banco Mexicali observed that during peak hours an average of 20 customers arrives per hour and that there is an average of four customers in the branch office at any time. How long does the average customer spend waiting in line and being serviced?

10. Paula Caplin is manager of a major electronics repair facility owned by Fisher Electronics. Recently, top management expressed concern over the growth in the number of repair jobs in process at the facility. The average arrival rate is 120 jobs per day. The average job spends 4 days at the facility.

   a. What is the current work-in-process level at the facility?

   b. Suppose that top management has put a limit of one-half the current level of work-in-process. What goal must Paula establish and how might she accomplish it?

Advanced Problems

11. Failsafe Textiles employs three highly skilled maintenance workers who are responsible for repairing the numerous industrial robots used in its manufacturing process. A worker can fix one robot every 8 hours on average, with an exponential distribution. An average of one robot fails every 3 hours, according to a Poisson distribution. Each down robot costs the company $100.00 per hour in lost production. A new maintenance worker costs the company $80.00 per hour in salary, benefits, and equipment. Should the manager hire any new personnel? If so, how many people? What would you recommend to the manager, based on your analysis?

12. The College of Business and Public Administration at Benton University has a copy machine on each floor for faculty use. Heavy use of the five copy machines causes frequent failures. Maintenance records show that a machine fails every 2.5 days (or $\lambda = 0.40$ failure/day). The college has a maintenance contract with the authorized dealer of the copy machines. Because the copy machines fail so frequently, the dealer has assigned one person to the college to repair them. The person can repair an average of 2.5 machines per day. Using the finite-source model, answer the following questions:

   a. What is the average utilization of the maintenance person?

   b. On average, how many copy machines are being repaired or waiting to be repaired?

   c. What is the average time spent by a copy machine in the repair system (waiting and being repaired)?

13. You are in charge of a quarry that supplies sand and stone aggregates to your company's construction sites. Empty trucks from construction sites arrive at the quarry's huge piles of sand and stone aggregates and wait in line to enter the station, which can load either sand or aggregate. At the station, they are filled with material, weighed, checked out, and proceed to a construction site. Currently, nine empty trucks arrive per hour, on average. Once a truck has entered a loading station, it takes 6 minutes for it to be filled, weighed, and checked out. Concerned that trucks are spending too much time waiting and being filled, you are evaluating two alternatives to reduce the average time the trucks spend in the system. The first alternative is to add side boards to the trucks (so that more material could be loaded) and to add a helper at the loading station (so that filling time could be reduced) at a total cost of $50,000. The arrival rate of trucks would change to six per hour, and the filling time would be reduced to 4 minutes. The second alternative is to add another loading station identical to the current one at a cost of $80,000. The trucks would wait in a common line and the truck at the front of the line would move to the next available station.

Which alternative would you recommend if you want to reduce the current average time the trucks spend in the system, including service?

Selected References

Cooper, Robert B. *Introduction to Queuing Theory*, 2nd ed. New York: Elsevier-North Holland, 1980.

Hartvigsen, David. *SimQuick: Process Simulation with Excel*, 2nd ed. Upper Saddle River, NJ: Prentice Hall, 2004.

Hillier, F.S., and G.S. Lieberman. *Introduction to Operations Research*, 2nd ed. San Francisco: Holden-Day, 1975.

Little, J.D.C. "A Proof for the Queuing Formula: $L = \lambda M$." *Operations Research*, vol. 9, (1961), pp. 383–387.

Moore, P.M. *Queues, Inventories and Maintenance*. New York: John Wiley & Sons, 1958.

Saaty, T.L. *Elements of Queuing Theory with Applications*. New York: McGraw-Hill, 1961.

Index

A

Absenteeism, 116, 118, 173-174, 200
Abuse, 130
Acceptable quality level, 149-150, 169
Accounting, 3-4, 7, 16, 18, 25-26, 29-30, 52, 73,
    79-80, 103, 106-107, 109, 145-146
    finance and, 3, 30
Accounting department, 16, 26, 146
accounts payable, 150
accuracy, 10, 47, 102, 145, 151, 170, 174, 221, 225,
    229, 237-239, 248
Achievement, 13, 149
Acquisitions, 143
Action plans, 120
Adaptation, 8
addresses, 11-12, 165, 196
adjustments, 34, 146, 224, 228, 236-238, 255, 257,
    259
Administrators, 171
Advances, 4, 224
Advantages, 18, 25, 83, 85, 89, 91, 99, 166, 263
Advertising, 32, 56, 64, 69, 124, 131, 145, 211,
    224-226, 246, 255, 262, 270, 291
    evaluating, 224, 262
    local, 131, 246, 270
    online, 255
    product, 32, 145, 211, 224-225, 255, 262
    retail, 211, 255
    types of, 69, 291
Advertising campaign, 56, 64
Affect, 2, 19-20, 30, 33, 46, 50, 67, 74, 90, 134, 145,
    154, 167, 181, 187, 190, 225-226, 242, 246,
    251, 262-263, 277, 281, 291-292
Africa, 1
Age, 254
Agencies, 47, 71
agenda, 22
Agent, 127
Agents, 22, 255
Aggregate demand, 256
agreement, 9, 18, 106-107, 211
Agreements, 256
Air pollution, 252
Aircraft, 14, 39, 116, 132, 214
    business, 132
Alabama, 248
Allocations, 80, 107
Allowances, 110
AMP, 97, 134
Animation, 164
anticipate, 29, 219
appearance, 74, 76, 145, 174, 269
Application, 33, 99, 118, 127-128, 131, 148-150, 166,
    177, 188-190, 201, 224, 229, 249
Applications, 4, 9, 18, 61, 128, 131, 177, 189-190, 296
arguments, 224
ARM, 85-86
Art, 3, 64, 146, 183, 228, 255
Asia, 1
Assets, 3, 18, 52, 108, 217
    current, 108
attention, 6, 13, 41, 50-51, 72, 75-76, 85-87, 91, 101,
    103, 105, 109, 114, 116, 120, 122, 148, 179,
    181, 214, 237, 289
Attitudes, 8, 75, 122, 151, 265-266
Attribute, 115, 146, 151, 153, 169, 176
attributes, 10, 47, 151, 154, 158, 167-169, 182
AU, 127
audience, 146
Auditors, 165
    compliance, 165
    external, 165
Audits, 32
Australia, 1, 17, 255
Authority, 34, 146
authorization, 131

Auto insurance, 22
    fraud, 22
Autocratic, 35
Automobile industry, 20
availability, 4, 8, 10, 12, 33, 41, 128, 137
    backup, 12
Available, 11, 16, 26, 29, 32, 53, 59-60, 64, 66, 70, 71,
    73-74, 76, 80, 83, 85, 88, 94-97, 104,
    106-107, 109, 112, 114, 118-120, 123,
    127-129, 135, 152, 164, 173, 186, 189,
    191-195, 200, 204, 206, 208-209, 211, 214,
    218-219, 222, 224, 229, 233, 238, 240,
    246-247, 254-255, 258, 264, 269-271, 275,
    277, 281-282, 287, 294-296
Average costs, 239

B

backup, 12
Balance sheet, 116
Bankruptcy, 127
Banks, 29, 108, 120, 158, 281
bar charts, 103, 114, 122, 149-150, 167
Behavior, 117, 144, 153, 165-166, 172, 179, 183, 230,
    238, 295
Benchmarking, 102, 119-123, 136, 144, 239
Benefits, 6, 20, 22, 26, 36, 73, 84-86, 105, 122, 127,
    129-130, 137, 144, 147, 166, 182, 239, 256,
    277-278, 296
    extended, 137
    service, 6, 22, 73, 84-86, 105, 122, 129, 144, 147,
        166, 182, 239, 256, 277, 296
Best practices, 70, 136
biases, 224
Bicycles, 83
Bid, 13, 77, 130
billing, 4, 15, 22, 59, 62, 73, 83, 107, 132, 142, 153,
    179
Bonds, 127
    completion, 127
brainstorming, 117, 119, 123
    online, 117, 123
Brand, 68, 85-86, 146, 181-182, 211, 215, 237, 247,
    254-255
    licensing, 211
    managing, 254
    packaging, 68, 85
    public relations, 255
Brand managers, 254
Brands, 18, 29, 136, 211, 228, 237, 254-255
    importance of, 211
    individual, 29, 136, 237, 254
    store, 254-255
Breakdown, 35-36, 53-54, 68-69, 104, 289
Break-even analysis, 91, 94, 261-265, 271-272, 275
Bribery, 20
    corporate, 20
Britain, 90
Broker, 69, 120
Budget, 26, 33, 47, 51-52, 70, 73, 79-80, 262
    defined, 26, 79
Budgeting, 7, 53, 277
    capital, 277
buffers, 201
Business cycle, 219
Business environment, 8
Business ethics, 183
business intelligence, 237
Business model, 210
business plans, 219
Business process, 98-99, 107, 139, 259
business process management, 99, 139, 259
business process reengineering, 98
business processes, 72-73, 90, 148
    definition, 148
Business review, 22, 30, 72, 99, 139, 259
Business services, 277
Business strategy, 3

Business Week, 2, 183
Buttons, 174
Buyers, 29, 211, 218
    Product, 29, 211, 218

C

Call centers, 9, 142, 145
Canada, 17, 19, 181
Cancellation, 123
Capabilities, 4, 7-8, 11, 14-15, 20, 23-24, 26, 70, 84,
    104, 145, 149, 196, 211, 215, 238, 270
Capacity, 12, 16, 19, 21, 25, 30, 32-33, 72-73, 80,
    84-85, 97-98, 103, 109, 113, 119, 127,
    134-136, 142, 164, 185-192, 194-196,
    201-203, 205-210, 212, 219, 239, 252,
    256-257, 266, 269, 274-278, 279-280,
    283-285, 288-292
Capacity planning, 12, 21, 33, 72, 103, 109, 142, 187,
    219, 279
Capital, 3-5, 9, 20, 39, 52, 72, 74, 78-79, 84-89, 91-92,
    94, 104, 187-188, 219, 277, 292
    customer, 3-5, 9, 20, 72, 74, 78-79, 84-89, 91-92,
        94, 104, 188, 219, 292
    fixed, 84-85, 89, 92, 94, 277
    human, 3-4, 52, 74, 79, 84-86, 219
    requirements, 4, 79, 84, 219, 277
Capital equipment, 78, 85, 277
Carbon footprint, 20
Career, 2, 23
Caribbean, 291
carrying costs, 213
Case study, 215, 218, 259
Cash flow, 52, 187
Cash flows, 17, 66, 187, 219
Catastrophic events, 19
Cause-and-effect relationships, 224
Cell phones, 19, 79, 141-142
Central Limit Theorem, 50
Certainty, 37, 50, 266-268
Channel, 47, 281-282, 284-286, 290, 294
Channels, 281-282, 289
    Service, 281-282, 289
Character, 33
checklists, 103, 114, 150
Checkout, 246, 286-287
Child labor, 121
Children, 1, 137
China, 10, 16-20, 30, 32, 137, 187, 255
    political environment, 10
Chinese, 10, 20, 79, 255
chipping, 119
Claimant, 22
Claims, 10, 18, 22, 145, 150, 165
Climate, 20, 241
Climate change, 20
clothing, 5, 12, 18, 63, 142
Clustering, 220
Clusters, 197, 220
Coaching, 21
collaboration, 214, 217, 238-240, 259
Columbia, 18
Columns, 80, 108, 113, 127-128, 267
Commitment, 25, 102, 105, 166, 182, 211-212
Communication, 25, 47, 79-80, 89, 94, 116, 118, 143,
    182, 194, 201
Companies, 4, 9, 11, 13, 18-20, 25, 29, 32, 47, 77, 83,
    91, 102, 117, 119, 127, 142-144, 151,
    165-166, 179, 195, 211, 220, 237
company policy, 212
compatibility, 265, 273, 277
Compensation, 7, 18, 73
Compensation plans, 7
Compete, 1-30, 31, 33, 72, 103, 142, 144-145, 187,
    219
Competition, 8, 10-11, 14, 16-20, 23-25, 146, 177,
    179, 211, 239, 256, 266
    transportation and, 18

Competitive advantage, 2, 4, 9, 23, 25, 30, 72, 85, 102, 166, 265, 273, 277
  positioning, 23
Competitive environment, 7
Competitive strategy, 30
Competitiveness, 21
Competitors, 7-11, 16-17, 25, 33, 47, 141, 182, 221, 276
  identifying, 8-10
complaints, 25, 98, 101, 114-115, 123, 131-132, 134, 136, 150, 160, 256, 280, 288, 295
  customer, 25, 101, 114, 123, 131, 134, 150, 256, 280, 288, 295
Compliance, 7, 68, 143, 165-166
Component parts, 98, 135
compromise, 34
Computer software, 41-42
Conditions, 8, 10-11, 17, 43, 84-85, 87, 127, 144, 161-162, 173, 186, 204, 221, 236, 255, 274, 284, 292
Confidence, 110, 181, 183, 255
Configuration, 86
  manufacturing, 86
Confirmation, 123, 127-128
Consideration, 44, 52, 76, 194, 211, 239, 285
Consistency, 13, 29, 85, 97, 104, 132, 135, 142
Constraints, 32, 52, 186-189, 192-194, 196, 199, 201-202, 206, 208, 210, 214-215, 273, 277, 282, 290
  changing, 186
  CHECK, 189, 196, 214-215
  creating, 32, 187
  implementing, 189, 215
  UNIQUE, 32, 208, 282
Construction, 35-36, 38-39, 47, 52, 68, 147, 152, 176, 197, 271, 277, 296
Consumer credit, 255
Consumer protection, 143
Consumers, 6, 85, 145, 166, 254-255
Consumption, 207
Contacts, 95-96, 108-109
Content, 132, 164, 172, 200
Continuous improvement, 87, 120, 127, 139, 143-144, 147-148, 163, 166-167, 169, 214
Contract, 27, 54, 108-109, 150, 211, 217, 296
Contracts, 11, 29, 73, 121, 226, 255
Contribution margin, 192-194, 206, 208-209
Control, 2-3, 34-36, 51-52, 73, 78, 83, 85, 103, 108, 116, 127, 132, 138-139, 141-142, 146-150, 152-161, 163, 167-171, 173-179, 181-183, 194-195, 230, 236, 249, 251, 255, 266, 290
control activities, 51
Control methods, 154, 167
Control systems, 195
Controlling, 32-33, 51-53, 69-70, 72, 158, 160, 246
Conventions, 37, 106
Conversation, 106
conversion, 112
Cooperation, 187
Coordination, 2-3, 6, 32-33, 35, 72, 108, 145, 240
  manufacturing, 2-3, 6, 32, 72
  systems, 3, 33, 72, 240
Copyright, 1, 30, 31, 71, 98, 101, 136, 141, 155, 185, 188, 217, 239, 261, 279
Core competencies, 7-9, 24-25
Core services, 13
Corporate social responsibility, 20, 30
  bribery, 20
  environment, 20, 30
Corporate strategies, 10
Corporate strategy, 2, 7-8, 11, 15, 20, 23, 30
corporation, 4, 10, 13, 19, 62, 101, 123, 172, 211, 226, 237, 240, 254, 270, 276
Corporations, 33, 120
  professional, 120
Corrective action, 150, 171
correspond with, 256
cost accounting, 109
Cost per thousand, 250
Costs, 8, 12, 14-16, 18, 22, 24, 26-27, 30, 34, 42-46, 53-54, 56, 61-63, 65-66, 70, 71, 79, 82-85, 87-89, 91, 94, 98, 105, 112, 120-121, 127, 135, 138, 142-145, 147, 151, 154, 163-164, 167, 169, 177, 182, 186, 190, 192, 196, 205, 207, 209, 213-214, 218, 239, 246, 255-256, 261-264, 266-268, 270, 272-277, 284, 287-289, 292-293, 295-296
  conversion, 112
  distribution, 24, 54, 120, 151, 154, 163-164, 218,

  255, 276, 284, 287, 289, 293, 295-296
  labor costs, 24, 26, 192, 205, 276
  licensing, 288
  product and, 12, 256
  product lines, 8, 255-256
  sales and, 30, 213, 218, 239, 246, 255-256
Countries, 1, 9-10, 16-18, 20, 25, 29, 32, 74, 127, 165, 185
  segmentation and, 10
courtesy, 10, 12-13
Creating value, 21, 33, 72, 83, 103, 142, 187, 219
Creativity, 117, 133
Credit, 9, 15, 24, 26, 73, 107, 131, 138, 148, 179, 189, 255
credit approval, 107, 131
critical path, 36, 39-46, 48, 50-51, 53-54, 56, 58-61, 64-66, 69-70
Cross-functional teams, 90, 120, 218
CSR, 124
Culture, 87, 102, 145, 182
  organizational culture, 145
Curves, 111, 122, 131, 153
Customer demand, 2, 18, 217, 219, 233, 256
Customer feedback, 111
Customer needs, 12, 148, 181, 279
Customer orientation, 90
Customer relationship management, 7
Customer satisfaction, 14, 20, 22, 72, 83, 91, 93, 101, 103-104, 113-114, 120, 142, 144, 148, 165-166, 168, 186, 188, 214
Customer service, 3, 5, 70, 73, 79, 84, 120, 147-148, 158, 177, 179, 214, 239, 256, 283-284
Customer value, 25, 73, 102-103, 166, 256
  logistics, 73, 103, 256
Customers, 1-2, 4-7, 9-18, 20-25, 27, 33, 36, 71-76, 82-83, 86-87, 90, 93-94, 97-98, 101-105, 108-109, 111-112, 114, 121, 123, 125, 127-131, 133-134, 136, 138, 141-145, 148-150, 153, 156, 158, 165-166, 173, 176, 181, 186, 188-190, 192, 197, 201-207, 210-212, 214-215, 218-220, 224, 227, 233-234, 236-240, 247-248, 251, 254-256, 262, 266, 275-277, 279-295
  business-to-business, 83
Customs, 10

D

Damage, 19, 22
data, 7, 9, 15, 19-20, 26, 28, 36-37, 43, 54-55, 59, 61-67, 80, 96, 101-103, 107, 109-110, 112, 114-118, 120, 122-123, 130-132, 141, 147-151, 153-156, 158-160, 163-164, 166, 169-171, 173-183, 189, 192, 206, 210, 218-221, 223-230, 232-233, 235-241, 243, 245-259, 266, 284, 288
Data collection, 114, 149
data processing, 19, 170
Database, 9, 33, 61-62, 107, 109-110, 120, 127, 238, 276
  characteristics of, 109
  examples of, 110
  purpose of, 109
  systems, 9, 33, 109
  uses, 109
Database design, 62
dates, 36, 42, 51-52, 88, 188
Deadlines, 33, 50
Death, 127
  premature, 127
Debt, 276
Debt service, 276
deception, 144
Decision criteria, 274, 278
Decision makers, 69, 82
Decision making, 21, 143, 261-278
Decision-making, 21
Deliverables, 34, 52
Demand, 2, 5, 10-12, 18-20, 25, 27, 83-85, 127, 136, 158, 186, 188-196, 201, 205-211, 213-214, 217-230, 233-240, 243-259, 261, 263-271, 273-274, 276-278, 279-280, 282
  aggregate, 191-192, 205, 207, 238-239, 255-256
  change in, 25, 27, 193, 208, 229, 261, 276
  derived, 11, 190, 221
  excess, 12, 136, 211, 274
  for labor, 85
  increases in, 219, 225, 239, 256
Dentists, 294
Department of Transportation, 246

Department stores, 89-90
Deposits, 158-159
Depreciation, 42, 262
design, 2, 4-5, 7-8, 10-13, 16, 19-22, 31-33, 47, 61-62, 68, 72, 74, 79-80, 82, 90-92, 95, 97, 99, 103-105, 108, 113, 115, 117, 119, 121, 123, 127-128, 134-135, 137, 142-144, 147-148, 150, 158, 161, 163-164, 172-175, 178, 187, 190, 211, 219, 256, 279, 281-282, 285, 288
  elements of, 90-91, 279
  principles of, 2, 20, 142, 144, 148, 187
diagrams, 29, 69, 102-106, 114-115, 122, 129, 136, 149-150, 197
  types of, 69, 104-105
Discipline, 30, 283, 285, 290, 294
Discount stores, 281
Discrimination, 20
Disposal, 165
Distance, 80-82, 85, 91-96, 112-113, 121, 125, 130
Distribution, 1-2, 19, 24, 48-51, 54, 59, 114, 120, 151-154, 157-158, 160-164, 168, 172-173, 178, 217-218, 220, 223, 255, 276, 283-287, 289-290, 293-296
  case study, 218
  supply chain management, 2, 24, 218, 255
Distribution center, 220, 255
Distribution centers, 217-218, 255
Distributors, 83
Diversity, 16, 19-20, 23, 76, 280
Division of labor, 3
DMAIC, 149, 181
Documentation, 68, 103-105, 109, 113, 117, 144, 165-166, 168
documents, 103, 147-148, 188-189, 212, 258, 294
Dollar, 17, 29, 34, 86, 128, 193, 285
Dollars, 17, 26, 30, 43, 47, 84, 127, 165, 206, 220, 237, 239, 246, 257, 263, 265, 273, 285
Downsizing, 121
Downstream, 85, 146, 195
drawings, 82
Drill down, 111
Drugs, 127, 283
Durable goods, 19
Duties, 51, 74, 84, 129, 136-137, 147, 149
Duty, 195
Dynamics, 279

E

Earnings, 17, 278
Earnings margin, 17
E-commerce, 16, 103, 254-255
Economics, 99, 259
Economy, 20, 219, 246, 256
Education, 1, 31, 61, 71, 79-80, 84, 91, 101, 107, 141, 182-183, 185, 217, 261, 279
  change and, 80
Efficiency, 12, 72, 84-85, 120, 181-182, 187-188, 198-199, 201-204, 206-207, 210, 284-285, 292
E-mail, 1, 22, 75, 83, 102
Empathy, 181-182
emphasis, 68-69, 88, 90, 229, 237
Employee involvement, 144-146, 166-167
Employee training, 118
Employees, 4, 7, 9-10, 15-17, 24-25, 27, 70, 71-72, 74, 79-80, 83-84, 93, 102, 104, 114-115, 117, 121, 128-129, 131, 139, 141, 143-145, 147-151, 153-154, 158, 166, 169, 172, 185, 189, 192, 199, 210, 248, 250, 276-277, 287
  organizational culture and, 145
  selection of, 80
Employment, 16, 84
  full, 84
Empowerment, 90, 147, 169
Encoding, 160
England, 3, 138
English, 47
Enterprise resource planning, 4, 103
enterprise resource planning systems, 4
Environment, 4, 7-8, 10, 20, 23, 25, 30, 37, 52, 68, 73, 79, 91, 98, 102, 121, 135, 144, 165, 215, 238
  natural, 4, 91
Environmental scanning, 8
Equity, 131
E-tailers, 1
Ethical behavior, 144, 165
Ethics, 20, 142-144, 167, 183
  Bribery, 20

Business ethics, 183
EU, 18-19, 119
Europe, 1, 3, 17, 19, 101, 255
European Union, 18, 165
   EU, 18
European Union (EU), 18
Evaluation, 36, 54, 81, 102, 108-109, 119, 122, 142, 165, 259
evidence, 68, 171, 259
Excess demand, 211
Exchange, 17, 183, 239
Exchanges, 94
Expansion, 20, 30, 219, 269
expect, 6, 13, 60, 128, 144, 202, 205, 236, 242
Expectations, 17, 29, 32, 101-102, 104, 121, 142, 144-146, 195, 235, 267
Expected return, 273, 277
Expenditures, 52, 70, 225-226
Expenses, 151, 187-188, 192, 255
Experience, 22, 29-30, 47, 52, 54, 68-69, 71, 74, 83, 85, 97, 99, 102, 118, 134, 138, 141, 144-146, 149, 166, 172, 182, 186, 202-205, 214, 218-219, 224, 235, 238, 267, 284
expertise, 9, 12, 34, 105, 136
Explanations, 150
Explosion, 185
External benefits, 166
External environment, 4
external failure costs, 143, 169

F
Facilitators, 104
Failure, 47, 52, 114-115, 118, 120, 123, 126, 132, 141, 143-145, 148, 160, 169, 182, 281, 289, 294, 296
fairness, 281
Family, 10, 85-86, 143, 165, 181, 190, 201, 215
FAST, 9-10, 14, 25, 74, 78, 102, 108, 131, 187, 210, 233, 238, 249, 264, 274, 281, 285, 295
Feature, 76, 107
Federal government, 246
feedback, 21, 104, 111, 122, 182
   giving, 122
Finance, 3, 25, 30, 33, 73, 103, 107, 121, 183, 214, 219, 237-238
   finance function, 121
Financial analysis, 119, 123, 272
Financial institutions, 4, 18
Financial markets, 10
Financial resources, 3, 7, 52
Financial services, 6, 25, 76, 87, 94, 99, 120, 148
Financial services industry, 76, 94
Fire, 113, 185, 212, 277, 293
Firms, 2, 4, 7, 9-11, 16-18, 21, 23, 31-32, 76, 78-79, 90, 93-94, 101, 120, 143-149, 151, 163, 166, 185-187, 194, 201, 211, 229, 239, 250, 259, 280
   case study, 259
   organizational culture, 145
   value chain, 2
Fixed costs, 84, 89, 94, 127, 192, 262-264, 272, 275-277
Fixed expenses, 192
Flexibility, 8, 11-12, 14-15, 24-25, 29, 33, 70, 72, 74, 77-78, 83-84, 86-89, 91-92, 99, 104, 200, 215
Flood, 277
flowcharts, 102-103, 105-108, 111, 113, 122-123, 127, 149
Focus groups, 6, 29
Food, 6, 9-10, 25-26, 29, 74, 78, 101-102, 115-116, 128, 132, 136-139, 142, 196, 233, 251, 264, 281-282, 295
   production, 10, 29, 78, 132, 136, 138, 196, 264, 281
Forecasting, 12, 21, 33, 72, 78, 83, 103, 116, 142, 187, 217-259, 266, 277
   sales, 33, 83, 103, 187, 217-219, 223-226, 228, 230, 236-239, 242, 246-249, 251-252, 254-257, 259, 266
Forecasts, 6, 79, 199, 211, 214, 218-221, 223-224, 226-230, 234-240, 242-243, 245-252, 255-257, 259, 262-263, 275
Forrester Research, 218
Foundations, 3, 30, 183
France, 19
fraud, 22
Free trade, 18
Freedom, 47

Frequency, 95, 114, 126, 131, 178
Fringe benefits, 129-130
Front office, 75-76, 87-89, 91-92, 99, 136
Full line, 254
Fund, 66, 76, 94, 128
Fund balance, 76, 94

G
Gantt chart, 41-42, 53-54, 67
Gantt charts, 41-42
general purpose, 29, 84
Georgia, 117, 195-196
Germany, 16, 19
Global sourcing, 254
Global strategy, 9
Global warming, 127
Globalization, 17-18
Goals, 2, 7, 17-18, 20-21, 23, 32-33, 46-47, 51-53, 72, 91, 102, 113, 120, 122, 142, 146-149, 166-167, 186, 198, 201, 218, 240, 261, 271, 279, 292
   definition of, 146, 148
Gold, 181
Goods, 3-6, 17-19, 85, 97, 121, 135, 149, 194-195, 219-220, 254-255
   free, 18
   private, 195
   public, 255
Government, 5, 18, 20, 79, 120, 224, 246
GPS, 1
Graphs, 114, 116, 123, 150, 173
Greenhouse gases, 20
Gross sales, 143
Group, 2, 5, 10, 50, 68-69, 79, 95, 104, 111, 117, 133, 144, 147, 173, 179, 207, 214-215, 224, 230, 237, 254, 266, 280
   behavior in, 179
groups, 6, 10-11, 22, 29, 47, 50, 86, 107, 143, 146-147, 207, 214-215, 220, 238, 240
   development of, 47
Growth rate, 22
Guidelines, 32, 165-166, 201, 235

H
Hazards, 19
   nuclear, 19
headings, 108
Health care, 18, 127, 144, 148, 186, 190, 237
Hierarchy, 35
Home country, 10, 17
Honduras, 18
Hong Kong, 20, 255, 281
Hospitals, 6, 93-94, 98, 190
HTML, 115, 117, 164, 186
HTTP, 22, 32, 47, 72, 85, 102, 117, 127, 142, 164, 186, 237, 259
Human resources, 3-4, 7, 25, 52, 73-74, 77, 103, 148, 219
Human rights, 165

I
Ice, 9, 27, 129-130, 249
III, 248, 250
illustration, 194
Image, 23, 53, 92, 123, 127, 145-146, 168, 172, 201, 211, 241, 246, 272, 293
   national, 168, 241
Implementation, 22, 33, 70, 99, 105, 122, 188, 215, 218
Import quotas, 18
Imports, 17-18, 258
   India, 18
Impression, 76, 145
Inc., 1, 10, 23, 25, 31, 60, 71, 83-84, 86-87, 92, 97, 101, 127, 132, 134, 139, 141, 146, 174-175, 179-180, 185, 188, 197, 217-218, 230, 237, 239, 250-251, 261, 277-278, 279
Incentive programs, 292
Incentives, 215
Income, 17, 138, 238
   market, 17, 238
Independent variables, 218, 221, 224-226, 240, 242
India, 3, 18, 20
Indonesia, 18
Industrial Revolution, 3
Industry, 3, 8-10, 13-14, 18, 20, 22, 76, 87, 94, 97-98, 108, 119-120, 127, 132, 134-136, 144, 158, 161, 176, 186, 211-212, 215, 250, 255-256

infer, 278
Information, 2-7, 9-10, 12, 14-16, 20, 22-23, 25-26, 29, 32-33, 36, 38, 41, 44, 47-48, 51, 56, 59-61, 64, 66, 69-70, 73, 75-76, 79-80, 83, 87, 90-91, 93, 95, 104-106, 108-111, 113, 119-120, 127-128, 130, 137, 142, 155, 166, 174-175, 177-178, 187-189, 197, 207, 209, 212, 214, 217, 219-220, 224, 226, 233-238, 256-257, 259, 261, 266, 268, 276-277, 279, 283, 291-292
Information system, 36, 38, 189
Information systems, 3, 7, 9, 25, 33, 73, 95, 109
Information technology, 4, 12, 16, 87, 90-91, 93, 120, 256, 259
Infrastructure, 32, 36, 38, 47, 103, 122
Initiative, 102, 217-218
Injury, 112
Innovation, 9, 20, 22-23, 30, 99, 121, 136, 183
Innovations, 3, 22, 103
   continuous, 103
inspection costs, 151
Insurance, 16, 18, 22, 28, 127, 150-151, 177, 262
   applications, 18, 177
   excess, 22
   gap, 18
   option, 151
Integration, 3, 12, 21, 33, 72, 99, 103, 120, 142, 187, 219, 239
Integrity, 20
intelligence, 237
Interest, 20, 33-35, 65, 69, 113, 122, 136, 147, 149, 179, 224, 262, 276
   credit, 179
Intermediaries, 4
Internal customers, 4, 11-12, 24, 93, 103, 121, 144-145, 219
internal failure costs, 143, 169
International financial markets, 10
International markets, 7, 19, 165
International Organization for Standardization, 165, 168, 172
International trade, 18, 165
International trade barriers, 18
Internet, 9, 16, 23, 25-26, 31, 53, 71, 83, 86-87, 92, 117, 120, 123, 168, 201, 238-239, 241, 272, 293
   defined, 26, 120
Interpersonal skills, 83
Interviews, 276
Intranet, 182, 255
Inventories, 6, 20, 52, 78, 83, 87, 108, 125, 188, 195, 218-219, 239, 254-256, 296
Inventory, 3, 5-6, 12, 21, 30, 33, 72-73, 78-79, 83, 88, 92, 94, 97, 103-104, 107-109, 112, 121, 135, 142, 187-188, 194-195, 197, 200-201, 213-214, 219-220, 239, 251, 254-256, 266, 279, 289-291
   management of, 3, 21, 30, 103, 201, 279
Inventory control, 3, 251, 290
Inventory management, 21, 33, 72, 103, 142, 187, 219, 254-255
Investment, 16, 52, 69, 83-85, 89, 94, 98, 120, 127, 135, 187-188, 265-266, 272-273, 276-277
   government, 120
   net, 83, 187, 276
   private, 69
Investments, 12-13, 20, 87, 90, 105, 119, 192
Investors, 3, 166
IRS, 174
ISO, 165-166, 169, 183
ISO 14000, 165, 169
ISO 9000, 165-166, 183
Italy, 17, 211

J
Japan, 16, 19-20, 90, 254
   automobile industry, 20
Job satisfaction, 201
Jobs, 18, 74, 77, 91, 105, 109, 111, 121, 144-145, 147, 172, 196-197, 256, 295
   causes of, 105
   levels, 74, 144, 196, 256
   measuring, 109
   service, 18, 74, 77, 91, 105, 109, 111, 121, 144-145, 147, 172, 196-197, 256, 295
Joint venture, 10
Joint ventures, 10

K

kaizen, 147
Knowledge, 3, 7, 69-70, 84, 136, 151, 166, 224
Knowledge management, 166
Korea, 18

L

Labeling, 165
Labor, 3, 5, 16-18, 23-28, 42, 46, 69-70, 72, 85, 89,
    98, 112, 121, 129-131, 136, 147, 165, 186,
    192-194, 205, 209, 212, 220, 250, 255, 262,
    276, 288-290, 292
    investment in, 16, 276
    trends in, 16, 23, 255
Labor costs, 24, 26, 192, 205, 276
labor force, 131
Labor productivity, 16-17, 24-28, 289
Lags, 229
Language, 281
Latin America, 1
Lawsuits, 47
Layoffs, 19, 90
layout, 29, 72, 74, 79-83, 91-97, 119, 134-136, 195,
    197, 279
Lead time, 9, 12, 15, 24, 97-98, 121, 135, 195, 198,
    278, 289
Leader, 83, 113
Leadership, 34, 90, 102, 166, 217, 254
lean manufacturing, 103
Learning, 2, 4, 9, 23, 32, 37, 53, 72, 85, 91, 102, 109,
    111, 122-123, 130-131, 139, 142, 167, 172,
    182, 186, 194, 201, 211, 218, 235, 240, 243,
    257-258, 261, 271, 279, 292
Learning curve, 37, 53, 109, 111, 122-123
Learning organization, 122
letters, 128-129
    application, 128
Leverage, 166
Liability, 47
Licensee, 211
Licensees, 211
Licenses, 10, 129, 288
Licensing, 10, 211, 288
Licensing agreement, 211
line charts, 115-116, 122
line length, 284
listening, 101, 183
Loading, 1, 296
Loans, 108, 131, 147, 187, 189
Local advertising, 270
Logistics, 4, 12, 19, 21, 33, 72-73, 103, 121, 142, 187,
    219, 256
    inventory management, 21, 33, 72, 103, 142, 187,
        219
    transportation, 12, 73
    warehousing, 12, 73
Logos, 211
London, 35, 53, 127
Loss, 3, 19, 47, 114, 143, 164-165, 169, 177, 213,
    262-263, 277
    assessment, 143, 165
    control, 3, 169, 177
    expected, 47, 277
    forecasting, 277
    frequency, 114
    known, 213
    prevention, 143, 169
    ratio, 164, 169

M

major points, 72
Make-or-buy decision, 264, 271
Management, 1-5, 7-9, 11, 13, 15-17, 20-25, 30,
    31-70, 71-73, 79-80, 82, 86-87, 89-90, 93,
    98-99, 101-105, 109-110, 115-117, 119,
    121-142, 144-145, 147, 150-152, 155-158,
    160-161, 163, 165-169, 172-173, 176-179,
    183, 185-215, 217-219, 232, 235, 240,
    247-251, 254-255, 259, 261, 263, 265-267,
    269, 274, 276-278, 279, 283-285, 287-288,
    290-292, 295
    activities of, 33, 60, 188
    functions of, 3
    organizational culture and, 145
Managers, 2-8, 10-11, 15-17, 20-21, 23, 27, 32, 34,
    36, 39, 41-42, 44, 46-47, 50, 52-53, 59,

72-74, 80, 84-86, 102-105, 108, 114-115,
    117, 120, 122, 142, 153-154, 161-162, 164,
    187-189, 192, 195-198, 200, 214, 219-220,
    224, 230, 235, 238, 254-256, 266, 273, 279,
    282, 284-285, 292
Manufacturers, 4, 6, 8, 18-19, 31, 71, 74, 78, 83, 85,
    97-98, 134-135, 141, 189-190, 211
Manufacturing, 2-6, 10-12, 16-20, 24-25, 27, 29-30,
    32, 62, 72, 74, 76-80, 85-86, 88-94, 97, 99,
    103-104, 107, 121, 127, 132, 135, 146, 148,
    163-164, 172, 177, 186, 188-191, 193-197,
    200-201, 205, 211-212, 214-215, 249-250,
    253-256, 272-273, 276, 278, 280, 288-289,
    296
Manufacturing employment, 16
Manufacturing firms, 2, 10, 76, 78-79, 93, 146, 194,
    201, 280
Manufacturing operations, 32, 86, 148
Manufacturing strategy, 30, 88, 99
Margin, 17-18, 192-194, 206, 208-209, 265
Margins, 15, 30, 192
Market demand, 186, 188-189, 194-196, 201
Market potential, 265
Market research, 5, 27, 224, 238, 242
Market segment, 10-11, 13, 15, 25
Market segmentation, 8, 10
Market share, 11, 13, 19, 32, 143, 146, 217, 239
Marketing, 2-3, 7, 9-10, 15, 23, 25, 30, 33, 73, 79,
    106-107, 148, 166, 188, 199, 211, 214, 219,
    236, 238-239, 256, 275
    defined, 79, 219
    global, 2, 9-10, 23, 25, 188
    ideas, 7
    of value, 73
    people, 9, 79, 219, 238-239, 256
    place, 7, 9, 238, 256
    value and, 148
Marketing strategy, 2, 23
Marketplace, 2-3, 8, 11, 13, 15, 23, 25, 145, 186
Markets, 3, 7, 9-10, 19, 21-22, 25, 72, 86, 165, 211,
    214
    thin, 86
Mass customization, 79, 92
Mass market, 10-11
Mass production, 4, 79, 92
Massachusetts, 47, 183
Material requirements planning, 103, 215
Materials handling, 85, 94, 111, 200, 254, 279
Matrices, 99
Matrix structure, 34
meaning, 24, 137, 198, 266
Measurement, 20, 102-105, 109-111, 122-123, 147,
    151, 154-155, 166, 181-182, 220-222,
    247-248, 250
measurements, 151, 177-178, 246
mechanics, 125, 173
Media, 143, 211
Medical care, 25, 190
medium, 246, 274, 278, 290
meetings, 29, 34, 47, 63, 80, 119, 238, 256
    conducting, 80
    online, 256
    types of, 34, 256
memos, 133
Merchant, 15
Mergers, 32, 143
Mergers and acquisitions, 143
message, 77, 93, 144
    ethical, 144
    producing, 77, 144
Metrics, 102, 104-105, 113-115, 117, 120-123,
    127-128, 186, 218
Mexico, 17, 19, 185-186, 215, 274
    and NAFTA, 19
Middle East, 1
MIS, 107
Modernization, 276
Mold, 97-98, 127, 134-136
Money, 2, 22, 69, 104, 119, 143-144, 175-176, 187,
    210, 266, 274, 282
    demand for, 274
Mortgage, 148, 150, 175-176
Motor vehicles, 129
Music, 123, 138
Mystery shoppers, 101, 105

N

NAFTA, 18-19
    North American Free Trade Agreement, 18

Nationalization, 18
Nations, 17-18, 20
Natural environment, 4
    sustainability, 4
Net income, 238
Net present value, 278
Net profit, 187, 278
New entrants, 8
New products, 111, 238
New Zealand, 1, 17
Newspapers, 6
Nominal value, 153-154, 161-162, 164-165, 169
North America, 1, 19, 136
North American Free Trade Agreement, 18
    NAFTA, 18

O

Objectives, 4, 8, 20, 33, 39, 90, 149, 165-166
    accounting, 4
Occupancy, 119
Occurrence, 48, 114, 150, 219
Offer, 6, 8, 18, 22, 26, 36, 47, 102, 106, 211, 220
Offset, 152
Oil, 8, 18, 69-70, 102, 124-125, 130, 174, 185-186,
    201, 249, 258
Operating expenses, 187-188
Operational planning, 2
Operations, 1-30, 31-33, 47, 68-70, 71-74, 77, 79-80,
    83-89, 91-92, 97-99, 101-103, 105, 107, 111,
    115-116, 119-120, 128-129, 132, 134, 136,
    141-142, 145-146, 148, 159, 166, 179,
    182-183, 185-188, 190, 192, 195, 197,
    209-210, 214-215, 217-219, 237-239, 249,
    254, 256, 259, 261, 265-266, 279, 281,
    283-285, 292-293, 296
Operations management, 1-2, 4-5, 8, 15-16, 20-25,
    30, 31, 33, 71-72, 98-99, 101, 103, 128-129,
    141, 183, 185, 187, 210, 215, 217, 219, 259,
    261, 279
    productivity improvements in, 16
operations plan, 218
Opportunities, 5, 8-9, 17, 21, 29, 68, 87-88, 103-104,
    211-212, 255
    e-commerce, 103, 255
Organization, 2-4, 6-9, 20, 23, 33, 52, 69, 72-73,
    90-91, 103-106, 108, 120, 122, 136, 142,
    144, 146, 165-166, 168, 172, 181-182,
    186-187, 201, 218-219, 238, 276-277
    definition of, 146
organization charts, 106
Organizational culture, 145
Organizational structure, 33-34, 73
Organizations, 2, 4-5, 9, 33, 72-73, 90-91, 108, 120,
    137, 165-166, 190, 195, 201
Orientation, 63, 90, 99
    performance, 90, 99
outlines, 187
Output, 5, 16-17, 23-27, 37, 53, 74, 82, 84, 109-111,
    122-123, 145, 148, 151-152, 155, 158,
    162-163, 165, 178, 183, 185-188, 196-199,
    201, 203, 207, 210, 219, 221, 240, 257, 262,
    265, 280, 291
    potential, 163, 165, 262, 265, 280
Outsourcing, 19, 73
overhead, 12, 16-17, 24, 26-27, 42, 65, 97, 135,
    192-194, 205, 207, 209, 262-263, 276
Overhead costs, 16, 24, 26-27, 42, 65, 192, 205, 207,
    209
Ownership, 35, 147, 255

P

PACE, 196, 224
Packaging, 17, 68, 85, 102, 126, 128, 178, 188
Panama, 42, 47
Parameter, 228-229, 235, 249
parentheses, 189, 202, 204-205
Particular risk, 108
Patents, 9
Payoff matrix, 267-269
payroll, 63, 73, 121, 136
Percentage of sales, 121
percentages, 114, 117, 206
Perception, 145
Performance, 4-8, 11, 16-17, 20-21, 29-30, 32-34, 69,
    72, 75, 80, 90, 94, 99, 101-105, 109-110,
    113-117, 119-120, 122, 130, 132, 139,
    141-183, 186-189, 195-196, 201, 211, 219,
    222-223, 235-236, 244, 247-248, 250-251,

259, 261, 265, 273, 277, 279, 295
Performance appraisal, 109
Performance evaluation, 165
Performance measures, 20, 101, 104, 113-114, 122, 132, 142, 148, 158, 186-187, 201, 235
performance metrics, 113, 120
Performance objectives, 149
periodicals, 250
Personal property, 129-130
Personality, 146
Philippines, 9-10
   licensing, 10
PHP, 85
pie charts, 116-117
Place, 5, 7, 9, 63, 69, 81, 83, 93, 102, 104, 111, 121-122, 124, 128-130, 138, 146, 154, 177, 179, 182-183, 238, 255-256, 281
planning and scheduling, 21, 33, 72, 103, 142, 187, 219
Plans, 7, 15, 20, 25, 36, 38, 46-47, 51, 68, 80, 92, 94, 120, 122, 127, 150, 168, 178, 194, 214-215, 218-220, 239, 249, 255-256
   business, 7, 15, 20, 25, 120, 218-219, 255
Policies, 16-17, 20, 28, 147, 177
Political environment, 10
Political risks, 18
Population, 119, 159, 172-173, 280-281, 284-285, 289-290, 294
Portfolio, 256
   Model, 256
Positioning, 23, 256
Power, 8, 19, 33, 83, 117, 127, 136, 235, 249, 252, 254, 256, 276-277
PowerPoint, 106, 123, 270
Premium, 102, 144
Premiums, 22
Present value, 263, 270, 278
Prestige products, 185
prevention costs, 143, 169
Price, 10-11, 13-14, 26-27, 29, 70, 73, 83, 85-86, 91, 101, 131, 145, 191, 193, 205, 207-209, 211, 214, 220, 242, 262, 264, 272, 275-277
   defined, 26, 193
Prices, 4, 7, 12-13, 18-19, 22, 33, 174, 211, 237, 242, 254, 256, 262
   break-even, 262
   custom, 174, 211
   input, 237
   minimum, 13
   reservation, 7, 174
   retail, 211, 254
Pricing, 9, 14, 83, 238, 263, 272, 275, 291
   new product, 238, 275
   strategy, 9, 83, 272, 275
   value, 83, 263
Pricing strategies, 263
Principles, 2, 20, 72, 142, 144, 148, 166-167, 187-190, 193-196, 201, 206, 215, 239, 259
privacy, 20, 137
Probability, 32, 37, 46, 48, 50-51, 53, 56, 59, 61, 63-65, 150, 152, 154, 160, 162, 236, 245, 266-270, 274, 277-278, 283-288, 290, 292-295
   subjective, 285
problem solving, 89, 147-148
problem statement, 294
Problem-solving teams, 147
Process control, 103, 147-150, 153-154, 161, 163, 167-169, 178, 182, 249
Process layout, 92
Process technology, 212
Procurement, 12, 142
product design, 97, 134, 144, 163-164, 178
Product development, 6-9, 12, 14, 24-25, 29, 47, 97, 103, 121, 134, 145, 186
Product life cycle, 219
Product line, 27, 30, 211, 257, 272, 275
Product managers, 255
Product mix, 186-187, 192-194, 196, 201, 206, 208-209
Product or service, 2, 111, 144
Product planning, 269
Product quality, 132, 144, 161
Production, 3-4, 10, 12, 16-20, 27, 29-30, 31-32, 64, 71, 78-79, 84-85, 88, 92, 97-99, 118, 121, 131-132, 134-136, 138, 143, 146, 149, 151, 156, 160-161, 164, 172, 175, 178-179, 185-186, 191-192, 194-197, 199-201, 205-209, 211-215, 226, 239, 253-256, 259,

262, 264, 275, 280-281, 288, 296
   centralized, 19
   globalization of, 18
   national, 16
Production costs, 213
production operations, 97, 134
production order, 280
Productivity, 16-17, 20, 23-28, 85, 87, 94, 99, 110, 119-120, 136, 139, 142, 147, 166, 197-198, 201, 210, 284-285, 289
   labor, 16-17, 23-28, 85, 136, 147, 289
Products, 2-12, 16, 18-22, 25, 27, 32, 35, 73-74, 77-79, 81, 83-86, 89-90, 103, 109, 111, 119, 121-122, 132, 142-146, 149-151, 158-161, 163, 165-167, 177-178, 185, 188, 190-196, 208, 211, 213, 220, 224, 228, 237-238, 249-250, 254-256, 262, 270-273, 275-276, 281
   attributes of, 10
   defined, 35, 79, 81, 143, 163, 193
   development of, 20
   labeling, 165
   levels of, 7, 9, 12, 143-144, 166, 262
   packaging, 85, 178, 188
   product life cycles, 85
   product mix decisions, 192
Profit, 15, 18, 20, 22, 30, 144, 187, 193-194, 206, 209, 213, 215, 261-263, 265-267, 273, 276, 278
Profits, 27, 30, 143, 145, 187, 192-194, 201, 206, 208-209, 211, 263, 266-268, 270, 272, 274-276
program evaluation and review technique, 36, 54
   PERT, 36, 54
Project cash flows, 219
Project management, 21, 31-70, 72, 103, 122, 142, 187, 197, 219
Project plan, 47, 52
Project scope, 47
projection, 218, 221, 230-231, 233-235, 240-242, 247-248, 250-251, 253, 257, 259
Promotion, 33, 224, 239, 256
   costs of, 256
Property, 18, 29, 68, 129-130, 136-137, 182
   removal, 136
   risks, 18
Property taxes, 129-130
proposals, 33, 82, 104
   producing, 104
   types of, 104
Protection, 20, 115, 143, 151
Prototype, 8
Prototypes, 255
Public relations, 64, 69, 144, 255
   campaign, 64
Publicity, 47, 230, 277
purchase order, 121, 255
Purchasing, 6-7, 16, 97, 135, 144-145, 149, 187, 192, 249, 256, 278
purpose, 4, 29, 33, 52, 84, 91, 109, 117, 145-147, 151, 169, 175, 225, 259, 262
   defining, 33
   general, 4, 29, 84, 145
   specific, 4, 52, 262
   statement of, 33

Q
Quality, 3, 5, 8, 10-15, 17-18, 20-21, 24-25, 27, 29-30, 33, 47, 52, 70, 71-73, 75, 83, 85, 87-88, 90-91, 94, 97-98, 101, 103-104, 113-114, 116-118, 120-121, 131-135, 138-139, 141-183, 186-188, 211, 219, 227, 237, 246, 249, 256, 265, 276-277, 285
quality control, 146, 155, 183
Quality issues, 114
Quality management, 103, 142, 144, 165, 167-169, 183
Quality strategies, 166
Quotas, 18
   import, 18
quoting, 98, 135

R
Radiation, 19
Rail systems, 18
Railroads, 3
Rates, 17, 37, 53, 69, 109-110, 113, 120, 122-123, 127, 148, 190, 266, 281, 286, 291, 295
   definition of, 148

reasonable, 266
Rating, 109-110, 130, 189, 218, 253-254, 273, 277
Ratios, 27, 163
Raw materials, 12, 18, 30, 97, 121, 135, 149, 165, 191, 205, 207-209, 212, 238, 254-255, 275-276
Raw materials inventory, 97, 135
Reach, 22, 110, 239, 257, 259
Real estate, 25, 277
reasonable assurance, 272
Recession, 219
recommendations, 52
Records, 73, 109, 112, 117-118, 129, 132, 170-171, 182-183, 256, 296
Records management, 73
Recruiting, 7, 26, 73
Recruitment, 26
Regional trading blocs, 19
Regression analysis, 225-226, 230-232, 240, 242, 249
Regulations, 7, 18, 92
   global, 18
Relationships, 3, 7, 9, 29, 36-38, 41-43, 47, 54, 59, 61, 68-70, 83, 88-89, 91, 187, 197, 206, 210, 224, 239, 256, 262
   cause-and-effect relationships, 224
   preferences, 9
Relative cost, 74, 84
Reorganization, 121
Repetition, 111
Replication, 33
reports, 5, 16, 34-36, 41, 52, 76, 94, 110, 118-119, 145, 162, 257
   accuracy of, 145
   length of, 41, 119
   organizing, 35-36
   producing, 145
   types of, 5, 34, 94, 118
Representations, 82, 105, 116
research, 5, 18, 27, 30, 73, 80, 97-98, 134, 215, 218, 224, 236, 238, 242, 296
   conducting, 80, 224
   planning, 215, 218, 242
   primary, 80
Research and development, 18, 73, 97, 134
   cost of, 18
   human, 73
Reserves, 8
Resource acquisition, 52
Resources, 2-4, 7-10, 16-17, 20, 23-26, 32-36, 39, 41-42, 51-53, 59, 72-74, 77-79, 84, 87, 89-92, 94, 101-104, 119-120, 122-123, 127, 143, 148, 151, 167-168, 173, 185-188, 190, 192-196, 201, 204, 206, 208, 218-220, 239-241, 247, 271-272, 275, 292-294
response time, 5, 117, 128
Responsibility, 20, 29-30, 35, 38, 46, 119, 147, 165, 280
Restricted, 50
Retail stores, 254
Retailers, 1, 4, 19, 83, 89, 217-218, 239, 254-255
Retailing, 2
Retention, 22, 120
Retirement, 286
Return on investment, 69, 98, 120, 135, 273, 277
   advertising, 69
Reuters, 18, 146, 164, 290
Revenue, 3, 24, 72, 94, 120-121, 193-194, 237, 246, 262-263, 273, 275
Revenues, 1, 29, 42, 68, 101, 261-263, 267, 270, 273, 275
revision, 82
Rewards, 87, 166
Risk, 1, 37, 46-48, 51, 54, 59, 108, 137, 144, 149-150, 177, 217, 265-266, 268-269, 271-273
   asset, 108
   business, 137, 144, 177, 272
   financial, 108, 266, 269, 272
   market, 47, 217, 265
   operational, 47, 51
   political, 47
   property, 137
   strategic, 46
Risk management, 46, 51
   monitoring of, 51
Risks, 18, 32, 35, 46-47, 51, 53, 119, 219, 271
   opinions of, 219
   patterns of, 219
   political risks, 18
Role, 2, 4-6, 17, 23, 35, 69, 83, 139, 142, 145, 167,

182, 201, 214
   interpersonal, 83
   managerial, 145, 167, 214
Russia, 17, 25

S

S corporation, 101
Safety stock, 218, 256
Salaries, 262
Salary, 94, 296
Sales, 2-3, 7, 9, 13, 16-17, 22-23, 25-27, 29-30, 31-33, 61, 69, 71, 73, 83, 86, 94, 97-98, 101-103, 105-107, 120-121, 123, 127, 129, 134-135, 143, 148, 166, 172, 178, 185, 187, 192, 199, 211, 213-214, 217-219, 223-226, 228, 230, 236-239, 242, 246-249, 251-252, 254-257, 259, 261-263, 265-266, 272, 274-276, 278, 279
Sales and marketing, 30
Sales data, 228, 246-247
Sales force, 29
Sales offices, 251
sales order, 121, 255
Sales potential, 32
Sales process, 105-107
Sales promotion, 33, 224, 256
   objectives of, 33
   tools for, 256
Sales taxes, 129
Sales training, 61
Salespeople, 224
   Inside, 224
   Outside, 224
Samples, 149, 151, 153, 155-158, 161, 163, 170-180, 182-183, 235, 249
Sampling, 80, 109-110, 122-123, 130, 149-154, 158, 160-161, 167-169, 178
Sampling distribution, 152-153, 160-161
SAP, 239
Saving, 85, 102
Scanning, 8
Scientific management, 3
scope, 33-34, 47, 72, 86, 91-92, 101, 103-104
SEA, 185
Security, 73, 290-291
security management, 73
Segmentation, 8, 10
Selection, 13, 34, 63, 69, 80, 84, 91-92, 230, 235, 257, 291
Selection process, 69
Self-improvement, 136
Self-managed teams, 147
Sensitivity, 34, 67, 263, 271-272
SEP, 253, 258
Service encounter, 75, 160
Service industries, 89
Service organizations, 4, 9, 190, 195, 201
Service provider, 6, 76, 83, 108
Services, 1-14, 16, 18-19, 21, 23, 25, 30, 32-33, 35, 73-76, 78-80, 83, 85-87, 89, 91, 94, 99, 103, 109, 111-112, 119-121, 124-125, 139, 141-146, 148-151, 158-161, 163, 165-167, 188, 190, 196, 201, 219-220, 224, 230, 237, 246, 262-263, 271-272, 276-277, 280-282, 289, 291, 295
   attributes of, 10
   defined, 35, 79, 120, 143, 163, 219
   international markets, 7, 19, 165
   levels of, 7, 9, 12-14, 76, 143-144, 166, 262
   quality management, 103, 142, 144, 165, 167
Shanghai, China, 20
shipping, 2, 18, 71, 83, 89, 94, 97, 135, 188, 194-196, 255-256, 279
Ships, 3, 142, 185, 255, 281
Shortage, 18-19, 186
SIMPLE, 22, 35, 55, 85, 90, 109, 151, 190, 195-196, 200, 227-230, 233, 235-236, 240-243, 249, 251, 254-256, 290
Simulation exercises, 53, 167, 201
Singapore, 31, 211
site preparation, 35-36, 38
Six Sigma, 30, 103, 136, 142, 144, 148-150, 162, 167-169, 181-183
Size, 1, 5, 24, 26, 35, 47, 82, 98, 109-110, 116, 131-132, 135-136, 151, 154-159, 163, 169, 175-176, 178-179, 181, 183, 185, 190, 195, 221, 249, 254, 256, 278, 280, 290, 293, 295
Skills, 5, 7, 18-19, 23, 33-34, 53, 74, 83-84, 91, 105, 119, 122, 138, 142, 151, 201, 240, 253, 271,

277, 292
skimming, 185
Slack time, 39, 51
Slope, 84, 225, 232
Small business, 272
Smartphones, 217
Smoke, 19
SOAP, 133, 179
Social responsibility, 20, 30, 165
Society, 8, 30, 139, 144
software, 18, 26, 41-42, 51-53, 59, 66, 94-95, 105-106, 115, 117, 127, 173, 196, 200, 204, 210, 228, 237-239, 247, 270, 275, 279, 290-291, 294
   custom, 26, 94, 127, 210
   tracking, 51
Sourcing, 73, 254-255
   retailers, 254-255
South Korea, 18
Sovereignty, 18
Spain, 19
Special events, 137
Special form, 201
Specialization, 89, 201
spreadsheets, 21, 113, 115, 279
Staffing policy, 295
Stakeholders, 34, 144, 238-239
Standard deviation, 48-49, 53-54, 151-152, 154, 157-158, 160, 162-164, 168, 172-173, 176, 178, 222-223, 225, 242
Standard of living, 16
Standardization, 77, 165, 168, 172
State government, 79
statistics, 49, 54, 151-152, 163, 168, 183, 223, 240, 248, 257, 291
   analyzing, 291
Status, 51, 68, 129, 195
Steam, 3
steering committee, 105
Stock, 9, 69, 78-79, 85, 88-89, 92, 101, 211, 217-218, 220, 238, 254-256
Stock sales, 9
Stockholders, 144
Stories, 276
Strategic alliance, 9-10, 32
Strategic alliances, 9
Strategic issues, 90, 104, 120
Strategic management, 30, 99
   competitive advantage and, 30
strategic objectives, 166
Strategic planning, 4, 166
Strategic plans, 25
Strategies, 8-10, 18, 21, 72, 74, 78, 88, 90-91, 93, 98, 166, 185, 187, 219, 259, 263
   corporate, 8, 10
   functional, 72, 90, 187, 219
Strategy, 2-3, 7-12, 15, 20-25, 30, 33, 69, 71-99, 103, 127, 142, 166, 187, 219, 256, 272, 275
   combination, 25, 86
   corporate social responsibility, 20, 30
   defined, 79, 81, 187, 219
   focus, 7, 9, 11, 25, 30, 33, 72, 76, 78, 85, 89-91, 142, 166, 219, 256
   global, 2, 8-10, 23, 25, 72, 83, 127
   multinational, 20, 97
   pull, 69
   push, 98
Stress, 141, 214
Students, 4-5, 24, 26, 59, 61, 94, 127, 129, 167, 173, 204, 247, 275, 294
Success, 2-4, 13, 20, 25, 29, 32-33, 46, 59, 80, 102-103, 145-146, 148, 166, 181, 183, 211, 218, 259, 272
Supermarkets, 83, 246, 251
Supply, 1-4, 6-8, 10-17, 19-24, 31-33, 46, 71-74, 83, 85, 91-92, 98-99, 101-103, 105, 120, 135, 139, 141-142, 149-150, 167, 185-187, 211, 214, 217-220, 225-226, 236, 238-240, 251, 254-256, 259, 261, 269, 279
   aggregate, 238-239, 255-256
   excess, 12, 22, 98, 211
   of capital, 85, 187
   of labor, 3, 16
Supply chain, 2-4, 6, 10-12, 17, 19-24, 32-33, 72-74, 83, 85, 91-92, 99, 102-103, 105, 139, 142, 149-150, 167, 186-187, 217-220, 225-226, 238-240, 254-256, 259, 269, 279
   defined, 186-187, 219
Supply chain management, 2-4, 23-24, 218, 240,

254-255, 259
Supply chains, 1-2, 4, 6-8, 10-11, 13, 15-16, 19-23, 31, 33, 71-72, 101, 103, 141-142, 185, 187, 217-219, 261, 279
   logistics, 4, 19, 21, 33, 72, 103, 142, 187, 219
Support, 3, 6-7, 10-11, 15, 20-21, 24, 26, 36, 38, 72, 97, 103-104, 120-121, 128, 134-136, 139, 145-146, 165-166, 182, 188, 224, 228, 239, 252
Surplus, 277
   total, 277
surveys, 6, 29, 68, 181, 220, 224
Sustainability, 4, 21, 23, 33, 72, 103, 142, 166, 187, 219
system, 4, 10, 18, 36, 38, 51, 85, 101-104, 119, 121-124, 127-128, 132, 137, 141, 148, 165, 177, 181, 186-190, 192, 194-196, 201, 214, 219-220, 228, 235-237, 239-240, 246, 255-256, 276-277, 279-282, 284-296
Systems approach, 70

T

Tables, 91, 96, 101, 104, 114-115, 152, 214, 236, 272, 291
   relationships in, 91
Taiwan, 211
Tangible products, 4
Target market, 13
Tax rates, 17
Taxes, 129-130, 262
   property, 129-130
   sales, 129, 262
teams, 36, 46, 90, 104, 120-121, 136, 146-149, 169, 182-183, 214, 218, 228, 236, 255
   effective, 236
   problem-solving, 147-148
   types of, 104
Teamwork, 145, 147
   culture and, 145
Technical competence, 34
Technological advances, 4
Technology, 2, 4, 9-10, 12, 16, 18, 20, 25, 29-30, 34, 47-48, 70, 84-87, 90-91, 93, 98-99, 105, 117, 119-120, 127, 146, 166, 168, 183, 212, 224, 256, 259, 278, 279
   advances in, 224
   information technology, 4, 12, 16, 87, 90-91, 93, 120, 256, 259
Technology management, 25
telephone, 5, 18, 22, 25, 69, 75, 86, 93, 102, 120, 123-124, 127-128, 174, 177, 182, 281
Termination, 108
Threats, 8-9, 68
throughput, 87, 186-190, 192, 194-196, 202, 204
Time dimension, 88
Time requirements, 200
Time value of money, 119, 266, 274
Time-series analysis, 218, 221, 226, 242
Timing, 1, 34, 46-47, 52, 69, 83, 109
tone, 99, 123-124, 146
Total cost, 43, 46, 56, 62, 84, 121, 262, 264, 266, 273, 276, 288, 296
Total costs, 84, 261, 263, 273
Total quality management, 103, 142, 144, 167-169
   TQM, 142, 144, 167, 169
Total quality management (TQM), 144, 169
Total revenue, 262, 273
Tourism, 246
Toyota Production System, 4
Trade, 18-19, 30, 35-36, 42, 53, 72, 120, 127, 165-166, 179, 235, 272
   deficit, 166
   domestic, 19
Trade barriers, 18
Trade deficit, 166
Trademarks, 86
Trade-offs, 30, 35-36, 42, 53, 127, 179, 235
Trading blocs, 19
Trailers, 1
Training, 7, 12, 18, 61, 73, 84, 102, 105, 115-119, 128, 132, 139, 143, 149-150, 152, 157, 174, 219, 284
Transactions, 9, 15, 93, 175, 179, 248, 280-281
   consistent, 15
Transfers, 255
Transformation process, 94
Transportation, 1, 12-13, 18, 25, 47, 73, 78, 86, 111-112, 168, 188, 218, 246, 277
   costs, 12, 18, 112, 218, 246, 277

networks, 47
Transportation costs, 218
trend analysis, 230
Trends, 2, 8, 16, 23, 116, 221, 239, 255, 266
TRIPS, 80, 92-95
Trucks, 1-2, 116, 195, 256, 280, 287-288, 295-296
Trust, 20
Turnover, 121, 200
typographical errors, 174

U

underscores, 72
Underwriting, 22
    cycle, 22
United Kingdom, 25
United States, 3, 12, 16, 18-20, 47, 68, 85, 87, 141,
        147, 181, 185, 190, 214, 254-255
    North American Free Trade Agreement, 18
Upstream, 86, 195, 200
U.S, 5, 13, 18-19, 22, 36, 102, 127, 166, 190, 195-196
U.S., 5, 13, 18-19, 22, 36, 102, 127, 166, 190,
        195-196
U.S. Air Force, 190
U.S. Postal Service, 5
Utilities, 36, 38, 86, 262, 277
Utility, 249, 252

V

Value, 2, 6-7, 16-17, 19, 21-25, 27, 33, 50-51, 59,
        72-73, 81, 83, 102-103, 108, 119, 121, 142,
        144-146, 148, 153-159, 161-166, 169-170,
        181-182, 187-188, 219, 221-223, 225,
        228-229, 237, 245, 256, 261, 263, 266,
        268-271, 274, 278
    building, 7, 72, 81, 119, 188, 270
    defined, 81, 162-163, 187, 219
    marketing and, 7, 33
Value chain, 2
Value-added, 188
    Product, 188
Variability, 10, 71-72, 78, 82, 93, 148, 152-158,
        161-164, 168, 170, 176, 181, 190, 192, 223,
        280, 283, 289
Variable costs, 84, 94, 112, 262, 264, 272, 275-277
Variables, 50, 74, 115, 151, 154, 167-169, 182, 186,
        218-219, 221, 224-226, 240, 242
Variance, 48-51, 53-54, 56-60, 151-152, 161, 178,
        283-284
Venezuela, 18
videos, 85, 91, 122, 285
Vision, 93, 102
Visualize, 197
Volume, 9-12, 14-15, 24-25, 29-30, 71-72, 76-78,
        83-89, 91, 104, 119-120, 127, 132-133, 151,
        186, 201, 211, 245-247, 256, 261-263, 272,
        276, 282
Volumes, 12-13, 15, 29, 74, 76, 78-79, 84-85, 88-89,
        196, 211, 263-264, 275

W

Wages, 16
Wall Street Journal, 30, 139, 142, 218
War, 147
Warehousing, 2, 12, 73, 83, 255
Warranties, 143
Warranty, 6, 73, 128, 143, 145, 169, 173
Waste Management, 73
Water, 20, 102, 128, 133, 138, 185, 295
Watercraft, 209
Weaknesses, 25, 68, 141
Web, 7, 15, 22, 25, 60, 72, 85, 101, 148, 237, 254-255
Web site, 22, 25, 72, 101, 255
    design, 22, 72
Web sites, 85, 254
West Virginia, 249
Wiki, 32, 47, 72, 259
Women, 20
Work, 2-6, 8, 10, 12, 15-16, 22-27, 30, 33-36, 38-39,
        42, 50, 53-54, 57, 67-70, 71-77, 79, 85,
        90-91, 97, 99, 102-105, 108-111, 114, 119,
        121-123, 125, 128-131, 135-137, 141,
        147-149, 166, 173, 181-182, 186-191,
        193-207, 209-210, 239, 255, 265, 271, 278,
        280, 284, 288-289, 292, 295
    attitudes toward, 8, 265
Work teams, 147-148
Workers, 4-5, 7, 16, 30, 32, 42, 77, 79, 84-85, 87, 89,
        111, 119, 146-147, 166, 172, 186, 190, 192,
        196-197, 201, 209, 212, 215, 253, 292,
        295-296
    skilled, 215, 296
    unskilled, 215
workforce, 9, 12, 16, 18-20, 25, 71-72, 74, 77, 84, 87,
        90-92, 119, 136, 166, 187, 219, 239, 277
Workforce diversity, 16, 19-20
    managing, 20
workplace, 147
World, 1, 3, 5, 9-10, 16-20, 29-30, 47, 72, 85-86, 101,
        127, 146-147, 181, 185, 196, 211, 228, 237,
        254, 279, 285
World War, 147
    First, 147
WWW, 2, 17, 22, 26, 47, 59, 70, 86-87, 94, 102, 106,
        115, 117, 120, 127, 146, 162, 166, 172-173,
        186, 204, 218, 237, 247, 259, 270, 275, 294

Z

Zoning, 68, 210